GREAT DEMOCRATS

GREAT DEMOCRATS

Edited by
A. BARRATT BROWN

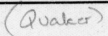

(Quaker)

IVOR NICHOLSON AND WATSON
FORTY-FOUR ESSEX STREET
LONDON, W.C.2
1934

First Edition . . . . *November, 1934*

Made and Printed in Great Britain by C. Tinling & Co,. Ltd.
Liverpool, London and Prescot.

CONTENTS

PREFACE

PREFACE

DEMOCRACY has had its leaders no less renowned than the Cæsars who exact obedience and worship from their followers. Greatness in human affairs is not to be measured only or chiefly in terms of military leadership or dictatorial domination. Force of character counts for as much as force of arms, and indeed in the course of time for infinitely more. Greatness is a relative term, and when applied to some of the Democrats included in this volume is bound to be a disputable one. There are great men who have also been Democrats, but the figures chosen for these pages are principally those of men and women who have been great *as* Democrats—great, that is to say, either in the extent to which they embodied in their lives and characters the democratic temper and attitude to mankind, or in the measure of their contribution to the democratic movement. I started by considering some seventy or eighty names, and I do not profess to have selected all who deserve a place in such a volume, even after fixing certain delimitations of time and place and quality. At one time I had thought of starting from the 17th century, and including men like Milton and Locke, and groups such as the early Quakers and the Levellers. But for the sake of whatever unity the volume may possess, it seemed well to confine the list to the last 150 years or so, during which the main growth of Democracy has taken place. Again, the majority of the names selected are those of Englishmen, though I have added a few American and one or two Continental figures, taking these few from different periods within the 150 years concerned. But the question of greatest difficulty was the application of a standard by which a Democrat should be defined. Should I only include those who have most fully embodied in their lives what I have called in the Epilogue " the democratic faith " ? Should I confine myself to champions of parliamentary government, or of individual freedom of expression and discussion ? It would have been a slenderer volume if I had rigorously

A*

applied such tests as these. But if I flung a wider net I was likely to land some strange fish of ill-assorted company.

Among the statesmen I hesitated over the names of Fox and Burke, of Lord John Russell and Sir Robert Peel, but decided to reject. Among the advocates of freedom I excluded more reluctantly such names as John Wilkes, Richard Carlile, George Jacob Holyoake, and Charles Bradlaugh. The final selection is made with a view to including representatives of different aspects of the democratic movement. Thus the range is wide enough to include an Anarchist like Godwin, a Tory Democrat like Disraeli, Socialists like William Morris and Keir Hardie, Liberals like Bright and Gladstone, Trade Unionists like Robert Applegarth and Joseph Arch, and pioneers of women's emancipation like Mary Wollstonecraft and Mrs. Fawcett, as well as poets and philosophers.

Here the difficulty was to select my representatives, and I would gladly have added many other names. I find on my supplementary list the names of Cobden and Fowell Buxton, Morley and Bryce, Tolstoy and Victor Hugo, Blake and Burns, Dickens and Meredith, William Lloyd Garrison and William Jennings Bryan, Daniel O'Connell and Arthur Griffith, Saint Simon and Lamennais, Lassalle and Bernstein, Francis Place and William Wilberforce, Harriet Martineau and Josephine Butler, Margaret MacDonald and Margaret Macmillan, Lord Shaftesbury and Sir Charles Dilke, Henry George and Bruce Glasier.

It has been difficult to refuse a place to many of these. It has been equally difficult to decide as to the claims of some of those I have included, and in particular of those whose faith in Democracy can be called in question. Thus I was considerably perplexed about both Karl Marx and Thomas Carlyle. Their influence upon the democratic movement has been unquestionably immense, but Marx, while defending parliamentary methods against the Anarchism of Bakunin, projected the notion of working-class dictatorship which has been developed by the Communists in our time, while Carlyle not only treated the people with a certain contempt, but propounded views on government that are not unlike those of present-day Fascism. None the less, I decided to include them both, and readers who turn to the chapters by Mr. Postan on Marx and by Dr. Jacks on Carlyle will, I believe, agree that the decision has been justified.

Howbeit, "there they are, my fifty men and women," and this volume will have fulfilled its purpose, if it enables Democracy to

> " Enter each and all, and use their service,
> Speak from every mouth "

to this age which indubitably needs to be reminded of their message.

A. BARRATT BROWN

Ruskin College, Oxford.
    September, 1934.

the chapters by Mr. Postan on Marx and by Dr. Jacks on Carlyle will, I believe, agree that the decision has been justified.

Howbeit " there they are, my fifty men and women," and this volume will have fulfilled its purpose, if it enables Democracy to

" Enter each and all and use their service,
Speak from every mouth."

to this age which indubitably needs to be reminded of their message.

A. BARRATT BROWN

Ruskin College, Oxford.
September, 1934.

ROBERT APPLEGARTH
1834–1924
by RAYMOND POSTGATE

ROBERT APPLEGARTH

1834-1924

by RAYMOND POSTGATE

ROBERT APPLEGARTH, when the writer of this met him, was a little old man with very white hair and beard, and blue eyes. He was weak with old age (he was nearing ninety) but still had a queer spry energy, and a manner of speaking and holding his head which reminded the hearer of a bird. He had settled himself into the position of being the Grand Old Man of the trade union movement, and his conversation was always calculated to give no offence. He seemed to radiate kindliness, and the occasional irrelevance of his remarks and his careful avoidance of any contested topic were legitimately enough put down to a desire to avoid any suggestion of patronage.

But a very old man is often not even the shadow of the young man that he was. Robert Applegarth, in the days of his vigour, was far from being a gentle and adaptable creature who was pleasant to all. He was a man of very firm and fixed principles, which he enforced upon the workers of his day by precept, example and pressure, and in contempt of the strongest opposition. He was not merely firm-minded; he was opinionated; he was, within the trade union world, a force as irresistible in his time as Napoleon was in the political world.

He was born on the 26th of January, 1834, and died on July 13th, 1924. Of the ninety years of his life only ten— the years between 1861 and 1871—are of importance to the history of England, but those years are of very considerable importance indeed. It may be doubted whether Applegarth himself realised how far more important they were than the rest of his life. It is true, however, that but for those years his name would not be remembered.

He was born in Hull, the son of an improvident and wandering sailor who, although he rose to be a quarter-master in an explorer's ship, was unable to give his son any adequate education. Robert went to work at the age of ten, and before long, though his father did not die until 1858, his mother was largely dependent on the boy's earnings. He moved to Sheffield when he was eighteen, and earned his living as a carpenter. He had four years before taken a job as a boy in a joiner's shop, but he was never regularly apprenticed. He married before he was 21. His wages at this time were never more than 24s. a week.

To "better himself" he decided to emigrate to the States. He landed in New York in December, 1854, and spent three years in America. He was fairly successful, but his wife was too ill to join him, and in 1857 he returned to Sheffield to start life again. The next year he joined the local union of carpenters.

He was one of the best of the children of the generation of Samuel Smiles. His enthusiasm for moral reform, self-improvement, and the programme of the Liberal Party was the most active principle of his character. It directed his kind heart and his abler head, and the certainty of his belief in Victorian principles gave him energy to operate a complete change in the structure of the trade union movement of this country. Only to-day, when all his generation is dead, can we say that the main lines of the building that he made are no longer plainly visible. The " amalgamated " unions that he and his fellows constructed were the most long-lived and rigid institutions in labour history in any country. When they were made they were a fortress : afterwards they became a prison : but as both their strength was formidable.

The society which Applegarth had joined almost at once excited his disapprobation for its inefficiency. It was a " Lodge " of the General Union of Carpenters and Joiners, but it was typical of the methods of that antiquated body that much doubt appeared to exist in the minds of the members whether it was not in fact an independent local society. It had sole control of its own funds ; there was no central fund or head office ; nor was there any co-operation between the Lodges which made up the society. Every Lodge made its own rules about subscriptions and about negotiations with the employers. As meetings were invariably held in public houses, the funds never attained any large proportions.

The method of organisation of the General Union of Carpenters (if it deserves such a phrase) was, with one exception, universal in Great Britain. The object of such a union was to carry on conflicts with employers, for the purpose of keeping wages up and hours down, and enforcing customary " working rules " which varied enormously from town to town. Funds were commonly raised only for that end. Later trade unions had an imposing list of " friendly benefits "—sickness benefit, accident benefit, out-of-work benefit, funeral benefit, superannuation benefit, etc. These were very rare at this time, and their payment rested upon the doubtful foundation of the solvency of the various Lodges. Later trade unions invariably had a paid general secretary, an elected Executive Committee, a book of rules which was enforced, and were administered efficiently from the centre. Such ideas would have been abhorrent to the trade unionists of 1858. They regarded the Lodge as everything, and the union as a mere federation of Lodges. A secretary, if elected by the whole society as was Richard Harnott of the Stonemasons, might by force of character exert great influence. But Harnott was an exceptional man, and had a genuine rule-book to which to appeal. Generally, the government of the whole society was left to one Lodge, and the powerful Lodges took it in rotation to be that Lodge. The committee of that Lodge became the committee of the whole society : the secretary of that Lodge, in the Carpenters' Union, became the secretary of the whole society.

Such a system astounded and disgusted a meticulous and efficient man like Applegarth. Membership was naturally very small—scarcely three thousand carpenters in all England held union cards. The Lodges were as reckless in starting conflicts as they were incapable in carrying them on. The society seemed merely to exist to collect carpenters' pence and give them in return nothing but a few convivial evenings in the local beerhouse. It did not protect their wages efficiently, and as an agent for education and self- improvement, in which Applegarth was even more interested, it was utterly useless.

Applegarth's perception of its defects was quickened (as were many of his colleagues') by a dramatic event which

occurred in 1859. The London master builders, vexed at
the various Lodges' agitation for a nine-hour day, locked
out all the building trade workers in July and announced
that they would not reopen their shops until all the
employees had signed a statement promising never to belong
to trade unions. The trade unionists, led by a gifted speaker,
a carpenter named George Potter, reacted vigorously, but
they were placed in a very difficult position. Their organisations instantly collapsed, for the most part. They had no
funds to face a struggle which had begun by putting 24,000
men on the streets.

They had to appeal to the workers of all England to save
them. Their appeal was answered. Trade unionists in all
the large towns, urged by local enthusiasts such as Applegarth, subscribed largely. Glasgow raised £257 and
Manchester £545. Moreover, a new union founded in
1852 called the Amalgamated Society of Engineers and
run on little understood new principles, contributed £1,000
every week for three weeks. This so astonished the
employers and encouraged the men that in February of
next year the master builders abandoned the lock-out. A
victory had been won, but at great expense. Many workers
were dissatisfied with the show that their societies had put
up and were anxious to know more about this strange and
powerful Amalgamated Society of Engineers. None was
more inquisitive than Applegarth, and the enquiries that
he made of the secretary, William Allan, made him decide
that the new principles should be adopted and extended
to his own craft.

He took part in the foundation of an imitative body called
the Amalgamated Society of Carpenters and Joiners,
brought the Sheffield Lodge into it, and in 1862 was chosen
secretary of the new union.

The principles upon which the new union was based were
these. The first was high contributions and high benefits.
Every sort of fund that could reasonably be held to be a
trade union function was to be started and membership
of all was to be compulsory. A " trade only " (i.e. strike
pay only) membership was regarded as a danger. Further,
as a natural corollary of this, the administration of all funds
and the direction of strikes and negotiations were to be all

put into the hands of the Executive. The Lodges lost at one cut all their funds and all their freedom.

The intention of this was double. The first was to anchor the membership firmly inside the union. There was to be no more of the old ebb-and-flow of members rushing in when a strike seemed near and flooding out when it was over. Once a man had paid a shilling a week for a few months he was not going to risk the loss of the benefits he had paid so much for. The second was to stop strikes almost altogether. Only men of a calm and clerkly type of mind, unsuited for industrial conflict—men like Applegarth, in fact—could administer the complicated business of such a union. They, and in the end their members too, would be most reluctant to risk their hardly-collected funds in rash conflicts. Consequently, strikes would before long become exceedingly rare things.

Applegarth was guided in adopting this policy by what amounted to a philosophy of society. He considered, along with most of the thinking young men of his day, that the interests of Capital and Labour were identical. Production for profit and all that we to-day call the capitalist system he believed had come to stay, and the duty of the working man was to make the best bargain for himself that he could : the efficient working of the system was to the advantage of both sides and the workingman should if necessary take the lead in co-operation. Strikes were an evil—they might be a necessary evil, as violence in self-defence might be necessary, but they should be used as rarely as a revolver is used in a civilised city. The union member should improve himself technically as a worker, and politically as a man. He should abandon the public-house and frequent the free library : he should make himself a skilled craftsman and indispensable to his employer. Very swiftly the employers would realise the necessity of coming to arrangements with trade unionists of this type. Conciliation and arbitration would have put an end to industrial strife.

Applegarth was not alone in advocating these principles. He was one of a group of powerful and strong-minded trade union officials who impressed them upon the whole trade union movement. William Allan has already been

mentioned; others were Edwin Coulson, secretary of the
Operative Bricklayers' Society, George Odger of the London
Trades Council, and Daniel Guile, secretary of the Iron-
founders.   Out in the provinces were men in less close
contact, but of the same mind, such as John Kane (Amalgamated   Ironworkers),   William   Dronfield   (Sheffield
Amalgamated Trades), and later Alexander MacDonald
of the Miners' National Union.

These men, who worked together for the same ends,
both in their unions and on the London Trades Council,
have been given by Mr. and Mrs. Webb the name of the
" Junta." Applegarth was their most eminent and influential
member : his interests were wider and his sphere of operations greater than many of his colleagues.   He entered
politics and took a large share in the International, for
example, but the principles by which he was guided were,
in these fields too, those of his colleagues.

The power which the "amalgamated " unions that they
led possessed was reinforced by the conditions of the time.
It would have been impossible to erect rich and closely
knit craft unions thirty years before.   The workers could not
have paid the subscriptions, and the employers would not
have tolerated them.   But since the days of Robert Owen
immense prosperity had descended upon the British capitalist
class.   The total amount of exports and imports in the
United Kingdom in 1831 is given as £97,623,332, whereas
in 1860 it was £373,491,000, which is an increase of 283
per cent. compared with a population increase of 43 per
cent.   Nor was the end of the age of Victorian prosperity
in sight.   The employers could, if they chose, give better
wages and better conditions : and it was soon clear to all
of them that a contented, docile and efficient trade unionist
movement was well worth a penny or twopence an hour
extra.   In the later Victorian age, when the "amalgamated "
unions were well established, it was recognised by the
majority of employers that it was not only foolish but almost
impossible to attempt to get efficient labour outside the
union ranks.

The amalgamated unions did not enrol the unskilled
workers, who had neither the money nor the temperate
meticulousness necessary to fit them for membership.

Moreover, as they were occupied in driving a bargain, they wished the supply of labour to be small and the demand great. They therefore fought with great bitterness the attempts of workers in other crafts to intrude upon their own craft. Indeed, the pugnacity which they had turned away from their employers seemed sometimes to be directed against their fellow-workers in other crafts.

The Junta's first duty seemed to be to break up the opposition within the trade union movement. Its chief enemy was the same George Potter who had made a name for himself in the building trade lock-out. He also ran the only trade union paper, called the *Beehive*, and was in favour of the old loose organisation and fighting policy for trade unionism.

In 1864, as a result of a quarrel between Applegarth and Potter, the *Beehive* began a campaign against the Junta. Its members were abused continually—on personal grounds almost wholly—and it replied by denouncing Potter as an irresponsible " strike-jobber." He was continually defeated in the London Trades Council, on which he soon lost his power. In the same year a trial of strength came in Birmingham. The master builders had forced a strike by introducing a " discharge note " for carpenters. Later it was announced that this had been withdrawn : the secretary of the General Union of Carpenters and Potter advised the men to hold out till this was officially confirmed. Applegarth rated them for this, telling his members they should have ignored the vote of the trade as a whole and gone back to work individually. " I tell you," he said, " that if I had been in Birmingham I should have been at my bench side on Monday morning . . . You are trying to humiliate the employers ; I will be no party to it." Applegarth won : the men went back.

Since the Junta, and not Potter, controlled both the London Trades Council and the only unions with funds, provincial unions in need came to it and not to him for assistance. This assistance was often granted only after severe inquiry showed that no trace of belligerence had been shown by the workers. The South Staffordshire colliers were severely rebuked for having provocatively played a brass band ; and a refusal of arbitration was enough to button up all pockets. The *Beehive* thundered, but strikers cannot live on thunder : control over funds and close knit unions, Potter found, was more powerful than newspaper rhetoric.

From 1864 Odger and Applegarth were engaged in an odd enterprise—the foundation of the International. As they conceived it, however, this was a meritorious and far from revolutionary action. The purposes of the International, in their view, were two—firstly, to stop the importation of foreign blacklegs, secondly to extend to the Continent the benefits of "amalgamated" trade unionism. Peace and ordered liberty would result : foreign employers and employed as well as British would live in concord, and the era of revolutions and repressions would pass. " We in England," said Applegarth kindly to the Basle Conference of 1869, " have no need to creep into holes and corners lest a policeman should see us." A great deal of unprofitable discussion did indeed occur at conferences, but this, as was well known, was a habit of foreigners and gave the Junta no alarm. Indeed, being preoccupied with home affairs, it gradually let the direction of the International slip into the hands of a German refugee named Dr. Karl Marx. It was only after the Paris Commune of 1871 that it discovered what he was doing with it. It then found the signatures of its members attached to a manifesto praising an attempt by an armed working class to tear down by force a democratically elected government. It repudiated its child at once.

Applegarth also took a prominent part in bringing the unions into the agitation by the National Reform League for the extension of the vote to the working class. The agitation came to its peak at a meeting in Hyde Park in July, 1866. The police forbade this meeting, but the Council of the League approached the gates, followed by a vast crowd, and demanded admission. The police and soldiers refused. The crowd, with Applegarth in its front ranks, then leaned against the railings, which (quite accidentally, as Applegarth too anxiously explained afterwards to all who would listen) happened just then to fall down ; and the meeting was held. The franchise was granted within a few months of this discreet display of strength.

Applegarth's greatest victory lay, however, in the legal sphere. In the year 1867 a Royal Commission was appointed to investigate into trades unionism as a result of a series of violent outrages in the Sheffield steel and Manchester brickmaking trades. It held an enormous enquiry which covered the affairs of nearly all the unions in Great Britain. Applegarth and his colleagues came out admirably from the ordeal. Their unions were shown to be efficiently run, pacific, devoted chiefly to friendly benefits, and incapable of any illegal actions. The older unions were shown to be disorganised, bellicose, unable to account for their money or their members, and quite conceivably tainted by violent practices. Public opinion, both working class and middle class, swung violently round. The government took no action to suppress the unions : on the contrary, it ultimately passed an Act giving protection to trade union funds and amending the iniquitous Master and Servant Acts which had given an enormous power for persecution into the hands of the employers. Next year Applegarth and a committee ran as candidate of the trade unions in Sheffield an employer named A. J. Mundella (to run a workingman would have been slightly indecorous). In this, the centre of the outrages, their candidate was victorious. Applegarth made it clear that the struggle was not only a defiance to the union-smashers, but also a defiance to the old unionism. " Who," he wrote, " is the candidate the Sheffield workers have selected ? Is he a firebrand from among their own ranks, a blind advocate of their own interests regardless of the interests of others ? No ! He is an employer of labour who has substituted for social warfare a system of even-handed justice . . . the system of arbitration."

The collapse of his chief opponent came in 1869. Potter came to the Junta and asked for its assistance in running the *Beehive* which was in danger of closing down. The Junta gave him a clergyman as superior editor and itself a majority on the board. The battle was over. Henceforward there was no organised opposition. Sooner or later all the trade unions adopted " amalgamated principles."

Consciousness that his work was done may have moved Applegarth to the decision that he now took. Or the cause may have been the recent death of his wife. For one reason

or another, he made up his mind in 1871 to cease his
secretaryship of the Amalgamated Society of Carpenters
and Joiners. He was hastened in his decision by a piece
of petty spite. A man named Cremer, jealous of his
power, had with certain friends secured a majority on the
Executive. They then proceeded to attack Applegarth
personally and endeavour to humiliate him. He had been
made a member of the Royal Commission on Contagious
Diseases (on which he was converted to Mrs. Josephine
Butler's views) and they ordered him to resign. Instead,
he resigned the secretaryship, with a telling letter of
reproach.

But this resignation was for public consumption only.
He did not intend to leave his union to be wrecked by
people like Cremer. He wrote round—most unconstitu-
tionally—to the General Council, a larger body representing
the whole society, telling the whole story. The General
Council, as he expected, came up to town and promptly
threw Cremer and company out of the office. However,
Applegarth did not withdraw his resignation. He preferred
to see the office taken up to Manchester and put in the charge
of a friend of his named J. D. Prior.

Now that he was a free man, he did not turn himself
into a politician. Respected and valued though he was by
the Liberal party, it was too early for workingmen candidates
to be popular. He only once was even nominated for a
seat : he never went to the poll. He took some part in
agitating for removing the tolls on London Bridge. He
also founded a short-lived " Industrial Education League."

But most of his attention was given to earning a living.
He sold quite successfully an apparatus called the Aerophore,
which was to be used on diving and in mining accidents.
It enabled fresh air to be blown to rescuers. He also sold
Jablochkoff's electric light, the first to be commercially
practicable in England. In 1898 he retired from commercial
life and took to poultry farming. Soon he gave that up also
and spent his life in watching the world around him and
giving friendly advice to his successors in trades unionism.

He found the unions in the process of violent change.
To the industrial unionists of 1901 he seemed like a survival
of another age. Their enemies were his successors—the

secretaries of powerful amalgamated unions, who declared
that strikes and conflicts with employers were wrong, that
Socialism was wrong, that trade unions without large
compulsory friendly benefits were wrong, that amalgamations
with other crafts and even more with the unskilled were
also wrong.   The Socialists and industrial unionists, to
whom all these things were desirable, were engaged in a
furious struggle with them.   The logic of events was with
them, but the strength and rigidity of the Junta's organisations were with their opponents.   They were continually
driven back ; only the lessons of the war and the passage of
time defeated their opponents.

Applegarth himself was by no means so sure of himself
as he once had been.   " Is it not time," he said in a public
speech, " that the workers dropped Amalgamated this,
Associated that, and Equitable the other, and all banded
in one giant organisation called the United Workers ? "
His words were not heeded ; nor, perhaps, did he heed them
much himself.   He was not, in his later years, concerned
deeply with trade union policy.   He was sunning himself
in the kindliness and respect with which he was universally
surrounded, and his chief wish was to respond by saying
what would please his audience and in general help the trade
union movement.

He died of extreme old age at the age of ninety, quietly
and without discomfort, on July 13th, 1924.

JOSEPH ARCH

1826–1919

by FRANCES EVELYN WARWICK

JOSEPH ARCH

1826–1919

by FRANCES EVELYN WARWICK

WHAT are the prime qualifications of a reformer? I think, when I look back over the many years of my active life and the many reformers I have encountered, that the two first are immovable convictions and a thick skin. The men or women who endeavour to leave the world a little better than they found it must first decide that what they seek is necessary and helpful to their fellow citizens. Then they must be prepared to stand up to every kind of opposition, including misrepresentation, abuse, calumny and the actual hatred of people who know them only by name. A reformer will win through in the end and the abuse will disappear giving way to praise or gratitude which may be posthumous, but if we will be honest with ourselves we have to admit that the last reward is as insignificant as the first penalty. The only thing that matters is the birth of a new form of progress, the betterment of the state of men and women, the realization of the principle, " Do unto others as you would have others do unto you."

To-day Joseph Arch is just the name by which we know a warm-hearted, brave and able man who did his work and went to his rest with the knowledge that he had used to the last his abundant gifts of vitality, health and energy. Thousands who have never heard of him are better off to-day because he faced every form of opposition on their behalf, and, knowing him as I did, I cannot help thinking that he would be perfectly satisfied with the result of his many sacrifices. We are celebrating this year the centenary of Tolpuddle, and when the men were sentenced by an unjust judge and by the connivance of a nervous Prime Minister, Arch was eight years old, living where he was born, at Barford in Warwickshire three miles from the Castle that was my home for so long.

He came of sturdy stock and used to say that his mother was the most wonderful woman he had ever known, so wide minded, open-eyed, resourceful. She would not stoop to squire or clergyman, she mingled a sturdy independence with her poverty. Where she was, no tyranny could thrive, and in her cottage where that forthright farm labourer, her husband, worked early and late to bring home a wage varying between nine and ten shillings a week, she could find time to read Shakespeare to her children and to instil into their young minds a spirit of independence that was never tainted with ill-will to those whose share of worldly goods had been granted on a different scale.

We talk of the pride of long descent, but the Parish Registers can often tell a better story than Debrett : and the farm labourers of to-day show direct descent from those whose names appear in Parish Registers when those registers were first established, centuries ago. A forbear of Joseph Arch had fought under Cromwell and the same fearless attitude towards life that animated the Ironsides was in the blood of Joseph Arch and his father. Squire or parson had asked the elder Arch to sign a petition against the repeal of the Corn Laws, and he refused to do so ; he lost his job as the price of standing out. In those days the labourer had no allotment, sugar cost 8d. a pound, tea 6s. or 7s. a pound, wages were so beggarly that soup and coal were given by squire and parson and others of the leaders of rural communities to enable labour to live and go on working. But in order that labour might be justified in living it must be obedient ; it must go through life touching its hat, it must adopt the ideas and principles of those who employed it. When Arch refused to sign a petition for repeal there was no soup or coal for his family, he had shown independence, he was a marked man, a rebel. Happily Arch could not be evicted ; the cottage he lived in was his own, he had inherited it ; and to help matters a little, young Joe went to work at the ripe age of nine years and earned 4d. a day under harsh farm hands who ill-used him. Four years later he was at the plough and, if I remember rightly, he told me he was earning 6s. a week. In his autobiography he tells how he would hurry out in the morning sometimes with an apple dumpling that was to serve him for dinner, how he could not resist the temptation of eating it on the way to work and how he would arrive at the farm with just a hunch of barley bread in his wallet and no better prospect than " a day's drudgery with perhaps a thrashing thrown in." It was a curious village life in those days, curious and ugly too. The labourers tried to start a Sick Benefit Fund and appealed to the parson to speak up for it in the pulpit ; he refused on the ground that it would make labour too independent—if they needed help they must ask for it politely.

It is quite clear that from early days the Arch family was a thorn in the side of the powers that were, but fortunately for him Joseph was very strong and very skilled, gifted with several kinds of manual dexterity. He studied his work with keen interest and a determination to succeed ; his hedge cutting, for example, was so good that he took many prizes and was ultimately proclaimed the hedging champion of England. He was an expert too with the scythe and presently became a mowing contractor, giving fair play to his gang and becoming more and more opposed to the reactionaries around him as he moved along the road to a freedom due to his own unaided exertions. It is well to remember that in those days the ballot was open—to vote for a Liberal was a crime in Tory-ridden rural England. Wages were kept so low that the farm labourer could not get enough to eat, many were reduced to stealing root vegetables and poaching rabbits, and needless to say there was no mercy for these offences at Petty Sessions before magistrates who took more thought for their hunters than for their farm workers. We cannot understand what life on the land was really like in mid and late Victorian days or how tightly the collar of serfdom gripped the toiler's neck.

A keen sense of the injustice that he saw all round him roused Joseph Arch to action, and when in 1872 three men came from Wellsbourne to ask him to start a Union he held his famous meeting under a chestnut tree in the village there. To his intense surprise, instead of an audience of thirty or forty he found 2,000 of whom about 250 agreed right away to combine. In that hour he became aware of the force that lay behind a movement to decent conditions of living.

Squire, parson and farmer were excited and alarmed. They even sent police to the next meeting, but there was nothing to be said or done. It was like lighting a heath fire this proclamation of a Union, this endeavour to raise

the farm labourer's wages from twelve to sixteen shillings
a week. In a little while Oxford, Hereford, Leicester,
Somerset, Norfolk, Essex, Northampton and Worcester had
joined in. Bucks and Dorset followed. There could be no
question about the men's vital needs, the loaf was 7½d. and
wages were as low as 9s. in some parts, but the reply of the
employer was a lock-out. At Easton Lodge, my grandfather,
Lord Maynard, stirred by his real sympathy for the farm
worker, mounted his horse and rode down to Dunmow to
plead for 10s. a week in place of 9s. He succeeded in his
efforts but only after expressing himself with memorable
vigour. Happily for the workless, public attention had been
called to the efforts of Joseph Arch and his colleagues,
the *Daily News* sent Archibald Forbes their famous war
correspondent to the lock-out area and his spirited statement
of the case reached the heart of the public. Money rolled
in to support the strikers. Men like Jesse Collings and
Auberon Herbert helped, then Charles Bradlaugh and
Annie Besant, ever to the fore to support the world's under-
dogs, lent their eloquence, and Cardinal Manning was with
the farm labourer. The railway companies were a great
help to the destitute farm hands and to many others, for
they absorbed nearly 5,000 out-of-work labourers in a year,
paying none of them less than 25s. a week. There was
migration, there was emigration, but while Joseph Arch
accepted these happenings and realized their present
significance, he was far-sighted enough to understand that
England was not bettering herself by impoverishing the
countryside. He did not approve of sending the best
workers to the United States. The figures of emigration
moved to a startling height and at last the National Agricultural Labourers' Union, which was his own creation,
sent him to Canada to enquire into the conditions prevailing
there. He made a very thorough survey in all directions,
maintaining his point of view in the most difficult circumstances because he was everywhere the guest of steamship
companies, railway companies, municipalities and rulers,
and there were many people who would have been glad to
mould his opinions. He was very human, that big, burly,
bearded man with the obstinate face and eyes that twinkled
kindly behind his spectacles. He would often say, " I'm

not ashamed to love a good dinner and I am very glad when
I get one ; an honest man should have an honest appetite."
So he enjoyed the hospitality he received to the full and
came back with a plain unvarnished account of everything
he had seen there, to the scorn and indignation of certain
jealous colleagues who felt that they should have been
chosen. It is typical of the man that he refused an appointment under the Dominion Government, though it would
have brought him in considerably more money than he
received from the Union ; I do not believe that even with
his travelling expenses (and they were considerable) Joseph
Arch ever had more than £1 a day while the Union lasted,
or that he had even two hundred a year to call his own. It
goes without saying that there were plenty of backbiters
and detractors waiting to injure him, people ready to say
that he lined his pockets. Men who had never known or
even seen him declared that he was robbing his Union and
drawing as much as £40 a week, and this at a time when he
had been a preacher for five and twenty years and claimed
to have walked 7,000 miles preaching his special gospel of
faith and unionism.

He was always making friends. His earnestness, his
sincerity of purpose, his plain blunt way and direct but
friendly speech had attracted men and women in all stations
of life. When certain libels were published and he was
told that if he would take an action he could recover considerable damages, his reply was characteristic. " If I have
to go into the Law Courts to prove that I am an honest
man," he said, " I must be in a bad way."

In the year following his return from Canada (1873) the
Suffolk farmers locked out 4,000 men, but in 1875 there
were 60,000 men in the Union, £7,000 in the bank, and
£21,000 had been spent on the relief of sufferers from strikes
and lock-outs. The public was standing by the farm
labourer, but the opposition to the Union continued.
" I had foes without and traitors within," he said, referring
to those years, a time of stern testing and unending anxiety.
It was not on his own account that he was troubled, he
could have found employment at good wages in any field
of farm work as organiser as well as worker ; his anxiety
was for those who looked to him.

B

The attitude of the authorities to Joseph Arch is shown very clearly in an incident that occurred about this time. His old father was taken ill. As I have said, Arch in spite of the libels of his enemies was a poor man. But he would not surrender his father to the workhouse and his wife undertook to look after him. It was still necessary in those days for her to go out charing to supplement the household earnings, so Arch went to the authorities and asked for an allowance of 1s. 6d. a week for his wife to make up in part for what she would lose by not going to work. He was told by the local Board of Guardians that he could send his father to the workhouse and contribute 1s. 6d. towards his support ! Arch thanked them for nothing, and managed to give his father the privilege of dying under his own roof. This incident occurred when the family income was at a very low ebb and there were young children to provide for.

I always thought that Joseph Arch endeavoured to see the other man's point of view and to be fair-minded. He had a strong feeling in favour of home production and was complaining in 1879 that this country was spending over £85,000,000 a year on the imported food that might have been grown at home ; I wonder what he would have said had he known the bill would have run up to £500,000,000 a year ! Surely he would have deplored still more the passing of England's sturdy children to the emigration ships and the far-off lands. He recognised the farmers' difficulties. " If the farmer lays out money on his land, he will probably be called upon to pay a heavier rent, and if he goes his landlord will give him nothing for unexhausted improvements." He saw the value of peace as a means of social improvement and did not hesitate to denounce both the Afghan and Zulu wars. It is well to remember that by this time when Joseph Arch spoke people listened. He could command an audience, not that he had any gift of eloquence or learning but because he was manifestly sincere and understood what he was talking about. Then too people knew nothing about the agricultural labourer and wished to be taught. He was stubborn, very stubborn ; compromise found no place in his scheme of things. In 1880 when he contested Wilton as a Liberal he would not canvass the electors. " I have no right to try and influence their opinion," he said to his exasperated advisers, " it is their business to think things out for themselves." He was defeated and at some of his meetings was howled down and stoned. " I had to fight land owners, tithe owners, farmers and clergy," he said, when he talked about this unavailing contest for which friends had found the money, but defeat left no bitterness and he busied himself in the attack on the tied cottage. He could find no word in favour of conditions under which a man may lose his home because he loses his job, even though he is a responsible tenant and pays his rent regularly. There was an injustice in this that Arch felt the more deeply because eviction had never been a terror in his life. His home was his own, his grandfather had bought cottage and garden for thirty pounds saved in service at Warwick Castle where, by the way, his mother acquired her domestic knowledge.

Through all these years, it is well to remember, the labourer had no vote. No politician cared what happened to him because he could not influence an election. It was only in 1884 after a long sustained effort to rouse the conscience of the country that the law was altered and then oddly enough, with the coming of the vote, the immediate appeal of the Farm Workers' Union passed and the affairs of that body became more involved and difficult. Men felt that they had reached their goal and those who wished to destroy the Union redoubled their efforts.

In 1885 when the Liberal Selection Committee was at work in North-west Norfolk, Arch was chosen as candidate over Sir Bampton Gurney, and he beat Lord Henry Bentinck at the poll and entered the House of Commons that had, I think, a dozen worker members in all. He was not there for long, the split on Home Rule brought about another election, and Lord Henry Bentinck secured the seat by a very narrow majority, a score of votes. Things were not good then with Arch. The resources of his Union were being drained by the Sick Benefit Scheme and by rumours put about that the Union was neither solvent nor honestly run. Finally, Mr. Walker took it up and succeeded in giving it a further lease of useful life. We have to remember that even to-day the agricultural labourer has no money to spare, villages are scattered, appeal is difficult, farmers remain hostile, labour is plentiful, it is no easy matter to keep a Union for farm workers in fighting trim. Arch was now on the County Council for Norfolk where he served for four years, and in 1892 he was back again in the House of Commons. By this time he was approaching his seventieth year, battered and bruised in an unending struggle on behalf of the class from which he sprung, and the rest of his days passed uneventfully. He was not destined to see the coming of the Old Age Pension which has left the worn farm labourer his place in the chimney corner when the evening falls. He had no visions of Agricultural Wages Boards, which, whatever their shortcomings, impose a measure of restraint upon those who would gladly, but with due salving of conscience and unctuous apology, reduce the worker to his old time state of penury. At least he left the farm hand better off than he found him, and he may claim to have been a pioneer of progress, the progress that the limited vision of his time could see. Those who did not like him would declare that he was self-satisfied and given to sounding his own praises, but this is not a just verdict. Arch came from a farm labourer's cottage and educated himself. By sheer force of character and honesty of purpose he came to the front and stayed there throughout his life, finding all manner of association of which he could not have dreamed in his early days. It is astonishing in truth that he remained so little affected and that from the first to the last he contrived to see so clearly all the essentials of the position he had taken up, the position that friends and foes alike endeavoured consciously or unconsciously to obscure. Many other men who have helped the worker have had the advantage of a fine education and a natural gift of expression. William Morris, for example, was working so to speak side by side with Joseph Arch, so were H. M. Hyndman, Mrs. Besant, Charles Bradlaugh, and scores of others who had entered into the arena armed with all the weapons of a sound education. They had not started their life's labour by earning 4d. a day at the age of nine, they had not given their early and middle age to tasks that provided no more than enough to give them food and shelter. Arch had a singularly big mind, but it had no room for either jealousy or hatred. He strove to understand his opponents and to be fair to them, and behind all the force of the political activities lay the simple faith of the Primitive Methodist, a faith that was ever to him a source of consolation and hope.

I think that if we read history aright, we shall find that all the great and helpful reformers have been men whose character has had a certain native simplicity. They have seen life truly, their minds have never been affected by current fable. History may have obscured their fame. All the friends of the people have been misinterpreted and derided in turn, but when the hour brings the man the evil conditions he was born to oppose yield to something better. The agricultural labourer's state to-day would have forced Joseph Arch to believe that the millennium had arrived ; we, looking at it perhaps with a clearer vision and aware of the enormous increased wealth of the world, hold that he is still living on the poverty line. We deny that any country can rightly consider itself civilized which leaves the farm worker in an insanitary cottage without a proper water supply or an effective drainage system, to bring up a family on the 30s. a week that is in many cases both the minimum and maximum wage. To be sure the toiler has his old age pension, the workhouse is no longer the reward of half a century's service to mother earth, but against this he is still without unemployment insurance and his cottage may be lost if he changes his job, because the farmer has only to say that he needs it for another worker and the law will come readily to his aid. He has proper medical attention and his children receive a better education than fell to the lot of Joseph Arch or even of his children ; we even have the beginnings of effective help in the shape of scholarships for farm workers' children. But we all know that more than half a million workers in this country do not get their meed of the necessities of life and that most of the little luxuries of normal existence pass them by. They must still plead in vain for allotments and small holdings, they get no really adequate return for their labours under the sun, and we of the Labour Party know that very much remains to be done before the man who produces the food by which we live can be held to have received his fair share.

There is nothing in this to diminish our gratitude
to Joseph Arch. Just as he fought against intolerable
conditions sixty years ago, so we are called upon to fight
conditions that are intolerable in a world that is sixty years
older and many times richer, a world in which transport
and inter-communication have given life new values of
which each one should have his portion. Nobody who
considers England as it was in the year 1826 when Arch
entered it, will be prepared to deny that we have made
progress in every direction. Our laws are more humane,
our social services have improved vastly, the national
conscience is more readily stirred, a feeling of brotherhood
is growing, however slowly. But all this is not enough,
the pace is too slow, there is no good and valid reason for
not accelerating. It is the duty of our Party to seek power
and having received it so to act that the reproach of the
hovel, the insufficient wage and the absence of all modern
conveniences shall be removed from our villages and those
who dwell therein. In doing this we shall put the roof to
the building of which Arch raised the foundations. We
have in this country literally more money than we know
what to do with; the honest three per cent. loan running
into millions of pounds will be over-subscribed in three
minutes. Why should we not have a National Regeneration
Loan to deal with town and country ? The former does not
concern me here, much though I may give of my waking
hours to its problems; the latter does. I say without
hesitation that it is within our power, if we will but strive
for it, to realize the dream of John Ball of whom
William Morris wrote, as well as the dream of Joseph Arch
who served generations yet unborn. When we too face
misrepresentation and obloquy, it is good to think of the
pioneer from the Barford cottage who started his life
unheeded outside the village street and so lived that when
he passed all men of good intent realized that he had been a
faithful servant of humanity. I am pleased to remember
after more than thirty years that when he set out the modest
story of his life he asked me to introduce it to the world.
None of the little services it has been my lot to render has
given me more pleasure. I honoured Joseph Arch.

JEREMY BENTHAM
1748–1832
by C. R. MORRIS

JEREMY BENTHAM
1748–1832
by C. R. MORRIS

JEREMY BENTHAM was not always a democrat. From his earliest years he was an enthusiast for the improvement of the conditions of life of the human race ; but it was only towards the end of a long life that he became a promoter of the idea of an educated democracy as the only practical solution of the problem of government. Yet it fell to him to exercise as great an influence as any thinker in history both on immediate reform in England and on the determination of the more permanent principles underlying the political development of the western world. This was not because Bentham is to be counted among the great philosophers or prophets. The real moral or philosophical insight contributed to mankind by him was negligible. His strength lay elsewhere. His indefatigable attention to the detailed application of his basic moral beliefs to practical issues exercised an extremely powerful influence in forcing men to recognise clearly what they really thought, and to see its bearing on actual problems of reform. The most striking thing about him was his genius for making the better side of public opinion operative and effective against obscurantism and insufficiently grounded conservatism. By this means he was enabled to be of the very greatest service to the cause of democracy.

Bentham was born at Houndsditch on 15th February, 1748. His great-grandfather was a prosperous pawnbroker in the city of London, where his grandfather and father practised as attorneys. His mother was the daughter of a shopkeeper at Andover. He was from the first a precocious child, beginning to learn Latin at the age of four. In 1755 he was sent to Westminster school, and in 1760 he was admitted to the Queen's College, Oxford. He had a very poor opinion of life at the University, the only sure effects of which on the students, he tells us, were " mendacity and insincerity." In 1763 he began to eat dinners at Lincoln's Inn, where he was called to the bar fifty-three

years later. The pleasantest memories of his youth were
associated with his life in the country when staying with
his grandmothers, at Browning Hill near Reading and at
a country house near Barking.

Bentham disappointed his father, an energetic and
pushing man, by his lack of success in his profession. He
held from the start that much of the money spent on liti-
gation would be better saved, and he did not conceal his
opinion from his clients. He began at once his speculations
on law and jurisprudence, and in 1776 he published
anonymously his *Fragment on Government*, in which he
offered a critical examination of the views about government
in general contained in the introduction to Sir William
Blackstone's *Commentaries on the Laws of England*. He
sought to expose a " universal inaccuracy and confusion "
pervading the whole of Blackstone's argument, and above
all to show up the author's complacency with existing
institutions and complete antipathy to reform. The
Fragment was but the first of a long line of papers which
flowed from his pen at short intervals, many of them unpublished and even unfinished, but all of them undertaken
in the passionate desire to demonstrate the practicability
and urgent desirability of particular reforms.

For the basic thing about Bentham was his conviction
that the new " science of human nature " could be applied
so as to improve greatly the conditions of human life.
Hume, he thought, had shown that it was possible to treat
morals like any other subject by the use of the experimental
method ; and that the growth of scientific knowledge in
this sphere was bound to bring with it a control over the
mind of man and the evils which afflicted the mind similar
to the control over physical nature brought by the discoveries
of Newton. This science, Bentham considered, had
demonstrated beyond question both the final aim of all
human endeavour and the means by which the achievement
of that aim was practicable. The aim he summed up in
the celebrated formula " the greatest happiness of the
greatest number," freely acknowledging the importance
of his personal debt to Hume. Speaking of the third book
of the *Treatise of Human Nature* he says : " No sooner had
I read that part of the work which touches on this subject

than I felt as if scales had fallen from my eyes. I then, for the first time, learnt to call the cause of the people the cause of Virtue . . . That the foundations of all *virtue* are laid in *utility*, is there demonstrated, after a few exceptions made, with the strongest evidence : but I see not, any more than Helvetius saw, what need there was for the exceptions."

Thus Bentham seems to have been delivered once for all from any danger of those doubts about the supreme end of man which have been the basic stimulus to the great philosophers. This freedom from fundamental doubt seems to be largely attributable, in him as in so many people to-day, to a faith in the credit of scientific method. Actually, of course, scientific method in the hands of Bentham served primarily, not to establish basic principles, but to work out in detail the conditions necessary to the production of happiness in general, and to determine what particular social conditions were likely to produce a maximum of happiness in a given society. But the philosopher —who has always been apt to look down on the speculations of Bentham—should not forget the significant fact that, in all the years in which he was indefatigably engaged in detailed applications, he never found cause for serious doubt about his general principle that happiness is ultimately the only thing of value. There seems little room for doubt that he really believed in it with his whole mind, and that he would have continued to believe in it in the face of any philosophical argument. And the success of his writings shows that he was writing to multitudes who believed in it no less than he did.

But what did Bentham understand by " happiness " ? He tells us that he learnt from Hartley to treat happiness as a sum of simple pleasures united by association. Happiness could thus be analysed into its simple component parts, and a calculus became possible of the capacity of particular actions and institutions to add to the sum of happiness in the world. The notion of pleasure can be made far more precise than the notion of happiness. The various kinds of pleasure found in experience can be distinguished and classified, as also can the conditions which give rise to the various kinds of pleasure. Moreover particular pleasures can be evaluated and compared by determining how much sacrifice of other pleasures people are prepared to make in order to secure them. A man will sacrifice five pints of ale to go to the theatre himself, and three or seven pints (as it may be) for the pleasure of enabling his wife to go to the theatre, and so on. The whole matter can be worked out experimentally.

We need not here examine the detail of Bentham's classification and calculus of pleasures. It will be sufficient to notice three things. First, he takes it for granted in his experiments for evaluating pleasures that every man is always pursuing his *own* pleasure. Secondly, he holds that what we ought to produce is the greatest possible *quantity* of pleasure, and that in order to achieve this every one must be treated as one, and no one—not even the agent—must be treated as more than one. Thirdly, he does not take seriously beyond a certain point apparent differences of *kind* in pleasures, since he holds the " scientific " view that they can be reduced by experimental investigation to differences of quantity, by finding out how much of the less intense will in practice be sacrificed for the more intense pleasure.

Now it is clear that in the hands of an industrious and able publicist this calculus of Bentham's is capable of becoming an extremely powerful weapon for organising public opinion in favour of specific reforms. And this is the use that Bentham made of it. Had he been of a different temperament, his utilitarian principle might have led him to become a defender of conservatism like Hume or Burke, to justify " Christian optimism " like Hartley, or like Godwin to bury himself in speculation about the society which ought to be. But actually his strength lay in the fact that he gave his attention always to the next step, whatever that might be, and turned the very powerful machinery of his philosophy on to the task of showing in the most compelling detail that a given particular reform was urgently necessary. In doing this he appealed not to men of goodwill, but to men of intelligence. And it was this which made his arguments so often seem unanswerable. If once his general standpoint was accepted, then the cogency of his ratiocination to particular conclusions could be effectively questioned only by those who were able and willing to go into the detail of the matter in hand with as much industry and ingenuity as Bentham himself had done. He offered both mathematical elaborateness and the most detailed and carefully chosen appeals to experience ; and this combination proved unassailable to all who accepted his general position.

Moreover, the important fact is that his general position was just sufficiently in line with the moral insight of his age. In a world which was emerging from the " age of reason " it was reasonable, intelligible rather than mystical ; for the Romantic it gave some priority to emotion and feeling ; in a world which was fascinated by science it based itself on a scientific investigation of human nature, and could use a scientific apparatus to apply its principles with the greatest precision to the remotest detail. Nor must we neglect an element within the Benthamite philosophy which unequivocally appeals to the deepest intuitions of the human heart, regardless of time and place and conditions : namely, its intransigent hostility to pain. There are many who will hardly stir themselves for the promotion of pleasure but will do a great deal for the alleviation of pain. And in so far as Bentham could sufficiently demonstrate that the absence of some particular reform was causing a large amount of unnecessary human misery, he had a case which would have proved a strong one if presented at the bar of any century or generation, particularly as his dispassionate investigations of detail and his elaborate calculations palpably acquit him of any improper sentimentalism.

The force of Bentham's appeal is well illustrated—to take only one case—by his impressive advocacy of reforms in English penal law. He condemned the complicated and haphazard nature of the existing law. In 1765 a hundred and sixty different crimes were punishable with death ; and according to Bentham there were a hundred executions for forgery between February, 1800, and April, 1801. England, which had been universally regarded as a model in juridical matters earlier in the 18th century, had since the French Revolution dropped behind continental countries. Abuses were due, according to Bentham, to the gradual and haphazard way in which judicial practice came to be determined by the actual procedure of a corporation of lawyers with wrong-headed " classical " notions based on no rational principle, and with a sinister interest of its own. What was wanted was codification. In the case of penal law Bentham worked out an elaborate classification of crimes and of punishments based on the principle of utility. Punishment ought not to be based upon feeling —upon hatred and the instinct for retaliation. Moreover, punishment of crime is not in itself a good, as the classical lawyer considers it. Being the infliction of pain, it is an evil ; and there should be no more evil in the world than is absolutely necessary—that is, the evil of the punishment must not be greater than the good of the resultant service to the community. Now the chief service which it renders to the community is the prevention of crime, by the incapacitation and deterrence of criminals. What is needed, therefore, is an exact calculation of the particular amount of punishment required to deter men from particular crimes. This calculation Bentham undertook and carried to great lengths with his moral arithmetic. He recognises four relevant qualities of punishment ; intensity, proximity, certainty, and duration. Like all enquirers who have closely considered the practical details he lays great stress on certainty. What is lost in certainty has to be made up in intensity and duration ; and this process soon fails to achieve its purpose, since when the punishment appears disproportionate to the crime juries will not convict. The general effect of Bentham's careful examination of the deterrent effect of punishments was that he for the most part advocated lighter penalties. But he was not a sentimentalist. The infliction of any pain, he held, offends against sentiment, and sentimentalism would therefore have to demand that there should be no punishment at all. Since there obviously must be punishment, we must put sentiment behind us altogether and approach the whole matter in a thoroughly detached, dispassionate, scientific spirit of careful exactitude. We should not aim at making punishments " mild," we should aim at making them " economic." Thus where temptation to crime is strong, the quantity of punishment must be increased—a thoroughly non-sentimentalist judgment. The beginning and the end of the matter must rest with a careful calculation of the pleasures and pains involved, carried through with the greatest attention to detail. No other principle must be allowed to interfere.

Thus, when we turn to his politics, we shall not be surprised to find that the temper of Bentham was not initially democratic. It was a very long time before he became convinced that there was any need for him to interest himself in constitutional questions at all. He had not considered that the application of the principle of utility to social questions pointed to the necessity of any one form of government rather than any other. Indeed in the early days he was really thinking in terms of paternalistic autocracies ; he was thinking of Catherine, of Joseph, of Gustavus, and of Leopold. He dreamed of all that could be accomplished by a benevolent despot with a Benthamite philosopher at his side. Similarly, he thought at first that the government of his own country had only to be convinced of the desirability and practicability of any reform in order to undertake it.

But in course of time, when all his philanthropic schemes seemed to be coming to nothing, Bentham became disillusioned in this regard. He was convinced that it was because of " sinister interests " that his obviously intelligent suggestions were not acted upon, and that the governing classes of this country did not want reform. Moreover, there had come meanwhile the French Revolution to shake the thrones of princes and to modify the ideas of philosophers regarding what could be achieved by autocrats. And Bentham perforce began to turn his attention to constitutional matters, and set his foot upon the road which led him inevitably to democracy. He took this direction in his enthusiasm to get something done, because he thought that an aristocracy would not do it. His was no visionary dream of a millennial society in which, just because it was a democracy, everything would be perfect and no government action would be required. He had the reformer's conviction that active government is essential on this earth. It is true that his philosophy taught that law, and obligation to obey law, is in itself evil since it necessarily restricts liberty : he had no patience with the view that obligation to obey law *is* liberty. But though

government action is at bottom an evil, it is, according to
Bentham, an absolutely necessary evil. In working out
his ideas of democracy, therefore, he was looking for a
form of government which should provide, not simply
a bulwark against improper action, but an organ for proper
action, to be undertaken with vigour at the dictates of
philosophic intelligence. What Bentham expected from
democracy was active good government.

In order that we may take Bentham's thought in its
proper order, we must first ask what he understood by
good government. Here Bentham was profoundly affected
by the economic theory of Adam Smith as well as by the
psychological theories of Hartley and of Hume. From
the former he learned, or thought he learned, that everything
would be for the best in this world if only every man
intelligently pursued his own interest ; from the latter he
concluded that an understanding of the mechanism of the
association of ideas would give to the legislators tremendous
power to educate citizens to recognise their true interests,
and so to control their actions and secure harmonious
collaboration in the pursuit of the welfare of everybody.
Of course, Bentham was not a mere disciple either of
Adam Smith or of Hartley. He took from them certain
doctrines which he considered their researches had
established and used them for his own purposes, sometimes
with results that can only strike the student as curious.

This is seen most clearly in the case of Adam Smith.
It has commonly been held that the theory of government
which is required by Adam Smith's economic doctrines
is the theory of *laissez-faire*, in the widest sense. The
Wealth of Nations seemed to show that the inimitable
laws of the universe would of themselves bring about
the greatest happiness of mankind, if only governments
would not interfere with the working of those beneficent
laws. If every man intelligently pursued his own good
by selling in the dearest market and buying in the cheapest,
the wealth, and therefore the welfare, of man would
automatically become the greatest possible, and the universe
would of its own motion bring itself to its own millennium.

Now it is obvious that when a thinker who essentially
believes in active government comes to turn to his own

use this *laissez-faire* doctrine, something curious is bound to happen. It is true that a reconciliation would be possible by distinguishing between the *interim* and the long run. Bentham might simply have argued that in the meanwhile sinister interests, for unfortunate historical reasons, do not allow the proper operation of these beneficent laws, and that vigorous government action is necessary for the time being in order to establish the conditions necessary for a free market. But it was not in accord with Bentham's temper to stop at this. He was primarily a rationalist and a reformer, not a romantic believer in naturalism or a democratic optimist. He believed not in some hidden power of human nature to secure the good of itself without legislation or government organisation, but in the power of science to enable the legislator to secure the good for man. Like Adam Smith he believed that the good of all can only be produced by men acting in the intelligent pursuit each of his own interest. But as a legislator he wished to take this into account in so manipulating the state of affairs that every man in pursuing his own good will also be pursuing the good of everybody. The world can be so arranged, he thought—the science of economics has shown this—that everyone can seek his own advantage without prejudice to the advantage of others. It is possible, of course, for it not to be so arranged : it is not so arranged at present. But it is the duty of the legislator, assisted by his knowledge of economics and of psychology, so to arrange it. In a word, Bentham believed, not that the interests of everybody are even naturally harmonised, but that they can be artificially harmonised by well thought out government action.

Such an arrangement of society, he thought, must commend itself to every intelligent man. Why, then, did not the Government, overwhelmed by his convincing arguments, embark with haste upon the necessary reforms ? The answer which Bentham gave to himself was this. As society is constituted at present there are important bodies of people, e.g. the legal profession, whose interests are bound up with things which are not to the interest of everybody. There is no need for this to be so, and in a scientifically ordered society it will not be so ; but in

the meantime these " sinister interests " cannot be induced
to be enthusiastic advocates of change. It might be easy
enough to convert that section of the people who are badly
treated by the existing conditions of society to support
reform ; but it is not easy to induce those who are comparatively well off in the existing state of affairs to take
the risk of advocating change. And unfortunately the
latter are for the most part powerful and intelligent, and
the former are uneducated and without influence. Hence
the difficulties which face the reformer. The solution
to which Bentham was driven was that an intelligent
social structure will never be brought into being except
in a community where everybody has an equal vote and
everybody is educated enough to understand his own
best interest. Even such a community will not go far
without its enlightened legislator, its Bentham. But with
his help it will be secure ; for when he puts forward a
demonstrably effective reform, it will not be deterred by
the influence of apparent sectional interests, but will press
forward at once to secure the interest of each and everybody.

Bentham's democratic faith will no doubt strike many
democrats as peculiar, in that he had no very great feeling
either for liberty or for equality. It is commonly said that
English democratic institutions bear the mark of having
been built up by men who passionately cared for *the liberty
of the subject* ; and it is often added that the Englishman,
who has so much of it himself, is singularly inappreciative
of what is meant by the *political liberty of the citizen*. If
this is so, Bentham is uncharacteristic in the first respect
and highly characteristic in the second. He was impatient
of any talk of political liberty in anything like the sense
of Rousseau, of Hegel, or of Green. He considered that
a man was free only when he was controlling his own
affairs. Restraint upon the individual by his fellows is
always restraint, no matter what the form of government ;
and as restraint it is evil. It is only justified if it produces
a greater good. As regards personal freedom itself
Bentham's disciple, John Stuart Mill, was, of course, a
passionate defender of such liberty for its own sake and
at any cost ; and great trouble it caused him when he came
to defend the philosophy of Utilitarianism. But Bentham

himself, true to his own principle, regarded personal
freedom as of relative importance only. Experience shows,
he held, that security is in the last resort more essential
to happiness than liberty. Therefore security is the pre-
eminent good, and, where necessary, the demands of liberty
must give way. Nothing, not even freedom, must stand
in the way of the production of happiness.

As for equality, here too Bentham maintained the integrity
of his utilitarian principle. But since he held it to be
demonstrable that the greatest possible happiness can be
produced only if in the distribution of happiness everyone
counts as one and none as more than one, it might appear
that Bentham sufficiently believed in equalitarianism
notwithstanding. But, it must be remarked, he did not
consider that the establishment of a regime of equality
of political rights would tend to establish economic equality ;
nor did he see any reason for thinking it desirable that it
should do so. Believing whole-heartedly, as he did, that the
price mechanism, if left to itself, exerts a beneficent influence
on production, and therefore on human welfare, he thought
the inevitable division into rich and poor to be a natural
and reasonable one, quite conducive to happiness. He
thought the influence of the rich over the poor capable
of being—what it should be—an influence of intelligence
over intelligence, not one of will over will. It would then
be part of the order of a beneficent nature, enabling the
less gifted of mankind to live in a wealthier, and therefore
a happier, world than they could have done if deprived
of the advantages accruing from an efficient division of
labour. Bentham did not anticipate that economic differences might of themselves operate to make a political
democracy incapable of being truly democratic. It may
be thought that in these matters experience has shown
Bentham to have been the victim of a shallow optimism.
But it should be remembered in his favour, for what it is
worth, that he never supposed true democracy to be
practicable without a thorough-going system of education ;
and that therefore experience has not yet been given a
proper opportunity finally to prove him wrong.

But, be that as it may, the most striking thing about
Bentham is that, when towards the end of a long life he

fully identified himself with the cause of democracy, he
did undoubtedly exercise a direct effect on the actual
development of political institutions in England. At the
time of the epoch-making election of 1807, when the
electorate of Westminster, tired alike of Tory and of Whig,
returned Sir Francis Burdett as a popular candidate,
pledged to electoral reform, Bentham had not been prepared
to extend the suffrage beyond those who paid rates. But
in 1817, when he published his *Plan of Parliamentary
Reform, in the Form of a Catechism with reasons for each
Article*, he argued plainly in his Introduction that any
" moderate reform " must prove insufficient and that
" radical reform " was absolutely necessary. In the following year—he was now seventy years of age—he drew up
twenty-six *Resolutions on Parliamentary Reform*, which
Burdett made the subject of a resolution in the Commons.
Herein he demanded secret ballot ; manhood suffrage—he
saw no reason why women should not be entrusted with
the vote, but he thought public opinion was not ready
for the change ; a fresh election at least once a year ; the
division of Great Britain and Ireland into six hundred
and fifty-eight districts as nearly as possible equal in
population, with further sub-divisions to facilitate expedition
in receiving votes ; and all elections to be begun and ended
on the same day. As usual, he worked out in great detail
the institutional changes, including those for local government, necessary to ensure effective democracy.

Of course, Bentham's adoption of the Radical cause
modified the character and reputation of Radicalism.
He was known never to have had any sympathy with
Jacobinism in any form, and, as we have seen, he was not
a believer in economic equalitarianism. He had held in
earlier days that the best form of government for a nation
is that which is fitted to the habits and temper of its people ;
and in his enthusiasm for democracy he did not forget
this. Arguing that universal suffrage, as advocated by
Radicalism on the basis of the principle of the artificial
identification of interests, was not dangerous, but was
in full accord with the spirit of English constitutional
tradition, he gave to the cause of thorough-going reform
a reasonableness and a respectability which perhaps did

more than anything else could have done to advance it into the sphere of practical politics. He followed in the tradition of Locke as an extreme advocate of free speech, holding that the temperate expression of any opinion whatever, if it was honestly held, might be abundantly justified on the principle of utility. In 1823 he sought to assist towards the education of opinion by financing the foundation of the *Westminster Review*, which exercised great influence for a time. Indeed, in his last years he bent all his characteristic conscientiousness and indefatigable energy to the promotion of the twin causes of education and of democracy.

He died on June 6th, 1832, two days after the Reform Bill had passed its Third Reading, and one day before it received the Royal Assent.

JOHN BRIGHT

1811–1889

by H. G. WOOD (Quaker Author)

JOHN BRIGHT

1811–1889

by H. G. WOOD

"I BELIEVE there is no permanent greatness to a nation except it be based upon morality. I do not care for military greatness or military renown. I care for the condition of the people among whom I live. There is no man in England who is less likely to speak irreverently of the Crown and Monarchy of England than I am ; but crowns, coronets, mitres, military display, the pomp of war, wide colonies, and a huge empire, are, in my view, all trifles light as air, and not worth considering, unless with them you can have a fair share of comfort, contentment, and happiness among the great body of the people. Palaces, baronial castles, great halls, stately mansions, do not make a nation. The nation in every country dwells in the cottage ; and unless the light of your constitution can shine there, unless the beauty of your legislation and the excellence of your statesmanship are impressed there on the feelings and conditions of the people, rely upon it you have yet to learn the duties of government."*

In this oft-quoted passage from the speech on Foreign Policy delivered to his constituents in Birmingham on October 29, 1858, we may find a summary of the principles which inspired the activity of John Bright from his earliest campaign for the abolition of the Corn Laws until his death in 1889. His claim to be a democrat rests not on his devotion to democracy as a form of government but on his concern for the moral and economic welfare of the common folk. From first to last he was preoccupied with the feelings and condition of the people—their freedom and self-respect, their happiness, and their material comfort and well-being.

When as a young business man John Bright began to interest himself in politics, two movements competed for his attention and active support, the Anti-Corn-Law League

* Speeches of John Bright, ed. Thorold Rogers ; Vol. II, p. 397.

and the Chartists' agitation. Had John Bright been primarily a theoretical democrat, he would have thrown in his lot with the Chartists. He was destined to gain for his fellow-countrymen the substance of the Charter in the campaign for Reform from 1858 to 1867, which won him the title of Tribune of the People, and which was carried to victory when Disraeli induced a Tory government to legislate along the lines laid down by John Bright. Yet when his first wife died in 1841, he did not seek relief from sorrow by becoming the champion of Chartism. At Cobden's suggestion, he took up the cause of securing cheap bread. He had already shown his interest in this question as early as 1839, and in that year in his own town of Rochdale he had undergone the rather humiliating experience of addressing an open-air meeting which adopted a Chartist amendment to the resolution which he had submitted in condemnation of the Corn Laws. The amendment stressed the futility of expecting a repeal of the Corn Laws from an unreformed Parliament, and declared that " the present Corn Law agitation is made up for the purpose of diverting the minds of the people from the only remedy of all political grievances."* John Bright's adhesion to the Corn Law agitation was not determined by any lack of interest in Reform and his action was itself a refutation of the construction which the Chartists put upon that agitation. But his judgment is characteristic. John Bright used to disclaim the title of statesman as being of a dubious honour, but he had the true statesman's sense for what is at any given moment practical politics. He rejected Chartism, because some of the six points were visionary and unwise, as, for example, the demand for annual parliaments, because the Charter was being advocated in a spirit of class-conscious revolution, because public opinion was not ready even for the sound elements in the Chartist movement, and because cheap food was a more urgent necessity than manhood suffrage.

John Bright was a manufacturer, and he felt the Corn Laws as a hindrance to the development of industry and commerce. This he never concealed. He entered on the campaign against the Corn Laws the more hopefully,

* Trevelyan, p. 31.

because the middle classes, especially mill-owners like himself, were as interested as the working classes in the repeal of the Corn Laws. Chartism had some middle-class supporters, but it did not unite class interests as did the cause of repeal, and it tended under the leadership of Feargus O'Connor to repudiate middle-class support. There was more hope of getting rid of the duties on corn, because every class in the community, except the land-lords, would gain by their removal. It is important to remember the way in which John Bright expected manu-facturers to benefit. The Chartists, taking their stand on Ricardo's principle that profits vary inversely with wages, and relying on the iron law of wages, by which it is assumed that wages tend always to subsistence level, denied that the workers would benefit by a fall in the price of corn. Wages would fall proportionately. The workers would be no better off, and only the industrialists would secure any advantage. Their line of reasoning was not sound, and, even if it had been sound, John Bright and the greater number of manufacturers and mill-owners who supported the Anti-Corn-Law League were not influenced by such considerations. They were not out to secure cheaper labour, but to find a better market at home and abroad. They calculated that if the workers could satisfy their fundamental need for bread more cheaply, they would have more to spend on clothes and the products of Lancashire mills. They also believed that if foreigners could sell more corn and foodstuffs to us, they would buy more manufactured goods from us. John Bright did not fail to press home these considerations, but his fundamental concern was the condition of the people. He was living through the Hungry Forties, and the relief of hunger was a first charge on his sympathy and energy. Moreover, the Corn Laws could be denounced as simply evil. They were a piece of class-selfishness, and of short-sighted class-selfishness. Here was an institution as indefensible as slavery itself, and John Bright could join in the agitation against the Corn Laws without reserve. The issues involved in Chartism were more complex, and whole-hearted support was not so easily given. A capacity to concentrate on clear issues is a great gift in democratic leadership, and John Bright showed he possessed this gift by his first essay in political propaganda.

The movement to repeal the Corn Laws owed its victory to the pressure of circumstances even more than to the weight of argument. The Irish famine of 1845 led Sir Robert Peel eventually to abolish the duties and to establish Free Trade in the fullest measure in which the country had yet known it. Bright was thus set free for other tasks. The improvement of the standards of living of the masses was still the lode-star of his political activity.

" Peace, Retrenchment, and Reform " were causes linked together in his mind by his concern for the welfare of the people. John Bright will always be remembered for his opposition to Palmerston's foreign policy, especially during the Crimean War. John Bright was a Quaker, but he did not base his criticisms of public policy on the ground that war is always wrong. During the Civil War in America at least he believed that it was better for the North to continue the conflict than to compromise with the South on the issue of slavery. But as a Quaker he distrusted the meddlesome pugnacity of Palmerston, to which John Bull appeared to respond so readily. He opposed consistently any proposals for this country to engage in war, because he was convinced that the objects for which the Government proposed to wage war were either unworthy in themselves or, if good and desirable, not such as to justify the costs of war. Moreover, the costs of war are certain and heavy, while the achievement of the desired ends is hazardous and improbable. John Bright was never tired of dilating on the wastefulness of war, alike in life and treasure. What do nations get out of war ? The evils of intolerable poverty and social unrest. Pleading for peace in 1853, and pleading in vain on the eve of the Crimea, John Bright reminded his hearers of the state of the country after the close of the Napoleonic wars. " War will find you all out at home by withering up the resources of the prosperity enjoyed by the middle and working classes of the country . . . You who lived during the period from 1815 to 1822 may remember that this country was probably never in a more uneasy position. The sufferings of the working classes were beyond description, and the difficulties, and struggles, and bankruptcies of the middle classes were such as few persons have a just idea of. There was scarcely a year in which there was not an incipient insurrection in some parts of the country, arising from the sufferings which the working classes endured."* As in the Corn Law agitation, John Bright stresses the community of interest, the community of loss and suffering, of the middle and working classes. I may note, in passing, that one reason for Fascist reactions in our post-war world is that Socialists so often ignore or deny this community of interest. It was part of Bright's strength as a democratic leader that he never forgot it, nay that he insisted on it and built on it. Yet once again be it observed that his fundamental concern was the burden of pauperism imposed by war on the workers.

In the same speech on Peace, he stressed the danger to existing institutions that inevitably results from war, and he would to-day no doubt argue the futility of seeking to make the world safe for democracy by war. In 1853 he spoke of the danger to the monarchy, to-day he would speak of the threat to Parliamentary government. " Rely on it, that injustice of any kind, be it bad laws, or be it a bloody, unjust, and unnecessary war, of necessity creates perils to every institution in the country. If the Corn Law had continued, if it had been impossible, by peaceful agitation, to abolish it, the monarchy itself would not have survived the ruin and disaster that it must have wrought. And if you go into a war now, with a doubled population, with a vast commerce, with extended credit, and a wider diffusion of partial education among the people, let there ever come a time like the period between 1815 and 1822, when the whole basis of society is upheaving with a sense of intolerable suffering, I ask you, how many years' purchase would you give even for the venerable and mild monarchy under which you have the happiness to live ? I confess when I think of the tremendous perils into which unthinking men—men who do not intend to fight themselves—are willing to drag or to hurry this country, I am amazed how they can trifle with interests

* Speeches of John Bright, ed. Thorold Rogers ; Vol. II, p. 368.

so vast, and consequences so much beyond their calculation."*

It may fairly be claimed that John Bright detected and exposed the *Great Illusion* before Norman Angell, though he did not deal with the difficulties of collecting indemnities —difficulties which our generation has painfully re-discovered. He perceived, however, that if wars are waged on borrowed money, a particular class of fund-holders may stand to gain. He perceived also that the gains of war, if any gains there be, whether in honour or power or loot, accrued to the governing and landowning classes. It is always easy for a class to imagine that policies which benefit itself benefit the nation, but the imagination is usually deceptive. As John Bright surveyed the foreign policy of Great Britain from the time of William III, he thought that the objects pursued were mistaken, and the outpouring of blood and treasure for the most part sheer loss. The maintenance of the balance of power in Europe seemed to him as futile as the pursuit of the will o' the wisp. Yet such fruitless efforts could hardly have been so pro-longed had not someone gained by them. To the question, " did nobody gain ? " John Bright returned a still famous answer. " Do you not observe at a glance, that, from the time of William III, by reason of the foreign policy which I denounce, wars have been multiplied, taxes increased, loans made, and the sums of money which every year the Government has to expend augmented, and that so the patronage at the disposal of Ministers must have increased also, and the families who were enthroned and made powerful in the legislation and administration of the country must have had the first pull at, and the largest profit out of, that patronage ?

" The more you examine this matter the more you will come to the conclusion which I have arrived at, that this foreign policy, this regard for ' the liberties of Europe,' this care at one time for the ' Protestant interests,' this excessive love for ' the balance of power,' is neither more nor less than a gigantic system of out-door relief for the aristocracy of Great Britain."* In the same speech in another well-known passage, Bright dealt with the fallacy

* Speeches of John Bright, ed. Thorold Rogers ; Vol. II, p. 369.

that a great revenue is a sign of national prosperity, and a
huge national debt an asset to the country. Lord John
Russell had coquetted with these dangerous sentiments
and Bright answered him thus : " Some people believe
that it is a good thing to pay a great revenue to the State.
Even so eminent a man as Lord John Russell is not without
a delusion of this sort. Lord John Russell, as you have
heard, while speaking of me in flattering and friendly
terms, says he is unfortunately obliged to differ from me
frequently ; therefore, I suppose, there is no particular
harm in my saying that I am sometimes obliged to differ
from him. Some time ago he was a great star in the northern
hemisphere, shining, not with unaccustomed, but with
his usual brilliancy at Liverpool. He made a speech, in
which there was a great deal to be admired, to a meeting
composed, it was said, to a great extent of working-men ;
and in it he stimulated them to a feeling of pride in the
greatness of their country and in being citizens of a State
which enjoyed a revenue of £100,000,000 a year, which
included the revenues of the United Kingdom and of British
India. But I think it would have been far more to the
purpose if he could have congratulated the working-men
of Liverpool on this vast Empire being conducted in an
orderly manner, on its laws being well administered and
well obeyed, its shores sufficiently defended, its people
prosperous and happy, on a revenue of £20,000,000. The
State indeed, of which Lord John Russell is a part, may
enjoy a revenue of £100,000,000, but I am afraid the
working-man can only be said to enjoy it in the sense
in which men not very choice in their expressions say that
for a long time they have enjoyed ' very bad health.' "*

The advocacy of non-intervention by Cobden and
Bright was in strict antithesis to Palmerston's habitual
policy of hectoring and bluff—a policy which was repudiated
later almost as emphatically by Lord Salisbury as by Bright
himself. It is probable that Bright's survey of British
foreign policy is unduly coloured by Palmerston's conduct.
The temper of foreign policy in the time of William III or
of William Pitt was not really so irresponsible as in the

---

* Speeches of John Bright, ed. Thorold Rogers ; Vol. II, pp.
387–388.

days of Palmerston. The dangers which some earlier
wars were intended to avert were not so remote or imaginary
as Bright suggested. Non-intervention might be tanta-
mount to selfish isolation, and to a refusal to participate
in a system of collective security. Yet in reality John
Bright was pointing to the abandonment of war as an
instrument of policy, and if non-intervention be so
understood, it is essential to the new international order.
Immediately Bright offered the much-needed corrective
to Palmerston. His stand against the war with Russia,
which brought on him the wrath of no lesser persons than
Tennyson and Martineau, in the end served to convince
the majority of his fellow-countrymen that Crimea was
an anagram for a crime. His fidelity during the Crimean
war gave him influence in stemming the demand for warlike measures in later years. When Palmerston seemed
ready to challenge his late ally Napoleon III over the
annexation of Savoy in 1860, Bright was able to strengthen
effectively the opposition. There was indeed good reason
to distrust Napoleon III, of whom Palmerston said that
" his brain is as full of schemes as a rabbit-warren is full
of holes." Like subsequent dictators, Napoleon III did
not inspire confidence abroad. But Bright was justified
in opposing the war with France on which Palmerston
would have liked to embark. In 1864 and in 1870, he
pleaded for non-intervention on the grounds that the
issues were not clear, and that no British interest was so
closely involved as to justify British participation in the
wars between Germany and Denmark, and between
Germany and France. He resigned from the Cabinet in
1882 rather than be a party to the bombardment of
Alexandria. To him, this coercion of Egypt might have
seemed little better than Palmerston's bullying of Greece
to collect the debts of Don Pacifico. Unless the interests,
the true, highest interests of the people were involved, there
could in Bright's view be no possible justification for a
country's engaging in a war. Though he would not have
England depart from the attitude of benevolent neutrality
during the American Civil War, yet he had no doubt
that the interests, the highest interests of the common
people were involved in the struggle, and he could not

wish the war to end except with the success of the North.

War then meant for John Bright the ruthless sacrifice of the welfare and progress of the people for no adequate end. Retrenchment claimed his support on similar grounds. Any government is liable to be extravagant with public money. Irresponsible military governments are almost invariably wasteful. His main criticism of the government of India is directed towards its excessive cost, which again is associated with the militarist policy of pushing forward the frontiers of empire. Like many others John Bright was attracted to Gladstone by the soundness and brilliance of the latter's handling of the national finances in 1859 and in the following years, when Gladstone was Chancellor of the Exchequer. Gladstone stood for economy in the spending departments, for reduction of the burden of taxation, particularly of indirect taxation. It was at this time that, in spite of the opposition of the House of Lords, Gladstone abolished the paper-duty, which constituted a tax upon knowledge. This action secured for democracy the possibility of a cheap press. We may now be more conscious of the disadvantages attaching to this boon, but that Gladstone's finance was a triumph for democracy cannot be questioned. At least one artificial barrier between the public and the securing of printed information had been swept away. Bright from henceforth recognised in Gladstone an ally and a leader.

His conduct of the campaign for Reform from 1858 to 1867 was probably his greatest single achievement. The details of Reform Bills no longer concern us. Bright's great aim was the enfranchisement of the workers. He was prepared to welcome any proposals for Reform, however inadequate, if they involved the addition of even a small number of workers to the electorate. Any recognition of the principle that the workers have the right to vote was better than their complete exclusion from the polling-booth. In a series of public speeches in the autumn of 1866, Bright outlined the case for Reform, and his exposition of the principles underlying representative government convinced the nation.

If we analyse these principles, we may put first the connection between the right to vote and the development

and maintenance of self-respect. Speaking in Glasgow
in 1858, Bright expressed himself thus : " But I observe
in some newspaper, I am not sure whether it was one in
your city—it is said that I have failed to show to the working
classes how giving them a vote could be of the smallest
advantage to them. I believe that it would be of one
advantage to them in the way of raising their self-respect.
I have seen thousands of men who have no votes, at the
nomination of candidates, attending polling-booths, with
looks of great anxiety, and often with looks of great
dejection. I believe that if the major part of those men
were enfranchised, the effect upon their minds and morals
and general condition would be obvious and signal. The
great secret of raising any man who has been brought
up to what may be called the inferior occupations of life,
is to find out something to increase his self-respect. If
a man becomes possessed with that feeling—if a man sees
any way among his fellow-workmen, and in your numerous
societies, benevolent or otherwise, by which he can make
himself of use—you will at once see the change in the
character of the man, and that what was before either
stupid or low in his nature seems to be removed and
diminished, and you will find that the man has become
wiser, and nobler, and happier. I believe that when you
admit the general body of our artisans upon the roll of
electors . . . you will do as much to raise their self-
respect, to give them at least the rudiments and elements
of the higher class of citizenship, as you can do by all the
other means that you now have in operation with a view
of improving the condition of the working classes."*
The possession of the vote establishes self-respect : the
withholding of the vote implies contempt for the people
or distrust of the people by the governing classes. Arguing
in the House of Commons in support of Lord Russell's
Reform Bill of 1866, Bright said, " Would it not be
infinitely better to show our trust in the people now ?
Of all the follies and crimes which Governments commit,
that of a constant distrust of their subjects, of their citizens,
of their country, is about the wildest and most foolish."†

* Speeches of John Bright, ed. by Thorold Rogers ; pp. 69–70.
† *ibid.*, p. 146.

The response of the working-man to his own clear and carefully thought-out appeals had convinced Bright of the honesty and soundness of judgment of the class for whose enfranchisement he was pleading. On the Corn Laws " the great minister of State had not comprehended the question . . . so well as the working-men of England comprehended it." Through the American Civil War, Lancashire operatives had remained loyal to the North and to freedom for the slaves, though their own economic interests attached them to the cause of the South. Working-men had understood the issues involved, while the governing classes in England had inclined to the wrong side, and even Gladstone had been misled. Bright believed in the good sense of British working-men. He resented warmly Robert Lowe's assumption that an extension of the franchise would only increase the elements of venality, drunkenness, ignorance and intimidation in the electorate. Bright deservedly stigmatised this assumption as the Botany Bay view of our countrymen. In the same spirit of respect for his fellows, he had on an earlier occasion rebuked British snobbery in dealing with our fellow-subjects in India. " I would not," he said in 1858, " I would not permit any man in my presence, without rebuke, to indulge in the calumnies and expressions of contempt which I have recently heard poured forth without measure upon the whole population of India."* The same fear and the same snobbery, which marked the attitude of the British governing classes towards the Indian people after the Mutiny, were apparent in the opposition to the Reform Bill.

John Bright's resistance to the Factory Act of 1847— a resistance which we now regard as mistaken—was in the main due to two considerations. He and his brother were model employers and on good terms with their own workpeople. So Bright underestimated the shortcomings of other employers. But, in any case, he thought the workers should defend and secure their own interests by direct negotiation with employers. The workers would thus maintain their independence and self-respect.

Curiously enough, John Bright did not at the latter end of his life support the women's suffrage movement. If

* Quoted in Trevelyan, p. 267.

pressed, he might have admitted that women no less than
the workers were entitled to such stimulus to self-respect
and such recognition of the respect due to them as the
possession of the vote may provide. But Bright's hesitation
about votes for women really sprang from the fact that
he had not the confidence in the judgment of women
voters which he reposed in working-men voters. On
this issue his judgment on a matter of democratic principle
was modified, not to say warped, by his judgment as a
practical politician. He thought women's suffrage " would
tend to strengthen the party which had opposed every
good measure for the last thirty years, and add to the
power of priest-craft."* If he had not been impressed
with the political good sense of working-men, we may
doubt whether he would have espoused the cause of Reform
so earnestly.

Perhaps the finest of his speeches on Reform was that
delivered in Glasgow on October 16, 1866. Here he
stresses Lord Acton's argument, that no single class is
fit to govern, and that a government or a House of
Commons in which every class is represented is most
likely to be the instrument of justice. For " justice
is impossible from a class. It is most certain and easy
from a nation : and I believe we can only reach the depths
of ignorance and misery and crime in this country by an
appeal to the justice, the intelligence, and the virtues of
the entire people." He analyses fairly the difficulty of
the rich in understanding the outlook of the masses and
in legislating for them, and he urges the advantages that
would come from combining the wisdom and experience
of different classes. " I am of opinion that the rich people
of a country, invested with power, and speaking generally
for rich people alone, cannot sufficiently care for the
multitude and the poor. They are personally kind enough,
but they do not care for the people in the bulk. . . . We
know very well all of us how much we are influenced by
the immediate circumstances by which we are surrounded.
The rich find everything just as they like. The country
needs no reform. There is no other country in the world
so pleasant for rich people as this country. But I deny

* The Diaries of John Bright, p. 379, n.

altogether that the rich alone are qualified to legislate
for the poor, any more than that the poor alone would be
qualified to legislate for the rich. My honest belief is,
that if we could be all called upon to legislate for all,
all would be more justly treated, and would be more happy
than we are now. We should have then an average ; we
should have the influence of wealth and of high culture,
and of those qualities that come from leisure, and the
influence of those more robust qualities that come from
industry and from labour."*

The extension of the franchise " would bring the
rich and the great more into contact with the people, and
into a better acquaintance with human wants and with
the necessities and feelings of their countrymen." He
desired to see the workers enfranchised, not because he
wanted to substitute the power of the workers for the
power of another class, but because he wanted the whole
nation to share in the responsibilities and tasks of government. This is the appeal of his peroration at Glasgow.
" I believe that ignorance and suffering might be lessened
to an incalculable extent, and that many an Eden, beauteous
in flowers and rich in fruits, might be raised up in the
waste wilderness which spreads before us. But no class
can do that. The class which has hitherto ruled in this
country has failed miserably. It revels in power and wealth,
whilst at its feet, a terrible peril for its future, lies the
multitude which it has neglected. If a class has failed, let
us try the nation. That is our faith, that is our purpose,
that is our cry—Let us try the nation."†

John Bright was a great Parliamentarian. At a time like
the present when representative institutions are at a discount
and the House of Commons is disparaged as a talking-
shop, it is well to weigh John Bright's judgment on the
House of Commons as being " in reality the only guarantee
we have for freedom." " You may have liberty with a
monarchy, as you have in this country, but you may have
a monarchy without liberty, as you see in many other
countries of Europe. You may have liberty, as we have
here, even with a portion of the legislative power in the

* Speeches of John Bright, ed. Thorold Rogers ; Vol. II, pp. 208–209.
† *ibid.*, p. 211.

hand of hereditary legislators ; but you might have hereditary legislators and no liberty whatever. But that branch
of the Legislature which we are about to discuss is not
only consistent with the existence of liberty, but it is
inseparable in this country from the existence of liberty."*
He pressed for the extension of the franchise because
he wanted the workers to enjoy to the full the guarantee
for freedom which is to be found in the House of Commons,
and because he had confidence that British working-men
would realise the importance of maintaining unimpaired
that guarantee of freedom for the benefit of every class
in the nation.

As we have already seen, Bright was no doctrinaire
democrat. He was accused of holding extreme opinions,
of setting class against class, of advocating a republic
in place of the monarchy. He did prefer republican
institutions, but he was not disloyal to the constitutional
monarchy in Britain. He was content to accept the wisdom
of our ancestors in this regard. He did criticise the landowning and governing classes, but there is no trace of
class-hatred in his appeal to working-men. So far from
being an extremist and a firebrand, he saw that to be
" moderate but irresistible in one's moderation " is the
mark of a practical politician. In his attitude towards
established institutions he is almost as conservative as
Burke. A shrewd sense of what is possible pervades all
his proposals for reform. Every measure of coercion was
distasteful to him, yet he did not decline responsibility
for the use of organised force by the State when the
necessity for its exercise seemed undeniable. When he
was offered nomination as Parliamentary candidate for
Birmingham in 1857, he was asked whether he would feel
obliged to resist the measures considered necessary by
the military authorities for suppressing the present revolt
in India. He replied by wire : " The success of the Indian
revolt would lead to anarchy in India, and I conceive that
it is mercy to India to suppress it. I should not resist the
measures considered necessary to suppress it. I should
insist on an improved Government for India for the future."†

* Speeches of John Bright, ed. by Thorold Rogers ; p. 54.
† Trevelyan, p. 261.

The great saying "Force is no remedy" seems to have been coined by Bright in 1880, and he had preached essentially the same doctrine since he first entered politics. It is not often remembered that he coined this saying and stressed this principle on occasions when he was actually prepared to sanction coercion as a temporary necessity. Thus he voted for a Coercion Bill to deal with agrarian crime in Ireland in 1847, and while recording his vote, urged the necessity of dealing with the twin grievances of the Land and the Church. "Until the feudal and ecclesiastical fetters were removed, there could be no diminution of poverty in Ireland and no peace for England."* In the same spirit he supported the suspension of the Habeas Corpus Act in Ireland in 1881. He would have reduced armaments to the small dimensions that might be necessary for police purposes, and he would have had the British Navy merged into an international police force to patrol the seas. He did not quarrel with the necessity of organised force to restrain crime and preserve peace.

The true remedies for injustice and oppression he believed could only be discovered by the democratic method and the democratic spirit. For John Bright, the essentials of that spirit and method included " the habit of looking for wisdom as the result of common debate." Hence his respect for Parliamentary procedure and discussion and his indignation at the misuse of Parliamentary procedure and privileges for party ends. He never forgave Parnell for the abuse of Parliament involved in the Irish Party's development of the art of obstruction. It would be difficult to say how much the conduct of the Parnellites damaged the prestige and effectiveness of the House of Commons. Bright was equally distressed at the disgraceful behaviour of the Tory party over the admission of Bradlaugh, behaviour which equally tended to bring Parliament into contempt. At the same time, Bright was not opposed to reform in procedure. He would probably have supported some of the modern proposals for expediting business and making the work of the House of Commons more efficient. The high level on which he always conducted his argument

* Diaries, p. 96.

alike inside the House of Commons and on the public
platform was another proof of his faith in democracy.
He was always at pains to make himself understood, but
he never talked down to a popular audience. He sought
to rise above party. " If we could divest ourselves of the
feelings engendered by party-strife " is a constant refrain.
This is of a piece with his rejection of appeals to purely
class interests. Democracy to Bright meant the co-operation
of the different classes of the community. He did not
believe any class could be the arbiter of justice. The aim
of representation is to secure a hearing for every class
and for every legitimate interest in the community. Parliamentary government is not a device to enable majorities
to get their own way. It is rather intended to compel
majorities to do justice to minorities. John Bright
himself believed that necessary reforms could and should
be effected without injustice to those most directly affected
by them. The Irish grievances might be redressed without
inflicting wrong and hardship on landowners. " What I
would propose would be to undo, absolutely undo, the
territorial and ecclesiastical arrangements of the last two
or three hundred years with regard to Ireland. But I
would do all this without inflicting upon any living man
the smallest act of injustice in connection with his interest
in the territorial and ecclesiastical arrangements of the
country."* Here he lays down a principle which should
be dear to every democrat. He was convinced that moral
obligations rest upon reformers, who once persuaded of
the justice of their ends are apt to be careless in their choice
of means. When Bright acknowledged moral limitations
in his methods of agitation, when he says for example,
" there is no effort *which the Constitution, which morality
permits us to use,* that we should leave unused and unmade
for the purpose of furthering this great cause," this is
no concession to a conventional piety. He could not
endure the comparison which the Irish " rebels " were
making between their Land League and his Anti-Corn-
Law League. He held up the crime and disorder promoted
by the one against the orderly and constitutional methods of
the other.† He was justified in so doing. There are things

* Trevelyan, p. 393.   † Diaries, p. 455, n.

a man may not do, even for his country or for a cause he deems sacred. The recognition of a moral law is essential to the life of democracy, as John Bright understood it.

Two qualities mark John Bright as a true democrat and reveal the secret of his power as an orator. For though he had natural gifts as a speaker, a fine personal presence and a clear bell-like voice, yet his influence on the public platform depended on his character. The first is his sheer humanity, his deep sense of the great simplicities in which men of every class and nation are united. His own experience of bereavement quickened his sympathy with his fellows. The undying appeal of the great passages in his Crimean orations depends on the directness and dignity with which he handles the theme of death itself. The sentences that won for him the esteem and affection of Queen Victoria have something of the same quality. " I think there has been, by many persons, a great injustice done to the Queen in reference to her desolate and widowed position. And I venture to say this, that a woman—be she the Queen of a great realm, or the wife of one of your labouring men—who can keep alive in her heart a great sorrow for the lost object of her life and affection, is not at all likely to be wanting in a great and generous sympathy with you."* Only a true democrat could have expressed himself in such terms, and anyone who lacks this sense of our common humanity does not deserve to be called a democrat at all.

The second quality is to be found in John Bright's moral courage, the honesty and independence of his judgment. He could the more easily speak out, since he cared nothing for office and was a poor administrator. But the secret of his moral courage as a democratic leader is not explained simply by the absence of personal ambition or by his possession of the leisure to think things through.

> How happy is he born and taught
> Who serveth not another's will :
> Whose armour is his honest thought
> And simple truth his utmost skill.

John Bright trusted in no other armour and desired no other skill. At a time when the possibility of such

* Trevelyan, p. 399.

C*

happiness seems to be fading out from Europe, it is imperative for Great Britain to retain the conditions that make the emergence of such leaders possible. But while democratic institutions are a condition favouring such freedom and happiness, the maintenance of democracy itself depends on the faith which lies at the basis of moral independence. John Bright was a free man because he had learned " in all his ends to look to God as judge and not his friends," and because he shared Cromwell's faith in toleration. Very pertinent in this connection is a quotation from Dr. Döllinger, in the present Master of Balliol's book on *The Essentials of Democracy*. " He who is convinced that right and duty require him to coerce other people into a life of falsehood . . . belongs to an essentially different religion from one who recognises in the inviolability of conscience a human right guaranteed by religion itself." John Bright adhered to the latter religion, the religion of the true God, and he never bowed the knee to Baal.

THOMAS CARLYLE

1795–1881

by L. P. JACKS

THOMAS CARLYLE
1795–1881
by L. P. JACKS

" Universal Democracy, whatever we may think of it, has declared itself as an inevitable fact of the days in which we live . . . The whole social wisdom of the Present Time is summoned, in the name of the Giver of wisdom, to make clear to itself and lay deeply to heart, with an eye to strenuous valiant practice and effort, what the meaning of this . . . may be."

(The Present Time, 1850.)

O N the question of admitting Carlyle into the ranks of the Great Democrats there is likely to be a division of opinion. If democracy means (1) universal suffrage (2) *plus* the decision of all national questions by majority-voting on that basis (3) *plus* the leadership of parliamentary orators, then Carlyle must be classed as an anti-democrat of the most pronounced and uncompromising type. But if the above system is not what " the people " really desire, but only what they have been " enchanted " (Carlyle's word) into believing they desire, their real and deeper demand being not for " representative self-government " but for *good* government by competent rulers—does it not then follow that a prophet who voices this deeper thing would be a truer interpreter of the popular will than an advocate of the sort of democracy so bitterly denounced by Carlyle ? And might we not on that ground acclaim him as the better democrat of the two ? And if we find him consistently advocating drastic reforms of democracy all in line with the deeper will of the people as thus interpreted ; and if further he himself is essentially a man of the people, a peasant by heredity and a worker by habit, not a lover of luxury and pleasure, not a seeker of " honours," but toiling through a long life to free his fellow-workers from the foul " enchantments " practised on them by speech-making demagogues, is not this an additional reason for putting him on the people's side ? So far as democracy connotes a real friendship for the people, as distinct from a desire for their votes, the present

writer thinks it is. He thinks that on all *human* grounds
Carlyle's claim to the democratic mind is fully as strong as,
if not stronger than, that of many persons who, on the
grounds of academic definition, claim to be better entitled
to it than he.

As a friend of the people Carlyle, indeed, is by no means
soft spoken. Again and again he takes the liberty of
informing them, as no seeker of their votes would ever
dare to do, that they are " mostly fools " ; mostly fools,
even to the extent of becoming " mere mesmerized cattle,"
under the malign influence of the political cant and clap-
trap abundantly poured forth by " stump-orators " of
many denominations, all intent on getting their votes.

Carlyle indicated the democracy of his own day as a
" sham," and in this sense, that what the people got out
of it was not self-government, as their orators informed
them, but misgovernment or no *government* at all, with
" anarchy " as the assured outcome unless it were reformed. *
And reformed in what direction ? In the direction, strangely
enough, of *aristocracy* ; but aristocracy created out of the
substance of the people, by a rigorous sifting out of its
best and worthiest elements, for the express purpose of
giving them the management of affairs—aristocracy, we
may say, on a democratic basis. Only thus would democracy
cease to be a malignant sham heading straight for
anarchy, and become the beneficent reality of good
government. One might define Carlyle as a democratic-
aristocrat. The language is paradoxical, but there are
many phenomena both in Europe and America to-day
which seem to show that the evolution of democracy in
the direction of such an aristocracy has at least entered on
the experimental stage.

Democracy, then, conceived as a method of settling
all questions by the counting of heads, was not only a
thing which Carlyle never believed in but one which he
positively, fiercely and continuously denounced as " the
high way to anarchy and the Bottomless Pit." Neverthe-

---

* Carlyle's prediction of anarchy as the certain outcome of sham
democracy will be found *passim* in *Latter Day Pamphlets* (1850), and,
more vehemently, in *Shooting Niagara : and After ?* (1867). Two years
later Matthew Arnold made the same prediction. He recommended
" culture " as the antidote. See his *Culture and Anarchy* (1869).

less he regarded his country and Europe generally—the Europe of his day—as irrevocably committed to Democracy of that sort. He called it " Shooting Niagara," not to be avoided when once you have got into the swirling current above the Falls, as England then was : and he predicted that the swift sequel of it would be a ruinous plunge into the whirlpools below, or as we now call it, a world-crisis. " Inexpressibly delirious seems to me," he writes in 1867 when extension of the franchise was in the air (a trifle in comparison with what has happened since), "inexpressibly delirious seems to me the puddle of Parliament and Public upon what it calls ' the Reform Measure ' ; that is to say, The calling in of new supplies of blockheadism, gullibility, bribeability, amenability to beer and balderdash, by way of amending the woes we have had from our previous supplies of that bad article . . . It accelerates what I have long looked upon as inevitable—pushes us at once into the Niagara Rapids ; irresistibly propelled, with ever increasing velocity, we shall now arrive—who knows how *soon* ! . . . For one's own poor share, one would rather have been shot than have been concerned in it. And yet, after all my silent indignation and disgust, I cannot pretend to be clearly sorry that such a consummation is expedited. I say to myself ' Well, perhaps the sooner such a mass of hypocrisies, universal mismanagements and brutal platitudes and infidelities *ends*—may it not be for the better ! ' . . . A superlative Hebrew Conjurer* spell-binding all the great Lords, great Parties, great Interests of England and leading them by the nose, like helpless mesmerized somnambulant cattle, to such issue—did the world ever see a *flebile ludibrium* of such magnitude before ? " † (*Shooting Niagara : and After ?*)

Such was Carlyle's prediction in 1867 for the " head counting " type of democracy, which gives high office, not to the man who is " ablest to do the work," but

---

* Disraeli, who, seven years later, offered him the Grand Cross of the Bath " the highest distinction of merit at Her Majesty's Command." He declined it in a memorable letter. In commenting on the affair to his brother John, Carlyle remarked " had they sent me ¼ pound of good tobacco the addition to my happiness had probably been suitabler and better ! " See *Carlyle in Old Age*, by D. A. Wilson, p. 321.
† In *Miscellaneous Essays*.

to the man who is "ablest to get himself elected for doing it."

This, I say, was in 1867, and sixty-seven years exactly have elapsed since these predictions were uttered. Have they been fulfilled ? Yes, certainly, so far as they concerned the inevitable extension of "head-counting" from the partial to the universal way of doing it. But has Niagara been "shot" ? Has "the plunge into Chaos" taken place ?

Well, we have been hearing a good deal of late about the present "World Chaos," and to judge by the number of "Guides out of Chaos" now being offered by "professorial persons" it would seem that Chaos had actually arrived, Chaos political, Chaos economical and, some say, even moral and religious. Is this, or is it not, the "arrival" predicted by Carlyle ? Is this, or is it not, the result of making Count of Heads ("mostly blockheads") "the Divine Court of Appeal on every question and human interest," and of leaving every man and woman "free to follow each his own nose by way of guide-post in this intricate world" ? Is the head-counting method of government related to the present world chaos as cause to effect ?

The reader will judge for himself whether Carlyle was a true prophet or a false. The present writer is concerned with something else. He aims to show, in fuller detail than the above quotations furnish, what Carlyle thought about Democracy. And he believes the upshot will be this : that Carlyle, while fiercely condemning Democracy as it flourished in his day and promised to flourish more abundantly thereafter (as indeed it has done) had, nevertheless, a profound belief in another kind of Democracy where the voting power would be used, not for electing "representatives" of the people, but for electing wise men to rule over them, and where the touchstone of fitness would be, not "ability-to-get-into-Parliament," but "ability-to-rule." To many this will seem only another name for apostasy from the democratic faith, and the question "Was Carlyle a democrat ? " will then become the academic one of defining our terms, a way of settling important matters for which Carlyle himself had a profound contempt. He called it " the exchange of small logic-shot." The present writer will try to avoid it.

It was not, however, on Democracy as a method of government by count of heads that Carlyle poured out his fiercest invective. This was reserved for its humanitarian or philanthropic pretension, as the appointed means for achieving the " brotherhood of man." A glance at his utterance on this aspect, copiously poured out in *Model Prisons* (1850), will help us to understand the peculiar quality of his friendship for the people and his attitude to Democracy in general.

Out of the Gospel of liberty, equality and fraternity there had arisen, as one of its by-products, a phenomenon known in Carlyle's diction as " Exeter Hall philanthropy " mainly devoted, again in his diction, to the creating of " universal-sluggard-and-scoundrel-protection-societies " and to " the indiscriminate mashing up of Right and Wrong into a patent treacle " for the healing of human woe ; the practical issue of it all being this : that hard-working and honest men must now be taxed to the bone for the support of sluggards and scoundrels, until they too, the hard-working and honest, succumbed under the burden, with no resource left but to turn scoundrels themselves and " enlist in the Devil's regiments of the line." " Away, you ! " he cries to the " sluggard-and-scoundrel " popula-tion ; " begone swiftly, ye Devil's regiments of the line : in the name of God and his poor struggling servants, sore put to it to live in these bad days, I mean to rid myself of you with some degree of brevity . . . Mark it, my diabolic friends, I mean to lay leather on the backs of you."

Some friends, it seems, had taken him to see one of the Model Prisons, then being attempted under the influence of " Exeter Hall philanthropy." " Surely one of the most perfect buildings within the circuit of London," he writes, " excellent all, the *ne-plus-ultra* of human care and ingenuity . . . airy apartments with glass roofs, of an agreeable temperature and perfect ventilation . . . The bread, the cocoa, the soup, the meat we tasted ; found them of excellence superlative . . . The Captain of the place, a gentleman of ancient military or Royal Navy habit, was one of the most perfect Governors . . . a man of real worth challenging at once love and respect." But (and here speaks the friend of the people) " all round this beautiful Establishment, or Oasis of Purity, intended for the Devil's regiments of the line, lay continents of poor and dirty dwellings, where the unfortunate, not *yet* enlisted into that Force, were struggling manifoldly—in their workshops, in their marble-yards and timber-yards and tan-yards, in their close cellars, cobbler stalls, hungry garrets, and poor dark tradeshops with red herrings and tobacco pipes crossed in the window—to keep the devil out of doors and *not* enlist with him. And it was by a tax on these that the barracks for these regiments of the line were kept up . . . My sublime benevolent friends, don't you perceive that here is a shockingly unfruitful investment for your capital of Benevolence ; precisely the *worst* that human ingenuity could select for you ? "

The inmates of this prison were twelve hundred in number, and they were being treated, so he was informed, by " methods of love." " Hopeless for evermore such a project ! " he exclaims. " False in the warp and false in the woof : about as false a problem as any I have seen a good man set upon lately ! To guide scoundrels by ' love ' is a method that will not hold together : hardly for the flower of men will love alone do : and for the sediment and scoundrelism of men it has not even a chance to do . . . Christian religion ? Does the Christian religion, or any religion, prescribe love of scoundrels ? Me, for one, it will not serve as a religion on those terms. Just hatred of scoundrels, I say ; fixed, irreconcilable, inexorable enmity to the enemies of God ; this, and not love for them, must, if you look into it, be the backbone of any human religion whatsoever. . . . Poor reader . . . if on returning to thy poor peaceable dwelling place, after an honest hard day's work, thou wert to find a brutal scoundrel who, for lucre or some other object of his, had slaughtered the life that was dearest to thee : thy true wife, for example, thy true old mother swimming in her blood ; the human scoundrel, or two-legged wolf, standing over such a tragedy ; I hope a man would have so much divine rage in his heart to snatch the nearest weapon and put a conclusion on said human wolf. A palpable messenger of Satan, that one ; accredited by all the Devils, to be put an end to by all the children of God. The soul of every God-created man flames wholly into one divine blaze of sacred wrath at the sight of such a Devil's messenger ; authentic first-hand monition as to what next is to be done."*

Carlyle's political philosophy, like Plato's, cannot be understood, much less evaluated, unless we consider it in the context, or perspective, of the much deeper and more comprehensive philosophy of which it formed an integral part.

The principle underlying this deeper philosophy, which turns up in different forms in all Carlyle's writings, according to the subject he is writing about, may be summed up as follows :

1. That the whole universe is the manifestation of a Reality which common sense recognizes as "the Fact" and religion venerates as God.

2. That this Reality, Fact, or God is dynamic, always in action, asserting itself irresistibly, and bringing to nought (in its own time) all who oppose or ignore it. The essential nature of the Fact is that of a *command*, not a thing which simply *is*, for men to look at and get knowledge of, but a thing that *has to be* and *will* be ; not merely a piece of information to be recorded but an *order* that must be obeyed at all costs. (*Latter-Day Pamphlets*, 21.)†

3. That this Reality, Fact or God may be called either " Truth " or " Right " ; " Truth " when we think of it as eternally *existing*, " Right " when we think of it as eternally *in action*. Right we may say is the dynamic, or imperative, name of Truth.

4. That the difference between Truth and Falsehood or between Right and Wrong (the imperative names of Truth and Falsehood) is infinite and therefore unspeak-

---

* It must not be said that all this is an echo of Darwin with his doctrines of Natural Selection and a generally ruthless Nature. The above was written nine years before the publication of the *Origin of Species*.

† The references throughout are to the Library Edition of Carlyle's Works ; Chapman and Hall, 1869.

able ; Truth and Right having the whole weight of the universe *with* them ; Falsehood and Wrong the whole weight of the Universe *against* them. (*ibid.*, 31.)

5. That veracity is a thing of many kinds, the summary of which is truth-*acting* ; truth-*speaking* being one, but no more than one, of the many ways in which truth commands us to act it. Every piece of dishonest work, such as a jerry-built house, is, therefore, an *acted* lie, marked with the sign of eternal reprobation ; every piece of honest work carries the approval of the whole universe and has its praises chanted in the highest heavens. Good workmen are God's friends ; bad, his enemies.

6. That all civilizations, nations, states and governments are doomed to perish, and all individual lives to end miserably, unless they are founded on the Law of God, which is simply the law of honest work, the Law of the Fact. (*ibid.*, 21.)

7. That there is only one kind of happiness to which human beings have any *right*—the kind which comes from getting their jobs well done. To the unearned kind, which consists in smooth-flowing pleasure, men have no right at all, making themselves contemptible when they claim it and being justly punished with misery when they seek it. (*Past and Present*, 195.)

8. That the universe is a hierarchy of values in which the greater good controls the lesser, and that any human constitution or social system based on another principle, such as majority voting, or human equality, is in opposition to the Fact, and must be prepared for the consequences. (*Latter-Day Pamphlets*, 20. See 2.) In other words, the universe is essentially an authoritative institution, not getting its orders from what the majority of its elements desire and vote for, but imposing its own orders (eternal law) on all its elements, whether they like them or not. The only social system which will *last* is one that is similarly constituted.

9. That the Fact has no fellowship with Liberty, Equality and Fraternity as understood at the French Revolution, but is flatly opposed to all three. The elements of the universe, whether human or other, have no liberty to do as they like ; their relations are all based on the inequality

of the better and the worse ; and the Fact, far from frater-
nizing with scoundrels and mutineers, condemns them
all to destruction. (*Model Prisons*, in *Latter-Day Pamphlets*,
passim.)

10. That the first right of man is the right to be governed
by somebody wiser and better than himself ; that human
nature hungers for such government, and that the wisest and
best of men, on whom all the others depend, are competent
only because they in turn are governed by the Fact, their
wisdom consisting in their obedience to its Everlasting
Laws, their reverence for its Majesty and their sense
of its Beneficence. "The great Soul of the World is
just."

We gather from this that Carlyle was, before all else,
a cosmically minded man. He was a good mathematician
and once (at the age of thirty-nine) offered himself to Jeffrey
for the Professorship of Astronomy in Edinburgh University.
I doubt if he would have been a success in that appointment, his interest in the universe taking the form rather
of cosmic reverence than of cosmic technique.* For him,
the Laws which govern the universe—and in his philosophy
they do *govern*, they are not mere " summaries of observed
phenomena "—are the laws which govern, or ought to
govern, human conduct, the same laws expressed in different
dialects ; Duty being nothing else than Fact translated
from the indicative to the imperative. It followed that
the Government of the Universe is the model on which
all human governments must be founded if they are to
stand, and all philanthropies guided if they are to benefit
mankind. The ideal statesman is one who, like Cromwell,
would make " the Laws of God into the Laws of England "
—the Rule of Fact.

" Of the continental nuisance called Bureaucracy I can
see no risk or possibility in England. Democracy is hot
enough here, fierce enough : it is perennial, universal,
clearly invincible among us henceforth . . . Democracy
clamours, with its newspapers, its Parliaments and all its
twenty-seven million throats, continually in this Nation

* Somebody once remarked in his presence that the starry heavens
were beautiful. " Man," he replied, " they're just *dreadful*."

for evermore. I remark too that the unconscious purport
of all its clamours is ever this ' Send us men skilled."
(*Latter-Day Pamphlets, The New Downing Street,* 173.)

A hundred passages could easily be collected from
Carlyle's writings which, in ever varying language and
distribution of emphasis, repeat the essential thought of
this statement. Some of them will be quoted in other
connections in the course of this essay ; but the above
passage carefully studied (as it deserves to be) will tell us
all we need know at this stage of Carlyle's attitude towards
Democracy.

In spite of all the hard things he has to say about the
proceedings of democracy as he observed them in his day,
it is clear from the above passage that he accepted it as a
form of political procedure which had come to stay, as
an established fact that had to be reckoned with—
at least in England. At no period of his long career
as a publicist, was there any question with Carlyle
of abolishing democracy in favour of aristocracy,
oligarchy, autocracy, bureaucracy, or anything else.
Any such proposal he would have regarded as flying
in the face of the Fact ; the Fact, in Carlyle's vernacular,
being, as we have seen, only another name for the Almighty.
To be sure, he has much to say in praise of Aristocracy,
also a sacred name when rightly interpreted, but the Aristocracy he recommends will always be found, when the
context is looked into, to be Aristocracy on a democratic
basis—an Aristocracy of the people, by the people, for the
people. The essential function of democracy is, then,
to evolve aristocrats, and having evolved them to submit
willingly, loyally and joyfully to their guidance. So long
as democracy fails to evolve an aristocracy, and a ruling
aristocracy at that—as it was visibly failing in Carlyle's
day—chaos and disaster will be the portion of society ;
but triumphant success will follow when the true aristocrats
emerge from its substance and begin to function as aforesaid. Needless to say, the aristocrat of democratic evolution
and origin will be a gentleman, but a gentleman of a different
stamp from the type evolved out of the amours of Charles
II and Nell Gwynn. He will be a gentleman, and have a
gentleman's habit of giving orders and expecting them

to be obeyed, democracy having evolved him for that very purpose.

All of which stands clearly indicated in the last sentence of the passage quoted above : " the unconscious purport of all its clamours is this ' Send us men skilled.' " The unconscious purport, be it observed. Deep beneath the conscious, deliberate and vociferous proclamation of liberty, equality and fraternity Carlyle thought he could discern in the heart of the Demos a " dumb, inarticulate " yearning for " skilled men " to guide, command and rule its stumblings in the darkness, and he looked forward to the time when this dumb unconscious yearning would become articulate and conscious, and so bring democracy to its goal. I think Mr. Roosevelt would fit in rather well, though not perhaps completely, with Carlyle's notion of an aristocrat democratically born, as Stalin clearly would not, nor any other dictator who owes his position to a revolutionary *coup d'état* or other accident which has given him command of the army and police force.* Here is the picture of the " skilled man " whom the peoples are dumbly seeking : " One noble man at once of natural wisdom and practical experience ; one Intellect still really human and not red-tapish, owlish and pedantical, appearing there in that dim chaos with word of command ; to brandish Hercules-like the divine broom and shovel, and turn running water in upon the place, and say, as with a fiat, ' Here shall be truth and real work, and talent to do it henceforth.' " (*Latter-Day Pamphlets*, 135.)

Let democracy concentrate all its energies and employ all its apparatus on the discovery and election of this man, sifting the whole population until he be found. Once found and definitely appointed as the people's choice for Captain-General, or Prime Minister, of the Nation, let him be given a free hand in the selection and appointment of his executive subalterns ; let the people leave *that* to him, not confining his choice to the six hundred or so whose only certificate of competence is " their ability to get into Parliament " (a worthless certificate according to Carlyle) but having for his field of selection the whole " twenty-seven "

---

* See Carlyle's *French Revolution* and his remarks on Napoleon, *passim*.

millions (now forty-five) of his fellow countrymen—the
assumption being that our Captain-General, himself a man
of pre-eminent worth and competence, and chosen by us
for that very reason, will have an eye for worth and competence in others, and must therefore be left free to find
it where he can, with twenty-seven millions to choose
from, and to employ as he deems best.

Let him also be furnished with a Parliament and a newspaper press. *But for the purpose of consultation only*, this,
according to Carlyle, being the original and proper function of a Parliament, since perverted, with disastrous
consequences, from the beneficent consultative body it
once was into the legislative body, anything but beneficent,
it now (1850) is. In a true democracy our chosen Captain-
General, surrounded by the wisest counsellors the nation
can find for him, he, and not his Parliament of counsellors,
shall be the lawmaker ; he shall bear on his Herculean
shoulders—for it was as a wise Hercules that we sifted him
out from " the twenty-seven millions "—the responsibility
of law-making ; and he shall hold his high office, or be
replaced by one worthier of it, so long as he proves himself
to be or not to be the wise Hercules we deemed him when
we chose him and gave him commission to guide us in the
way. *Vox populi vox Dei* ? Yes—*when it speaks in this
language*, which is language according to " the Fact."
But not when it goes off into the " wind and smoke " of
" parliamentary eloquence " and " Hansard debatings "
—on all of which a wise man has only one comment to make
—" stop that noise ! "

Such is the programme of democracy in the Gospel
according to Thomas Carlyle. All its tasks, functions,
duties and " problems " sum themselves up into the one
duty and problem of finding its man, its Captain-General,
and loyally following his leadership when found. This
problem solved, all other problems will be on the way to
solution ; " otherwise, not."

" Is not this Proposal," our prophet asks, " the very
essence of whatever truth there is in Democracy ; this,
that the able man be chosen, in whatever rank he is found ?
That he be searched for as hidden treasure is ; be trained,
supervised, set to the work which he alone is fit for. All

Democracy lies in this ; this, I think, is worth all the
ballot-boxes and suffrage movements now going. Not
that the noble soul, born poor, should be set to spout in
Parliament, but that he should be set to assist in governing
men ; this is our grand Democratic interest. With this
we can be saved ; without this, were there a Parliament
spouting in every parish, and Hansard Debates to stem the
Thames, we perish—die constitutionally drowned in mere
oceans of palaver . . . Let us brush the cobwebs from
our eyes ; let us bid the inane traditions be silent for a
moment, and ask ourselves, like men dreadfully intent on
having it *done*, ' By what method or methods can the able
men from every rank of life be gathered, as diamond grains
from the general mass of sand . . . and set to the work
of governing, contriving, administering and guiding for
us ? ' It is the question of questions. All that Democracy
ever meant lies there : the attainment of a truer and truer
Aristocracy, or Government by the *Best*. . . . One true
Reforming Statesman, one noble worshipper and knower
of human intellect, with the quality of an experienced
Politician too ; he, backed by such a Parliament as England,
once recognizing him, would loyally send, and at liberty
to choose his working subalterns from all the Englishmen
alive ; he surely might do something ! "

This picture of a workable democracy is, at least, easily
comprehensible. In the centre stands the figure of our
national Captain-General, popularly chosen as the mouthpiece and instrument of the unconscious demand of all
men (not to govern themselves, but) to be well governed.
Round him and acting under his orders stands a sufficient
corps of " working subalterns," freely chosen by him,
irrespective of their " ability to get into Parliament," on
the sole ground of their *ad hoc* competence for their business.
Behind him stands a consultative Parliament elected on
the ground of ability to give counsel, i.e. on the ground
of *intellect*,* but with no mandate to make laws. Are
we to go off the gold standard or to keep on ? Are we to
have free trade or protection ? Is there to be a legal limit
to the speed of motor cars, and if so, what ? No submission

* " Human Stupidity, the accursed parent of all our sorrows : Human
Intellect the exact summary of Human Worth." (*Downing Street.*)

of such things—nor of others yet more difficult—to the
majority votings of " twenty-seven millions " incompetent
to settle them, with the certainty that the real issue will
be lost in political manœuvrings and finally drowned in
" oceans of palaver ! "   Not that way, which leads no-
whither, but another which aims at " the Fact ! "   Let
our " working subalterns " get busy—finance subalterns
in the one case, traffic subalterns in the other.   Let our
Captain-General then lay the matter before his consultative
Parliament and hear all sides.   Finally let *him* decide what
is to be and stand or fall by the wisdom of his decision.
Such is Carlyle's notion of the way a democratic people
should get itself governed.

How far would this differ from " the Continental nuisance
called bureaucracy ? "   Not at all if we assume that our
Captain-General is himself a bureaucrat and his " working
subalterns " satellites of the same order.   But very considerably if he is the " wise Hercules " of Carlyle's picture.
All hinges on that.   And if the objection be raised that
no such " wise Hercules " can be found, Carlyle's reply
would be—have you ever tried to find him ?   " The whole
British nation, learned, unlearned, professional, practical,
speculative and miscellaneous is at your disposal.   In the
lowest broad strata of the population, equally as in the
highest and narrowest, are produced men of every kind
of genius ; man for man your chance of genius is as good
among the millions as among the units."   The material
is there, there in abundance ; the man able-to-govern can
be found—though perhaps in hiding.   But your methods
of finding him are all wrong, and likely to drive him into
deeper hiding still.   You have confused " ability to get
into Parliament " with ability to govern and made the first
to do duty, as it never can, for the second.

This " ability to get into Parliament," what does it at
present amount to ?   Stump Oratory !   Proficiency in
that and little else !   Your Great Man, judged by present
standards (1850) is the man who can make you the Finest
Speech—with the result that the Government you get is
Government by Speechmakers, by Stump Orators, a very
different thing from Government by Wise Men, who are
mostly of a silent disposition, and with this result—" the

Fact " gets drowned in oceans of palaver. " He who well considers will find this same ' art of speech ' . . . the saddest of all the curses that now lie heavy on us. With horror and amazement one perceives that this much celebrated ' art ' is the chief destroyer of whatever good is born to us and the grand parent-manufactory of evil to us—as it were, the last finishing and varnishing workshop of all the Devil's wares that circulate under the Sun . . . Words will not express what mischiefs the misuse of words has done and is doing, in these heavy-laden generations . . . Considered as the whole of education or human culture, which it now is in our modern manners . . . the art of Speech is probably definable as the short summary of all the Black Arts put together." (*Latter-Day Pamphlets, Stump Orator*, 219 and 222.)

What wonder then that " the man able-to-govern " cannot be found, our final test of human greatness being the Art of Speech, with its consequent " ability to get into Parliament." Found by other methods he can be, for he is there. But not easily found : " him it were vain to try to find always without mistake ; alas, if he were in the majority, this world would be all ' a school of virtue,' which it is far from being. Nevertheless to him, and in all times to him alone, belongs the rule of this world.

" Friend, I am perfectly deliberate in calling this the truest doctrine of the constitution you have ever heard. And I recommend you to learn it gradually and lay it well to heart, for without it there is no salvation. Where he reigns all is blessed, and the gods rejoice and only the wicked make wail." (*Latter-Day Pamphlets, Parliaments*, 302-3.)

Carlyle's essay on *Parliaments* leaves it transparently clear that in spite of his blazing scorn for the loquacity of " honourable gentlemen " he believed firmly in the necessity of an elected Parliament. Equally firm and clear is the support he gives to Free Speech, to the Public Discussion of Public Affairs. But he fiercely attacked the conversion of Parliament into an institution for affording " honourable gentlemen " an opportunity " to grimace oratorically " before the public. Public discussion—yes ; *but let all that go on outside of Parliament.* Is not the open forum of the Press (and, he might now add, the wireless) sufficient for that ? If you want a Grand National Palaver, or Universal Debating Society, are there not " stumps " to stand on in every corner of England and printer's type available by the waggon load ? Has any " honourable gentleman " or " noble Lord " so much steam to blow off that it cannot be blown off elsewhere than in the House of Commons or the House of Lords ? Blow it off by all means, but not *there* ! Let Parliament as a whole conduct its proceedings *behind closed doors*, as it did in Cromwell's time (and as they do in Cabinet Meetings), with no opportunity given to any honourable member for winning public applause in the speech-making department or for boring other honourable members to death by his interminable steam-blowing operations. Let the House of Commons promptly convert itself into a gravely deliberative body assembled, not for the purpose of getting speeches made, reported and admired, but for the purpose of getting business transacted. Let the good old practice of " no reporters present " be restored. Keep your Parliament sacredly immune from all temptation to practise the black arts, the monkey tricks, the balderdash and the " buncombe " of stump oratory ; for this it is, and not any fault in your " rules of procedure " which has reduced Parliament to its present (1850) condition of impotence and futility and made it a derision to wise men, who can only cry, as they listen to its debates, " stop that noise ! " Such were Carlyle's ideas for " the Reform of Parliament."

" The poor Parliament," he writes, " has had to distort and pervert its activity in many ways ; and has at length diffused itself into oceans of windy talk reported in Hansard ; has grown, in short, a National Palaver, one of the strangest entities this Sun ever looked down upon. A National Palaver, recognised as Sovereign, a so-called Convocation of all the Stump-Orators in the Nation to come and govern us, was not seen in the earth till recently. I would fain hope that it can only be a transient phenomenon ! . . . I am told there is not, once in the seven years, the smallest gleam of new intelligence thrown on any matter, earthly or divine, by an honourable gentleman on his legs in Parliament. Nothing offered you but wearisome, dreary, thrice-boiled colewort . . . Honourable gentlemen have

complained to myself that under the sky there is not such
a bore . . . Let honourable gentlemen who can print
their own stump oratory, by all means do so." (*Parliaments*,
268.)

" The tragic experience is dimly but irrepressibly
forcing itself on all the world that our British Parliament
does not shine as Sovereign Ruler of the British Nation ;
that it was excellent only as Adviser of the Sovereign Ruler ;
and has not, somehow or other, the art of getting work
done ; but produces talk merely . . . and in vortexes of
talk is not unlike to submerge itself and the whole of us,
if help come not." (*Parliaments*, 272.)

" The sad conclusion . . . appears to be, that Parliaments, admirable as Advising Bodies, and likely to be in
future universally useful in that capacity are, as Ruling
and Sovereign bodies, not useful but useless or worse
. . . smitten with eternal incompetence for that function
by the law of Nature itself . . . We may take it as a fact
. . . that no Sovereign Ruler with six hundred and fifty-eight
heads, set to rule twenty-seven millions, by continually
talking in the hearsay of them all, can for the life of it
make a good figure in that vocation." (*Parliaments*, 273–5.)

" Men have come to imagine that the Laws of this
Universe are decided by voting . . . It is an idle fancy.
. . . My friend, do you think, had the united Posterity of
Adam voted, and since the Creation done nothing but
vote, that three and three were seven—would this have
altered the laws of arithmetic ? . . . I consider not. And
is arithmetic, think you, a thing more fixed by tne Eternal
than the laws of Justice are . . .? No pin point can you
mark within the wide circle of the All where God's laws
are not . . . Wretched being, do you hope to prosper
by assembling six hundred and fifty-eight poor creatures
in a certain apartment and getting them, after debate, to
vote that what is *not*, is ? . . . Confess it, you have some
cowardly notion to this effect, though ashamed to say so.
Miserable soul . . . you are become an enchanted human
ass." (*Parliaments*, 284–5.)

In the light of all this, and remembering the ten
" principles " which form the background of it, I think
we shall not be far wrong in naming Carlyle " a Great

Democrat " in the sense of his own understanding of
Democracy, which was not the popular notion of it in 1850
and is not the popular notion of it to-day. More exactly
I would define him as the prophet of a Democratic Labour
Party which, so far, has not appeared on the earth, but
may appear hereafter—a Democratic Labour Party, *devoted
to the promotion of honest work*, as the only " policy " the
Fact is at all likely to honour, all the other objects of the
Party being strictly subordinated to that. On the formation
and growth of the present Labour Party I think he would
have looked with mingled emotions of hope and despair ;
with hope, at every sign it showed of fulfilling the promise
of its name by developing into a Party of Honest Work
and evolving, on that basis, a New Aristocracy of Competence ; with despair, so far as it succumbed to the
speech-making habit and measured its progress by the
head-counting triumphs consequent on the practice of
that " Black Art."

Carlyle's conception of a workable democracy is closely
related to his conception of social discipline. The two
conceptions indeed are so closely interwoven that neither
can be understood without the other. Social discipline
without a Captain-General would be an orchestra without
a conductor. A Captain-General without social discipline
would be a conductor without an orchestra. Each implies
the other.

The figure of orchestra and conductor is my own. Had
Carlyle used it—and I am not suggesting that he should
have done so—and spoken of " orchestration " instead of
" regimentation," his views of social discipline would
probably have excited less prejudice, and been less misunderstood by the pacifically minded. As it is, his doctrine
of discipline can be best described as a " transfigured
militarism," though with considerable emphasis on the
word " transfigured." He would set up for civil life, and
especially for the industrial side of it, a system of discipline
analogous in efficiency, though not in *form*, to the discipline
of an army. Is it not obvious that our Captain-General
with his " working subalterns " will be wholly unable to
get their job done and their plans carried out if the " twenty-

seven millions " who are to execute the plans are *untrained
in the co-operative art of working to pattern?* As well
might the Commander-in-Chief at Aldershot proceed to
execute his autumn manœuvres with a mob of raw recruits
swept up from the streets the night before. As well might
the conductor of an orchestra expect to get his symphony
played by people with no other qualification for playing it
than a general agreement with him (after due speechmaking)
that it was a very fine symphony indeed ! Without discipline,
then, discipline habitual, spontaneous and willing, like
that of the manœuvring regiment or the playing orchestra,
our Captain's plan, be it what it may, cannot be made to
march, to yield any order visible to the eye, or any harmony
audible to the ear. How is our Captain to get discipline ?

Not by " making speeches to his constituents." Not by
practising the Black Art of stump oratory, not even with
a pulpit for " stump." Not by proclaiming from the
housetops that discipline is necessary (except as a general
warning that our Captain means to have it). Not by *telling*
the raw recruits that they must " change their minds,"
or get into more orderly ways, or acquire the habit of
" subordinating their private interests to the interests
of the community "—not indeed by " telling " them
anything, except by way of the general warning aforesaid.
Our conductor does not bring his orchestra players to
symphony point by lectures on the Art of Music or the
Life of Beethoven. He *rehearses* them continually. Our
Commander at Aldershot has little use for propaganda,
or for eloquence (except occasionally in fuliginous outbursts) when training his raw recruits *out* of their slouching
go-as-you-please habit, *into* the habit of efficient marching
men, instant in their response to orders and infallible in
the execution thereof—no use for these talking methods,
or next to none. But he has much use for *drill*.

Our Captain-General of the Nation will proceed in like
manner. His " System of Education " will be largely a
System of Training in the Co-operative Art. Chosen by
us, mark you, for the express purpose among others of
giving us discipline, of giving us social *drill*, he will have
among his " working subalterns " one highly competent
and greatly honoured (nay, not one, but many) whom

we will call " the Social Equivalent of the Drill Sergeant "
—" just as Rhadamanthus " but efficient as Cromwell or
Frederick the Great. He it is who will make it his business
to turn us all, not into civic *servants* (too much
" buncombe " about " service ") but, primarily, into
civic *soldiers*, able to keep step and direction *together*, able
to execute whatever social manœuvre is required of us
without getting tied up into bundles and mobs ; able
moreover to stand up to fire without impulse to run away.
We have asked our Captain-General to make us an omelet,
elected him for the purpose ; our muddled, slouching,
go-as-you-please habits are the eggs to be broken ; our
" Social Equivalent of the Drill Sergeant " is the man who
will break them. If we dislike him for his name and suspect
that his " drill " will include the bayonet exercise, let us
call him " conductor of the orchestra," who is also a man
to be obeyed, and continue the substitution as we read
the following :

" That of commanding and obeying, were there nothing
more ; ought not all to have it ; and how many ever do ?
I often say. The one Official Person, royal, sacerdotal,
scholastic, governmental, of our times, who is still thoroughly
a truth and a reality, and *not* in great part a hypothesis and
worn-out humbug, is the Drill Sergeant who is master
of his work and will perform it. By Drill Sergeant understand not the man in three stripes alone ; understand
him as meaning all such men up to the Turenne, to the
Friedrich of Prussia . . . Ask your poor King's Majesty,
Captain-General of England, Defender of the Faith and
so much else ; your poor Lawyer, sacred dispenser of
Justice ; your poor Doctor, ditto of health ; they will all
answer, ' Alas, no, worthy Sir, we are all of us fallen not
a little, some of us altogether, into the quasi-humbug
condition : he alone of the three stripes, of the gorget and
baton, *does* what he pretends to.' That is the melancholy
fact ; well worth considering at present."

" But now what is to hinder the acknowledged King
(Captain-General) in all corners of his territory to introduce
wisely a universal system of Drill, not military only, but
human in all kinds, so that no child or man born in *his*

territory might miss the benefit of it—which would be immense to man, woman and child ! I would begin with it, in mild, soft forms, so soon almost as my children were able to stand on their legs, and I would never wholly remit it until they had done with the world and with me." (*Shooting Niagara*, 384.)

At this point, perhaps, the freeborn Briton, for whom Discipline is the very Devil, will resolve to read no further. Let him have patience ! Carlyle is not yet at the end of his parable. We have now to learn that this same Discipline, which no Stump Orator dare propose to his constituents, thinking, foolish man, that he would lose every vote if he did, is, in reality, the very thing which all his constituents are secretly hungering for, and will enjoy to the top of their bent when they get it. Thus :

" This of outwardly combined and plainly consociated Discipline, in simultaneous movement and action . . . is one of the noblest capabilities of man, most sadly undervalued hitherto ; and one he takes the greatest pleasure in exercising and unfolding, not to mention the invaluable benefit it would afford him if unfolded. From correct marching in line to rhythmic dancing in cotillon or minuet, and to infinitely higher degrees, there is a natural charm in it ; the fulfilment of a deep seated, universal desire to all rhythmic social creatures . . . A richer mine than any in California for poor human creatures ; richer by what a multiple, and hitherto as good as never opened ! . . . It is strange to me, stupid creatures of routine as we mostly are, how in all education of mankind, this of simultaneous Drilling into combined rhythmic action, for almost all good purposes, has been overlooked and left neglected by the elaborate and many-sounding Pedagogues and Professorial Persons we have had, for the long centuries past. It really should be set on foot a little ; and developed gradually into the multiform, opulent results it holds for us. . . . To all children of men it is such an entertainment when you set them to it."

So he goes on, pleading for Discipline both in work and in play, pleading for it as the most enjoyable thing going, and finally winding up with what may be considered,

D

though he does not call it so, " a contribution towards
solving the Problem of Leisure," perhaps the gravest
" problem " industrial democracy has now to grapple
with.

"I believe the vulgarest Cockney crowd, flung out
million-fold on Whit Monday, with nothing but beer and
dull folly to depend on for amusement, would at once
kindle into something human, if you set them to do almost
any regulated act in common. And would dismiss their
beer and dull foolery, in the silent charm of rhythmic
human companionship, in the practical feeling, probably
new, that all of us are made on one pattern, and are, in
an unfathomable way, brothers to one another." (*Shooting
Niagara*, 383–6.)

Shooting Niagara (1867) is the last deliverance of Carlyle
on this question of Democracy. It summarises a message
otherwise spread over thirty volumes ! After that he fell
silent and would often say sorrowfully to his friends " no
man has believed my report." Perhaps he was mistaken
in thinking so.

EDWARD CARPENTER

1844–1929

by HENRY W. NEVINSON

EDWARD CARPENTER
1844–1929
by HENRY W. NEVINSON

" O Democracy, I shout for you !

Back ! Make me a space round me, you kid-gloved, rotten-breathed paralytic world, with miserable antics mimicking the appearance of life.

England ! for good or evil it is useless to attempt to conceal yourself—I know you too well.

I am the very devil. I will tear your veils off, your false shows and pride I will trail in the dust—you shall be utterly naked before me, in your beauty and in your shame.

For who better than I should know your rottenness, your self-deceit, your delusion, your hideous grinning corpse-chattering death-in-life business on top ? (and who better than I the wonderful hidden sources of your strength beneath ?)

Deceive yourself no longer."

THAT was the cry of Edward Carpenter when he published the first edition of *Towards Democracy* in 1883, he being then in his fortieth year. I met him first very soon afterwards in Toynbee Hall, and then described him as " what is called a ' charming ' man, with mild brown eyes, grey-brown hair and short beard, fine, irregular face, grey flannel shirt-collar ; altogether pleasing, earnest, sweet-tempered, modest and clever." But that is too gentle a description for " the very devil." And so indeed is a fuller and truer note in my diary after hearing him talk to an assembly at St. Martin's Town Hall upon new ideas in science (October, 1896). He had a worthy audience—Sydney Olivier, Bernard Shaw, Henry Salt, Fred Evans (the enthusiastic bookseller), Mrs. N. F. Dryhurst, Mrs. Arthur Wilson (noble-hearted Anarchists), and almost the whole gang of the rebellious leaders in the vanguard of what I have called " the Stage Army of the Good." For indeed there is in England a band of high-spirited people who can always be depended upon to fight for every good cause, and, having worked their way round behind the scenes, to reappear at any new front.

Of the man himself I wrote a description which, though

it omits the devil in him, would stand fairly well for him
at any time during the remaining thirty-three years of
his life, when at frequent intervals I was with him and
came to know him very intimately :—

" He is certainly a very beautiful and attractive person ;
tall, slim, and fairly straight ; loose hair, and beard just
grizzled ; strong, dark eyebrows, dark brown eyes, straight
nose, and thin cheeks palish brown ; the whole face very
like Carlyle's at forty-five—a Carlyle rather fined down
and ' cultured.' He was dressed in loose greys, with a
blue shirt, and tie in a large bow ; voice soft but strong
enough without effort ; spoke from a few notes and went
slowly ahead in almost perfect grammar, and with apparent
composure ; not many ' points ' and hardly any laughter ;
perhaps an intentional avoidance of such things. His
main purpose was to show that Science, owing to its
limitation, is apt to leave out many vital sides. The study
of it should teach increased perception like that of savages ;
it should be intellectual, but also dwell on the moral or
emotional relations of the object to ourselves. He illustrated this by a passage from a scientific treatise which
described the heart as ' a common pump '—the heart
that throbs and vibrates to every emotion of love and fear
and happiness. The study of medicine, again, should
not be of drugs, but of health, until the body becomes so
pure as to be conscious of its internal states and changes,
as certain Indians are."

That denunciation of unimaginative science had been
already expanded in *Civilisation* : *its Cause and Cure* ; and
England's Ideal had also been published and was selling
by thousands. To myself they rank among his very best
works, perhaps because they were written in plain, straightforward prose. But *Towards Democracy* was better known,
and it is as the writer of that extraordinary rhapsody that
Carpenter is best still remembered. For, though on one
occasion he had himself to wheel a lot of the unsold copies
around on a barrow, it had an immense circulation and
profound influence at all events up to 1914, when the
wretchedness of the Great War wiped out all hopeful
enthusiasm.

After his terms at Cambridge and his happy escape from Holy Orders, he had lectured about the country upon mathematics and astronomy, and had visited the United States to enjoy converse with Walt Whitman, whose Titanic poetry possessed him. Finding that, with small savings and a small inheritance, he had enough to live upon for a time, he then stayed with a friendly farmer at the little village of Bradway, and there began to write like one inspired :—

" I never hesitated for a moment. Day by day it came along from point to point. I did not hurry. I expressed everything with slow care, and to my best ; I utilised former material which I had by me ; but the one illuminating mood remained and everything fell into place under it ; and rarely did I find it necessary to remodel, or rearrange to any great extent, anything that I had once written.

" What sweet times were those ! all the summer to the hum of the bees in the leafage, the robins and chaffinches hopping around, an occasional large bird flying by, the men away at work in the fields, the consuming pressure of the work within me, the wonderment how it would turn out ; the days there in the rain, or in the snow ; nights sometimes, with moonlight or a little lamp to write by ; far, far away from anything polite or respectable, or any sign or symbol of my hated old life.

" Then the afternoons at work with my friends in the fields, hoeing and singling turnips or getting potatoes, or down in Sheffield on into the evenings with new com-panions among new modes of life and work—everything turning and shaping itself into material for my poem."

He was sick of civilisation as it existed during the third quarter of last century. He had known it in Brighton and London and Cambridge. He had known it in Society, in the upper middle classes, and among the dons. It was the wretchedness of comfortable women's life that moved him most. One may find what he thought of it in canto XXIV of the poem. It is a terrible description of the English middle classes as we all knew them then, and as most of us accepted them without much question. He starts with the misery of the poor, but he goes on to the spiritual misery of the well-to-do—" the avenues of young girls and women, with sideway flopping heads, debarred from work, debarred from natural sexuality, weary to death with nothing to do " :

" When I see, flickering around, miserable spectrums and nostrums of reform—mere wisps devoid of all body—philanthropic chatter-boxes ; when I see and hear the droning and see-sawing of pulpits ; when the vision of perfect vulgarity and common-placeness arises upon me —of society—and of that which arrogates to itself the sacred name of England."

So he continues with his scathing vision of the country and people around him, with whom he was compelled by his education and comfortable means to associate.

In the midst of a complacent society which counted the growth of wealth as progress and a quadrupled population as national glory, he uttered his denunciation of the age, and pointed to an ideal far beyond its practice to fulfil. Before he was mature, Carlyle, Ruskin, and Dickens had shaken the faith of commercial Liberalism, and Carpenter stood as a priest in heretical succession to them. He opened his attack through evidences of physical and spiritual sickness. The very numbers of our medical and spiritual doctors proved what invalids we are. Crawling phenomena like policemen showed the rottenness of our state. Compared with the cat, we are degenerates of nature, who have lost our unity. Compared with the fox or the Bushman, we are self-conscious, distracted, and ugly. As to our civilization, he wrote :—

" The civilised man disowns the very breasts that suckled him. He deliberately turns his back upon the light of the sun, and hides himself away in boxes with breathing-holes, which he calls houses. He muffles himself in the cast-off furs of the beasts, each century swathing himself in more and more layers, till he ceases to be recognisable as the Man who was once the crown of the animals, and presents a more ludicrous spectacle than the monkey that sits on his own barrel-organ."

Before he was forty Carpenter had given up all desire

for the intellectual life in cloistered academies. It seemed
to him a fraud and weariness. I like to remember his
poem on the British Museum Library in Part IV of
Towards Democracy :

" How lovely !
All the myriad books—wellnigh two millions of volumes—the
interminable iron galleries, the forty miles or so of closely packed
shelves ; "

And then further on, he suddenly exclaims :

" How lovely !
To think there are all these books—and one need not read
them."

But the inspired value of *Towards Democracy* does not
lie in its denunciation of civilised English life, hampered
by conventions and all the stress and inequality of acquisitive society. It lies in its brilliant little pictures of common
human life, of natural labour, of sex, and all the natural
desires of men and women. There is a passage in *Jean
Christophe** which reproduces so exactly Carpenter's mood
and manner in this his most famous work that I may quote
a few of its sentences :

" Show the life of every day to the men and women
of every day ; that life is deeper and more vast than the
sea. The smallest among you bears the infinite in his soul.
The infinite is in every man who is simple enough to be
a man, in the lover, in the friend, in the woman who pays
with her pangs for the radiant glory of the day of child-
birth, in every man and every woman who lives in the
obscure self-sacrifice which will never be known to another
soul ; it is the very river of life, flowing from one to another,
and back again and round.

" Write the simple life of one of these simple men ;
write the peaceful epic of the days and nights following,
following one life to another, all sons of the same mother
from the dawning of the first day in the life of the world.
Write it simply, as simple as its own unfolding. You are
addressing all men ; use the language of all men . . .

* *Jean Christophe*, IV, 58 (quoted by Sir Arnold Wilson in his *Walks
and Talks*, page 6).

D*

There are only styles which say or do not say exactly what
they have to say. Let the rhythm of your heart prevail
in your writings."

Such sentences might be extracted from *Towards
Democracy* itself. It is hard to realise that Romain Rolland,
the author of them, had probably never even heard of
Edward Carpenter.

It was for natural life in the open air, in community with
nature and simple men, that he longed. Rousseau, Thoreau,
Ruskin and Walt Whitman had known the longing, and
to some extent had fulfilled their desire. Carpenter was
their follower, but in passing one must notice that those
other true lovers of nature had only a very limited knowledge of what nature really is. They knew nothing of
the stifling heat and innumerable pests of the tropics,
nothing of the deadly cold with which nature surrounds
the Poles. To dwell in community with nature in Savoy,
or the Lakes, or Massachusetts, is enviable and may be
holy, but in those charming regions praise of nature as
a whole may go too far, and that gives a certain weakness
to all such famous and influential thinkers. For their
adoration of nature is narrow and closely bounded.

But Carpenter for a brief interval did at all events attempt
to extend his knowledge of nature beyond the limits reached
by his great predecessors. In 1890 he abandoned his
temperate and beneficent valley in Derbyshire for the
widely different scenes and climate of Ceylon. His book
Adam's Peak to Elephanta tells the story, but if you would
realise how vast the difference was, you may learn it from
Jungle Tide by John Still, whose knowledge of Ceylon
was gained by a generation of years. It was not only to
a more savage aspect of nature that Carpenter was then
introduced. All through the years when he was something
over forty and at the height of his powers, the minds of
such English people as cared for thought were much
exercised by impalpable visions and ghosts of Oriental
philosophy.

We were at that time rather overwhelmed by mystic
seers, mahatmas, holy precipitators, and devotees guided
by their own self-assured intuition to the neglect of reason.

In the utterances of most among these maundering prophets and prophetesses, as of Mme. Blavatsky, for instance, Carpenter could discover only " general rot and confusion," and indeed, as being a sane person, I have found it hard to discover anything else, for such utterances were perhaps not intended for the sane. At all events, at the invitation of a thoughtful Sinhalese, the same who had previously sent him a copy of the *Bhagavat Gita*, the most definite of India's sacred scriptures, Carpenter set out for Ceylon, and was there introduced to a certain Gñani, whom he came to regard as " a high type of pre-civilisation man."

Few Englishmen are visionaries or mystics, but the thoughtful among us are often conscious of a desire to pierce behind this outer world into the hidden " realities " of which all phenomena may be but the shadows. The diversity of life in its innumerable forms and degrees— the gulfs fixed between the personalities of man and man— such diversities are obvious to us all. But Carpenter had from the first, or at all events since his meeting with Walt Whitman, maintained the essential unity of all life, and in this Gñani, he tells us, it was a matter of absorbing interest to feel himself in contact with the root-thought of all existence—the intense *consciousness* (not conviction merely) of the oneness of all life—the germinal idea which in one form or another has spread from nation to nation, and become the soul and impulse of religion after religion.

After a space of ten years, he tells us, he came to realise that the true line consists in combining and harmonising both body and soul, the outer and the inner. They are the eternal and needful complements of each other, and perhaps he may have thus recalled to himself the prayer of Socrates to the rural god Pan that his inward and his outward life might be made one. If carried to excess, he says, the Eastern methods result in over-quiescence, and even torpor ; but the Western habits tend to over-activity and external distraction of the mind, which may result in disintegration. As recognising the necessity of the Eastern side of thought, Carpenter may perhaps be called a mystic, but he maintained the balance of the visionary life as against the practical with enviable exactness.

After Ceylon he returned to a life in the healthy nature of England, which to him was almost irresistible. But at least equally strong was the attraction of manual work. For a time he had already attempted to get into touch with the workers of the factory cities by lecturing, and even miners listened to him fairly well, though with their backs turned to the lecturer ; I suppose to show that what he said was not of much importance to them. But lecturing was not sufficient. He tells us that once on his way through France it suddenly flashed upon him, with a vibration through his whole body, that he would and must somehow go and make his life with the mass of the people and the manual workers. For a time he had lived in a Sheffield attic practising ironwork, as far as such a nature could, in association with railway men, porters, clerks, signalmen, ironworkers, coach-builders, Sheffield cutlers ; and from the first, he tells us, he got on excellently and felt fully at home with them—" and I believe," he adds, " in most cases they with me." It must have been very difficult, for he always remained " very much the gentleman," and owing to our inequality of life and food and education there yawns a disastrous gulf between the worker and the gentleman. Strive as I may to be one with them, I have always felt that gulf, and the workers have felt it too. But Carpenter possessed a share of a faculty described by Colonel T. E. Lawrence as the secret of his own power among the Arabs :—

" Among the Arabs there were no distinctions, traditional or natural, except the unconscious power given a famous sheikh by virtue of his accomplishment ; and they taught me that no man could be their leader except he ate the ranks' food, wore their clothes, lived with them, and yet appeared better in himself."*

I think that in England even Carpenter never quite succeeded in attaining to that height of equality with the workers. He could not even swear naturally. But in 1883 he made his next gallant attempt. He purchased the freehold of three fields, about seven acres, at Millthorpe, between Sheffield and Chesterfield, and that was his home

* *Colonel Lawrence,* by Liddell Hart, p. 11.

for forty years. As he says, the strange gadfly (he uses
the Greek word *oistros*) of hard manual work, and digging
down to the very roots of things, spurred him on :

" I hardly know how to account for it," he writes in
My Days and Dreams. " It possessed me. Every habit,
every custom or practice of daily life—house arrangement,
diet, dress, medicine, &c., was overhauled and rigorously
scrutinised. I worked for hours and for whole days
together out in the open fields or garden, or digging drains
with pick and shovel, or carting along the roads ; going
into Chesterfield and loading and fetching manure, or to
the coalpit for coal, grooming and bedding down the
horse, or getting off to market at 6 a.m. with vegetables
and fruit, and standing in the market-place behind a stall
till 1 or 2 p.m. ; I was not satisfied but I must do everything
that was necessary to be done myself."

Those of us who have felt that stinging gadfly driving
to active or manual work, can appreciate and envy. Though
I did not go to stay with him at Millthorpe myself till
1917, while I was for a time away from the War, many
were naturally attracted to such a man, leading so unusual
a life and writing books of such influence in prose and the
irregular but rhythmic forms adopted from Walt Whitman's
manner.

In his proposed solitude he was beset by earnest and
innocent reformers, cranks and faddists of every degree,
advocates of theoretic systems, public benefactors (of
whom he was particularly shy), freelovers, mystics, tee-
totallers, vegetarians, nudists, the charming worshippers
of nature whose knowledge was limited to idyllic literature
and week-ends in the country, worshippers of himself,
both male and female, adorers even of his self-made sandals
as symbols of nobly uncivilised existence. I noticed with
pleasure that he met their adulations or even their simple
praise with low growls like a suspicious dog or even with
outspoken barks of " Wow, wow, wow." As he grew
older, he said that excessive cleverness and all that sort
of thing bored him rather than otherwise, and it comforts
me to know that when I stayed with him at Millthorpe
after my return from the Dardanelles and Salonika, he

found no cleverness in me at all, but wrote to his friend
Charles Sixsmith that I was always "so natural and
homely."

For a long time he found the country people around
him suspicious and aloof, for in England they are accustomed to regard every "gentleman" as allied to the squire
and the parson in enmity against them. "But by slow
degrees," he writes, "the rustics accepted me as almost
one of themselves, and gave me, some of them, their warm
friendship" :

"Despite the great differences between them and the
town-workers, and the greater intelligence and alertness
of the latter, I admire the character of the country-folk
most—their extraordinary serenity and good humour,
their tenacity, sincerity, and real affectionateness. Even
their silent ways—though irritating at times—are a relief
from the eternal gabble of the cities."

I remember with what pleasure he told me of a farm
woman with whom he condoled upon the departure of
her daughter from home, only to be answered : "Yes,
I do miss her, especially on washing days !" It was the
saying of people who live very close to the rocks of reality,
and also of the English nature always so careful to conceal
the commonplaces of emotion. As to the gabble of theorists
and doctrinaires, he must often have disappointed them
because he refused to take the oath of allegiance to any
party or definite cause. Though abstemious in his own
way of daily life, he was not even a teetotaller or a vegetarian,
when such peculiarities might give his hostess or his
companions trouble. "Is not the life more than meat,
and the body than raiment?" And in higher matters too
he refused to submit to rules and definitions of thought
or action :

"That neither Hyndman in his time, nor Morris in his,
nor the Fabian Society in theirs, nor Keir Hardie, nor
Kropotkin, nor Blatchford, nor any other individual or
body, succeeded in capturing the social movement during
these years and moulding it to his or their heart's desire,
must always be matter for congratulation."

By temperament, if not by conviction, he was a complete anarchist, detesting all commandments, authority, and forms of government. Most ethical teachers allow the Mosaic Decalogue to pass, but Carpenter writes :

"The Decalogue may have been a rough and useful ready-reckoner for the Israelites; but to us it admits of so many exceptions and interpretations that it is practically worthless."

When I objected that anarchism had not worked even among the angels of heaven, and that man was a little lower than the angels and did not seem in any hurry to catch them up, he admitted that even in Kropotkin, so courageous and attractive an anarchist, he perceived a charming naïveté which summed up all human evil in the one word "government," misleading by its apparently simple solution. But still he hoped that Russia might one day lead the great European reaction towards a freer and more voluntary state of society. When I observed that the day of freedom was still far from dawning in Russia, he replied with his great saying, "History is a difficult horse to drive."

In "practical politics" he took little interest, though he strongly supported Women's Suffrage as a symbol of deliverance from the idle and unsatisfied existence in which he had seen his sisters languishing at Brighton. His ideal of the great city was (to borrow Walt Whitman's phrase) where the men and women think lightly of the laws. "External law," he proclaimed emphatically, "must always be false," and he could not have existed under a dictatorship which superseded freedom by compulsion, as in the Russia, Germany and Italy of to-day. The Internal Law of self-expression was the only motive of behaviour which he acknowledged. At a public meeting in London soon after the war he took as his text, "To thine own self be true," and when I suggested that the quotation came from the stupidest old fool in Shakespeare, and that if a politician whom I named were true to his own self, the resulting man would be a devil indeed, he replied that even in that politician there must be a core of good which he could follow as his own true self. So unfailing was his optimism.

He retained it even when in his later years at Guildford,
George Merrill, his friend and attendant, would return
from the town in a state of maudlin drunkenness in the
afternoon.   Carpenter would look a little anxious, but I
never heard a word of reproach, and he never recovered
from his grief at the death of George.

Like most of us Carpenter was much occupied with all
the problems and variations of sex, and in the middle nineties
he published, or rather distributed, two or three pamphlets
upon that irresistible subject. Owing to the prosecution
of Oscar Wilde opinion was much agitated about sex in
those years, and the pamphlets were banned at first.
Collected afterwards under the title *Love's Coming of Age*,
they had a wide circulation, and probably exercised greater
influence than any of Carpenter's works except *Towards
Democracy*. As in his other works he here denounces the
shame and secrecy which were then still attached to the
body and all relations of sex :

" Until these subjects," he writes, " are openly put
before children and young people with some degree of
intelligent and sympathetic handling, it can scarcely be
expected that anything but the utmost confusion, in mind
and in morals, should reign in matters of Sex. That we
should leave our children to pick up their information
about the most sacred, the most profound and vital, of all
human functions, from the mere gutter, and learn to know
it first from the lips of ignorance and vice, seems almost
incredible and certainly indicates the deeply rooted unbelief
and uncleanness of our own thoughts."

He warns married people against the boredom and
vulgarisation of love where sex has been the only bond :

" The weary couples that may be seen at seaside places
and pleasure resorts—the respectable working-man with
his wife trailing along by his side, or the highly respectable
stock-jobber arm in arm with his better and larger half—
their blank faces, utter want of any common topic of conversation which has not been exhausted a thousand times
already, and their obvious relief when the hour comes
which will take them back to their several and divided
occupations—these illustrate sufficiently what I mean."

But it is possible for sex to lead to a higher plane of intercourse :

" In all men who have reached a certain grade of evolution, and certainly in almost all women, the deep rousing of the sexual nature carries with it a romance and tender emotional yearning towards the object of affection, which lasts on and is not forgotten even when the sexual attraction has ceased to be strongly felt."

Or for a finer and more poetic expression of his idea one may read the passage in *Towards Democracy* headed " The Ocean of Sex " :

" To hold in continence the great sea, the great ocean of Sex within one,
With flux and reflux pressing on the bounds of the body, the beloved genitals,
Vibrating, swaying emotional to the star-glint of the eyes of all human beings,
Reflecting Heaven and all Creatures,
How wonderful !

" Scarcely a figure, male or female, approaches, but a tremor travels across it.
As when on the cliff which bounds the edge of a pond someone moves, then in the bowels of the water also there is a mirrored movement,
So on the edge of this Ocean
The glory of the human form, even faintly outlined under the trees or by the shore, convulses it with far reminiscences ;
(Yet strong and solid the sea-banks not lightly to be over-passed !)
Till maybe to the touch, to the approach, to the incantation of the eyes of one,
It burst forth, uncontrollable."

He did not limit this sense of romance and tender emotional yearning to the love between man and woman. He found it possible and indeed frequent between members of the same sex, as it certainly existed in ancient Athens and other Greek states. His volume on *Intermediate Types among Primitive Folk* describes a kind of men who willingly undertake domestic and similar services usually deputed to women. But his insistence is not upon these rather abnormal types. It is upon the affectionate comradeship that he had found in such examples as Walt Whitman, and, as he believed, in Shelley, and had certainly experienced in his own life and relationships. Knowing that I did not share these feelings but was always passionately in love with women only, he observed to me once rather sadly, " You know I am rather heavily weighted on that side." But he did not regret it.

What, then, is the upshot and consummation of such a man ? How should we rank him among the Democrats ? He belonged to the class of men that England produces from time to time—men like Cromwell, Byron, Shelley, Charles Gordon, and T. E. Lawrence ; aristocrats by birth or by nature, but always standing on the side of the common people, the side unpopular with their own class. To him the expression of Self was not only an aim ; it was a necessity. But Self could find expression only in what he calls Democracy. In a great passage which brings us to a natural conclusion, he said :

" Of that which exists in the Soul, political freedom and institutions of equality, etc., are but the shadows (necessarily thrown), and Democracy in the States or Constitutions but the shadow of that which first expresses itself in the glance of the eye or the appearance of the skin. Without these the others are of no account, and need not be further mentioned."

Or, to take a further passage from *Towards Democracy* itself :

" To realize Freedom or Equality (for it comes to the same thing)—for this hitherto, for you, the universe has rolled ;

" For this the heroes and lovers of all ages have laid down their lives ; and nations like tigers have fought, knowing well that this life was a mere empty blob without Freedom.

" Where this makes itself known in a people or even in the soul of a single man or woman, there Democracy begins to exist."

Whether Carpenter will be much read in future, or is much read now, does not greatly matter. He does not rank among the few supreme poets or writers of the world's history. He is not one of the Twelve (for indeed there have been no more). We must remember him as a noble and characteristic type of our English nature—individualist, active, thoughtful, courageous, polite, but capable of burning indignation at the sight of cruelty or distress. Few may read him now, few can remember him, but in our souls he lives, he moves. Like a benignant ghost, unconsciously he haunts our steps. That is what I attempted to say over his grave in the Guildford cemetery when we buried him on July the 1st, 1929.

JOHN CARTWRIGHT

1740–1824

by H. L. BEALES

JOHN CARTWRIGHT
1740–1824
by H. L. BEALES

FRANCIS PLACE found Major John Cartwright an amiable bore. " When he was in town," said Place, " he used frequently to sup with me, eating some raisins he brought in his pocket, and drinking weak gin and water. He was cheerful, agreeable and full of curious anecdote. He was, however, in political matters exceedingly troublesome, and sometimes as exceedingly absurd. He had read but little or to little purpose, and knew nothing of general principles. He entertained a vague and absurd notion of the political arrangements of the Anglo-Saxons, and sincerely believed that these semi-barbarians were not only a polished people, but that their ' two-fold polity,' arms-bearing and representation were universal and perfect."

Place did Cartwright less than justice. If that was all that could be said for him, he would have deserved to be forgotten. If his career has not been made the subject of a biography since the two-volume *Life and Correspondence* published by his niece in 1826, shortly after his death, the democratic trend of political organisation and political thought since his day have established his claim beyond cavil to a resting-place in the pantheon of democratic heroes. Place's thumb-nail sketch of Major Cartwright is superficially true and no more. Cartwright was at times a bit of a political nuisance ; in Place's schemes he was even a misfit. He was a tedious writer, too, though he never wrote anything so abysmally dull as Place's worst efforts. But his dullness has been exaggerated. It was mainly the dullness of consistency and repetition. He kept on hammering away at the same theme. It really did not matter that his notion of the political arrangements of the Anglo-Saxons was vague and absurd. It did matter that he saw the defects of the political arrangements of his own day, measured their consequences in corruption and misuse of power, stated alternative arrangements and spent half a century in trying to force them into being. It

would be easy to substantiate Place's strictures against
Cartwright's scholarship. Easy but unprofitable. People
make their legends, political or theological or racial, because
of their own needs, not for any devotion to historical truth.
Our St. George has grown out of a meat-purveyor, it is
said, and legendary Nordics have generated sundry current
greatnesses. If Cartwright romanticised our Anglo-Saxon
ancestors, he did it in good faith and for a good cause.
It was the cause that mattered, not the scholarship. After
all, all history is contemporary history in some measure.

Cartwright sprang from the substantial middle rank
of eighteenth-century society. He spent his vacations
in a whig nobleman's family ; he served as midshipman
under Lord Howe in the Seven Years' War and attained
a lieutenancy in 1762 ; he gained experience of colonial
government in Newfoundland when that war was over ;
he became a Major in the Nottinghamshire militia in
1775 and took vast pains in making his unit efficient. Thus
summarised, his early career sounds ordinary enough for
one of his station. Yet there were already signs of an
unusual quality. On the Newfoundland station he found
it necessary to take steps to protect Irish fishermen from the
dishonest cupidity of their employers, and Red Indians
from the brutal cruelty of the fishermen. In 1772 he drew
up a plan for the supply of English oak for the navy and
worked for ten years to get it adopted—with little prospect
of success, for corruption reigned supreme in the
timber department of our public life. In 1774 he took
to speculation in politics, publishing, anonymously because
he still looked for a career in the navy, his *American
Independence : The Interest and Glory of Great Britain.*
He had already begun to expect that his professional
career would suffer. " The subject of my (American)
letters," he wrote in 1774, " and other considerations
have of late caused me to consider the voting for Members
of Parliament as a very serious duty, not to be sacrificed
to interest ; and whatever I may consider as my duty,
I trust that I shall always have resolution to practise."
Whither his mind was tending was made clear by his
comment on Wilkes, " I will agree with you in hanging
Mr. Wilkes, if he can be *legally* tucked up ; but no reflections,

I beg of you, upon the cap of liberty." His view of his
duty as a militia-man was not one that all his colleagues
would accept. "The militia," he wrote to his brother,
the inventor of the first power-loom, "by its institution
is not intended to spread the dominion or to vindicate in
war the honour of the crown, but it is to preserve our laws
and liberties, and therein to secure the existence of the
state." When he designed a badge for his regiment
he set on it "a cap of liberty resting on a book, over which
appears a hand holding a drawn sword in its defence.
The motto is *Pro legibus et libertate.*"

Cartwright was public-spirited. He hated injustice.
His mind had a conservative bent. He was religious by
temperament, bound by conscience to follow his vision
of what was right. He was entirely free of the extravagance
and corruption of so many of the leaders of his age. He
never betrayed the least sign of the petulance or the un-
reliability or the inability to co-operate of the disappointed
man, though no man to all appearance spent half a century
of devoted effort more fruitlessly than he. He ought to
have been, things being as they were in his day, a nearly
obscure pillar of social and political orthodoxy, or at most
a minor public figure, a good county member, say, resisting
the onset of change, or a just landlord contending for the
welfare of the tenants on his estate. His extraordinary
pertinacity, his energy and organising power, his singleness
of mind, his simplicity, his lack of guile, his courage, his
positive goodness would have gained him general respect
and some influence, but he would never have made a
political leader. He would have been passed over when
offices were being distributed, and ignored when intrigues
were being hatched. He had no political finesse. He was
too honest to be included in any bunch at whom a Walpole
could sneer with his "all these men have their price."
He would have made a first-rate naval commander, as he
did make a first-rate major of militia. But politics was not
his natural field. How was it then that he became a father
of parliamentary reform, a radical prophet, and the original
author of the political programme adopted by the Chartists?

Political history is a tantalizing pursuit. It has to be told
in terms of personalities whereas the personalities are little

more than marionettes. They have their day and cease to be ; that day is big and exciting and " significant " (blessed word !) according to their closeness to the spirit and movement of their age. If they render articulate the aspirations of the public, if they are in line with the historical tendencies that brought them into political being, if the dynamic forces of their day (including its historic past) become incandescent in their words and actions, whether positively or negatively, their name is writ large on the historian's pages. In truth those pages are but a form of algebra. So-called facts are no more than relationships, and the political equations require solution in terms of non- or mainly non-personal causation. If then we seek explanation of the transformation of the excellent Major Cartwright into a radical democrat, and of the posthumous triumph of his devoted and selfless labours in a temporarily hopeless cause, we must find it not on the stage where the actors strut but in the audience for whom the play was made.

The remorseless movement of historical forces brought the disruption of the first British Empire when Cartwright was in his middle thirties. If ever a cycle of events deserved the term " inevitable "—a term of whose use the historian should be sparing—that did which culminated in the Declaration of American Independence. It was the American problem which determined Cartwright's political attitude and which brought to an end his naval career. Cartwright's proposal for the solution of the American problem was a federal league of Great Britain and the colonies each with two independent legislatures. He came to this solution by the two-fold process of examining the colonists' grievances and analysing the principles of the English constitution. " It is a capital error," he wrote, " in the reasonings of several writers on this subject, that they consider the liberties of mankind in the same light as an estate or a chattel, and go about to prove or disprove their right to it, by the letter of grants and charters, by customs and usage, and by municipal statutes. . . . But the liberty of mankind is not established on such rotten foundations. 'Tis not among mouldy parchments, or in the cobwebs of a casuist's brain, we are to look for it ; it is the immediate gift of God, and the seal of it is that freewill which he hath made the noblest constituent of man's nature. It is not derived from any one, but it is original in every one ; it is inherent and unalienable. . . It is utterly impossible that any human being can be without a title to liberty, except he himself have forfeited it by crimes which make him dangerous to society. . . . All the subtleties and refinements, all the arguments that the wit of man can invent, will never be sufficient to justify any species of arbitrary dominion, while we retain a knowledge of this short and simple proposition, ' The good of society is the end of civil government,' nor will they ever justify a discretionary taxation by a prince or government, the people being unrepresented, so long as we know that ' a man hath no property in that which another can take from him without his consent.' " Holding such beliefs, Cartwright refused to serve against the insurgents, forfeiting thus his professional career at the very moment when advancement in it would have made marriage possible for him.

In studying the American question Cartwright was forced to reflect on English politics. In his *American Independence* he touched slightly on the subject of parliamentary reform, expressing the hope that Lord Camden would " frame a proper bill " with that object. It was for him, however, to show what was required, and he did so in his treatise, at once argument and programme of reform, entitled *Take your choice* ! *Representation and Respect* : *Imposition and Contempt. Annual Parliaments and Liberty* : *Long Parliaments and Slavery.* If the style of this work is ponderous, .. yet contains memorable sentences. " It is liberty, and not dominion, which is held by divine right. . . . A man hath by birthright a property in the English constitution. . . . Personality is the sole foundation of the right of being represented, and property has in reality nothing to do in the case. . . . We might as well make the possession of forty shillings per annum the proof of a man's being rational, as of his being free."

It has often been pointed out that the year 1776 was a veritable *annus mirabilis.* The American Declaration of Independence, Adam Smith's *Wealth of Nations,* Bentham's *Fragment on Government* all gave it lustre.

Cartwright's *Take your Choice!* may not be giant's work like these, but it had virtue all the same. It gave meaning and definition to the democratic idea, which was being formulated, bit by bit, in the political incidents of which Wilkes and the Society of the Bill of Rights and Horne Tooke were the central figures in England. Cartwright passed beyond their theories to the full statement of political equality. He affirmed the principle of personal representation and so demanded universal suffrage—an age limit of eighteen and one man one vote only—secret voting, annual parliaments with all elections on the same day, and equal electoral districts. Thus he sketched the programme of radicalism. Already the American Revolution was clearing the air. Political discussion, the formulation of first principles, was driven to the consideration of realities. Cartwright cut no great figure as a philosopher. He was no Bentham and no Rousseau. But he stated for the first time the principle of personal representation and so became the vehicle of the democratic impulse which was conceived in the Puritan and born in the " Glorious " Revolution, but which was still adolescent when George III tried to revive the power of the Crown.

Cartwright's later writings added nothing to the doctrines of *Take your Choice!* He composed, for the Society for Constitutional Information to distribute, a *Declaration of Rights*, and had it embellished with symbolical ornaments of his own designing. General Oglethorpe reported to the Major and Granville Sharp that Chatham had praised it in his presence. In 1780 he published *The People's Barrier against Undue Corruption*, in which he claimed not only the Englishmen's inherent right but their historical right to annual parliaments, and shows both how corrupt practices had grown up and how reform could be attained. The *People's Barrier*, like Cartwright's other writings, would have a bourgeois flavour to the democrat of to-day, but it was radical enough in its own setting. The *Bill of Rights and Liberties* of 1817 contained an introduction in the form of a dialogue between Lord Henry Hotspur, Sir Francis Folkright, Sir Samuel Citiman and John Hampden Firelaw, Barrister, which summarises the arguments of the earlier treatise, and shows in detail how representation

would be redistributed, and how the ballot would be worked
(with ceremonial prayers, polling apparatus, and all the
rest in most complicated form !). It contained, all the same,
nothing new, unless a greater awareness of the interest of
the labouring class in parliamentary reform be new. So
it is with the other books and pamphlets published at
frequent intervals in the intervening years. *The Legislative
Rights of the Commonalty Vindicated* (1777) is an enlarged
edition of *Take your Choice!*. *The Commonwealth in Danger*
(1795) contains a trenchant reply to Arthur Young's
unworthy attack upon him and an explanation of his views
on the French Revolution, but is otherwise a re-statement of
his ideas and proposals. *The State of the Nation* (1805) again
appeals for a restoration of the constitution in both its
branches, civil and military, with a commentary from the
reformer's angle on history, old and recent, and on current
events and dangers.

Cartwright was a man of undeviating pertinacity, and
his whole life became a crusade for parliamentary reform.
He never flinched at the cost, whether obloquy, suspicion,
humiliation or conflict with authority. He had to suffer
from all of these things. In his *Letter to a Friend at Boston*
(1793) he complained that he had been " marked out for
obloquy by persons not very friendly to public freedom.
No sooner was my back turned a few weeks ago, in order
to accompany my wife in paying the last filial duties to a
dying parent, than calumny, with her thousand tongues,
instantly filled the country with unnumbered reports . . .
as malicious as they were false. According to some I had
been apprehended for sedition and treasonable practices
and lodged in Newgate. . . One report stated that I had
fled northwards ; and another that I had escaped to France.
Two other reports have come to my knowledge. By one
of them, it was said that I was ruined in my affairs ; by the
other it was positively asserted that I was become insane, and
was sent to a mad-house." Rebutting, in *The Commonwealth
in Danger* (1795), Arthur Young's accusation that he
welcomed the execution of the French King, Cartwright
declared that Young's " hobgoblin absurdities " were
inspired as a " preparative " to legal attack upon him.
" As a preparative for legal attack, it is necessary that in

the public mind, including the minds of future juries, the cause of these men (private men aiming at reforms essential to freedom) should if possible be brought into distaste or contempt, their intentions misinterpreted, their characters destroyed, and their names made objects of detestation and abhorrence." Humiliation was thrust upon him when in 1792 he was passed over for one of lower rank in the appointment of lieutenant-colonel to his regiment of militia, and then removed from the regiment. His *Letter to the Duke of Newcastle* (1792) did not mince words to and about His Grace, and even accused him of commissioning spies to report his political behaviour. The *Letter* contained, beside a statement of his attitude to the French Revolution, an interesting revelation of corruption—" I never, my Lord, was in the habit of putting my signature to the lower corners of blank sheets of papers by dozens as I once saw done by an auditor of national money accounts " —as well as his plan for providing the navy with English timber. It contained, too, a blunt observation that " amongst the discoveries of these pregnant times, it has been found out that men may live and thrive without Lords ; that the sun will shine and the dew will descend, where there are none but equal citizens to partake of these blessings ; and that even good laws can be made, and justice well administered, without either hereditary legislators or hereditary judges." What stung Cartwright about the Duke of Newcastle's action in excluding him from his regiment was its unjustness rather than its foundation in dislike of his politics. Cartwright had been an exemplary officer, respected and liked by fellow-officers and rank-and-file. And he regarded his militia-work as definitely a part of his duty of citizenship. Standing armies he regarded as a menace to liberty ; the militia of King Alfred was the only constitutional force a free country could employ or need. Given such a free force of free men, no unnecessary wars of expansionist adventure would occur, and no needless and unwise extensions of the war with France would be possible. To drive Cartwright out of the militia was to deny him the functions of free citizenship. Though wounded deeply in 1792, Cartwright was not attacked by legal process till 1819. He was accused

then, with Wooler (of the *Black Dwarf*) and others, of
conspiracy against the constitution—fomenting discontent
and disaffection by seditiously conspiring to elect a representative (Sir Charles Wolseley) for Birmingham and force
him into the House of Commons in which Birmingham
was unrepresented. For his part in that incident Cartwright
was fined £100, his age saving him from imprisonment.
The sentence might have been more severe had he not
run to earth a subterranean issue of inflammatory placards
which would have compromised him and other reformers,
and which was the work of the *agent provocateur* Fletcher
alias Franklin *alias* Forbes.

To a man of Cartwright's stamp thought and action
went together. He was no mere intellectual. There was
no divorce between written word and effort to implement
it. He was well enough off to devote himself actively
as well as verbally to the cause of reform, and he spent
generously of his substance in the cause. His fortunes
underwent some vicissitudes in the course of his life—as
in 1788 when a woollen-mill at Retford failed, and when a
friend's misfortune left him with a debt of honour of
several thousand pounds to meet, though, being usurious,
it need not legally have been paid—but he showed skill
in managing his estates, first in Nottinghamshire and then
in Lincolnshire, and earned the cordial approval of Arthur
Young. He was a successful producer of woad, and he
persuaded his fellow-producers to regulate their production
in concert with him. " In agriculture," he wrote in 1793,
" I give constant employment to near fifty families, exclusive
of occasional multitudes ; in manufacture, I am the largest
proprietor of a large work, employing some hundreds of
persons ; and on these foundations I have in commerce a
considerable capital afloat." Thus he could finance the
Black Dwarf, which Wooler conducted with ability,
organize his various reform societies, and run up and down
the country on speaking tours.

The reform movement, of which Cartwright's work
was a conspicuous part, went through three phases in his
political life-time. The first, to which the prelude was the
" Wilkes and Liberty " struggle, might be described as
the American Independence phase, though in truth the

American and the English events sprang from the same impulses and were inter-connected. The second was the French Revolutionary phase, and the third the post-Waterloo phase, which issued after Cartwright's death in the great reform victory of 1832. Cartwright's own labours were continuous, but both the associates who worked with him and their influence were conditioned by the seeming urgency of the issue and the immediate prospect of success.

In the American Independence phase, the lead was taken by the Yorkshire freeholders under the leadership of the Rev. Christopher Wyvill. Yorkshire had some 16,000 freeholders represented by two members. They looked with critical eyes at the 400 borough members who had to consider a total electorate of less than 100,000. They were sensitive, naturally enough, both to high taxation following an unsuccessful war, and to the excessive corruption which was habitual over their borders. They called their press and gentry together at the close of 1779 to petition the House of Commons against public extravagance and corruption. Half the counties of England were induced to follow their lead, and county associations were organised in a movement to demand reform not only of proved abuses but of parliamentary representation itself. The Westminster electors, under the influence of Charles James Fox, proclaimed a striking programme, which comprised equal electoral districts ; annual parliaments elected on a single day ; universal male suffrage, exercised by all inscribed on the electoral register and effected by secret ballot ; the exclusion of placemen from the House of Commons ; the payment of members ; the eligibility of all voters to be candidates for Parliament. The Gordon riots came to the rescue of the advocates of reaction, but the disasters of the American War enabled a reduction of the pension list and the sinecures to be secured. Wyvill and his associates enlisted William Pitt's interest, and it became clear to all that the whole system of representation was under attack by men who would not be fobbed off with a mere pruning of Treasury patronage. To enlist wider support for the reform movement the Society for Promoting Constitutional Information was formed in 1780, and in two years it had a membership of a hundred, including

men of distinction in several fields.   The Society produced
a useful pamphlet literature and petitions to the Commons.
Pitt divided the House on a series of moderate reform
proposals which were rejected by large majorities both
in 1783, and, when Prime Minister, in 1785.   From that
defeat the first reform movement did not recover.

Cartwright's part in this first phase was important.
He interested people in the cause ; he stirred up his county
of Nottingham to send petitions to Parliament ; he founded,
with Dr. Jebb and Capel Lofft, the Society for Constitutional
Information, taking a most active part in its meetings
and writing its *Declaration of Rights* ; he composed a series
of books ; he co-operated with Wyvill ; he promoted meetings
and conferences, wrote letters to the papers, corresponded
with reformers in Ireland.   The reformers' programme
was his programme and none among them was more
zealous than he.   But the movement was narrow, confined
to the middle class and divided on such issues as a policy
of gradualism, and compensation to the owners of
rotten boroughs on their disenfranchisement.   Dr. Jebb
was the farthest-sighted of the enthusiasts when he
declared, " I am persuaded that a reform, when effected,
must take place in consequence of the active energy of the
people."   How could the substantial folk, even though
they drank toasts to " The Majesty of the People " and
declared that all civil authority issued from them, win the
labouring classes save by working with them ?

The French Revolution rekindled and democratized
the reform movement.   At first it shocked the conservatives
and stimulated the radicals : later it shocked the radicals
and stimulated the conservatives.   Cartwright's influence
remained on the side of the constitutionalists.   He gave
testimony to Horne Tooke's character in his trial in 1794 ;
he joined the Society of Friends of the People, though
they wanted to expel him when his radicalism came into
conflict with their whiggism ; he continued to write books
and organize petitions ; he tried to bring reformers together,
whether they were members of the London Corresponding
Society paying a subscription of a penny a week, or of the
middle-class societies paying a guinea or upwards a year.
It may well have been Cartwright who was mainly

E

responsible for the petition presented by Charles Grey in 1793, which contained so effective a presentation of the case for reform. But while he was anxious to work with anyone who would support the great cause, he was disturbed by Paine's republicanism and religion, and not the sort of man, yet at any rate, to be a leader among the artisans into whose hands the main impetus of the movement was passing. In any case the movement was effectively damped down by 1796 when Fox, with some truth, said that " the whole country seems dead." Cartwright's part in the second phase of the reform struggle was useful but not dominating.

The third phase of the reform movement is associated with Cobbett, Burdett and Place, with Spa Fields and Peterloo. Its chequered history is familiar right up to its successful issue in the Reform Act of 1832. Yet its prelude is largely forgotten and is mainly Cartwright's work. He refused to give up the struggle, even though disillusion and governmental repression denied all prospect of immediate success. He may have seemed an amiable bore to Place, but the old fighter's last efforts were not without effect. His candidatures for Boston in 1806 and 1807 were hopeless, but his astonishing speaking-tours in 1812, 1813, and 1815 did much to keep alive the reform movement among working people. His Hampden Club, founded in 1812, was composed of highly respectable members and it expired in 1819, but it fostered the formation of political clubs in the provincial towns. Some of them got into trouble with the authorities, but they helped to give the political leaders the popular backing which made the movement at last irresistible. Cartwright was never a better reformer than when at last he carried his efforts for the people to the people themselves.

There is no need to perorate about Cartwright. He was not a great man or a great writer as these things are ordinarily reckoned. But no cause ever had a cleaner or more devoted advocate, and no essentially second-rate figure ever accomplished more. The history of the struggle for Parliamentary reform cannot be written without recognition of the great part he played in it in its pioneer and formative stages. No great democrat was ever more selfless than John Cartwright.

WILLIAM COBBETT

1762–1835

by G. D. H. COLE

WILLIAM COBBETT
1762–1835
by G. D. H. COLE

THERE are certain Englishmen who, being memorable for much besides, make one think, whenever they come into one's mind, of England. Not of England as a nation, much less a Great Power, or of England as a political unit, or of England with any other special qualification, but purely and simply of England. It is not merely that these men are " so English," though they are : it is that they have in some sort the quality of being England, and of expressing in whatever they do or say something as unmistakably English as the burr of an Oxfordshire (not, be it noted, an " Oxford ") accent. They have an English burr ; and it goes without saying that, having this, they are none of your desiccated townsmen, remote from the life of field and village, but countrymen in mind, wherever they live. For the heart of our urbanised England is still in the country.

Cobbett was an Englishman in this very special sense. Carlyle called him " the pattern John Bull of the century " ; and the phrase sticks in the mind. Bluff, egotistical, shrewd, capable of meanness as well as of greatness, positive in all things and desperately wrong in some—but also devastatingly right in many more—no theorist till he could see with his own eyes the human stuff of which problems are made, quick to anger and indignation but also infinitely friendly ; didactical and often overbearing, and yet full of human sympathy ; very well satisfied with himself and ever ready to hold his own experience up as an example to others ; and therewith possessed of a singular power of identifying himself with the country he loved and the people for whom he fought—there, as nearly as I can paint it in a few words, you have the portrait of this tall, gawky, florid, exuberant farmer, who looked like a farmer, and did more than any other man to bring hope into dark places where hope was needed even more sorely than meat and drink.

Above all else, I think of Cobbett as the man who, at a wretched time in the history of the English people, put hope into their hearts, not by telling lies or painting fancy pictures, either of this world or of the next, but by good solid cursing that never degenerated into a whine or a mere vapouring of despair, but bade men gird up their loins and struggle for the right. No matter whether he was talking at the moment to a gathering of farmers in some country town on market day, or to a crowd of half-starved labourers assembled on some Hampshire heath, or to the journeymen and factory workers in one of the new industrial towns, he knew how to speak comfortable words, even if all he said was of men's wrongs and miseries, and nothing at all of their compensations. He had a wealth of righteous indignation always at command, not vamped up to suit his hearers, but coming naturally out of him—felt and swelling within him too strongly to be bottled up. There were so many things to arouse that indignation ; and, if he expended some of it on the wrong objects, that mattered very little, as long as his anger flowed like a sea over the inhumanity and injustice of the times.

Yet Cobbett was not only an angry man, finding everywhere he went ample cause for his anger. If he had been only that, his passion would have been far less compelling. He was angry, exceedingly angry ; but there was always love as well as anger in his words. He loved the people on whose behalf he made crusade ; and, equally with the people, he loved the land they lived in—the villages and churches, the great houses with their parks of orderly trees, the birds and beasts, the downs and valleys and rivers and streams, the crops that grew out of the earth and, last but not least, the earth itself. The smell and feel of the countryside were his tonic ; and, though much of his life was lived in towns, he had to be coming back always to the open country for refreshment and inspiration. In the town, he often seemed to be only guessing : in the country, he knew.

Not that Cobbett's love of the country was just like mine, or probably yours ; for I at any rate am a town-dweller, and not a countryman. The country is a place to which I go, not with the sense of going home. But to

Cobbett the country was home, and his eye for it was the eye of a countryman. He wanted it to be useful, and not merely ornamental. The barren heath of Hindhead stirred no pleasure in him ; and the sight of a field full of thistles put him quite out of humour for a morning. Gentlemen's parks he could bear with, for he loved a good tree, above all if it was one of his favourite *locusts*. He had, moreover, a feeling for the old squire that never forsook him even when he was most roundly denouncing the squire's political opinions. The squire was a part of Old England : he had been there so long that, equally with the village church, he fitted into the scene. It was another matter when the park belonged to a stockbroker, or an army contractor, or any of the new-fangled money-spinning class. Then indeed Cobbett had a good look at the man's park and house, very ready to find fault. But the old squire had, if not his agreement, at least his sympathy, extended the more readily because, in Cobbett's opinion, his chance of survival was poor enough in the bad new times.

For Cobbett was one of those evangelists who see the future by looking back to the past. Maybe the past they think they see is not quite what really was ; for they are as ready to pick out from it the things they love and value as to pick out what is bad in the present. That is nothing against them ; for every age needs men to tell it in good homespun language what is wrong with it, and a touch of exaggeration does not come amiss either for stirring the imaginations of the victims or for shaking the complacency of the smug. Nor is there any harm in idealising the past, in the sense of seeing its virtues more plainly than its faults ; for that is one way of giving men heart to set about mending present wrongs. Or, if it be a fault not to see all things steadily and whole and in the correct perspective, it may be a fault that is inseparable from a certain sort of greatness. To be always cool may be a virtue ; but to lose one's temper at injustice may be a virtue too, even if loss of temper always distorts the vision.

The past that Cobbett saw in this idealised way was sometimes nearer, and sometimes more remote. At times, it was a past beyond the Reformation, when monasteries recognised the obligation to care for the poor, and the tithe was a charge on property for the relief of the poor, and not itself a form of property. Under the spell of that vision he produced his *History of the Protestant Reformation*, which roused the Evangelicals to the height of fury, as he fully meant it to do. At other times the past was nearer, in the glorious days before the Bank of England, founded to help Dutch William's wars, had saddled the country with the National Debt. Or again the past would draw nearer still, to the days of his own childhood, before Pitt had ruined the country with his villainous " system," or the stock-jobbers enriched by the war had bought up the old estates, or " the Wen," London, had been swollen to its present monstrous size. Those were the days—the days when Cobbett was a boy scaring crows in a field, or weeding the garden paths at Waverley Abbey, or watching the fine gentlemen—who could afford it then—ride out to hounds. But now, he tells us again and again, all that is gone—or going. The stock-jobbers are putting up their ugly big houses all over the countryside, or shoving the old decaying gentry out of their homes : the peasants, who used to be cheery souls, with good healthy appetites and a healthy respect for the State, are shivering in rags at the gang-work set by the parish, or gone away to work long hours in the suffocating misery of the new factory towns. The old squires, where they are left, wear long faces because of the rates and taxes ; and they are thinning fast. It is their fault, too, that they are being undone, because they backed up Pitt and his " system," and never lifted a hand to save the labourers from ruin. And they lived fine too, when they couldn't afford it. There's Squire Ridge, ruined with fox-hunting, and Squire Somebody-else, who tried to hold up his head among a pack of stock-jobbers, spending pound for pound. All the old glories fast departing ; and in their places lords of the loom and steam engine, brokers from Change Alley, and the pestilent fellows who make the paper for the Bank to print its filthy notes on.

You would get tired of this quite soon ; but suddenly, in the very middle of his tirade, Cobbett sees something else in his mind's eye, and in a minute he is off after that. Perhaps it was only the really excellent crop of Swedish

turnips he saw when he was riding past Mr. Acres'
farm to-day, or perhaps it was a pretty girl in a field with
whom he exchanged the glad eye. Whatever it was, you
hear about it, as soon as the picture comes into his vision ;
and then you are in the fields with him, in sun or rain,
seeing what the Swedish turnips looked like, or giving
the girl the glad eye yourself. Or perhaps what comes up
in his mind is a remembrance of his own life ; and then
too you hear about it. " When I was a soldier in New
Brunswick," "when the swindling Americans robbed me
of five thousand dollars," " when Pitt offered me one of
the Government newspapers," " when I was in Newgate
gaol "—all vastly egotistical, all much to Cobbett's honour
and glory, and for an example for all good citizens in the
middle way of life to follow, but withal immensely vivid,
racy, diverting, and altogether human.

In *Rural Rides* you get this expansive, discursive,
objurgatory, preaching, reminiscent, but above all *noticing*
William Cobbett at his best. Here is writing dashed off
quickly, often on the morrow of a long day's ride over the
country, while the impressions were fresh, and sent post-
haste up to London to be printed in that most personal of
all periodicals, Cobbett's *Political Register*. Their fascination lies a good deal in this impressionistic quality, or rather
in their absolute naturalness and spontaneity. As you
read them, you follow his racing thought and roving eye,
never knowing what either will light on next. They are the
perfection of political journalism, because they weave
politics into the texture of normal living ; but they are also
literature that has long survived our minding about many
of the persons and controversies with which they deal.
Cobbett rode over southern England, and as he rode he
wrote ; and no book was ever written that was more
England's own book, getting the smell and feel and look
of the English country and the English country people
down in print, so that the reader can smell and feel and see
as well as Cobbett. Usually I set no store by first editions ;
but my first edition of *Rural Rides* always seems to have a
country smell. Perhaps that is only because it is a little
mouldy.

Or take *Advice to Young Men—and Young Women*, for

E*

they are both on the title page, though the book is generally
spoken of discourteously without the young women. Here
you get less of the vivid pictures of field and farm ; for here
Cobbett is writing not a journal, but a sort of tract. You
will probably not take Cobbett's advice ; for his standards
and habits are not yours. You will hardly choose your
wife by deciding that she is the very woman for you when,
on a second meeting, you find her scrubbing out a washing-
tub in the snow, in the half-light of very early morning,
on a bitterly cold day, out of doors. Nor will you, probably,
insist on doing your writing-work on a stone floor, or obey
Cobbett's precepts about rising early and going early
to bed. You will not, I think, agree fully with his views
on education, or find your wife, when you get one, willing to
be written about quite as Cobbett wrote about Anne Reid,
though assuredly he never said anything about her that
was not vastly complimentary as he meant it. But, though
on many points you will not quite share Cobbett's views
—for, whatever your opinion may be, it is pretty certain
you have twentieth century habits of mind—I think you
will enjoy *Advice to Young Men—and Young Women*,
above all else the bits that are about the author's own life.
If you do not enjoy it I am inclined to say, that is your
fault ; for it means you do not know and like racy, redolent
English writing when you meet it.

Then there is the *Political Register*, which Cobbett conducted as a weekly for well over thirty years, writing the greater
part of it himself, and basing its appeal practically to the
exclusion of all else on his own personality. Others
contribute to the *Register* now and then : there are screeds
by the old prosy Radical, Major Cartwright, who was, for
all his prosiness, the salt of the earth, and whole pages of
reports of current events, or important documents reprinted,
or extracts from parliamentary papers and debates. But
no one bought the *Register* for the sake of these : men bought
it to see what Cobbett was saying now, whom he had chosen
to pillory this week, what particular feature of the iniquitous
" system " he had chosen this time to denounce, or perhaps
where he had been riding last, and what he had seen and
thought by the way. The *Register* was *Cobbett's* Register—
the weekly register of Cobbett's impressions, reactions, and

ideas derived from what he had been seeing and hearing
and doing during the past week. His leading articles were
enormous : often they took up most of the paper. But they
were read—read aloud by poor men at coffee-houses and
ale-houses where other poor men gathered who could not
read, or at least could not afford to buy, and read no less
in rich men's clubs round Westminster ; for Cobbett's
political opponents always wanted to know what he had
to say this week. The *Political Register* was a power.
Sometimes it barked up the wrong tree, but never up the
wrong wood. And whether Cobbett chose the right or the
wrong tree, men always attended to his barking. For a
man cannot write like Cobbett, and not be attended to,
even if he happens on occasion to be talking nonsense.

The *Political Register* went through strange metamor-
phoses. It was founded as an extreme patriotic journal,
to back up Pitt and the French war policy, to denounce
Jacobins and Radicals and to shout down the demagogues
on the other side. Within a few years it was shouting down
the very groups that had supported its establishment, and
Cobbett was bellowing as loudly for Radical Reform as he
had bellowed against it. He did not change sides again ;
for he had found out by then where his allegiance really
belonged. But the *Register* went through many queer
changes after that. For two years Cobbett edited it from
Newgate Gaol, where he had been sent for saying libellous
things about the flogging of soldiers. For two more he
edited it from the other side of the Atlantic—in days when
there were no telegraphs or steamships, and letters could
come only as fast as a sailing ship could travel. That was
when he had fled to the United States partly from Lord
Sidmouth's " Gagging Acts " of 1817, but also from his
creditors, who had become far too pressing in their
attentions. At different times the *Register* was sold at the
most varied prices—from a shilling or more down to twopence, according to the changing exigencies of the Stamp
Duties—those " taxes on knowledge " which were deliberately used to hamper the activities of Radical journalists.
Its appeal was widely different from year to year. At one
time it was full of appeals to the farmers, and plainly
addressed to them as its principal audience. That was

when Cobbett had gone a-crusading among the farmers to raise up support for an " equitable adjustment " of the monstrous burden of the National Debt, as well as for Radical Parliamentary Reform. At other times, it was written to and for the agricultural labourers—victims of a Poor Law which condemned them to semi-starvation and to serf-labour under the Speenhamland arrangement. Or again, it would be filled with *Addresses to the Journeymen and Labourers* of the towns, adjuring them to join manfully in the cry for Radical Reform, and painting a lurid picture of their exploitation by the financial power. Whatever the direction of the appeal might be, there in the *Register*, week after week, you had Cobbett talking about every conceivable sort of thing that wanted doing or undoing, in language that even the plainest readers could readily understand. Perhaps Cobbett's predilection for stone floors helped him to write fast. Assuredly he did write fast : so that no other journalist, save Daniel Defoe, has ever approached his output, and certainly none has ever sold a paper for more than thirty years, almost exclusively on the strength of his own person-ality. The circulation of the *Register* ebbed and flowed with changes in political interest or tension. But no other paper on the same side ever came near equalling the influence of Cobbett's weekly diatribe.

This account of the *Political Register* has taken me back to Cobbett's early days when, so far from upholding the cause of Radical Reform, he made his bow as the most violent of all the anti-Jacobin pamphleteers. Cobbett's first published work, unless we accept the view that he had a hand in an earlier pamphlet written to uphold the rights of the common soldier, was a violent diatribe against that estimable Radical Reformer, Dr. Joseph Priestley, whose house had been burnt down not long before by the Birmingham mob. Priestley, finding liberty at a discount in an England at war with France, had come to look for it in the brave New World that had so lately flung off the tyrant's yoke. He had landed in the free United States, to a salvo of congratulatory addresses from American Societies, whose members, fresh from singeing the King of England's beard, were eager to wish the Jacobins the same good hunting. Cobbett himself was in the United

States because of a little disagreement with the powers that were in England ; for he had used his experience as sergeant-major in the British army to collect imposing evidence of corrupt practices on the part of his officers, and this excess of zeal had made England too hot to hold him. But Cobbett in exile was very much the Englishman ; and the revolutionary Societies' addresses to Dr. Priestley were altogether too much for him. His *Observations on Dr. Priestley's Emigration* were neither polite nor profound ; but they were undoubtedly pungent, and the British diplomatic representatives in the United States were not long in seeking out so doughty a champion. During the remaining years of his sojourn in America Cobbett, not without encouragement from official quarters at home, laid about him with a will, defending the British cause through thick and thin, and lavishing upon the American people a wealth of home truths and home untruths that made them at all events sit up and take notice.

Philadelphia, where Cobbett was living, was strongly pro-French. Cobbett opened a bookseller's shop there, after a series of entertaining quarrels with the regular booksellers ; and, just to teach these rebel dogs their place, filled his shop-window with all the things most calculated to annoy the American public. Pictures of his Sovereign Lord the King, George III—not an American hero— a fine battle-piece of Lord Howe routing the American fleet, and so on. As Lewis Carroll said, " He only does it to annoy, because he knows it teases." That was always apt to be Cobbett's way. His *History of the Protestant Reformation* was written in just that spirit.

That was not the end of Cobbett's American escapades. He accused Dr. Rush, who was not only a famous physician, but also a political figure, of bleeding George Washington to death ; and there were unpleasant consequences of the libel, especially as Cobbett went on to say just what he thought about the judge who tried the case and, in *The Rushlight*, to devote a whole periodical to further unpleasantness about Dr. Benjamin Rush. Cobbett had gone to America because he found England too hot to hold him ; he returned to his native country because the American continent also blistered at his presence.

He came back, however, in the odour of political sanctity, to be greeted by Tory politicians in search of a journalist with enough punch to put the lousy Radicals in their place. The anti-Jacobins put up enough money to start the *Political Register* as an organ of the extreme right. It was to set about all Radical traitors in the same spirit as Cobbett had shown when he blackguarded Dr. Priestley or wrote his scurrilous life of the " impious " Tom Paine. The *Register* began in that spirit ; but, if the spirit lasted, the heroes and the villains soon exchanged rôles. Cobbett did indeed damn the Peace of Amiens up hill and down dale : he had his windows broken for refusing to illuminate in celebration of the peace. But before long he was causing his backers serious anxiety ; and in a few years they became well aware that they had received a serpent into their bosom. Cobbett began by taking a rooted dislike to Pitt, and probing inconveniently into the financial abuses of what he began to call " the Pitt system "—the very last things which even Pitt's political opponents wished to have exposed. He was then still all for war with France ; but he wanted the war to be run cleanly, without pandering to stock-jobbers and handing out pensions and sinecures to the cousins and aunts of the important people. What a hope !

In 1806 Pitt died, leaving behind him an unresolved ambiguity about his dying words. Some say they referred to the fate of England, and others that they were about pork chops ; but there was no doubt that Pitt left behind him a fair microcosm of the National Debt in the form of private obligations of his own ; and these debts a grateful nation, eager to honour " the pilot who died without weathering the storm," elected to pay. Cobbett celebrated the occasion by some candid words about Pitt, following his own maxim " *De mortuis nil nisi verum*—and then some." But when his own friends, including William Windham, succeeded to office, there was at least a lull in hostilities. The Ministry of All the Talents—except Cobbett's—was to be given a chance. Cobbett only remarked that Fox was not quite such a scoundrel as he had hitherto always made him out to be, and offered a few simple proposals for the new Ministry's acceptance. For example, Windham, now at the War Office, might begin by cleaning up military corruption.

William Windham thought otherwise—for, like most politicians, he regarded public corruption as an " act of God." Cobbett admonished, expressed pained surprise, threatened, and finally fulminated. Of a truth, the new lot was as bad as the old. New minister was but old Pitt writ large ; and within a year of Pitt's death, Cobbett was decisively of the Opposition, clamouring for Radical Reform to end the " Pitt system," and, before long, as determined to end the war that bred corruption and national decay as he had been a while before to pursue it to the bitter end. The infidel Tom Paine had been right after all. Cobbett soon loved to quote his *Decline and Fall of the English System of Finance* against the transgressors. Soon, he was rubbing salt into the wounds of orthodoxy by quoting with approval irreligious pamphlets that followed up the ideas of Paine's *Age of Reason.* He did not abandon the Church ; but he loved to quote a refutation of orthodox Christianity, and fling out a challenge to the parsons about it. " Answer that if you can, you lazy, tithe-eating dogs. What are you paid for, if not to answer ? "

This political Odyssey of Cobbett's needs a word of explanation. In his American exile, during the years that followed the Revolution in France, Cobbett was, as we have seen, the extremest of anti-Jacobins. How does that square with his later attitude ? I think the answer must be that, almost from a boy, he had seen little of England. Still a youth, he had fled from his incarceration in a lawyer's office to go for a soldier ; and his years of service in the army had been spent in Canada, largely among those " Yankee Loyalists " who had settled there after the War of Independence. From them he had doubtless learned to think of the Americans as a pack of rebels. His *penchant* for attacking corruption in high places and for defending the weak had been with him already ; and on his return to England he tried hard to bring the officers of his regiment to book for defrauding the soldiers. But while he was in England his " case " occupied all his time, except what he spent courting Anne Reid ; and though he had cause to find himself " agin " the Government over the court-martial proceedings, he saw nothing of the country, and found no reason to modify his general political outlook. Failing to get a fair chance of proving his case against his officers, he fled to France, then in the throes of Revolution, but not yet at war with England. But he did not go to France for politics, or to a part of the country where political excitements ran high ; and it seems likely that when, on the outbreak of war, he escaped from France to the United States, he carried with him no clear political convictions at all. He was not a man who theorised easily : it needed actual sights and experiences to stir his mind to thought.

In America, he found himself surrounded by anti-British feeling, strongly on the side of France. John-Bullishly, he revolted in exile against the abuse of his country, and became by reaction a fervent patriot. In his vigorous pamphlets denouncing and trouncing Priestley and Tom Paine, there is not a trace of political thinking. They are simple scurrility, carried off by the sheer vigour of the writing. Having found his trade, Cobbett stuck at it ; but he developed no new ideas except by reaction against his American surroundings. He came back at length to his own country, knowing nothing of it, except the Farnham of his youth.

Plunging at once into English journalism as a writer on the patriotic side, he was kept hard at it in London for some years, writing with plenty of vigour, but developing few new ideas. Stuck in London and seeing nothing of the countryside, which alone he thoroughly understood, he found nothing to stir his imagination, or to make him think, until his own friends came to office in 1806, in the Ministry of All the Talents. Then he expected things to begin to happen ; and when they did not, he was in a mood to look at the situation for himself, and form an independent judgment. Moreover, after years cooped up in town, he felt the longing for the country coming upon him ; and he began to go and look again at the places he had known in his youth. He was shocked, appalled. He saw everywhere signs of the intense misery which high prices and economic change had wrought upon the country people ; and at once his reaction against the " Pitt system " turned into a full-blown Radicalism. He rallied to the defence of his own people against their oppressors, and learnt a new hatred of the stock-jobbers and war financiers whose great houses he found everywhere scarring the country. Their opulence seemed to him to affront the misery of the starveling labourers. His case against " Pitt finance " became in an instant not merely an intellectual case, but a belief charged with intense emotion. These were the devils who were responsible for the labourers' miseries : down with them and all they stood for to the nethermost hell !

Thus Cobbett, converted, became the foremost of Radical agitators—foremost, because he was so like in mind to those on whose behalf he stood forward that the poor people readily recognised him for their own, as no merely intellectual leader of revolt could ever have been. Cobbett was a luckier, cleverer, more forcible peasant, who, thanks to his luck and brain and force of character, was able to stand forward to present the poor men's case. Knowing their own, they acclaimed him. Knowing that the English poor had at last found a representative leader, the wiser heads among the enemies of the poor were alarmed, and took counsel together against him.

It took but four years or so after Cobbett's full conversion to Radicalism to land him in Newgate gaol. There, cooling his heels not uncomfortably, he had time to get ready for a fresh onslaught on the " thing." For gaols in those days were not as gaols are now. A prisoner with money in his pocket could do well enough in gaol, living in a hired apartment of his own, much to the gaoler's profit, writing pamphlets and articles which he could send out and publish freely, having his family to stay with him in the prison, receiving visits of sympathy from one of His Majesty's judges, dressed in his full robes in order to mark his protest at the sentence, and last but not least entertaining his friends, whenever he chose, with steaks and porter within the precincts of the prison. It was not so bad to be gaoled in those days, provided only that you could afford to pay through the nose. Cobbett paid, and lived in Newgate like a fighting cock ; but his publishing business and his farm at Botley went to rack and ruin the while, and a few years later he paid the penalty with his bankruptcy.

The occasion of Cobbett's gaoling need not much concern
us here. He had written in the *Political Register* an article
about the flogging of English soldiers on which the Government was able to base a successful charge for sedition ;
and for this he was put in prison, after a tangle of negotiations
in the course of which he decided at one point to stop
publishing the *Register* altogether, as the price of being
let off. But the negotiations fell through, and the
Register went on. Cobbett was able to write its main
article regularly from prison, though he had to be careful
not to provoke a further prosecution, which might have
ruined him once and for all. To this circumstance, and
to the opportunity for thinking things over that his term
in prison afforded him, we owe his *Paper against Gold*—
the first of his long series of books published in parts and,
apart from the *Register*, the first of his Radical writings
of importance. From this time paper money is seldom
long out of Cobbett's mind. It becomes for him the symbol
of the " system," and by his denunciation of it he becomes
the first of the long line of English popular monetary
reformers, or shall we say, " currency cranks " ?

The root idea of *Paper against Gold* Cobbett got from
Tom Paine, whose pamphlet, *The Decline and Fall of the
English System of Finance*, he never wearied of quoting
with the strongest approval. A large part of the sorrows
of England was to be scored up against the wretched Bank
of England ; for the foundation of the Bank had been also
the origin at one and the same time of the accursed National
Debt and of paper bank notes, the twin plagues that were
dragging the country down. The Debt was piling up to
such a height that it would be impossible ever to repay it,
and ruinous even to meet the interest charge ; and as the
Debt grew, the curse of paper money grew with it, for how
else could the Debt grow ? These were the days of the
famous Bullion Committee, which demonstrated plainly,
despite the Government's denials, the depreciation of the
Bank's paper in relation to gold, as a consequence of the
attempt to finance the long war by borrowing instead of
taxation. Pitt had chosen the easy way of inflation because
he wanted to make the war popular among the swindling
fraternity of stock-jobbers and speculators, who profited

handsomely by the manipulation of government loans. The paper money had meant high prices, and starvation conditions for the unfortunate agricultural labourers, who were unable to raise their wages. It had meant temporary prosperity for the farmers, who had taken to new-fangled habits on the strength of it—buying pianos and educating their daughters to behave like gentlefolk. It had meant high rates for the landlords, but high taxes as well, as the burden of the poor rates increased, and as the long war had to be financed more out of taxes, even to meet the annual charges of the mounting debt. The landlords had profited for the time, like the farmers ; but both these classes were beginning to pay, and for both there was coming a real day of reckoning, when they would be called upon to meet the postponed costs of the war. Only the money-spinners were in clover, with their ceaseless jobbing of inflated money-values. Only they throve and multiplied as the mass of paper money grew greater and greater with each year.

Holding these views about the curse of paper money, Cobbett might have been expected to be found on the side of the " sound money men " when the war was over, and the sages were once more urging the return to the gold standard. But not a bit of it ! Cobbett, the arch-enemy of paper money, took the field as the strongest critic of the Bank Bill of 1819, under which the restoration of the gold standard was finally carried through. He did so without abating one word of his denunciations of the paper system, but arguing that it was manifestly unfair and ruinous to repay in gold a debt which had been contracted in inflated paper money, and that before a resumption of cash payments could properly be allowed steps ought to be taken to scale down the debt, and the interest on it, to a figure corresponding to the changed value of money. Cobbett demanded an " equitable adjustment," by which he meant a lowering of the interest burden of the debt, by means of a forced reduction in the rates of interest, as a necessary preliminary to putting back the gold standard.

To this struggle we owe Cobbett's famous " gridiron " prophecy. If he were wrong in predicting that a return to the gold standard without an " equitable adjustment "

would mean collapse, he gave leave to Lord Castlereagh
" to put me on a gridiron and broil me alive, while Sidmouth
stirs the fire, and Canning stands by making a jest of my
groans."   Cobbett always claimed that his prophecies
had come true, on the ground that, though the gold standard
was put back, and the interest on the Debt was not reduced,
the events of the financial crisis of 1825, when the Bank was
compelled to reissue the small notes abolished a few years
earlier, justified what he had said. He held, in 1826, his
" Feast of the Gridiron," to celebrate his rightness ; and
he developed a habit of putting a gridiron as a sort of crest
at the top of the front page of the *Political Register*. The
" gridiron " became a recognised symbol among the
Cobbettites : it turned up again in Chartist days as the
motto of John Cleave's Cobbett Club. Cobbett himself
lived long enough to offer strong opposition to Attwood's
paper money projects when they were put forward by the
Birmingham Political Union, and to conduct at Birmingham
with Attwood one of those prodigious debates to which
huge audiences seem to have been ready in those most
enduring times to listen all day and most of the night.
On this occasion Attwood spoke for four and a half hours,
and his supporter, Charles Jones, for I forget how long,
before Cobbett got a word in. Cobbett then went at it
for two hours, and Attwood took two more to reply. There
were giants in those days.

This discussion of Cobbett's views about currency
has taken me far away from his enforced residence in
Newgate from 1810 to 1812, when he was still only at the
beginning of his career as a Radical leader. His great
period as a leader did not come till the war was over, and
the great wave of economic distress which followed the
peace had swept over the industrial districts. Till then the
Register had been read mainly by gentlemen and farmers :
it had hardly reached the working class. But in 1816
Cobbett, conscious of the rumblings of unrest all over the
new industrial areas, suddenly altered his appeal and began
to talk directly to the working classes in the north of England.
Knowing the country far better than the town, he had till
then been far more alive to agrarian than to industrial
grievances and hardships ; but now, in his *Addresses to*

the Journeymen and Labourers, he began to make a vigorous
call to the miners and factory workers to rally to the cause
of Radical Reform.   In order to do this, he started producing off-prints from the *Register*, containing no news
that would have subjected them to the Newspaper Tax,
for sale at a penny and twopence a time ; and these special
off-prints, started as purely occasional pamphlets, soon
turned into a regular twopenny edition of the *Political
Register* for popular consumption.   The success of his
vigorous appeals was immediate.   It is said that, at the
height of their popularity, Cobbett was selling sixty thousand
copies a week.   Undoubtedly Cobbett's cheap *Register*—
called " Twopenny Trash " first by its enemies, though
he joyfully adopted the name—had a great deal to do with
bringing over the factory workers to the cause of Radical
Reform of Parliament.   " At this time," writes Bamford,
the Lancashire weaver, " the writings of William Cobbett
suddenly became of great authority : they were read on
nearly every cottage hearth in the manufacturing
districts . . ." Bamford attributed to Cobbett's influence
the abandonment of rioting, and the creation instead of
an organised Reform movement among the weavers.
Whether that be true or not, certainly Cobbett leapt of
a sudden to an outstanding position anong the leaders of
the working class.

He had soon to pay the penalty of his success.
Sidmouth's " Gagging Acts " of 1817, followed up by the
Six Acts of 1819, suppressed his cheap *Register*, by imposing
upon it the high newspaper tax, and so making cheap
publication impossible.   Moreover, knowing the Acts of
1817 to be largely aimed at him, and having also serious
private embarrassments of his own, Cobbett escaped the
prison which was the fate of most of the other working-
class leaders by flight.   In 1817 he took ship secretly to the
United States ; and there he stayed for the next two years.
He was accused of cowardly desertion of his post in the hour
of danger ; and there is no doubt that he did run away.
Whether he should have stayed, to face gaol for debt, or
sedition, or both, is a moot point.   We at any rate can afford
to be grateful for his flight ; for with it begins the sequence
of books by which he is best remembered.   Away from

the constant battle of journalism and political agitation, Cobbett found leisure to sit down and write books—though, with his passion for the land, his first thought when he reached the United States was to get land to farm as well as a political asylum. For two years he farmed, and wrote ; and when, late in 1819, he came back to England to face the repression, just as the Six Acts were being passed into law, he brought back with him the stock of ideas that went to the making of a whole series of books that will not easily die.

Two of these books, *A Journal of a Year's Residence in the United States of America* and *A Grammar of the English Language*, appeared while he was still away from England. Cobbett's *Grammar* is, I think, still an admirable grammar, for the sort of person for whom Cobbett meant it. I have tried it on grown-up students to whom their teachers had omitted to teach their native language at school, and the results of using it have been excellent. Nor is it worse as a grammar for being at times a political tract as well. For just as in *Rural Rides* Cobbett mixed his politics with the affairs of the countryside, till the Swedish turnip became a political weapon, so in his *Grammar* he bombarded his political adversaries unmercifully with the parts of speech. " The nominative is frequently a noun of multitude ; as *mob, parliament, gang.*" " The gang of borough-tyrants *is* cruel, and *are* also notoriously as ignorant as brutes." " Amongst a select society of empty heads, ' moderate reform ' has long been a fashionable expression ; an expression which has been well criticised by asking the gentlemen who use it, how they would like to obtain *moderate justice* in a court of law, or to meet with *moderate chastity* in a wife."

In 1819, despite the Six Acts, which intensified the repression, Cobbett came back to England, and resumed his place among the outstanding Radical leaders. Thereafter his books followed one another in quick succession. *The American Gardener* appeared in 1821 ; and in that year he also began publishing his series of *Rural Rides* in the *Political Register*. His *Sermons*, including one on *The Sin of Drunkenness*, pointedly directed at George IV, followed in 1821, in the midst of the Queen Caroline case ; and

Cottage Economy appeared the same year. Part I of his *History of the Protestant Reformation* followed in 1824 ; and a succession of lesser books led up to *Advice to Young Men* in 1829, and the first collected issue of *Rural Rides* in 1830. Cobbett's best books are thus the work of his middle age. He was nearing sixty when he began *Rural Rides*, and sixty-six when he published *Advice to Young Men*. Like Defoe, who alone can dispute his claim to be the greatest of English journalists, he wrote all the better as he grew old.

All this time he was vigorously pursuing his political campaigns. In 1820 and thereabouts he became absorbed in the case of Queen Caroline—the best of all sticks for beating a reactionary Ministry and a profligate King. Cobbett, who was perhaps induced to espouse the Queen's cause mainly for this reason, became Caroline's most devout champion, writing her manifestos for her in most uncarolinian prose, and building up behind her an immense popular agitation throughout the country. When the Queen's death knocked away the foundations of the movement, Cobbett was ready for a new cause. During the next few years he headed a revolt of the farmers against high taxation, working up among them a big movement in favour of Radical Reform. But returning agricultural prosperity caused the tide of agrarian unrest to ebb for a time ; and the circulation of the *Register* went down till the country, now under milder and more hesitant Ministers, began to warm up for the struggle over the Reform Bill.

Into this struggle Cobbett put the whole of his energy. He felt a profound distrust of the various groups of parliamentary reformers—from Whigs bent on " moderate reform " to the " feelosophical villains " from north of the Border who were determined to transfer power to the middle classes in such a way as to leave their working-class allies out in the cold. Throughout the campaign he denounced the Whigs and Lord Brougham with impartial vigour, urging the working-class Radicals to get control of the Political Unions throughout the country, in order to press forward their own nominees to Parliament and so dish the Whigs. In this contest, Cobbett's followers were usually worsted, and the Whigs and " feelosofers " between them captured most of the nominations. The Reformed Parliament of 1832, when it came at last, contained Cobbett, as member for Oldham. But he had only a handful of followers to face a powerful Whig majority with which the Tories were usually ready to make common cause when really Radical measures were at issue. It was said by his parliamentary contemporaries that old Cobbett did not make much of a politician, and never demeaned himself as a proper "House of Commons man." He has, however, apart from his violent attacks on Peel and on the Speaker, at any rate one very memorable House of Commons speech to his credit. He spoke it in the course of the debates on the Factory Bill of 1833. Though it has been quoted often, I feel I must quote it again—the one longish quotation from Cobbett's writings I have introduced into this paper :—

" Sir, I will make but one single observation upon this subject, and that is this : that this ' reformed ' House has this night made a discovery greater than all the discoveries that all former Houses of Commons have ever made, even if all their discoveries could have been put into one. Heretofore, we have sometimes been told that our ships, our mercantile traffic with foreign nations by means of these ships, together with our body of rich merchants —we have sometimes been told that these form the source of our wealth, power and security. At other times, the land has stepped forward, and bid us look to it, and its yeomanry, as the sure and solid foundation of our greatness and our safety. At other times the Bank has pushed forward with her claims, and has told us that, great as the others were, they were nothing without ' PUBLIC CREDIT,' upon which not only the prosperity and happiness, but the very independence of the country depend. But, sir, we have this night discovered, that the shipping, the land, and the Bank and its credit, are all worth nothing compared with the labour of three hundred thousand little girls in Lancashire ! Aye, when compared with only an eighth part of those three hundred thousand little girls, from whose labour if only we deduct two hours a day, away goes the wealth, away goes the capital, away go the resources, the power, and the glory of England ! With what pride and what pleasure, sir, will the right hon. gentlemen opposite, and the honourable member for Manchester behind me, go northward with the news of this discovery, and communicate it to that large portion of these little girls whom they have the honour and the happiness to represent ! ''

Cobbett was not destined to have a long or distinguished parliamentary career. He was an old man when he was elected ; and, proud as he was of being there to represent the common people, the House of Commons was by no means his spiritual home. He sat assiduously through the debates, though the late hours did not suit him and he had very little respect for most of the proceedings of the '' honourable House.'' But his letters show him pining for the country and for his farm ; and he was happiest when Parliament was in recess, and he could get back to his crops. For throughout his life, whatever he was doing—and that was usually a great deal—he was never really happy without a patch of land to look after. He made one farm after another—his Botley farm, on which he lavished many years of labour, only to be ousted as a result of his bankruptcy, his farm on Long Island during his two years' exile in the United States from 1817 to 1819, his seed farm at Kensington, his farm at Barn Elms, and in his last years Normandy Farm, Ash, near Aldershot. There he made his agricultural experiments, with acacia trees or *locusts*, as he called them, with Cobbett's corn, Swedish turnips, straw plait, and a host of other things ; and he was always eager to pass on his knowledge to his fellow-farmers and labourers. He wrote and edited agricultural manuals, from Jethro Tull's famous *Horse-hoeing Husbandry* to his own *English Gardener*, *The Woodlands*, and *A Treatise on Cobbett's Corn*. Farming and education were blended together in his mind. He must always be turning over land, and tilling the soil of other men's minds as well.

Yet for formal educational systems he had for the most part a great contempt. His references to Oxford are uniformly derogatory : he loved nothing better than to see a professor caught out ; and his most outrageous diatribes were poured out against the '' feelosofical villains '' like Brougham, who set out to teach the poor the blessings of the new industrial system. He had no use for the Society for the Diffusion of Useful Knowledge, Brougham's favourite, which Thomas Love Peacock aptly nicknamed '' The Steam Intellect Society.'' The kind of education

he believed in firmly was the sort he had got himself, and
was ready at every opportunity to impart to others—the
kind a man picked up not at school, but by sitting over
Cobbett's *Grammar* or Cobbett's *History* or even Cobbett's
Register before or after a hard day's work. If you read
Advice to Young Men you will soon realise that the young
men who set out to follow it were not in for an easy time.
They had to be up early, and abed late. They were to
live sparingly ; and plenty of hard work was recommended
as a means to keeping fit. Beer they might have—especially
home-brewed ; but they had better keep off other intoxi-
cants, and certainly off such noxious brews as tea. Cobbett
had learnt in a hard school ; and he was thoroughly well
satisfied with the results. Let others go and do likewise,
if they wanted to make their way in the world.

This egoism of Cobbett's is everywhere in his work. I
can imagine that his contemporaries often found it offensive
as well as laughable. Certainly they were always on the
look-out for weak points in his armour, of which there were
not a few. It is laughable still, because of its *naïveté* ; but
it is no longer a source of offence. For it is only the prig,
like Marcus Aurelius, whose self-satisfaction continues to
offend when the possessor is centuries dead and gone.
Cobbett's self-satisfaction is not priggish. It rests not on
an interest in saving his own soul, but on an assertion that
he is as good a man as anyone else ; and it is preserved
from self-centredness because he also made it an assertion
of the rights and claims of the common people from whose
ranks he had come. " Hate me, hate my class," Cobbett
seemed to be always saying ; and it was to a great extent
his egoism that enabled him to go on throughout his life
thinking and feeling as one of the country folk among whom
he had been born, and thus able to speak to them, far more
than any of his contemporaries, as one of themselves. The
common people of England have not had so many inter-
preters that they can afford to forget Cobbett.

When Cobbett died, in 1835, the *Times*—the " bloody
old *Times*," as he had often called it—said that he was an
" episode." The *Times* meant that, with all his doing and
saying, he had never understood or formed part of the main
stream of the development of English life. He had lived,

battling against an unwelcome and unintelligible present in
the cause of a romanticised past. Therefore, it was predicted, he was destined to have no successors. On that
last point the *Times* was right ; for Cobbett was the last—
and indeed also the first—articulate voice of that English
countryside, which, even in his own day, the rising tide of
industrialism was swiftly drowning. He belonged to an
age that was dying ; and, as he saw the sufferings and
injustices that the birth of the new age brought upon his
own people, it was natural for him not only to revolt, but
to look romantically at the ages that had been swept away.
This explains his attitude to the old squires ; and it also
explains his views of the Protestant Reformation.

It was fitting that Cobbett's last crusade should be made
on behalf of the village labourers for whom he had been
fighting hard the best part of his life. In the agricultural
troubles of 1830-1, which Mr. and Mrs. Hammond
have called " The Last Labourers' Revolt," he stood up
manfully on behalf of the unfortunates whom the Whig
Government was putting down with so savage a severity.
He was put on trial himself, on the charge of responsibility
for fomenting the revolt ; and doubtless his speeches about
the labourers' wrongs had helped to stir up the spirit of
resistance in them, though Cobbett had certainly not incited
them to actual rioting. He was acquitted, for the jury
disagreed ; and his acquittal was regarded as a bad blow
for the Whig Government. But the labourers, though they
had behaved with a singular absence of violence, were put
down ruthlessly ; for the Whigs were determined to show
that, though they were parliamentary reformers, they were
as devout upholders of law and order as the Duke of
Wellington himself. Cobbett's hatred of the Whigs was
greatly fanned by the events of 1831 ; and his last crusade
was against a further Whig blow at the rights of the poor.

In 1834 the Poor Law Amendment Act was passed, to
sweep away the " Speenhamland " system of poor relief in
aid of wages in the rural areas, and to make an end of out-
door relief for the unemployed in the industrial regions.
In the early months of 1835—he died in June, 1835—
Cobbett was trying to stir up the whole country to a revolt
against the new Poor Law, which he had fought hard, with

only a handful of supporters, while it was before the House of Commons. His last articles are a summons to this crusade to preserve the right of the poor to maintenance. But he died just as the new Poor Law Commissioners were beginning their work ; and in fact the agricultural labourers had been too heavily beaten down four years before to have strength left to respond to his appeal. The response came in 1837 among the industrial workers, when the " Three Bashaws of Somerset House," having completed the introduction of the new Poor Law into the agricultural areas, turned to applying it to the industrial districts. The outcome of that response was the Chartist Movement. But before the advent of Chartism Cobbett was dead ; and Feargus O'Connor was left to lead it.

Whether Cobbett was an " episode " or not, he was certainly an Englishman. I know of none so English, so much of that England which was not a nation of shopkeepers, but a nation of farmers and sailors and adventurers over the face of the earth. Not that Cobbett scorned shop-keeping. He kept shop for many years, first in Philadelphia, and latterly at his shops in London. In the Strand and at Bolt Court he sold not only books and newspapers and pamphlets, but also seeds and trees, and even patent fire-grates of a type which he was trying to introduce from the United States. Cobbett kept shop ; and he had a very good idea of the value of making money, though he never mastered the art of keeping it for long. But for him shop-keeping was an incident ; and the wares he sold were mostly of his own making. He delighted in making things, and was never happy unless he had plenty of work on hand. Whatever he was doing, his day was like a farmer's day. I have a diary of his, written at the end of his life, in which jottings about the crops and the weather appear all mixed up with notes about Parliament and politics and family affairs, and anything that happens to need noting down. Its jumble of activities gives an extraordinarily clear impression of the ceaseless round of doing and making that was Cobbett's life.

Much of that round I have left out—far more, indeed, than I have put in ; for this is an essay, and not a biography. But I have at least tried to suggest the sort of man William

Cobbett was.   If you want more, I have written a life of him.   But, best of all, go to his own books, and of these, above all others, to *Rural Rides*.   For there you will find Cobbett himself, talking about all manner of things as he rides over the country he loves and seeing in it only too much to hate.   *Rural Rides* is Cobbett; and it is also a not inconsiderable part of England.

THE CHARTISTS
by ALFRED PLUMMER

THE CHARTISTS

by ALFRED PLUMMER

IN England almost a century ago it was becoming quite clear that industrial capitalism and the factory system had come to stay. It was no less clear that a great tide of popular discontent was sweeping in. The Grand National Consolidated Trades Union had just collapsed. Hope had run ahead of power, leaving high aspirations unsatisfied by achievement ; and the working people were turning, as they have often done since, from industrial to political action. Numerous Radical Associations voiced the working man's deep disappointment with the Reform Bill of 1832 ; and the " New Poor Law " of 1834, with its demoralising " bastilles," the workhouses, was arousing the fiercest resentment. The moment was ripe for the unenfranchised masses to make a fresh attempt to attain democratic rights and institutions, and gradually, after some four or five years of unco-ordinated preliminary organisation and struggle, the Chartist Movement emerged.

Chartism was a working-class political agitation on a national scale, arising largely from economic distress coupled with a strong sense of social injustice, and aiming at parliamentary reform as a means to the ultimate improvement of the lot of the working masses. The movement drew the bulk of its recruits from the new industrial proletariat, but it included also many of the more enlightened artisans of London, Birmingham and other large cities. From the earlier Radical reformers the Chartists gleaned six " points " —manhood suffrage, vote by ballot, the abolition of the property qualification for membership of Parliament, payment of members, equal electoral districts, and annual parliamentary elections. This was the framework of the famous " People's Charter," and to inscribe its " points " upon the Statute Book was the Chartists' immediate objective. This done, the newly constituted Parliament was to set to work to create a New Jerusalem ; for the agitation was a revolt not against a particular injustice, but against the general injustice of the whole economic and

F

political system. It was not the momentary outbreak of a
misguided mob, but the expression, over nearly two decades,
of working-class discontent, rising to three peak points—
in 1839, 1842, and 1848—when giant petitions were prepared
and presented to Parliament. Broadly speaking, the
Chartists knew much more about the causes of discontent
and the possibility of removing them than the governing
classes ; for the reformers were more deeply thoughtful and
more forward-looking than the rulers. The reformers really
desired to create a great democracy ; the rulers, fearing the
advent of any such thing, loudly protested that the act of
creation had already taken place when the Reform Act was
passed in 1832. But the working classes were sceptical,
and Radical writers soon appeared to give form and direction
to the workmen's criticisms and aspirations, chiefly through
the penny pamphlet and the cheap propagandist periodical.
Consequently, the anti-reform forces tried to cut off these
supplies of " political information," using heavy stamp
duties as their principal weapon. It is significant that the
most decisive phase of the struggle against these " taxes on
knowledge," as they were called by the reformers, immediately preceded the Chartist Movement and provided the
Chartists with many of their leaders.

Since 1816, when Cobbett cast his *Twopenny Trash* in the
teeth of a reactionary government, a great struggle for
freedom of the press had been proceeding in England.
Until 1831 the contest consisted chiefly of a series of attacks
upon Radicalism by the forces of reaction. The law,
especially the law of libel, was exploited to the full by the
government. Radical journals were constantly harassed,
often suppressed, but never defeated. Although frequently
crippled, they could not be crushed. If prosecutions before
packed juries often resulted in imprisonment for their
leading journalists and heavy legal expenses, they also meant
advertisement and increased circulations. Thus the dour
struggle continued until, in the early thirties, under the
almost fanatical leadership of Hetherington, the Radical
press passed from the defensive to the attack.

Henry Hetherington (1792–1849), a compositor by trade,
was one of the earliest pupils of the London Mechanics'
Institute, and from this beginning he developed into a most

resolute, indomitable democrat and champion of cheap periodicals, quite a number of which he owned, printed and published himself. In 1829–31, when the working-class Radicals of London used to hold regular meetings in the *Rotunda* at Blackfriars, Hetherington took a prominent part, with William Lovett and others, in founding the Metropolitan Trades Union, subsequently transformed into the National Union of the Working Classes, which aimed at securing for every working man " the full value of his labour and the free disposal of the produce " of it, protection against " the tyranny of masters and manufacturers," radical reform of the House of Commons and the dissemination of " sound moral and political knowledge amongst the mass of the community." There were at that time over 150 working men's clubs in London, and the meetings at the *Rotunda*, which could accommodate 1,000 people, were always crowded to the doors and sometimes beyond. Here Hetherington met many other active Radicals, some of whom were destined, like himself, to become leading Chartists. Later he became treasurer of the London Working Men's Association, founded in 1836, and during the Chartist revival in 1840 he was the leading figure in a new London society called the Metropolitan Charter Union, formed to unite Chartists and other Radicals and to keep the principles of the Charter before the public by peaceful and persuasive means such as lectures, discussions, distribution of tracts, the sale of a penny weekly paper and the opening of reading rooms, coffee houses and co-operative stores. In the following years Hetherington became the first secretary of a somewhat similar society—the National Association for Promoting the Political and Social Improvement of the People. But among all his incessant activities, that by which he is chiefly remembered is his remarkable leadership of the Radical forces in the great " Battle of the Unstamped Press."

In 1830 the stamp duty on newspapers and periodicals selling at less than 6d. was 4d. per copy, which greatly hindered the dissemination of political ideas among the poorer classes.* Towards the end of 1830 Hetherington

---

* Francis Place tells us that the hire of a morning paper " for a time scarcely sufficient to read one-half of it " cost twopence.

decided openly to join issue with the authorities by publishing a weekly called *The Poor Man's Guardian*, unstamped, in order " to try the power of Might against Right." " No more evasion," he wrote, " we will not trespass, but deny the authority of our ' lords ' to enclose the common against us." With this declaration of defiance he began a struggle in which for over five years he cheerfully sacrificed money, personal freedom and future prospects until at last the duty was reduced to one penny per copy. From December 25, 1830, to December 26, 1835, *The Poor Man's Guardian* appeared regularly in spite of incredible difficulties and dangers. Its weekly circulation rose to 16,000 copies in less than three years, while the circulation of *The Destructive*, also produced by Hetherington, reached approximately 8,000.

Although the enterprise was highly perilous, Hetherington was soon joined by strong allies, all publishing unstamped journals. In 1833 Carlile's *Gauntlet* had an estimated circulation of 22,000, and five other leading unstamped weeklies taken together were selling some 30,000 copies. There was Cleave's *Weekly Police Gazette*, and Watson's *Working Man's Friend*, Lorymer's *Reformer* and *Bonnet Rouge*, Lee's *Man*, and Detroisier's *Cosmopolite*. Hetherington, a giant among giants, led the van of these determined forces. Often, says a contemporary,

" he had to leave his shop disguised and return to it disguised —sometimes as a Quaker, a waggoner or a costermonger . . . To distribute his paper, dummy parcels were sent off in one direction by persons instructed to make all resistance they could to constables who seized them ; in the meantime real parcels were sent by another road. His shopmen were imprisoned, his premises entered, his property taken, and men brought into the houses by constables . . . broke up with blacksmith's hammers his press and his type."

On one occasion the indentures of his apprentice were declared void on the ground that he was employed upon an illegal publication.

Hard as it was to maintain steady and punctual production of unstamped papers,* it was even more difficult to dis-

* A MS. note gummed inside a copy of the first number of the *Bonnet Rouge* (Feb. 2, 1833) states that " Application was made to several

tribute them over a wide area.   The following advertisement from the *Poor Man's Guardian* speaks for itself :

" WANTED.   Some hundreds of poor men out of employ, who have nothing to risk, some of those unfortunate beings to whom the distress occasioned by a tyrannical government has made a prison a desirable home.   An honest and moral way of finding gaol bread and shelter and . . . earning the thanks of their fellow-countrymen now presents itself to such patriotic Englishmen as will, in defiance of the most odious ' Laws ' of a most odious tyranny, imposed upon an enslaved and oppressed people, sell to the poor and ignorant *The Poor Man's Guardian* . . .

" N.B.—A subscription is open for the relief, support and reward of all such persons as may become victims of the Whig Tyrants."

Many bold and desperate men responded, and many of the volunteers became " victims."   Some of them sincerely desired to help Hetherington and his allies ; others were attracted by the prospect of the gift of a stock of papers and £1 for every month's imprisonment they might incur by selling them.*   There were also many secret sellers who coveted the profit but feared the punishment.   Meantime, police pressure increased.   At every turn the editors, printers, publishers and vendors of unstamped journals were subject to espionage.   Numerous copies of *The Poor Man's Guardian* and other papers were collected by police agents and sent in to the Home Office where they were labelled " Seditious."†   At a time when the vigilance of the authorities was greatest, large numbers of Cleave's *Police Gazette* were carried out of an undertaker's shop

---

printers to print this Number, but they refused owing to its very strong destructive principles ; it was ultimately printed by a man living in a garret in Holywell St. (Strand) who was drunk at the time, which may account for the misplacing of the pages."   The misplaced pages run 1, 6, 5, 2, 3, 8, 7, 4 !

* The money for the Victims' Fund was raised mainly by taking collections at meetings.   Between August 13 and December 8, 1831, subscriptions totalled £76 13s. 3d., to which was added 14s. from the sale of tracts.   Of this sum nearly £70 was disbursed chiefly in grants of £3 each to men who had been sent to prison for three months.   During the six months ending March 8, 1833, over £82 was spent in relief of victims.

† See *Home Office Papers*, 64 (17) and (18).

near the printing office, packed in coffins. The ruse succeeded well until people became alarmed at the apparently appalling rise in the death-rate in that particular parish !

Hetherington indefatigably toured the country seeking support, addressing meetings and making such adequate arrangements for the sale of the unstamped papers that, in spite of every obstacle, they were widely distributed throughout London and the provinces. " I hear a good deal of the circulation of ' Cobbett ' and the *Poor Man's Guardian* in this district (Hampshire)," wrote the Duke of Wellington to Lord Melbourne in November, 1832. " In the large towns," says another contemporary observer, " there were certain places where people dropped their pence into narrow apertures, and papers to the amount made their appearance immediately, as if by magic." A reputable contemporary Radical writer stated that in the middle of 1835 the weekly sales of unstamped papers reached 7,000 copies in Birmingham alone.

As for Hetherington, the police were always upon his trail. He was convicted four times and twice imprisoned for six months for publishing the *Poor Man's Guardian*. When arrested and brought before the magistrates he told them bluntly that he was determined at all costs to resist the attempts of a corrupt government to suppress the voice of the people. In March, 1832, shortly after his release from prison, Hetherington told an audience that he did not expect to be long at liberty, but he would " continue to agitate most desperately while he had the opportunity," and when he was caught again he would have six months' rest " and then come out like a giant refreshed with new wine." In 1834 Hetherington scored a success even in the Law Courts, by securing an acquittal from Lord Lyndhurst and a special jury in the Court of Exchequer. This gave his opponents pause and marked the gradual turn of the tide of battle in Hetherington's favour. Within two years a bill was before Parliament reducing stamp duties to 1d. per copy. The *Poor Man's Guardian* closed its troubled, but triumphant, career on December 26, 1835, its place being taken by the *Twopenny Dispatch*, edited by James (Bronterre) O'Brien, who had been editor of the *Poor Man's Guardian* since the latter part of 1832.

James (Bronterre) O'Brien (1805–1864) was a native of Granard, Co. Longford, Ireland. He was educated at the Edgeworths' new school at Edgeworthstown, and at Trinity College, Dublin, where he graduated with the highest honours. In 1828 he commenced legal studies in the King's Inns, Dublin, whence he proceeded to Gray's Inn, London, in 1830. Almost immediately he was swept into the Radical reform movement. Young and inexperienced though he was, he seems to have been regarded as a desirable acquisition by the Radical leaders. O'Brien had not long been in London when he met Henry Hunt, probably, the best mob-orator of the day, and shortly afterwards William Cobbett. He went regularly to the meetings of the London Radical Reform Association where, in all probability, he and Hetherington first became acquainted. O'Brien himself tells us that he " soon got sick of law " and decided to give all his soul to Radical reform. Although he afterwards developed into an orator of no mean capacity, his early work in the cause of the working classes was done as a journalist. He commenced by writing, under the *nom-de-plume* " Bronterre," a series of three articles in Carpenter's *Political Letters*. Then, in the spring of 1831, he became editor of the *Midland Representative and Birmingham Herald*. Subsequently he edited Hetherington's *Poor Man's Guardian*, the *Twopenny Dispatch*, *Bronterre's National Reformer*, and the *Operative*; and was joint editor of the *London Mercury* and the *Southern Star*. Moreover, in an attempt to present the French Revolution to the British public " in a point of view as novel . . . as it will be true to reality " and so to redeem " the glorious cause of democracy from the obloquy and bad odour it has incurred," he translated Buonarotti's *History of Babeuf's Conspiracy* and wrote the first volume of an entirely sympathetic biography of Robespierre. O'Brien also planned several other works, including *A Real History of the French Revolution*, *A History of the English Commonwealth*, and an essay on *The Existing State and Future Prospects of Society*; but before he could complete his *Life of Robespierre* his home and books were seized and sold for debt. " I discontinued the work," he wrote, " only after I had been literally turned into the streets with a young and helpless family, without

a roof to shelter them, a chair to sit on, or a bed to lie on."
Furthermore, his participation in the Chartist Movement
left O'Brien little time for historical writing.

From 1838 to 1841 O'Brien was one of the most energetic
and prominent of the Chartist leaders, but after 1841, owing
largely to his bitter quarrel with O'Connor, his influence gradually declined. During 1839 O'Brien gave himself so completely to the cause, and was so incensed at the indifference
and contempt of Parliament, that he rapidly lashed himself
into a violent and revolutionary frame of mind. Like a
whirlwind he threw himself into all departments of the
Movement, and his prodigious activities approached, if they
did not excel, those of O'Connor himself. Besides editing
the *Operative*, O'Brien toured England and Scotland,
addressing innumerable meetings, large and small, on
weekdays, and delivering Chartist " sermons " on Sundays.
When he was not on the road he regularly attended the
sittings of the Chartist National Convention in which he
represented no fewer than five separate localities. He spoke
frequently, served upon committees, drew up voluminous
manifestos and resolutions, and occasionally took the chair.
All this in an age when travelling was still very slow and
arduous, and when speeches were expected to be much
longer than they are to-day. In June, 1841, O'Brien was
nominated as a parliamentary candidate for Newcastle-
upon-Tyne, and although he was imprisoned in Lancaster
Gaol at the time, he sent forth a lengthy election address in
which he declared for " peace founded upon liberty for
all—for law founded upon justice for all—for order founded
upon contentment for all," and for giving the people " every
facility " to alter and improve the laws " in conformity with
the will of the majority." He advocated the amendment of
the electoral system " upon the plan and principles of the
People's Charter," and strongly condemned " every species
of monopoly, whether of wealth, power or knowledge."
Apparently the Sheriff ignored O'Brien's candidature, no
poll was taken, and one Whig and one Tory were returned.

All O'Brien's speeches and writings were marked by
intense dissatisfaction with the existing social and political
order and bitter hostility to all who wished to preserve it.
He was an admirer of Robert Owen ; but he was never an

Owenite, for Owen had no faith in political action, while
O'Brien held that until the common people could gain
control of the law-making power, through universal manhood suffrage, no real Radical reform, no improvement of
the parlous economic position of the working classes,
would materialise.   In 1837 he wrote :

" . . . the end I have in view is social equality for each and all,
to obtain this we must first have political equality for each and
all.* To obtain political equality we must have a more extensive
and effective organisation of the working classes, and of that
portion of the middle class which is immediately dependent on
their custom, than has hitherto been even thought of, much less
accomplished. It will, therefore, be an object of mine to
promote such . . . organisation, and, as the best means of
promoting it, I will never cease to recommend and encourage
among those classes knowledge and union ; a full and accurate
knowledge of their wrongs and of their rights ; and a steady
union of purpose to redress the one and obtain permanent
enjoyment of the other."

Among the many obstacles in the way, O'Brien saw firstly,
the various vested interests of the aristocracy and the
moneyed middle classes—the " capitalists, stock-jobbers and
other gamblers," and secondly, the ignorance of the working
people. The latter could be released from tyranny and
oppression only by the diffusion of knowledge and the
extension of the franchise : hence his ardent advocacy of
the " People's Charter." He did not condemn competition
and machinery as such, but rather the abuses connected with
competition and machinery in a " cannibal civilisation."
Machinery owned and operated by the workers, and competitive effort directed to noble ends, such as emulation in
the field of scientific research, would assuredly increase

*" Political Equality " was defined by another Chartist writer (J. C.
Combe) as follows : " Political equality means that every individual in
any given state has the right not only to take part in all political proceedings whatever, whether it be to give a vote for a member of Parliament
or for a parish officer, but also that he has the right to fill any office of
state, if the majority of his fellow citizens will and approve that he
should do so—in other words, political equality means that no one
individual man is better than another one, unless the majority of his
fellow citizens declare him to be so. Political equality means that the
minority must submit to the will of the majority, at the same time that
freedom of speech and opinion is secured to all."

F*

human welfare. But all such beneficial possibilities were stultified by that " overwhelming evil . . . the profit-hunting system, *alias* the unjust power of capital over labour." As a result of the exercise of this power crafty individuals were able to profit by the honest labour of others without yielding up a just equivalent. " If everyone were paid the full value of his services," said O'Brien, " there would be no unjust accumulations " ; but he does not tell us how the " full value " is to be discovered or determined.

O'Brien was the chief pre-Marxian exponent of class-war doctrines. Among the various usurpations of the upper and middle classes, he assigned a leading place to the private ownership of the land by the rich, and the dispossession of the poor. His opinions upon this subject were based upon a study of the writings of Spence, Ogilvie, Hall and Paine, and he was the chief Chartist advocate of land nationalisation. He held that there never should be, and never should have been, private ownership of the land ; for if mankind had refused to tolerate this in the past, " they would have prevented ninety-nine parts out of a hundred of all the woes and crimes that have hitherto made a pandemonium of the world." His practical proposal was gradual State purchase of estates upon the decease of existing owners. Thus, the State would become trustee in perpetuity of the land of the nation, which it would let to cultivators " in such quantities as the law and local circumstances may determine," and every tenant-farmer would be able to get from the State sufficient temporary credit to enable him to stock and crop his farm.

This burning question of land ownership and occupation is to be found also in the speeches and writings of Feargus O'Connor (1794–1855), who had an Irishman's natural affection for agriculture and the small farm. Feargus O'Connor was the son of Roger O'Connor, an Irish Nationalist and land owner of County Cork. Nurtured in a political atmosphere, Feargus entered political life under the banner of Daniel O'Connell, " The Liberator," and in 1832 he was returned to Parliament as member for his native county. It was not long, however, before he quarrelled with O'Connell, and, having been unseated on petition in 1835, he transferred his activities to the cause of Radical reform in England.   At first he was not cordially welcomed.   On the death of Cobbett in 1835, O'Connor contested Oldham but received only 31 votes.   It is true that in the following year he was elected an honorary member of the London Working Men's Association, but his speech at a meeting attended by 3,000 of the élite of the London working men, in February, 1837, was coldly received.   Yet, in little more than two years he was, for good or ill, at the head of the Chartist Movement.   He soon removed from London to Leeds, and from 1837 to 1852 he owned and controlled *The Northern Star*, which rapidly became by far the most widely circulated and successful Radical newspaper of the period.   O'Connor was endowed with a commanding presence, a powerful voice and a private income.   He had the gift of oratory ; he knew how to play upon the emotions and prejudices of an audience, and could with great facility adapt his discourses to suit his hearers.   His apparent sincerity and disinterestedness, together with his humour and pugnacity, appealed especially to the workmen of the Midlands and the North. Thus it was that he became the most popular and conspicuous of the Chartist leaders, wielding through the press and from the platform more power over the rank and file than any other leader.   He felt strongly and talked untiringly.   He was capable of great feats of endurance and as a travelling agitator he was almost ubiquitous. Eloquence and personal magnetism were his : but he had neither the power of clear, profound and original thought nor wise and consistent leadership.   O'Connor was a Radical, but never a Socialist, and he quite definitely repudiated Communism.   In the end he turned to a sort of agrarian individualism.

" I have generally found [said he] that the strongest advocates of communism are the most lazy members of society—a class who would make a division of labour, adjudging to the most pliant and submissive the lion's share of work, and contending that their natural implement was the brain, whilst that of the credulous was the spade, the plough, the sledge and the pickaxe. Communism either destroys wholesome emulation and competition, or else it fixes too high a price on distinction, and must eventually end in the worst description of despotism—the despotism of self-surrender and non-reliance on self; whilst upon the other hand individual possession, and co-operation of labour, creates a wholesome bond between all classes of society, which none can push beyond the will or requirement of his neighbour . . . if horses and machines were common property, such is the perverseness of human nature, that all would continue to require the use of both horses and machines precisely at the same time. I am even opposed to public kitchens, public baking-houses and public wash-houses. In fact, I am for the principle of *meum* and *tuum*—mine and thine."

O'Connor did not succeed in returning to Parliament until 1847, when he won Nottingham against Sir John Cam Hobhouse. Five years later he was pronounced insane and placed in an asylum.

The Radicals of London, having published the *People's Charter* in May, 1838, turned immediately to consider the best means of urging Parliament to pass a law based upon it. The idea of a great conference of delegates from all parts of the country had been canvassed in London in 1831, and again in May, 1833, when large bills headed " A National Convention the only proper remedy" were distributed at Westminster. But no national convention was held until the Chartist Movement began to gather impetus early in 1839. Already the agitation was sweeping strongly through the North of England.

" Reaching Newcastle," says Thomas Devyr, a reporter on the staff of the Radical *Northern Liberator*, who had exceptional opportunities for observation, " I found myself among a body of Reformers, remarkable indeed for their zeal, activity and single-ness of purpose . . . the Northern Political Union, which had been discontinued when the Reform Bill became law, was revived, and I was elected its Corresponding Secretary. This was in the spring of '38. It was a time of great depression and scarcity of money . . . The workers crowded everywhere to hear the new evangel [and] the movement thus vigorously commenced rolled southward. Sunderland, the two Shields, the collieries, were . . . stirred up . . a ' Political Methodism ' seized upon the leaders. At six o'clock, throwing down their implements of toil, those true—not mock—noblemen would hasten home, lunch on bread and cheese and a glass of ale, and [go] off on foot to a meeting generally one or two, sometimes six or seven miles off . . . the forward reformers all round were steadily exchanging a little silver for a little steel and lead.   There were some neutrals, not very many, and whatever neutral had an unused ' shooting stick ' found a sudden market for it . .   In obedience to the law of demand, one case of fifty muskets and bayonets came along from Birmingham . . ."

When the first Chartist National Convention of 49 delegates, elected at public meetings in all parts of the country, met in London on February 4, 1839, it soon became clear that although all were agreed as to the objective, there existed fundamental differences of opinion as to the method of proceeding towards it.   Broadly, the cleavage was between the " physical force " section, led by O'Connor, who favoured insurrectionary and militant methods, at least in the last resort, and the " moral force " section, led by William Lovett, who advocated a policy of political instruction and peaceful propaganda.

William Lovett (1800–1877) was a native of Newlyn, Cornwall, where he was brought up by his widowed mother upon strict Methodist lines.   He was apprenticed to a ropemaker, but lack of employment, combined with a natural bent for woodwork, caused him to enter the cabinet-making trade.   He was honest, industrious and highly intelligent ; yet as a young man he had a hard struggle to get a living.   In 1821 he migrated to London and was soon at the hub of working-class Radicalism at a time when that movement was emerging from the shadow of the Napoleonic Wars and when doctrines and methods were being hammered out anew.   He became the first store-keeper of the London Co-operative Society, founded in 1826, and later, in the thirties, we find him supporting the unstamped press agitation, which was, he said, one of the most important political movements with which he was ever associated. He took a prominent part in the formation and activities of the London Working Men's Association and in the Chartist Movement from the very beginning.   In February, 1839, he was elected secretary of the first Chartist National Convention, in spite of the opposition of O'Connor and O'Brien.   A staunch trade unionist, he eventually became President of his union, the London Cabinet-makers.   Lovett is described by a contemporary as " a tall, gentlemanly-looking man with a high and ample forehead, a pale

contemplative cast of countenance, dark brown hair, . . .
in manner quiet, modest, unassuming, speaking seldom
. . ." He had a sensitive spirit, keenly attuned to the
sufferings of others, and this temperament made him liable
to extremes of high enthusiasm and deep depression. He
was no orator; but in small gatherings or at the nerve-
centre of a movement he was invaluable. He was
methodical, accurate and business-like; an excellent
secretary and a good administrator—qualities rarely to be
found in the working-class movement of those days. Also
he possessed great moral courage. In 1831 he was "drawn
for the Militia," but he would neither serve nor buy himself
off (although he could have raised the money easily), nor
provide a substitute,

". . . on the grounds of not being represented in Parliament,
and of not having any voice or vote in the election of those
persons who made those laws that compelled me to take up
arms to protect the rights and property of others, while my own
rights and the only property I had, my labour, were not
protected."

Needless to say this plea was rejected, and Lovett's household goods to the value of between £15 and £30 were seized
and sold.

Lovett was a great lover of good books and had an
unshakable faith in the power of education—" the instrument of mental freedom and national progress "—to
emancipate the working classes, mentally, socially and
politically. Yet with all his idealism, he was essentially
level-headed and always an opponent of precipitate and
violent courses. He wished to see the franchise extended
to all men *and women*, except those incapacitated by mental
deficiency or crime. Believing, as he did, that this reform
could be obtained through the steady pressure of an
enlightened public opinion, he felt compelled to contend
strongly against all attempts to curtail the right of citizens
to express their opinions.

" The principle of democracy, " he wrote, " accords to every
individual the right of freely putting forth his opinions on all
subjects affecting the general welfare, the right of publicly
assembling his fellow-men to consider any project he may

conceive to be of public benefit, and the right of being heard patiently and treated courteously, however his opinions may differ from others."

He was opposed to all forms of autocracy or aristocracy, holding that " irresponsible power, vested in one man or in a class of men, is the fruitful source of every crime " against the toiling masses. In addition to the reform of the House of Commons along the lines set forth in the *People's Charter*, Lovett advocated the public examination of all persons wishing to become parliamentary candidates ; the delegation by Parliament of a limited and carefully defined number of matters to " district legislatures " ; and the restriction of the obstructive powers of the House of Lords. Dissension and increasing weakness within the Chartist Movement confirmed Lovett in his views on the vital necessity of education, and especially the importance of the study of Social Science " as forming the chief and secure basis of morality, of individual prosperity, and national happiness." Communism, Owenite Socialism, and nationalisation of the land did not commend themselves to him ; but he held that " great benefits may yet be realised by a wise and judicious system of co-operation in the production of wealth." He proposed to check accumulations of wealth by abolishing primogeniture and entail, and imposing heavy taxation upon inherited wealth and unearned increments : he also advocated the abolition of all indirect taxes. Throughout his life Lovett was an internationalist. He held that the interests of the toiling masses of all countries were identical, and he embodied his views in several voluminous addresses to the working men of other lands. War he regarded as " a pernicious waste of the fruits of . . . industry," an " instrument for perpetuating national feuds and political slavery " ; and as a first move towards its final abolition he proposed a " Congress of Nations " and " a court of judicature for nations " ; the former to devise a code of international law and to declare the outlawry of the instigators of wars ; the latter to effect rational settlements of disputes between nations.

Lovett had actually joined issue with O'Connor upon the physical force *versus* moral force controversy before the

meeting of the first Chartist Convention. In a characteristic and almost prophetic reply to O'Connor as early as
December, 1838, Lovett declared that :

"The whole physical force agitation is harmful and injurious
to the movement. Muskets are not what are wanted, but
education and schooling of the working people. Stephens and
O'Connor are shattering the movement in setting secondary
demands in the foreground. Violent words do not slay the
enemies, but the friends of our movement. O'Connor wants
to take everything by storm and to pass the Charter into law
within a year. All this hurry and haste, this bluster and menace
of armed opposition can only lead to premature outbreaks and
to the destruction of Chartism. If Stephens, O'Connor and
their adherents cannot realise this, many will leave the movement."

But this view, sound as it was, was accepted only by the
more moderate artisans of Lovett's type, not by the
"unshorn chins and fustian jackets," the less enlightened,
less fortunate workers of the Midlands and the North.
The rank and file of the Chartist Movement was, like its
leaders, composed of diverse elements, and this accounts for
the failure to find and follow a common policy. The
stockingers who could earn but 4s. or 4s. 6d. a week, the
handloom weavers who earned only 5s. 6d. a week, and the
miners of South Wales were in more desperate straits than
the skilled artisans of London, and therefore were drawn
towards more desperate remedies. A policy of education
and the patient building of a political party must have
seemed to them as utterly useless as making a step-ladder
to reach the moon. Great demonstrations and monster
petitions to Parliament, reinforced, if need be, by the
threat of an armed rising or a general strike, seemed much
more appropriate.

A plan for a general strike (or "sacred month") on a
national scale as an instrument of political reform was
published at the beginning of 1832. The author, William
Benbow, originally a Manchester cobbler, had lived an
exciting, if precarious existence as a Radical agitator in the
troublous times of the Hampden Clubs, the anti-democratic
"Six Acts," and the "Peterloo massacre" of 1819. By
1832 he had become a confirmed revolutionary firebrand.

In the Chartist National Convention in February, 1839, O'Connor urged that the best way to impress the members of Parliament would be to go with the Petition in one hand and "ulterior measures" (which included the general strike) in the other. O'Brien, on the other hand, deprecated the use of threats, for, said he, "no set of men like to be bullied." On various occasions the general strike was discussed by the Chartist leaders as one among several methods—such as refusal to pay taxes and a run on the Savings Banks—of putting pressure on the government if Parliament rejected the National Petition. On April 22, 1839, O'Connor made a speech in the Chartist Convention in favour of the general strike ; if the need arose, he said, the workers could "meet the cannon with the shuttle." O'Brien was now in favour of the discussion of "ulterior measures." The other members of the Convention were divided, and many were undecided. The "physical force" men regarded the general strike as an excellent way of commencing an armed rising ; but the moderates and "moral force" section thought that the response to a general strike call would be disappointing. Hetherington was prepared to go forward with the project of a general strike, after the rejection of the Petition, if the results of an exhaustive investigation of its nature and possibilities seemed to justify such a course. Lovett, who was really opposed to the idea, urged delay pending the collection of an adequate strike fund, and proposed that, if the Convention decided to proceed, one or two trades only should be called out on strike on a certain day, while all other workers should be asked to contribute money to a strike fund. The Commons rejected the Chartists' Petition on July 12, 1839, and, in disgust and desperation, the Convention, now reduced to half its original numbers, fixed August 12 for the beginning of a general strike. But they were ill at ease and far from unanimous, and in the end, on the advice of an investigation committee of seven (including O'Connor and O'Brien), they cancelled the strike call and urged that a number of "grand moral demonstrations" should be held instead.

Meantime, an attempt to break up a meeting of working men at Birmingham on July 4, 1839, by means of police imported from London, resulted in a riot in which several

Chartists were arrested. The next day the Chartist Convention met and Lovett moved a resolution protesting against the " wanton, flagrant and unjust outrage " upon the people of Birmingham " by a blood-thirsty and unconstitutional force from London." The resolution was passed unanimously and ordered to be printed and posted about the town. All the delegates were ready to sign, but Lovett, fearing the consequent arrest of all the Chartist leaders, volunteered to be the sole signatory. The protest was published during the afternoon of July 5th ; on the evening of July 6th Lovett and Collins were arrested. A month later they were tried. Lovett, conducting his own defence, stood by the resolution he had signed and stoutly maintained that the people had a right of assembly and free discussion. He was sent to prison for one year.

This marked the beginning of a series of prosecutions. The government, thoroughly alarmed by the talk and reports of drilling and arming and by the threats of a general strike and other " ulterior measures," embarked upon repressive action, and by the end of 1840 the majority of the more prominent Chartist leaders, including O'Connor and O'Brien, had been prosecuted to conviction and imprisoned. But Chartism did not die. Indeed, on his release from prison in 1841 O'Connor found a Chartist revival already in progress, and he soon revealed his determination to run and rule the second phase of the Movement—a shrewd bid for personal power which coincided with a strong desire among the rank and file for unity and decisive leadership. In the course of a whirlwind tour, O'Connor addressed numerous monster meetings in the chief industrial areas, delighted his worshippers, put heart into those whose faith was flagging, and gathered in new recruits by the score. *The Northern Star* flashed more formidably than ever. No shift or manœuvre was neglected in order to tie likely lieutenants firmly to O'Connor's chariot, and no quarter was given to Lovett and his like, who refused to do homage to " the leader."

Among these new recruits of 1841 was a remarkable man named Thomas Cooper. Cooper (1805—1892) was the child of poor parents and had been a shoemaker, a teacher, a musician, a local preacher and a newspaper reporter, before he joined the Chartists.   Hovell's sketch of him is worthy of quotation :—

" He was an entirely self-taught man.   He acquired an incredible amount of learning under the most disadvantageous circumstances.   Latin, French, Greek, Mathematics, Music, English Literature . . . all came alike to him . . . Like most self-taught people, Cooper lacked that balance of judgment which comes largely by contact with other minds, and he was apt to act hastily upon half-truths.   He also had no little opinion of himself, as a glance at his autobiography will show.   A brilliant but impulsive intellect, Cooper flared up suddenly in the Chartist world, and as suddenly disappeared.   But in the years 1841–2 there was no leader so successful as he."

While acting as a reporter, Cooper discovered deep distress and starvation among the stockingers of Leicester and district who earned less than a penny an hour ; and his intense indignation carried him into the Chartist Movement.

" His conversion was quickly followed by the loss of his situation, and he thenceforward devoted himself wholly to the cause of the stockingers.   He ran several newspapers in succession, conducted innumerable meetings, and rapidly acquired an immense following which he proceeded to organise.   He took a large hall of meeting, and christened his flock the ' Shakesperean Association of Leicester Chartists.'   By the summer of 1842 he claimed 2,500 members.   He divided them up into classes . . . devised a kind of uniform, gave to his adherents a pseudo-military organisation, and proudly bore the title of ' Shakesperean General " . . . By these means—the magic of uniforms and badges—Cooper developed a really ferocious *esprit de corps* among his followers, who idolised him. But he was not content with demonstrations.   He took pains to give his disciples education in an adult school and amusement of the right sort."

Cooper in his turn idolised O'Connor and turned against all who opposed his attempt to dominate the movement.

" We still held by the People's Charter," says Cooper in his autobiography, " and fondly believed we should succeed. Feargus O'Connor, by his speeches in various parts of the country and by his letters in *The Northern Star*, chiefly helped to keep up these expectations.   The immense majority of Chartists in Leicester, as well as in many other

towns, regarded him as the only really disinterested and
incorruptible leader . . . Common sense taught me that no
cause can be gained by disunion. And as I knew no reason
for doubting the political honesty and disinterestedness
which O'Connor ever asserted for himself, and which people
believed, I stuck by O'Connor and would have gone through
fire and water for him. There was much that was attractive
in him when I first knew him . . . The fact of his having
been in the House of Commons and among the upper
classes also lent him influence. I do not think half a
dozen Chartists cared a fig about his boasted descent from
' Roderick O'Connor, the king of Connaught and last king
of all Ireland ' ; but the connection of his family with the
United Irishmen and patriotic sufferers of the last century,
rendered him a natural representative of the cause of
political liberty."

In 1842–3 Cooper was tried twice in connection with
his activities as a Chartist leader in the Potteries in the
summer of 1842. On the first charge—arson—he secured
an acquittal ; but a few months later he was convicted of
conspiracy and sedition, and imprisoned for two years.
While in prison he wrote his well-known work, *The
Purgatory of Suicides*, and many of his vivid descriptions of
the misery and starvation prevalent during the " hungry
forties," subsequently published in his book *Wise Saws and
Modern Instances* (1845). Like O'Brien, Cooper ceased to
advocate physical force after his release from prison. Also,
like O'Brien and many others, he quarrelled with O'Connor
and gradually drifted from the main stream of Chartism into
literary work.

The chasm between O'Connor and other leaders, such as
Lovett and O'Brien, was clearly revealed and greatly
widened in 1842 by an attempt to build a bridge between the
Chartists and certain middle-class Radicals led by the
Quaker, Joseph Sturge.* This *Complete Suffrage
Union*—" a sort of middle-class Chartism "—was at
first regarded favourably by O'Brien, Lovett, Cooper and
other Chartist leaders in the hope that the proposed
alliance would place the Charter more speedily upon the

* See the study of Sturge by Stephen Hobhouse in this volume,
pages 640-3.

statute book. It was attacked tooth and nail by O'Connor who saw in it a threat to his supremacy. But the *Complete Suffrage Union* was destroyed not so much by O'Connor and *The Northern Star* as by the Sturgeites' refusal to use the term " Charter " and the Chartists' refusal to accept " Bill of Rights " as an alternative. Upon this rock the Union split. Lovett in particular stood stoutly for the Charter in name as well as form. Cooper made an eleventh-hour attempt to save the second conference in December, 1842; but he failed, and the " respectables " parted from the Chartists, much to O'Connor's delight.

In the same year (1842), after the rejection of the second National Petition, the Chartist leaders attempted to make use of a series of strikes which broke out in the industrial north-west of England by persuading the strikers to remain " out " until " the Charter became the law of the land." The strike movement, originally directed against reductions of wages, spread from Lancashire to the Clyde and Tyne and into the Midlands. It seemed possible that the proposed general strike " to paralyse the government " would come about after all. But Chartist leadership was poor, and many of the strikers could not be won over from industrial to political action. Cooper addressed numerous meetings in the Potteries, urging the men to strike, and then hurried to a Chartist conference in Manchester, where he declared himself in favour of a national general strike, although he felt certain it would lead to fighting. O'Connor voted in favour of the extension of the strike, but did not really intend to do anything to further it. Indeed, *The Northern Star* discouraged the whole movement on the ground that it was not, and could not be, sufficiently national in scope. Eventually the strikes fizzled out, but not before the government had begun to bring to book scores of Chartists, including O'Connor and Cooper. O'Connor was tried and convicted, but luckily for him the conviction was over-ruled on technical grounds. Cooper, as we have seen, was less fortunate.

Although its strength fluctuated a good deal, the Chartist Movement never really recovered from the failures of 1842. In the following years O'Connor, now the complete autocrat of Chartism, sought to revivify the movement by improving the organisation of the National Charter Association, and by launching a back-to-the-land scheme of small holdings for Chartists. Towards the close of the eighteenth century and throughout the first half of the nineteenth century it was frequently asserted in pamphlets and periodicals* that the cultivation of small farms mainly by the spade was both socially desirable and economically sound. The Chartists were always drawn towards the land as one possible means of economic salvation, of release from a doomed handicraft or the toils of the new factories, and in 1843 O'Connor decided to form a company for the purpose of buying large estates and dividing them into small holdings of two, three or four acres.

Upon these he proposed to settle working men who had subscribed for a certain number of shares, priority being determined by ballot. At the same time he wrote a manual upon the *Management of Small Farms*, and painted an alluring picture of the happy, independent life available to a man " with a spade, a hut to cover him, and as much land as he can cultivate by his own industry." Such a man " dreads not the sound . . . of the factory bell. He is not deprived of the comfort of the society of his wife . . . He is not reduced to the humiliating necessity of shaking his slumbering babe into a kind of artificial life in order that she may obey the capitalist's morning summons. He sees no cripple at his board, no dwarf in his family . . . He is master of himself and of his time . . . He seeks no refuge for his wounded feelings in the beer shop or gin palace."

O'Brien, now at daggers drawn with O'Connor, attacked the land scheme chiefly on the ground that all such projects tended to destroy the unity of the working-class movement by luring men away from the steady pursuit of radical political and economic reforms, and fixing their attention upon small selfish objects. Even if the National Land Company proved a success, it could benefit only a minority of the workers, while its operations were an active acquiescence in those existing laws and institutions of property which every honest Chartist ought to repudiate.

* See, e.g., Thos. Wright, *The Monopoly of Small Farms a Great Cause of the present Scarcity* (1795) ; and D. Davies, *The Case of the Labourers in Husbandry stated and considered* (1795).

In short, every man who supported O'Connor's futile and pernicious " land-lottery " was in effect enlisting himself with the government against his own class, and was helping to drain away essential funds which ought to be devoted to agitating for the Charter.   In one week in May 1847, said O'Brien, subscriptions to the National Land Company totalled £641 18s., while the National Charter Association received only £1 2s.   Lovett also thoroughly disliked and distrusted both O'Connor and his scheme, but did not accept O'Brien's alternative, land nationalisation and administration by a state department, because he feared that the result would be an inefficient and intolerable bureaucracy.   Cooper " felt sure the scheme would bring ruin and disappointment . . . upon all who entered into it " and urged O'Connor to give it up.   There were other critics of the scheme, both inside and outside the Chartist Movement ; but no amount of criticism could destroy the strength of its appeal to the rank and file.   Within ten months from the provisional registration of the company the " land fund " reached the astonishing sum of £50,000 ; and the final total was over £90,000 in three years.   Five estates were actually bought and a contract of sale was executed in respect of a sixth.   Had this purchase been completed, the six estates would have covered 1,618 acres, acquired at a cost of nearly £60,000.   In all, 250 substantial brick bungalows, containing three rooms and a kitchen, and four school houses were built.   With tremendous optimism O'Connor aimed at settling 24,000 families upon the land in five years ; but he under-rated, *inter alia*, the fact that his settlers knew practically nothing of the skilled business of agriculture, and therefore were likely to come to disaster before they had had time to learn.   Moreover, the legality of the Company, which had been provisionally registered as a friendly society, and the efficiency of its internal management, were called in question from time to time, until finally in May, 1848, the House of Commons ordered an enquiry.   Finlaison, the noted statistician, found that 19,331 members had subscribed £74,406 for 57,236 shares, paid in full ; while 150,025 shares had been partly paid for, 50,669 members having subscribed £16,348—an average of only 2s. 2d. per share or less than 6s. 6d. a member.   Actually 230 members, owning 681 fully paid shares, had been put in possession of small-holdings, so that there still remained over 19,000 unsatisfied subscribers. The Select Committee of Investigation reported that the Company was an illegal scheme " not consistent with the general principles upon which Friendly Societies are founded," and that as it could not fulfil the promises held out to the shareholders it should be liquidated. The accounts and other records had been badly kept, but no suspicion of fraud fell upon O'Connor. Indeed, it seems that he had put into the Company about £3,300 of his own money, During the following four or five years nearly all O'Connor's original settlers abandoned their holdings, which were gradually acquired by agricultural workers.

Among those named as trustees of the National Land Company was a certain Ernest Jones, who also acted with O'Connor as joint editor of *The Labourer*, a periodical published mainly for the purpose of popularising the land scheme. Ernest Charles Jones (1819-1869) was not a child of the people. He was born and educated in aristocratic, military circles in Germany and England, for he was the son of Major Charles Jones of the 15th Hussars, a Peninsular and Waterloo veteran, and equerry to the Duke of Cumberland who later became King of Hanover. In the thirties Ernest Jones came to England and in the early forties we find him settled in London writing verses, novels and newspaper articles. He moved in " fashionable circles " and was presented at court in 1841 ; but his sympathies were always strongly with the oppressed, and it is said that when he was a boy he was so fired with admiration for the Poles during their great struggle in 1829-30 that he set off with a bundle under his arm, and was eventually found in the middle of the Black Forest " on his way to help the Poles." In English politics in the forties he was attracted almost irresistibly by the cause of the unenfranchised working classes. In 1846 he joined the Chartist Movement and in the following year he began to write in *The Northern Star* and *The Labourer*. Although Jones was not in the Chartist Movement during its earlier stages, he quickly realised that dissensions among the leaders had been a serious source of weakness which must be removed if final failure was to be avoided. Accordingly he did his best to work with O'Connor, although this made him unpopular with the anti-O'Connorites. In the general election of 1847, when O'Connor sprang a surprise on the country by winning a seat at Nottingham, Jones stood for Halifax, but in spite of much acclamation at the hustings he polled only 280 votes.

Both O'Connor and Jones made speeches at the mass meeting which accompanied the despatch of the last great Chartist petition to Parliament in April, 1848. Parliament's shelving of the petition incensed Jones and confirmed him in the opinion, which he expressed at more than one public meeting, that no further headway could be made without a display of force. A Chartist Convention which met on May 1st, 1848, dissolved on the 13th in complete confusion and disagreement ; and when Jones, refusing to admit defeat, was making a desperate effort to rally the broken forces, he was arrested at Manchester, with five other Chartists, and eventually sentenced to two years' imprisonment for seditious speaking.

By the time that Jones was released from prison, the embers of Chartism as an organised movement were nearly cold. O'Connor, quite harmlessly installed in the Commons, was beginning to fail in physical and mental health. To the working men of the early fifties the trade union and co-operative movements seemed to hold out more hope than Chartism. When Jones stood again for Halifax in 1852, he polled only 52 votes, and he was unable to win a seat at Nottingham in the following year. He continued his *People's Paper* for six years, but it never approached the success of *The Northern Star*. Although he can scarcely be called a Socialist, Jones remained a Radical democrat until he died in 1869. He had great faith in the franchise coupled with political education as the gateway to all social and economic reforms, contending that the wider the extension of the franchise, the safer would be the institutions of the country. He believed that the Charter would bring about a better distribution of wealth as well as political power. " I am," he wrote, "wed to no particular form of Government for theory's sake. Systems should be made for men, men were not made for systems. I pity those persons who compose constitutions in their closets, founded on abstract rights, but totally unfitted for the requirements of the age

. . . The way to make a happy future is to make a happy present . . . I am for solid, practical reform ; and no reform is solid that is not adapted to the actual wants of the people." And again, in defence of democracy, he said, " Democracy means not the rule of a class, but of a nation—it embraces all—it tempers one class with another . . . We have been invited to condemn democratic institutions upon several grounds. First because they are asserted to have failed in various countries and ages. I join issue with the conclusions drawn from these precedents . . . [for] it is requisite to show that the conditions in both cases are the same . . . and I protest against demanding from the infancy of nations that which their maturity alone can achieve. I protest against measuring the child by the standard of the man." Within the democratic state, Jones argued, every human being had a right to full and free development of every power and capacity of his nature, consistent with the exercise of the same right by others.

For more than ten years Jones tried to revive the failing forces of Chartism by public speaking, by journalism and by writing political poems and songs ; but in the end he was forced to turn, like other Chartists before him, towards the idea of a middle-class alliance. In 1858 he formed, in place of the Chartist Movement, a Manhood Suffrage Association of both middle and working classes, and so helped to start the movement which resulted in the Reform Act of 1867.

The decline and decay of the Chartist Movement did not end the distresses, problems and aspirations of English working people. The end of the Chartist Movement was not the end of Chartism. The organisation withered and was gone ; the essence remained. Deep in the recesses of working-class life there lingered heterodox views, advanced opinions, a desire for social and economic improvements and an obstinate belief in " the rightness of democracy," which provided an excellent jumping-off ground for the next advance. To the creation of this situation and these opinions and beliefs, each of the Chartist leaders mentioned in this essay had, in his own way, contributed something. Men like O'Connor, O'Brien, Hetherington, and Cooper, stirred the imagination of the English masses—a people not easily moved—by speech, writing and example, until thousands of the workers ceased merely to " think of themselves with a shilling or two more in their pockets," but " were swept along by the rhetoric which described their place in society, degraded and insulted, their lives spent in the cold and dark in a world of luxury and wealth. Their indignation was fired by this picture of society as it was : their imagination was touched by a picture of society as it might be."

Hetherington spoke from Radical reform platforms for over twenty years ; he was a staunch and leading Chartist from the inception of the movement until his death in 1849 ; but his chief service to the democratic cause was rendered when he fought triumphantly against the newspaper stamp duties. Among all the pioneers of Chartism he was probably the most sincere, courageous, energetic, ingenious and successful ; " one of those men," said Francis Place, "whose peculiarities fit them for martyrs."

O'Brien exerted a many-sided influence upon the democratic movement. His essential and efficient co-operation with Hetherington, as editor of the *Poor Man's Guardian* during the unstamped press struggle, has been too often overlooked. It was O'Brien who created the " soul " of that remarkable little journal. Unfailingly in every issue appeared his editorials in which he struck shrewd blows at his enemies, while he encouraged his friends. " The protests and pressure of a few law-abiding citizens," says Dr. Holland Rose, " would have effected little but for the persistent efforts of the editors of unstamped papers who slowly but surely undermined the position of the authorities." Although O'Brien's ambitious literary programme was never carried out, he was one of the chief channels through which the influence of the French Revolution reached the working people of his day. He made no systematic attempt to build up a body of Socialist doctrines but he was indefatigable in the propagation of political ideas, of criticism of the social system, and of analyses of the causes of the " present distresses " ; and indeed the failure of several of his independent journalistic ventures is attributable to his over-keenness in this direction, for he allowed the news to be completely outweighed by political argument and

propaganda.   He was no economic fatalist : on the contrary
he was desperately anxious to add reform to reform rapidly,
for he saw more clearly than most men the heavy human
or " real " costs of British industrial pre-eminence.   Like
O'Connor, he was a good orator and was very active in the
Chartist cause in 1839, but by playing with the fire of
revolutionary physical force he misdirected his powers.
O'Brien was much indebted to the writings of other reformers,
especially the early English Socialists ; and in his turn he
exerted some influence upon later writers, including Karl
Marx.

O'Connor must receive credit for his energy and
power on the platform, and for his successful, if not
particularly scrupulous, conduct of *The Northern Star*, the
only Radical paper of that period which was really a power
in the land.   But against these things we must set his
inconsistency, his toying with violent methods, his egotism
and itch for personal supremacy, his quarrelsomeness and
inability to work for long with other leaders.   O'Connor
wanted the centre of the stage all the time, and all the stage
most of the time.   Moreover he completely lacked the
foresight and political judgment of contemporaries like
Cobden and Bright.   It may well be argued that, on balance,
O'Connor and his paper did Chartism more harm than good.
Such was certainly the opinion of Lovett, who regarded
O'Connor as " a trader in political agitation " and the " chief
marplot " in the Movement : a man who by his personal
conduct and his handling of *The Northern Star* set a blight
upon the cause of democracy " from the first moment he
opened his lips as its professed advocate."   O'Connor is also
severely judged by Francis Place, who calls him an arch-
agitator who, " by his volubility, his recklessness of truth, his
newspaper, his unparalleled impudence . . . triumphed over
every other agitator."   Allowing for some exaggeration and
prejudice in these judgments, O'Connor's faults were
enough to solidify the opposition of the ruling classes, strip
Chartism of most of its leaders, and bring the Movement to
the final fiasco of 1848.

Between Feargus O'Connor and William Lovett the
contrast is complete.   Lovett had all that O'Connor lacked
of wisdom, foresight, constancy, and depth and originality

of thought.   He was largely responsible for the initiation and organisation of several important bodies, like the London Working Men's Association, but owing to his steadfast repudiation of violent methods and his preference for peaceful persuasion and education he was never influential or popular among the majority of Chartists.   " While I am bound to confess," says a contemporary, " that I came to London much prejudiced against Lovett and all who belonged to the Working Men's Association, looking upon them as no better than tools of the Whigs . . . I will unhesitatingly affirm that no . . . man [could] have surpassed William Lovett in talent, in energy, and in honesty."

Thomas Cooper came into the Chartist Movement in its second phase and stayed about five years, two of which he spent in prison.   Impulsive, but intensely loyal and thorough once his sympathies were captured, he worked for Chartism with all the enthusiasm of a religious convert ; and when he passed over from the left wing to the right—from courageous advocacy of physical force to an equally courageous preaching of moral force and popular education,* his conversion was entirely sincere.   During the Chartist revival of 1841-2 Cooper built up at Leicester one of the largest and best local organisations in the Movement.   He found the Leicester workers a listless and depressed multitude ; he transformed them into a solid, forward-looking brigade of determined Chartists.   By keeping their minds occupied he preserved many poverty-stricken workmen from the worst depths of despair.   His writings in verse and prose touched a wider circle, and although these came too late to do much for Chartism, they were not without effect upon the next phase of the democratic movement.

Lastly, we come to Ernest Jones, who was in effect the commander of the rearguard of Chartism now in retreat.   Although Jones had many weaknesses and no outstanding gift of leadership, he was one of the most steadfast and single-minded of all the leaders of Chartism.   He notes in his Diary the fact that domestic troubles and the disappointment of his literary hopes had left him " as enthusiastic of mind, as ardent of temper, as fresh of heart

* See his *Eight Letters to the Young Men of the Working Classes* (1851).

and as strong of frame as ever . . I am prepared to rush fresh and strong into the strife and struggle of a nation, to ride the torrent or guide the rill, if God permits.'' At first he tried to infuse a militant, class-struggle spirit into the Movement ; a policy in which he was probably confirmed by his direct contact with Marx in the early fifties. Jones numbered many other political exiles among his friends, and, like Lovett, he helped to create among English working men an interest in international affairs and a sense of international solidarity which the Labour Movement retains to this day. When the mantle of O'Connor fell upon him, Jones inherited a legacy containing more of failure than success ; but, quite undismayed, he strove gallantly against heavy odds for over ten years to keep Chartism alive, and although in the end the body of the Movement died in his arms, he was able to bear its banner and its spirit onward into the manhood suffrage movement which secured the franchise for urban workers in 1867.

THE CHRISTIAN SOCIALISTS
by G. C. BINYON

THE CHRISTIAN SOCIALISTS
by G. C. BINYON

" THE notion of the Christian Church is associated, in the minds of many, with the notion of priestcraft and kingcraft ; of the slavery of the intellect, persecution, and tyranny ; and it would be ridiculous to deny that they have cause enough for connecting the thought of it with those fearful sins of man against man. The history of the Church, in every age, is full of sad tales of the sins of the clergy against the people.

" But the honest and thoughtful man who reads such tales, whatever just indignation he will feel against the doers of them, will pause before he condemns and throws away from him the Church and Christianity itself, for the sins of the men who had the preaching thereof.

" He is bound, by every law of fairness, to ask himself— These tyrannies, persecutions, enslavements of the intellect, trucklings to the rich and powerful of the earth, were they in accordance with the spirit of the Church, or were they contradictory to it ? Were men Priests in as far as they did such things ; or may they not in doing them have been acting exactly contrary to their own calling, denying their own Orders, and making themselves no Priests at all by the very act of tyranny and bigotry ?

" I assert the latter.

" I assert that the business for which God sends a Christian Priest in a Christian nation, is to preach and practise Liberty, Equality, and Brotherhood, in the fullest, deepest, widest, simplest meaning of these three great words : that in as far as he so does, he is a true Priest, doing his Lord's work, with his Lord's blessing on him : that in as far as he does not, he is no Priest at all, but a traitor to God and man : and that if he perseveres in his mistake— and a wilful mistake it must be—about his own work, the Lord of that Priest will come in an hour that he thinketh not of, and will, in fearful literalness, cut him asunder, and appoint him his portion with the unbelievers, where will be weeping and gnashing of teeth."

That is how Charles Kingsley began his famous sermon, " The Message of the Church to Labouring Men " (on the text, St. Luke iv, 16–21) in St. John's Church, Fitzroy Square, London, on the 22nd of June, 1851—the year of the Great Exhibition.

Among the thousands who thronged to the Exhibition, there was circulated a Trade Union leaflet which called attention to the grim misery beneath the magic brilliance. To those who were more conscious of the grim misery than the magic splendour, Charles Kingsley attempted to justify God to the People.

To the Vicar of St. John's, Fitzroy Square, however, much of Kingsley's message seemed to be dangerous and untrue ; and he did not scruple to say so in church when the sermon was over. And the Bishop of London, having heard some garbled version of Kingsley's sermon, forbade him to preach in London. His working-class supporters then invited him to start a free church outside the jurisdiction of Bishops, and promised him a large following.

. No one who had really understood the sermon could have thought of making such a proposal ; and Kingsley did not entertain the idea for a moment. He was a Christian Socialist ; but a Christian first and a Socialist derivatively as a consequence of his Christianity ; and he was not simply Christian, vaguely, but a Churchman.

Kingsley—Rector of Eversley from 1844 till the year of his death in 1875, Professor of History at Cambridge, and later Canon of Westminster—has, for some reason, often been associated with " muscular Christianity " and even with non-dogmatic religion : but that is to do him no sort of justice. It is as popularizer of the theology of Maurice that he should be thought of ; for he never felt thoroughly at home either with Tractarians or the Protestants of his day, and regarded Maurice as his master. So, too, did Ludlow ; born in India, and educated in Paris, he could only hear of one clergyman in England who appealed to him, Arnold of Rugby—until, at Lincoln's Inn, he met Maurice, then Chaplain there, towards whom, at once and

for always, he felt the deepest reverence. These three—
Maurice, Ludlow and Kingsley—were the leaders of the
Movement; and it is important to note that Maurice never
professed to be anything but a Church reformer; so that
the Christian Socialist Movement should be regarded,
primarily, as one of restoring the social teaching of the
Church.

. . . . .

In this volume the Christian Socialists appear as
Democrats, and are even given a place among Great
Democrats. Whether they have any right to such a place
could be questioned ; and it might even be denied that
they have any title to be called Democrats at all. But it
must be remembered that the word " Democracy " has
not had, at all times, the same associations ; it has carried
with it different assumptions and suggestions.

For example, it may be supposed, by some, that if the
People are to govern themselves, then they must not look
outside themselves for guidance, for if they were to do so
that would be government from outside and not self-
government at all. On that supposition, the People must
never look upon Christianity as a Revelation giving guidance
for human affairs ; if Demos reigns, God cannot. If
Democracy is understood in that way, all the Christian
Socialists were so far from being Democrats that they were
vehement opponents of Democracy.

Theo-crats would really be a better description of them
than *Demo*-crats ; that is to say, they believed in God's
Government of the world and of man, rather than in
self-government of the People. The belief that dominated
all their thinking and doing was the belief in the Kingship,
Reign, or Kingdom of God and His Christ.

But each of the three leaders, even before the Movement
started in 1848, had, through his study of the Bible, come
to understand God's Government of the world and of man
in a way that might fairly be called " democratic."

In these days, the notion of the Bible seems to be
associated in the minds of many with the notion that the
Old Testament contains nothing but records of wars of
Israel with Amalekites, and should therefore be disregarded,

and that the New Testament contains nothing of importance except the precept " Whatsoever ye would that men should do unto you, even so do unto them," so that once that has been memorised, the New Testament can be disregarded too. In those days, both Evangelicals and Tractarians found in the Scriptures an ampler Revelation. It was not, in either case, one that could be called " democratic." But these men found in the Bible what Maurice called " the great principle of a theocracy."

This principle, he maintained, had never been so power-fully asserted as it had been by the French Revolution— although that Revolution had in words denied God's Government. Did not God, he asked,

" in that awful judgment upon the kings, the nobles, and priests of France, declare that every man in a nation which professes to acknowledge His name, must and shall be treated as something more than a mere animal, to be used for the services of other and more powerful animals, to be kept down and tamed by the awful sanctions of law; that every man must and shall be treated as His child, as formed to bear His image; or if not, that in His hand is a cup, and the wine is red, and the lords of the earth shall drink it to the very dregs ? "

That great *theocratic principle* strikes the keynote of the Christian Socialism of Maurice and his associates ; is it not in perfect harmony with " Democracy ? "

They got this principle from the Bible ; for in the Old Testament they found the story of how Israel in Egypt cried by reason of their taskmasters, how that cry came up unto God, how He came down to deliver them, led them out of Egypt, through the wilderness, towards the Promised Land ; they found also a Law which meant (as Kingsley put it) that " all systems of society which favour the accumulation of capital in a few hands, which oust the masses from the soil which their forefathers possessed of old, which reduce them to the level of serfs and day-labourers, living on wages or on alms, which crush them down with debt or in any wise degrade or enslave them, or deny them a permanent stake in the commonwealth, are contrary to the Kingdom of God " ; in the New Testament they found the Gospel of Christ's Kingdom, not as some-thing in a future world, nor yet in the future of the world, but as a present reality which actual wrong-doing may defy but cannot abolish and so is doomed to eventual destruction ; while in both Testaments they found God executing His judgments for the correction of His People through the agency of men who denied Him.

What they had learned from the Bible was reinforced by experience of life ; Kingsley, as a boy of thirteen, had been deeply impressed by the truly horrible sights he had seen at the Bristol riots of 1831 ; by pondering on them, he slowly learned his first lessons in Christian Socialism. Ludlow had seen with his own eyes something of what slavery meant in Martinique ; and he had had first-hand experience of revolutionary movements in France between 1830 and 1848 ; he had already reached the position that Socialism and Christianity were not in their nature hostile, but akin. And the thinking of Maurice had, of course, been stimulated by the Chartist Movement.

It was, then, quite natural that they should see in the contemporary ideals and principles—Chartism, Democracy, Co-operation, Socialism, Communism—evidence of God Himself at work asserting the great principle of a theocracy.

Thus they were all three ready to strike out a new line when the Chartist Movement ingloriously disappeared from public view on the 10th of April, 1848. The decline of the popular movement gave them their opportunity to proclaim Christian Socialism.

Accordingly, in the late evening of that tenth of April and in the small hours of the next day, they planned how to tell their message to the workmen of England : " You say that you are wronged. Many of you are wronged ; and many besides yourselves know it. . . . You think the Charter would make you free—would to God it would ! The Charter is not bad ; *if the men who use it are not bad !* But will the Charter make you free ? Will it free you from slavery to ten-pound bribes ? . . . Who would dare refuse you freedom ? for the Almighty God, and Jesus Christ, the Poor Man who died for all poor men, will bring it about for you, though all the Mammonites of the earth were against you. . . ."

It is plain that they did not regard democratic self-government, the possession of a vote and representation in

Parliament, as a cure-all for the wrongs they saw around them. The kind of " self-government " they really believed in was that which enables a man to govern himself, control his lower nature, and submit himself to the laws of God's Kingdom.

.   .   .   .

From the point of view of Liberal political democracy, the Christian Socialists may be disappointing.

Maurice at one time spoke of the Church as the only protection against Democracy. That was because he regarded Monarchy as a theocratic institution (are not kings anointed by archbishops ?) and assumed that Democracy must necessarily be anti-monarchical, revolutionary, and anti-Christian : his vision of the future did not include a glimpse of Labour politicians in court-dress ; nor did he think that Democracy would ever become associated with slow and timid measures of advance, still less that one day Christian opinion would rally to Democracy as a protection against something worse.

At a later time, he recognised that Democracy had rendered good service in countering oppression and subjection, by insisting on the value of each single person.

He was never quite happy about Democracy ; but he became content to acquiesce in a democratic constitution with a wide franchise as a form of government in a Christian country on condition that the power of the vote or office in government were accepted as a ministry, an obligation, a vocation, with a full sense of responsibility ; in that case, the People would be looking outside themselves for guidance, they would be governing themselves by becoming willing subjects of Christ the King. But if the People in any country felt themselves free, in the name of self-government, to repudiate Divine authority ; if the power of the vote or of office in government were to be grasped at merely as power ; then—Maurice insisted—the voice of the People would not be the Voice of God, but the devil's voice. He was as much afraid of the tyranny of the majority as of the tyranny of the few or of one.

All through his life, Maurice felt an abhorrence for " the *mere* democrat " ; and as for the doctrine that power proceeds from the People, he would have none of it. He always taught that the will of the natural man is self-will, and that the human will must find its freedom in the Will of God.

Similar views about Democracy, with some variation in emphasis, were held by all the Christian Socialists.

Kingsley may always have attended too much to people's rank in society, but for all that he always saw the man beneath. He thought that Democracy must be accepted as a fact, and he was ready for all extensions of the franchise ; but to be of any real value it must be accompanied by education, and christianised, that is, provided with that vision without which the people perish.

Ludlow and Maurice seem never to have thoroughly understood one another on this topic. Ludlow attributed to Maurice " a horror of democracy " ; Maurice replied that this imputed horror was one in the interests of the people ; he thought that Ludlow played into the hands of the mere democrat. But the difference between them was really slight. Maurice was, before all else, a theologian and a seer ; and Ludlow had a clearer perception of the practical training and education afforded to persons by actually trying, however faultily, to manage their own affairs, whether in the industrial world or in the larger field of national politics.

Neale was, from a theological point of view, *in* rather than *of* the Movement ; but a statement of his made out of intimate practical experience and observation could no doubt have been agreed to by both Maurice and Ludlow : " social institutions stand to morality somewhat in the relation in which machinery stands to labour. The machine does not make the care and thought, the attention and skill, of the worker needless. Far from it. What it does is to make this thought and care and skill more effective for the end proposed than they would be without its aid." None of the Christian Socialists attached great importance to the machinery of political democracy ; they were more concerned to create the will and the skill to use it properly.

Thomas Hughes (born in 1822) was the youngest of the five Christian Socialists : educated under Arnold at Rugby, the scene of his famous *Tom Brown's School Days*, he was early attracted by the idealist aspects of Democracy ;

he was even, at one time, tempted to become a physical-force Chartist. He was called to the bar in 1848, and he alone of these men entered Parliament, as member first for Lambeth and afterwards for Frome. Speaking in the House of Commons in 1866, in support of the Representation of the People Bill, he described himself as an advanced or extreme Liberal ; but his speech was one which would now be called Labour or Social-Democratic. He found fault with the Bill for its " excessive solvency " ; it was impossible for those living in luxury or affluence to represent those with no accumulated property except Trade Union funds and the like. His ground for supporting the Bill was his hope that it would open entrance into the House of Commons for the expression of principles hitherto un-represented in that assembly. He spoke of the philosophy of Samuel Smiles and self-help, and said that the really representative men among the working-class were animated by quite other ideas. The Trade Unions and Co-operative Societies had proved that the working men were ready to make sacrifices for their principles, and that the strong were ready to help the weak ; their desire was not to leave their class but to lift it.

Hughes was not under the illusion that all who would be enfranchised by this Bill were animated by these ideas ; and he was obviously far more interested in the will and the skill to use the machinery of representative government than in that machinery itself. He desired to see it used for the furtherance of Christian Socialism and Co-operation, that the people might be better housed, fed, and educated.

As political Democrats, all the Christian Socialists were but half-hearted ; Democrats pure and simple—" *mere* democrats "—they never were. Not for a moment could any of them accept that kind of Democracy which (as a modern writer has put it) " asserts that man can do what he likes, since there is no power greater than man." They had no idea that the will of the People was the final arbiter of political wisdom ; if they hearkened to the voice of the People, it was because they heard in it the Voice of God. But they could distinguish between the Divine accents and the language of those who humble themselves before the captains of industry and thereout suck no small advantage. If Democracy could serve as a mouthpiece for the Voice of God, and could herald and unveil His Kingdom, they were ready to be Democrats ; but they were ready also to defy the will of the People, if it were the devil's voice.

Their belief in the Reign of God as an ever-present fact governed their whole outlook. They did not think that man has to make God's Kingdom come ; he has, they taught, only to discover that he already lives under God's Rule, and so to *realise* His Kingdom.

Thus they were free alike from the fanaticism and the disappointments of those who think that justice is to be established by men who have steeled their wills to an inflexible determination ; they were saved from the dis-illusionment that awaits those who put their trust in princes or any child of man, or in any institution, system, party, or movement. Such men are not confounded when any of these fail them ; nor are they without hope when there is no leader who inspires confidence ; for they share Kingsley's faith that " though man hold his peace, yet God will speak ; to the poor there will always be in the Church a message from their Heavenly Father—in the Bible, which proclaims man's freedom—in Baptism, which proclaims his equality—in the Supper of the Lord, which proclaims his brother-hood—and that not as dim and distant possibilities, for which he is to crave and struggle of his own self-will, but as his absolute and eternal right, which God the Father has given him, which God the Son has bought for him with His blood, and which God the Holy Spirit will give him strength and wisdom to take possession of and realise whensoever he casts himself humbly and loyally under the guidance of the God who made him."

The Christian Socialists were Great Democrats because they were more than Democrats.

* * * * *

They were always less interested in politics than in economics, and less interested in economics than in morals. They were unrelentingly opposed to the prevalent belief in Competition as the ruling principle of trade and industry ;

G*

in opposition to that belief, they advocated Co-operation as a truer principle. And they were not content to preach it in words only ; they determined to assert it in action. For this purpose, they promoted working-men's associations, to exemplify Co-operation in practice. Three foundation-principles were laid down : Human society is a brotherhood, not a collection of warring atoms ; true workers should be fellow-workers, not rivals ; a principle of justice, not selfishness, should regulate exchange.

" Co-operation " goes back to the eighteen-twenties or earlier. Robert Owen visualised whole communities in which the people provided themselves as consumers with the results of their own labours as producers ; and a vision of that kind floated before his followers as they took practical steps to realise their ideals.

These practical steps took the form of establishing, not complete " Villages of Co-operation " such as Owen had dreamed of, but Co-operative Societies or Associations. The Co-operative stores that are so familiar to-day may be traced back to the initiative, example, and influence of the Rochdale Pioneers of 1844 ; these men were inspired by the Owenite ideal, and, as a first step, formed themselves into a Co-operative Society in which they banded themselves together *as consumers*.

The Working-men's Associations which the Christian Socialists promoted were Co-operative Societies *of producers*. This was due to the influence of Ludlow. He was perfectly aware of the difference between producers' co-operation and consumers' co-operation ; and he was also aware that it is a more difficult course to associate first for producing and then have to search round for a market for the goods produced, than it is to begin at the other end, that is to say, with the requirements of consumers. He deliberately chose the more difficult course, on principle ; for he believed that consumption was merely consuming, but that there was something creative and godlike about producing.

The associations which he and the others promoted soon came to nothing, for reasons which have been a good deal discussed and have been variously explained. But Ludlow never regretted his choice, nor abandoned his preference.

Kingsley was also quite aware of the distinction between

the two kinds of Co-operative Societies ; and he came to look to the method of Rochdale with far higher hope than to the other.

It does not appear that Maurice was much interested in this question. He had seen the associations, which he had helped to promote, fail ; he knew what the Rochdale Pioneers had accomplished, without anyone to promote the association for them ; and he concluded that he would do better not to meddle in such matters. He turned to work that suited him better, that of the Working Men's College. This was founded by the Christian Socialists for the purpose of " training men as citizens of a country in which justice shall rule in every department of the national life, and brotherhood be aimed at as the true condition of men." Its foundation was a direct result of the failure of the working-men's associations, and it is characteristic of the humility of Maurice—then Professor of Theology at King's College, London, and later Professor of Moral Philosophy at Cambridge—that he said, " We and they want educating."

Neale and Hughes were both active for many years in the cause of Co-operation. It should perhaps be explained that Ludlow, Neale, and Hughes were not so foolish as to imagine that associations of producers were all that was needed to realise their ideal of Co-operation ; they saw quite clearly that a market for the goods produced must be organised. But they did not at all agree with the view that the producer should be entirely subordinated to the needs of the consumer. They repudiated any such " Consumers' theory of industry " ; they believed in what they called self-employment. This " Self-employment " theory is their version of Industrial Democracy.

They were continually troubled by the question about what place the workers (producers) employed by Co-operator consumers ought to have. Opinions may differ as to the wisdom of their utterances on this point ; but whether they were right or wrong in what they actually advocated, they were certainly right in protesting against anything that could make it seem to the men and women employed by the Co-operative Wholesale Society or in the " Co-op." shops that they might just as well be working for a profiteering capitalist. The inadequacy of the

" Consumers' theory of industry " is a point stressed to-day by the Co-operative Productive Federation, which is, of course, a Federation of associations *of producers*.

Neale's services have won him the outstanding place among the five Christian Socialists in the esteem of the Co-operative Movement ; in its present status and success, of which we see evidence all around in the " Co-ops " where one buys C.W.S. productions, it recognises his monument.

He devoted his energy and his fortune, to the extent of many thousands of pounds, to the cause. He acted as General Secretary of the Co-operative Union from 1875 to 1891. No disappointment and no financial loss discouraged him. In the course of his long life, he disciplined his natural impatience into a patience that was truly Christian, that is to say, a perseverance which could go on and endure, yet not grimly but with hope and confidence. He died, at the age of eighty-two, young in heart ; a true leader, because himself a follower of his Divine Master. " There lies his secret," said Hughes, " and it must be ours too, if we are to hold our place as pioneers of our people out of the competitive wilderness in which all nations are wandering, into the promised land of industrial peace, to which we do not doubt that at some time, under some leaders, a way will be found."

.   .   .   .

The nations are still wandering in the Egyptian darkness of a decaying capitalism which has brought the production and distribution of the means of life into a condition of semi-paralysis.

When Kingsley wrote his poem

> " The Day of the Lord is at hand, at hand,
>   Its storms roll up the sky ;
>   The nations sleep starving on heaps of gold ;
>   All dreamers toss and sigh . . ."

he did not know that three-quarters of a century later, the nations, though possessing heaps of gold, would consist of would-be producers and sellers and would-be buyers and

consumers confronting one another, apparently helpless—
with the international armaments industry supplying them
impartially with the means of self-destruction.

But to the prophetic mind, the Day of the Lord is always
at hand, and Kingsley could compare his generation to
the dwellers in the doomed Cities of the Plain—hence his
nickname " Parson Lot "; he felt himself facing a crisis
in world-history which found the Church all unprepared
to meet it.

The principal aim of the Christian Socialists was not
to build a new social order, but to bring to light God's
Eternal Order as the only true foundation for man to build
on. Maurice perceived that that foundation had been
overlaid by a misinterpretation of Christianity which left
the world " to regulate itself upon the most selfish,
tyrannical, hateful maxims "; so long as that is so, he
declared, " the most vague dreams of the fancy, which
have a show of freedom, or the most terrible despotism,
which has a show of government, will be preferred to it."
His life-work was that of restoring, from the Bible, from
the Creeds, and from Church History, the social teaching
of the Christian Church.

The Christian Socialism of Stewart Headlam of the
Guild of St. Matthew, of Westcott of Durham, of Gore
and Scott Holland of the Christian Social Union and the
Church Socialist League—which pioneered the way for
the Christian social teaching of to-day—can be traced
back to these Christians who dared to call themselves
Socialists.

From this point of view, Maurice stands pre-eminent;
Ludlow was his prompter, Kingsley his popularizer; and
if the Church to-day is in any degree better equipped than
the Church of the eighteen-forties to meet the crises of
world-history, it is due to the Word of the Lord which
He spake by the mouth of His prophet Frederick Denison
Maurice.

EUGENE DEBS
1855-1926
by NORMAN THOMAS

EUGENE DEBS
1855-1926
by NORMAN THOMAS

EUGENE VICTOR DEBS was born November 5th,
1855. He died October 20th, 1926. In the seventy-
one years of his life he had been five times candidate
for the Presidency of the United States, and twice the
prisoner of the United States: once for his bold assertion
of the right of labour to organize and to strike, and the
second time for his eloquent, steadfast and intelligent
opposition to the hysteria of war and his demand for a
negotiated peace. The record of his colourful and crowded
years was not the record of what men call success in America
or, indeed, anywhere else in our Western world. Yet to-day
in his own country the memory of no man who has achieved
pomp and power is dearer to masses of his fellows than his.
Over and over it has happened to me in widely scattered
cities and towns that after a meeting men have come up
and told me with a kind of awe in their voices: " I
knew 'Gene Debs," or " I was a friend of 'Gene Debs."
On inquiry I found that often their knowledge of Debs was
confined to one of his hearty handshakes. It was a thing
they always remembered. It is experiences like this which
illustrate the statement that no American of his generation
—perhaps no American of any generation—was ever better
loved than 'Gene Debs, or in his day better feared and
hated.

The man so loved and hated was not a great Socialist
philosopher, theoretician, maker of platforms and programmes, or even, in his later years, an organizer. He was
a man of eloquent words and a doer of great deeds. Yet
the unique thing about him is not what he did for the
labour movement or for Socialism but that he was in himself
a kind of incarnation of the flaming spirit of the labour
movement and of Socialism.

'Gene Debs's passionate identification with the working
class was voluntary. He was not born into a class from
which he could not rise. It was by choice he insisted

that he did not want to rise from the ranks but with them. He was a good Socialist, an avowed Marxist and a true internationalist. Although he never visited Europe he had an understanding of international problems and he was the hero, almost the idol, of many of the immigrant workers of New York and other cities. Nevertheless, he came to Socialism by a characteristically American road.

He was born in the great central Mississippi valley in the days when Abraham Lincoln was the authentic expression of its spirit at its best. He was a native of that region happily called the Valley of Democracy, a country which had not yet outgrown its pioneer days. His father and mother were Alsatians, thrifty and energetic folk who soon became substantial and respected citizens in the little town of Terre Haute on the banks of the Wabash, Indiana, where they made their home. They had more than average love of music and books. 'Gene's middle name, Victor, attests the family devotion to Victor Hugo. As is so often the case with great men, 'Gene's mother was an unusual woman of much force of character and a graciousness which won the everlasting devotion of her children. Ten children in all were born to these immigrants who had left an older culture for a rough but rapidly growing frontier town. Four of them died in early infancy. The fierceness of summer heat and winter cold were not easy to endure in those days and the then little clan was afflicted with what was commonly known as " the Wabash Shakers," apparently an acute form of malaria. 'Gene and his younger brother, Theodore, who later in life was to prove more than brother to him, both remembered how intensely they suffered from those evils. It is rather remarkable that fever left no mark on their strong constitutions. It was in the earlier years a rather primitive life that the children knew. But Jean Daniel Debs's grocery business flourished and there was always plenty of food. Moreover, the son, 'Gene, was given the best education the town afforded in what was called the Old Seminary. It was not good enough to satisfy either father or son. The lad wanted to go to work and at last got his father's permission. So before he was fifteen 'Gene left school.

His first job was in the Vandalia paint shop at Terre

Haute where railroad cars were painted. 'Gene went to
work with a borrowed scraper for the vast sum of 50 cents
a day. He put the wages of the first two days into his
own scraper which he bought for one dollar. He cherished
it to the end of his life as another man might have cherished
a less honourable coat of arms.

In the paint shop he worked for about a year and, as he
afterwards said, " It almost killed me." To him as to
thousands of American boys of his generation the railroad,
and especially the railroad engine, stood for romance and
liberation. It was for 'Gene a genuine escape when for the
first time, before he was sixteen years of age, he fired an
engine. By the end of 1870 he got a regular job as fireman.
His hours permitted him to go on with a little schooling, and
in particular to listen to the political speakers of his time,
to study their arts, and to practise speaking. This job he
kept for about four years. Then, because of his mother's
great anxiety, born of the long chapter of railroad accidents
of those days of little rocking engines, 'Gene threw up his
job and went to work in the wholesale grocery house of
Hulman and Cox.

But his heart was still with the railroad men. In February,
1865, before he was of age, 'Gene Debs took the stand which
determined his life's work. He joined the newly formed
lodge of the Brotherhood of Locomotive Firemen, and their
national organizer, Joshua Leach, picked him out as a leader.
From that time on, though he might make a living in the
grocery warehouse by day, his heart was in the work of the
union, of which he was the secretary.

The next twenty-two years of the life of the " long,
tow-headed boy from Terre Haute " were interesting, but
of themselves they would never have given 'Gene Debs a
place among earth's greatest. He developed rapidly into
an efficient labour organizer, speaker, and editor. As the
country emerged from the dreadful panic years of the '70s
which were marked by violent labour upheavals he saw
his Brotherhood grow to power. Indeed, he was the chief
factor in helping it grow to power. He was popular at home.
For two terms he was City Clerk of Terre Haute and his
salary came in handy to help him in the work of organizing
the firemen. In 1884 he was elected as a Democrat to the

Indiana Legislature and in the same year he was married to Kate Metzel. His chief biographer, McAlister Coleman —to whom I am indebted for most of the material in this paper, truly says : " It was his first love affair and his last and it lasted until 'Gene's death." The couple had no children and perhaps the extraordinary warmth of affection which 'Gene bestowed so freely on his fellow men was in part an expression of a love which other men concentrate less upon the comrades of their spirits than upon the children of their bodies.

In these years both 'Gene's union and 'Gene himself belonged definitely to the respectable school of labour organization and politics. He had a vigorous tongue and personality with which to fight the battles of his union, but the organization itself was anything but Socialist.

'Gene's capacities were generally recognized and more than once he had a chance to leave the work of a labour organizer for fields more remunerative financially. If he had not been well fed up with his first experience in the Legislature he easily could have gone far in American politics. As it was, the passage of the years found him the best loved man and one of the most powerful officials in the Brotherhood of Firemen. He was the editor of their paper and a famous orator—of a rather flowery, rhetorical sort—especially in labour circles. Only in one respect did the years bring him disappointment. His pet plan of federation between the different railroad workers' organizations was repeatedly baulked. Moreover, it was chiefly the so-called transportation men—that is to say, the men working on the trains—who were organized. The great mass of men engaged in maintaining the road beds and doing other necessary tasks was virtually unorganized. Thinking on these things Debs came to a momentous decision. At the 1892 convention of his Brotherhood in Cincinnati he suddenly announced that he was resigning from the Brotherhood. The next year he began the organization of the American Railway Union. The date of its birth was June 20th, 1893. Debs and fifty other carefully picked men drew up a constitution and elected officers. 'Gene as president of the A. R. U. set his salary at $75 a month. He had been receiving $4,000 a year with the Brotherhood of Locomotive Firemen. The union was to include all railroad workers. 'Gene was definitely set on eliminating " the aristocracy in labour which unfortunately exists." It was in this connection that he first enunciated the sentiment to which I have already referred and which in various forms he was to repeat so often. " If I rise it will be *with* the ranks, not *from* them."

The American Railway Union had a meteoric success. Almost miraculously, early in 1894, it won its first strike against that formidable builder of a railroad empire, Jim Hill, of the Great Northern. 'Gene and his faithful brother and comrade, Theodore, were received with ovations by the workers not often matched in American history. And then came the Pullman strike.

George M. Pullman was the maker of the American sleeping-car. He had established a town of his own in Pullman, Illinois, not far from Chicago. He had equipped this town with some of the show features which might be expected under a benevolent feudalism. Behind this façade were three-storey tenement blocks where the foreign-born workers lived and at the south end of the town long rows of wooden shanties which were built at a cost of $100 apiece, and were rented by Mr. Pullman's company for $96 a year. In the panic of 1893 men were laid off wholesale and wages were slashed to a starvation level. By the spring of 1894 the Pullman workers were in debt to the company for their so-called model housing, and the like, to the extent of more than $70,000. It was against this hypocrisy and these intolerable conditions that at last the strike was declared. At once the Pullman workers on strike sought the support of the railroad workers who had to handle the Pullman company's cars. They appealed to the A. R. U.

Debs was an experienced labour official. He knew the tremendous odds against victory. He knew that in spite of his victory over Hill his A. R. U. was still a pretty green army. Therefore he opposed the strike. But at the meeting of the A. R. U. members in Chicago the Pullman workers told of their suffering in words so moving that the men voted to support them by a strike. Into that strike Debs threw himself heart and soul. It began on June 26th with a boycott on Pullman parlour cars, and soon became a general railroad strike involving at least 125,000 railroad workers on twenty roads. The Knights of Labour, which had not yet gone to its death, pledged support to the strike, and the trades and labour organization of Chicago even went so far as to offer to call a general strike in support of their brethren on the railroads. Debs and the responsible leaders did their best—and with a high degree of success—to preserve order and to prevent violence. The brave and genuinely democratic Governor of Illinois, John P. Altgeld, watched the situation with every intention to preserve order but with no intention to use the militia for purposes of crushing the workers. Under these conditions, for the first time in American history on any considerable scale, the federal government used its power to break a strike. The first weapon brought into action by the government was an order directly from President Cleveland sending federal troops into Chicago, ostensibly to protect the mails. Not only was federal help not asked by the Governor of the State—as had previously been the rule—but the Governor sent a dignified, cogent and powerful protest—all to no avail. The second weapon was an injunction against Debs and some of his associates invoked under the Sherman anti-trust Act which had been passed in 1890 to check monopoly. Its purpose was to prevent the A. R. U. from " in any way or manner interfering with, hindering, obstructing, or stopping " any of the business of a list of 21 railroads in the Middle West. The injunction was not wholly without precedent. Its use on so large a scale was new and ultimately supported by the Supreme Court. Debs was twice arrested: first on June 15th, when he was soon released on bail, later on July 17th. He was arrested the second time for contempt of court, in that he had violated the injunction. With Debs and other leaders in jail the strike was soon broken. Before long the A. R. U. disappeared as a practical force in railroad affairs. It left behind it a burden of some $40,000 in debts. Later on 'Gene Debs without a salary paid off this debt from the proceeds of the speaking engagements which poured in upon him during the next few years. It is characteristic of the man that in his endless travelling on these speaking engagements, and later for the Socialist Party, for some ten years he refused to ride in Pullman cars. This meant that he sat up at night in day coaches and slept as best he could. The reason he gave was that the strike against Pullman was not officially ended. It was well on in the twentieth century before a Socialist Pullman car conductor persuaded him that " even a righteous boycott had to end some time."

To go back now to the legal cases. The first efforts of the railroad managers and their allies in the government had been to convict Debs and his associates on a general blanket charge of conspiracy to commit various wrongful acts. This charge came to trial early in 1895. The principal counsel for defence was Clarence Darrow, who began his tremendous reputation as a labour lawyer in this trial. He carried the war into the enemy's camp. He let it be known that he was going to examine members of the General Managers' Association and, above all, his Majesty King Pullman himself. At this dramatic juncture mysteriously a juror was taken ill. The presiding judge, a man named Grosscup, declared a mis-trial. The case was never called again ; and the bosses fell back on the injunction to which I have already referred. Debs, under it, was sent to jail at Woodstock for six months for contempt of court. A great deal of public feeling was aroused on behalf of Debs and his comrades, but to no avail. Conditions in Woodstock, unlike conditions in the unspeakably vile Cook County (Chicago) prison, where Debs had been confined on his arrest, were decent, and Debs was allowed much time to read or write. It was there that his conversion to Socialism was finally completed, largely under the influence of that famous American Socialist, Victor Berger, later to be Congressman for Milwaukee, Wisconsin. Nevertheless, since the truth must be told, although Debs always said that he was finally converted to Socialism in Woodstock, he did not immediately become active in Socialist politics. Instead he was one of the supporters of William Jennings Bryan in the famous campaign of 1896, fought largely on the money issue. It was only after Bryan's defeat that he finally saw the need of a new party. On June 18, 1897, 'Gene and his friends formed the Social Democracy. The bulk of his followers were drawn from the American Railway

Union which was at about the same time formally dissolved. Around this labour phalanx was an odd assortment
of free-lances of various kinds. The first platform of the
Social Democracy contained the astonishing and chimerical
proposal that one State of the Union should be selected for
the establishment of co-operative industries which ultimately would extend to the whole Union. Other demands of
the platform, both immediate and more ultimate, were more
truly in line with the usual Socialist proposals.

About the time that 'Gene Debs and the middle-westerners
were forming the Social Democracy there was a split in
the old Socialist Labour Party in New York City and the
East. This split was provoked largely by the rather
despotic tactics of that brilliant and able thinker and leader,
Daniel De Leon. De Leon's tactics tended to draw workers
out of the regular trade unions into a Socialist union rather
than to inspire them to convert their comrades in the labour
movement. For these and other reasons Morris Hillquit,
Abraham Cahan and many another of the most promising
younger Socialists broke away. Naturally, they sought
alliances. So there came together this Eastern group with
its Marxist and European background and the native
American Social Democratic group which, as a whole, had
what is called in America a Populist background. Out of
the union the present Socialist Party was made. The final
unity, however, was not consummated until July 29th,
1901, at Indianapolis, after 'Gene had made his first race
for the Presidency in 1900 and received 96,878 votes.
His biographer truly tells us concerning this campaign that
" 'Gene contented himself with Socialist generalities couched
in Ingersollian* phrases—with talk of a new world, the
emancipation of the workers and the happiness of the little
children of the future." This remained Debs's style of
speaking, except when he was aroused by some specific
wrong.

From 1901 the history of 'Gene Debs was to a large
extent the history of the Socialist Party. He lost none
of his interest in the organization of labour on the economic
front and did some brave preaching of labour unionism in

*R. G. Ingersoll, the freethinker and popular orator of the later half
of the nineteenth century.

difficult places. In 1905 he was one of the organizers of the Industrial Workers of the World, better known by its initials, I. W. W. He was not content, however, with the development of that organization along syndicalist lines which utterly repudiate political action, and was not long active in it. He was to the day of his death a thorn in the side of the shrewd and able Samuel Gompers, president of the American Federation of Labour, and his conservative labour advisers. Nevertheless, the general policy of Debs and the Socialist Party was one of working within the organized labour movement on fair and democratic lines. Debs himself, however, never could abide the tendency to racial discrimination in the A. F. of L., its over-emphasis on craft unionism, and some other features which he had regarded as undemocratic ever since the day when he resigned his own well-paid job with the Brotherhood of Locomotive Firemen.

While the history of Debs is the history of the Socialist Party in its activities and enthusiasm, it seems in the retrospect a somewhat extraordinary fact that a man who had been so active in building labour organization for more than twenty years was not, in the Socialist Party, primarily an organizer any more than he was a theoretician. He was instead the voice, sometimes the pen, always the soul and conscience of the Party. He was its candidate for the Presidency in 1904, in 1908 and in 1912. Every year saw the Socialist Party grow in organized power, in membership and, above all, in the number of its votes. 1908 was the year of the famous train, the Red Special, which carried Debs and a few comrades all over the country in such a campaign as America has rarely seen. 1912, without the Red Special, but with better organization, was the year which saw the Socialist Party receive its highest percentage of the total national vote. This was also the year of the famous Bull Moose or Progressive campaign when Theodore Roosevelt temporarily became the leader of the forces of a mild revolt. The Progressives stole and mutilated a good many of the Socialist immediate demands, but they remained definitely capitalist and nationalist in outlook. Neither their liberalism nor the liberalism of the Democrat Woodrow Wilson served to prevent the growth of Socialism.

This growth continued apace during the early years of the World War while the United States was trying to remain neutral and yet make money out of the blood of the youth of Europe. It was at this period that the Socialist Party, and Debs with it, wrote some of the most creditable pages of their history. In the retrospect it is surprising that a comparatively small party succeeded in diagnosing so correctly the true causes of the war and in advocating so intelligently a programme of negotiated peace behind which it urged the United States to put its moral and economic force. In the midst of the war came the presidential election of 1916. Debs was no longer young and he was tired. He insisted that some younger man should run. His insistence was probably a mistake. Allan Benson who was nominated had been an able Socialist writer. He proved not to have the temperament for the human contacts and the arduous programme of speaking which an American presidential campaign requires. Moreover, a great many Socialist sympathisers, while they were very suspicious of President Wilson's type of pacifism, nevertheless voted for him because in the words of the campaign slogan "He kept us out of war." The whole world knows for how short a time Wilson kept us out of war. Inevitably America's benevolent neutrality to one group of contestants with whom it carried on a most profitable trade forced the country into war when it became evident that the profits of the merchants, manufacturers and bankers might be in danger. There were plenty of good slogans lying around to sanctify the war and plenty of sincere idealism which that eloquent phrase-maker, Woodrow Wilson, was able to exploit. Doubtless he had first fooled himself.

But the Socialist Party of America kept the faith. The St. Louis declaration of the Party, adopted after America had entered the war, is the most vigorous anti-war declaration adopted by an official Socialist Party during the whole World War.

Each day saw the war passion and hysteria grow apace. With the German attack upon revolutionary Russia even Socialists began to wonder if this might not be a necessary war. Probably these months were the most trying in Debs's whole life. Even his townsmen who knew him best and had loved him most, irrespective of politics, began to turn against him, and there were times when there was actual danger of physical attack upon him and his home.   America was mad with war hysteria.

Out of comparative inactivity, the increasing persecution of Socialist and other disbelievers in war aroused 'Gene Debs.   He took the stump again, urging civil liberty in America, the recognition of the Bolshevik Government in Russia and a negotiated peace.   He once told me that he had delivered in substance the famous speech, which later got him into jail, some sixteen or seventeen times before finally he went to the State Convention of the Ohio Socialists. This Convention was held in Canton, Ohio, not very far from Cleveland.   On his way to the Convention, Debs stopped off to visit three Cleveland Socialists—Charles E. Ruthenberg, Alfred Wagenknecht and Charles Baker—in jail for their anti-war stand in 1917.   Fired by his contacts with them, he stepped on to the Convention platform and made the speech which, together with his later speeches to the jury which tried him and the judge who sentenced him, rank as his greatest.   The Department of Justice was waiting for him.   He was arrested under the espionage law. Many years later a prominent Democrat told me that when President Wilson first heard of Debs's arrest under this law he was shocked and said that he had never meant the law to be used in a case of that sort.   In a few days, however, Wilson had changed his mind in resentment because of the uproar that went up on the arrest of Debs.   By all radicals and many liberals Wilson was held responsible for the law of which 'Gene had fallen foul.   From that moment Wilson was Debs's implacable enemy.

At last came the trial.   It was marked not only by the eloquence of Debs, but by one or two characteristically kindly acts.   A girl carrying a bouquet of red roses, intended for 'Gene, fainted at his feet.   He picked her up and carried her into the ante-room.   One of the witnesses against him, a young stenographer, was obviously much discomfited by the testimony he had given.   After this young man had finished his testimony and the court had adjourned for the day, 'Gene walked over to him and patted him on the shoulder : " Never mind, sonny," said he, " you did the

best you could under the circumstances." 'Gene's eloquence was in vain. A jury of farmers found him guilty.
They could hardly help it in view of the fact that the judge
had charged them that it was unnecessary to prove that the
Canton speech had actually caused insubordination, mutiny
or refusal to accept military service. All the jury had to
decide was whether it was 'Gene's intention or a possible
result of his work that these things should happen. The
case was appealed and dragged the weary length of appeals
in American courts, Debs remaining free on bail. Finally
it was unanimously affirmed by the Supreme Court, the
so-called liberals on the bench uniting with the conservatives.
'Gene did not actually begin his jail sentence until April,
1919, five months after the Armistice. His first place of
confinement was the Moundsville Penitentiary in West
Virginia. His statement on entering its doors was this :
" I enter the prison a flaming revolutionist—my head erect,
my spirit untamed, and my soul unconquerable." Somewhat later he was transferred to Atlanta. Many of his
friends regarded this as a persecution. By this time Debs
was not well, his heart was in bad shape, and the heat of
Atlanta was terrific. The Atlanta Penitentiary was—and is
—no model prison. Nevertheless in it 'Gene Debs made a
place for himself unique in prison annals. On account of
his health he was relieved from heavy prison work and in a
short time became a kind of unofficial personnel officer
among the prisoners—this with the full consent of the
Warden. When he left jail men wept. A hardened negro
" lifer " said of him : " 'Gene Debs is the only Jesus Christ
I ever knew."

Debs was not pardoned in any hurry. Thousands of
those who loved him, although they were not Socialists,
joined in repeated requests for his release. President
Wilson was adamant against it. It was one of Wilson's
weak points that he was inclined to regard every sharp
difference of opinion with him as a kind of sin against the
Holy Ghost and therefore unforgivable.

When Harding succeeded Wilson in March, 1921, the
situation changed. Harding was a mediocre politician
whose administration wrote some of the blackest pages of
American history. Nevertheless he was not vindictive. I

happened to have known Harding, because as a boy I lived in the town from which he came. Therefore, on two occasions I saw the President in behalf of Debs. It was easy enough to read between the lines of what the President said and to see that with him the problem was purely political. He would pardon Debs when he became convinced that the pressure for release was greater or, at any rate, more intense than the pressure to keep him behind prison bars. The post-war hysteria had not yet subsided to the extent that Debs's release was a matter of indifference to thousands of so-called patriots. Finally the President took the extraordinary step of sending for Debs to come and see him in Washington. No publicity was given to this trip. Debs left Atlanta Penitentiary, called on the President and returned to the Penitentiary. Not for years would he speak of his visit and then only with reserve. The respective characters of the two men make that meeting a dramatic footnote to history. Not Harding sat in judgment on Debs but Debs on Harding. He made no appeal for himself. He told the President of conditions in Atlanta that needed immediate remedy, and his last words with the President were a plea for the pardon of a fellow prisoner. Finally on Christmas Day, 1921, the President commuted Debs's ten-years term and he left Atlanta a free man.

In this brief description of Debs's imprisonment I have omitted reference to his political activities. He kept in fairly close touch with political events through letters and occasional visits from friends. In the presidential campaign of 1920 he was the candidate of the Socialist Party. Of course he was completely inactive. Even his writing was restricted. The party was feeling the destructive effects not only of the war which was over but of the post-war hysteria and the Communist split. Debs got a great many personal and protest votes. Something like a million votes were counted for him, the highest number he had ever received, but not the highest proportion of the total vote. 1920 was the year in which for the first time women voted for President all over the country.

Debs came out of prison into a very confused political situation. All his revolutionary instincts were on the side of the Bolsheviks in Russia. He at once declared : " I am a Bolshevik from the crown of my head to the tips of my toes." Nevertheless the stories of Bolshevik persecutions and denial of civil liberty greatly disturbed him. His closest friends were loyal to the Socialist Party. Debs stayed with his party. He found a country that was feeling all the effects of the new issues and new attitudes which had been developed in the war and the post-war years. In 1921 the post-war boom receded into depression from which America made a rapid recovery, and soon Debs with the rest of his party found themselves engulfed in the extraordinary current of one of the maddest periods of gamblers' prosperity on record.

To all this Debs brought his own great personality but less than his old leadership. Once more at Terre Haute he received a great ovation from a crowd which included hundreds of those who during the war had turned against him. He was never embittered by the fickleness of crowds. He brought out of prison that which he had taken into prison; namely, a capacity for prophetic wrath against wrong combined with an almost infinite love for individuals, the weakest and stupidest of them. He was the same lanky, bald-headed, affectionate, magnetic Debs. But he had definitely lost in health. The years did not make easier for him or for his friends the struggle which he had to make against over-dependence on alcohol. Like many others of his temperament, 'Gene was more susceptible than most men to the effect of liquor. It was not this, however, but ill-health and the fact that he had been removed from intimate contact with public affairs and party controversies during critical months which affected his post-war leadership. Much of his energy he threw into a campaign for better prison conditions. He left the direction of party affairs largely to that able lawyer and thinker Morris Hillquit. He went along without enthusiasm but without protest when in 1924 the party nominated Senator LaFollette of Wisconsin, a courageous progressive but not a Socialist, and entered a coalition in his support out of which it hoped that a genuine labour party might emerge. Probably the party was justified in taking this particular gamble, although in the light of hindsight it might have taken it in a way somewhat better to have protected its own interest and its own future.

It lost on the gamble. LaFollette got about 5 million votes.
His followers had expected more. Organized labour had
co-operated rather reluctantly. The A. F. of L. leadership had
never abandoned its old non-partisan political policy.
After the election the convention, which Debs and the Socialist
Party had hoped might give birth to a true labour party,
buried the LaFollette movement. Representatives of the
Railroad Brotherhoods and some other unions listened with
respect, but unmoved, to Debs's eloquent plea at the
convention for the formation of a genuine labour party. The
Socialists had to begin again.

Into this new beginning Debs threw himself gallantly.
He became the National Chairman of the party and was only
restrained in the amount of his speaking by the state of his
health. But there was always an element of pathos about his
post-war meetings. Crowds turned out to honour the man,
and to pay a kind of pious tribute to their own past. There
was about these meetings a memorial quality. Men paid
to the living Debs the tribute that usually they reserve for
the dead.

But they did not pay him the one tribute he wanted;
namely, the tribute of consecration to the Socialist goal.
His own pleas to them had much of their old eloquence, but
he made in effect the same speech he had been making
before the war. He had little to contribute to an analysis of
post-war conditions and the fallacy of the tinsel prosperity
of the Coolidge epoch.

Yet the brave warrior went on unclouded in spirit and
vibrant with hope. In the summer of 1926 he was forced
to go again to a sanitarium which he had visited before.
He never left it alive. He read, talked occasionally with
friends who were allowed to see him, reminisced of the
past. In October he was obliged to take to his bed. His
biographer writes :

" He went unwillingly. Whenever there was no one
about he walked the halls. One day he found a girl, whose
case had been pronounced hopeless, weeping near his room.
He tried to comfort her. He spoke of Henley's brave *Invictus*.
She begged him to write some lines of the poem for her.
Theodore Debs brought her this verse written in 'Gene's
graceful longhand :

It matters not how strait the gate,
How charged with punishments the scroll :
I am the master of my fate,
I am the captain of my soul.

'Gene fell into a coma.   For five days they bent anxiously
above that great heart of his, the physicians certain that it
had stopped.   On the fifth day, October 20, 1926, the heart
beat no more.   'Gene died with his hand in Theodore's.''

BENJAMIN DISRAELI
1804–1881
by D. C. SOMERVELL

H

BENJAMIN DISRAELI
1804–1881
by D. C. SOMERVELL

M R. BALDWIN has declared, not once but many
times, that Disraeli not only was the founder but
is still the major prophet of the British Conservative
party, that his policy is still the party's policy, that the
political gospel he preached with singular consistency
through a career of nearly half a century is as alive and
appropriate to-day as when it was delivered. To-day the
British constitution is, what it never was in Disraeli's time,
completely democratic, and if we take the results of the last
five elections, those of 1922, '23, '24, '29 and '31, we find that
in three of them the Conservatives secured more seats
than all other parties combined, and that in one of the
remaining pair—that which provided the first Labour
Government, they were still the largest party. It may be
said that these results are misleading. Let us, then, turn
from the distribution of seats to the distribution of voters.
If we do so, we reach the surprising result that not in three,
nor in four, but in all five of these general elections more
votes were cast for Conservative candidates than for the
candidates of any other party.

If we take these two facts together—that Disraeli is still
the prophet of post-war Conservatism, and that post-war
Conservatism has secured the substantial support of a
completely democratised electorate—we have established a
fair claim to the inclusion of Disraeli in a volume of essays
on Great Democrats. Yet he was a democrat with a
difference. He sometimes, though not always, used the
term " democracy " to describe a danger which should
be shunned. He invariably used the term " aristocracy "
to describe a system he desired to revive and to preserve.
Indeed there are many respects in which he stands somewhat apart from most of the other " Democrats " in this
book. Many of them were voices crying in a wilderness,
preparing the way for a democracy that was to be. Disraeli
was never that. He was never an agitator, never a dema-

gogue in either a good or a bad sense of those disputable
words. He was a parliamentary politician, in days when
the conditions of success in politics were still fundamentally
aristocratic. His work in life was to recreate and inspire
a political party which both in his life-time and after his
death should give effect to his statesmanship, to his political
ideas. He led that party for twenty-six years in the House
of Commons and for four years in the House of Lords.
He served in five Governments, three times as Chancellor
of the Exchequer under Lord Derby, twice as Prime
Minister. In the course of his parliamentary duties he
had occasion to handle a great many questions which have
no direct connexion with the subject of democracy.

If we were in this essay to review the whole career of
Disraeli we should not only find the material too much for
the space at our disposal but we should write much that
is irrelevant to our subject, which is Disraeli's contribution
to democracy. We will therefore do nothing of the kind.
None the less, it may suit the convenience of those readers
who have not got the history of Victorian politics at their
fingers' ends, if we give a brief summary of our man's
career from start to finish.

He was born in 1804, son of a Jewish scholar and writer.
Though a Jew by race young Disraeli was in boyhood
baptized a Christian and was all his subsequent life a
regular member of the Church of England. After writing
several clever and successful novels, the first published
when he was only twenty-one, he stood for parliament in
1832 as an opponent of the Whigs who had just triumphantly
carried through their Great Reform Bill. He called himself
a Radical, though he claimed, not without some success, the
support of the Tories also. He was defeated, and several
subsequent defeats convinced him that his only chance was
to toe the party line. In 1837 he was elected as a Tory,
but he soon proved in the House that he was still something
of a Radical by defending the Chartists and condemning
the new Poor Law.

In 1841 Peel, the Conservative leader, became Prime
Minister. He gave office to young Gladstone, but not to
young Disraeli, possibly because he thought the latter
was one of those brilliant talkers who are more of a hindrance

than a help in the practical conduct of business. Every House of Commons contains some men of this type, and Peel may be forgiven for his mistake. In any case he was punished for it. Peel was one of those " practical " men who live intellectually from hand to mouth. Elected by the land-owners' party to support the Corn Law, he lost faith in it and decided to repeal it. His inarticulate back-benchers, the " Gentlemen of England," only needed a leader to rouse them in rebellion. Disraeli gave the lead, and though the Corn Law passed, Peel and the " Peelites " (including Gladstone) were driven out of the Conservative party.

The " Gentlemen of England " found a figurehead for their party in Lord Stanley, afterwards Lord Derby, but he was in the House of Lords, and it was only after some delay, with manifest reluctance, and with long continued grumblings, that they accepted the leadership of " the Jew " in the House of Commons.

For the next twenty-four years, 1850-74, it was Disraeli's laborious task to " educate " his party, to fashion this Party of the Past, this collection of disgruntled Die-Hards and Protectionists, into a Party of the Future, inspired by his own broad, statesmanlike ideals. Three times during this period his party held office, for less than a year in 1852, for less than two years in 1858-9, and for about two years in 1866-8. It was during the last of these spells of office that he succeeded Lord Derby as Prime Minister. But all these Governments, like the Labour Governments of our own day, commanded the support of less than half the House. Their performances were tight-rope performances and gave little opportunity for unhampered statesmanship.

At last, in 1874, came the belated reward of all Disraeli's patient labours. He found himself the head of a brilliant Cabinet, and leader of a loyal and united party with a substantial majority in the House. He was in his seventieth year, and his health had already begun to fail, but he held on his course for six years, in the course of which he was able to set a deep mark upon the social, the imperial, and the foreign policy of his country. At the end of it he was, when already a dying man, decisively defeated by Gladstone, but it is not irrelevant to remark that the party he had

fashioned held office for sixteen out of the twenty-five years
that followed his death.

The career of Disraeli falls very obviously into three
periods. There was a first period in which he was free-
lance, free to set forth in speech and pamphlet and political
novel the full range of his ideals. Then followed a long
middle period during which our idealistic statesman was, in
Pauline phrase, an " ambassador in chains." He can,
indeed he must and will, pursue the task of " educating "
his party, but since he is also its leader in the House of
Commons he cannot afford to give his followers more than
at the particular moment they can swallow. He is, in this
middle period, primarily a politician, and everything that
he says and does must be said and done with one eye on
the needs of the moment. If sometimes the eye swerves,
and he launches forth unguardedly and flutters his dove-
cotes, well, that is pleasant proof for posterity that the idealist
was there all the time, but it is really to his credit that the
eye does not often swerve. In the last period he is in
enjoyment of power. Even a Prime Minister with a
majority cannot enact all the ideals of his youth, but at
least he can prove, as we shall show that Disraeli abundantly
proved, that the Radicalism and " Tory Democracy " of his
youth had been something more than wild oats, and that,
to vary the metaphor and quote a contemporary, " his wheat
was as good as his chaff."

It is obvious that, for the purpose of this essay, we need
say very little about the middle period. It is full of entertaining politics, but that is not our purpose. Our purpose
is to elucidate, in so far as they concern democracy, the
ideals of Disraeli's youth, and then to see what he made of
them long afterwards in his days of power. The material
for such a study is easily accessible. The six-volume *Life
of Disraeli* by Monypenny and Buckle is not only the longest
but about the best biography of any British statesman. It
contains copious quotations from Disraeli's own words, and
they are, after all, the only evidence. The passages here
quoted come from a variety of sources, speeches, pamphlets
and novels, and cover a long span of years. Dates have
curiously little importance in this connexion. However
much Disraeli might twist and turn in the sphere of tactics,

his fundamental ideas were formed early and for life.

In one of his earliest election speeches as an independent
" Radical " candidate he says : " Rid yourselves of all that
political jargon and facetious slang of Whig and Tory—two
names with one meaning, and used only to deceive you—
and unite in forming a great National Party which can alone
save you from destruction." It was not long, however,
before he discovered that Whig and Tory were words with
very different meanings. The Whigs, in his view, had just
" enfranchised as much of the nation as it was convenient
for them to enfranchise." They had created a new House
of Commons which was no more, indeed less, representative
of the nation than the House of Lords. The latter represented the landowners in person, the former the shopkeepers by deputy. Such a House of Commons was bound
to sacrifice national to class interests, and Disraeli, who was
nothing if not a romantic, had less sympathy with the
" solid middle class " than with those either above or below
them in the social scale. And what of the Tories ? Under
Peel's guidance they were a party " who, without any
embarrassing promulgation of principles, wish to keep
things as they find them as long as they can. Whenever
public opinion, which this party never attempts to form, to
educate, or to lead, falls into some violent perplexity, passion,
or caprice, this party yields without a struggle to the impulse,
and, when the storm has passed, attempts to obstruct and
obviate the logical and, ultimately, the inevitable results of
the very measures they have originated, or to which they
have consented."

Of the two parties, then, one, the Whigs, had a principle
and a wrong principle, namely government in the interests
of the commercial middle classes. The other party, the
Tories, had at present no principle at all except negation,
and was engaged in fighting a losing battle against the
Whig advance. As soon as Disraeli realised that he could
not effect anything practical from outside the party system
it was obvious that he would choose the party which was
opposing the principle he held to be wrong, and that he
would attempt to give it principles of its own. " If the
Tories indeed despair of restoring the aristocratic principle,
and are sincere in their avowal that the State cannot be

governed with the present machinery, it is their duty to coalesce with the Radicals, and permit both political nick-names to merge in the common, the intelligible, and the dignified title of a National Party."

The term National was to be reserved for a very much later political occasion, and it was dropped in favour of "Tory Democracy." But both terms deserve consideration, for each implies an aspect of Disraeli's statesmanship. By a National Party he meant the opposite of a class party, the "opposite also of a party trading in nostrums imported from abroad." Speaking many years later when leader of his party in the House of Commons, he said : "What is the Tory party unless it represents national feeling ? If it does not represent national feeling, Toryism is nothing. It does not depend upon hereditary coteries of exclusive nobles. It does not attempt power by attracting to itself the spurious force which may accidentally arise from advo-cating cosmopolitan principles or talking cosmopolitan jargon. The Tory party is nothing unless it represents and upholds the institutions of the country. . . . I cannot help believing that because my Lord Derby and his colleagues have taken a happy opportunity to enlarge the privileges of the people of England [by the Reform Act of 1867] we have done anything but strengthen the institu-tions of the country, the essence of whose force is that they represent the interests and guard the rights of the people." Disraeli saw the nation as a richly varied organic unity. He was "Unionist" in the sense in which the party he once led now calls itself Unionist, as standing for common interests and against class warfare.

"Tory Democracy" brings us to the crucial issue of Disraeli's claim to be a Democrat. He certainly did not believe, as the men discussed in most of these essays believed, that an unlimited extension of the franchise was a thing to be desired for its own sake and in all circum-stances. The possession of a vote was, he held, not a right but a privilege, and it should be given only to those who were likely to make good use of it. He certainly did not hold with a Liberal Prime Minister of a later day who said that self-government is better than good government. He was not prepared to trust a majority of ignorance. It

was hard to believe in " the remedial qualities of a government carried on by a neglected democracy who, for three
centuries, had received no education." He refused to
accept the doctrine that only by universal suffrage could
you escape the danger of class government, for no class
government would be so dangerous as one controlled by
the largest and most ignorant class of all. " You would
find a locofoco* majority as much addicted to class
legislation as a factitious aristocracy."

What then was to be done ? This was a question to
which Disraeli had no very direct answer. The mistake
made in 1832 was that it took property, and property alone,
as the qualification for the vote. But if one rejected manhood suffrage, what other qualification was possible ?
In the middle of the century both political parties were
contemplating the possibility of extending the franchise
beyond the limits of 1832, and in his own Reform Bills of
1859 and 1867 he proposed what were ridiculed as " fancy
franchises." Votes were to be given to possessors of £10
a year from Government stock, of £60 in the Savings Bank,
of a £20 Government pension, to graduates of Universities,
ministers of religion, lawyers, doctors, and schoolmasters—
persons who in many cases were already voters. These
fancy franchises were swept out of the Bills in which they
had been inserted, by the combined votes of democrats and
anti-democrats, and there is no evidence that Disraeli took
them very seriously. On the whole his answer to the
question " Who should vote ? " would be that it was not a
matter of the first importance. No doubt he envisaged a
gradual advance to complete democracy ; he did nothing
to delay it and something to hasten it, and he correctly
forecasted that a democratic electorate would be less
favourable to Gladstonian Liberalism, and more favourable
to Disraelian Conservatism, than the electorate of 1832.
But though he was, somewhat accidentally, the principal
author of the Second Reform Bill, which established
household suffrage in the boroughs in 1867, he thought
that there were many questions more important than the
extension of the franchise.

---

* Locofoco, an ephemeral term for a " red-hot " Radical. Locofocos
were an early brand of matches, also called Lucifers.

H*

One of these more important questions was the character
of the men whom the vote returned to parliament. And
here Disraeli was an unrepentant aristocrat. He believed
that the best material could be found in the old landowning
families. He believed that the holders of inherited wealth
and the heirs to old traditions of rulership and public
service were capable of taking a more disinterested view of
the needs of society as a whole than either the newly
enriched magnates of commerce and industry or the leaders
of working-class agitation. It may be said that the main
effort of his life was to teach these " Gentlemen of England "
to rise to the occasion and to realise their national duty.
Noblesse oblige. That is Tory Democracy in a nutshell, the
old traditional England of Lords and Commons against the
new machine-made England of the Manchester School,
which captured Peel and Gladstone and finally collapsed
before the onset of the Labour party.

This is the subject of the two most important of the
novels, *Coningsby, or the New Generation*, and *Sybil, or the
Two Nations*, both of them written during the years when
Disraeli was entering upon his great battle with Peel for
the possession of the Conservative party. In *Coningsby* a
group of young men of noble birth, sketched from the
" Young England " group which was already gathered round
the author, discuss their dissatisfaction with existing party
politics and their ambition to strike out a new line. In
Sybil we are shown the problem they have to solve, the
problem of giving unity once again to the Two Nations, the
Rich and the Poor, which the avarice of mill-owners, the
crude revolutionism of demagogues, and the frivolous
indifference of the gentry were driving ever further apart.
" The People," says the hero, who is of course an aristocrat
of Disraelian ideals, " never can be strong. Their
attempts at self-vindication will end only in their suffering
and confusion. . . . It is increased knowledge of themselves that teaches the educated their social duties. There
is a dayspring in the history of this nation, which perhaps
only those who are on the mountain tops can as yet recognise.
The new generation of the aristocracy of England are not
tyrants, not oppressors, as you persist in believing. Their
intelligence, better than that, their hearts are open to the

responsibility of their position. But the work that is before them is no holiday work. It is not the fever of superficial impulse that can remove the deep-fixed barriers of centuries of ignorance and crime. Enough that their sympathies are awakened ; time and thought will bring the rest. They are the only natural leaders of the people ; believe me, they are the only ones."

But at the end of *Sybil* we are really no nearer an answer to the question what precisely the new Tory-Democratic party is to *do*. At the end of the book the hero has no positive achievement to his credit except his marriage to the heroine who, though the daughter of a Chartist foreman, turns out to be, by one of those melodramatic genealogies in which the old novelists delighted, herself an aristocrat of the deepest dye. This lack of precision in social programme is characteristic of Disraeli, whose interest in the social problem was always more general than particular. Of course, a novel is not the proper place for the details of a legislative programme, and very soon after writing these novels the author was immersed in the delicate task of recreating the Conservative party. We have to pass on to the last period of Disraeli's career to discover his social programme. But something may first be said of his historical position in this matter.

The fundamental doctrine of the mid-Victorian Liberals, and of the Benthamites and Cobdenites from whom they took their ideas, was *laissez-faire*. England entered the nineteenth century encumbered with the remnants of an already obsolete system of paternal government. A mass of legislation hampered the free action of the individual in relation both to God and to Mammon. One set of laws penalised thought, another restricted trade. The generation that occupied itself in striking off these shackles became enamoured of the view that the duty of government was to govern as little as possible, to leave as much as possible to the free play of individual initiative, on the assumption that everyone was the best judge of his own interests, and that what was best for each could not fail to be best for all. In fact, individualism.

This philosophy was very well suited to the industrious and bustling middle class which took its lead from its own most successful members, the new industrialists. The same men who played the leading part in the movement for the abolition of the Corn Laws were the strongest opponents of the Factory Acts, which were the expression of a purely philanthropic impulse opposed to the established doctrines of the age. But Disraeli had realised, long before he wrote *Sybil*, that *laissez-faire* individualism was of very little use to the masses. What they needed was not to be left alone to enjoy their destitution in perfect freedom, but help which should enable them to escape from it ; not freedom but organisation. As the century passed its meridian, as the great Victorian expansion of the fifties and sixties passed into the " slump " of the seventies, individualism began to give place to collectivism. Government began to intervene in one social problem after another to help, to direct, to control ; until in the early nineties it was possible for a belated survivor of the old Liberalism to look around him and ruefully exclaim " We are all Socialists nowadays ! "

In 1872 Disraeli addressed a great gathering of his party, for which he had recently established a national organisation on lines afterwards copied by Chamberlain's Birmingham " caucus." It was the speech of a statesman who realised that power was soon coming his way, and in it he gave his party a new slogan. " A great scholar and a great wit three hundred years ago said that in his opinion there was a mistake in the Latin Vulgate, which as you all know is the Latin translation of the Holy Scriptures, and that, instead of saying ' Vanity of vanities, all is vanity '—*Vanitas vanitatum, omnia vanitas* —the wise and witty King Solomon really said *Sanitas sanitatum, omnia sanitas*. Gentlemen, it is impossible to overrate the importance of the subject. After all, the first consideration of a minister should be the health of the people."

To-day it is certainly the first consideration, but so little was it so in 1872 that a Liberal speaker poured scorn on Disraeli's public health programme as " a policy of sewage." Disraeli replied that it was, for the working-man, " a matter of life and death." The subject, he said, had many branches. " It involves the state of the dwellings of the people, the moral consequences of which are not less considerable than the physical. It involves their enjoyment of some of the chief elements of nature; air, light, and water. It involves the regulation of their industry, the inspection of their toil. It involves the purity of their provisions, and it touches upon all the means by which you can wean them from habits of excess and brutality."

When Disraeli took office in 1874 he selected Richard Cross as his Home Secretary, and the fruits of the policy of *sanitas*—or sewage—soon began to appear : an Artisans' Dwellings Act, which for the first time called in public authorities to remedy the defects of private dwelling-houses. When a weakness was found in the operation of the measure, an Amending Act stiffening its provisions was carried before Disraeli left office. There followed a Friendly Societies Act, a Trade Union Act, which stood as the charter of trade union liberties for thirty years, a Public Health Act, a Factory Act, a Rivers Pollution Act, and an Enclosure Act designed to promote free access to commons and their use as public playgrounds. In commendation of the democratic character of these measures it is enough to quote Alexander Macdonald, one of the first Labour members to enter the House of Commons, who said in 1879, " The Conservative party have done more for the working classes in five years than the Liberals in fifty." It may of course be said that Cross, and not Disraeli, was the author of this legislation. Up to a point that is true, but it was Disraeli who secured for Cross his opportunity. " When Cross explained to the Cabinet," he writes, " his plan [for the Artisans' Dwellings Act] many were against it and none for it but myself ; and it was only in deference to the Prime Minister that a decision was postponed to another day. In the interval the thing was better understood."

But it would be wrong to think of these measures of social legislation, significant as some of them were as first steps along roads that have now been extensively explored, as anything like the principal claim of Disraeli to inclusion in a list of Great Democrats. His principal service was simply his forty years of membership of the House of Commons. Though he sometimes in his early days allowed his whimsical fancy to play over the

" drollery " of that institution, imagining that it might be
superseded in course of time by the authority of a revived
Royal power or by the representative activities of " a pure
and intelligent press," his whole career is evidence that
these fancies should not be taken too seriously. If the
British parliament has been more successful as an organ
of democracy than the parliaments of other countries—
and there is little doubt that it has been more successful—
the reason is that it has attracted to its service a greater
proportion of the best brains and the best characters in
the country. In this service Disraeli and Gladstone, rivals
in all else, are on the same side. It is impossible to estimate
the extent to which the prestige and the efficiency of
parliament have been maintained and enhanced by the life-
long service of such men, by the interest their performances
added to its activities, and by the example both of them
set of punctual and regular attendance at its debates.
" Unless you are always there," Disraeli was wont to say,
" how can you lead the House of Commons ? How can
you feel their pulse ? How can you know the men ? "

What he would have thought of the Labour Party it is
idle to speculate, for it was after his time. But from his
attitude to the very few working-class candidates who
secured election in his lifetime it is safe to assume that he
would have thought neither better nor worse of any
man by reason of the fact that he had done manual labour
or was a member of the most numerous social division of
the community. He would have judged Labour members
as he judged his " Gentlemen of England," by their capacity
to rise above the prejudices of their class and envisage the
national welfare. But he certainly did not think that the
wage-earners of the country would be likely to be better
represented by a fellow wage-earner than by an Old
Etonian. He held that the best parliamentarians were
most likely to be found in the class with the most abundant
leisure, and in the class least tempted to pursue politics as a
means of livelihood and as a road to notoriety.

Let us be frank. Disraeli attached immeasurable
value to the conception implied in the term " a gentleman,"
and in his generation the term had a more restricted and
aristocratic significance than is generally attached to it

to-day. If to believe in the leadership of gentlemen—
and Sir Philip Sidney, who passed the cup of water to a
common soldier, was his ideal of a gentleman—if to believe
in the leadership of gentlemen is to be no Democrat, then
Disraeli was no Democrat. If, on the other hand, the
conception of a gentleman is of permanent value, if the
vigorous survival of democratic parliamentary government
in this country, in an age which has seen the same system
brought to dishonour or destruction in so many other
countries, is mainly due to the living force of traditions
which our parliament has inherited from a more aristocratic
past, then Disraeli's service to this country is not yet
exhausted. And if, rejecting Fascism and its rivals, we hold
that the maintenance of parliamentary institutions in full
vigour is the best safeguard of democracy, then Disraeli's
services to parliament were services to the democratic cause.

But nothing about Disraeli is so democratic as his own
career. He was the first Prime Minister to " climb to the
top of the greasy pole " (the phrase, however regrettable,
is his own) from a starting-point quite outside the classes
then recognised as eligible for such honour. All previous
Prime Ministers had come either from the landed gentry,
or were, like Peel and Gladstone, sons of very rich men
and had enjoyed the Eton-and-Oxford type of education.
Disraeli was, no doubt, a gentleman according to our
easier standards of to-day, but he was certainly not recognised as one of themselves by " the Gentlemen of England "
when they reluctantly accepted his leadership. In cricketing
jargon his first Government was described as " the
Gentlemen, with one Player." With infinite difficulty
and patience he blazed a trail that others have more easily
followed, and he is in this respect the forerunner of Lloyd
George and Ramsay MacDonald.

THE EARLY FABIANS
by S. K. RATCLIFFE

THE EARLY FABIANS

by S. K. RATCLIFFE

ON alternate Friday evenings through the winter, during a period of twelve years from 1894, the little hall of Clifford's Inn, a few steps east of Temple Bar, offered a scene which was a good deal nearer to the centre of political England than the stranger who looked in could have imagined. The small square interior had been furnished, by the Art Workers' Guild, with rush-bottomed chairs, and it was warmed by a wide open fireplace kept generously filled. An audience of a hundred made a full meeting, but when topic or speaker gave a particular interest to the occasion many more were crowded in. The discussion was not unlikely to be carried on by a few of the keenest debaters in England, and there were some evenings of intense excitement. Or alternatively, the inquiring visitor might come upon an affair of not more than forty or fifty people, closely engaged with technical matters of local government or industry, of education or taxation.

The differing types of meetings were equally typical, for this was the Fabian Society at work in its creative years, when statesmen were being coached by its experts, and Fabian Tracts in surprising numbers were playing their part in educating the new municipalities.

The forces which brought the Society into existence were concentrated within the early 1880's, when the deeper social stirrings among the English people were hardly at all reflected in political events. Gladstone had been returned to power at the head of a triumphant Liberal host, but—as we have lately been reminded by the marching narrative in Mr. Garvin's Life of Chamberlain—the still dominant Whigs in the Government had no contact with the restive democracy of the industrial centres, and in domestic affairs the Old Man's force was spent. The Cabinet was taken up with Ireland, Egypt, South Africa; the House of Commons alternated between Irish scenes and the absurd and interminable squabbles about Bradlaugh and the oath. The school boards had laboured through the

first decade of compulsory education. The urban wage-
earner had been enfranchised since 1867, and the vote was
shortly to be granted to the rural worker. The Radicalism
that had found its plangent voice in Birmingham held out
a considerable hope for the people of England, but that was
destined to be broken by Chamberlain's change of party
and the bitter wrangle over Home Rule.

There was no Socialist movement at that time in Britain,
but there were many indications of a revival of Socialist
sentiment and activity. English Socialism had virtually died
out with the memories of Robert Owen, whose influence,
along with Chartism, was spread widely among the working
classes. Continental Communism had been drowned in
the Paris blood-bath of 1871. Karl Marx was dying in
London just as the founders of the Fabian Society were
beginning to find one another. Few English Socialists can
have known anything about him or have formed a conception of his stupendous significance. Hyndman's *England
for All* (1881), the first product of a new national Socialism,
was written to popularise Karl Marx's ideas. But it contained, to Marx's disgust, no mention of his name, and
Hyndman did not add the word " social " to the title of
his Democratic Federation until a few months before
William Morris seceded to establish the Socialist League.
There prevailed in England, and on the Radical side almost
as generally as elsewhere, a large ignorance of all social-
democratic thought and a lamentable indifference to the
grim side of industrialism and the appalling misery of the
great towns.

The direct stimulus to Fabian Socialism came from across
the Atlantic, although the entire Englishness of the movement has never been open to question. In 1883 Thomas
Davidson, a gifted Aberdonian of an itinerant habit, a man
of fine intellectual vitality who had become an American
citizen without losing his special quality as scholar and
teacher, was in London starting an experiment in ethical
perfectionism—the Fellowship of the New Life. This was
inspired by the purest idealism. The disciples dreamed of
devoting themselves to " the cultivation of a perfect character
in each and all," and to the reconstruction of society " in
accordance with the highest moral principles." A few of

them played with the project of a chosen community, which was no less remote from the actualities of modern England than the Pantisocracy of Coleridge and Southey had been from the England of William Pitt. Davidson attracted a number of exceptional men, Edward Carpenter and Havelock Ellis among them ; but it speedily became apparent that the New Fellowship was one thing, and the enterprise which the more positive members of this little company had in mind was quite another. As an admirable American writer says of a group geographically far from the Fabians, " they were not timeless like the Utopians."

A second and very definite force in their direction was already operating in London. It came from the one powerfully seminal essay in sociology so far thrown up by the American West. Henry George had published *Progress and Poverty* in 1879, but the book did not appear in England until two years later, to be followed almost immediately by the author in person. There is no doubt that a deal of practical enthusiasm was set going by his platform addresses. More than half a century later, in his single speech on American soil, Mr. Bernard Shaw acknowledged his own specific debt to Henry George, as many years earlier he had declared that among the men with whom he worked in the '80s four out of five had been stirred to action by *Progress and Poverty*. But the prophet from California was no leader for England. The men who within a few months were to be the first Fabians were not converted to the Single Tax. Henry George, they pointed out, was generalising from what he knew of the Western States, and his panacea seemed to have little relevance to English conditions. But there was one definite piece of illumination in his programme of action. *Progress and Poverty* dealt with the misery of the wage-earners as a class, and Henry George treated it as an evil to be swept away. His English admirers thought he had seen with greater clearness than any other reformer (though Chamberlain was not far from the same view) that the political method could be employed for the removal of social ills ; and this was precisely the guidance they were looking for.

The distinctive objects of the Fabian group were manifest from the start, and they could hardly have been more unlike the aims so earnestly confessed by the founders of the Fellowship of the New Life.   Nevertheless, the one movement arose directly out of the other, and nearly all the original members of the Fellowship were also Fabians. In October, 1883, we find a small number of like-minded people coming together at 17 Osnaburgh Street, Regent's Park, in the rooms of Edward R. Pease, who was to be the Fabian Secretary for close upon thirty years.   In December the Fellowship is formally constituted—with its " cultivation of a perfect character " and all.   Curiously, however, and without warning in the record, it is only four weeks later (January 4, 1884), and in the same rooms, that we have a different Society created and christened.   Frank Podmore moves that it be called the Fabian Society—in allusion, as he explains, to the victorious policy of Fabius Cunctator ; and the resolution is adopted by the impressive vote of nine to two.   The Society is not at first described as Socialist. Its purpose is declared to be that of reconstructing the existing social system " in such manner as to secure the general welfare and happiness."   Three months pass, a few more members are gathered in, and then the committee orders 2,000 copies of Tract No. 1 to be printed, with the title of *Why are the Many Poor?*   This was destined to remain in circulation for half a century ; and on the whole, one may say, the initial Fabian Tract was the actual starting point of the Fabian movement.

It was a four-page leaflet, and was drafted by W. L. Phillips, a house-painter who did not abandon his trade. Some years afterwards it was revised by Bernard Shaw, who sharpened the wording and cut down the rhetoric ; otherwise the substance was little changed—a notable tribute to the sound quality of the first Fabians' only genuine workman colleague.   Two sentences stood on the front page by way of epigraph, and they were printed within quotation marks.   The second ran thus :

For the right moment you must wait, as Fabius did most patiently, when warring against Hannibal ; but when the time comes you must strike hard, as Fabius did, or your waiting will be in vain, and fruitless.

This fragment of wisdom was not found in any classical

author.   It was composed by Frank Podmore, the biographer of Robert Owen and an energetic early Fabian.   In later years Mr. H. G. Wells was not by any means the only critic to point out that Fabius was never known to strike hard, and to assert that the time for a decisive blow seemed never to arrive for his modern followers.   However that be, we may admit that the style and title adopted by the high-spirited young architects of middle-class Socialism was one of the oddest, and the tactics announced were perhaps the most peculiar, ever associated with a plan for the reshaping of a social order.   But, as a matter of fact, the temporising motto did not make any difference to the Society's chances, while the name was seen to possess the higher merits of nomenclature.   It was not too definite ; it was sufficiently unfamiliar to catch the public attention, and it was unfor-gettable.

The Society's beginnings could not have been humbler than they were.   But the members were ready to proselytise, and Tract No. 1 gave them a decisive start, for it fell almost at once into the hands of the one man through whose genius and audacity the Fabian Society took colour and shape.

In 1884 George Bernard Shaw was twenty-eight years of age.   He had come over from Dublin nine years earlier, and was still adrift in London—a raw, angular, defiant young Irishman, whose characteristics he has himself described with humour and verve in several chapters of autobiography.   He had somehow contrived to keep himself afloat during the seedy interval, writing incessantly but earning by his pen almost nothing.   He was completely aware of his own powers, but was making only the poorest headway towards persuading editors and publishers to believe in them.   He had been aroused by Henry George, and since the reading of *Das Kapital* had convinced him of the central truth of Socialism he had known himself to be a man with a mission in life.   He was looking about for a group or association with which to throw in his lot ; and in the London of that day, as we can well believe, there was no embarrassing choice of such.   Bernard Shaw knew nothing so far of William Morris and his artist friends.   It was plain enough that the one avowed English Marxist, H. M. Hyndman, was impossible as a colleague for him, while the comrades of the Social Democratic Federation lived and moved on a different plane of interests and habits.

Why are the Many Poor? seemed to point to the answer. That headline was an inspiration. It made Bernard Shaw a Fabian ; and his discovery soon afterwards of a young civil servant with several London University degrees proved to be an event that made possible the Fabian Society as the world came to know it. Fifty years ago, if London had been combed for a pair of opposites more extreme than these, the search might have been regarded as a forlorn hope. Yet they were in point of fact uncommonly well suited as fellow-workers amid the conditions of that time. Mr. Shaw has described the occasion of their first meeting : the appearance, at one of those debating societies which he and his associates were turning to unmerciful use for their own purposes, of a small dark man (looking, he might have added, rather like a neat Frenchman of the Second Empire) who knew more about the subject of the evening than the opener and spoke from notes with an unmistakable air of mastery, ticking off his points as he passed rapidly down the paper. On the instant Bernard Shaw recognised the indispensable man. " Quite the cleverest thing I ever did in my life," he said long afterwards, " was to force my friendship on Sidney Webb, to extort his, and to keep it." We need not doubt the accuracy of this statement.

The contrasted companions did not enter the infant Society together. Bernard Shaw turned up within the first half-year. Sidney Webb was elected in May, 1885, along with his colleague in Whitehall, Sydney Olivier, who at that time shared with him the duties of Resident Clerk at the Colonial Office. Mr. Webb remained in the department only until 1891. His colleague passed on through knighthood to the highest grades of the Service, and ultimately to the House of Lords and a Secretaryship of State in the first Labour Cabinet. In 1885 also Annie Besant joined the Fabians. Graham Wallas came in twelve months later. Hubert Bland and William Clarke were foundation members.

The company of original Fabian apostles was now complete. They could not be described as a unitary group.

On the contrary, they were seven displaying a striking variety of talent, temperament and personal interests. Granted that the most famous of them had to be taken from the beginning for what he is, an immitigable individual, we have to recognise that among the remaining half-dozen the nearest to a pair of intellectual companions were the Oxford friends, Graham Wallas and Sydney Olivier. Sidney Webb at twenty-six was essentially what he is at 75 : encyclopædic and inexhaustible, untiring, wholly devoted to his chosen public causes. William Clarke was a moralist and a solitary. His fine spirit was marred to some extent by a habit of passing severe judgment upon his associates, and an inclination to quarrel. Bland was a man of the world, with a peppery disposition. Annie Besant was an *exaltée*. The task of keeping the peace fell continually upon Bernard Shaw, who said the hardest things and indulged in the wildest extravagances, but was free from rancour and would neither take offence nor allow any of the others to do so. It is probably true that without the constant play of the Shavian temper the dominant personalities of the Fabian Society would have flown apart within the first few years.

They started straightway upon those enterprises which progressive organisations soon learned to think of as peculiarly Fabian. That is, they produced a large number of tracts, and conducted an original platform campaign. They would go anywhere to lecture or debate. No place was too obscure for a visit, no association so modest or so cranky that they would not look it up. Sidney Webb always excepted, they were in need of political and economic education and they made no secret of the fact. More than one discussion society was kept going for their benefit. It was at an economic circle in Hampstead that Bernard Shaw encountered Philip Wicksteed, who combined mathematical economics with profound mediæval studies. Wicksteed convinced him of the truth of Jevons's conception of value, at the expense of Marx's ; and the Jevonian theory was adopted as an article of Fabian orthodoxy. There were no free-lances to rival the Fabians in mobility and dash. And they made a perfect stage army, for many years were to pass before they had any numbers. It was as a body of some forty members that they went out to the assault upon the strongholds of *laissez-faire*. They were not more than 150, and they had not yet acquired an office, when in 1890 they ventured upon a collective manifesto.

The publication of *Fabian Essays in Socialism* was an event, and the reception of the book was altogether unlooked for. Of the seven authors one alone, and that one the least Fabian in attitude and temper, was known to the public. By a happy accident the Society decided to be its own publisher at the start. The first edition of 1,000 copies went off within a month. It was at once repeated, and a cheap re-issue through a regular publisher carried the sales in the first year beyond 25,000. The volume has remained in print and in demand. Mr. Shaw has written three prefaces, the latest bearing date 1931. The *Essays* have never been revised. The Fabians were not tempted by their success to set out upon a second series ; and it will always be regarded as singular that the governing group of the Society, never without writers and sociologists of distinction, has at no time undertaken a further compendious statement of Fabian Socialism.

No manifesto of the past half-century can be better known than this, so that the briefest note upon its eight chapters will here suffice. The papers were delivered as lectures at Willis's Rooms in St. James's, a historic hall bearing memories of Coleridge, Carlyle, and other eminent amateurs of the platform. Although issued as the considered product of a group, with Bernard Shaw as editor, the *Essays* make an impression of considerable variety and here and there, oddly enough, of sheer utopianism. The discourse on the historical basis of Socialism by Sidney Webb is a foretaste of the monumental work with which the names of the two Webbs have since been associated, and one noteworthy characteristic feature of it is the section that describes how large a measure of practical Socialism was already embodied in the British State and municipal system. William Clarke's exposition of the industrial basis, still one of the most interesting to read, contains what was probably the first well-informed summary for English readers of the results to date of the swiftly growing trust-monopolies in the

United States. Sydney Olivier, discussing the moral basis of a Socialist community, reveals an imaginative mind (he was the poet of the group) playing about a subject which was at that time unexplored and must have seemed curiously unfamiliar.   Graham Wallas, dealing with property and the future organisation of society, is seen to be already coming within hail of the absorbing group of problems to which his mature thought was devoted, although then manifestly hampered by lack of knowledge.   Annie Besant's paper reads to-day like what the early Fabians must have known it to be—the sermon of an impassioned social preacher, knowing little of modern industry, which she was endeavouring to forecast, and therefore gloriously confident in predicting the swift transformation of our competitive anarchy into the co-operative commonwealth.   It appeared to this glowing evangelist a simple thing for the new municipalities to become big employers of labour, so enterprising and unrestrained that they must quickly drive the private employer from the field.   Annie Besant's essay, we may be sure, was not subjected to any editorial revision.   No doubt her caution was an imperious " Hands off ! "

Hubert Bland, who tries to compass the outlook, announces that the Fabian permeation of Liberalism is already at an end and predicts the advent of a Socialist Party.   Mr. Shaw has two contributions in the volume : his initial Fabian essay in which the essential nature of Socialism and its economic doctrine is set forth, and a paper on the transition to social democracy which had been read before the British Association.   These two chapters make an instructive contrast for the reader at a distance of forty-five years.   The first is a lesson in elementary economics, making use of the orthodox terms, and leading off with a lucid but far from effortless exposition of the Ricardian law of rent.   It works up to a restrained peroration, a piece of eloquent writing that foreshadows in its cadences and choice of words the long and brilliant succession of the author's speeches that were to come in essay and drama.   The paper on the transition is an example of pure Shavian prophecy and declamation, in the style which, startlingly new in 1890, has since become familiar to readers in every quarter of the world.   Forty years later, in his third preface, Mr.

Shaw wrote : " Everything that is contained in the *Essays* should by this time have become part of the common education of every citizen." Well, not quite everything.

If any reader of this book, finding the early Fabians in the honoured roll of the Great Democrats, has felt impelled to deny their right of admission, he may be advised to renew his acquaintance with *Fabian Essays.* The seven contributors are all democrats. They are not partial or apologetic democrats, but thoroughgoing. Each one of them makes a clear confession of faith—theoretic, prophetic, or commonsensible. Mr. Webb moves over the historical field without intimating the least doubt as to the possibility of democracy's being stayed in its march to a socialistic fulfilment. And, in view of the long interval of speculative development through which he has since passed, Mr. Shaw's early creed has a most particular interest. He is found here accepting all the postulates of political democracy, and even proclaiming that the old Radical expedient of annual parliaments is no less certain of adoption than adult suffrage and the payment of M.P.s. The truth is, of course, that at the stage of the *Essays* and for a good many years to come it had not occurred to him or any others in the Fabian camp to challenge the assumptions of the popular faith or to doubt the efficacy and adequacy of the parliamentary system. All alike were innocent of any wish to examine the instruments of representative democracy. They took the methods for granted, and awaited without scepticism or misgiving the fulfilment of the democratic process.

The adhesion of Annie Besant (1847–1933) was rather singular. She brought with her a unique notoriety. In 1885 she was an extraordinarily vital and attractive woman of thirty-eight. For ten stormy years she had been the colleague of Charles Bradlaugh in Radical politics and the atheist assault upon bibliolatry. Their joint names and energies aroused a passion of anger and loathing such as our generation would find it difficult to realise ; but, on the other hand, they enjoyed together the support of a huge working-class public. Under Bradlaugh's tuition Annie Besant had become an efficient journalist and pamphleteer, and her power of sustained work was equal to that of almost any man or woman in public life. Her oratory, before it became clotted in occultism, was a surpassing gift.   She was a dauntless champion of the working man, and still more of his wife and daughter.   As a young woman of thirty, separated from her husband the Fenland vicar, she had stood beside Bradlaugh in the dock of the Old Bailey during the celebrated birth-control trial of 1877, conducting to admiration her own defence.   In the East End of London and the North of England the working people rewarded her with an affection that had in it a touching note of worship. By the time she met the Fabians, Annie Besant had turned away from Bradlaugh's declamatory individualism, and his atheism was leaving her unsatisfied.   But it was not until four years after her break with him in social doctrine that she gave up her joint-editorship of the *National Reformer* and with it all the associates of her defiant young woman-hood.

To the Fabians her reputation and her matchless eloquence were undeniable assets, and for herself their companionship was invaluable during the four years of her pilgrimage from secularism to mysticism.   But it must have been manifest from the beginning that the Fabian Society was no place for Annie Besant.   As Bernard Shaw put it, she was a tragedienne, while the Fabian note was comedy.   She was out of her element in their ironic tabernacle.   Shortly before the appearance of *Fabian Essays* she had capitulated to H. P. Blavatsky and plunged headlong into theosophy, and was thus losing interest in the body of political and social reforms upon which the ardours of her temperament and her dazzling gifts had been expended.   Her new religion swept her away and she was lost to the Fabians, just as the Society was entering upon its first stage of success and influence.   After *Fabian Essays* there remained to Annie Besant forty years of voyaging over the strangest seas. Midway in her fantastic quest she returned to the old field of political agitation, resumed her membership, and spoke again from the Fabian platform.   But this was a voice from the grave.

William Clarke (1851-1901) was the only one of the Fabian seven who, unknown in 1890, failed afterwards to achieve a reputation equivalent to his abilities.   An East-Anglian who as a non-collegiate student had taken honours at Cambridge, he gained his early platform experience as an itinerant speaker for the Liberal Party. There was a note of unusual authority in his speaking as in his writing. He was an exceedingly competent journalist—a leader-writer on the *Daily Chronicle* during the brilliant editorship of H. W. Massingham, and a writer of middles in *The Spectator*. William Clarke was probably better informed on American affairs than any journalist in England. He lectured widely in the United States, and he had a strong spiritual kinship with Emerson and Whitman. There were few more effective speakers. His mind was orderly and dogmatic, and every sentence came from him, as one of his colleagues said, like an ultimatum. Financial misfortune and an incurable malady contributed, with the intolerable snail's pace (as he thought it) of social progress, to darken his spirit. His outlook became one of settled gloom, and long before his death, in Herzegovina, he had ceased to be an active Fabian.

Hubert Bland (1856-1914), an excellent Fabian judged by practical services, was an incongruous member of the group. His training and habits were those of the City, and he was a figure of no little flamboyance. Like Hyndman, he kept to the frock-coat and silk hat long after they ceased to be obligatory for a professional man ; but while the leader of the S. D. F. looked like a stockbroker, Bland added a cravat and broad-ribboned monocle, so that he seemed to cross the company-director with a West-End actor or a Royal Academician from St. John's Wood. Along with his clever wife, Edith Nesbit, of the popular children's books, he was the centre of a semi-bohemian coterie at Blackheath (and later at Well Hall, Eltham). He was a steady colleague, a useful lecturer, an incisive debater, and valuable to the Fabians as bringing into their mainly civil-service and university atmosphere the standpoint of the City man, frankly imperialist and Tory when the plain implications of his Socialist creed were not involved. He became a skilled literary journalist, with a talent for reviewing fiction, and his later energies were expended in that field rather than in Fabian propaganda.

Upon Graham Wallas (1858-1932) there had been bestowed an enviable endowment of gifts and graces which

placed him among the most highly esteemed university
teachers of the world.   The son of a North Country clergyman who later held a rectory in Devon, he had been a
scholar of Corpus Christi, Oxford, and was a master in a
suburban school when he met with the Fabians.   No one
of them took more enthusiastically than he to open-air
speaking and hole-and-corner debating, and none could
have turned that hard training to better account.   He had a
sparkling platform style and an unfailing good-humour
which made him acceptable to every kind of audience.   The
London School Board attracted him as soon as he was free
to become a member of an elected body ; and, since anti-
clericalism was a passion with him, he plunged into the
attack upon the Anglican zealots who, as he held, were
ruining the schools.   As chairman of the Board's School
Management Committee he had for several years the
responsible direction of the elementary schools system.
Among the Fabians, Graham Wallas was the authority on
modern democratic movements.   He would doubtless have
become the historian of Chartism, which he knew through
and through, had he not been diverted by a rediscovery of
the Place manuscripts and thus impelled to write the Life
of Francis Place.   This find opened a fascinating new field
of research for his younger contemporaries.

It was common form to twit the Fabians with their
neglect of social psychology.   They were, it was said, so
taken up with programmes and tactics that they had no time
for the individual citizen and voter, for his feelings and his
funny ways.   But they could take pride in the fact that the
very first English inquiry into such phenomena was the
task of one of themselves : that it was Graham Wallas and
no other who taught people to look at the man behind the
vote.   He produced *Human Nature in Politics* out of the
abundance of his own experience, just when intelligent men
and women everywhere were beginning to be worried about
the puzzle of democracy in action : about the absurdities
of our electoral machinery, the obscure workings of the
citizen's desires and superstitions, the demoralising effect
of his family troubles, and the mysterious tempests of mob
emotion into which he was swept.   Wallas was the first
to turn the light upon all this, as he was the first in

England to utter a considered warning against the excesses
of contemporary irrationalism in public life. For twenty
years there was no more ardent or consistent Fabian than
he. But the Society did not hold him. Differences
with his colleagues on educational and fiscal policy led
to his resignation in 1904, without, however, any personal
breach or loss of good-fellowship. The Fabian period
furnished Graham Wallas with a store of material for discussion and illustration in his lectures at the London
School of Economics, which were attended by men and
women students from almost every land ; and the Society
was enabled to call upon his services to the end of his happy
and fruitful and extraordinarily valuable life.

The *Essays* started something of a Fabian boom. The
conditions of the time were specially favourable to the new
lead. The Trafalgar Square calamity of 1887 was a disturbing comment upon the glory of Britain in the year of
jubilee. The great Dock Strike of 1889 (fought, incredibly,
to establish the dock labourer's claim to casual pay at the
rate of sixpence per hour) was a shock in itself, and a greater
shock when the men won. The creation of the new County
Councils helped the public to realise that the long night of
English local government was coming to an end, and the
new councillors were not unwilling to put their ignorance
to school. The first elections to the London County Council
gave the Fabians a splendid opportunity, of which they
made the fullest use in the creation of the Progressive Party.
For a short time, too, there was scope for Fabian permeation
in politics, but the short-lived Liberal Government of
1892 was too weak to break new ground, except in the
notable Harcourt Budget of 1894. At the end of 1893
Sidney Webb sounded a retreat from Westminster in a
Fortnightly Review article with the title of *To your Tents,
O Israel !* and the effort was officially over. It was something more than a coincidence that a few months earlier the
Fabians had come out with the first definite project for a
political Labour Party and the I. L. P. had been founded
at Bradford.

Meanwhile there had occurred the most important
personal event in the history of the Society. In 1892

Sidney Webb married Beatrice Potter, one of a famous family of sisters, already an authority on Co-operation and perfectly trained in the new technique of social investigation by work for Charles Booth's great London Survey. Thus began a unique partnership, which was destined to be wholly fulfilled, chiefly in three directions : first, through a series of indispensable books—massive in structure and of pioneer quality as regards both method and subject-matter ; secondly, through consistent and unremitting devotion to the public concern and to the principles of social reconstruction with which the Webbs were especially identified ; thirdly, in their generous encouragement of young people entering public life, and the record of democratic hospitality that distinguished their house in Westminster. During thirty years the best of England found its way to No. 41, Grosvenor Road. The ironic necessities of a Labour Government adjusting itself to an unreformed House of Lords created Lord Passfield for a season ; but it is to Sidney and Beatrice Webb that honour and affection belong.

All that followed these events lies outside the scope of this chapter, but mention must be made of two crises, one connected with national affairs, the other an exciting personal episode. The first befell at the outbreak of the South African War in 1899. A considerable body of members felt strongly that the Society could not avoid the duty of coming out in condemnation of the war policy. But every organisation in the country was gravely divided upon this issue, and the majority of Fabians accepted the view of the Shaw-Webb group on the committee, holding that a declaration would mean an irreparable schism. This led to a small number of resignations, the most conspicuous of which were those of J. Ramsay MacDonald, Walter Crane, and Mrs. Emmeline Pankhurst.

The second affair was precipitated by an explosive man of genius who joined in 1903. Becoming a member of the executive, Mr. H. G. Wells made a demand for a new and aggressive policy which would have involved resources never within reach of the Society. There ensued a year of inquiry and manœuvre, which ended in the defeat of Mr. Wells and his young disciples. They had grown

I

suspicious of the Old Guard, who, however, were safe within the defences of their experience and Mr. Shaw's platform skill. The insurgents also were contemptuous of Fabius, who to be sure had not been much heard of during the years of the Society's initial success. Mr. Wells, however, does not seem to have drawn the obvious and rather amusing moral provided for himself in the later behaviour of that dubious commander. Fabius, we learn from Plutarch, tended in his old age to become morose and to show jealousy of the younger men, especially of Scipio. Mr. Wells could never have been a Fabian leader ; but his incursion was certainly not without its effect. It put a term to the second clearly marked period of the Society's history, while Fabian characters are prominent or incidental in several of the novels between *Tono-Bungay* and *The Bulpington of Blup*.

There is a notion abroad that the Fabians of the first generation were a band of brothers unequally divided between sharpshooters and doctrinaires. That is an absurd misreading. Their aims were clear. They worked hard and with a fine disinterestedness towards a stage of national development which they saw to be inevitable. They built up a body of positive socio-economic thought, and coupled it with a method that could hardly have been better suited to the time, and they displayed an astonishing eagerness for certain kinds of work too often shunned by theorists and practical reformers alike. The fortune of the field and the time was with them. They had vitality, variety, and exceptional powers of speech and persuasion. And they had the supernatural luck of possessing two leaders of unrivalled quality ; one, a man of the largest intellectual grasp, with a power of accumulating and mastering his material exceeding that of almost any contemporary ; the other, beyond all question, the greatest master of expression produced in the English world during the modern age.

Si monumentum requiris, circumspice. In public and institutional life, in social and economic thought, Britain has been largely remade within a single generation. Our local government, our technical education and university system, the great range of social services that has gone far to make this country to a large extent the accepted standard of democratic enterprise and administration—these have proved themselves to be the most positive and vital actualities of present-day society. The social historian, when tracing the origins and the personal and other influences which shaped the new institutions in the formative period, will find himself in continual contact with the work of the early Fabians and their immediate successors. Indeed, he may well be driven to the conclusion that this England of the twentieth century would not have evolved as it has done without the labours of the men and women who came together in 1884–5 and so quaintly took the name of the least heroic Roman in the Plutarchian galley.

MILLICENT GARRETT FAWCETT

1847–1929

by RAY STRACHEY

MILLICENT GARRETT FAWCETT

1847–1929

by RAY STRACHEY

"TO promote the improvement of the condition of women is a great and noble cause to devote one's life to. Success in such a cause is a goal worthy of the noblest ambition ; failure in such a cause is a better thing than success in any meaner or paltrier object."

These words formed the peroration of a speech in the Birmingham Town Hall in the year 1872, and they were uttered by a young woman of 25, who, although she was defying all the conventions and outraging all the proprieties by appearing on a public platform, seemed as gentle, as composed and as much at ease as if she were in her own drawing-room. Mrs. Henry Fawcett, the young woman in question, spoke with a simplicity and directness which disarmed criticism, and she looked so quiet and pretty and so exquisitely neat that she allayed fears, even though the substance of her thought was revolutionary, and the strength of her purpose was all too abundantly clear.

Millicent Fawcett came to her convictions, and to the life work which grew from them, by a path which was as straight and clear as her own nature. She was born at Aldeburgh in Suffolk in 1847, and was the seventh child and fifth daughter of Newson and Louisa Garrett. Descended on both sides from families of the eastern counties, she was happy in all the circumstances of her childhood, both in the places and in the people among whom it was passed. Her father was a merchant, shipbuilder and maltster, a man of abounding energy and charm, who swept his train of ten sons and daughters with him into all the adventures of the countryside—the shipwrecks, the railway constructions, the elections or the news from the Crimea, infusing everything with a concrete reality which found a congenial echo in his daughter's mind.

During Millicent's childhood her sister Elizabeth (later Mrs. Garrett Anderson) was conducting her long and bitterly opposed campaign to qualify as a doctor, and the ins and outs of this struggle were eagerly followed by the whole family. Elizabeth had the hearty support of her adventurous father, but her mother could hardly bear what she felt to be the shame of the notoriety, so that it was not only the external opposition, but also the shrinking of women themselves which were familiar to Elizabeth's small sister. She grew up with the assumption that the position of women must be enlarged, whatever the cost might be, and she was early familiar with the pioneer efforts in this direction.

At the age of twelve Millicent was sent, for three years, to a school at Blackheath. At this school, and still more at the town house of her elder married sister Louie, where she often stayed when her school days were over, she began to come into contact with the general movements of thought of the day. She was taken to hear Frederick Maurice preach, and she met many of the philanthropists and radical thinkers, and was above all influenced and impressed by the writings of John Stuart Mill, whose whole outlook and philosophy seemed to chime in exactly with her own mind. The structure of the State, and the adjustment of men (and women) to society were the problems which seemed to her interesting and important, and as she grew to be a young lady she thought and read much upon these subjects. In 1865, when she was seventeen, she had the good fortune to hear Mill speak at one of his election meetings at Westminster, and his convinced advocacy of Women's Suffrage enchanted her. Here, indeed, was a cause worth working for ; a cause which combined the general advancement of the female sex with a fundamental principle of political progress ; here was a step which was right in itself, and which would be productive of untold future development—" a noble cause to devote one's life to." From the time of that meeting Millicent Garrett's course in life was fixed.

The year 1865 was an important one in her life in another way also, for it was then that she first met Henry Fawcett. He was then thirty-two, and had been blinded by an accident eight years before ; but, with a courage and strength of purpose which were characteristic, he had not allowed his misfortune to interfere with his life or work. He was a Professor of Economics at Cambridge, and had recently been elected a Member of Parliament, and was one of a group of Radicals who were working with Mill in the House. Everything in his way of looking at life and duty corresponded with the outlook of Millicent Garrett, and when, two years later, they were married, they brought to their partnership a community of tastes and a similarity of conviction which formed a basis for their deep happiness.

The years which followed their marriage were full of work and interest for both of them. Part of the year they lived in Cambridge and part in London ; and in both places they had a congenial society, and were in contact with all the radical and reform movements of the day. Their only child, Philippa, was born in 1868, and what with her two houses and her baby and her large circle of relations and friends, Millicent's life was filled with occupation. Her husband's blindness, too, caused her to work unusually closely with him, reading to him, summarising documents and writing speeches, lectures and articles, and the political training which this gave her reinforced and deepened her interest in the problems of political and economic theory. Millicent, however, was not one to be content with being interested, nor was she satisfied by being fully occupied. The cause to which she had given her allegiance remained supremely important to her, and even during her busiest years she worked steadily for it.

1867, the year when the Fawcetts were married, was the year when the first Women's Suffrage petition was presented to the House of Commons, and the first of the Parliamentary debates took place. This debate, which Mrs. Fawcett heard from the Ladies' Gallery, was on an amendment to the Reform Bill to omit the word " man " and substitute the word " person," and it brought the subject for the first time into the range of real political questions. Ridicule, indeed, still attached to it, and there was a long and weary spell of effort ahead ; but the approach which Mill made on that first Parliamentary occasion was so serious and so profoundly reasoned that, in spite of their traditional jocularity, the members were deeply impressed. Mill's argument was that without the enfranchisement of women democracy was incomplete. He claimed, indeed, that there

I*

were reasons, based on the inequality of the laws towards women, and on their false position in the world, which made their enfranchisement especially desirable, and argued that none of these things could be properly adjusted until women themselves shared in the national life. But this was special pleading. To his own mind the whole case followed from the basic democratic principle that free institutions were better than the best of despotisms, and he maintained that the representation of women was merely a particular case of the desirability of establishing representative government.

Logic and political theory are not the forces which act most immediately in public life, and Mill's amendment was defeated ; nevertheless a very real advance had been made, and the Women's Suffrage Movement definitely began when that vote was taken.

During the next two years Women's Suffrage Committees came into existence in London, Manchester, Bristol, Birmingham, and Edinburgh, and Mrs. Fawcett was an original member of the first of them. She attended the first public meeting which was organised, and on this occasion made—with great trepidation—her first public speech. It was a very short little speech, but it showed the plain good sense which was to characterise all her subsequent work.

" A great many things combine," she said, " to make us forget what a small minority we are . . . The members of this Society have a great deal to do so long as ' I never heard of such a thing ' is the particular objection urged."

This first public meeting was followed by others in different parts of the country. It was nervous work at first for the early pioneers. No one knew whether a woman's voice could carry to an audience, nor whether so shocking a thing as a woman public speaker ought to be countenanced. Chairmen were afraid to preside, audiences were prepared to scoff, and it was most uncertain how it would all go off. By degrees these fears subsided, but for a long time the country propaganda was a good deal of an ordeal.

Mrs. Fawcett took her share of this effort, but was, of course, too busy to devote her whole time to it. She did, however, work regularly with the Committees, and soon came to be regarded as the one to whom all the more delicate and difficult tasks could safely be left, and the one whose counsel it was wisest to follow.

For the seventeen years of her marriage Mrs. Fawcett lived this busy active life. She and her husband both advanced the women's cause in every way they could, not only by direct support for the suffrage, but also by advocacy of the Married Women's Property Bills and of the movement for higher education. With this latter, indeed, they were very closely involved, and it was at their house in Cambridge that the first decisions were taken which led to the establishment of Newnham College. To all these occupations Mrs. Fawcett added yet another when she prepared and published in 1870 her text-book *Political Economy for Beginners*. In her writing, as in her speaking, she was lucidly clear, and this book was so straightforward that it became immediately popular, and went into ten editions.

Henry Fawcett was a Liberal, of the Radical wing, and during the years up to 1873 he was a critic of his own party. While the Liberals were in opposition his party orthodoxy was less strained, and when Gladstone became Prime Minister in 1882 he offered the position of Postmaster-General to Fawcett. It was during his tenure of this office that the Reform Bill of 1884 came forward, and the women suffragists naturally entertained great hopes from this measure. The Bill proposed to enfranchise agricultural labourers ; and if such a wide and democratic extension of the franchise came, surely women could be brought in at the same time ? So they argued, and so they hoped ; but nothing of the kind occurred. Mr. Gladstone announced that if the women's amendment were carried he would withdraw the Bill, and in the face of this threat most of his followers, even those deeply pledged in its favour, voted against the amendment, which was lost.

This set-back marked a definite stage in the suffrage movement. Until then there had been hope that the extending basis of the franchise might carry women along without the need of much special propaganda. The general democratic case, which was becoming so integral a part of the system of government, did, in fact, cover the women's suffrage point, as Mill and Mrs. Fawcett saw. But its implications were far wider than politics, and it was because of those implications that enmity arose against it. Others besides its supporters could see that the vote was the key to all sorts of other changes in the position of women ; and it was the fear of these changes which hindered progress.

With the defeat of 1884, therefore, the suffragists realised that they would have to " convert " the country. Their task was nothing less than the creation of a changed public opinion about women ; and though they quailed not a little at its magnitude, no one dreamt of giving it up. After all, the change of public opinion was as much part of their ultimate object as was the franchise itself.

In Mrs. Fawcett's personal life the year 1884 was of the gravest importance, for in November, after an illness of barely a week, her husband died. This was a crushing sorrow, but neither her nature nor her judgment would allow her to be prostrated. Instead of dwelling on what she had lost, she dwelt on what she had had, and turned again to the causes they had worked for together, and to the good and needful things which still remained to be done ; and in this way she found comfort.

1885 was the year of the publication of the articles by W. T. Stead on the subject of prostitution which were known as the Maiden Tribute. These articles, and the subsequent trial and imprisonment of Stead, roused Mrs. Fawcett's passionate indignation, and for some years she did a good deal of work for the Vigilance Association. The more she saw of its work, however, the more clearly she perceived that the enfranchisement of women was the necessary first step in every reform which touched their status, and she finally came to the conclusion that she would concentrate all her efforts for the women's movement upon this one cause alone.

It was impossible, however, to do nothing but suffrage work. Mrs. Fawcett had been living in the very centre of the political world, and she held views of the utmost clarity and positiveness. It was part of her women's suffrage creed to believe that women were as intimately concerned with political happenings as men, and she was neither able nor willing to abandon all these interests and convictions. When the question of Irish Home Rule came forward, Mrs. Fawcett, who vehemently opposed this measure, joined the group of dissentient Liberals, and soon became one of the leaders of the Liberal Unionist party.

Her opposition to Home Rule was, in her eyes, a part of her general democratic faith. She did not believe that democracy was served by every sub-division of authority, and was convinced that, in this case, Home Rule would have meant the abandonment of the rights of a loyal majority to the violence and force of a turbulent few. This view, which was strengthened by her frequent visits to Ireland, enlisted her democratic enthusiasm against Home Rule, and from 1886 to 1902 she took a prominent part in this agitation.

In spite of this active work, however, Mrs. Fawcett went steadily on with women's suffrage propaganda, making her appeal to men and women up and down the country. Sometimes she met with real hostility, and always with ridicule, but both melted away before her reasonable approach ; and her travels were marked by pleasant little tributes which greatly lightened her way. In Birmingham, for example, she was met outside one of the meetings of this period by two working women who had waited to speak to her. " Thank you, ma'am," was what they said, " you have made us feel two inches taller."

While Mrs. Fawcett pursued the uneventful course of propaganda work which marked the end of the eighties, her daughter Philippa passed through her college days at Newnham, and in 1890 she sat for the Mathematical Tripos. At that date women were allowed to take the papers, but they were not given degrees, nor placed in their competitive order in the lists. Accordingly when the results were known, and Philippa was found to be the first on the list, she could not be styled Senior Wrangler, but had to be placed " Above the Senior Wrangler "—a position which has never been awarded before or since ! This triumph, which of course gave her mother the most acute pleasure, was of very great service to the higher education of women. It was so sensational that it became news all over the world ; and it proved without the possibility of further question that women were not by nature disqualified from the highest successes in the most abstract branch of human thought.

The outbreak of the South African war put an end, for the time being, to propaganda work. Mrs. Fawcett had followed South African affairs closely through her cousin Edmund Garrett, who was editor of the *Cape Times*, and she strongly supported the British side. When the reports of the mismanagement of the Concentration Camps reached England, and it was decided to send out a Commission to investigate them, she accepted the position of its leader, and sailed for South Africa in July, 1901. Although this Commission was known to the Pro-Boer party as the " White-washing Commission," its activities really followed a different course. Mrs. Fawcett and her companions found a great many things seriously wrong with the camps, and before they left they secured far-reaching reforms.

With the end of the war the women's suffrage campaigns began again, and now with renewed vigour. The young generation which had profited by the opportunities for education were coming into the movement, and developments followed quickly. In 1897 the existing independent Suffrage Societies had joined together into a National Union with Mrs. Fawcett as President, and she now devoted a great deal of care to the basis of its organisation. Her belief in democracy, which inspired her belief in the cause itself, was no remote academic theory, but a very practical reality, and she determined that the society which she led should itself be truly democratic.

The task was no easy one, for the societies were attracting thousands of women of varied experience and strong character, whose willingness to pull together in one united body was threatened by the very intensity of their enthusiasm. Mrs. Fawcett might, indeed, have established an autocratic system, and used the devotion of her followers to their cause as a lever to keep them in order. But she did not contemplate such a course. Instead she took the utmost pains to establish a constitution which was not only democratic in theory but workable and efficient in practice, and alive in every part. When it was first evolved the constituent societies were only 16 ; within eight years they were 305, but no radical change was required. The system which the suffragists worked out for themselves was capable of indefinite expansion, and so thoroughly did they assimilate the spirit of their leader that they came to attach the utmost importance to the efficiency of their own machine, and to have the most scrupulous regard for its internal self-government. No one who lived through those stirring years, and who was trained in the methods of Mrs. Fawcett's society, could ever believe that democracy and efficiency were incompatible, or doubt that freedom could be fully combined with order and unity.

The development of the National Union of Women's Suffrage Societies coincided with, and was greatly stimulated by, a parallel movement which began in 1905, when Mrs. Pankhurst founded the Women's Social and Political Union and adopted militant tactics. Mrs. Fawcett was not herself connected with this movement, but in its early days, before a policy of violence was adopted, she did not altogether disapprove of its methods. She herself believed in convincing public opinion rather than in startling or coercing it; but she appreciated the great value of the advertisement which militant methods gave to the cause, and it was not until the suffragettes definitely adopted unconstitutional expedients that she felt it necessary to dissociate herself from them.

Between 1905 and 1914 the suffrage agitation grew to very great dimensions. Thousands of women devoted their time and money and their energy to it, and already by 1910 more than two hundred meetings were being held every week. Processions, deputations, petitions, and every conceivable form of agitation multiplied, and even an unwilling House of Commons was forced to take notice, though the Parliamentary deadlock seemed very difficult to break. All this mass of activity involved for Mrs. Fawcett not only a great rush of work, but a heavy burden of responsibility, but she took it all with great calmness, and was neither cast down by reverses nor unduly elated by success. She knew, all the time, that the ultimate victory was assured, and though there were moments of great difficulty she was never at all discouraged.

In 1903, when the revival in the movement began, Mrs.

Fawcett was 56 years old, and although the volume and the pace of the work increased at an accelerating rate for eleven years she showed no sign of wearying. Indeed her power seemed to increase, and her speaking, which had always been at a high level, grew yet more statesmanlike and convincing, while her grasp of the essentials of the political situation and her realistic wisdom only grew with practice.

The turmoil of activity which centred round the suffrage societies went on without interruption until the very outbreak of the European War in August, 1914, and then came to an abrupt standstill, or rather, abruptly changed its character. Within a few hours of the declaration of war Mrs. Fawcett had issued to her societies the call to take their share in the national effort. " Let us prove ourselves worthy of citizenship, whether our claim be recognised or not," she said, and immediately the whole of her great organisation responded.

The four years which followed were sad and difficult for Mrs. Fawcett, as for everyone. She had not, indeed, any trouble of conscience, for her country's part in the war seemed to her inevitable and right ; but she feared that the cause in which she so steadfastly believed would be put back for a whole generation. This belief, however, was mistaken. The enthusiasm and success with which women threw themselves into every kind of war work, and the immense variety of occupations in which, as time went on, they replaced the men who were called to the front, brought about the wholesale conversion of almost every one of those who had resisted the women's suffrage movement. The consequence of this was that when, in 1916, the question of the franchise was re-considered with a view to the position of soldiers and sailors, no one seriously opposed the claim which Mrs. Fawcett put forward for a simultaneous re-consideration of the claims of women. In 1917 the Representation of the People Bill, with a clause giving votes to women of thirty who were either householders or the wives of householders, was passed through the House of Commons by a majority of seven to one, and early in 1918 the Bill passed the House of Lords and received the Royal Assent.

After this victory Mrs. Fawcett retired from the Presidency of the National Union, which, however, she encouraged to continue in existence until the vote should be secured on fully equal terms. She was seventy-one and, though full of health and vigour, she felt that she had had enough of meetings and committees, and would like to be released from the burden which she had carried for over fifty years ; and so she withdrew, as much as her colleagues would let her, into private life. In 1924 she was made a Dame Grand Cross of the British Empire, in recognition of her work for women, and she was known thereafter as " Dame Millicent."

The years of semi-retirement were very tranquil and happy, and lasted from 1919 until her death in 1929. During that decade she saw the beginning of all the good things she had expected to follow from the granting of the vote. She saw the spate of legislation which adjusted so many of the legal disabilities of women, and she saw the election of women to the House of Commons, and the inclusion of one of them in the Cabinet. She saw, too, the final women's suffrage measure of 1928 which gave women the vote on the same terms as men, and she was present in the House of Lords when the Royal Assent was given to it, as she had been present, sixty-one years before, when John Stuart Mill had brought the first amendment before Parliament. She saw, too, the new generation of young women who were growing up to their rights and responsibilities without the need to struggle, and she was delighted with them, and with the effect which their share in the national life was having upon the subject matter of politics. Health, Housing, Infant Welfare, Social Services and International Peace were all things which she knew men cared for ; but she had expected, and now she saw, that a new urgency attended these questions, and it rejoiced her heart.

" I look upon this cause," she had written years before, " as one of the very greatest things that has ever happened in the history of the world, immensely larger and more important than any merely national movement. It is the greatest step towards freedom which the human race has ever yet made, because it is not confined to any one nation or to any one rank or class in society ; it is the uplifting of our entire sex all over the world."

This had been a very high claim ; but Dame Millicent did not retreat from it. She had seen her fight through from its beginning to its end, and nothing which followed mitigated or even clouded her faith.

JOHN GALSWORTHY
1867–1933
by ST. JOHN ERVINE

JOHN GALSWORTHY

1867–1933

by ST. JOHN ERVINE

I

HIS inclusion in a collection of biographies of social and political reformers would have puzzled, even if it had pleased, John Galsworthy, for he was not a reformer in the sense that Robert Owen, John Bright, Richard Cobden, Lord Shaftesbury, and, to take a far different example, Shelley, were reformers. His advocacy was seldom deliberate or direct ; his reforms were almost always achieved by accident. It is difficult to think of him, as one can think of Shelley, sending up fire-balloons with exhortatory messages attached to their tails or casting on the tide bottles containing appeals to reason in the hope that mankind everywhere would instantly and nobly respond to them. It is even more difficult to think of him addressing monster and emotional meetings or taking a place at the head of a crowd. A sense of the ridiculous is disabling to one who wishes to lead the public in clamour against wrong. Galsworthy had that sense in a very high degree, joined to a marked and middle-class distaste for eccentricity or any departure from correct standards. He was, in his bones and blood, a Forsyte. He was too reticent and nervous and fastidious to be successful on platforms, although he was an excellent speaker—at his best, too, when he spoke spontaneously, though this was a fact he could never admit. He believed himself to be an indifferent orator, at his worst when he was asked to deliver an impromptu speech. In spite, however, of his hatred of florid demonstrations and his inability to cut a dash on platforms, he had habits that, if he had allowed them to develop, might have made him as eccentric as Shelley. Mr. Ford Madox Ford, in a volume of reminiscences, asserts that he was once infuriated by his failure to make the Inland Revenue Department accept a larger amount of income tax than they thought was due from him. In making his return, he had accidentally omitted to include a large sum, and, on discovering

his omission, had written to the authorities offering to pay
the additional amount due to them. They replied, according
to Mr. Ford, who is a romantic writer and impatient of fact,
that their accounts were now closed and could not be re-
opened, a statement which, if it be true, will be refreshing
and grateful to multitudes of persons liable to the tax.
Galsworthy thereupon sent a cheque for the sum due to
the Revenue, and it was returned to him, together with a letter
in which he was informed by the Lords Commissioners
that this correspondence must now cease. Enraged
by their arbitrary refusal of his money, Galsworthy continued
to worry the Commissioners for a long time ! . . . The
story, even if it be apocryphal, is true in spirit. A Forsyte
would have acted in that manner, a Forsyte with a touch
of Shelley in him, and that, to an astonishing extent, is
what John Galsworthy was. He was honourable and just
and immeasurably compassionate. His sentiment at times
overcame his intelligence and left him at the mercy
of his emotions, so that he was not able to distinguish
between the oppressor and oppressed, and was inclined
to think that " the little 'un " must be in the right, and
" the big 'un " in the wrong. If he had walked into the
Valley of Elah on that morning when the fair and ruddy
youth, David, encountered the great, hulking and un-
circumcised giant, Goliath, he would almost certainly have
run to David's aid, although Goliath was the weaker of
the two, the more in need of help.

II

He was born at Coombe, near Kingston Hill, in Surrey,
on August 14, 1867. His father, also John Galsworthy,
was a London lawyer of some renown and chairman of
several companies, a fierce man, according to Mr. Ford,
who lived next door to him for a time, and married to a
woman who was " young for her age " and flighty and
wore bright coloured ribbons in her bonnet. These two
" separated, tired of seeing one another, at very advanced
ages." " There was," Mr. Ford adds, " something pixyish
and hard about those old people . . . It was not a
usual stock, that from which Galsworthy came." Unusual,

indeed, and obvious material for a son who wished to
make a Saga about it. His parents were well-to-do. Their
son had no need to earn his living, a piece of luck, no doubt,
for a young man about town, as Galsworthy at first seemed
likely to become, but a piece of ill-luck for a man who,
suddenly becoming serious, took to his pen and attempted
to transcribe life. He spent four years in a private school
at Bournemouth, and five years, 1881–1886, at Harrow,
where he established a reputation as " the neatest and one
of the best football players and runners " who had ever
attended the school. "His neatness of movement," said
the Rev. E. Stogdon in a letter to *The Times*, which was
published a day or two after Galsworthy's death,

" was due to a beautiful figure, which he retained till the end, and
his neatness of dress seemed to be the expression of a character
which loved beauty and artistic things. Galsworthy won the
school half-mile in 1885 and 1886, and M. G. Glazebrook, the old
Oxford Blue, who was judging when he won by a foot in 1885,
said that he had never seen such pluck. In 1886 he won the
school mile in 4.43, but he, honest man, wrote to me in 1921 that
he remembered it as 4.48, and that he owed it to a very good
monitors' dinner he had had the night before at Welldon's
with champagne and port. He wrote, too, that he was always
nervous before a race and hated it, and he had spent the afternoon
of the "house" miles, from 2 to 4, sitting in his room eating
oranges and reading *David Copperfield* before the fire. The oranges
and *David Copperfield* and central heating brought about a collapse
half-way through the race. Galsworthy was captain of the school
football XI. He was a beautiful dribbler and full of pluck, but
he would be the only boy to climb the hill after a match without
a spot of mud on him."

From Harrow he went to New College, Oxford, where,
in 1889, he took an honours degree in Law, but, although he
ate late dinners in Lincoln's Inn, he did not practise at
the Bar. He took a trip round the world and spent two
years in wandering. In the course of these travels he met
and became the friend of Joseph Conrad, who was then an
officer on the *s.s. Torrens*, bound from Australia to South
Africa. In 1895, Galsworthy began to write, and three
years later, his first work, entitled *From the Four Winds*,
was issued under the pseudonym of John Sinjohn. It

was afterwards withdrawn from circulation. This book was followed by two " John Sinjohn " novels, one entitled *Jocelyn*, which was withdrawn, and another entitled *Villa Rubein*. The latter was subsequently re-written and acknowledged as a Galsworthy book. In 1904, when he was thirty-seven years of age, his first mature novel and the first to be issued under his own name, *The Island Pharisees*, was published. In 1906, he won renown and opened the Forsyte Saga with *The Man of Property*. In that year, too, his first play, *The Silver Box*, was performed. The social critic, who was to be mistaken for a social reformer, had begun his career. Thereafter, he worked with immense industry, and every year, almost until he died, he produced a new novel or a new play, sometimes a novel and a play. Success attended him, and he became, in the horrid jargon of the publisher, a " best-seller." Several of his plays, for example, *Loyalties* and *The Skin Game* and *Escape*, enjoyed long runs, although his best plays were too stern for the popular taste. One of them, indeed, *The Forest*, received short shrift in the theatre, in spite of its excellent quality. In 1922, three novels, *The Man of Property*, *In Chancery*, and *To Let*, were issued in one volume, under the generic title of *The Forsyte Saga*, which was originally intended to be the title of *The Man of Property*. The volume was instantly a very great success, not only in Great Britain, but in America and on the Continent, especially in Germany, where it was avidly read in the belief that it illuminated English character. It was followed, in 1929, by a companion volume of three novels, *The White Monkey*, *The Silver Spoon*, and *Swan Song*, in which the fortunes of the younger generation of Forsytes were followed under the generic title of *A Modern Comedy*. This volume was as popular as its predecessor, and Galsworthy accumulated honours and world renown. The University of St. Andrews made him an Honorary LL.D., and that of Manchester an Honorary D.Litt. In 1929, he was admitted to the Order of Merit by His Majesty the King, and in 1932, a few months before his death, he was awarded the Nobel Prize for Literature. On January 31, 1933, he died at Grove Lodge, The Grove, Hampstead.

III

His sense of Pity and his sense of Property joined to a sardonic Determinism, were the points on which John Galsworthy's philosophy turned, if, indeed, the word " philosophy " is not too large to describe his feelings. One night, as he and I left his dining-room, I stopped to look at Max Beerbohm's cartoon of him engaged in conversation with his philosophy, a grim looking lady, if I recollect aright, in a drab dress. " I don't know what my philosophy is," he mournfully remarked to me. That was not, as it might seem to some, a modest disclaimer of anything so grave as a philosophy of life ; it was, I think, an exact statement of fact. Galsworthy acted, as he wrote, from impulse rather than from deliberation. On more than one occasion he stated that when he sat at his desk to begin his day's writing, he had no idea of what he was about to put on paper. The fact that he had no plan in his head was, in a sense, useful. His novels are records of impressions made on his mind by people with whom he came in contact, and if he had drawn a plan of a book, he might have found himself gravely embarrassed by it, since he must then occasionally have come under the necessity of adapting his people to his plan, instead of putting them down as they appeared to him. But his inexperience of life outside a very restricted society made his impulsive method of composition a dangerous one ; for it left him at the mercy of his sentimental imagination. He indulged in Pity, and tended to treat weakness as if it were a virtue. He had few checks on his emotions, and his seclusive and withdrawn nature made such checks difficult for him to obtain. He could not easily, if at all, relax, and was not a good mixer. He knew very few people, even in his own world. A Harrow man once said of him that he sometimes attended cricket matches at his old school, sitting apart and speaking to no one, departing as he came, recognised but ungreeted. Those who have written about him assert that he was hard to know : he himself might have said that he found his fellow creatures unapproachable. He was immensely kind and he was eager to be amiable, but he could not unstiffen,

nor could he use the easy language of friendly intercourse.
He kept himself to himself, and may be said to have been
the last of Dr. Arnold's pupils, the Englishman who had
been frozen into Good Form. His shyness and diffidence,
his "neatness," as Mr. Stogdon calls it, added to his
upbringing in which there was no hardship, no struggle,
scarcely any need for effort, made it difficult for him to obtain
any knowledge of people outside his own circle. Poor
people almost entirely eluded him, and in his accounts of
them and their lives he substituted sentimentality for
knowledge. He derided the sense of property in everything he wrote, but his own sense of it was so acute that
he could not believe it was possible for a man to be happy
and hard-up. He seems, in all his books, to be saying,
"How can this man be happy. *He's poor!*" He hated
the Forsyte obsession with property, but he could not
conceive of life without property. St. Francis of Assisi
must have been an insoluble puzzle to him.

The Forsyte Saga may be said to be a book of reminiscences, and the pleasure it gives to its readers is the
result of its excellent portraiture. He paints admirable
pictures of people with whom he is familiar, especially if,
as in the case of Soames Forsyte, he dislikes them. Soames,
indeed, is the acid test of Galsworthy's artistry. This
character, intended by his creator to be unlikeable, grows
steadily in the affection of the reader until, at the end of
the Saga, he is the only Forsyte whose end is regretted.
It is plain from the preface to *A Modern Comedy* that
Galsworthy was puzzled and almost appalled by the
affection which Soames had inspired. "The chronicler,"
he says, and I invite the reader's attention to that significant word *chronicler*,

"catechised (as he often is) concerning Soames, knows not precisely
what he stands for. Taking him for all in all he was honest,
anyway. He lived and moved and had his peculiar being, and,
now he sleeps. His creator may be pardoned for thinking there
was something fitting about his end ; for, however far we have
travelled from Greek culture and philosophy, there is still truth
in the old Greek proverb : ' That which a man most loves shall
in the end destroy him.' "

How grudgingly Galsworthy pays his small tribute to

Soames! "He was honest, anyway." He resents the
affection people felt for the upright old man, and, although
he does not confess as much, except in an oblique manner,
is angered by their indifference to Irene, Soames' first wife,
to whom Galsworthy is sentimentally tender. Many
readers of the Saga have acknowledged their affection for
Soames Forsyte, but no one has ever acknowledged any
affection for, or even interest in, Irene, that prig, with the
cold, uncharitable heart and long, venomous memory,
overcharged with hate, who brings misfortune on every
person with whom she comes in contact. He was well
aware of the public disinterest in, even dislike of, Irene,
for he is at pains, in the preface to *The Forsyte Saga*, to
justify her actions. "The figure of Irene," he says,
"never, as the reader may possibly have noticed, present,
except through the senses of other characters "—a statement
which is not strictly correct—" is a concretion of disturbing Beauty impinging on a possessive world." But
his readers have noticed also that Irene is a morbid miser,
hoarding her body as if it were a museum piece, and displaying a sense of possession as acute as that of the most
acquisitive Forsyte :

"In criticism of the last phase of the Saga one might complain
that Irene and Jolyon—those rebels against property—claim
spiritual property in their son Jon. But, in truth, it would be
hypercriticism of the story as told. For no father and mother
could have let the boy marry Fleur without knowledge of the
facts ; and the facts determine Jon, not the persuasion of his
parents."

That is, perhaps, as good a case as can be made for Irene,
but it is of the nature of special pleading and leaves the
reader unimpressed. Irene remains eminently dislikeable.
"One has noticed," Galsworthy remarks a little plaintively
in the preface to *The Forsyte Saga :*

"that readers, as they wade on through the salt waters of the
Saga, are inclined more and more to pity Soames, and to think
that in doing so they are in revolt against the mood of his creator.
Far from it ! He, too, pities Soames, the tragedy of whose life
is the very simple, uncontrollable tragedy of being unlovable,
without quite a thick enough skin to be thoroughly unconscious

of the fact. Not even Fleur loves Soames as he feels he ought to be loved. But in pitying Soames readers incline, perhaps, to animus against Irene. After all, they think, he wasn't a bad fellow, it wasn't his fault ; she ought to have forgiven him and so on ! And, taking sides, they lose perception of the very simple truth, which underlies the whole story, that where sex attraction is utterly and definitely lacking in one partner to a union, no amount of pity, or reason, or duty, or what not, can overcome a repulsion implicit in Nature. Whether it ought to, or no, is beside the point ; because in fact it never does. And where Irene seems hard and cruel—as in the Bois de Boulogne, or the Goupenor Gallery—she is but wisely realistic, knowing that the least concession is the inch which precedes the impossible, the repulsive ell.''

But the reader, even if he be moved by this argument, is still aware of the irrefutable fact that the intense Irene married Soames for his money, and that she bilked him !

IV

The theme of the Saga is the devitalising effect of a strong sense of property, but that is as far as Galsworthy goes in stating his theme, and he continually overstates its effect. He does not propose the abolition of personal property, for he was no Communist, nor does he advocate the nationalisation of the means of production, distribution and exchange. He was not, as superficial persons some-times suggested, a Socialist. (The single occasion on which he exercised the franchise was in 1931, when he voted for the National Government !) His politics, so far as he had any, might be described as those of a Liberal with Tory tendencies. He could not easily contain himself in the presence of people to whom property was a sacred institution, and in his abhorrence of them, he satirised them unjustly, robbing them, in some instances, of all reality. The Rev. Mr. Boms, a shareholder in one of Old Jolyon's companies, is made to oppose a resolution to grant £5,000 to the widow of " our late superintendent," one Pippin, who had committed suicide through the mental strain induced by excessive devotion to the Company's affairs. " We all desire, I should hope, to be charitable. But I feel sure . . . that he will in some way, by some written expression, or better perhaps by reducing the amount, record our grave disapproval that so promising and valuable a life should have been thus impiously removed from a sphere where both its own interests and—if I may say so—*our* interests so imperatively demanded its continuance. We should not—nay, we may not—countenance so grave a dereliction of all duty, both human and divine." This is *jejune* satire, and the sentiments are incredible in the mouth of any man, even a Galsworthy parson—for Galsworthy was seldom just to the clergy. Poor Mrs. Baynes cannot snap a pair of large bracelets on her white wrists without being accused of revealing her sense of property. When Annette, Soames' second wife, gives birth to a daughter, Fleur, his only child, " his heart felt queer, warm, as if elated. . . . The sense of triumph and renewed possession swelled within him. By God ! this— this thing was *his !* " One of the Forsyte women loves the statement of Christ that " In My Father's house are many mansions," because it comforts her sense of property. All the Forsytes are obsessed by property. Even those members of it, like young Jolyon, who break with the family tradition, concentrate on this property point. They only differ from the rest of the family in being anti-, rather than pro-, property. As the late Victorians watched the funeral procession of their Queen, they were solemnised by the " dusky pomp and pageantry." " Never again would a Queen reign so long "—though how they felt so sure of this is hard to tell—" or people have a chance to see so much history buried for their money." The Victorian era comes off hardly in Galsworthy's opinion :

" Sixty-four years that favoured property, and had made the upper middle-class ; buttressed, chiselled, polished it, till it was almost undistinguishable in manners, morals, speech, appearance, habit, and soul from the nobility. An epoch which had gilded individual liberty, so that, if a man had money he was free in law and fact, and if he had not money he was free in law and not in fact. An era which had canonised hypocrisy, so that to seem to be respectable was to be. A great Age, whose transmuting influence nothing had escaped save the nature of man and the nature of the Universe."

The judgment seems as unsound as it is severe. Its

author shows no signs of knowing that the age of
"canonised hypocrisy" and accumulation of capital in
upper middle-class hands was the era in which, among
many others to whom these epithets cannot be applied,
Carlyle and Ruskin and William Morris, Lord Shaftesbury,
William Booth, Cardinal Manning and the later Tractarians, Kingsley and Maurice, Annie Besant and Bradlaugh
and George Jacob Holyoake lived and moved and had their
influential being. It is, perhaps, natural that a man to
whom a life of ease and security was an inheritance should
despise the means by which he lived in ease and comfort,
and should attribute to those who uphold the system of
private capital a preoccupation with property which is
almost dehumanising; but the ordinary reader of the *Saga*,
who is unencumbered by so sharp a sense of property as
Galsworthy possessed, has difficulty in believing that
Soames Forsyte's first thought on beholding his newly-
born baby was that he had increased his great possessions.
These are, no doubt, the superficials of Galsworthy's
horror of property as a decisive factor in human life, but
they are characteristic of the sentimentality with which he
thought of that factor. What, the reader enquires, is to
be done about property ? Galsworthy is singularly un-
helpful to those who seek an answer to this question. The
most he can say in reply is that " the generation which
came in when Queen Victoria went out . . . has decided
that everything requires re-valuation :

"And, since there is, seemingly, very little future before
property, and less before life, is determined to live now or never,
without bothering about the fate of such offspring as it may chance
to have. Not that the present generation is less fond of its
children than were past generations—human nature does not
change on points so elementary—but when everything is keyed
to such pitch of uncertainty, to secure the future at expense of
the present no longer seems worth while."

Galsworthy is here, surely, treating a transient mood,
arising out of a local situation, as if it were to be a permanent
feature of universal society. Is there " very little future
before property," and what does Galsworthy mean by his
addition, " and less before life " ? If life is to peter out

or dwindle to " less " than " very little," then the question of property will scarcely require answering. It will have been settled by the extinction, or reduction to " less " than " very little," of life itself. Dead men, or men in a state of suspended animation, are not likely to need property. Does Galsworthy, in this passage, finally renounce hope of any improvement in the conditions of life ? Does he believe that life is about to be extinguished and that any attempt " to secure the future at the expense of the present " or in any other way " no longer seems worth while " ? The conclusion appears to be pessimistic, but is merely ill-considered. He tells his readers that " the fundamental difference between the present and the past generations " is that the latter had some certainty about the future, whereas the former have none. " People will not provide against that which they cannot see ahead." What was there " ahead " that was visible to the past generation, but is invisible to the present ? Galsworthy does not say. Galsworthy does not know. He is using words, a little gloomily, that have just come into his head and without in the least attempting to connect them with reality.

" All this, of course, refers only to that tenth or so of the population whose eyes are above the property line ; below that line there are no Forsytes, and therefore no need for this preface to dip. What average Englishman, moreover, with less than three hundred a year ever took thought for the future, even in Early Victorian days ? "

How amazing it is that a man able to observe and record with so much skill the superficial aspect of society, should be capable of putting down, in circumstances of seriousness, sentences so destitute of truth as these ! Are there no Forsytes below the property line ? Were the first Forsytes, the yeomen to whose home in Dorset Soames, shortly before his death, made a pilgrimage, without the acquisitive faculty ? If they were, how did the sense of property enter the Forsyte family ? Must one have more than three hundred pounds a year to feel concerned for the future ? Can we believe that husbandry is unknown among those with less than that sum, that there are no spendthrifts " above the property line "?

V

Galsworthy's views on property were those of a sensitive man who had never had to earn his living. His unreasoning compassion, which caused him to suppose that any person less well off than himself must be an object of pity, compelled him to hate the system of society which is founded on a basis of property, but prevented him from appreciating the fact that a man can be happy although he is poor. He could see no way out of the tangle in which his thoughts had tied him, and so he slipped into a form of soft determinism which allowed him to indulge in the luxury of despair. He threw up his hands, but took care to put on his gloves. There is not one workman in the Galsworthy literature with moral force or high, unquenchable character, or irrepressible vigour. Jones, in *The Silver Box*, is a muddle-headed, drunken fool, incapable of putting up a fight of any worth, and David Roberts, in *Strife*, who is the most emphatic artisan in Galsworthy's work, is merely obstinate, a man who mistakes contumacy for strength and supposes himself to be seeing visions when he is only seeing enemies. At the end of *Strife*, Tench, the Secretary of the Company which is at odds with its workmen, remarks to Harness, the Secretary of their Trade Union, as he reads the terms of settlement of the strike, " D'you know, sir— these terms, they're the very *same* we drew up together, you and I, and put to both sides before the fight began ? All this—all this—and what for ? " To Tench's pathetic enquiry, Harness cynically answers, " That's where the fun comes in ! " In those sentences, Galsworthy's vision of society is brilliantly and succinctly stated. He sees the world distracted by obstinate and emphatic men who will not listen to the proposals of unemphatic, almost insignificant, men of reason. If John Anthony, the leader of the employers, and David Roberts, the leader of the workmen, had only listened to Henry Tench, the Secretary of the Company, and Simon Harness, the Secretary of the Trade Union, how nicely and neatly all their differences would have been removed and their troubles settled. It is a prime defect in Galsworthy's work that his able and reasonable men always appear to be flabby and uninfluential, insignificant and incapable of imposing their opinions on the obstinate and the obtuse. But it is a more serious defect in Galsworthy himself that he seems never to have known a workman of fine quality. The Tolpuddle Martyrs, if he had ever heard of them, appear to have left no impression on his mind. He seems never to have read Graham Wallas's *Life of Francis Place* or to have known anything of the Chartists. The entire Trade Union Movement with its host of able and upright leaders, such as Joseph Arch, Richard Bell, Mary Macarthur, J. R. Clynes and J. H. Thomas, eluded his observation. It was not in his tradition. He saw labourers only as driven men, and appeared not to have noticed that they, too, can drive.

VI

He had as little knowledge of artists, although he could claim to be one, as he had of artisans. If his men of reason are flabby, his artists are flabbier. They are highly emotional, always striking attitudes and making impotent gestures, and they display a tendency, in times of trouble, to wander about the streets in a sort of delirium, expounding at great length and with immense detail to the circum-ambient air the entire story of their troubles. Bosinney, the architect, in *A Man of Property*, who is also portrayed as Malise, the journalist, in the play, *The Fugitive*, is typical of them all. He has his author's sympathy, but it is hard to understand why. The man is inconsiderate and a bungler beyond belief. Why should Soames Forsyte be branded as a Philistine fool because, having commissioned Bosinney to design a house to cost £8,000, he complains on finding the cost carelessly increased to £12,000 ? Soames was comfortably off, but he was not rich enough to bear an unexpected expenditure of £4,000, and he was entitled to think himself seriously aggrieved by an architect so casual about his client's affairs, that he lets him in for a large sum of money without even informing him that he is to be let in. Bosinney, indeed, is a suburban miss's idea of an artist, a person who, one feel's sure, invests himself in the evening in a velvet coat, is indifferent to hours of meals and the convenience of other people, is disorderly in his personal

K

habits and untidy in his home, and floridly eloquent on
the need of the artist to express himself, by which he means
only that he may indulge any whim that comes into his
head, however upsetting and even disastrous it may be
to his neighbours. After Soames Forsyte enters an action
against Bosinney for breach of contract, Bosinney wanders
round the West End of London in a fever of emotion,
followed by George Forsyte, Soames' cousin; and as he
wanders through the fog, Bosinney, the readers are informed,
but have difficulty in believing, utters aloud the tale of
Irene's marital troubles. " George understood from those
mutterings that Soames had exercised his rights over an
estranged and unwilling wife in the greatest—the supreme
act of property." Gregory Vigil is equally emotional and
equally futile. He constantly clutches his forehead and
tilts his face towards the sky and adopts attitudes of despair
until one is impelled to cry out in protest against so much
posturing, so little common sense. Galsworthy, it seems,
had less perception of men and women than the careful
collection of details in his novels would cause one to suppose.
He saw the surface of things remarkably well, but seldom
saw beneath it.

VII

He had pity, but not affection, for mankind. He did
not love his fellow-creatures, but he was very sorry for
them. He was of that order of Liberals and humanitarians
who are eager to have ills removed so that they may not
themselves be perturbed by their presence. But, those
ills removed, he had no wish to have anything more to do
with mankind. That is a common characteristic of many
Liberals and humanitarians. They do not like human
beings : they are interested only in causes and in reforms
and improvements. They love mankind in the abstract
so much that when they contemplate mankind in the
concrete they lose their temper. They are repelled by
the joys of common people, and they abhor crowds. Black-
pool and Margate and Bangor and Rothesay are places of
which they cannot speak with sufficient scorn. They
loathe Hampstead Heath on a Bank Holiday. Their

single desire, when they find a place of beauty, is to keep it to themselves. It is no longer a place of beauty if they have to share it with other people. These morose solitaries will occasionally condescend to the crowd, always, however, with an effort and some distaste, but will never in any circumstances whatsoever be matey with it. " And the load of their loveless pity," as G. K. Chesterton says in *The Secret People*, " is worse than the ancient wrongs." An American author, Mr. J. Brooks Atkinson, in a charming work called *East of the Hudson*, remarks on the illiberalism of liberalism as a professed creed :

" It was intolerant of any part of you that did not fit its intellectual plan. As a conservative you still enjoyed personal freedom ; you could be as revolutionary as you pleased in regard to persons, politics or art. No one gave a damn. But as a liberal, you had to subscribe to the whole program, horn-rimmed and pince-nezed ; liberalism governed not only your political and economic tenets, but your reading, your playgoing, your week-ends and your friendships. There was no slack for the free play of mind or emotions. Liberalism had become more formal than conservatism ; it was plainer and more thin-skinned.

Nothing was more humiliating than the incompetence of the liberals in any natural circumstance. Ordinarily they led a fairly enjoyable life, quarrelling among themselves over the significance of dull books or the shallowness of entertaining ones and over the precise quality of stupidity in all public men. On the essential points they agreed ; they devoted their time to discussing the unessential ones intelligently. They were not up to the task of grappling with simple things.

During the Lindbergh carnival, for instance, *The New Republic* applied the old, tired formulas to a fresh public uprising. For the first time in my experience New York had surpassed itself in an expression of genuine enthusiasm for a lad who had not truckled once. So disinterested was the response, in fact, that those who had tried to commercialize it were lost in the festive fray. Even the scavengers who tried secretly to gossip about Lindbergh domesticities found themselves overwhelmed. For the public shouting had nothing to do with private misfortunes. It merely celebrated a beautiful action, dramatically performed and simply expressed.

Everyone in New York—even the dull people—saw the point. But the liberals, who had been disillusioned before, sat up late at night to protect their special privileges. Well, it was

hard and thankless labor. All *The New Republic* could find to say
was interesting but gratuitous : that the newspapers had erred
in their estimation of the numbers of the crowd, that New York
staged the celebration as a sort of nose-thumbing at Paris,
Brussels, London and Washington, and that ' every country,
every city, every business, every individual, and every cause
which saw an opportunity of exploiting his popularity had done
it to the best of their ability.'   Nothing about the common
exhilaration of the event ; nothing about a public expression of
feeling that needed no artful propaganda to achieve a release.
Nothing about the poetry of the flight. The intellectual formulas
that were so perfect in defining terms and discovering hidden
crises, always proved inadequate in a simple situation. Through
their inability to see a simple issue in terms of human action—
even when, as in the Sacco-Vanzetti case, every fact played into
their own hands—the liberals steadily lost caste and became as
superfluous as the statesmen, the capitalists and the buncomen
whom they regularly deplored."

Is that charge not justly delivered ?   John Galsworthy might
have pleaded guilty to it, despite his genuine kindness
of heart and of his generosity.   He would give money to a
man in need : he could not so easily give his hand.

VIII

He took immense pains to verify his statements of wrong,
even submitting his accounts of legal procedure to lawyers
to be vetted, although they did not always save him from
the censure of other lawyers, such as Sir Chartres Biron.
He visited prisons and studied penology very closely while
he was writing his tragic play, *Justice*, which, so it is said,
confirmed Mr. Winston Churchill in his intention to remove
some of the barbarity from our prison system.   In the
War, he financed an agency of relief in Austria, an endowment of which few people are aware.   It was not his
custom to let his benefactions be known.   But he carried
his emotions with him wherever he went, and allowed his
Pity to overwhelm his Reason.   On one occasion, while
visiting slaughter-houses in London, to collect information
for a series of articles on the use of the humane-killer, he
encountered a distinguished novelist in the Hampstead
Tube.   The novelist enquired what he was doing, and

Galsworthy replied, " I'm doing a strange thing. I'm visiting all the slaughter-houses ! . . . " He then explained the purpose of his visits. " Do you know," he said, " that every sheep that is killed suffers half a minute more pain than it need. Multiply all those needless half-minutes of pain by the number of sheep that are slaughtered, and you have a lifetime of agony ! " To which the novelist replied, " No, my dear Galsworthy, you haven't. Each sheep suffers half a minute of needless pain. That is all ! " In that scrap of dialogue, the quality and defect of Galsworthy are apparent. He was always imagining that individual experience could be multiplied into crowd experience, and that the multiplied misery which he imagined to be felt by the crowd was also the extent of the individual's misery. He sentimentalised and was lost. His most direct suggestion of reform was made through the mouth of Michael Mont in *The Silver Spoon,* when he pleads for " Foggartism," a system of solving the population and poverty problem by exporting children to the Antipodes, something after the fashion associated with the famous Fairbridge Farm School in Western Australia which was founded by the late Kingsley Fairbridge, the model, perhaps, for Galsworthy's Sir James Foggart. Michael, unabashed by the failure of his advocacy of Foggartism, later turned his attention to housing ! . . . Such schemes as these were as far as Galsworthy went. It was not his business to create : his business was to criticise and to call attention to wrong ; and that, as best he could, he did. But his heart, though it was gentle and good and well-bestowed, had no hope of any betterment. " The conviction that the forces of the universe are beyond our knowing seems to persist throughout the earlier works," says Mr. Hermon Ould in his book, *John Galsworthy.*

" It is mockery to talk of justice. There is no justice for men, for they are forever in the dark. Small, of no import ; insects to be crushed and made an end of when the machine comes full circle. The blackness of this pessimism, not laboured, is not dispelled by *Fraternity,* the book which followed *The Man of Property.* Determinism still colours the author's thought. We are like flies caught among the impalpable and smoky threads of cobwebs ; so men struggle in the webs of their own natures, giving here a start, there a pitiful small jerking, long sustained, and tailing into existence . . ."

So does Mr. Ould interpret Galsworthy's belief. But if that was his belief, and, indeed, it seemed to be, he denied it by his own actions, for he constantly strove to obtain that justice for men which he thought was unobtainable. Why should anyone attempt to obtain what he believes to be non-existent ? Were Galsworthy's mind and emotions in a state of confusion ? Or was he so sentimental that he could not act on his own belief and let the world, so far as he was concerned, peter out ? The Forsytes, in the *Saga*, dwindle and diminish. All their strength was in those of them that their chronicler least esteemed, the tough old men who had a strong sense of property and worked hard for the increase of their possessions. The later Forsytes, living on rent or interest, lost their vitality and dribbled away to nothing. The *Saga* is a tale of a drooping family that grows thinner and weaker with each generation, until, at last, as their chronicler himself weakens and comes near to his death, the whole family seems to collapse. In the last year or two of his life, John Galsworthy visibly faded. His hands and face aged and became drawn and tired, and his fine, candid eyes lost their brightness. He had had enough. By a singular irony of fate, he, who was extremely sensitive and full of emotion, so that he had continually to clench his fists and button up his lips lest he should betray his feelings, came to be regarded as an example of the cold and self-contained Englishman. The legend of the cold, unemotional and reserved Englishman will not easily die, yet what legend is so little related to the facts ? Neither the aristocracy nor the working-class at any time in English history have been reluctant to reveal their feelings, and our statesmen, even in our own time, weep well and easily. Our literature is full of emotional outbursts and displays of warm feeling. Elizabethans, apparently, saw nothing unmanly in Romeo's tears and frantic griefs, nor were they embarrassed when the young lover flung himself on the ground and rolled about the floor in distress. They did not attribute his uncontrolled emotion to the fact that he was a foreigner. Galsworthy had all the Englishman's emotional quality, but he endeavoured to conceal it, lest it should be used as evidence against him. He would have done better to show it and accept the consequences. Bigger than his books and plays, he was innately noble, a kind and generous man, with a heart that never failed to beat in sympathy for suffering men and women, even although, in the depths of his mind, he regarded them as lost. He could scarcely be called a democrat, since he had no faith in the average man's ability to make himself better, or in the essential sanity of the crowd, and was assured that we should all be much better dead. But it is hard to know what he could be called, since he had little or no faith in any other form of government. He pitied people too much to have any belief in their power to look after themselves, and he seemed to think that we were making the worst of a bad job. In his despair, he said, " Let's be as kind as we can," and left life at that. The vague young clergyman in *A Bit o' Love* says that we must go on and on until we love every living thing, and that, apparently, was the sum of Galsworthy's own belief. But it is a counsel of sentimental despair. We cannot love every living thing, because every living thing is not lovable. *That* motive for living is the poorest of all, since it invites us to work for a world inhabited only by those we like, a world which is an extension of our own personality, a reflection of our own ego. But of what use is a world of echoes, a world of prolonged repetitions, a world which is a vast Hall of Mirrors in which we see ourselves endlessly reflected ? If there is any virtue in democracy, that virtue lies in its unending diversity. " In My Father's house are many mansions," and the mansions, we may believe, are of many shapes and sizes. If Galsworthy had pitied people less and liked them more, he would have been a greater man. But he could not like them : he could only be sorry for them.

WILLIAM EWART GLADSTONE

1809–1898

by RAMSAY MUIR

к*

WILLIAM EWART GLADSTONE

1809–1898

by RAMSAY MUIR

I

GLADSTONE'S long political career covered the whole of the nineteenth century transition from oligarchy to democracy. He was born in 1809, when the proud Tory aristocracy of England was engaged in a death-grapple with Napoleon, and with all the revolutionary ideas he represented. The son of a rich Liverpool merchant who owned slave-worked plantations in the West Indies, he was educated at Eton and Christ Church in an atmosphere of high Toryism, and was early absorbed in the High Church movement, which regarded with abhorrence the ideals of Liberalism. He came of age in 1830, when the agitation for the great Reform Bill was beginning. He entered the reformed Parliament in 1832, as Tory member for Newark, which was (in spite of the Bill) practically a pocket-borough of the Duke of Newcastle. Some of his first speeches—on the abolition of slavery in 1833—were made in defence of his father's slave-property. His absorption in an almost mediæval conception of the relations of Church and State made him appear a natural and instinctive Tory reactionary—in Macaulay's overworked phrase (without which no essay on Gladstone would be complete) he was " the rising hope of the stern unbending Tories."

The career which began in this way covered sixty-three continuous years in Parliament; and between the age of thirty-three, when he first held office as Vice-President of the Board of Trade, and eighty-six, when he took farewell of his last Cabinet, he held high office for no less than twenty-seven years, more than ten of them as Chancellor of the Exchequer, and more than twelve as Prime Minister. In the last twenty or thirty years of his life he was regarded, not only in England, but throughout Europe, and indeed throughout the world, as the supreme spokesman and representative of Liberalism, of democracy, of pacifism,

and of political idealism.   He was as much the protagonist
of these ideals as his great contemporary Bismarck was of
the rival creed of authority, militarism and *realpolitik*.

The astonishing transition from the High Church Toryism
of 1830 to the advanced Radicalism of 1890 was in some
sense an echo of the change that was passing over the
outlook of Britain and of Europe ; and Gladstone was in
many ways one of the most representative figures of the
nineteenth century.   But the surprising thing about this
remarkable intellectual pilgrimage is that Gladstone never
underwent any sudden political conversion.   He never
" crossed the floor," in the sense of deliberately transferring
his allegiance from one political party to another.   He was
never a theorist : he was not one of those who form a theory
of the way in which the state ought to be constituted, and
then devote themselves to bringing it, as far as possible,
to realisation.   Like his master, Peel, he never made up
his mind about the way in which a problem ought to be
solved until he was brought up against it in practice.   He
was an empiric, not a doctrinaire.   " It has been experience
which has altered my politics," he said himself—experience,
not theory.   His business through life was, in his own
phrase, " to work the institutions of his country," not to
theorise about them ; and he confessed that he had never
been able " to adjust the proper conditions of handling
any difficult question until the question itself was at the
door."

This habit of mind explains, among other things,
the ambiguous and evasive forms of speech to which he
was prone.   Challenged, as all politicians are apt to be, to
express his judgment upon subjects on which he had not
yet reached a definite conclusion, he drew upon his immense
command of language to wrap the matter up in a way that
seemed to give an answer, yet left sufficient loopholes.
But when he did face up to a problem, he never ran away
from, or attempted to conceal or to compromise, the conclusions to which his powerful intellect and his unflagging
industry led him.

The guiding principle of his life was the profound
religious belief which was his anchor.   This it was which
made him a Tory ; but this it was, also, that later made

him a Liberal. For his own belief was so real and so important to him that he presently found it unendurable to interfere with the beliefs of others. And as the essential root of his Christianity was a belief in the equal value of all human souls in the sight of God, it was natural that he should become a democrat.

Although his passage from one attitude of mind to the other was so gradual as to be almost insensible, it is possible to trace the course of the change, which was most rapid in the ten years following 1841. In that year Peel, when forming his great ministry, with uncanny insight chose the young ecclesiologist for what seemed the singularly inappropriate office of Vice-President of the Board of Trade, and gave him the exacting task of working out the details of the fiscal changes which he had taken in hand. Gladstone had always hitherto accepted the traditional Tory and Protectionist view. He threw himself with all his intellectual power and all his industry into this new field; and emerged a convinced and uncompromising Free Trader. Throughout his life this was one of the subjects on which he never wavered, and was never ambiguous. It was to be his task, as Chancellor of the Exchequer under Aberdeen and Palmerston, to complete the work which Peel had begun.

This was the first great breach with his Tory traditions, and it loosened the whole structure. When the Conservative party was broken by the repeal of the Corn Laws, Gladstone naturally followed his leader, Peel; and for some years he and his fellow Peelites occupied a detached position, considering themselves to be still Conservatives, though for the preservation of Free Trade they supported a Whig government. In these years of detachment from strict party allegiance, Gladstone's outlook changed rapidly. In the years 1850 and 1851, in particular, he is found expressing opinions on religious freedom, on colonial government, on the misgovernment of the continental despotisms, on Ireland, which show a rapid departure from the standpoint of his youth. By 1851 he was already a Liberal, though he scarcely recognised the fact. Perhaps the best expression of the changed direction of his thinking was given in a letter on church questions to the Bishop of Aberdeen (1851). " I am deeply convinced," wrote this

quondam Tory, " that all systems, whether religious or
political, which rest on a principle of absolutism, must of
necessity be feeble and ineffective systems ; and that
methodically to enlist the members of a community in the
performance of its public duties is the way to make that
community powerful and heathful." The essential idea
of democracy is implicit in this sentence. The man who
wrote it was manifestly a Liberal. He had rejected Authority
for Liberty as his guide. Long afterwards, looking back
at his life, he recognised that this was his fundamental
change. " I was brought up to distrust and dislike liberty,
I learned to believe in it. That is the key to all my changes."

From the detached position of the Peelites it was an
easy transition, through the Peelite-Liberal coalition under
Aberdeen, to the Liberalism of Palmerston. Under the
Palmerston régime, indeed, Gladstone found himself
far more Liberal than his chief and than most of his
colleagues. His succession to the leadership of the Liberal
Party after Palmerston and Russell has often been
regarded, indeed, as marking the transition from
Whiggism to Liberalism. Whatever else he was, Gladstone
was never a Whig : the cool and compromising Whig
temper was not for him. If he was often slow to make up
his mind on a subject, he was all ardour once his mind was
made up.

II

Gladstone has often been described as an apostle of pure
individualism and of *laissez-faire*. It is true that his
enthusiasm for Free Trade brought him into close alliance
with Cobden, Bright and the Manchester School of Liberals,
who were always a small minority within the Liberal Party,
But unqualified individualism was far too doctrinaire a
creed ever to capture him. At the end of his life he claimed
that under his leadership the Liberal Party had never been
identified with *laissez-faire*; and the claim was justified.

This supposed devotee of individualism was actually the
first English publicist to advocate the nationalisation of the
railway system, as the best means of ensuring that this
new method of transport should be scientifically organised

on a " national plan." This was in 1843 ; and when he failed to win acceptance for this view, he worked out, in the Railways Act of 1844, a system of State regulation of the railways, whereby they were required to publish their accounts in great detail, as a safeguard against abuse, while the State reserved the right of fixing railway rates and fares, exercising this right through the Railway and Canals Commission. This was a method of regulating monopolies or quasi-monopolies, through publicity of accounts and a reserve power of fixing prices, which might well be applied to other monopolies ; but nobody has ever ventured upon so bold an experiment.

Gladstone's Irish Land Acts, again, which gave fixity of tenure to the tenant, and provided for the determination of fair rents by the courts, was an exceedingly bold departure from the theory of free contract. At the end of his life, he faced, for the first time seriously, the land problem in England. His conclusions were that the labourer must be given land ; that to this end landlords must, where necessary, be expropriated by the State ; and that, if land nationalisation became necessary, it must not be ruled out on merely theoretical grounds.

Of this supposedly *laissez-faire* politician a commentator in the *Spectator*, writing in 1864, when the ascendancy of *laissez-faire* ideas was highest, observed that " Mr. Gladstone does not hesitate to apply the full powers of the State to ameliorate social anomalies, as he showed by creating State banks, State insurance offices, and State annuities for the very poor." To-day he would assuredly have been an ardent Social Reformer ; but he could never have adopted a theory so abstract and doctrinaire as Socialism.

It is true that Gladstone shared the reluctance of his contemporaries to bring about any sweeping enlargement of the powers of the State over the individual. But he never erected this distrust into a principle ; he examined every question on its merits, when it was forced upon his attention ; and if his powerful intelligence told him that direct State action offered the best means of dealing with a difficulty, he had no hesitation in calling it into play. The notion that Gladstone was a devotee of *laissez-faire* is as false as any other sweeping generalisation about this great empiric.

Unhampered by an abstract theory as to the proper constitution of Society, he grappled with one problem after
another as it presented itself, guided only by a growing
ardour for liberty, and a deepening sense of what liberty
implies.

III

It is not possible to measure or to value the contribution
made by Gladstone to the transformation of British social
life which took place during his lifetime. This generation
is apt to undervalue it, being engrossed in the process of
economic reconstruction, in which Gladstone's activity
was perhaps least felt. Anything like a narrative of his long
career would be wholly out of place in a short essay such
as this : even an analysis of the principal measures of the
three main governments over which he presided could be
no more than a bald and *jejune* catalogue. We shall obtain
a clearer idea of his achievement by surveying in turn the
main spheres in which his work attained important results.

His own contemporaries thought of him primarily as
a great master of public finance ; but our post-war ideas
about public finance have undergone so great a change that
the Gladstonian tradition in this sphere has become for many
a subject of scoffing. His first object as a financier was to
reduce government expenditure to a minimum, to keep
down the level of taxation, and to leave as much as possible
of the total earnings of the nation " to fructify in the pockets
of the citizens." The post-war generation has adopted
very different views. We have become accustomed to
gigantic expenditures. The State has assumed huge and
costly new functions of social service which had not been
thought of in Gladstone's time. Taxation has been used
as a means of reducing inequalities of wealth. There are
many who hold that the State can use the national income
better than individuals ; and, almost without a qualm,
we have seen State expenditure expand until it engrosses
nearly one-third of the total earnings of the nation. We
think nothing of spending £5 millions here and £10 millions
there on subsidies to particular interests at the cost of the
community at large. Amid all this lavishness the meticulous

watchfulness of Gladstone to prevent all waste has come
to seem almost absurd. We shall probably never return
to his hatred of any unnecessary extension of public
expenditure. But a revival of his anxious parsimony about
the use of public money, his determination not to spend
a penny without being sure of getting at least a penny's
worth, his feeling that the obligations of a public financier
were even more sacred than those of a private trustee,
his hatred of the waste of public money as a crime, his
insistence that the Treasury must always be a watch-dog
over the spending proclivities of the other departments of
State—a revival of these methods and of this spirit would
be of infinite benefit ; and it is certainly one of the elements
of Gladstone's greatness that by unwearied labour he
succeeded in establishing this standard.

Gladstone's supreme achievement in the financial sphere
was the perfecting of the system of Free Trade. A generation which has abandoned Free Trade, and convinced
itself that all countries can make themselves richer by
refusing to buy one another's goods, is not likely to value
this achievement highly. Free Trade did not create the
manufacturing supremacy of Britain, which was due largely
to other causes ; but for nearly half a century it enlarged
and strengthened this supremacy, and, when the inevitable
challenge came, it enabled British manufacturers to hold their
own and more, by making available to them unlimited
supplies of all their requirements at the lowest price, and thus
enabling them to compete on favourable terms with the
manufacturers of other countries who were penalised by
the taxation of their requirements. It secured for the
working-people of Britain the highest standard of living
of any country in the world ; for the comparative figures
worked out by the League of Nations show that (apart
from new countries with unexhausted resources) the real
level of wages is highest where tariffs are lowest, and lowest
where tariffs are highest. It turned Britain into the world's
central market, where the products of all the earth could be
obtained, by home and foreign buyers, at the lowest prices.
It made Britain the great carrier of the world's goods, the
owner of more than half of the world's shipping, so great
was the inward and outward stream of goods to and from

her harbours. It gave to Britain the main share in financing the movement of world-trade, because she was the world's central market ; and bills on London became the principal currency of international traffic. It made Britain the chief banking and insurance centre of the world, and, in effect, the manager of the world's monetary system. It made Britain the principal purveyor of capital for the development of the world's undeveloped resources ; she was able to perform this immensely valuable function because, under Free Trade, she readily accepted payment of the obligations due to her in the products of the debtor countries ; and in return she naturally enjoyed a very great advantage in the markets of these countries. The time will come—perhaps it is even now arriving—when these benefits of the system with which Gladstone was peculiarly identified will not seem so contemptible as they are now held to be.

Like Cobden, Gladstone hoped that the whole world would see the wisdom of a Free Trade policy ; and would by its means be welded together in a great partnership of mutual advantage which would banish war from the face of the earth. In the sixties it seemed as if this hope would be realised. It was killed by the nationalist venom sown by the Franco-Prussian war. But Gladstone's belief in this system was no more dependent than Cobden's upon its being universally adopted. As a Free Trade country in a Protectionist world, Britain was not so happy as she would have been in a Free Trade world ; but she was happier and more prosperous than she would have been as a Protectionist country in a Protectionist world, wherein trade is regarded not as an exchange of mutual benefit but as a form of warfare.

To Gladstone the moral aspect of a political problem always counted for more than its material aspect ; and he would have been a Free Trader on moral grounds, if on no other. Being a Christian, he wanted Britain to do unto other countries as she would like them to do unto her. This was, in truth, the keynote of his foreign policy, as we shall see. In trade matters, we should like other countries to give free entry to our goods. If all countries acted on the Golden Rule—which is, when all is said, the only sound rule of life—universal Free Trade would be established to-morrow. They all prefer to wait for the others. Gladstone and Cobden saw that the Golden Rule is, in trade matters, not only sound morals, but good business. This generation, having persuaded itself, on very inadequate grounds, that it may possibly not be good business, has scrapped it without regard to its moral aspect.

One further aspect of Gladstone's financial policy deserves mention, especially in considering him as a great democrat. When he began his political life, the bulk of the national revenue was raised by indirect taxation, covering almost the whole range of articles of consumption. The burden therefore fell with disproportionate severity upon the poor. The whole tendency of Gladstone's finance was to abandon taxes upon articles of common consumption, with the exception of a few semi-luxuries such as tobacco, beer and spirits, and tea. A large part of the burden was transferred to direct taxation, which is proportioned to the means of the taxpayer. This change was to be carried much further in the generation after Gladstone's death ; but it may fairly be claimed that he, following Peel, began the process whereby the burden of taxation has been more and more transferred from the necessities of the many to the superfluity of the few. The process has now been reversed.

IV

We may next turn to consider the part which Gladstone played in democratising the institutions of the country. So long as Palmerston lived, no advance beyond the system of middle-class government established in 1832 was practicable. Indeed, there was no very loud demand for a change in that period of complacent prosperity, as John Bright found when he tried to awaken the country to a demand for a more democratic franchise. Before Palmerston's death, however, Gladstone had definitely committed himself to the democratic position, in a characteristic sentence : " Every man who is not presumably incapacitated by some consideration of personal unfitness or of political danger is morally entitled to come within the pale of the constitution." It will be observed that the sentence is by no means an uncompromising declaration for universal suffrage—which then existed only in France, and had been the means of establishing the dictatorship of Napoleon III. As usual, it left loopholes. But it did imply a substantial enlargement of the limited franchise of 1832. The Bill of 1866, which was defeated by a revolt of timid Whigs, was its outcome. This failure gave his chance to Disraeli, who "dished the Whigs" by introducing the Bill of 1867, in the hope of winning for his party the allegiance of the new electorate. But this Bill, as it emerged from the House of Commons, was quite as much the work of Gladstone as of Disraeli : it was Gladstone who got rid of the "fancy franchises" and other safeguards with which Disraeli had qualified the concession to democracy. For the later Reform Act of 1884, with its corollary, the Re-distribution Act which established the single-member constituency, Gladstone was directly responsible. Thus the democratic franchise with which Britain entered the twentieth century was predominately the work of the statesman who had begun his career as a fierce opponent of the first Reform Act of 1832. With these measures must be linked the Ballot Act of 1870, which was intended to put an end to the influencing of the voters by fear or favour, and the Corrupt Practices Act of 1880, which made bribery at least dangerous. Thus the electoral system of the pre-war period was mainly the work of Gladstone's governments.

As for the House of Lords, Gladstone's innate Conservatism, and his reluctance to raise any issue before it became practically necessary to do so, made him tolerant of its survival. He put on the soft pedal when some of his followers, in 1884, were for starting a campaign to "mend or end" the hereditary chamber. In truth, the House of Lords had wielded its powers with great moderation during the half-century following 1832. But after the Home Rule split of the eighties, when the Whig peers who had hitherto been loyal to Liberalism swung over to the other side, the House of Lords became bolder, and in Gladstone's last ministry (1892-4) rejected every important measure sent up from the House of Commons. This at last convinced Gladstone that a hereditary second chamber was an anomaly in a democratic system ; and it was with difficulty that the old warrior of 85 was restrained by his cooler-headed colleagues from setting forth upon a campaign against the House of Lords.

Not less important—perhaps more important—than the changes for which Gladstone was responsible in the structure of Parliament was his contribution to the purification and improvement of the Civil Service. He was primarily responsible for the system whereby posts in the public offices are filled by a Civil Service Commission, independent of parties, and selecting its nominees by competitive examination. Before these reforms were made (1855) Civil Service posts were filled by nomination, and as each party looked forward to rewarding its supporters by these means, neither party was willing to change the system : " a certain amount of corruption and inefficiency," it was said, " was the price that had to be paid for representative government." In just the same way, party managers to-day are reluctant to carry out a reform of the electoral system, because each hopes to have the luck of the gamble in a future election. With this sort of argument Gladstone had no patience. Once he had made up his mind that a certain course of action was right, no consideration of this kind could have any weight with him ; and he put through a reform which everybody agreed to be desirable, but which nobody was willing to undertake. It is scarcely possible to exaggerate the importance, for a democratic system, of an uncorrupt and efficient Civil Service, such as we possess in this country, thanks largely to Gladstone. Without it, the great enlargement of State activities which has taken place since his time would have been impossible.

Again, democracy needs for its efficient working not only a free but a cheap press : Gladstone's struggle with the House of Lords over the " taxes on knowledge " made this possible. Nor is democracy in any real sense possible without a general system of education : the Education Act of 1870, for which Gladstone's first ministry was responsible, created such a system for the first time. Finally, before democracy could be made real, old established privileges of class and sect had to be finally swept away. The Army, a stronghold of privilege, was at least partially democratised by Gladstone's War Minister in his first government, Lord

Cardwell, particularly by the abolition of the purchase of commissions. And no one played a greater part in the overthrow of sectarian privileges than this High Churchman, once a zealot for a mediæval conception of the relations between Church and State. He had a great part in the removal of Jewish disabilities ; he helped to destroy the religious tests which barred a University career to Dissenters ; he made it possible for the atheist Bradlaugh, whose opinions he detested, to take his place in the House of Commons ; and, by the Disestablishment of the Irish Church, he destroyed the privileges of his own Church when these privileges were identified with injustice.

Gladstone was not a theoretical democrat ; he thought of democracy largely as the machinery through which the ablest men might find their way to power without regard to class or wealth—as the means, in short, to the creation of a true aristocracy ; and, taking this view, he had no doctrinaire belief in the equal right of everybody to a vote. But by twice enlarging the franchise, by introducing the ballot, by creating the machinery of popular education, by facilitating the growth of a cheap press, and by waging war against privileges of class and sect, he did more than any other man to make democracy in Britain possible and real.

V

In his own lifetime, Gladstone's foreign policy was regarded, even by many of his own followers, as the weakest side of his statesmanship. To-day it may well be regarded as his greatest title to honour and remembrance ; and this though he was never Foreign Secretary, never negotiated a great treaty, and never took part in an international conference. For he was the promulgator of a new conception of foreign policy, which sought primarily not for national prestige, but for international justice and peace.

In the famous debate on the Don Pacifico case in 1850, in which Palmerston's high-handed treatment of Greece was unsuccessfully arraigned from many different points of view, Gladstone spoke rather as what we now call " a good European " than as a flamboyant " patriot." " Let us do as we would be done by : let us pay all the respect to a feeble State and to the infancy of free institutions [in Greece] which we should desire and exact from others towards their authority and strength." The Golden Rule as the foundation of international relations ! Is that a wholly impracticable dream, as it seemed to Gladstone's contemporaries ? Some approximation to it, as we now know, is the only possible foundation for international peace, perhaps the only means of saving civilisation from ruin.

During the years before he became Prime Minister and assumed a more direct responsibility for foreign policy, Gladstone's interventions in foreign affairs were invariably inspired by a desire to protect the weak and the oppressed. His vehement protests against the tyranny of the Bourbons in Naples gave an immense stimulus to the Italian *risorgimento*. At every stage in the development of Italian unity, his voice was heard on the side of those who were struggling to throw off ancient tyrannies. Sent out as Commissioner for the Ionian Islands (which had been occupied by Britain since the Napoleonic War) he was responsible for the transfer of these islands to Greece—the only instance in which a Great Power has voluntarily transferred territory to a small Power without asking for any consideration in return.

In his first ministry (1868–74) two important episodes illustrated the spirit of his international policy. The first was the reference to arbitration of the exaggerated claims of the United States for compensation for the damage done by the *Alabama*, and the payment of the very excessive damages awarded. This was the greatest triumph for arbitration as a method of settling international differences that had yet been seen. It was a recognition of the necessity of substituting law for force. Gladstone was sharply criticised for accepting the award, as a lowering of British prestige. His critics would apparently have thought it more patriotic to spend ten times the money, and thousands of lives, in upholding national prestige.

The second episode was the prompt action which was taken to safeguard the neutrality of Belgium when the war between France and Prussia broke out. The two belligerents were challenged to give a pledge that they would observe the neutrality of Belgium. Both of them gave the pledge, and observed it. But if they had failed to do so, Gladstone, much as he hated war, would have thrown the strength of Britain into the field against the aggressor. He would have been ready to fight for the defence of international law, and for the protection of the weak against aggressive strength.

The most noteworthy illustration of Gladstone's courage and originality in the sphere of foreign affairs was afforded by the famous Midlothian campaign. For a century past, the traditional foreign policy of Britain had been to uphold Turkey against Russia; Gladstone himself had been a member of the Government which had fought the Crimean War for this purpose. Revolts against the Turkish authority broke out in various parts of the Balkan peninsula. They were suppressed, especially in Bulgaria, with more than customary ferocity. This brought on a war between Russia and Turkey, in which a complete collapse of the Turkish Empire seemed to be imminent. Russia forced a treaty upon Turkey which would have freed all the Christian peoples in the Balkans from Turkish control. Thereupon the Great Powers intervened : the Balance of Power was being disturbed, and Russia was becoming too strong. Austria made an agreement with Russia whereby as the price of abstaining from war she took the province of Bosnia. Britain—now under the government of Disraeli— pursued the traditional policy of supporting Turkey against Russia, and obtained from Turkey the island of Cyprus as the price of her support. For a moment war between Britain and Russia seemed imminent. There was a Conference at Berlin, in which the Russo-Turkish treaty was revised in a sense favourable to Turkey; and Disraeli returned from the conference in triumph, bringing " peace with honour."

All this was in accord with the normal traditions of European diplomacy. There seemed no reason why Gladstone should intervene. He had retired from the leadership of his party in 1874. His former colleagues were for the most part quite content with what Disraeli had done. They were exasperated by Gladstone's intervention. But Gladstone was in a state of flaming indignation. For him the issue was not a question of Balance of Power ;

it was a question of right and wrong. The Bulgarian Atrocities had stirred all his hatred of oppression. The Power that was guilty of them had no right to exercise sovereignty over subject peoples. The Great Powers, instead of bargaining for their own advantage, ought to have united to free the Balkan people from the iniquity of Turkish rule, and to clear the Turk "bag and baggage" out of Europe. It was intolerable that Britain should constitute herself the protector of Turkey, and still more that she should acquire territory as the price of doing so. There could be neither peace nor justice in the world so long as international politics were conducted upon such principles.

Single-handed he started out upon a crusade against this kind of politics, at first with articles and pamphlets, then in the famous Midlothian campaign, and in wayside speeches at every railway station. This expedition of his at the age of nearly seventy was the most heroic enterprise in Gladstone's career. He faced unpopularity, the anger of the London mob, the chill disapproval of his own colleagues. Single-handed, he changed the course of British policy. He appealed to the moral sense of the people. He went behind Parliament to the nation. The Liberal victory in the election of 1880 was directly due to the spirit which he aroused. Events proved that he was right. Disraeli's "peace with honour" lasted for only a few years. Lord Salisbury, who had been engaged in the negotiations, later admitted that "we had put our money on the wrong horse." If the course which Gladstone advocated had been adopted, peace might have been created in the Balkans, instead of the seeds of future wars ; the results of the Balkan wars of 1912–13 might have been anticipated ; the incessant Balkan unrest which kept Europe in disturbance and ultimately led to the Great War might have been conjured away.

These remote calculations were not in Gladstone's mind. He was concerned only with what seemed to him a broad issue of right and wrong. But it was a novelty that such standards should be applied to international politics ; to the majority of practical politicians, Gladstone seemed to have become the prey of sentimental idealism. By being

" practical " and realistic, they had lost the chance of bringing peace in the most vexed region of Europe ; just as they have to-day lost the chance of making the League of Nations a reality.

In the course of this great campaign, Gladstone defined what seemed to him the true principles of British foreign policy, in a speech at West Calder, delivered to a small gathering of Scottish farmers, miners and labourers. He laid down six principles, of which the first was that the supreme interest of the nation was the maintenance of peace. By peace he meant much more than mere abstention from war ; he meant co-operation with other countries to maintain a system of peace throughout the world. Gladstone was no absolute pacifist ; as we have seen, he was ready to fight if need be for the defence of the " law of nations," as in the case of Belgium. The second principle was that peace can only be maintained by an organised co-operation of nations, through the concert of Europe, which was then the only possible organ of international co-operation ; but a League of all Nations for the preservation of peace would have been the true expression of what was in Gladstone's mind. The third principle was that Britain ought to avoid all specific alliances or entanglements such as we had been involved in with Turkey ; our only engagements should be with the whole Concert of Powers, not with any group of them. The fourth principle was that in this co-operation the influence of Britain should always be used for the extension of liberty ; the fifth that we should recognise that we have no right to dictate to the world the course to be pursued, but that joint action must be based upon real consultation ; and the sixth that in this consultation all nations ought to be treated as equals— not equals, of course, in power, but equals in the right to be consulted.

Here is a statement of policy more lofty, more clear-sighted, more noble than anything that had yet been heard in the discussion of international affairs. It was, in effect, an anticipation of the ideals and system of the League of Nations. It was the counterpart, in the political sphere, of Free Trade in the economic sphere. It was an attempt to base international politics upon the Golden Rule ; an

attempt to substitute discussion for dictation, and reason
for force, and thus to extend the essential principle of
democracy to the international sphere. In adopting this
attitude, Gladstone was far ahead of his time. He was a
prophet of the future. No one can doubt what would have
been his attitude on the problems of to-day. If that high
courage and zeal had been enlisted in its support—if the
British Government could have spoken with the voice of
Gladstone—the League of Nations and the world's peace
would to-day be in a very different position.

VI

Nothing has yet been said about Ireland. Yet Ireland
was, during more than half of his life, from 1850 to the
end, one of his chief preoccupations, and at the end his
supreme concern. It was in 1850 that he was first fired
by a realisation of the intolerable injustices that had been
inflicted upon the Irish people during three centuries, and
of the necessity of redressing them. A sudden outburst
in a letter to his wife in 1850 shows how the theme had
already taken hold of his imagination. " Ireland ! Ireland !
That cloud in the west, that coming storm, the minister
of God's retribution upon cruel and inveterate and but
half-atoned injustice."

Irish measures dominated his first ministry (1868–74),
which disestablished the Irish Church, introduced an Irish
Land Bill, and tried to deal with the Irish University
problem. In his second ministry (1880–1885), which was
distracted by so many difficulties in Egypt, in South Africa,
in India, Ireland still dominated the scene : the Irish
members under Parnell were making Parliamentary
government unworkable ; the Land League was bringing
chaos in Ireland itself ; the murder campaign, and especially
the murder of Lord Frederick Cavendish, was making it
more and more difficult to maintain order. Gladstone did
not allow himself to be deflected by these things. Outrages,
disorder, obstruction were themselves the products of
injustice, and the more troublesome they became, the
clearer became the need for reforming measures. The

new Land Bill of 1881 prepared the way for the destruction of landlordism in Ireland. The failure of coercion prepared the way for the conclusion that self-government alone could restore peace. Once converted to this view by the logic of events, Gladstone never wavered. He broke his party ; he lost many of his dearest friends ; he was the object of insults and of envenomed hatred. Nothing could bend him. In the records of Parliament is there any episode more heroic than that of the great fight for a lost cause when the second Home Rule Bill was introduced in 1892, and the unconquerable old man of eighty-four fought on through all-night sittings, never sparing himself in a cause that he believed to be the cause of justice ? He was defeated in his last great fight—the only cause he had ever espoused in which his steadfast courage did not in the end win victory. Is there anybody to-day who does not recognise that he was right, who does not know that if he could have carried his proposals through, Ireland and Britain and the British Empire would have been saved from many miseries ? This was a noble end to a noble career.

VII

It has been said that the inspiration and interest of British politics in the days of Disraeli and Gladstone sprang from the fact that Disraeli had brought romance into politics, and that Gladstone had brought religion and the quest of righteousness into politics. There is truth in this saying. There is truth also in the saying that Gladstone had a way of reducing the most complicated and debatable issues into simple questions of right and wrong. No doubt he often over-simplified the issue. He laid himself open to the charges of hypocrisy and of self-righteousness, which were often levelled against him. There have been few public men immersed in the often sordid business of politics with whom the moral issue has so completely dominated all calculations of material interest. This was, in truth, his greatest contribution to the building up of a democratic system. It was the secret of the devotion he inspired in half the nation, as of the contempt which he aroused among those who believe that the open profession of high moral aims must always be hypocritical. But the kind of leadership he gave was the kind of leadership which democracy needs. Spurgeon expressed the view of millions when he wrote to Gladstone in 1882 : " You do not know how those of us regard you who feel it a joy to live when a Premier believes in righteousness. We believe in no man's infallibility, but it is restful to be sure of one man's integrity." And the more one studies the records of this full and active life, the more one feels that, amid all its shortcomings, these are its outstanding notes : integrity, and a passion for righteousness. Could there be greater gifts to democracy ?

WILLIAM GODWIN
1756–1836
by H. N. BRAILSFORD

WILLIAM GODWIN
1756–1836
by H. N. BRAILSFORD

WILLIAM GODWIN enjoys in our day a parasitic immortality. Two women keep his name alive, for he was the husband of Mary Wollstonecraft and the father of Mary Shelley. Everyone has read of Godwin's money debts to Shelley, while only the few realise Shelley's intellectual debt to Godwin. The oblivion that has fallen on him as a thinker does injustice to a powerful and daring intellect ; worse still, it renders unintelligible one of the most stirring chapters in the history of English literature and thought. Tom Paine was the knight-errant of the democratic revolution that had made the United States and re-made France. He was also the pamphleteer who brought to the masses of the people the practical conclusions of its "philosophy"—its republicanism, its humane programme of social change, its militant Deism. But Paine was fighter rather than systematic thinker, and it was chiefly the studious weaver and the reflective cobbler who cherished his vivacious books on their meagre shelves. Godwin, on the other hand, was the prophet of the revolutionary "intelligentsia." To him they turned, when the fury of Burke or the gloom of Malthus oppressed their minds. Two generations of poets drew from him their first views of life and society. He sent Wordsworth as a revolutionary pilgrim to France. Southey and Coleridge planned the foundation in America of a "pantisocratic" community based on his prescriptions. Shelley, reading him first at Eton, re-read him every year of his life, and some of his earlier poems contain passages that are merely Godwin versified. It was from this sage —for youth looked up to him with veneration—that the progressive fraction of English society, in the last years of the eighteenth century and the first years of the nineteenth, derived its knowledge of the French "philosophy" of the Encyclopaedists. This industrious student had digested it all, from Voltaire to Condorcet. But he was

much more than a skilled interpreter.   He englished it by
giving to it a characteristically ethical turn.   He built it,
moreover, into a system more solid and comprehensive than
any of his French predecessors had attempted or achieved.
He lacked, what some of them possessed to excess, a sense
of humour, and thanks to this precious deficiency he carried
their premises remorselessly to their logical conclusion,
and by so doing blew up the erection he had raised with
such ambitious care.   He made explicit the anarchism that
lies latent in individualistic liberalism.   His writing was
always lucid and often eloquent, at first in an elaborate
periodic style that recalls Gibbon, later in an easy and
graceful prose that reminds us that we have entered the
generation of Hazlitt and Lamb.   Much as Voltaire's
prestige rested in his own day on plays that are now forgotten, so Godwin's popularity reposed on novels that
seem to modern taste, with the exception of *Caleb Williams*,
intolerably tedious.   Yet a critic of Hazlitt's distinction
could struggle to persuade himself that they were better
than those of the Tory Walter Scott.   His chief work,
Political Justice, was issued at the monstrous price of three
guineas, yet it ran through three editions and sold four
thousand copies.   It was a book that men not only read
but remembered, and the progressives throughout the
early years of the nineteenth century—Robert Owen is
a notable instance—had a way of reproducing in their
own writing not only its substance but its phraseology
and illustrations.

For this generation philosophy meant Godwin, as for the
mid-Victorians it meant John Stuart Mill.   The difference
lay in this ; that Godwin's fame was buried under a
mountain of obloquy in the reaction that froze all generous
thinking during the Napoleonic wars ; whereas it was
Mill's good fortune, in an epoch of peace, to inspire
a triumphant Liberal Party.

The man who was to mature into this thinker who
impressed himself so deeply on his generation, was born
in 1756 at Wisbech in the Fens.   His father and grand-

father were Independent ministers, and he was reared
in the Calvinist tradition. The child was brought up on
the *Account of the Pious Deaths of Many Godly Children*,
and he would move his school-fellows to tears by his
sermons on the Last Judgment. At seventeen he went
to the Theological College at Hoxton and emerged from
it still an ultra-Calvinist in his religious beliefs and a Tory
in politics. These early influences shaped his mind.
Calvinism is not an English mode of thought : it is a French
creed, Latin in its systematic completeness, its logical
courage and its disdain for sentiment. This habit of mind
Godwin retained long after he had shed every one of
Calvin's dogmas. No Methodist and no Churchman
could have written *Political Justice*. The terrors of his
pious nursery explain the peculiarities of Godwin's
reaction against Christianity. He was not content to discard
a personal God as an unnecessary hypothesis. He revolted
against Him as a tyrant whom he would depose.

Godwin, however, matured slowly. He filled several
positions as a dissenting minister, and published a volume
of sermons before he drifted into Unitarianism and the
Whig view of politics. It was as much lack of success as
a pastor as his growing unbelief that set him to earning his
living as a pamphleteer and novelist. His life at this period
differed from that of other young men who live by
journalism and aspire to literature, chiefly by his methodical
industry.

Godwin might never have risen above this respectable
level, had not friends and the ferment of the French
Revolution stimulated him to a brief exercise of his latent
powers. Through the greater part of his long life he was
merely an industrious literary craftsman, who wrote sale-
able novels for a living, conscientious school books and
several historical works of some pretension. His was a
ponderous, slow-moving mind, that could excel itself only
under the influence of some unusual intellectual excitement. This came to him first through his friendship with
Thomas Holcroft, his senior by twenty years. Starting
life as stable boy and cobbler, Holcroft was by turns actor,
schoolmaster, translator, journalist and for a time a most
successful playwright. He had more experience of life

than the sedentary, introverted Godwin would ever have acquired, even if he had realised his own dream of over-coming death and sleep by the exercise of the " powers of the mind." He had indomitable courage, the zest of a never-aging youth for adventure among ideas, a hot temper and a passion for argument. He had lived in Paris and absorbed the new " philosophy," and he set himself to pummel Godwin out of his compromising moderation. It was Holcroft who drove him from whiggery to anarchism, and turned the Unitarian pastor into an atheist. But above all, Holcroft was a leading member of the London Corresponding Society, which aimed, after the first dazzling successes of the French Revolution, at the introduction of its democratic principles into our island.

We who lived through the excitement of the Russian Revolution can dimly understand the effect of the French upheaval on contemporary England. Its influence, how-ever, both as a stimulant and a begetter of terror was vastly greater. This revolution occurred among our immediate neighbours. It befell a land that was at that period un-questionably the leader and pattern of European civilisa-tion. It had been preceded by a flowering of imaginative and reflective literature, in a language which most educated Englishmen understood, that dazzled men's minds even before the fall of the Bastille presented its ideas in action. This revolution, moreover, made itself instantly respected or feared by its startling military victories. By comparison, Russia was distant and unfamiliar : it ranked as a backward and almost barbarous land : its language was little known, and its great literature seemed exotic. Its revolution was dwarfed, when it happened, by the events of the Great War, and finally, the visible demonstration of Russia's new power and success came, not in the early years of struggle, but very much later, after the adoption of the Five Years Plan. For all these reasons our ancestors were moved, some to sympathy and others to abhorrence, very much more powerfully by the French than were we by the Russian Revolution. The effects, none the less, were in varying degrees the same—for a big but rapidly dwindling minority an imaginative exaltation, a sense that a new era of hope had dawned, for the immense majority a horror of its

violence and a dread of its innovations that drove them
into a furious defensive reaction.

Godwin attended the dinners of the Society for com-
memorating the Revolution that was long since over—
that of 1688. It heard that celebrated sermon of Dr.
Price, which drove Burke to rhetorical fury. This was an
eminently respectable society, which counted several nonconformist doctors of divinity and at least one Whig earl
among its patrons, but even in its sermons it welcomed
the contemporary Revolution. The London Corresponding
Society was bolder, and even after the Terror, in 1794, the
band at its dinner played *Ça ira* and the *Marseillaise*, and
its guests drank the toast of " the Armies contending for
Liberty "—by which it did not mean those of King George.
In its more sober moments it worked for a reformed
franchise and annual parliaments, and counted in the little
London of that day its 30,000 members, backed by
numerous provincial branches and a strong Scottish
society. It started among shopkeepers and mechanics,
with the godly Thomas Hardy for its leader, but it soon
attracted a rash crew of intellectuals who talked " hanging
matters " at its meetings—Horne Tooke, Tom Paine,
William Blake, Ritson the vegetarian, Thomas Holcroft,
and finally Sinclair, Thomas Muir, and Joseph Gerrald who
were soon to make the journey to Botany Bay. On the
fringes of this group, cautious, critical, yet in his cold way
stirred in every fibre of his tightly-knit intellect, moved
William Godwin.

In this atmosphere Godwin wrote his one great book,
the *Enquiry concerning Political Justice*, of which the first
edition appeared early in 1793. It is usually classed as an
answer to Burke, but Godwin's real purpose was, by
correcting Montesquieu, to " place the principles of politics
on an immovable basis." To do this he had to traverse
rapidly the whole field of psychology and with lingering
steps to journey to and fro and back again across the whole
territory of ethics. In reality the book is a preface to all
future progress, an elaborate study of the conditions under
which mankind may gird up its loins for the " generous
race to perfection." A second edition betrayed a growing
caution and commonsense, while a third (dated 1798) was

so heavily revised that it lost much of the vivacity with the extravagance of the first draft. It is a book of astonishing daring, not merely in its enthusiastic prescriptions for an anarchist-communist millennium, but still more in its unsparing onslaughts on every pillar of the Constitution—king, church, landed aristocracy and courts of justice. It teemed with " hanging matters," but Pitt refrained from prosecuting the author because " a three guinea book could never do much harm among those who had not three shillings to spare."

With this book Godwin leapt into instant popularity and fame. For a brief moment Englishmen did not resent his flattering suggestion that they were demi-gods who might rapidly achieve perfection, if they would but shed a few such outworn rags as their monarchy and their Constitution. This cold, methodical man enjoyed sunshine, lived for a few years or two at high pressure in this state, and wrote (1794) his one novel that deserves to live. *Caleb Williams* illustrates, with a stirring plot in the romantic manner, the criticism of society and government that is the basis of *Political Justice*. As a melodrama (the *Iron Chest*) it survived in humble theatres within my memory.

The reaction, however, was now breaking in a pitiless panic on reformers and philosophers alike. It did, indeed, receive a check when a London jury acquitted the twelve leaders of the Corresponding Society, Holcroft among them, on a charge of high treason. It is probable that a formidably reasoned and powerfully written plea in their defence from Godwin's hand contributed not a little to this defeat of the Government. It may have saved their lives, but henceforward the movement was broken ; the timeservers turned against it, and those of the philosophers who lived by their pens, at first Holcroft and later Godwin himself, were compelled to write under pseudonyms. Some were assailed by Church and King mobs ; some fled to America or the Continent ; reform was delayed for nearly forty years.

Godwin's was a placid and unaggressive courage. He would defend a friend at no small risk to himself, but he was not by temperament a fighter. He repeated the main argument of *Political Justice* once again in a series of essays entitled *The Enquirer*, written in a lighter style with some approach to ease and charm of manner (1797); but thereafter, save for a pamphlet or two, through the remaining forty years of his life he was virtually silent.

The career of Godwin, the leader of thought, ends here. The rest is the private life of an unfortunate man on whom the world weighed too heavily. His happy union with Mary Wollstonecraft ended in sudden tragedy. His second wife, the widow Clairmont, was a vain and worldly woman, who persuaded him into publishing—and bankruptcy. He went on writing good school books, bad novels and worse plays. He met no enemies more worthy of his pugnacity than duns and bailiffs, and the struggle broke and degraded him. His last years were spent serenely, as a pensioner of the Government, in defiance of all his anarchist principles. His posthumous work on religion which might have done good service had he dared to publish it in his own lifetime, for it ranks with his more effective writings, was wasted, first by his own timidity, and then by that of Lady Shelley. He died in 1836. When at length these last *Essays* appeared in 1873, a new generation found them but moderately interesting and no longer shocking. Agnosticism had become respectable.

* * * * * *

Godwin's service was that he started in England a fruitful debate on the conditions of progress, or as he phrased it "perfectibility." It is not finished: it never will be finished, for it shifts with every advance in physiology, psychology and the social sciences. Godwin did much to clear the ground and state the problem. Progress was a new idea: classical antiquity had not grasped it: it began to appear only as the thinkers of the eighteenth century made their first attempts to reach a scientific view of universal history. What, broadly, are the conditions that determine the character and destiny of mankind? Scholastic philosophy supposed that innate ideas are implanted in our minds, sovereign and immutable. Montesquieu had laid especial stress on climate as the external condition that

chiefly moulds us. On neither of these foundations could
one base a doctrine of perfectibility : one cannot by taking
thought alter either innate ideas or the climate. Godwin
therefore followed the Encyclopaedists in their psychology.
Man is under the empire of his impressions : through
every hour from birth, experience is moulding him ; his
whole environment shapes him ; he is the creature in this
broad sense of " education ". These philosophers came,
in their headlong argument, to think of human nature as
an infinitely malleable raw material, which may indeed be
bent and distorted, but may equally be trained in any
desired direction. This was a comforting conviction, and
Godwin went on to confirm it and apply it.

He asked from his readers, before he swept them along
with him, only one further admission, which looked, at a
hasty glance, innocent enough. He asked us to concede,
in the old Socratic sense, that man is a reasonable being.
He acts on a reasoned view of his own advantage : show
him by cold argument that he is mistaken, that he has
miscalculated as to his own interests, and he will alter his
ways. Even vice is merely error. In brief, men's voluntary actions originate in opinion. Of course they do, one
answers, but when, if ever, are they wholly " voluntary "
and self-conscious ? But one need not bring to bear on
this proposition the formidable batteries of modern
psychology. It is enough to point out that Godwin has
quietly taken his stand on a position of the extremest
individualism and intellectualism. He has made action
an affair of the lonely individual, tightly enclosed in his
own skin ; and further he has assumed that the process
that leads up to action can be, and should be, wholly
rational.

Grant him this, and in a few pages he will rush you,
bound hand and foot, into philosophic anarchism. All
action ought to be voluntary. By effort, education and
persuasion it can be made so. It follows, then, that sound
reasoning, when adequately presented, is invincible.
Truth is omnipotent (as from the dock the heroes of the
London Corresponding Society would tell the judge who
sent them to Botany Bay), and the vices and weaknesses
of men, which are but our names for their faulty reasoning,

can certainly be overcome. It follows that man is
perfectible.

Is this a pulpit platitude ? On the contrary, it is a
charge of dynamite warranted to blow up any and every
government. For if truth is omnipotent, why trust to
laws ? If men will obey argument, why use constraint ?
The difficulty is that in our society truth goes trammelled.
Sincerity, therefore, is the first virtue that the new philosophy inculcates. We should perpetually argue with
one another, criticise and correct one another, with a
Roman boldness. Polite lies must be scorned. The law
of libel should be swept away. If we all were to tell every
knave at his first transgression what we thought of him,
we might dispense with prisons and gallows. Censorships,
established religions and even state systems of education
are all abolished in the name of this first indispensable
condition of progress—unfettered opinion.

Authority, constraint and any form of terror must be
brushed aside without hesitation. Godwin scorns any
morality that rests on the pains and punishments of the
after-world. To terrify men is a strange way of rendering
them judicious and fearless : it is to leave them indolent
and unbraced by truth. Authority in any form makes
dwarfs of men. What is punishment ? You and I differ
in opinion, and you tell me that you must be right, since
you have a more brawny arm. The case is no better, if
without waiting to be coerced, I bow to authority. If
one must obey, at least one should do it without reverence.
To surrender my conscience to another man's keeping,
even if he masquerades as my lawful ruler, is to annihilate
my individuality as a man.

Government, then, has lost all justification. It is harmful, it is unnecessary, and it has no rational basis—for
Godwin disposes very neatly of the myth of a social contract.
His elaborate criticism of " positive institution " (his odd
term for government) is interesting, because of the
characteristic ethical turn that he gives to the familiar
case against monarchy, aristocracy and even a republican
constitution of the American type. They make for moral
corruption ; they subvert our standards of value ; they
promote ostentation and luxury by which we wrong the

L*

"labouring millions." They are linked, moreover, with the delusion of patriotism and the institution of war. Defensive war he reluctantly tolerates, but he will have no standing armies : and sincerity forbids stratagems and secrecy. Nor will he hear of colonies.

Government, then, is an evil, and he will not even call it a necessary evil, save in some brief transitional phase. His idea of a constitution is shadowy. He hates the overgrown national State, and turns to the parish, as Tolstoy and Gandhi turned to the village, as the true unit of society. At most he would allow a Parliament that met for one day only each year. Within the parish public opinion is sovereign and would express itself through juries, deciding each case on its merits without laws. They would never punish, but they would censure the wrongdoer. Godwin's argument against the folly and immorality of punishment is perhaps the most impressive thing he wrote. He was here a century ahead of his contemporaries. Coercion annihilates the understanding, alike of him who suffers it and of him who exercises it. At the most Godwin would tolerate imprisonment to restrain a violent criminal, but against solitary confinement he argues fiercely. How can a man learn to exercise virtue, if he be shut out from the society of his fellows ? How shall he exercise benevolence or justice in a cell ?

When one asks how mankind is to rid itself of kings and governments, Godwin's answer is explicable only when one reviews the circumstances of the time. He wrote amid the Terror, which was to prepare the reaction in England. Violent revolutions he condemns, though the folly of rulers may render them inevitable. Nor will he advise "constitutional" agitation. He loathed public meetings, poured his scorn on elections and even condemned the process of deciding issues by a majority vote. He will sanction only the unorganised pursuit of truth in intimate gatherings of friends. The moral beauty of the spectacle, as they meet for candid enquiry and persuasion, will render it contagious. Organised political associations—he had watched the Corresponding Society— will mean only tumult, intrigue, cabal, declamation, and the ascendancy of artful and intemperate men. This argument of Godwin's was perhaps his most fateful contribution to history, for it helped in a time of stress and danger to keep the young and generous generation that hung on his words from any active participation in politics. Godwin, it may be, did as much as Pitt to delay reform. It is true that in this way he saved many poets and idealists from Botany Bay. Incidentally he saved his own skin. He stood firm, admiring the irresistible march of Truth, and Pitt was content to leave him standing. The doctrine was, however, a perfectly consistent deduction from his individualist position. Not only did he object to political association, he regarded any form of co-operation as an offence to human dignity. He marvelled that men would demean themselves to play concerted music, or to act another man's play.

The positive expression of Godwin's ethical teaching was his doctrine of " universal benevolence." Reason forbids that I should make any distinction among my fellows because some are my countrymen, my kindred or my friends. I owe to each the same perfectly impartial benevolence, and a stranger may have a clearer call to it than my own mother. My mother may be a fool, a liar or a thief. Of what consequence is it, then, that she is " mine " ? Gratitude has no place in morals, and reason refuses to recognise the private affections. Justice deals with beings all capable of pleasure and pain : all have a common nature and a like capacity for enjoyment. Justice requires of us that we shall exercise our capacities, our talents, and resources so as to produce the greatest sum of benefit for sentient creatures. Property, Godwin holds, should be sacred—that a good man may give it away. For justice assigns a destination to all I possess. It must go where it will produce the greatest good.

The family under this analysis melts away, as the State has already done. Marriage is a curse, not merely because it is an extreme form of co-operation, but also because it involves a promise, and all promises are unreasonable ; for they are undertakings to suspend the free exercise of one's judgment. Property, however, will flow in a steady stream, actuated by universal benevolence, from him who hath to him who needs. In a rational society wealth would lose its distinction, and a man who amassed wealth would hide his treasures as carefully as to-day he displays them. So we approach the vision of a society in which equality is automatically achieved. Food and clothing will spontaneously flow from the quarter in which they abound to the quarter that is deficient. So, even without the family, will the needs of the children be met. Something will always turn up for nobody's child. Finally, in this easygoing Utopia, half-an-hour's toil should suffice to provide every man with necessities. We may hope too for great physical changes. We must get rid of sleep. Life too can be prolonged by intellect. We are sick and we die because we consent to suffer these infirmities. The vision of perfectibility ends with the overthrow of death itself.

One does not criticise so strange an amalgam of caution with extravagance. Its merit lay in its unflinching logical courage. Godwin set out from his individualist and intellectualist assumptions, and plunged forward with the sincerity of a reasonable machine, caring nothing what he overthrew in his course. Down went every ninepin that stood in his way, State and family, Church and King, motherland and law. One regrets that he ever compromised, as on occasion he did—for in later life, after some experience as husband and father, he condescended to reinstate the " private affections." The merit of it all was that his honesty provided the perfect refutation of his premises. The reasoning was sound, but the conclusions were impossible. Clearly then, the premises were at fault. *Political Justice* is the *reductio ad absurdum* of individualism.

The argument is worth following, if only because it discovers to us the advances we have made in social analysis and the interpretation of history, since the eighteenth century philosophised. Godwin leaps, with a motion habitual among reformers, though it is rarely so athletic or so prompt, from an absolute condemnation of the past to the serenest confidence in the future. History is nothing but a chronicle of oppression and wrong, priestcraft and superstition. It has not dawned on him that priests and kings are zoological facts, and that man is precisely the sort of being who breeds these creatures. Because his reading of history is so naïve, he fails to find the dynamic factor in it, the spring of change, the causative element in progress. To the whole chapter of economic causation in history he remained totally blind. Writing in London, while the North was rushing into the industrial age, he never guesses the significance of capital or machinery, nor perceives that it must regiment " the labouring millions " in enforced " co-operation." The limitations of any purely ethical view of history and society proclaim themselves from every page. He was the last of the ancients. But when this is said, much that is stimulating remains. We are obsessed to-day by a physiological and economic determinism. It is bracing to read these pæans to the powers of the human mind. It is salutary to be reminded that we can control our environment, and set our wills to perfect ourselves. Because self-conscious beings can criticise themselves, they can react against history. Nor is there in our language a writer who has analysed with equal humanity and power the degradation that overtakes every society that props inequality by coercive violence.

THOMAS HILL GREEN
1836–1882
by J. H. MUIRHEAD

THOMAS HILL GREEN
1836–1882
by J. H. MUIRHEAD

I

THE sixties and seventies of last century were a turning point in the history both of the practice and theory of democracy. In the name of the freedom of the individual Liberalism since the first Reform Act had gone from victory to victory. In 1867 it obtained the greatest triumph of all in having its " clothes stolen " and itself " dished " by the new Franchise Act passed by Disraeli. At last the fetters seemed to have been struck off and the people freed from the tyranny of minority rule. If the older democrats Priestley and Paine, Bentham and James Mill had been alive they might have been ready with their *Nunc dimittis*. But the men of the day had no such easy confidence. Already in 1858 " elective and responsible government had become," in John Stuart Mill's words, " subject to the observations and criticisms which wait upon a great existing fact." It had begun to be perceived that there might be such a thing as the " tyranny of the majority," and that there must be " a limit to the legitimate interference with individual independence."* Two years later Herbert Spencer wrote an article in the *Westminster Review* on " Parliamentary Reform, the Dangers and the Safeguards " to be later expanded in his celebrated essay *The Man versus the State.* What answer had current political theory *alias* philosophical radicalism to this menace ?

Three lines were open to it : to declare war against all invasion of the natural rights of individuals by the State ; to try to draw a line of demarcation between what the State might legitimately do in matters that concern the interests of " others " and what it might not do in matters that concern the " individual alone " ; or to revise the whole philosophic basis of Liberalism in harmony with the

* Mill's *Liberty*, c. I.

deeper insight into the whole situation that experience was bringing. The first, as afterwards became manifest in Spencer's essay, was to play into the hands of whatever was reactionary in current politics ; the second was what Mill tried to do in chapter IV of the earlier and not less famous essay *On Liberty*, needless to say with complete want of success, seeing that the whole distinction between self-affecting and others-affecting conduct is illusory. If Liberalism was to survive as a creed that had any claim to be called philosophical, its whole theoretic basis had to be revised. Whence was the revision to come?

If any one had told Jeremy Bentham that it was to come from Oxford, that abyss of corruption and home of lost causes, we can imagine the derision with which he would have received the information. Even in the fifties it would have seemed incredible to John Mill. Yet this was what was actually to happen, and the place of Thomas Hill Green among " Great Democrats " can only be understood in the light of the service he did democratic theory in this the hour of its trial. Green was not merely a great man who happened to be a democrat, nor merely great, like so many others who are commemorated in this volume, as a sincere and ardent reformer. He was all this. But his peculiar claim was that he brought a whole new order of ideas and with it a new inspiration to the workers in the field of democratic politics.

II

T. H. Green was born on April 7th, 1836 at Birkin in the West Riding of Yorkshire, where his father was rector. He was related by descent to Oliver Cromwell, of whom in his lectures on the English Commonwealth he gives perhaps the profoundest study we have in the language.* At school at Rugby he showed himself " slow and easily puzzled." But he showed also a sturdy independence amounting to what an old school friend described as a " certain grave rebelliousness." From Rugby he went to

* Characteristically he saw in the story of the Great Rebellion an instance of the " tragic conflict between the creative will of man and the hidden wisdom of the world which seems to thwart it."

Balliol College, Oxford, in 1855. While still an under-graduate we find him writing on National Life and Loyalty in the spirit of his hero John Bright, and already a pene-trating observer of current events. He hated Louis Napoleon as no better than a successful brigand. Palmers-ton he thought " did about as much harm as it is possible for an individual Englishman to do." On the defeat of his Conspiracy Bill of 1858, Green describes himself as " quite off his head with joy." On the formation of a rifle corps in the University " to keep down the Chartists," he wrote that he " should like to learn the use of the arm in order that he might desert to the people if it came to such a pass." Elected a Fellow of the College in 1860, he put aside the temptation to take orders, repelled by the system of social and ecclesiastical privileges with which he associated the English Establishment. " Saving souls," he held, " is one thing, making a fuss about an institution and a creed quite another." At the outbreak of the American Civil War he espoused the cause of the North, describing the South as " a slave holding, slave breeding and slave burning oligarchy on which the curse of God and humanity rests."

In 1864 he accepted an assistant commissionership on the Royal Commission to inquire into the education given in the schools available for the children of the middle class people of limited means, and threw himself for the next year and a half into the congenial task of improving what was called the " education of a gentleman," and so putting it within the reach of all that the phrase would have lost its original meaning. This ambition remained with him to the end. In the last years of his life he took a leading part in the establishment of the Oxford High School, and in connection with this, in one of his last public utterances, he expressed a hope that " as it was the aspiration of Moses that all the Lord's people should be prophets " so it might be ours that English society should be one " in which all honest citizens will recognise them-selves and be recognised by each other as gentlemen."

In 1870 he was elected tutor of Balliol—the first layman apparently appointed to the office in the College. From the first we are told he attracted as his pupils " men in whom radicalism was seeking for a meeting point with loyalty, scientific theory with religious faith." When we remember the names of some of the men who during the next ten years came under his influence, Arnold Toynbee, H. H. Asquith, Alfred Milner, Charles Gore, Scott Holland—all leaders in their own fields, all inspired with a burning zeal for social improvement through legislative enactment on democratic lines—we can understand the place that his teaching has had in the life of the nation. In 1871 he married Charlotte Symonds, the sister of John Addington Symonds, a contemporary of his own in Balliol. In 1874 was published the " Introduction " to Hume's *Treatise of Human Nature*, by which he took rank in the great line of British thinkers from Locke to his own time. In the following year he came to Glasgow to receive the degree of LL.D., and it was there in the house of his old college friend Edward Caird that the present writer, about to proceed to Balliol as an undergraduate, first met him.

In appearance he was rather short and square built, with thick black hair, dark eyebrows, brown eyes of a steadfast look and with a general air of quiet strength. His wife once told him that he was like Sir Bors in the Holy Grail :

" Sir Bors it was
Who spake so low and sadly at our board."

and Nettleship remarks on the completeness of the resemblance :—

" A square-set man and honest ; and his eyes
An out-door sign of all the warmth within."

His usual dress of black or sober grey suited his character, which allied him, as a colleague said, " with plain people of the working or middle class rather than the upper, the puritans of the past and the nonconformists of the present, Germans, and all that is sober-suited and steady-going." There was as yet no Labour Party, and Socialism had not yet invaded the Universities. But no university man had ever a truer love of social equality or realised more fully that the advance to it was an integral part of the advance to any true liberty.

As a junior undergraduate I naturally saw little of him, but, with other " Greats " men, I had a standing invitation to his fortnightly at-homes and the opportunity of taking essays to him.   On these occasions one was struck by his extraordinary sympathy with one's difficulties and by what a pupil once described as his " almost confounding humility." It was in 1878 that he delivered the second of his two *Sermons* on " Faith," not, like the first in 1870 on " The Witness of God," to a few pupils in his own room, but to the senior members of the whole college in the Lecture Room in the front quad.   Those of us who heard it are not likely to forget the profound impression it made upon us.

His own faith in democracy was known by its works. In 1876 he was elected to the Town Council—the first to establish this link between Town and Gown.

In 1878 he was appointed Whyte's Professor of Moral Philosophy and gave during the following years the lectures which were the foundation of his two best known books, the *Prolegomena to Ethics* and the *Lectures on Political Obligation*, both published after his death.   He had built himself a new house in the Banbury Road and was looking forward to many years of useful work, when he was taken suddenly ill of blood poisoning and died on March 26th, 1882.   " We shall never know a nobler man," wrote one of his friends.   The following is a translation of the Latin inscription on the beautiful copper tablet in Balliol Chapel :— " In memory of Thomas Hill Green, Fellow and Tutor, Professor of Moral Philosophy.   While dedicating himself to the study of all philosophy, he made it his special task to determine with what justice men hold their beliefs on right and wrong and on the nature of God.   In the high tone of his discussion of these subjects and the illustration he gave of his own teaching in his life and character he was a leader and example to his college and to the whole University.   Elected to the Town Council he strenuously exerted himself to further the prosperity of his fellow citizens, and both in thought and deed made it his constant aim that no man should be deprived of access to a fuller life."

III

Writing in 1881* Green noted " the difference between the present position of political reformers and that in which they stood a generation ago." While formerly they had gone forward in the name of individual liberty and freedom of contract, they were now apparently engaged in initiating legislation which had for its direct object the limitation of the rights of the individual by the enforcement of new regulations in factories and workshops and of statutory hours for women workers and by the institution of compulsory education. All this we have seen was viewed with suspicion by philosophical reformers as a departure from older and sounder principles. Not so by Green. He maintained that while the immediate objects of reformers and the form of persuasion by which they seek to advance them vary much in different generations " the nature of the genuine political reformer is perhaps always the same. The passion for improving mankind, in its ultimate object, does not vary." This ultimate object is best described as freedom. But we must understand what we mean by freedom. It consists not merely in the absence of external compulsion in the matter of our actions and enjoyments. It includes also the positive capacity, in the first place, of doing and enjoying something worth while doing and enjoying, and, in the second place, of doing and enjoying it in common with others. " When we measure the progress of a society by its power of freedom, we measure it by the increasing development and exercise of the whole of those powers of contributing to social good with which we believe the members of society to be endowed ; in short by the greater power on the part of the citizens as a body to make the most and the best of themselves." Here was an entirely new note in the philosophy of Liberalism and the theory of democracy. Could it be substantiated as a principle which should take the place of the old one, whether as put forward in the name of natural rights of the individual, as it was by Locke, or in the name of utility and the greatest happiness of the

* Lecture on Liberal Legislation and Freedom of Contract, delivered at Leicester.

greatest number, as by Bentham and Mill ? Or was it only a mystical, ultimately reactionary, appeal to moral and political prejudices, as it was in Burke—the writer whom Green used to incite us to read in preference to Bentham ?

Needless to say, in Green's mouth it was not this. On the contrary it was the application by a singularly clear-sighted Englishman to the circumstances of his time, of ideas he had derived from a study, deeper than that of most of his contemporaries, of the great classical tradition inherited from the free air of Greek ethics and politics, expanded in the light of what he had learned from Kant on the freedom of the will, from Fichte on the vocation of man, from Hegel on the objectivity of reason in nature and social life.

Only the barest statement of his central principle is here possible. It is contained in the title of the opening section of the constructive part of the *Lectures on Political Obligation* : " Will not Force is the Basis of the State." So stated, it might seem sufficiently unilluminating. What, it might be asked, is the difference ? No one supposes that States grow on mulberry trees or are precipitates of electric forces. They are creations of the will. The only question is, whose will ? One school held that they are the creation of the will of forceful men or groups of men seeking their own interest. Another that they come into existence by the will of the members of the whole community, freely contracting themselves into the obligations of law and order for a limited purpose. Another still that they have grown by a kind of unconscious will under pressure of external circumstances, forcing men into larger and larger unions. Which, if any, is the will that Green means ? The last comes nearest to his meaning. But the definition only raises the deeper question of the nature of this unconscious will. We only know of the unconscious through what we know of the conscious ; and it is in the light of the fresh analysis to which Green was one of the first in this country to submit the will, or what Kant called the practical reason, that his whole theory of morals and politics must be understood.

In spite of its boasted enlightenment the current philosophy of the subject in England had not advanced beyond

Hobbes's definition of the will as " the last appetite in deliberating," or Hume's statement of the relation between reason and passion in the often quoted words : " Reason is and ought only to be the slave of the passions and can never pretend to any other office than to serve and obey them." Both will and reason were, according to this view, in essence self-seeking and represented nothing in the universe except themselves. To Green on the contrary will in man was something entirely different from anything that could be called mere appetite, owing to the presence in it of the idea of an object in the attainment of which a conscious subject sought satisfaction. Reason, similarly, in its practical sense, meant " the capacity of such a subject to conceive a better state of itself as an end to be attained by action " and thus to control and redirect appetite and passion. Such a subject moreover from the beginning is a social being whose satisfaction is bound up with that of the group to which he belongs ; and the " better state " is that of the group as a whole, as something more comprehensive and permanent, and claiming therefore a greater loyalty, than anything that is merely private to himself. Social progress means advance in two main directions : a widening of the range of persons who have a right to share in the better state, and a growing consciousness of that in which it consists as the development in each of the members of his distinctively human capacities. " Our ultimate standard of worth," Green wrote, criticising current Positivism, " is the ideal of *personal* worth. All other values are relative to values for, of, or in a person. To speak of any progress or improvement or development of a nation or society or mankind except as relative to some greater worth of persons is to use words without a meaning." As he was under no delusion as to the value of the abstraction called " humanity," so he was under no delusion as to the road by which the " religion " of it had to travel. " There is no other genuine ' enthusiasm of humanity,' " he wrote, " than one that has travelled the common highway of reason—the life of the good neighbour and honest citizen—and can never forget that it is still only on a further stage of the same journey."

In one further respect—the most characteristic of all—

he went beyond anything contained in the current teaching as to the basis of progress and democracy : in his belief, namely, that all these elements could only be held together and exert their full influence over men's lives when conceived of as the action of a Spirit which is progressively communicating itself to them through nature and the institutions of civilized society, but is more than is contained in either. It was on the ground of this last addition that R. L. Nettleship claimed for him the title not only of a " philosophical " but of a " religious " radical. "It was because he saw in history the self-development of an eternal Spirit, because he regarded religion as the highest form of citizenship, because he believed reason to be at once the most human and the most divine thing in man, that he could be comprehensive without vagueness, reverent without superstition."

Such in brief outline was his account of the nature of the " will," in which he found the true basis at once of moral and political obligation. Human consciousness as such means freedom and self-determination ; self-determination means the will to betterment of the self as will ; for its full development such a will requires rights ; rights demand the State. But he was well aware of the paradox that might seem to be involved in all this. Where, it might be asked, could any of those fine things, any trace of the consciousness of having willed them in the State, be found in " the untaught and underfed denizen of a London yard with gin shops on the right hand and on the left ? " Where, even in the larger class to whom the rate and the tax collector, the policeman and the bailiff are the chief forms in which the State is known ? Yet it was one of his profoundest convictions that, if the ordinary man's consciousness of the interests and rights he has in common with his neighbour, even if they be only such as consist in getting his wages paid at the end of the week, his money's worth at the shop, or protection for his wife and his family, failed to make him at least a loyal subject, it was " a sign that the state was no true state." But it was also his view that to make " loyal subjects " was not enough. The true State wanted in its citizens not merely loyal subjects but " intelligent patriots," and for this it was necessary to

assign them a part in the working of the State. It was
here that democracy found its deepest root and justification
as the completion of the man and the citizen.

IV

Returning from this account of the basis of the State
to the controversy as to its function in the life of the
individual, it could be seen at a glance how the entire
issue was changed by it. It was no longer a question of
atomic individuals with their closed circle of natural rights,
on which Government by an unfortunate necessity has to
infringe. Rather was the individual to be conceived
as a centre of radii going out in all directions representing
the human interests that connect him with other individuals
and embody themselves in organisations and institutions—
family, society, trade unions, which at once protect and
foster them. Beyond all these is the State, " the nation
organised in the form of a self-governing community,"
the " society of societies " related to them not as that which
creates individual rights (as Bentham would say), nor as a
standing threat to them (as Spencer held), but as the
power that sustains the general conditions, under which
the rights that belong to men as possible contributors to
the common good alone can become actual. Limits
certainly there are as to what the State can legitimately
attempt to do. But the principle of the limitation was
entirely different from that which Mill had proposed in
the illusory distinction between self-regarding and other-
regarding actions. It rested on the completely valid
distinction between outward acts which are necessary for
the maintenance of rights and which can be secured by
outward force and inward motives that, just because they
are inward, can be secured by no outward force. While
therefore " the citizen must never act otherwise than as a
citizen," the State can never do more than provide favourable conditions for the free exercise of his citizenship. It
can never " compel men to be free " in the only sense in
which freedom has moral worth. But to say this is not
to say that the State has no moral purpose. Its whole

purpose from beginning to end is moral. If it abstains from the attempt to " make men moral," it does so in the interest of morality itself.

It is impossible here to follow Green in his detailed application of this theory to the particular problems of private property, war, the right of resistance, punishment, sovereignty, as they appeared in his time. Sufficient has been said to indicate its relation not only to theories current in England in his day but to those from which it derived its inspiration. It is the Greek idea of the State as consisting essentially of " equals and likes " extended from the narrow limits of Athens or Sparta to the modern nation. It is the German idea purified of the dangerous element of mysticism which saw in the State " the footstep of God upon earth " and set it above all moral law.* It is in a word the " idealist " theory stated in the most attractive form that it had yet assumed by a man imbued in a singular degree with an essentially British devotion to the liberty of the subject, but at the same time with a profound religious conviction of the supreme reality of the great positive ends of truth and beauty, justice and charity, which alone give value to the possession of liberty.

In the half century which has intervened between Green's time and our own the political world has moved on into an entirely new phase. Can events be said to have confirmed or weakened the view for which he stood ? *Prima facie* it might seem even more paradoxical than it seemed then to speak of States, rent with the violent factions that have brought democracy into disrepute, as based on Will in Green's sense of the word instead of on Force. That some States have failed to live up to the opportunity that deliverance from former subjection to tyranny of one kind or another offered them at the end of the war to organize themselves on a democratic basis, resting on a truly general will, is undeniable. But what

---

* This might seem inconsistent with what has been said above on Green as a " religious " radical. As a matter of fact his view is the exact opposite of the mystical dogma that worked such devastation in pre-war political speculation in Germany. While the latter took the State out of the moral order and set it above it, Green placed it in it as deriving the whole of such authority as it possesses from the extent to which it makes the good life possible for all.

we have to ask is whether democracy in this sense has
really had a chance in nations with so little training as these
have had in the disinterestedness and the will to live and
let live on which the success of it depends. If in this
country, as we may hope, things are different, it is from
no special merit of our own, but because, by the grace of
God, for the last three centuries we have been spared the
terrors both of civil war and of foreign invasion, while at
the same time in the colonies we have had a safety-valve
for the more rebellious spirits in the home population,
and have thus enjoyed an atmosphere in which the will
to the good of the whole had a chance of normal development. But even though this were less true than it is, the
history of internal politics is not the whole of the story.
If there is little evidence of the development of the idea of
a common good within nations, it may still be said that
never before has the idea of a common good as between
nations taken so deep a hold on the peoples of the world.
If Green were alive to-day, I cannot doubt that he would
find consolation for what to others (though not to himself)
might appear the disproof of his theory in the case of some
of the leading States, in the support it is finding in the
aspiration of good men in all quarters of the globe towards
a real brotherhood of nations, " the dream," as he called
it, " of an international court with authority resting on
the consent of independent States."

J. KEIR HARDIE

1856–1915

by KATHARINE BRUCE GLASIER

J. KEIR HARDIE

1856–1915

by KATHARINE BRUCE GLASIER

KEIR HARDIE—" Queer Hardie " as the cartoonists twisted it. For a full quarter of a century, from the Mid-Lanark by-election in 1888 to the outbreak of the world war in 1914, in political, social and religious circles, throughout the British Empire and far beyond it, in the English-speaking world, there was no other name that excited such violent outbursts of emotion.

For it was no mere difference of opinion that Keir Hardie roused. Instinctively men and women felt that he was calling them to a new way of life. He was challenging them to accept the truth, the full truth of human brotherhood against their most cherished traditions and privileges. And he incarnated his creed.

How his followers loved him ! How his opponents hated him !

Such men have always been accused of turning the world upside down. But they create movements. They are makers of history. The progress of humanity is in their hands.

But, those who hated him might interrupt : " There is a rake's progress downhill to destruction as well as a pilgrim's progress upward."

In 1897, after his first ten years of political life, a cartoon, drawn by Carruthers Gould, appeared in a Liberal paper representing Keir Hardie as a railway guard, red flag in hand, gaily waving off the Socialist I.L.P. train, loaded with working men and their leaders, J. Ramsay MacDonald in a corner seat facing the engine. Destination—" Ruin."

Similarly ten years later, in 1907, he appears in *Punch*. Keir Hardie was then M.P. for Merthyr Tydfil in South Wales, and had been elected chairman for the second time of the Parliamentary Labour Party. Broken in health, " banished " by insistent friends on a world tour that he might regain strength, he visited India. And the *Punch* cartoonist drew a majestic, Roman-helmeted, most imperial Britannia, with coat of mail beneath her flowing robes, using her titanic strength to eject from an India, represented by a Moslem mosque and a few palm trees, a comparatively diminutive Keir Hardie, clad in Scottish miner's rig of rough homespun, with ill-fitting, ill-matched trousers and coat, waving aloft in his hand a firebrand, labelled twice over, on stick and far-swirling smoke,

" Sedition ! "

Yet in both these hostile cartoons the splendid head and face of the man Keir Hardie is in all essentials the same as that drawn by his devoted friend Jordie Christie for the *Labour Leader* when he represented Keir Hardie as entering the House of Commons, after his return for South West Ham, carrying " The Unemployed," broken, ragged and footsore, upon his back.

In this cartoon Keir Hardie has the unmistakable majesty of the man who has made other men's sorrows his own : the straight, fearless, forthright gaze of one who, to use Robert Burns' phrase, has " derived his patent of nobility direct from Almighty God."

All three of these cartoons with many others are reproduced in the volume of *Keir Hardie's Speeches and Writings*, edited by his son-in-law, Emrys Hughes.

The most malignant of his cartoonists if he had artist power at all could not rob Keir Hardie of his lion-like head or make him look afraid. Even when Æsop's fable of the bull and the frog was drawn to suggest the Liberal Party's view of the rise of the Labour Party, Keir Hardie as the frog more than holds his own.

The *Punch* cartoonist's suggestion that Keir Hardie out in India in 1907, just after the blunder of the arbitrary partition of Bengal, was an irresponsible firebrand, inciting his downtrodden fellowmen to bloodshed in the pursuit of either political or economic freedom, was denied at the time by the Indian Government authorities on the spot and by his whole life's record.

If he had left no other writing, his little book *India : Impressions and Suggestions*, based on the journey-pictures he had sent home to the *Labour Leader*, is a complete testimony to the real Keir Hardie. The Home Rule for India League published a second edition in 1917.

Its warmly human pages of description have a stern framework of carefully attested facts and figures to sustain its indictment of the bureaucratic Government of India with quotations from authorities as far apart as Max Müller, Ludlow and Sir Thomas Munro, and Lord Cromer. Like his far too little known booklet *From Serfdom to Socialism* it combines clear and documented historical statement with quiet persuasive argument and practical political suggestions. Both books reveal an almost yearning solicitude for the needs of the ill-equipped British workers who were flocking to his standard. As an artist in words understood by the common people, he lent them his eyes to see India and the Indian peoples, with all their differences of race and caste and their helpless poverty, as he had seen them, and won their passionate affection.

It is a simple deduction from present-day history to claim that, had Keir Hardie been able to lend the British Raj his eyes in 1907, the British Commonwealth of free, self-governing nations with the United States of India its centre in the East might have been to-day an accomplished fact.

His real offence was his consistent mingling with all classes and castes on terms of frank equality. Both in India and later in South Africa he brushed indignantly aside every suggestion of a colour bar to full human right. In South Africa, where three months later he landed at Durban, he gave the fearless advice to the white Trade Unionists that they should throw open their membership to the coloured men and so prevent their competition as cheap workers.

" It will scarcely be credited," he wrote home, " that this produced as much sensation as though I had proposed to cut the throat of every white man in South Africa." He was howled down in town after town, and in Ladysmith and Johannesburg was met with showers of stones. The Boer farmers on whose behalf he had been pelted in British towns during the Boer War made no effort to protect him. But he splendidly stood his lonely ground and had a great

M

meeting in the Albert Hall, presided over by J. Ramsay
MacDonald, to welcome his return home.

" I am an agitator," he confessed to them. " My work
has consisted of trying to stir up a divine discontent with
wrong. With what remains of my life I intend to follow
the same course."

But from his earliest boyhood he had a deeply religious
horror of every kind of violence. Belief in bloodshed as a
method of human progress was to him a hideous superstition. " We are all members of ONE body," he would
cry to the great crowds who gathered to hear him, and it
was manifest to the most cynical among his hearers
that to him at least the words were no worn-out religious
phrase but a living, burning consciousness.

The basic principles of International Socialism seemed
to Hardie as to Bishop Westcott the only possible economic
and political expression of the Sermon on the Mount or
of any other complete ideal of human brotherhood. But
to dogmatise and quarrel about the exact form which the
Socialist State would take was " to play the fool."

In democratic countries let the workers of hand and
brain, they who are the vast majority and the source
of the nation's life, learn to trust and love one another
enough to vote solidly together for everything that would
help forward Socialism and, if meantime intolerable conditions prevailed, or above all if they were called upon to
make war upon each other, let them strike together—tactics
must be determined in every country by circumstances
and events. Teach everyone to hate capitalism as a system.
But to organise hatred of one's fellow human beings
and to prepare deliberately for a class, or a national or
a racial war was to destroy the hope of Socialism at its
root. " If men won't vote right they certainly won't shoot
right," he used to tell us. " Our job is to get behind the
guns and then melt them down as fast as possible."

Keir Hardie's unshakeable faith in democracy was
founded on his life-long experience of the bedrock
honesty and goodness of the average man and woman in
every clime, ennobled by the discipline of work, " work
that demands not mastership over one's fellow men but
mastership over material and tools—tools which never

fawn or yield to fear or flattery." But democracy was also to him the only alternative to the brute force which he loathed.

At the Edinburgh Conference in 1909 (when the Independent Labour Party, "the child of his life" as he wrote of it, endorsed by a careless vote Victor Grayson's "broken bottles" speech, made in Dublin during the dockers' strike, and his slipshod lead, supported by Robert Blatchford in *The Clarion*, for a revolutionary Socialist Party separated from the Labour Party), Keir Hardie resigned from the National Administrative Council of the party with his three colleagues, J. Bruce Glasier, Philip Snowden and J. Ramsay MacDonald, and became a rank and file member that he might fight the question out in the branches.

" We must test the question whether the I.L.P. is to stand for the consolidation of the working class movement or follow some chimera called Socialism and Unity, spoken of by men who do not understand Socialism and are alien to its very spirit."

At Geneva in the same year he attended a Conference of the Young Egyptian Party as a representative of the British Labour Party.

" Beware," he said, " of secret organisation and of all thoughts of an armed rising for the overthrow of British authority. Such organisations are sure to be honeycombed by spies and traitors. Work openly and in the light of day for the creation of public opinion in Egypt and Great Britain and have no fear of the result."

But it must be confessed that from his first entry into politics Keir Hardie had an almost uncanny power of infuriating his opponents. " Keir Hardie is the point of the Labour Movement's spear." So in an article in *The Workmen's Times* as far back as 1892 I strove to explain it.

His lifelong friend and colleague J. Bruce Glasier gave the deeper explanation. He was writing in 1915, after Keir Hardie's death, a Memorial for immediate use among his friends and comrades, knowing that his own death was not far distant :—

" Men were influenced by Keir Hardie far more than they were aware of," he wrote. " Certainly far more than they cared to

acknowledge. The very readiness with which on certain
occasions . . . men raged against him was but an expression
of that feeling which urges men ' to resist the spirit within
them ' and to persecute the upholders of principles which prick
their consciences to the quick."

I will add here three other introductory passages from
the same Memorial. They have a tragic aptness to the
present hour.

"Keir Hardie was the greatest agitator of his day. He stood
in many respects unprecedented as a working-class leader in
our country. He was the first man from the midst of the working
class who completely understood them, completely sympathised
with them, completely realised their plight and completely
championed them.

He was the first working-man who fought his way to Parliament for them, with no badge but that of Labour and Socialism
on his shield.

He was the first working-man who, having entered Parliament,
never deserted them, never turned his back on a single principle
which he had professed, never drifted away from his class in
thought, in feeling or in faith.

Never did he insult them or speak harshly or scornfully of
them. Nothing in modern democratic politics is more noble than
his unbroken affection and respect for the working class, his
untarnished loyalty to them, his championship of them, his
enduring faith in their cause."

.   .   .   .

In the early days of our Socialist movement in Britain,
Edward Carpenter, the Admiral's son and Cambridge
graduate, had been wont to teach his disciples that the chief
need of respectable Victorian society was a new shame, the
shame of being rich, "with the sickly white hands of idleness."

J. Keir Hardie, born 15th August, 1856, in a one-room
cottage in Legbrannock, a village in the Lanarkshire mining
area, knowing from his earliest childhood the extreme of
physical poverty, both by example and precept proclaimed
to his fellow working-men that their chief need was a new
pride.

"So long as men are content to believe that Providence has

sent into the world one class of men saddled and bridled, and another class booted and spurred to ride them, so long will they be ridden—but the moment the masses come to feel and act as if they were men that moment the inequality ceases."

That ringing sentence sounds the keynote of Keir Hardie's lifelong message. It was written for *The Miner*, a penny monthly, in 1887. He was its Editor and chief contributor. The whole of the £75 a year he was then drawing as Organising Secretary for the Ayrshire Miners' Union, itself struggling for existence, went to maintain the paper. His home in Cumnock had to depend upon his meagre salary as acting Editor of a little local Liberal paper *The Cumnock News*. From first to last, if ever a man of genius identified himself with " the least of these " and gave his all for their cause, it was Keir Hardie.

From wife and child, friend and follower, he demanded a similar devotion. He made no apology and took the devoted service he evoked as a matter of course.

At the start of his political career in the Mid-Lanark by-election in 1888 when he stood as an Independent Labour candidate, the first in British politics, the officials of the Liberal-Labour Electoral Association made a determined effort to persuade him to stand down and not to " split the Liberal vote." He was offered a safe seat at the General Election, the Liberal Party paying his expenses and guaranteeing a yearly salary of £300, as it was doing for others. But as Keir Hardie had demonstrated in detail in *The Miner*, out of the 72 members of Parliament sent from Scotland, not one represented the working class.

Whilst taking part in Trade Union deputations to Parliament to plead with members for support for such measures as the prohibition of boy labour in the pits under 12 years of age and a legal eight hours day for miners, Keir Hardie, who had himself gone down the pit in Lanarkshire as a trapper at ten years of age, and for ten years had worked as a miner for ten hours a day, had found himself in active conflict with the miners' leaders, Burt, Fenwick and Abraham, all Liberal-Labour M.P.s. To Hardie therefore it was clear that a stand must be made, and the Liberal-Labour Electoral Association's offer was sternly refused.

The ensuing by-election was fought with incredible

bitterness. Liberal working men and their leaders, complacently content with their own party's methods of
payment, raised wild accusations against Keir Hardie of
" Tory Gold." The official Liberal was easily returned
with 3,847 votes, mainly by miners. The women were not
yet enfranchised. The Tory had 2,917 votes and Keir
Hardie (Labour) only 617.

With a dramatic sense which often stood him in good
stead, he immediately issued a manifesto to the " Gallant
Six Hundred." Only its opening paragraphs can be given
here :—

> " Men, in my own name and that of the poor and needy
> everywhere, I thank you for your votes. You have shown that
> there are still a remnant left of those whose hearts beat true for
> humanity's cause.
>
> At Balaclava, six hundred men faced five thousand. To-day
> the name and fame of the six hundred live in song and story,
> but the five thousand——?
>
> Your vote marks a turning point in history. You have
> raised the ' condition of the people ' question to a first place.
>
> The meaningless drivel of the ordinary politician must now
> give place to the burning words of earnest men whose hearts
> are on fire with love to their kind, men who believe in the Father-
> hood of God, the brotherhood of man."

Those words on Keir Hardie's pen were no empty
flourish. He had had to fight his way to the faith they
represent.

His mother, Mary Keir, a domestic servant before her
marriage to David Hardie, a ship's carpenter, was undoubtedly the chief influence of his early years. No woman
I have ever met, not even Louise Michel, so embodied
the spirit of revolt. In the midst of a rigid Calvinist
Presbyterian world she hugged the brand " atheist and
republican " to her breast and quoted passages from Tom
Paine and Charles Bradlaugh with a zealot's heat. She
knew alike the fiercest and the tenderest poems of Robert
Burns by heart and told me that she had taught many of
them to Keir before he was able to read.

Tough in frame as a tempest-torn hawthorn tree on a
mountain side, even in old age she breathed a tireless
courage. Her dark eyes flashed fire, and her work-worn

hands tossed incessantly as she recounted in a kind of
torrent story after story of what life had meant to her.
The experiences she unfolded of heartless treatment as a
servant girl, one specially ugly instance occurring in a
clergyman's household, would have darkened Dickens'
darkest pages and given point to the pens of the Brontë
sisters.

It is difficult for those who have been born into the
humaner atmosphere of the twentieth century in Britain,
with its broader outlook on religion and its quickened
social conscience—so much of it due to Keir Hardie's
inspiration, with its great national Labour Party firmly
established and continually gathering strength both in
Parliament and the municipalities, with its network of
Social Services, its Workmen's Compensation Acts, its
Old Age and Unemployed Insurances and Compulsory
Education up to 14 years, even to conceive of the dire
distresses which compelled Keir Hardie's mother after
her marriage to David Hardie to let her passionately loved
first-born son leave school and start work as a message
boy at seven years old.

" I taught the lad to read and write at hame in the evenings, aye and to think for himsel'," she told me with a kind
of bleached pride. " He went to Sunday School and to
Night School after he went down the pit, but he aye thocht
he could teach himself the best and he was aye a fule ower
religion."

As a speaker Keir Hardie served his apprenticeship as
an active member of a little evangelical chapel in Lanarkshire and took earnest part in its mission work, especially
on its temperance platform. It was here he met his wife,
Lillie Wilson, whom he married when he was 23 years old.
She was temperamentally unfitted for the storms and
vicissitudes of her husband's public life but bravely did
her part as thrifty wife and mother of four children, one
of whom died at two years old. The simple cottage home
and garden which they established at Old Cumnock in
Ayrshire is still a place of pilgrimage for Keir Hardie's
disciples.

The Manifesto to " The Gallant Six Hundred," already
referred to, was dated, Cumnock, 28th April, 1888. Many

years of fierce trade union fighting had gone before it. Conditions in both the Ayrshire and Lanarkshire mining areas were at their lowest ebb. Horror of wrong coupled with a hatred of hypocrisy had burned within Keir Hardie ever since a terrible experience of both when he was a boy of nine years old, that, to use his own words in telling of it, " changed his whole outlook on men and things."

His own written story of it is quoted in full in the opening chapter of the excellent official biography by William Stewart. In the face of wrong henceforward burning words came to his need with a courage to utter them that grew with his sense of the strength of the wronger and the defence-lessness of the wronged. Continually his fellow-miners, men twice and thrice his age, put him forward to voice their grievances. Inevitably he was victimised.

Reading incessantly, Carlyle, Emerson, John Stuart Mill, Mazzini, Charles Kingsley and Ernest Jones, he discovered journalistic powers sufficient to support his little family. But he was soon to lose that refuge—respectable Liberal editors could not tolerate his conduct in Mid-Lanark. Before the autumn of the same year, he was appointed secretary of the newly formed Scottish Parliamentary Labour Party, with Cunninghame Graham as President and Dr. Clark Vice-President, and a statement of principles that Hardie himself described as " commonsense Social-ism." Men and women who shared his views and admired his courage were by this time supporting his lead all over Britain. The Independent Labour Party with Keir Hardie as its first Chairman was formed in 1893.

No propagandist can ever have toiled more selflessly, either with voice or pen. The bulk of his writing was done for papers which could not afford to pay their contributors. He consistently preferred the hospitality of the simplest homes to any other. He continually spoke in the open air.

" Give to every one who asketh of thee," he quoted with one of his rare smiles when friends protested against a week's programme of ten huge meetings and three committees entailing two night-mail journeys, added to all the anxieties of editing *The Labour Leader*, for which he took full financial responsibility from 1889 to 1903. His health had begun to give way under the strain long before he was fifty.

Yet it was never stale patter that he gave. Always his written or spoken words sprang from deep well-springs of sympathy as well as conviction. Continually he amazed his enemies as well as his friends with his swift intuitive capacity to grasp the essential facts of some special industrial or political situation, and the unfailing power with which he could present them. From his first speech which deplored the absence in the Queen's speech of any mention of the unemployed he compelled the attention of the House of Commons.

The actual dates of his parliamentary life may be usefully inserted here. He was elected M.P. for South West Ham in 1892, was defeated at the General Election of 1895, was returned for Merthyr Tydfil in 1900 and remained its member until he died, September 26th, 1915.

The correspondent of the *Leeds Mercury*, writing a descriptive report of one of his speeches, declared him " one of the most cultured speakers the present House of Commons can boast." George Bernard Shaw appraised him as " the damnedest natural aristocrat in the House of Commons."

It is literally true to say that when he was first returned to Parliament he was so happy in his supporters' happiness and so absorbed in the work that lay before him that he was as unconscious of the wild offence which the cloth cap he habitually wore would create in " the most exclusive gentlemen's club in Europe," as he was of the Salvation Army cornet hidden under Frank Smith's coat. He was no wrecker of Parliament.

His work, as he saw it, was to seize every opportunity which the rules of the House allowed to give publicity to the wrongs of the workers. Day after day he did it with relentless thoroughness and a courage that never failed. Standing alone he fulfilled his promise to form an Independent Labour Party in the House and proved in a score of historical scenes on behalf of the workers how one man convinced of the righteousness of his cause can become a host.

No man in our modern political world has ever more consistently " despised the gain of oppressions." In 1892 when he was standing for West Ham, Andrew Carnegie

M*

as a fellow Republican sent a substantial donation to his
election fund. But the steel workers at Pittsburg, U.S.A.,
were out on strike against shameless conditions of hours
and wages, with all the forces of the Pinkerton gang, or
hired gunmen, of the Carnegie firm arrayed against them.
Keir Hardie promptly and publicly dispatched Carnegie's
money to the Strike Fund.

What a scandal it made at the time, in a Britain dotted
over with Carnegie Libraries !

Two years later again Keir Hardie was making a hurried
lecturing tour in the United States, strengthening the
hands of Eugene Debs and his followers. Debs was in
prison at the moment for alleged incitement to riot of the
unemployed. But he was allowed to see his great Scottish
comrade, by this time Chairman of the new-born Independent Labour Party, and its solitary representative in the
House of Commons. Debs delighted Keir Hardie by his
cheery invitation from the prison steps to " Come right in
and make yourself at home."

Frank Smith was travelling with Keir Hardie. At
San Francisco, a Presbyterian minister, the Rev. Mr.
Scott, brought the Mayor of the town, known as " The
Silver King," to interview them. Quite coolly the financial
magnate proceeded to offer Keir Hardie 100,000 dollars
(£20,000) if as Chairman of the I.L.P. he would persuade
the Party to make a declaration in favour of bimetallism,
or even himself make a speech supporting it. The Mayor
possessed great silver-mining interests and was supporting
Bryan in his U.S. Presidential campaign because he was
making bimetallism a chief plank in his programme.

To his bewilderment his offer was met with laughter.
A labour leader had refused £20,000 for a speech ! Nay
more, Keir Hardie was speedily reported as publicly
regretting that wholehearted reformers were fighting such
side issues as the silver question instead of going straight
for the Socialist ticket.

The Mayor could only imagine that " the other side "
had got in before him. Yet within the week both Hardie
and Frank Smith were stranded without funds in Butte
City and were thankful to a friendly Scottish piper for
drawing them a crowded audience in the Opera House

and a collection which left them 75 dollars after paying all expenses.

The adventure was one of Keir Hardie's favourite stories. He did not use the old-fashioned religious phrase of " answer to prayer," but his Celtic nature blazed with conviction that the means would always be found where the will was strong enough for the right.

In the notorious incident of Lord Overtoun, the great religious philanthropist who gave away £10,000 a year in support of evangelical missions at home and abroad, while he was the head and virtual owner of great chemical works in Glasgow where the men worked twelve hours a day for seven days a week, for less than 3d. an hour, with no meal-hours or sanitary or protective arrangements of any kind to save the men from hideous injury, Keir Hardie's scathing articles in *The Labour Leader* in 1899, reprinted as pamphlets, were sold by the hundred thousand and worked like a volcano under the foundations of complacent Victorian Christendom.

Further, among those who had joined the movement, if he thought that anything in the nature of riches existed, he was wont to commandeer them for the movement's urgent needs so cavalierly that I recall one friendly victim's rueful confession that whenever he saw Keir Hardie coming up to his front door he forthwith fled by the back. " The man would have had me risk my family's livelihood," he told us. But it was only what Keir Hardie had habitually done with his own.

As Robert Smillie, the Scottish miner leader, one of the oldest and most revered of Keir Hardie's colleagues, proudly chuckled over his pipe, " Not only did Keir Hardie never tak' a bribe. They kent they couldna bribe him." The saying became a household word in the movement.

It cannot be too often insisted upon that to Keir Hardie human solidarity was a living consciousness, not a phrase, and the foundation of all Socialism as well as of religion worthy the name. His tenderness of sympathy extended to every form of life—to the countryside ravaged by industrialism and to all dumb animals. His stories of Donald the pit pony and of the two slum dogs, written for the children of the Socialist Movement, are classics of humane literature.

His steady and persistent upholding of the right of women to complete freedom and equality was blent with his life-long practice. It was one of his rigid rules of conduct that no woman should be allowed to clean his shoes. Many a quaint excursion he made in consequence into the Mary Ann backs of the (to him) entirely undesirable mansions in which he was sometimes quartered. But always his reverent courtesy and cheery chivalry bore down the prejudices of the most hide-bound mistresses and maids. His personal cleanliness of thought and deed (like his love for homespun clothes that could be washed) was as instinctive as John Woolman's.

How delighted he was when he first discovered the diary of the grand old Quaker and learned of his refusal to eat out of the silver dishes of the slave-owner !

It was in keeping with Keir Hardie's whole career that when the Independent Labour Party with his untiring help and guidance had safely brought a strong and powerful Labour Party into being, uniting the trade union, the co-operative and the Socialist organisations into one great Parliamentary party, he should turn a chief part of his time and now alas ! fast failing strength to the support of the movement for Women's Enfranchisement. And again it was natural that his fullest sympathy should be enlisted by the despised and rejected East-end Section, led by Sylvia Pankhurst and her *Woman's Dreadnought*.

But the war and the failure of the workers here in Britain as in the other countries of Europe to withstand the call of their militarist rulers broke his heart.

" I have said both in writing and from the platform many times that the impetus which drove me first of all into the Labour Movement and the inspiration which has carried me on in it has been derived more from the teachings of Jesus of Nazareth than from all other sources combined."

The words were taken from a stirring address delivered by Keir Hardie on " Labour and Christianity " at the Browning Hall Settlement in London in 1910.

Herbert Stead left on record a further saying, nearer the end of Keir Hardie's life in the accumulating tragedies of the war. " I am sometimes sick at heart with politics and all that pertains thereto. If I were a thirty years younger man methinks I would leave all to preach the whole gospel of Jesus Christ."

But from whatever side he had worked it would have been the same Keir Hardie, loving all mankind, hating every form of hypocrisy and wrong—striving, to use his own phrase, " to make Socialism the handmaid of religion," and to separate forever both the Cross and the Red Flag he loved from the Sword.

JEAN JAURÈS
1859–1914
by HENRY DE MAN

JEAN JAURÈS
1859–1914
by HENRY DE MAN

THE leaders of international socialism who had risen to eminence about the end of the last century seem to have included quite a number of really remarkable and even uncommonly big men. Amongst those I have myself known well, I will mention only the German August Bebel, the Austrian Victor Adler, the Swede Hjalmar Branting. To those militant members of the Socialist International who, like myself, were still under thirty when the World War broke out, they may have seemed even bigger than they were. The question is open to argument, and will probably not be settled until a good deal more historical perspective has been gained. But Jean Jaurès, who belonged to that generation, is in a class by himself.

Whenever the mental image of Jean Jaurès flashes across my mind, no matter how transiently and hazily, I experience a kind of feeling that I can compare only with the sudden widening of the " inner " angle of vision by which one subconsciously prepares oneself to look, say, at a mountain, after having looked at ordinary-sized things or beings. I have found that many men who have known Jaurès, even amongst those who were hardly younger than he, experience a similar feeling. One of them once expressed it by telling me that to him Jaurès seems to have been the last living representative of an extinct race of giants.

Of course, that feeling is founded on a sense of spiritual, not of physical, qualities. Yet, in the physical appearance of Jaurès, there was nothing to contradict that impression. True, he was only middle-sized, and his sturdy build, broad chest, and big bearded head sometimes made him appear rather smaller. But there was something in the *tout ensemble* that, even physically, seemed appropriate to fill a much bigger space, just as a " reduced " drawing of, say, a Michael Angelo statue, calls for an enlarged scale of vision. Perhaps the upward tilt of the head had something to do with it—for Jaurès usually carried his head thrown backward on his steer-like neck, as if he were gazing at a distant region far above the horizon. May be, also, the powerful range of his voice even in ordinary conversation—and the impression of uncommon physical strength and energy he gave one. Furthermore, his attitude denoted, to an extraordinary degree, aloofness from irrelevant things and equally extreme awareness of big things, as if he filled a much larger " lifespace," as the Germans say, than ordinary mortals.

But these are the things which made me say that in his appearance and bearing there was nothing to contradict the " outsize " impression ; yet in the main, that impression must have rested on something else. To put it in a nutshell, I should say it was the feeling that he seemed to radiate thoughts that represented something much bigger than the mere output of a single brain, something much more perennial, too, than the contents of a single life-span— something human rather than individual, something connected with mankind as a whole rather than with a particular person.

On second thought, I feel that the word " radiate " fits the essential idea I wanted to convey : Jaurès struck one, not as a man who " produced " or " had " ideas, but as a man in whom ideas were alive and active, a carrier less than an embodiment. And perhaps one should say, not " ideas," but " an idea " ; and this would go a step further to explain the amazing impression of bodily and spiritual identity that connects the image of his personality with the feeling of a super-personal size.

To understand the full meaning of this, however, one must try to define, in concrete terms, what one might call the actual contents of Jaurès' mind, or, in other words, the peculiar quality of his socialism.

To describe that fitly, I think there is no better way than to call him " the humanistic socialist." A man like Bebel, who at one time faced Jaurès as the typical representative of " German " as opposed to " French " socialism, indisputably incarnated the mind of a class and of a big national party ; but where Bebel embodied a class, Jaurès embodied a nation ; and where Bebel represented a party, which after all stood but for a moment in a long historical process, Jaurès represented a civilisation—the mind, or at least the result of the workings of the mind, of many generations of men. And we shall see presently to what extent he was inspired by the belief in the oneness of human values and socialist aims, arising from a still more fundamental belief in the oneness of all things, cosmic and human.

He was at the same time a leader and a thinker. And he was a thinker before he became a leader. The story of his life is essentially that of a man who, having reached the highest level of human culture to which his epoch could give access, tried to make socialism the application of the postulates of this culture to the condition of his time.

Jaurès was born in 1859 in Castres, a small town in the south of France. His family belonged to the local *bourgeoisie*, of small wealth but high respectability, and with strong strains of peasant blood. Among his relatives higher education was the rule, and quite a few rose to eminent positions in liberal professions and the public service. His brother and two other relatives were admirals in the French Navy.

Jaurès' father died early, leaving very little fortune, and Jean might have had some difficulty in pursuing his studies to the end, if he had not been helped along by a series of scholarships as an " exceptionally brilliant pupil." This took him right up to the *École Normale Supérieure*, the super-University where the French Republic gives the most promising of her sons, picked out by competition and supported by scholarships, what is probably the most intensive classical and philosophical education that can be acquired anywhere. The *Normale* is practically the training school for prospective University professors of the Literary and Philosophical Faculties. At the age of twenty-four, Jaurès thus found himself what amounts to a " don " at the University of Toulouse, where he specialized in the teaching of Plato's philosophy.

But Jaurès obviously was something more than a brilliant scholar. What saved him from being nurtured to death on the hotbeds of the French academic system, with its super-intensive and unilateral methods of intellectual

training, was something more than his exceptional intelligence and what one of his friends called his "monstrous"
memory. For all his scholarly zeal and concentration,
Jaurès was not born to be a book-worm. The all-devouring
curiosity that drove him arose from what he once himself
termed his *appétit de vivre*—his "life-hunger." One must
have accompanied Jaurès on walks or travels to know how
immediately and intensively he reacted to the outer world.
He "took everything in" to an amazing degree, whether
it was a picture in a museum, a trembling leaf above a
brook or a human incident in the streets.

He once pleaded guilty to being nothing but a *paysan
cultivé*—a cultured peasant. And indeed, he was primarily
a peasant—a peasant with a poet's soul. The chief quality
that made him—by general admission—the greatest orator
of France was fundamentally poetic. The strength of
what psychologists would call his "verbo-motor impulses"
exactly corresponded to the strength of his innate instincts
and emotions. And this explains why, even in his highest
oratorical flights, and in spite of the "latin" abundance
of metaphors and classical reminiscences he often indulged
in, he never gave one the least impression of priggishness
or "oiliness." There was no trace of cant or *cliché*
about his eloquence, just as there was no trace of sentimentalism about his emotional raptures.

His sense of humour had no kinship with what the French
call *esprit*, a quality bred of court-gossip and drawing-room
repartee. It might rather be described as Shakespearian,
and I might almost say plebeian, in the sense in which
everything fundamentally human flows from sources
common to all people.

For all his idealism, he undoubtedly had what the French
call *malice paysanne*—peasant shrewdness—and he knew
how to make the best of it when dealing with a difficult
audience or with the intricacies of a tactical situation.
But even where his intuition thus helped him to "adapt"
himself to a situation, this adaptation never appeared as
if he were sheltering behind something that was not really
and fundamentally himself. Even where he used tactics,
it all happened above board. For he then showed but a
few of the many sides of an amazingly comprehensive

personality, yet without thereby showing anything that was not genuinely his own.

From the beginning of his career, Jaurès' urge toward verbal self-expression and combativeness in the service of ideas drove him to political activity. In 1885, at the age of twenty-six, he stood for Parliament in his native district and was elected a member of the Chamber of Deputies. He took his seat on the left of the House, as an advanced liberal, but without joining a party. Between that time and 1902, he was alternately beaten and re-elected at successive elections, so that on the whole he spent about half of those fifteen years as a deputy and the other half as a professor, and, incidentally, as an alderman of the city of Toulouse and a regular contributor to the well-known radical daily *la Dépêche*. From 1902 until his death in 1914, he was re-elected a deputy at each poll.

During the first term of his parliamentary career, he slowly developed from a man with general political ideas into a man with special political and economic knowledge. At first he spoke only on academic topics such as the educational system ; but he soon discovered the importance of social and economic questions. He studied them so earnestly that from the third year of his term he succeeded in impressing the Chamber not only by his eloquence as a speaker and debater, but also by his competence as an authority on social problems.

At the same time, he evolved from a *bourgeois* radical into a socialist labourite. In 1890, he publicly announced his adhesion to socialism. This attitude was emphasized by the energetic way in which he supported the strike of the miners of the neighbouring Carmaux district in 1893, which was one of the outstanding social struggles of that early period in French trade unionism.

As a socialist deputy, Jaurès played an authoritative part in most of the great parliamentary debates of the nineties, such as those that exposed the financial corruption of a large section of politics after the so-called Panama scandal. It was not until 1898, however, when the Dreyfus case began to capture public attention, that Jaurès rose to national eminence.

The heroic struggles of those times, which re-determined

the grouping of the main political forces in France down almost to the present day, also crystallized the position of Jaurès both as the chief representative of the " Left " with regard to the country at large and as the leader of a particular tendency in the labour movement with regard to the Socialist Party.

The " *Affaire* Dreyfus " practically brought about the birth of Jaurèsism, which to this day puts its peculiarly national stamp on French republicanism and socialism.

The opposite tendency was Guesdism, so named after Jules Guesde, the leader of the *Parti Ouvrier* that competed with the *Parti Socialiste*. Guesde was practically responsible for the introduction of Marxism into France. A particularly extreme and uncompromising kind of Marxism at that, since the Marxist conception of the class struggle could not be popularized in France without putting an exception-ally strong emphasis on its opposition to *bourgeois* democracy. France being a country of peasants, artisans and *petits bourgeois* rather than of industrial workers, and French socialism having arisen from the first as a continua-tion of the *bourgeois* revolutionary movements of 1789, 1830, and 1848, Marxism could not have been born but elsewhere. As soon as it began to be imported into France, it appeared that its growth was practically limited to the few regions with a developed factory system, such as the mining and textile districts of the Nord and the Pas-de-Calais. These hotbeds of French industrialism were also the hotbeds of Guesdist socialism.

In most of the rest of France, however, conditions were different. They made socialism appear less as a class attitude of the proletariat than as the general concern of all those who wished the maxim of 1789 " *Liberté, Égalité, Fraternité* " made as true with regard to the domination of the rich as it had been made true with regard to the domination of the nobility and the clergy. As the miners and factory hands of the industrial north listened to the new watchword of the class struggle, the artisans, peasants and intellectuals in France at large continued to respond to the old watchwords of " *Republican defence*," Democracy and the Rights of Man. To them, socialism meant an idea, common to all the true heirs of France's old revolu-

tionary tradition ; to the Guesdists, it embodied the economic
interest and the political will-to-power of a new class of
society. In order to make the proletariat class-conscious,
the Guesdists felt compelled to denounce the democratic,
humanistic and idealistic conception of socialism as a
" *petit bourgeois* deviation," a snare to entrap the workers
into fighting the battles of their class enemies, an illusion
to be exposed in the light of the materialistic conception
of history.

Nowhere more than in France, therefore, was the dual
soul of socialism, as a humanistic idea adopted by a proletarian class, to appear as a living antithesis, which had to
manifest itself in its full strength before any kind of synthesis could be successfully attempted.

Jaurès' task was to be, first to affirm the antithesis to
Guesdist Marxism, and then to bring about its absorption
into a new synthesis.

The clash reached its climax over the Dreyfus case.
From the beginning, Guesde had taken the uncompromising
position that the fate of an army officer, rightly or wrongly
court-martialled as a spy as the result of an anti-Jewish
officers' intrigue, was no concern of a workers' party.
True, Guesde held that Dreyfus was innocent and that
he deserved a new trial, but that, he said, was a private and
not a political issue. Socialism, he argued, had nothing
to gain by joining the movement that had received its
chief impetus from Émile Zola's open letter *J'accuse*. The
class-consciousness of the workers could only be confused
by a movement that splits, not *bourgeois* and workers,
but Dreyfusards and anti-Dreyfusards, republicans and
anti-republicans, pacifists and militarists.

Jaurès, however, threw himself heart and soul into the
movement for the revision of the Dreyfus case. Socialism
to him meant more than a class struggle for the overthrow
of capitalism. It necessarily implied, he thought, the
defence of the Republic against the reactionary forces of
Cæsarism and clericalism, the safeguarding of civil liberties
against military authoritarianism, the broadest human
solidarity with the victims of any kind of oppression and
injustice. Class interest itself does not mean much if it
does not identify itself with the claims of justice and human

dignity. Even in a capitalist state, the function of law is not, as the Marxists say, merely to defend capitalism ; law is also the means to safeguard certain elementary rights common to all men, such as the right to a fair trial, without any racial or religious bias. Captain Dreyfus, to whom this right had been denied, must therefore cease to be considered as a military servant of the *bourgeois* state ; as the victim of an abominable miscarriage of justice, he represents " mankind itself, in the worst state of dejection and despair that imagination can picture." So " we need not be unfaithful to our principles of class action in order to lend our ear to an appeal for pity ; we may be revolutionaries without ceasing to be human beings ; we need not, in order to remain within the bonds of socialism, free ourselves from the bonds of humanity."

No wonder, therefore, that when Jaurès had to choose a name for the daily paper which the Socialist Party of France launched in 1904 under his directorship, he called it *l'Humanité*. And his first leading article thus justified this title :

" The name of this paper, in all its conciseness, expresses exactly what our party strives for. All socialists work to realize humanity. Humanity hardly exists thus far. It is being frustrated and outraged, within all nations, by class antagonisms, by the unavoidable clash between the interests of a capitalist oligarchy and the working masses, and, between the nations, by the passions of nationalist egoism and chauvinist pride. The task allotted to socialism is to resolve those antagonisms by suppressing the classes through socialisation of the means of production and by making of each nation, restored to its own unity, a constituent part of humanity."

Humanity, after having been the watchword of the antithesis to Guesdist class bigotry, was to become the keyword of the synthesis that ultimately created a united French Socialist Party, devoted at the same time to the interests of the workers and the claims of an ideal of justice for all.

For this is the superiority of the broader humanist view of socialism over the narrower view represented by Guesde's Marxist orthodoxy, that the former could understand and therefore absorb the latter, whilst the narrower view could only be absorbed or remain aloof, but never provide room for the other.

The unification of the various fractions of French socialism, which culminated in April, 1905, in the foundation of the United Socialist Party, was chiefly Jaurès' achievement, because of this broadness of vision. Moreover, it was in the very nature of Jaurèsism to include a fundamental striving towards unity. From his earliest writings on metaphysical problems, Jaurès appears to have considered the universe itself as a " continuous striving towards oneness." His pantheistic optimism was based on the belief that the whole cosmic order meant " unity in the making," a slow but progressive resolution of antagonisms, aimed at oneness between Man and God, mind and matter, nature and civilisation, instinct and reason, just as the meaning of history was to resolve classes and nations into the higher unity of mankind redeemed by socialism.

What Jaurès called his " idealist conception of history," therefore, was meant less as a denial of the truth of the Marxist " materialist " conception of history, than as an attempt to show that it was merely a half-truth, and required insertion into a broader frame. In a series of brilliant academic debates with defenders of the orthodox Marxist faith such as Jules Guesde and Paul Lafargue (Karl Marx's son-in-law), Jaurès outlined these theoretical foundations of his socialist faith. Marx, he argued, was right in emphasizing the importance of technical progress, economic interests and class motives in the making of history. His economic interpretation of history is correct as far as it goes, viz., as far as it gives us the key to the understanding of the growth and decay of capitalism, and generally speaking of all social states based on class hierarchy, as a consequence of the class antagonisms engendered by economic motives. But there is more than that in history, even in the history of socialism. Apart from the causes we see at work in economic developments, we must consider ends that are inherent in the nature of mankind and in the living world at large. There is a perpetual striving for other values than economic values, there is an evolution of ideas that transcends even class interests, because it represents the need of mankind to understand the world, to grasp truth, to realize equity and unity.

In several volumes devoted to the history of the French Revolution, Jaurès showed that economic motives, important though they were, did not explain away the enormous influence of those individual achievements Thomas Carlyle ascribed to his " heroes," nor the all-permeating action of ideas. Even the French *bourgeoisie*, in preparing its economic revolution, he said, would not have succeeded if it had only had in mind its material interests, if it had not been " inspired by the belief that it was fighting the battles of mankind at large." And in the long process of intellectual fermentation that prepared the Revolution, " philosophy was at work, not only or not even chiefly amongst the oppressed classes, but amongst all, and in favour of social changes that appeared necessary to the conscience of all thinking men before they promised any advantage to a particular class."

Similarly, to-day, " every thought that arises trying to meet the future meets one of the currents of socialist thought." Hence, the big intellectual advantage of the working class is that, alone of all classes, it " has no need of lies," whilst its opponents fight " with the sun of truth blinding their eyes." Hence, moreover, socialism, even in its most revolutionary aspects, is heir to a millenarian tradition of intellectual progress, of which Greek philosophy, mediæval catholicism, Renaissance humanism, eighteenth-century anti-clericalism were but previous stages. Therefore, even the chief intellectual opponent of the French Revolution, Roman Catholicism, viewed as the incarnation of a great historical force that has perhaps not spent all of its creative energy, can be met by socialism " without genuflexion but without anger." Socialism, in short, is nothing but the contemporary form of a perennial movement of humanity towards its self-realisation, its emancipation from primeval fear, age-long ignorance, internecine dissension, the horror of war and the injustice of poverty.

French socialism thus having, according to Plato's image, " taken over the torch " from the hands of the *bourgeois* revolutionaries of 1789, essentially means the continuation of their task, by transforming political democracy into social and economic democracy.

Applied to the field of political strategy, these principles resulted in the following main postulates, which might be considered the essential tenets of Jaurès' political faith as a party leader :

(1) Socialism, though it naturally appeals in the first place to the industrial working class as the chief victim of capitalist oppression, must extend its appeal to all men, and especially to the peasants, lower middle classes and intellectuals ;

(2) It may never separate its cause from the maintenance and development of the Republic, as the embodiment of the constitutional liberties won in the victory over monarchism, feudalism and clericalism ;

(3) The natural allies of the Socialist Party therefore are those " radicals ", viz. " *bourgeois* democrats," who, without yet agreeing to go so far as social democracy, at least remain faithful to the *défense républicaine*, the maintenance of the Republican and democratic State against the offensive return of Royalism, Cæsarism or Popery ;

(4) In a case of emergency arising out of such a reactionary menace, the solidarity with *bourgeois* republicanism may extend to participation in a coalition government ;

(5) Socialism demands democratic self-government of nations as well as world unity, the Socialist Party therefore must strive for peace whilst accepting the duty of taking part in the defence of democratic nations against aggressive military powers ;

(6) To achieve that double aim, the Socialist Party must demand the organisation of the army on a democratic and defensive basis, viz. the " *nation armée* " as opposed to a professionalized standing army with a long term of service, whilst actively pursuing its opposition to entangling alliances with reactionary powers, the solution of international conflicts by negotiation and arbitration, and active resistance of the workers against " wars of aggression " by means of the general strike.

These were, indeed, the leading principles of French socialism under Jaurès' guidance, that is to say from the Unity Congress of 1905 till 1914.

In actual practice they meant that, with regard to home politics, the Socialist Party tried to take liberalism in tow for the realisation of social reforms, whilst in foreign politics it put itself at the head of a pacifist policy, based simultaneously on labour internationalism as a check to wars of aggression and on " *bourgeois* pacifism " as a means to reconcile national defence with a policy of international conciliation and arbitration.

For ten years Jaurès fought heroically to realize that programme, in the teeth of growing warlike nationalism, even in his own country. The chapter of the history of Europe that closed in August, 1914, tells the story of how he failed, and why he was bound to fail.

A year before the unification of the French Socialist Party, at the Congress of the Socialist International held at Amsterdam in 1904, Jaurès had said, in his famous oratorical duel with August Bebel, the leader of the German Social-Democratic Party :

" There is a menace that hangs over Europe and the world, a menace to peace, to our liberties, to the development of the socialist and labour movement, to political and social progress at large. . . . This menace is the political impotence of German social-democracy. Certainly, you are a great and admirable party, which has given international socialism some of its most powerful and deepest thinkers, and the example of methodically co-ordinated action and progressively strong organisation. . . . Yet, the more your power increases, the more manifest becomes the contrast between your apparent political importance, as measured by the increasing figure of your votes and your representatives in public administration, and your real influence, your real force of action. On the day after the June elections, when you polled a three million vote, it became clear to all that you had an admirable recruiting power, but that neither the traditions of your proletariat, nor the mechanism of your constitution put you in a position to utilise this apparently colossal strength. . . . Even if you gained a majority in your Reichstag, your country would be the only one where socialism would remain out of power in spite of its parliamentary majority, for your parliament itself is powerless."

But France itself reacted to the menace of the growing international antagonisms and the accelerated race of armaments by strengthening the links of its alliance with Tsarist Russia, and by steadily increasing its standing army, going as far as extending the term of compulsory military service to three years.

Jaurès' last big political fight was against the so-called three-year-law. His pacifism may have been *bourgeois* or have lacked the uncompromising radicalism of the post-war peace movements, but, such as it was, it was genuine and unyielding. The reactionary and nationalist newspapers branded him as a traitor to his country and an agent of her enemies, and some of them hardly disguised their appeals to assassination.

In July, 1914, as the shadows of death that hung over Europe grew closer and more menacing day by day, Jaurès had forebodings that he himself already stood on one of the darkest spots. I heard him say so, in the almost jocular tone of a man to whom duty means so much that fear means nothing besides, on July 28th, the last day of the last executive conference of the Socialist International, where an eleventh-hour appeal had been made to the workers of Europe to check the war preparations of their governments. The two next days in Paris convinced him that the odds against that appeal being heard had become well-nigh overwhelming. On the evening of July 31st, on leaving the office of *l'Humanité* for a quick meal before writing another desperate appeal to the French government, he said to his friend, Captain Gérard : " We are in for war, and this war is going to awaken bestiality in men as no war has done before ; we must be prepared to be shot down at any street corner." A few minutes later, as Jaurès sat down to a sandwich at the *Café du Croissant*, with his back to the open street window, a shot rang and a bullet pierced his brain from behind. It had been fired by a half-witted maniac, whom the jingo papers had convinced that Jaurès was the worst enemy of France.

On the 23rd of November, 1924, his body was translated to the Panthéon, France's Westminster Abbey, dedicated to the greatest of her sons, under the inscription : " *Aux grands hommes la Patrie reconnaissante.*" The coffin was borne on the shoulders of a group of miners of Carmaux.

If he had needed a personal epitaph, this could have been found in a sentence that was spoken at one of the last big parliamentary debates Jaurès took part in, by a conservative member of the Chamber of Deputies, one of his most determined opponents. Jaurès had made a desperate effort in speaking in favour of a motion that, according to party lines, could rely only on the support of a minority. But he so carried away the whole House that, when he began a sentence with the words "*La majorité de cette Chambre, Messieurs* . . .," his opponent could not help interrupting : "*Mais vous êtes, à vous seul, la majorité !* "*

And indeed, on that occasion, as on many others, Jaurès appeared as " a majority by himself." That is, no doubt, an uncommon tribute to the persuasive power of his eloquence, and even more to the truth of his own saying that the cause he fought for put its adversaries in the position of having to fight " with the sun blinding their eyes." But it is also a highly significant tribute to democracy. For though a democratic constitution does not necessarily mean that truth, justice and progress must win every single battle, it means that they cannot be prevented from fighting their battles on a field where they must in the long run prevail. For on this field the stake is the minds of men, and the mightiest weapon, in the end, is the argument that appeals to feelings and values no one can deny without turning his own conscience and his own reason into enemies of those who " have no need of lies."

---

* But you are a majority by yourself !

THOMAS JEFFERSON

1743–1826

by GEORGE E. GORDON CATLIN

THOMAS JEFFERSON
1743–1826
by GEORGE E. GORDON CATLIN

IN less than a decade, the bicentenary celebration will occur of Thomas Jefferson's birth at Shadwell, in Virginia, in 1743. The period of his life is that of the hey-day of Whiggery and the transition from Whiggery into Liberalism. He is the especial hierophant of the natural rights of man. An epoch of material change succeeded of which Jefferson and even Franklin never dreamed. The consequence has not altogether been the progress for which they hoped. By the time of the centenary, in 1926, of Jefferson's death, a reaction had already spread against most of the principles for which he stood—natural rights of liberty, free discussion and toleration, the superiority of the legislature, opposition to centralisation, preference for an agricultural civilisation. Those who fear for the future of democracy will be well advised to re-examine the origin and history of the Jeffersonian principles.

Thomas Jefferson, liberal democrat, was a landowner by inheritance and related on his mother's side to the great family of the Randolphs of Virginia. When he left college it was his good fortune to enter the chambers of one of Virginia's most eminent lawyers, George Wythe, where he was to be followed by John Marshall, the great Chief Justice, and by Henry Clay.

His political life began at the age of twenty-two when he heard Patrick Henry take up, for Virginia, the challenge that the New Englanders had passed over, and denounce, in 1765, Grenville's Stamp Act. One of Henry's resolutions declared that the General Assembly of the colony had " the sole right and power to levy taxes and impositions upon the inhabitants of this colony." The issue between the Virginian House of Burgesses and the Parliament of Britain was squarely set.

In 1767, Jefferson was called to the Virginian Bar ; in 1769, he became a member of the House of Burgesses. Appointed to draft the address of welcome to the new

Governor, his production, despite its expression of " our firm attachment to His Majesty's sacred person," was thought unsuitable and was rejected. His bill to enable slave-owners to manumit their slaves was defeated. " During the regal government," he writes bitterly, " nothing liberal could expect success." It should be added that under the republic, as Jefferson found, liberal projects did not always attain it. The House, having passed resolutions on the subject of no taxation without representation, was dissolved abruptly by the Governor.

On May 17th, 1769, in the Raleigh Tavern, at Williams-burg, George Washington, Patrick Henry, Jefferson and others met to discuss an embargo on British goods so long as the Townshend duties remained in force. The American Revolution was beginning. Events had launched the political career of Thomas Jefferson.

In 1774, the Boston Port Bill, the British Government's reply to the Boston Tea-Party, resulted again in a resolution by the Virginian House of Burgesses, a further dissolution and another meeting in the Raleigh Tavern. Jefferson already stood out as one of the originators of the Committee of Correspondence which organised collective action in the colonies. In the same year, Jefferson drafted his *Summary View of the Rights of British America*. In January, 1775, he was elected, at the head of the poll for his county, on to its Committee of Safety and as a member of the Virginian Convocation. The fight at Lexington occurred in April. In June, Jefferson was draftsman of the address of the Virginian House of Representatives to the Governor of Virginia.

In this address, " His Majesty's dutiful and loyal subjects, the Burgesses of Virginia," expressed pleasure at the " benevolent tender " towards " ending our unhappy disputes with the Mother Country " ; but declared that the Resolution of Parliament " only changes the form of oppression without lightening the burden." The reply to Lord North, drafted by Jefferson, was adopted in July, 1775, by the Congress at Philadelphia. In 1776, Jefferson sketched a " New Model Constitution for Virginia," of which part was embodied in the final draft ; and moved to the scene of Federal action in Philadelphia. When, on

June 10th, Congress appointed a committee to draw up a Declaration of Independence, Jefferson was the committee's obvious draftsman.

The rest of the career of Thomas Jefferson belongs to the public history of his country—his work for reform in Virginia ; his governorship there from 1779 to 1781 ; his embassy to France from 1784 to 1789 ; his tenure of the Secretaryship of State, and his quarrel with Alexander Hamilton ; and his Presidency of the United States from 1801 to 1809.

After he retired from public life, leaving his work to be carried on by his younger friends Madison and Monroe, he occupied himself with completing his library at Monticello (later sold to Congress), with entertaining his friends, and with the foundation of the University of Virginia. This last, the beautiful university at Charlottes-ville, along with the Declaration of Independence and the Statute of Virginia for Religious Toleration, he regarded as among his three claims to fame. At his direction, upon his gravestone was placed an inscription that " by these as testimonials that I have lived I wish most to be remembered." He was a great Virginian gentleman. In these respects he was more.

He rode his horse until within three weeks of his death at the age of eighty-three. He died in the early morning hours of July 4th, 1826, having lived until the jubilee of the Declaration that he fashioned.

The full responsibility of Jefferson for that Declaration can be taken as established. John Adams, one of the drafting committee, in his old age wrote, " the essence of it is contained in a pamphlet, voted and printed by the town of Boston, before the first Congress met, composed by James Otis, as I suppose in one of his lucid intervals, and pruned and polished by Samuel Adams." To this charge Jefferson had the effective reply that he had never seen Otis' pamphlet. He added, in words that carry conviction : " I did not consider it as any part of my charge to invent new ideas altogether, and to offer no sentiment which had ever been expressed before." Jefferson's statement is that the Declaration was written without consulting books or pamphlets. His debt, however, in thought to Locke and Algernon Sidney, champions of "natural liberty," is obvious and acknowledged.

On the other hand, it is a popular error to suppose any debt to exist upon the part of the authors of the American Revolution to Rousseau or the Encyclopædists. The debt is all the other way. This Lafayette symbolically acknowledged when he placed a copy of the Declaration of Independence conspicuously in his library, with a vacant space beside it for a comparable French Declaration. The debt of the "Patriot" group personally to Jefferson is indubitable.

Already, in the *Summary Review* of 1774, Jefferson had struck the distinctive note of the Declaration. The detailed and legalistic arguments of John Dickinson are abandoned. The right, admitted even by Washington, of the British Parliament to tax the Colonies in specific cases, "with moderation," is no longer conceded. "The young," writes Edmund Randolph, "ascended with Mr. Jefferson to the sources of these rights." Jefferson substituted, for a temporary quarrel, eternal issues. That is his fame.

King George, "as Chief Magistrate of the British Empire," is invited to hear "the united complaints of His Majesty's subjects in America." Deputies from "the other states in British America" were invited, in the *Summary View*, to concert in presenting an address. The jurisdiction of the British Parliament over these states is denied. The King rules in Virginia, by the same title, although in a different fashion, as he rules in Hanover. The union with Britain is a dynastic union and no more—but he is yet the King of free Englishmen who, exercising the natural right of free emigration, have brought with them to the shores of a new country those liberties that they had enjoyed since the days of their Saxon ancestors. The quarrel is with the British Parliament. But the King does not, in the *Summary View*, escape censure. "Open your breast, Sire, to a liberal and expanded thought. Let not the name of George the Third be a blot on the page of history."

When Jefferson came to write the Declaration of Independence he pursued, with more emphasis, the same policy. Fundamental claims are substituted for legal complaints.

Again he " ascends to the source of rights." This source is no longer historical or traditional but a fount of truths esteemed to be self-evident. The complaint against the Parliament of Great Britain has been broadened into an indictment also against its King. The indictment, however, is framed, not in the legal and constitutional terms of a petition of right, but as an inevitable deduction from the first principles of all political philosophy. Rebellion cannot be supplied with a legal permit—nor would the French Foreign Ministry have been interested in a dispute that was to remain domestic.

Jefferson framed an argument that could appeal to men of all nationalities in a candid world. It was not merely one that might have force with Englishmen trained in the free traditions, and acquainted with the legal principles, of their country. The Declaration is an international document in conception and appeal. Like the Germans with Lenin in 1917, so the French, in 1776, demanded a sweeping policy—which in the event, damaged the empire of Britain but demolished the social system of France ; just as the plotters of the Wilhelmstrasse, with their " sealed train," destroyed the monarchy of Russia but swept away that of Germany.

There were many who were prepared to say, with such a Tory as John Lind, that Jefferson had " put the axe to the tree of all government." Charles James Fox could claim that the Americans " had done no more than the English had done against James II." It was, however, clear that Congress had advanced, in fact even if reluctantly, to the enunciation under Jefferson's guidance of philo-sophical and practical principles much more far-reaching than those to which the Whig Revolution of 1688–9 had committed itself. It was not for nothing that Condorcet exhorted the French to consider the principles of liberty and " to read them in the example of a great people " or that Mirabeau referred to the way in which the claims of the Declaration were " very generally applauded."

The Parliamentarians, in the days of James I and the early days of Charles I, had made humble pleas as subjects to their rightful sovereigns. The Whigs, in 1689, had effected a constitutional compromise with an executive magistrate who was also their liege lord. The Declaration placed, not only laws above men, but irrefragable principles of society above positive laws. It thereby prepared the way for the French Revolution that made magistrates the delegates and functionaries of the general will. But, of the two, the Declaration, by exalting the laws of human nature rather than the arbitrary will of a majority, adhered to the sounder principles.

Jonathan Mayhew, in 1766, wrote : " Having been initiated, in youth, in the doctrines of civil liberty, as they were taught by such men as Plato, Demosthenes, Cicero, and other renowned persons among the ancients, and such as Sidney and Milton, Locke and Hoadly among the moderns, I liked them ; they seemed rational." Mayhew is representative enough of the average. There must have been many among those educated in the American colleges in the mid-eighteenth century, impressed by the radicalism of Locke and the rational system of Newton, who would have echoed Mayhew's judgment and approved his taste. Certainly Jefferson was among them. The writings of Cicero, Sidney, Locke, Montesquieu, Priestley and Malthus are all on the short list of books he later recommended to a grandson. Among these, Locke must count first in influence.

In his brilliant *Declaration of Independence*, Professor Carl Becker summarises the attitude of Locke towards the problem of governmental authority. " Government ought to have the authority which reasonable men, living together in a community, considering the rational interests of each and all, might be disposed to submit to willingly." Primary among these rational interests are what the Lockians called men's " natural rights." Professor Becker happily quotes from the writings of William Ellery Channing, the great Unitarian and opponent of Slavery, to show what the men of the generation after Jefferson understood to be the character of these natural rights that Hooker adumbrated, Locke enunciated, and Jefferson proclaimed. " Man has rights by nature. . . . In the order of things they precede society, lie at its foundations, constitute man's capacity for it, and are the great objects of social institutions."

To-day, when it is popular to describe both the theory of natural rights, preceding civil government, and the more mature theory of natural law as being discredited, we hear of the rights of women, urged on more than utilitarian grounds, and of the ordinary man's " right of continuous initiative " as the basis of a workers' democratic movement. Substantially these claims are not different from those urged by Jefferson on behalf of life, liberty and the pursuit of happiness.

The points in which Jefferson marks an advance upon Locke, in the history of thought, are that he discards any reference to an original social contract, and that he derives all " just powers " of government solely from the consent of the governed.

In the Lockian theory there is a double contract—the contract between members of society to conduct themselves as social and civil beings, and the contract with a ruler or legislative for purposes of authoritative government. In the Jeffersonian theory no ruler stands out, over against the people, as an independent party to some contract, tacit or avowed. In the first draft of the Declaration man is described as being born " equal and independent." He is untied by any traditional or " original " social contract. The men of each generation maintain a government for its utility. They recognise no obligation to any government that claims to derive its powers from a non-popular source or that endeavours to negotiate or enforce a contract, as a party independent of the people. They admit no vice-regent of God, or symbol of the eternal nation, or group claiming to rule others " for their good, as a moral obligation." Executive officers are functionaries entrusted with power by the people.

Jefferson, as is well known, carried this rejection of any tradition or " original contract " so far as to maintain that no generation was entitled to bind its successor. Statisticians assured him that a new generation arose every nineteen years. After each such period, therefore, he demanded a " revolution," an entire overhauling of the constitution, in order that it should again receive popular authorisation. Force was given to this demand by the restriction imposed, in the American States, on the will of democratic legislatures by written constitutions. Such " revolutions," he held, like thunderstorms, cleared the

air. " A little rebellion, now and then, is a good thing. . . .
The spirit of resistance to government is so valuable on
certain occasions that I wish it to be always kept alive."

The objections to Jefferson's and Channing's theories
of man's natural equality and independence are clear on
the surface. " All men are born free ? . . . No, not a
single man," says Bentham, " not a single man that ever
was, or is, or will be." In the days of the slavery issue
in the United States, reverend gentlemen could point out
that these were notions tainted by French infidelity, and
that " a God-fearing people " would reject them. To-day,
every biologist, without calling in God's curse upon Ham,
can riddle the argument about human equality. Every
critic of Whiggery and Liberal individualism can point
out the folly of regarding men as born, or as living, " independent." They are born as babies—and live as men—
dependent and social beings.

The argument, however, dies hard—and properly so.
The Cynics and the Stoics, who first elaborated the theory,
did so as a protest against artificial and irrational inequalities,
which had no basis in such values as sincere men could
accept. It was on this basis that the theory was maintained
by the Church, as true " according to the law of nature."
A rigid doctrine of predestination and of original corruption
tended to undermine it. If all men were worms, it might
well be that the more miserable worms had no ground of
complaint against God's will which condemned them to
servitude as children of damnation. It was the great work
of Locke to free men from this bondage by declaring that
the mind of each man at birth was *tabula rasa*, instead of
bearing blazed upon it, with other innate ideas, the adverse
decree of fate. Sensations, environment, enlightenment,
education, would determine the future. Thomas Jefferson, no
less than Robert Owen, was to draw the deductions. Men
were to be assumed equal until it was known what a
favourable environment could do to improve them, or an
adverse environment had done to retard them. Equality,
for Jefferson, was no herd-levelling, but an elaboration of
the full meaning of liberty.

When he is discussing education, Jefferson states his

principles in a form far less sweeping. In his proposals for elementary instruction in Virginia he writes : " Of the boys thus sent in one year, trial is to be made at the grammar school for one or two years, and the best genius of the whole selected, and continued six years, and the residue dismissed. By this means twenty of the best geniuses will be raked from the rubbish annually, and be instructed at the public expense." Repeatedly, however, Jefferson insists that the common man can be trusted : he " was not one of those who held fourteen out of every fifteen dishonest."

" The form of government which we have adopted," he writes in 1826 (in perhaps his last letter), " restores the free right to the unbounded exercise of reason and freedom of opinion. . . . The general spread of the light of science has already laid open to every view the palpable truth that the mass of mankind has not been born with saddles on their backs, nor a favoured few booted and spurred, ready to ride them legitimately, by the grace of God." At the back of all Jefferson's metaphysic of inalienable rights, of which the only true grounding is to be found in the permanent qualities of human nature, lie a practical common-sense and an anticipation of the importance for liberty of the right of experiment.

Jefferson's doctrine of equality, in brief, is one more protest against unjust equality, on behalf of a condition in which innate ability may be able to take its just place. There is, however, in the Jeffersonian doctrine little of the harsh ill-manners of a society where the open career is being avidly seized upon by self-made men of talent. The social atmosphere desired is one that places the burden of proof upon the man who requires pre-eminence and unequal rights. A happy tale illustrates well Jefferson's conception of good manners. A negro bowed to the ex-President when he was out riding with his grandson, Thomas Jefferson Randolph. Mr. Jefferson returned the bow : the grandson did not. " Turning to me, he asked," records Randolph, " ' Do you permit a negro to be more of a gentleman than yourself ? ' "

Jefferson's attitude towards the Slavery issue shows his

N*

own interpretation, as statesman, of the principles of
liberty he had proclaimed to the world. His autobiography
records the failure of his attempt to procure the manumission of all born, in Virginia, after a certain year. " It
was found that the public mind would not bear the proposition, nor will it bear it even at this day " (1821). " Yet
the day is not distant when it must bear and adopt it,
or worse will follow. Nothing is more certainly written
in the book of fate than that these people are to be free ;
nor is it less certain that the two races, equally free, cannot
live in the same government." Throughout, Jefferson's
remedy was the deportation of the emancipated slaves to
San Domingo or Africa.

Again, in 1784, Jefferson's Report to Congress suggested
manumission for all slaves born after 1800. The adoption
of the Report was lost by a single vote. " The voice of a
single individual," writes Jefferson, " would have prevented
this abominable crime from spreading itself over the new
country . . . Heaven was silent in that awful moment ! "
The Missouri Compromise of 1820 he regarded as
" a reprieve only." " Justice is in the one scale, and self-
preservation in the other." Self-preservation came first.
Economic change would, in due course, issue in slave-
emancipation.

" The opinion that the negroes are inferior in the faculties
of reason and imagination must be regarded with great
diffidence. . . . To our reproach it must be said that,
through a century and a half [during which] we have had
under our eyes the races of black and red men, they have
never yet been viewed by us as subjects of natural history."

The tempered preoccupation with liberty which
characterised his attitude towards national independence
and towards slavery, also showed in his attitude towards
governmental authority. It is displayed in his insistence
on the importance of freedom of the press, *habeas corpus*
and trial by jury.

Liberty, for Jefferson, was the liberty of " the embattled
farmers "—of landowners and lawyers, such as himself.
He praises an agricultural civilisation. He desires to
develop local government in " wards." Although no man
worked more for the united front of the Colonies in the War

of Independence, he is yet the very patriarch of the doctrine of State rights. He has the Whig distrust of " the government " as such. Administration should be " wise and frugal." He dislikes energetic government because it will be oppressive government. If it encroaches, it is to be resisted. " What signify a few lives lost in a century or two ? The tree of liberty must be refreshed from time to time with the blood of patriots and tyrants."

Although he makes the people the sole source of power, divides mankind into the Whigs who trust the people and the Tories who fear them, and proclaims the duty of absolute acquiescence in the rule of the majority, this notion of " the people " remains unanalysed. There is no discussion of how a majority vote may be courted. There is no apprehension of the dangers of demagoguery. There is no comment upon the inner meaning of Bonapartism. Bonaparte is a brilliant soldier but no more—substantially, a stupid fellow, " supplying ignorance by bold presumption "—calculating ; not perhaps without insight, but lacking a reasoned sense of direction ; anyhow " a moral monster."

The tendency towards centralisation and infringement of State rights which showed itself in the financial and executive policy of Alexander Hamilton and, on the side of the judiciary, in the judgments of Chief Justice Marshall, found in Jefferson a determined opponent. Even against the Hamiltonian policy of settlement of private debts to Britain, he complains that " the British commercial regulations lessen our means of payment." It should be added that Jefferson's own interpretation of the meaning of the division of powers was sometimes odd. Thus, when President, he held it to be within the power of the executive to release individuals imprisoned by the Federal Courts under the Sedition Act on the ground that the President held the law to be unauthorised by the Constitution and null. The analogous British legislation he briefly described as " Mr. Pitt's Bill against democratic societies."

Jefferson's devolutionist and self-sufficient ideals in domestic government are not unconnected with his isolationism in foreign affairs. The purchase of Louisiana, during his

Presidency, is not so much an essay in imperialism as a considered step to this self-sufficiency.

President Monroe was a tried friend of Jefferson's and himself a thorough Jeffersonian. It was natural that he should consult the elder statesman about the policy to be pursued towards the revolted South American colonies of Spain. In October, 1823, two months before the enunciation of the " Monroe Doctrine," Jefferson wrote to the President words that emphasised and underlined Washington's farewell exhortation.

" Our first and fundamental maxim should be, never to entangle ourselves in the broils of Europe." " They are," he adds elsewhere, "nations of eternal war." " Our second, never to suffer Europe to intermeddle with cis-Atlantic affairs. . . . While [the Europe of the Holy Alliance] is labouring to become the domicile of despotism, our endeavour should be, to make our hemisphere that of freedom. . . . . With her [Britain] we should cherish a cordial friendship ; and nothing would tend more to knit our affections than to be fighting once more, side by side, in the same cause. . . . If, to facilitate this [regional peace, for the Americans] we can effect a division in the body of the European powers, and draw over to our side its most powerful member, surely we should do it. But I am clearly of Mr. Canning's opinion, that it will prevent, instead of provoking, war."

No man has ever been more entitled to speak on the meaning of the rights of man, and on the revolutionary defence of liberty, than Thomas Jefferson. In his last years, he wrote : " I shall not die without a hope that light and liberty are in steady advance." He was a great revolutionary. His judgment, therefore, upon one of the greatest of European revolutions is of the highest present importance to us who live in what is, again, a great revolutionary age. The judgment, which he has placed on record for us, is to be found in his autobiography.

" I was much acquainted," writes Jefferson of his days when he was ambassador to France, " with the leading Patriots of the Assembly . . . I urged, most strenuously, an immediate compromise ; to secure what the government was now ready to yield, and to trust to future occasions for what might still be wanting. They thought otherwise, however, and events have proved their lamentable error. For, after thirty years of war, foreign and domestic, the loss of millions of lives, the frustration of private happiness, and the foreign subjugation of their own country for a time, they have obtained no more, or even that securely."

Jefferson continues, however, " the appeal to the rights of man, which had been made in the United States, was taken up by France, first of the European nations. From here, the spirit has spread over those of the south. The tyrants of the north have allied indeed against it ; but it is irresistible. Their opposition will only multiply its millions of human victims ; their own satellites will catch it, and the condition of man, through the civilised world, will be finally and greatly ameliorated."

The theoretical basis upon which Jeffersonianism was built appeared to have been destroyed, before Jefferson was dead, by Jeremy Bentham. " Natural Rights is simple nonsense : natural and imprescriptible rights, rhetorical nonsense—nonsense upon stilts." Substantially, however, the dogma that " each man is to count for one " rests upon no better basis than other natural rights, such as the rights to liberty and the pursuit of happiness. On the contrary, Jeffersonianism, in its whole temper, its democratic quality, its respect for majority rule, its hedonism, is compatible with Utilitarianism and " the greatest happiness principle." The influence of Priestley, scientist, Unitarian and precursor of the Utilitarians, is detectable upon both.

Jeffersonianism is weakened by a shallow belief in what can be accomplished by " enlightenment," apart from consideration of the economic condition of those to be enlightened. More than Utilitarianism it tends to exaggerate the independence of man's " rights " from the social surroundings under which he lives. But it does not fall into the error of T. H. Green of deriving those rights from some society or its particular social order. That fact is very relevant to any judgment that is passed to-day upon

Jefferson's theories. It is important, moreover—in these days of pseudo-socialistic, "organismic" and "totalitarian" views of society, with their false analogies, misapplied biology and subordination of the nature of man to his civilisation, its social forms and political fanaticisms.

The moral rights of man are no other than the fundamental psychological demands of rational man upon his environment. They derive, not from any particular society, but from the nature of man himself, and from the common human nature shared by each human being. This Thomas Jefferson was concerned to affirm, although he adopts the individualistic terminology of natural rights, and not the more effective terminology of natural law. Final authority does not lie in some infallible doctrine or divine right or absolute political dogma. The institutions of man are to be judged by their proper accordance with the basic nature and impulses of man, and not with the arbitrary will of individuals or groups, dictators or doctrinaires or dynasts—this is the meaning of those opening clauses of the Declaration of Independence, which are Jefferson's title to remembrance as a great democrat. The source of the eternal demands of humanity lies in the permanent qualities of the nature of man, and is grounded upon hopes that this nature, and not any government, limits and determines.

ABRAHAM LINCOLN

1809–1865

by BRUCE BLIVEN

ABRAHAM LINCOLN

1809–1865

by BRUCE BLIVEN

ABRAHAM LINCOLN was born February 12, 1809, in what was then a remote American frontier region, a few miles from Hodgensville, Kentucky. His ancestry on his father's side was English, but the family had lived in America for several generations. Little is known of them, and certainly nothing which would adequately account for the extraordinary qualities Lincoln displayed. His father, Thomas Lincoln, was the common, rather happy-go-lucky type of the American frontiersman ; his mother, Nancy Hanks Lincoln, seems to have been of unusual character. Certainly she made a deep impression on the child, Abraham, before her death which occurred when he was nine years old. Lincoln himself believed, without any positive evidence, that she was illegitimately descended from an aristocratic Virginia family, also of British blood. He had one sister, four years older than himself ; and after his mother's death his father married again, the stepmother being a widow, Mrs. Sarah Johnston, with children of her own. In his seventh year, his father moved to another equally unsettled region in the State of Indiana at what afterward became the town of Gentryville, and here Lincoln grew to young manhood. In 1830, when he was twenty-one, the family moved again —this time, to New Salem, Illinois. In that State he continued to live until he had been elected President.

Lincoln's childhood was spent in deep poverty, with hardly any formal education. Every American is familiar with the stories of his reading, in the few books available to him, by the light of a flickering pine-knot, or stretched out on the floor beside the fireplace in the rude cabin which was his home. The list of his books is known : the Bible, *Pilgrim's Progress, Æsop's Fables, Robinson Crusoe*, a *History of the United States*, and Parson Weems' highly-coloured *Life of George Washington*. His life as a child was on the whole like that of his playmates ; it contained a good deal of hard work, as well as the boisterous recreations of the time and place.

But he was unusual in that through some native tenderness he never shot either wild fowl or game. He was, however, extremely strong, and more than held his own in the athletic contests of the frontier. In particular, he was a famous wrestler. In early youth he grew to be unusually tall—nearly six feet, four inches. All his life he had a naïve pride in this fact, and whenever any strikingly tall man came into his presence, he would insist on their measuring heights, back to back—a habit which sometimes offended an important political personage, who feared that he was being ridiculed. Lincoln's unquestioned popularity among his neighbours perhaps resulted, first of all from his personality, second from his physical prowess, and third from the fact that he was a famous story-teller. All his life, he delighted in telling tales, most of which grew out of his own early experiences. With these brief humorous anecdotes he would reinforce an argument, or convey an unspoken rebuke. Many of these stories which he told to exclusively male audiences were " improper "—though of course much less so by the easier standards of our day than by those of the strongly religious small frontier settlement of America a hundred years ago.

Tradition has made much of Lincoln's early occupation as a " rail-splitter," but this was only one of many sorts of work which he did in his youth, and he deprecated the attempt of professional politicians to romanticize this fact about his early life, which they had begun to do even as soon as his first Presidential campaign. More important in every way were his river voyages. Both of the places where his family lived during his childhood and youth were near the Ohio, an important navigable tributary of the Mississippi ; and it was not at all surprising that in his late teens he should have made two long voyages, all the way down to New Orleans, drifting down the river with a boat whose cargo was there sold for whatever it would bring. Indiana, where Lincoln lived from his eighth to his twenty-first year, was territory where slaves were not permitted ; and it was not until these trips to New Orleans that he came into contact with the institution whose mortal foe he was thenceforth to be. The story is told that, seeing slaves exposed for sale in the market place, he exclaimed to one of his comrades, " By God, boys, let's get away from this. If ever I get a chance to hit that thing, I'll hit it hard." Whether the incident be true or not, the frame of mind indicated by it is in accord with the historic facts.

On his return from the second of these voyages down the Mississippi, Lincoln left the parental roof and began to shift for himself in Illinois. For the next twenty-five years, his life was by his own estimate of it a failure. He " kept store " for a short time, certainly without any conspicuous success. He spent a few months as captain of a volunteer company in the " Black Hawk War," an unimportant military campaign against an Indian chief who had " gone on the warpath." Lincoln saw no fighting and ever after ridiculed his own experience. About this time he studied law, chiefly by the old-fashioned, simple procedure of reading law books, and for many years thereafter he practised in a rather desultory fashion, earning small sums which were, however, adequate for his extremely modest needs. In 1834 he was elected to the Illinois State Legislature, where he served until 1842, without particularly distinguishing himself. In 1847–8 he was a member of the national House of Representatives in Washington, where his service was also far from noteworthy. Thereafter he continued his law practice, in and near Springfield, Illinois, until after his election to the Presidency in 1860.

Lincoln's personal relations with other people were never very happy, and least of all with women. He was incurably awkward and shy ; he believed, and during most of his life community opinion agreed with him, that he was one of the ugliest men who ever lived. He was subject to fits of profound melancholy, regarding which science knows much more to-day than it did then ; these periods of depression sometimes caused serious fears among his friends that he might take his own life. Despite his shyness and uncertainty—or perhaps partially because of them— Lincoln was three times engaged to be married. The first of these episodes was with Miss Ann Rutledge, who died not long after the beginning of the engagement, in 1835.

There is no doubt that Lincoln was deeply attached to her and that her death contributed to the shadow which lay over the rest of his life. Three years later, he became engaged again, to Miss Mary Owens, but he was the most unenthusiastic of lovers and seems to have been quite satisfied with her decision that the engagement had been a mistake. A year later he met Mary Todd, whom he married in 1842. What is chiefly remembered of her to-day is her ungovernable fits of temper, her unceasing though futile efforts to teach Lincoln the small social amenities, and the fact that her mind was definitely clouded toward the end of her life. Of their four children, only one, Robert Todd Lincoln, survived to manhood. He had a modestly distinguished career, chiefly in the field of business.

During the whole of Lincoln's life, negro slavery was the outstanding public issue in America. The nation which had begun with a few States along the Atlantic seaboard was rapidly extending itself westward into the vast territory of the Mississippi Valley and it was now plain that this process would continue until the Pacific Ocean had been reached. The importation of Negro slaves from Africa had been forbidden a year before Lincoln's birth, but this did not mean, of course, that slaves already within the United States were set free. Broadly speaking, slavery was firmly established in the South, was not practised in the North, and was practised to some extent in the border States between the two. As additional territory was incorporated into the United States, the question of over-whelming importance was whether it should be " slave " or " free." Each side feared that the other would obtain an overwhelming preponderance in Congress, and pass legislation adverse to its interests, and as new territory was added to the United States, the struggle became ever fiercer. By the famous " Missouri Compromise," passed in 1820, when Lincoln was eleven years of age, Missouri was admitted as a slave State, but it was agreed that slavery should henceforth be banned in all territory north of an east-and-west line at latitude 36 degrees 30 minutes north.

In 1854, Stephen Douglas (afterward famous for his participation in the Lincoln-Douglas debates) managed to obtain the repeal of the Missouri Compromise. The result was that the new territories of Kansas and Nebraska became the battleground between advocates and opponents of slavery, who sometimes actually engaged there in guerrilla warfare. Another development which was hastened if not caused by the repeal of the Compromise, was the formation of the Republican party, on a platform of opposition to slavery. It elected Lincoln as President in 1860, and has dominated American political life most of the time ever since. The repeal of the Compromise was re-enforced in 1857 by an extraordinary decision of the United States Supreme Court in the famous Dred Scott case, which held that all attempts to forbid Negro slavery in any part of the United States were unconstitutional—a decision which was equally bad as law and as morals. The effect of this decision was to cause the opponents of slavery to despair of attempts to confine it to the South, and to make them feel that it must be destroyed root and branch.

In the foreshortened view of history, many persons have come to believe that Lincoln was all his life an Abolitionist, but this is not true. The moral crusade against slavery was conducted by a small minority of the population, and he was not in its ranks. William Lloyd Garrison started the struggle in 1831, in Boston, when he published the first issue of his famous paper, *The Liberator*, and for many years he found comparatively few followers. Lincoln disapproved of the gallant, if utterly hopeless raid of John Brown at Harper's Ferry, Virginia, in 1859, which the South looked upon as the beginning of a slave rebellion and for which Brown was promptly hanged. He stood aloof from the men who conducted the " underground railway," whereby fugitive slaves were aided in escaping into the free Northern States, and he was not outspoken against the laws whereby many of these Negroes were caught and returned to the South.

Lincoln was opposed to slavery, on personal and moral grounds, and he never faltered in this position during the whole of his life ; but he would have educated the South to see the error of its ways, and would never have committed any overt act in the effort to enforce his views. The Civil War was to him a war to save the Union, as he indicated in his famous letter to Horace Greeley, editor of *The New*

*York Tribune.** The Emancipation Proclamation was not
issued until the War was a year and a half old, and was
intended primarily as a War measure, to induce the Negroes
in the South to rally to the Northern cause. Lincoln himself
recognised that it was of doubtful legality, and needed to
be confirmed by an amendment to the Federal Constitution,
which was afterwards done.

It was his debates with Stephen Douglas, in 1858, which
first brought Lincoln to the attention of the whole nation,
and thereby led indirectly to his being chosen for the
Presidency. He had for some years before that had a good
reputation in Illinois ; but this was only one State, and a
remote one on the frontier. The debates were in fact
part of an electoral campaign between the two men, the
prize being a seat in the United States Senate. Senators
were then (and for many years afterward) chosen by the
State legislatures, but the voters could decide the matter
by sending to the legislature members pledged in advance
to one senatorial candidate or another.

It would have been difficult to choose two opponents
more strikingly dissimilar than these. Douglas, so short
and stocky in build that he was nicknamed " the little
Giant," was a florid, self-confident, dynamic individual,
an opportunist in politics, a good deal of a demagogue, with
the gothic oratorical style which was so popular in the
America of that day. Lincoln, tall, awkward, shambling,
was slow in movement and speech. His face was deeply
lined and tragic ; and few of his early audiences had the
acumen to perceive the dignity, the nobility of his expression.
He was perhaps the finest orator America ever produced,
one of the little handful of the world's greatest ; but his
gift was not always uniformly present, and even when it
was, his hearers often failed until afterward to realise the
beauty and power of his utterance. (This was notably
true of his masterpiece, the Gettysburg address, which
passed unnoticed at the time, both his hearers and the
newspapers giving all their attention to a perfectly worthless

---

* " My paramount object in this struggle is to save the Union and is
not either to save or destroy slavery. If I could save the Union without
freeing any slaves I would do it ; and if I could save it by freeing all the
slaves I would do it ; and if I could save it by freeing some and leaving
others alone I would also do that."

two-hour address by Edward Everett.) Lincoln's gift consisted in beautiful, simple—often almost Biblical—English, charged with deep emotion ; a masterly economy of phrase ; utter sincerity and candour, and the assumption in his hearers of an intelligence and goodwill equal to his own. On certain occasions, his power over the crowd seemed simply superhuman ; at least once, he so enthralled even the shorthand reporters that they forgot to write down what he said.

The debates with Douglas no longer have any reality for the reader, because in retrospect the difference between the two men no longer seems important. Lincoln was about half way between the Abolitionists and Douglas, Douglas half way between Lincoln and the out-and-out slavery men. Stephen Douglas, indifferent to the rights of the Negro as he was to their suffering as human beings, was concerned only that each section of the North, and the newly-opened West, should have local autonomy, with the right to accept or reject slavery as it chose. Lincoln felt that there were deep principles at stake, that conscience dictated a course of unalterable opposition to the further extension of slavery into new territory *plus* a steady long-continued pressure for its amelioration and ultimate removal even in the South. The debates ended inconclusively ; Douglas won the necessary majority of the State legislators and became Senator ; but Lincoln's part in the contests had been widely published, and had commanded deep attention. Almost overnight he became a possible nominee for the Presidency.

His " availability " was increased in February, 1860, through his speech in Cooper Union, New York, where he was heard by all the intellectual leaders of the day and made a profound impression by an address simple, closely-knit, deeply moving because the speaker was himself so deeply moved by the principles he enunciated. He now appeared the most obvious candidate for the Republican nomination in a year when it was evident that the choice of that party would be elected (the Democrats having split into a Northern and a Southern wing). After a short but intense struggle, involving some political sharp practice of the sort all too familiar in American political life, Lincoln was nominated.

The election was bitterly contested, but Lincoln had more votes than either of the Democratic candidates, or the nominee of the inconsiderable Whig party. He took his seat as President on March 4, 1861, and a month and eight days later the Civil War had begun.

Neither Lincoln nor any other individual made the American Civil War; it is altogether likely that neither he nor anyone else on earth could have prevented it. It was the culmination of what was truly called an "irrepressible conflict," extending over many years, a conflict which seemed incapable of any reasoned solution. Modern historians have tended to emphasize the economic origins of this struggle; they point out that cheap slave labour put the South in a position of advantage which the North found increasingly onerous. To be sure, the South was predominantly agricultural, and much of its chief crop—cotton—was sent abroad to Lancashire; but industry was growing in the area, and the low cost of slave labour tended to force down the wages of free white workers.

When the war began, however, neither this nor any other aspect of the slavery question was much to the fore. True, nine years earlier, in 1852, Harriet Beecher Stowe had published *Uncle Tom's Cabin*, a romanticised version, in "popular" novel form, of all the worst aspects of slavery. It swept through the nation with tremendous force, and it is perhaps true, as has been said, that it had more political effect than any other book (except the Bible) ever written. Yet its consequence was chiefly to inflame the fury of the South and to re-emphasise the determination of the Northern Abolitionists, who in fact needed little urging. When the War started, the one overwhelming issue was the right of the Southern States to secede from the American Union. Lincoln, and the North generally, denied that any such right existed, and fought to maintain their contention.

Their vehemence is somewhat hard to understand at the present day, and it puzzled most Europeans at the time; but it must of course be considered in the light of antecedent conditions. The United States was not then the unquestioned world power it is to-day. The desperate struggle by which it had achieved national unity was still sufficiently recent to make the idea of internal division seem an overwhelming calamity. Despite the Monroe Doctrine, then forty years old, European Powers still wielded great influence in the western hemisphere, and were feared and respected proportionately. To-day it is easy for us to hold that perhaps no great harm would have been done if the North and the South had formed separate nations. Slavery would have been abolished at once in the former and within a short time, undoubtedly, in the latter, since at that time it was in the process of being repudiated throughout the civilised world (even the Russian serfs were emancipated in the year when the Civil War began). One can only say that at that time very few in the North were prepared to accept such a development, and that to-day, seventy years after the War, the whole South accepts its outcome as having been for the best.

Before such a conclusion could be accepted, however, America was to go through the darkest years of its whole national history, to be followed by decades of acute misery in the South during the agonies of " Reconstruction." There is no point in telling here, even if space permitted, the military history of the War. In general, the more closely one studies the record, the more completely does whatever glamour might be attached to it disappear. Like all wars, everywhere, it was a series of blunders, hesitations and timidities alternating with reckless pouring out of human life either in hopeless efforts or for almost valueless objectives. On paper, the North was so overwhelmingly superior that it should have brought the War to a victorious conclusion within a year or two at most. The South had the advantage, however, of fighting a defensive struggle in a terrain which gave them the advantages in such an operation. The average Southerner, moreover, was more likely than the average Northerner to be an outdoor sort of person, skilled in horsemanship and firearms. The South had several military commanders available from the beginning of the War who were of the first rank in ability ; the best men on the Northern side came into power late in the struggle, and some of the men in command at the beginning were timid and vacillating to the point of pathological weakness.

President Lincoln found himself beset all at once by an

extraordinary list of pressing difficulties. His Cabinet included some able men ; but the ablest of them were inclined at first to be contemptuous of his abilities, and to act against his wishes. His force of character soon overcame this tendency ; but he found it necessary personally to supervise all details of policy, both domestic and foreign, to an extraordinary degree. The situation was made more difficult by the fact that both Great Britain and France on the whole were on the side of the South during the early part of the War, and the blockade which the North established over the Southern ports led to several " incidents " with Great Britain, at least one of which led the two countries dangerously near to the brink of war.

The President of the United States is legally the commander-in-chief of all its armed forces, but as a rule this relationship is only a nominal one. In Lincoln's case, however, it had a desperate reality. During the first two years and more of the conflict, President Lincoln had the utmost difficulty in compelling the Northern generals to conduct an aggressive campaign. Several times the Southern troops came within a few miles of Washington itself, and some of the most important engagements in the War took place far to the north of that city. When the President demanded that the Northern troops should fight, his generals told him that the strategic position made this inadvisable. In order to answer them, he was obliged in the midst of all his other duties to undertake an impromptu reading course in military science. Later on, brilliant commanders like Ulysses S. Grant and William T. Sherman came to the fore, and took much of this burden from the shoulders of the President. It is true, however, that in the end the South was starved out, exhausted and made bankrupt, rather than defeated by pure military science.

What history will undoubtedly regard as the most important event of the War, and of Lincoln's whole career, is, of course, the Emancipation Proclamation of September, 1862. As I have already indicated, this was primarily conceived as a War measure and not as an act of justice to the Negro. There were millions of slaves throughout the South who could render extremely valuable assistance to the Union cause ; and by declaring that in Northern eyes they were legally free, the President aided greatly the chance of a Northern victory. Many thousands of Negroes escaped from their masters and made their way into Northern territory where they were organized into labour battalions, or in some cases into troops.

Lincoln had planned to announce the emancipation of the slaves some months earlier but was dissuaded from doing so by the members of his Cabinet. They pointed out, when he first brought the suggestion forward, that the Northern cause was not going well, and argued that the proclamation would then be regarded as a gesture of weakness, not of strength. They feared it would be interpreted in the South, and perhaps in Europe, as an invitation to the slaves to rise in a Spartacist rebellion against their masters, and that this would alienate European opinion, already hostile to the North. The President yielded to this view, but only temporarily. As soon as things were going somewhat better for the North, in September, he announced that the slaves would be freed on January 1 of the following year. The proclamation was carefully worded to avoid the suggestion that the emancipated Negroes should offer any violence to their late masters; and at the time there was, in fact, very little trouble from this cause.

While the North, on the whole, thought of the War as being a struggle for human liberty, it was accompanied, like other conflicts conceived in the same way, by many incidents of an undemocratic character. The North found great trouble in obtaining by voluntary enlistment the number of soldiers it required, and speedily resorted to the draft. To-day, the system used seems shockingly unfair. No attempt was made to select men with any reference to the number of their dependents or their other social responsibilities. Instead, they were designated at random, and were permitted to buy their way out of the army by hiring a substitute. It was also possible to escape service by making a flat payment of $300 to the Government. This system, which obviously forced the poor man to risk his life while those a little more well-to-do escaped, was accompanied by even grosser scandals. Men hired themselves out as substitutes, enlisted, deserted and hired themselves out again, repeating the process many times.

Other men were kidnapped and virtually sold into the service, including some Canadians. Dissatisfaction with conscription came to its head in the riots in New York City in July, 1863. Considering themselves unfairly treated, a huge mob of men, composed largely, it is believed, of Irish immigrants, paraded the streets of New York for several days. They burned down the houses of prominent citizens and lynched a number of negroes. Federal troops arrived in the city after four days of this, and restored order.

Despite Lincoln's faith in Democracy, he curtailed civil liberties during the War in a fashion which brought many and bitter protests. The writ of *habeas corpus* was early suspended and in many instances civilians were tried in military courts with a denial of substantial justice. Like other great democrats in wartime, the President considered that winning the conflict was all-important, and sacrificed everything else to that end. On the other hand, his humanitarianism expressed itself, during the War, in one of the most touching aspects of his career. There were many cases where Union soldiers were arrested for falling asleep on sentry duty, or for other similar infractions of military rules ; and often the military courts sentenced these soldiers to be executed. The President had the power of pardon, and, not unnaturally, the family and friends of a condemned man almost invariably sought to obtain his intercession. In many cases there were extenuating circumstances ; the soldiers were very young, were unaccustomed to military life, and not infrequently were forced to perform sentry duty when completely exhausted by other labours. Very often Lincoln intervened to save the life of a condemned man. His action was bitterly resented by the military authorities who claimed that he was destroying army discipline, but it made him tremendously popular with the civilian population.

In 1864, while the War was still in progress, Lincoln had to stand for re-election. That he would win was probably a foregone conclusion ; the North recognised that whatever his merits or demerits, a change of administration at such a time was undesirable. He won without difficulty, and to-day the election is chiefly memorable because of his second inaugural address, whose closing passage is rightly regarded as a masterpiece of English prose.* The inaugural was delivered on March 4, 1865.

By this time, the end of the War was in sight. The South's man-power was sadly depleted, and food and all military supplies were running desperately short. The Northern blockade of Southern ports was so successful that commerce with Europe had practically ceased. Southern paper money had depreciated enormously, and even if it had not, there was little to buy. The death knell of the Confederacy was sounded when General Sherman and his army struck down in a south-easterly direction from Tennessee to Atlanta, Georgia, the most important industrial city of the Confederacy, and then moved eastward to the Atlantic Ocean, thus cutting the South in two. General Robert E. Lee, the chief Southern general, and one of the great military geniuses of all times, was operating in Virginia endeavouring to protect Richmond, the Confederate capital. He was opposed by General Grant, the outstanding military hero of the North, a man whose achievements afterward caused him to be elected President. A month after the President's second inaugural, it was apparent to everyone that the South's gallant fight had become completely hopeless. On April 9, 1865, Grant and Lee met near Appomattox Court House, and in an impromptu fashion arranged the terms of surrender.

It is one of the great tragedies of American history that Lincoln did not survive the War to aid in the difficult days of "Reconstruction" which lay ahead. Had he done so, there is little doubt that much of the abject misery and the mismanagement of Southern affairs by stupid, venal and often brutal Northerners would have been avoided. On April 14, only five days after the end of the War, the President was assassinated by John Wilkes Booth, a fiery young Southerner, an actor and a brother of the famous Edwin Booth. As everyone knows, Mr. and Mrs. Lincoln were sitting in a box at the theatre, attending a performance

---

* " With malice toward none ; with charity for all ; with firmness in the right, as God gives us to see the right, let us strive on to finish the work we are in ; to bind up the Nation's wounds, to care for him who shall have borne the battle, and for his widow, and his orphan—to do all which may achieve and cherish a just and lasting peace among ourselves, and with all nations."

of *Our American Cousin*. Shortly after ten o'clock in the
evening, Booth slipped into the box, shot the President,
and leaped down to the stage. He tripped as he did so
(breaking a small bone in his leg) but quickly recovered.
Shouting *sic semper tyrannis* (the State motto of Virginia)
he dashed out of the stage door, mounted a horse and
galloped away. Lincoln was taken to a house nearby,
where he died a few hours later. Booth remained at liberty
for some days, and was then surrounded while hiding in a
barn, and shot by his pursuers. (A persistent American
myth, for which there seems no historic foundation, is that
someone else was killed in his place and that he survived
and lived for many years in the south-west.)

Lincoln's body was sent for burial to his home city of
Springfield, Illinois, to which he had not returned since
leaving it four years earlier to assume the office of President.
Great crowds assembled along the route of the funeral
train, demonstrating their grief over the loss of the martyred
President. The tomb in Springfield is still a national
shrine, visited every year by thousands of Americans.

When Lincoln became President, he was unknown,
with hardly any reputation outside his own State, Illinois ;
when he died he had already been recognised, even by the
South and to some extent in Europe, as one of the greatest
Americans of all time. Since his death, his fame has
continued to increase until to-day there is no doubt that
he is by far the most deeply venerated of all Americans.
An important reason for this is, of course, the fact of his
martyrdom. After his death, his memory continued to
carry much of the patriotic emotion which was centred
about him in wartime, as well as the heroic quality attached
to one who laid down his life for his country. The adulation
with which he is regarded might have been less if he had
been forced to grapple throughout the four years of a second
term in office with the heartbreaking problems which
developed after the end of the War.

To an extraordinary degree, Lincoln satisfied the popular
American ideal. His modest origin, the deep poverty in
which he was reared, his lifelong unpretentiousness and
even humility, all helped to fulfil the fundamental American
requirements for heroic leadership. When one who came

from such a background was able to meet and dominate
men of wealth, aristocracy and formal education, every
common American felt that his own life was thereby
vindicated to some extent.

Another element in his character which seemed to set
him on a pedestal was the deep sadness which marked all
his adult years. Modern psychologists have indulged in
much speculation as to possible concrete causes, either
physical or mental, for this air of tragedy which hung over
him. To be sure, the responsibilities of office during his
Presidency were enough to sadden any man ; but Lincoln's
melancholy had been marked for many years before that,
and cannot be associated with any explicit external cause.
Certainly it helped to deepen the reverence with which
the mass of the population regarded him, the half-conscious
feeling that in some way he was taking upon himself the
burden of all his fellow-countrymen. The fact that his
sombreness was from time to time shot through with gleams
of robust humour did not at all destroy this general
impression.

Finally, we must return to the plain fact that he was in
truth a great man. The power, simplicity and directness
of his thought were matched by the dignity and beauty of
the words in which he clothed it. His tenderness for all
suffering humanity was amply proved by his deeds as well
as his words. It is a hallmark of greatness to continue to
grow ; and Lincoln's development during the last years
of his life was as remarkable as in any earlier period. He
was the product of his own generation, and necessarily
marked by the limitations of his own time ; but certainly
very few men in history have come closer than he to breaking
all temporal bonds and emerging into that timeless region
where greatness speaks to greatness unfettered by the
years.

MARY MACARTHUR

1880–1921

by MARY AGNES HAMILTON

o

MARY MACARTHUR

1880–1921

by MARY AGNES HAMILTON

ON a day now nearly thirty years ago, a politician, walking along the Embankment, found his way blocked outside the Army Clothing Factory by a dense crowd of workers, mostly women, standing with intent faces lifted to a young woman mounted on a chair. She was " only a fair-haired slip of a girl," but she was speaking " with uncommon fire and persuasiveness." He stood to listen. The simplicity and directness, as well as the emotional force of her appeal, struck him : an unusual combination of shrewdness and magnetism : with now and then a delightful stroke of humour. Her audience, dull at first, was coming to life. She was trying, it seemed, to persuade them to come into a Trade Union ; nothing very new in that, yet this girl somehow made it seem new ; new, and rather exciting. No generalities from her ; she seemed to know all about their conditions, their wages, hours and fines. Bread and butter stuff, in the main ; yet connected, all the time, with something bigger, very real to her, which, somehow, she also made real to them.

" Who is she ? " he asked a man, standing by : a workman who had paused, as he had.

" Why," he replied, " that's Mary Macarthur. She's waking 'em up, proper. Bit of all right, she is." He nodded. Had he been a Dundonian, instead of a Cockney, he might have added, " She's a nicker."

Of that name, the politician, and other persons, whether or not they normally took much interest in politics, were to hear, continually, in the course of the next years. Working women were coming into the news. There were strikes, and successful strikes, among the jute workers in the North, the corset makers in the Midlands : stories of a " Girls' Parliament " among the London work-girls ; a sense of general stir and movement, with, behind it all, a captain who seemed to know her job. In the papers were letters, interviews, articles by this same Mary Macarthur : pieces,

simply and yet vividly written, which woke the reader up
to facts he had forgotten or never known about the conditions under which women were working, and the wretched
wages they were paid for making the common articles
of daily use in every household. If they were beginning
to revolt, they were right ; but what was one to do about it ?

Sweating—horrible word for a still more horrible thing
—confronted the Londoner in terms from which he could
not escape when the *Daily News* organised a great Exhibition,
with the women workers actually there. That, too, it
appeared, was the work of Mary Macarthur. One day she
had burst into the office of the editor, Mr. A. G. Gardiner,
and poured out to him a torrent of burning words about
the grim under-payment of women workers, in factories
and in their wretched homes : told him how, in one factory,
a girl had dropped dead, only the other day, from sheer
exhaustion : how, another, sickening with diphtheria and
too poor to afford bed-clothes, covered herself at night
with the fine baby linen she was stitching at one penny
per finished garment, and so, all unwitting, spread disease
and possible death to the infants for whom her work was
bought by mothers who would have shuddered away
had they any conception of the conditions under which it
was made : how women chain-makers, toiling for fifty
hours a week at the heaviest work in their own forges, were
lucky if they brought home seven or eight shillings at the
end of the week. She stormed at him, burst into tears,
appealed to him, passionately. What was more surprising,
however, was that she had an idea, a plan, and a superbly
practical plan—the organization of an Exhibition. She
had worked it all out ; there was no resisting her. The
Exhibition came into being : daily, she was on duty there,
giving short, pithy lectures, with here and there a touch of
humour, in which she explained how and why the flower,
hook and button, ball and sack, shirt and fur, box and jam,
match and dress makers, and hundreds of others, actually
toiled and starved. How she found time to do it was a
puzzle, for she was secretary of the whirling office of the
National Union of Women Workers, as also of the Women's
Trade Union League, and the task of bringing women
into unions kept her busy, addressing meetings from very

early morning till very late at night : never failing when
she was billed to speak, no matter how small the meeting,
nor how dreary the street corner at which it was to be held.
Had she not stood for an hour at the appointed pitch in
a snowstorm so blinding that her one companion could
hardly see her, while shadowy figures darted by, none
heroic enough to stay to make a meeting ? One day, the
papers reported her as making, at the Guildhall, a speech
which converted the organised Trade Unions to the principle
of a minimum wage ; on the next, she was in Scotland ; on
the day after in Yorkshire ; on the day after that, guest of
honour at a dinner in the House of Commons, with Keir
Hardie in the chair, preparatory to her departure for
America.

Yet it was neither the agitator nor the orator, but the
quick-witted, long-sighted, and completely equipped
practical organiser who appeared before the Select Committee on Home Work set up by Parliament in 1907, in
direct response to the public feeling aroused by the
Exhibition, and the pressure of the new Labour Party in
the House of Commons. The broad-cloth-coated men
sitting round the semi-circular table in the sombre committee
room were, some of them, vaguely sympathetic, but none
saw his way through the tangled mass of evidence that had
been put before them. This matter of women's work
seemed to be a jungle : they felt baffled, overwhelmed. Yet
this young woman of twenty-seven, very attractive looking,
with her fair hair, blue eyes and slim figure, speaking
quickly and yet so clearly in tones that betrayed the fact
that she hailed from across the Border—one parent a
Highlander, the other from Aberdeen—seemed to have got it
all quite clear in her head. She not only woke them up ;
she put the whole question suddenly into focus. Nothing
emotional here ; hard facts, logically marshalled by a clear
head. Women generally, earning an average wage of seven
shillings a week : home workers an average of four and
sixpence. This average concealing the fact that, for women,
there was no sort of standard rate ; so the " good " employer
was being penalised and under-cut by the bad. Willing
to pay a decent, living rate, he could not in practice do so,
because there was no machinery for imposing that rate on his

competitors. This she gave them as their thread through
the maze ; this view she drove home by a mass of actual
illustrations. Thus, in the Cradley Heath chain-making
area she had visited a number of employers, and in every
case the employer

" admitted to me that the rates were scandalously low, and said
that if only we could get a meeting of all the employers, he was
sure that a 15 or 20 per cent. rise could easily be given. The
difficulty is to get a meeting of the employers."

In another case, at an ammunition works in Edmonton,
the demand for a fifty per cent. cut caused a strike. A Trade
Union was formed, and the firm consented to arbitration.
Then, however, they showed that competing firms were
paying even lower rates.

" It is impossible to describe the anguished impotence with
which we sat listening to the statistics of the rates and wages
paid by these unrepresented firms. Had we been able to
command their attendance, and could the decision of the arbi-
trator have been binding upon them—as would have been the
case, had we been a Wages Board, and not a voluntary Arbitration Board—there would have been a general levelling up of
wages, instead of a levelling down."

At the end, a member of the committee, a previously
hostile " realist," said to her in set terms : " Your evidence
has brought Wages Boards within the sphere of practical
politics." The matter was clinched when, as the result
of the profound impression created by her evidence, she
was asked to bring a number of the actual workers before
the committee at a private session. Then the committee
reported in favour of giving statutory Wages Boards power
to fix minimum rates ; the House of Commons agreed ;
and on January 1, 1910, the Trade Boards Act received
Royal Assent. Four trades were scheduled, in the first
instance : chain-making, machine-lace making, paper-box
making, and wholesale and bespoke tailoring. In these
trades, Boards were to be set up, constituted from representatives of employers and employed, the employed, in
view of their known weakness, being permitted the aid of
assessors.

Mary Macarthur had got the machinery into existence.

Next, she had to make it work. The first and crucial test
came in the chain-making area, at Cradley Heath. There,
conditions were so bad, and the exploitation of the women
so terrible, that it was the first industry to be scheduled.
After long and difficult negotiations, in which as assessor
to the workers' representatives she finally brought the
Associated Employers to agreement, minimum rates for
various classes of work were at last fixed by the Board.
They represented a vast improvement from the workers'
point of view. Under the Act, however, three months'
notice of these rates had got to be given ; those three months
were feverishly utilised by the employers, contractors and
middlemen—and women—to pile up stocks by overtime
working, and so prepare a slump in the industry for which
the blame could then be cast on the new rates. Moreover,
the employers outside the Association got great numbers
of their workers—ignorant, illiterate, and terrified—to
affix their marks to a paper contracting out of the operation
of the Act. The situation was dangerous in the extreme.
Mary at once called a conference of the Associated Employers
and finally got from them an undertaking that they would
stand by the Board's rates, on condition that they were
not under-cut by the outside firms and middlemen. This
condition she prepared to secure, by a bold stroke—so bold
that it almost frightened her colleagues. She called the
workers to whom less than the Board's rate was being
offered to repudiate the signatures and marks got from them
under false pretences, and come out on strike. Such was
the hold she had established over them, such was their
faith in her, and the warming effect of her personality,
that, to a woman, out they came, although, as far as they
could see, they were faced with sheer starvation. There
was no money in Cradley Heath, and although her National
Federation of Women Workers made itself responsible
for a strike fund, it had hardly any money either. She,
however, at once turned her genius for publicity into collecting the sinews of war, and rousing public opinion on the
side of the strikers. She gave interviews, she wrote letters,
she addressed meetings of all kinds ; she even employed
the new power of the cinema to show what the life of the
chain-maker was like ; she got the newspapers to open

funds. In the end, it was public opinion, mobilised by her, that settled the strike. It took ten weeks of grim endurance, but in the end the outside employers had to come in and give way. The final meeting is described by J. J. Mallon, who was there, as " not like a strike but a prayer meeting ; " at the close the women crowded round to kiss the hands of their deliverer. The Board was safe ; the minimum rates were paid. As the local paper put it at the time : " For years the chain-makers have been working for miserably inadequate wages, and, until Miss Macarthur came upon the scene, they were powerless successfully to ask for more."

The fight thus won at Cradley Heath had to be fought out in each of the three other scheduled industries ; and it was fought with the same vision, courage, generalship, and unstinted giving of herself. To the workers whose cause she championed, she gave something more than the minimum wage she secured for them. Mr. Mallon has described some of the street meetings held in Nottingham, among the lace workers. He says :

" I am not sure that Mary Macarthur's most moving speeches were not made at some of these queer, unreported assemblies. Something moved in her when the poor faces of the home-workers looked up at her as she held forth on a chair at the street corner, and still more when she noted the raggedness and malnutrition of the children. She spoke amazingly ; like a compassionate angel . . . On one memorable evening—she was feeling the strain of her continuous exhortation, and was a little over-emotional—she plunged a large audience of home-workers into tears and kept them there. Though they wept, they were happy. Poverty and suffering had cut them off from the world, but Mary Macarthur had *re-established communication, and made them feel that they were still members of the human family.*"

In this last sentence is indeed the key to her work ; her unfaltering devotion and remarkable success in it. Her sense of the " human family " was active, constant, passionate. Injustice, whenever, wherever she met it, set her on fire. She could feel the wrongs and sufferings of others as her own, and never got used to them. She felt them as a call to action. Action—swift, practical action— was her element ; for it she had all the gifts : the power to plan, as well as the power to strike. She wrote, of course, abundantly ; but writing was, for her, merely a means of getting something or other done. She had little or no æsthetic sense ; a pen, so her friends told her, she handled like a walking-stick. For two hectic years—1906-8—she wrote most of the lively paper she founded, *The Woman Worker* ; and would, at times, dash out of her office to sell it in the streets. In her writing, she had the knack of throwing off phrases just enough removed from the commonplace to serve as slogans ; there, she had the humour and much of the vitality of which she had complete command on the platform ; but the platform was her element, to a degree to which the desk never was. As a speaker, whether at conference, mass meeting, street meeting, or committee, large or small, she had every kind of skill, from sheer oratory to subtle wangling : a power, almost uncanny, of " getting " her audience, whatever its composition. But neither in speaking nor in writing do general or abstract ideas, like Democracy or Socialism, figure prominently. She was a Democrat through and through ; she was also a Socialist ; the existence of a purpose, bigger than herself, was always with her ; so much with her, that she had no need to talk of it.

She lived, and will live, as the champion of the working woman. To women everywhere her service is indeed incalculable. She gave them self-respect : by her personality as by her achievement she broke through the sense of isolation and helplessness. On the freeing of the woman worker she concentrated : for it, up to the autumn of 1911, she made the major sacrifice of refusing to marry the man who loved her and whom she was learning to love ; it, she saw as " fundamental work " in her own phrase. In her concentration, however, was no hint of narrowness. Always her work for women was part and parcel of the wider struggle for human freedom and for a society based on justice. She knew the sufferings of the exploited of her own sex ; she also knew, from direct experience, how limited and stifling the lot of even the most " comfortable." When, in 1903, she left her home in Ayr, she exchanged ease for hardship, the secure position of the " lady " for incessant toil and drive. After a stormy and not very educational

o*

schooling in Glasgow, she had come back from a year in
Germany to an effort to fill her life by being a Primrose
Dame and a contributor to the local paper. It would not
do. Then she got her father to take her in as book-keeper
to his big drapery establishment, where she came for the
first time into contact with the girl who must work to live.
To write a skit for the paper, she went with the girls to a
meeting of the Shop Assistants Union. " Going to scoff,
I remained to pray." The words are apt : the idea behind
the Trade Union movement, as put by John Turner,
seized her, then and there, with the force of a revelation.
Very soon, she was President of the Ayr branch : then of
the Scottish Council of the Union. In that capacity she met
and made friends with Will Anderson and Margaret
Bondfield, both moving spirits in the Union, and persons
for whom its work was joined on to the larger issues of
Socialist politics ; made her mark at Conferences. The
first sharp break with her father's point of view came
when she insisted that she must support Robert Smillie,
standing as a Labour candidate in Mid-Lanark. It was an
action significant of the immense movement away from its
old moorings her young mind had taken, and of its sense
of the ocean in which, native, it was to swim. In the
summer of 1903 she left Ayr for London, to find her work
in life.

It was waiting for her. Margaret Bondfield, to whom
she went, was searching for a secretary for the Women's
Trade Union League. Unless a new organiser could be
found who would rouse women who, as Mary Macarthur
was to put it later, " are badly paid and badly treated
because they are not organised, and not organised because
they are badly paid and badly treated," it seemed as though
the League, founded thirty years earlier, must peter out.
Here, in this electric girl, Lady Dilke and Gertrude Tuckwell believed that she had been found. And so it proved.
For Mary, the little, dreary office in Club Union Buildings
wore already the air of the theatre of adventure, and the
sense of it filled and thrilled her. She was not going to
wait for Unions to join the League ; she was going out to
make them. And she did. Made, she was going to keep
them—a far harder task. Ground won was, for her, as

she put it later apropos of Lady Dilke, " never a place of rest but a place of arms, a foothold whence we may fight our way to positions yet more commanding." Within three years of her taking over, she not only made unions where none had been before ; she got the various scattered little unions, by 1908, into a single organisation, the National Federation of Women Workers, with seventeen branches and over two thousand members. The actual figures were never very imposing, but she was past mistress in the art of bluffing, with something about her that made it impossible to call her bluff. As a shrewd observer put it, she and Miss Tuckwell, her devoted and very able President, " with all their camp followers were no more than a stage army, but they said that they were the women workers of Great Britain, and they made so much noise that they came to be believed." Certainly, she missed no chance.

The sudden revolt of the women working in the food and other factories of Bermondsey, in the hot days of the summer of 1911, called her at once to the spot. There were actually twenty separate strikes, involving as many separate factories and sets of conditions ; there was also the tremendous problem of feeding the workers, few of whom were in any kind of organisation. That she met by launching an appeal, through the press, not for money but for loaves and milk ; she poured workers into Bermondsey, for practically continuous meetings, designed to hold the women together : she herself carried through the complex negotiations with the various groups of employers. She won ; her personality diffused enthusiasm and the sense that here was a great adventure ; her practised statesmanship commanded the respect of the most obstinate employer. An essential element in that statesmanship was her clear realisation that the jam makers and the tea packers, the sweet stuff makers and the box makers, were part and parcel of a common industrial army, and cheap women's labour must not, to their own destitution and the under-cutting of the men's rates, be allowed to drag living standards down. Her own battalions, large or small, were always part of the much greater army fighting for Socialism and Democracy.

Thus, while she worked for women, year in and year out, amid scenes and drama—some of it wearing to her associates :

much of it costing real personal sacrifice from herself—she
was never in the narrow sense a feminist, always an equalitarian. Her realism, her sense of humour, her strong belief
in comradeship and co-operation between the sexes, and
the passion for justice that brought her out on the side of
the weak, wherever they were to be found, gave a wider
basis to her industrial and her political effort. A pungent
sanity colours her remarks about her own sex. " Women
are not all wise, any more than they are all beautiful."
" A woman matured in stupidity is the most intractable
material that could be found." " The future woman must
have the masculine steak and beer standard, instead of the
feminine one of buns and tea. But man need have no fear
of the woman of the future if he will only realise that his
interest and hers are one." Here was her central conviction
—" his interest and hers are one." A keen advocate,
therefore, of adult suffrage, she was never interested in the
limited Bill which would enfranchise only a handful of
middle-class women. When she herself, in 1918, stood for
Parliament—the first woman to be nominated as a candidate
—she stood, not as a woman, but as a representative of the
Labour Party. " I do not believe that any woman ought
to be returned simply because she *is* a woman. But I
hold equally strongly that no woman should be excluded
for the same reason." In her Election address, she stated
that " it takes a man and woman to make the ideal home
and I believe that neither can build the ideal world without
the help of the other."

She stood, of course, as Mary Macarthur—and had
trouble with the returning officer about that. But, by 1918,
her experience of life had been deepened by marriage and
motherhood : her first baby lost, to her bitter grief, but
Nancy, the second, born in 1915, was the light of her eyes.
In 1911, Will Anderson's loyal and unswerving devotion,
and the perfect friendship he had schooled his heart to
give her, at last convinced her that their common work
might be more effectively done together than apart. In
1918 she could talk of the ideal home as one who knew it.
Uncomfortable housekeeping, hers, no doubt : too much
office about the house ; a feverish temperature, often, and
too many domestic upheavals : " treasures " announced

with enthusiasm, proving all too often to be " devils " :
a rush and pressure that slower blood might have found
intolerable ; but genuine companionship between husband
and wife, flowering into authentic happiness ; a personal
attachment that grew stronger as each learned to know
the other with the intimacy only shared life can bring.
Will Anderson satisfied the deep emotion of her passionate
nature and its need of hero-worship : in him, she found a
mate of strength equal to her own, and of a calmer wisdom.
Years back, in 1903, when he asked her to marry him, and
she, full of her new work in London, said " No," he had
said to her that she " had not yet been attuned to her deepest
and sweetest music," was not yet, " wonderful woman as
she is, so rounded and complete as she will be." He was
right, and she knew it. Her work, after her marriage, had
a new ripeness and a deeper range. There is genuine social
imagination in the memorandum she wrote in 1913 for the
Committee set up to consider the sickness claims of women
under the Health Insurance Act, on which she had fought
Mr. Lloyd George so long, while it was passing ; while
her argument for the establishment of a State medical
service, on preventive lines, is as relevant and as forceful
to-day as when she penned it. During the war years she
showed qualities of genuine statesmanship, such as marked
her out, no less than her husband, as a future member of
a Labour Cabinet.

The war was for both a shattering catastrophe. Throughout its hideous course they worked like lions : he in the
House of Commons, to which he was elected at a by-
election in 1914, as a member of the small pacifist group ;
she outside, as the fearless, tireless champion of the
working woman and, no less, of the working man. Her
first and instant task was to protect the mass of women
thrown out of employment in the early months ; about
their case, she felt so keenly that she was ready to lead a
procession to Buckingham Palace. Instead, she was called
into the consultations that led to the setting-up of the
Queen's Work for Women Fund ; and, in connection with
this, won from Her Majesty herself, as from the great ladies
and eminent civil servants associated with it, the respect
and the affection that had, before, been given her so freely

by the simple working woman. Soon, however, a different
emergency called her : women of all sorts were being drafted
into the munition factories to take the places of the men
called to the colours. Understanding the impulse of
service that made gentle and simple rush into war work,
her whole energy was bent to prevent its being exploited,
and, in the long run, turned against their husbands and
their brothers. There was to be a world after the war :
she never forgot it. Women must not be sacrificed, or
used as blacklegs, in the new munitions establishments that
were hastily being rushed up on every hand.

With the tenacity of the lion, and something of the
wisdom, on occasion, of the serpent, she fought the battles
of the women and of the men ; by sheer force of personality, she compelled Ministers, State Departments, and
Trade Unions to recognise human claims the women
themselves could not put forward and the pressure of the
hour made it easy, and apparently patriotic, to overlook.
Patent enough, the weakness of her constituents. Organised
women were but a tiny fraction of the vast army of women
workers mobilised within the first year of the declaration of
war ; that army, constantly growing until it reached figures
over two millions, composed in the main of women new to
industry, with no tradition of organisation, and quivering
with heroic impulses, was in no sense a fighting force. Yet
she bluffed employers and Ministers into believing that it
was. She claimed to speak for two million women, of
whom nearly one and a half million had never worked for
wages before and were hardly aware of her existence : and
her word prevailed. Before long, the engineers, the most
exclusive craft union in the country, were glad to have her
as their champion ; and one Minister of Munitions after
another had to concede her demands. In her tenacity,
Mr. Lloyd George met something he could not charm away ;
against her, wiles, eloquence, nimbleness were of no avail ;
she knew all his dodges, and could work them, when she
chose, as well as he could. She knew every turn of the
game and played it, with firm wrist, keen eye and unyielding
purpose. When argument would not serve, she used her
charm, or, if that did not work, frankly resorted to bullying.

To tell the story in detail is not necessary, although the

more it is studied in detail, the greater is the admiration compelled by her generalship. In the upshot, she not only secured decent conditions for the war-worker ; she established certain facts, now more or less taken for granted, which would not have been so taken, but for her. First, and not least important, that long hours are detrimental to the out-put, as well as to the health, of the worker. Second, that women's wages are not a separate chapter, but part and parcel of the wages of men. At the end of the war, thanks to her, the wages and general status of the woman worker, and of the man, were definitely better than they were before ; a standard was set, which it has proved hard to break down. The notion that any standard should, in fact, be a living standard, is now accepted, if not always acted upon. She was, as were all who stood for the maintenance of Trade Union conditions, bitterly attacked, at the time, by the short-sighted, who thought, even about the war, in terms of weeks and months ; but she won a new kind of respect for all who came into contact with her. For personal recognition, personal honours, she cared not at all ; the substance of achievement was what she valued, and that, for her, was ever only a starting-point for fresh effort.

During the 1918 Election campaign, she in Stourbridge, Will Anderson in Attercliffe, had to meet the full tide of calumny. She was, of course, defeated, though her vote was a magnificent one ; that she did not mind. His being out of the House was a harder blow : she would not have stood herself had she not felt sure that he was—as was no Pacifist—safe. Together, however, they prepared for a new and harder fighting than any that had gone before. She, with her old dash and energy, organized the women for whom the sudden closing down of munitions factories spelt disaster ; led them, in procession as of yore, to Whitehall : forced Ministers to make provision for them, and to keep their pledges, when given to her. He threw himself into the campaign, in which her heart was with him, for a Peace of reconciliation. Neither was yet forty ; little could either guess how near the end of the struggle was for them both.

Early in February, 1919, he spoke at a meeting in Bradford ; caught a chill on the way home, and, within a fortnight, lay dead of pneumonia. For two more years she,

literally heart-broken, worked on, resolutely fighting to the
very last. She went to Washington, for the first Conference
of the new International Labour Office, and carried the
brunt of the work for the Maternity and Child Welfare
Convention. She spoke, with her old fire and force, at
Labour Party Conferences and meetings. She organised the
transformation of the National Federation of Women
Workers into a district of a great general Labour Union, the
National Union of Municipal and General Workers, in
consonance with her firm conviction that " her interests are
the same as his." More serious, however, than the grave
physical mischief, which compelled her to undergo two
operations in the year 1920, was her inner desolation.
After the second operation, her friends knew that the hurt
was mortal ; on New Year's Day, 1921, she died.

The years that have passed since her death have changed
the colour and dimmed the brightness of many reputations.
Hers has submitted to no fading. Men of good will
everywhere agree that the only loss comparable to that of
Will Anderson is that of his wife. Her, no description fits
so well as that which Carlyle wrote of John Sterling :
" You could see, here looked forth a soul which was winged ;
that dwelt in hope and action, not in hesitation and fear."
Sterling's candour and purity of heart she had ; in her
however, these lovely qualities were allied to a burning
purpose and an unfaltering will, which translated hope into
action. A brain of admirable hardness lay behind a personality of compelling force and charm, whose enhancement
was never her aim. Not for herself did she labour,
rejoice and agonise. She gave, unstintedly, that disinterested service that is the hope of Democracy and its
guarantee, asking only for fuller opportunities of being used
in the common cause.

KARL MARX

1818–1883

by M. M. POSTAN

KARL MARX
1818–1883
by M. M. POSTAN

I

IT has been said of Marx's personality that it was a mixture of the humdrum and the heroic, heavily weighted on the side of the heroic. His life was a similar mixture, heavily weighted on the side of the humdrum. Much of what Marx did, and most of what was done to him, had its parallel in hundreds of other German lives in the first half of the nineteenth century ; and the typical incidents, as distinguished from the exceptional ones, were evenly distributed over the whole of his life. He was born in 1818 in the town of Trier, into the family of a Jewish lawyer, and his early life and education were those of hundreds of other middle-class youths in Western Germany. On the material side there were the solid comforts of a society which had already recovered from the troubles of the Napoleonic wars and had not yet been thrown into the turmoil of the industrial revolution. Gymnasium and university followed as a matter of course ; a professional and even a professorial career seemed to be pre-destined. On the cultural side there was the intellectual and artistic abundance of the eighteen-thirties. The period was one of transition, which, like many other periods of transition, enjoyed the best of both worlds ; and it was on the best of both worlds that young Marx was reared. From his father, a person of considerable culture, he obtained his knowledge of, and attachment to, the main tenets of eighteenth century rationalism. A great friend of the family and his own father-in-law to be, Baron von Westphalen, introduced him to the new Romanticism. The resultant mixture equipped him well for the circle into which he fell in Berlin during the second year of his university studies. The intellectual fashions at the University of Berlin in the late thirties were dictated by men who still considered themselves followers of the Hegelian tradition, but were in reality engaged in a revolt against the great idealist masters.

The group of Hegelian left-wingers, led by men like Bruno Bauer, Ludwig Feuerbach and Karl Koppen, was trying to liberate the Hegelian logic, essentially one of flux and change, from subservience to philosophical and political conservatism. Into this group Marx fitted as a matter of course. The mixed composition of his own youthful ideas enabled him to swallow easily Bruno Bauer's love-hatred of Hegelian philosophy, and it was under Bruno Bauer's influence and supervision that Marx pursued his somewhat irregular preparation for a learned career in Berlin and Jena.

If the promise of a learned career failed to materialise, the failure was due to forces outside Marx's own control and was shared by most of his friends. By 1840 political events succeeded in diverting the bulk of German youth from their intended vocations into a life of political struggle and adventure. The year 1841, when Marx was completing his doctorate thesis in Jena, witnessed the final extension of the official Prussian reaction to the universities, and with the reaction at its height there was as little chance of Marx entering the academic profession as there was of any of his friends remaining there. Bruno Bauer and most of his friends were chased out of universities and all had to take to journalism, politics and the life of professional *frondeurs*. And the life of journalism, politics and professional *fronde* had also to become the fate of young Marx. In 1841 he accepted a post on the *Rheinische Zeitung*, and his work on that left-wing paper was his first introduction to the life he was going to lead thereafter. As an introduction it was brief and highly ominous. In March, 1842, Marx was forced to resign and almost immediately afterwards the newspaper was suspended for what the Government considered its extreme opinions. With the end of the *Rheinische Zeitung* Marx, like most of his friends, emigrated abroad and, like most of his friends, took up his residence in Paris.

In Paris Marx moved yet another step further in the direction of political and social radicalism. It was there that he for the first time began to formulate the doctrines which eventually separated him from the rest of the young Hegelians and formed the basis of his future social and economic theory. It was above all in Paris that he became

an avowed socialist. Even before his emigration he had
shown some sympathy with the early manifestations of the
French working-class movement. His residence in France
enabled him to conceive for that movement something
stronger and more definite than mere sympathy. Paris in
the forties was all a-bubble with that political discontent
and speculation out of which the new socialism was to rise.
Disappointment in the false liberalism of Louis Philippe
and his *haute bourgeoisie*, the intellectual exhaustion of
eighteenth century doctrines, the progress of the industrial
revolution and the rise of the industrial proletariat—all
these factors combined to produce in the France of the
forties a veritable cataract of socialist activity. Into that
cataract the bulk of the young German *émigrés*, and Marx
among them, were drawn with irresistible power. His
expulsion from France in 1845 and three years of residence
in Brussels could do nothing to avert the progress of his
socialist evolution. The publication of the *Heilige Familie*,
written in collaboration with Engels, and the *Misère de
la Philosophie* were important landmarks, leading directly
to the Communist Manifesto, which he and Engels were to
submit to the International Communist League in 1848.
And it was in Paris that he met for the first time his
life-long friend and collaborator, Friedrich Engels, now
also moving towards a socialist point of view.

So when, in the spring of 1848, the revolution broke out
in Germany and Marx was able to return to his native
Rhineland, he arrived there as a fully-fledged socialist. Yet
even now his destiny was not yet clear. It is difficult to
say what exactly his life or his chances would have become
had the democratic *régime* in Germany been established
there and then, and had Marx been allowed to become one
of its leaders. For while the revolutionary movement was
still on the upgrade, he took up a very moderate attitude,
refusing to join the separate communistic organisations and
representing in the office of the *Neue Rheinische Zeitung*,
which he was editing, the unity of the German radical left.
But fates decreed that German democracy should not continue and that Marx should not become a republican
statesman. In 1849 the Prussian reaction returned triumphant, and all the radical elements of German society—

and Marx among them—had either to retire from journalism and politics or once more to emigrate abroad.

Thus we find Marx for the second time in exile, this time in London, concentrating on the preparation of the world's future, through sheer inability to affect Germany's present. From this time onwards his life ran its predestined course. From 1849 to 1855 there were the years of abject poverty in the slums of Soho, relieved by furious reading in the British Museum and work for the modest International (in reality, German) Communist League and the German Working-Men's Society in London. From 1855 to 1865 the material privations became less severe and the intellectual activity of the hunger years began to bear abundant fruit. The main outline of his economic and social doctrine took shape and the first International was finally established. And then from 1865 to 1875 there came the decade of fulfilment, with the first volume of *Das Kapital* out, the international movement strong and yet subservient to his views, all rivals in socialist theory and politics defeated and destroyed, he himself famous, feared and lionised. It was only after 1875 with the loss of his wife, ill-health and the demise of the International, that the constant progression of his life was arrested. Death came in 1883.

Thus all his life Marx travelled along a road which, however far it took him, always remained a highway, and never deteriorated into the solitary track of genius in the wilderness. Hundreds and thousands of other men and women, mostly young Germans, were travelling in the same direction, being converted to the same ideas and drawn into the ranks of the same movement. If Marx's life before 1846 followed the familiar pattern of a young German radical, his life after 1850 was shaped in the equally common mould of a cosmopolitan revolutionary anɗ communist.

Yet Marx's was not an ordinary life. Into an existence which, for all its adventures, was often commonplace, he crowded a record of exceptional achievement—indeed so exceptional as to baffle all attempts at simple explanation. The lovers of the simple (and nearly all Marx's biographers fight shy of subtleties) find it easy to derive Marx's greatness from his intellectual genius. But the quantity and quality of his genius is very easy to exaggerate, for his intellectual greatness was largely relative to the mediocrity of his rivals and competitors. The only man in his *entourage* comparable with him in ability and knowledge was Engels, and Engels refused to compete. There is no denying that in his capacity for constructive generalisation, in his logical powers, and in his intellectual vitality Marx had few rivals in his generation, and that these qualities alone would have given him an exalted place among the sociological writers and political agitators of the mid-century. But he was more than a sociological writer or a political agitator ; he was the prophet of a faith, and the leader of multitudes. And this he would never have become through his genius alone. There was a drive behind that machine which made it go further than its intellectual powers alone would have taken it. That drive came from the inner recesses of his character and will, and owed more to his emotions than to his intelligence. The lovers of the simple would perhaps describe it as " ambition." But however it is described and docketed, its origin need not be in doubt. Marx was a Jew, and a Jew in a community which had only just been emancipated from the mediæval disabilities. Of this fact Marx always remained conscious, but it was not so much a conscious as an unconscious preoccupation with his racial origin that influenced his life. It was to this preoccupation that he probably owed his constant striving for the highest pinnacles of achievement. The first independent action of his life, his marriage to Jenny von Westphalen, had in it something of a daring aspiration. Jenny was older than Marx, very beautiful, rich, and above all, very highly born, and his wooing and winning of Jenny was symbolical of the rest of his life. He attempted things which a man of less insatiable ambition would have shirked. He was not content just to write a book on political economy ; he was going to produce a new science of economics. He would not merely improve upon the social philosophy of his predecessors ; he was going to do for social philosophy what Darwin's *Origin of Species* did for biology. It was not his intention to lead a political party on behalf of a political reform ; he was going to create an international movement that would shake the foundations of the world. Some of these designs were too vast to be achieved by any man, however great his genius. But they were sufficiently great to give a heroic scale to whatever Marx did achieve. He did not produce a new intellectual revolution, for his ideas were neither as new nor as revolutionary as he thought; but he came near enough to producing it to rank as one of the greatest social writers of all time. He did not shake the world as quickly and as profoundly as he hoped, but he came near enough to doing it to be considered as one of the greatest political leaders of the nineteenth century.

No doubt the combination of that peculiar genius with that extraordinary ambition had its shadowy side. The purely relative nature of Marx's genius was even more obvious to Marx himself than it is to us, and he was even more inclined to exaggerate the distance separating him from his fellow human beings than he had a right to do. His overwhelming and overweening conceit, his contempt for his adversaries, knew no bounds. They led him into innumerable almost legendary struggles against all other established leaders. His desperate battle with the German hot-heads in the fifties, his battle with Proudhon in 1867 and 1868, and with Bakunin from 1868 to 1872, filled his life with the continuous clash of arms; and if it is true that Marx's existence was one of unceasing struggle and war, the struggle was as much against adversaries as against adversities and the war was more against friends than against enemies.

Yet even the dark side of Marx's character was a help to achievement. But for his ruthless and unscrupulous handling of men, he might not have been able to impress his doctrines on his followers. Sometimes, indeed, he even impressed them on his enemies. There is nothing more moving in the history of communist leadership than the spectacle of Bakunin, after years of vicious and extremely painful attacks on his character by Marx and his friends, writing to Herzen to record his admiration for Marx's greatness and for his services to the socialist cause. There is more than a touch of pathos in the fact that in the later years of his life Bakunin was working on the Russian translation of *Das Kapital* and died with the work unfinished.

II

Marx's ideas were similarly a mixture of the generic and the individual, of things borrowed from the spirit of his age and things created anew. Least individual of all was his general philosophical outlook, and above all the scientific optimism and the evolutionary pre-suppositions inherent in his " dialectical materialism." Marx's materialism involved a belief that the laws of social life were as definite and as capable of being discovered as the laws of matter : a belief which he shared with all the scientific enthusiasts of his age. The characteristic mental state of advanced mid-Victorian thought was one of intellectual hope. Great as were the scientific achievements of the age, its scientific expectations were greater still. Men expected science not only to overcome the practical difficulties of existence, hunger and disease, but also to solve the accumulated multitude of intellectual problems, and to penetrate all the ancient mysteries of mankind and the universe. These expectations Marx shared to the full. In accordance with the spirit of the age he set out to discover the habits of society as a scientist discovers the habits of nature, to forecast and anticipate the action of social laws as a scientist forecasts and exploits the action of natural laws—in short, to create a new science of society, and thus to convert politics into a form of engineering, in which every action could be calculated, measured, foretold and controlled. Thus viewed, Marx's materialism was merely a variant of nineteenth century " positivism " : a philosophical justification of his search for social laws.

It was not only in his search for social law in general but also in his predilection for a special kind of law that Marx proved himself to be a true son of his age. If the scientific pre-occupation of the seventeenth and early eighteenth centuries was with physics, the great scientific novelty of the nineteenth century was biology. Newton and Darwin each represented the most characteristic scientific achievement of their respective epochs. Just as the concept of the field of forces, thrust and counter-thrust, were the characteristic notions of the Newtonian age, so the evolutionary concepts, the laws of origin and transformation, were characteristic of the age of Darwin. The thought of that age, its politics and phraseology, were as full of evolution as ours is of relativity, and to this evolutionary mentality Marx paid a joyous tribute. The scientific laws which he tried to lay bare were evolutionary laws ; he sought to fit every situation that he was studying into an evolutionary curve : to enumerate the stages through which it passed, and to envisage its life-cycle as one of origin, maturity and decay. True, in common with most German evolutionary thinkers of the mid-nineteenth century, he tried to express his evolutionary notions in Hegelian phraseology, that is to say to represent the successive stages of evolution as parts of the Hegelian order of thesis, antithesis and synthesis. But, shorn of its cumbrous and barbaric phraseology, this Hegelian logic, as employed by Marx, merely expressed the evolutionary nature of the social process. All it meant was that every stage of development rested on the preceding stage and itself formed the starting-point for any stage to come. It is, therefore, no wonder that Marx regarded himself as the Darwin-in-chief of sociology and his own " dialectical materialism " as an evolutionary re-interpretation of social life.

From this philosophical position, typical of his age and common to most of his contemporaries, Marx proceeded by steps of his own towards the social theory and political programme that bear his name. The link was provided, not by his much discussed and now exploded " labour theory of value," but by his " economic interpretation of history." In spite of the enormous amount of space given to the theory of value in *Das Kapital*, it was in reality outside his main body of doctrine and unnecessary for the logical sequence of his ideas. The economic interpretation of history, on the other hand, followed most naturally from his general outlook. To a materialist in search of a materialist interpretation of society, economic phenomena offer an obvious opening. There is nothing easier than to assume that what matter is to animal life and the physical world, economic realities are to society and culture. They are concerned with elementary facts of human existence and thus also with the most essential conditions of social life.

It was therefore in full consonance with the accepted materialist attitude that Marx made his famous distinction between the economic basis of society and its " ideological superstructure " : the organisation of production and distribution on the one hand and legal institutions, religious beliefs and philosophical ideas on the other. Of course Marx was too much of a philosopher and too much of a historian ever to have alleged, as he is sometimes accused of doing, that non-economic phenomena had no effect on the course of history. In most of his historical examples he was careful to show how the political facts and ideas affected those very economic relations from which they were derived. But that they did derive he never doubted. Behind the complexity of historical events he always saw the great economic cause, the one source from which everything else sprang and to which everything else could be reduced and related.

This original economic source Marx sometimes described in its simplest and crudest form. Every element of society and culture and every important movement in history could directly be explained by the material needs of men and their instruments of production. But on the whole, this cruder and simpler version of economic materialism is more typical of *epigoni*, of the followers and vulgarisers of the Marxian theory, than of Marx himself. He himself, oftener than not, used the word " economic " in a sense far subtler than that implied in the vulgar versions of economic determinism. The economic factor determining history and society is something more than the animal urges of hunger, thirst and lust, or the inanimate matter employed in their satisfaction. What Marx had in mind is the economic activity of society, the way society organises its production and distribution. In the process of production and distribution different economic functions are assigned to different groups of producers ; their shares of the profits are apportioned and their mutual relations ordered. It is through the " social relations of production " that economic factors shape history and culture. And it is the social relations of production that are implied in the term " economic" in Marx's own version of economic materialism.

This concept of social relations of production links Marx's sociology to what is probably the most important of his generalisations, that of class and class war. Social relations of production are essentially relations between classes. Marx assumed that men performing the same economic functions and thus occupying the same economic positions in the productive system fall into natural groups or, as he called them, social classes. And as every new system of production rearranges and redistributes the economic functions of men, it also creates a class structure of its own. The economic system of mediæval agricultural production was characterised by a feudal structure of society ; the emergence of capitalism was accompanied by the appearance of a modern class structure, the *bourgeoisie* and the proletariat. In the process of historical transformation the ruling classes of old disappear, new ruling classes emerge, the orders of superiority and inferiority, subordination and superordination, change and reverse. A state of constant class war is therefore inevitable, for rising classes must fight their way to domination, ruling classes must fight to maintain their positions. And in that war legal institutions and constitutional forms are but weapons, political and legal changes are but battles won and lost.

With this final twist, with the substitution of class war for social relations of production and for production itself, the Marxian theory of history merges into his political programme. It offers immense opportunities for political application, and in these opportunities its real originality is to be found. By explaining the social mechanism of historical change Marx was able to envisage the mechanism of the changes to come, or, to be more exact, to construct the mechanism of the changes to be brought about. What Marx himself endeavoured to bring about was the establishment of a socialist order in the interests of the working classes, and to this endeavour the class theory of history offered a certain hope and a direct indication for action. To present history as an endless record of the rise and fall of classes, was to raise hopes before the subject classes of the age. But what converted the hope into a certainty was Marx's insistence on the youth of the proletariat and on its connection with the modern industrial system. Doctored up in the Hegelian way this insistence became a prophecy. It revealed the proletariat as that new power which, in accordance with the " dialectics of the historical process," was maturing in the womb of the very system it was destined to destroy. In other words, the economic interpretation of history, and with it the rest of Marxian philosophy, became a way of assuring the working classes that they were bound to win.

Even more important from a political point of view was the immediate bearing which this version of economic materialism had on the problem of socialist tactics. If all fundamental historical change is wrought by class war and if the transition to socialism necessarily involves a struggle between capitalists and the proletariat, then socialism can be achieved only by a proletarian victory in the capitalist class war. The attempts of the earlier socialists to achieve a socialist society by the immediate and piecemeal establishment of socialist communities or workshops within the present social system were, from Marx's point of view, utopian and dangerous. Under capitalist conditions they could not survive, and they could not affect the social system even if they did. What is more, they diverted the working classes from the concentration on class war, which should be the chief object of a truly socialist movement.

In this way the Marxian social and political theory became a justification for the objects and strategy of the socialist organisation which Marx was directing. Of course it would be unjust to Marx to regard his theories as a mere adjunct to a political programme. Shorn of its political implications the Marxian philosophy still remains a doctrine of great intellectual and scientific force, capable of holding its own by the sheer breadth of its generalisations and the power of its logic. Yet it is not its scientific generalisations or its logic that have given it its unique place in the history of modern times. On intellectual and scientific grounds alone it would hardly have outshone or outlived, as it certainly has done, the multitude of political and sociological theories of the mid-nineteenth century. If Marx is still a leading force to-day, while men like Comte and Spencer are mere fodder for the sociologist, it is because he did not confine himself to science and philosophy, while Comte and Spencer did. He hitched his science to a star, and it was his great fortune that the star was Aurora herself, the morning star of a rising political faith.

III

The political implications of Marxian philosophy, however, are too inconsistent to give him a secure seat among the nineteenth century democrats. Democracy as a political creed benefited relatively little and suffered a great deal from Marx and his followers. Yet there is one sense of the word " democracy " and one aspect of Marx's activity which entitle him to a place in the gallery of great democrats. Democracy may mean several things. It may mean the belief in certain forms of government : government by the majority, representative institutions. It may also mean a certain conception of the functions and power of the state : government by consent and aversion from compulsion and force. Neither of these two variants of democracy derives much support from Marx's writings and activity. Belief in the absolute value of representative government is inconsistent with the view of all constitutional forms as a mere expression of class power, while belief in government by consent is inconsistent with the view of historical progress as a product of class war. It is, therefore, no wonder that Marxian theory has so commonly been used as an armoury of arguments against the political tenets of liberal democracy. Much of the cynical attitude of modern communists towards parliament and elected majorities and much of the argument in favour of proletarian dictatorship derives naturally and easily from Marx's writings.

Yet it would be wrong to represent Marxian thought as anti-democratic. Useful as it may have been to the advocates of communist dictatorship of our own age, it has many affinities with the liberal and democratic faith of the age of Marx. For democracy can have yet another meaning, more general and in a sense more fundamental

than either the belief in representative institutions or the
dislike of government by force. Democracy is not only
a theory of government, but also a scale of moral values.
As a scale of values it belongs to the European tradition
of humanitarian individualism. It accepts human personality and individual man as an end in themselves, the sole
purpose and the only justification of a social system. It
judges political actions by the good or evil they do to
individuals, rather than by their effects on the collective
super-individual entities of race, state, church and society.
Between this view of life and the political programme of
democracy there is a natural connection. Majority rule,
representative institutions, government by consent and
respect for opinions, are merely broad applications of
humanitarian ethics to problems of state government.
Nevertheless, the link, natural as it is, need not always
be accepted. It does not require more than the usual
allowance of inconsistency to believe in the ethical principle
of democracy without subscribing to its political applications,
or to accept its political forms without believing in the
underlying ethical principle.

This is exactly what Marx did. His allowance of inconsistency was if anything above the average ; and it not
infrequently enabled him to travel far and fortunately
beyond the logical confines of his theory. Sceptical as he
was of the absolute virtue of democratic forms and prone
as he was to take a realist view of government, he yet
betrayed over and over again his unquestioning and almost
instinctive dependence on the ethical principle of modern
democracy. This principle he owed to his father and
to his father's friends, to the whole of the enlightened
humanitarian influences to which he was exposed in his
childhood. He shared it throughout his life with his
friends of the Prussian left, the neo-Hegelians, the liberals,
radicals, and socialists, and he handed it over to the first
generation of German social-democrats. It was deeply
embedded in the whole of the social thought of the time
and was taken for granted to an extent which made its
public and conscious avowal by Marx as unnecessary as
it was difficult.

It was this liberal and humanitarian predisposition which

threw him in his early student days into the company of the philosophical radicals in Berlin, which led him at the very beginning of his adult life into opposition to the reactionary government of Prussia, and which assisted in his conversion to socialism. We know from his articles and correspondence that what for the first time attracted his attention to socialism was the pity and the pathos of the unsuccessful working-class movements in the forties. If in the course of the subsequent years he moved a great deal further in the direction of socialism, he was led as much by a fervid compassion for down-trodden humanity as by intellectual conviction. The fervour may have been prophetic and Hebraic in its origin; but the pity and compassion were wholly German, sentimental and nineteenth century, something alien to the callous century that preceded it and almost equally alien to the century which followed.

Nowhere, however, does the liberal inspiration of Marxian ideas emerge more fully than in his conception of the future socialist order. Unlike the utopian socialists, Marx was very careful not to construct imaginary schemes of the socialist state. In his adumbration of the socialist society he confined himself to a few vague ideals. But vague and general as these may have been, they were ideals. They represented Marx's standard of values: his final measure of good and evil. It is therefore doubly significant to find that the Marxian image of the socialist paradise embodies the essentials of a liberal and democratic order. The transition from capitalism to socialism will be the transition from the kingdom of necessity to the kingdom of freedom. The kingdom of freedom will be that state of classless co-operation, social harmony and fulfilment of individual personality, which simple liberals hope to achieve within the confines of the present economic system. In other words, where Marx differed from the common run of liberals was not in his conception of the democratic ideal, but in its timing. If Marx denied the democratic programme, his denials were all qualified by an implied " for the time being." From the point of view of his final objects, democracy was not only consistent with socialism, but was its purpose and justification.

Nevertheless, had this democratic faith been confined to

the realms of final objects, had it remained mere *Zukunfts-musik*, critics would still have been justified in regarding Marx's message as unrelated, if not inimical, to the democratic movement in the modern world. Marx's democratic outlook, however, revealed itself in ways more definite and more immediate. It influenced some of his political utterances and decisions in direct opposition to the dictatorial and anti-democratic tendency in others. We know that Marx's chief contribution to modern socialist tactics was his advocacy of the participation of the proletariat in the politics of the modern state. To him the struggle for unrestricted franchise and the exercise of political power which that franchise offered, was the most urgent part of socialist action. True, he usually represented this political activity as a mere extension of class war and the preparation for the socialist revolution ; but on more than one occasion he emphasised the fact that the political emancipation of the working classes was to be desired for its own sake.

It is this happy inconsistency in Marx's attitude to the democratic politics of the day that gives special significance to his struggle against the revolutionary adventurers in the socialist movement. The struggle began in earnest in 1847 when Marx was opposed by Weitling, a German working-man conspirator, and continued in 1848 when Marx thwarted an insane project of Herwegh (a revolutionary poet who put more poetry into his revolution than into his poems) to invade Prussia at the head of a legion of German revolutionaries. It was resumed in 1850 during the conflict with the party of direct action in the International Communist League. It was taken up again in the successive clashes with Mazzini, the French anarchist Proudhon, and above all, the Russian anarchist Bakunin. In all these recurrent struggles Marx was doubtless led by a whole medley of motives. There was, in the first place, the natural caution of a shrewd observer, sceptical of the outcome of the revolutionary attempts and anxious to save the young communist movement from inevitable failures. There was also a motive which can, with a certain amount of circumlocution, be described as a personal dislike of physical adventure not untinged with emotional aversion from danger. There was, above all, the insistence on the inexorable

P

march of economic events and on the futility of political action in advance of economic evolution. But in addition to all these motives there was a definite opposition to the political outlook of the revolutionary wholesalers. He was often prepared to assume that " to-morrow will be finer than to-day," and that the gifts to-morrow may bring must not be spurned. This assumption stood in curious contrast to his economic theory of the growing insecurity of capitalism and the impoverishment of the working classes. In some moods he would argue that that very impoverishment would facilitate the coming of a socialist revolution, but in others he seemed to think that the progress of which capitalism was capable was facilitating, if not the establishment of a socialist order, at any rate a greater measure of political and social action by the working classes.

When in this mood Marx invariably found himself adhering to the liberal and democratic opinion of his day. Some of that adherence was unconscious and unintentional ; some of it definitely was not. On more than one occasion Marx openly allied himself with the other progressive forces. There was not a single liberal cause in the sixties and seventies which he did not make his own. He was an enthusiastic and steadfast admirer of Lincoln. Remote as his own class doctrine was from Lincoln's grandiloquent idealism, and difficult as he found it to represent the Yankee war against the South as an incident in the proletarian struggle, he nevertheless remained to the last a supporter of the great president. He was caught in the wave of humanitarian sentiment raised by the anti-slavery issue, and on the crest of that wave he remained until the end of Lincoln's days. To realise what this attitude meant it is enough to compare it with the attitude of a modern communist to Franklin Roosevelt, or to any other leader of the liberal and democratic movements of our own day. And what is true of his attitude to Lincoln is true of his attitude to the other liberal causes of his time. Thus his interest in the Irish movement was unflagging. Though he sometimes tried to dress up his pro-Irish attitude in the phraseology of the Communist Manifesto, no ingenuity, not even his own, could represent the possible triumph of the nationalists in Ireland as a contribution to the proletarian class war. What in reality commended that movement to Marx was its liberal aura, its struggle for freedom and its connection with the humanitarian issues to which every democrat in Europe responded as a matter of course. And what is true of his attitude to Ireland is also true of his attitude to the liberal movements in Italy and Hungary and Russia. He disliked Gladstone as a personification of middle-class hypocrisy and a sanctimonious humbug, yet the party which was to become Gladstone's, the liberals and radicals of England, often received from Marx a measure of support as unexpected as it was unsolicited.

It goes without saying that these excursions into democratic camps could be matched by similar excursions in the opposite direction. We know that towards the end of his life Marx was engaged in a desperate fight to prevent the adoption by the German social-democratic party of the so-called Gotha programme in which parliamentary and democratic politics were regarded as almost equal to the socialist purposes of the party. In the course of this fight Marx gave expression to points of view which were far nearer to the pure substance of his original class theory than most of his other political declarations and which have been used since to great effect by modern communists and anti-democratic socialists. The nature of that attack can very easily be misunderstood, for, like most of Marx's other charges, it was directed against more than one objective. A wounded sense of proprietorship must have played an important part. The movement which he had nurtured to life, and which he had come to regard as his own, suddenly began to frame its policies for itself and to disregard its maker's orders. But there is no doubt at all that Marx found himself alarmed by the political possibilities of the programme. He feared that the striving for immediate political and social reforms, which the Gotha programme sanctioned, might lead the movement away from its final objectives. The fear arose naturally from Marx's social philosophy, and was nearer to the letter of his doctrine than were his democratic policies. Judged by the letter of his doctrine Marx's humanitarian presuppositions and liberal sympathies were mere inconsistencies. But then in his attitude to the state, as in his character and life, there was

a great deal of inconsistency. It is owing to his inconsistency, as much as to his greatness, that we can rank him
among the democrats of the nineteenth century, and indeed
among that century's truest sons.

GIUSEPPE MAZZINI

1805–1872

by GWILYM O. GRIFFITH

GIUSEPPE MAZZINI

1805–1872

by GWILYM O. GRIFFITH

FIVE years after Mazzini's death, Swinburne wrote
of him as " the man for whom I would very gladly
have given all the blood of my body and all the
power of my heart and mind and soul and spirit." It was
Swinburne, too, who hymned Mazzini as " the fair, clear,
supreme spirit beyond stain," the " soul beloved beyond all
souls alive." But it was another English poet, not given
to Swinburnian rhapsody, who wrote of him as working
miracles upon the wills of men and of " live confederations
yet to be "—

> " The hidden founts of gathering river-floods,
>   To bear one day the music of his name
>   Through lands of harvest to the boundless sea."

Such tributes read a little strangely in this later age, in which
we psychologise our great men instead of worshipping them.
But even in those earlier times there was always material
with which one might balance an excessive laudation. For
example, it was no secret that Pope Pius and Count Cavour
had an ill opinion of Mazzini, and Karl Marx, among
later contemporaries, vehemently despised him.

The fact seems to have been that you had either to
dislike Mazzini very much or else yield him an admiration
akin to worship. Alexander Herzen once described him as
the Calvin of modern Europe, but he venerated him with
a warmth of affection which Calvin rarely excited ; and
Carlyle, not given to an excessive adulation of his contemporaries, testified in a celebrated letter to the *Times* that
Mr. Mazzini, if ever he had known one such, was a man
of genius and virtue, worthy to be called a martyr-soul.
John Morley ranked him as the most morally impressive
man he had known, or that his age knew ; and once, at
least, Garibaldi, momentarily disentangled from controversies that warped his judgment and embittered his

spirit, paid to the Maestro a tribute that was representative
of a whole generation of Italians :

" I want to-day to do a duty which I ought to have done long
ago . . . When I was a lad and was full of vague longings, I
sought a man to be my guide, the counsellor of my youth. I
sought him as a thirsty man seeks water . . . I found him.
He alone was awake when all around were slumbering.
He became my friend and has remained my friend. . . . In
him the holy fire of love for fatherland and freedom has never
dimmed. That man is Giuseppe Mazzini. I drink to him, to my
friend, to my teacher."

For it was true of Mazzini as it was of Lincoln that he
symbolized the soul of an entire people ; and of Mazzini
it was true even more than of Lincoln that he became a
mythic and legendary figure within his own lifetime.
One thinks of Dall' Ongaro's *stornello* :—

> " Where is Mazzini ?   Ask the pines
> Upon the Alps and Apennines.
> He is wherever traitors cower
> In terror for their fatal hour ;
> Where'er men wait impatiently
> To give their blood for Italy."

And not in Italy only, but among all the struggling
democracies of Europe, his name was for a while a flag of
hope and defiance, and his writings the holy writ of in-
surgent liberalism. His appearance, it is true, seldom
swept the multitude with that tornado of enthusiasm which
blew around Garibaldi. Mazzini's influence was more
elusive ; it worked silently in the region of thought and
faith, and it was most potent with elect minorities ; but in
its own sphere it was creative and supreme.

It is strange, then, that so impressive and memorable a
figure should be so generally forgotten. Historians, indeed,
cannot neglect, however much they may underestimate, his
influence ; and there are little groups throughout the world
among whom, as a sort of spiritual free-masonry, the
Mazzinian cult still flourishes. Nevertheless, to the
multitude his name is unknown. Who has not heard of
Lincoln, John Brown, Bismarck, Garibaldi ? Who has heard
of Mazzini ? Yet it was Jowett of Balliol who said of him :

" I think his reputation will increase as time goes on, when that of most statesmen disappears." And, after all, it is still too early to declare that Jowett's judgment has been falsified.

I

It may stimulate our imagination if we glance at one or two portraits of this strange being who was once so much in the eye of the world.

Take Giovanni Ruffini's description, who knew him in his young manhood :—

" He had a finely shaped head, the forehead spacious and prominent and eyes black as jet, at times darting lightning. His complexion was a pale olive, and his features, remarkably striking altogether, were set . . . in a profusion of black hair . . . . The expression of his countenance, grave and almost severe, was softened by a smile of great sweetness, mingled with a certain shrewdness, betraying a rich comic vein. . . . When he warmed upon a subject there was a fascinating power in his eyes, his gestures, his voice, his whole bearing, that was quite irresistible."

George Meredith's portrait of him in middle-life (as " the Chief " in *Vittoria*) is better known :—

" He was a man of middle stature, thin, and even frail . . . with the complexion of the student, and the student's aspect. The attentive droop of his shoulders and head, the straining of the buttoned coat across his chest, the air of one who waited and listened . . . detracted from the promise of other than contemplative energy, until his eyes were fairly seen and felt. . . . . In them lay no abstracted student's languor, no reflex burning of a solitary lamp, but a quiet, grappling force. . . . The chin was firm; on it, and on the upper lip, there was a clipped growth of black hair. . . . He had the English manner; a remarkable simplicity . . ."

And this for a picture of Mazzini in old age (quoted by Mrs. Hamilton King in her *Recollections*) :—

" Were it not for . . . [his] unhealthy pallor . . . and the excessive emaciation of the whole form, this would be the very handsomest man I ever set eyes on. And even as he is, so worn and wasted that he seems rather like a moving shadow than

P*

flesh and blood, the face has a strange and powerful attraction ; there is a sort of fascination about the man . . . The hair is scanty, a sable silvered, and the beard and moustache, which are closely cut, are white as snow."

Add to these descriptions such human details as that he invariably dressed in black, with a black scarf in lieu of a collar ; that he made pets of dogs and cats, and that uncaged canaries flitted about his room ; that he could never resist a beggar or a street-singer, and adopted a girl-waif of the London streets ; that he would pawn his cloak rather than do without cigars ; that among his intimates his gift of mimicry and playful humour was irresistible ; and that from youth to old age his one pastime was his guitar.

II

Giuseppe Mazzini was born in Genoa, June 22, 1805, the year that saw Napoleon assume the iron crown of the Lombards and the title, King of Italy. He was thus still a child when the Napoleonic dream faded, the Holy Alliance made the world safe again for the dynasts and despots, and Italy was once more reduced to a patchwork of kingdoms and petty States under Austrian domination. Mazzini's father, Dr. Giacomo Mazzini, was a physician of local repute and Professor of Anatomy in the University of Genoa. Dr. Mazzini was a self-made man, an ex-republican (he had taken part in the republican revolution of 1797) and a confirmed political pessimist. He comes out badly in most Mazzinian biography, but in spite of his dourness he appears to have been a man of high character and genuine kindness ; he was beloved by the poor and received the thanks of his sovereign for heroic devotion to duty during the cholera epidemic of 1836. Mazzini's mother was a woman of striking presence and natural intellectual gifts. A devout Catholic of the Jansenist school, she saw to it that her children (there were three daughters and Giuseppe) were trained in the Jansenist faith. The Calvinist element in her Jansenism comes out strongly in her letters. (When Mazzini is in hiding in Switzerland and involved in the " tempest of doubt " she writes : " You lack faith ; I have it to the full. You are the elect of God. Your name is destined to shine forever among the benefactors of mankind. . . . For me this is an article of belief. It is decreed.") For the first five years of his life Giuseppe was bed-ridden through spinal weakness—a circumstance which contributed to his intellectual precocity and brought about the ears of his parents much solicitous advice on the future training of the little " philosopher in Lilliput." In those years, and for long afterward, his mother's influence was supreme, and something of her Calvinism can be traced in his later thought.

Mazzini graduated from the University in 1827, and in the same year joined the secret revolutionary society of the Carbonari. He practised law, gained immediate popularity as an advocate and a wider reputation as a contributor of brilliant essays to the *Antologia* of Florence ; but in 1830, betrayed by his Carbonaro chief, Raimondo Doria, he spent three months in solitary confinement in the fortress of Savona, and then (January, 1831) entered upon his long career of exile. Of his Savona experience his mother declared : " I knew from that moment that Pippo's [Giuseppe] spiritual course was marked out." It was, in fact, the turning-point of his life ; for, as she discerned, all that hitherto had been more or less vague and romantic in her son's mind now took definite form and consistency. In this period he arrived at all his fundamental conceptions, political and philosophical, and it may be said that after he had reached the age of thirty he added very little to the body of his thought, except in the sphere of economics. Thus his career virtually began with his imprisonment in Savona in 1830, and ended with his imprisonment in Gaeta in 1870. He died in Pisa, March 10, 1872.

The first period, then, of Mazzini's political activities— roughly from 1830 to 1837—centres in the society of " Young Italy," which he founded in Marseilles in 1831. This, the first of modern political Youth movements, aimed at the regeneration of Italy through an " apostolate of ideas." Mazzini preached the democratic unification of Italy as part of a larger democratic movement for the reconstruction of Europe as a whole, and for this, he believed, the initiative must proceed from a reformed and republican Rome. Consistently with this belief in the European character of the movement he founded the affiliate-societies of " Young Switzerland," " Young Germany," and " Young Poland," and co-ordinated them in the Association of " Young Europe " (Berne, 1834).

As an educational movement " Young Italy " achieved immense and immediate success ; so much so that the story of it remains as the very poetry of revolutionary politics. For Mazzini, armed only with his dream, and challenging the wealth of kingdoms and all the forces of tyranny and privilege, did in fact accomplish the seemingly impossible. His writings, smuggled into Italy and reproduced by secret presses, were eagerly read, and while his society spread its agencies from Lombardy to Sicily his ideas spread like invisible flame against which " black cabinets " and police and cordons of scaffolds were no effective barrier. Garibaldi, then a young sailor, was one of the recruits. He has described his enlistment : " There arose in my mind strange glimmerings by the light of which I saw in a ship no longer a vehicle charged with the exchange of [merchandise] . . . but a winged messenger bearing the word of the Lord and the sword of the Archangel." Mazzini had appealed to his Italians in the name not of rights but of duties, not of interests but of principles, not of racial egoism but of nationality dedicated to the service of humanity ; and they had responded. And at a time when statesmen were dismissing the notion of Italian Unity as a childish dream (Cobden's phrase for it, a few years later) and when individual patriots who, like Manzoni, secretly cherished the dream, nevertheless feared to confess the guilty secret, even among their intimates, lest they should be regarded as utterly mad—at such a time Mazzini set the idea on fire and kindled men's souls with it from one end of Italy to the other. That was his *métier*.

Only in the field of revolutionary action " Young Italy " failed ; but there it failed disastrously ; comrades flung away their lives upon rash enterprises for which their leader was not without responsibility, and Mazzini's own death sentence was proclaimed " in high and intelligible voice " by the Genoa bell-man outside his parents' house. Nevertheless this first period, as we have noted, saw the full orientation of his thought, and the " tempest of doubt " through which he passed in 1835-6 left him with a confirmed and veteran faith.

The second period (1837-1848), rich in its history of philanthropic work and of engaging friendships with the Carlyles and others, covers his first sojourn in London. Here, burdened with ill-health and debt and never out of the hands of moneylenders, he began anew. He founded and taught in his famous night-school for Italian organ-grinder boys, organised an English society for their protection from exploitation by villainous *padroni*, established an Italian Working Men's Association, and re-knit the severed threads of his political plans. He wove a conspiratorial web which stretched from London and Paris to Corsica, Malta, Cuba, the two Americas and wherever exile congregations could be gathered ; and he founded propagandist journals that went to the ends of the earth. His dour father was restive. He had advanced money to his son for a timber business in Switzerland, an olive oil business in Soho, but could gain no satisfactory information about the investments. He importuned Pippo to abandon politics (" your ideas are ulcers ") and write lucrative plays of the Harlequin-Pantaloon order (" *Caro*, it is well to reflect upon this ") ; and while the old Professor attacked him at long range Carlyle raked him with thundering monologues on the imbecility of democracy and the ballot. He could only hold on his way. His mother secretly supplied him with a monthly allowance ; he spent it on charity or on his schemes. And when (1844) the British Foreign Office gave him unexpected advertisement by opening his letters in the post and (ineffectually) counterfeiting the seals, he used the publicity to plead his country's cause.

And then in 1848 the revolutionary storm broke over Europe and the third period of his career began. After eighteen years of exile he returned to a tumultuous Italy that received him with torchlight processions and royal honours but could not unite upon his national-democratic programme. Nevertheless the incredible dream of a republican Rome came true, and in the important hour he was summoned to its head as Triumvir and virtual President

(1849). It was the climax, though not the end. " Mazzini," wrote Pisacani, " soared above the other two [Triumvirs] on the wings of genius and his opinion prevailed in every department ; his intelligence shone resplendent, an absolute element, this, of grand conceptions. No one contested his superiority." Palmerston declared that Mazzini gave Rome a better government than she had enjoyed for centuries, and that oracle of British sentiment, *Punch*, broke into poetry :—

> " Though brutish force the game has won,
>   Triumvir, thou hast nobly done
>
>   •   •   •   •   •   •   •
>
> And Rome's old heroes from their spheres
>   Shout, chiming in with British cheers,
>   ' Bravo, Mazzini ! ' "

" Brutish force the game had won," for a fugitive and outraged Pope at Gaeta had summoned the Catholic Powers to the rescue of Rome. They had responded with expeditionary forces from Austria, Naples, Spain and France ; Newman, in far off Birmingham, was able to celebrate the victory of a meek Hierarchy over the " haughty clarion and black artillery " of the Mazzinian hosts ; and with the collapse of the revolution and the fall of Rome the Triumvir returned to exile and to England. His English friends urged him to abandon politics and give himself to literature, but he would not, perhaps could not. As Herzen declared, the worse things went with him the higher he felt he must hold the flag. " If Mazzini loses friends and money and barely escapes one day from the chains and the gallows, on the next he takes his stand more obstinately and resolutely than ever, denies himself everything, even sleep and food, ponders whole nights over new plans, and every time actually creates them, flings himself again into the conflict, and again beaten, sets to work once more." It was so now. He had aged and was grown prematurely grey, but he was indomitable. But the world had changed and Italy was turning from the Messianism of the earlier years and looking for redemption through diplomacy.

Thus the fourth and last period (1850–1872) found him sadly at odds with the Italian movement itself. The initiative had passed from him to Cavour and he saw the *Risorgimento* degenerate into something *bourgeois* and prudential, an affair of royal marriages and foreign alliances. He lost the upper classes to Cavour, he found the nation turning from republicanism to the monarchy, he saw the materialistic doctrines of Marx " corrupting " the working classes, and he beheld the Papacy, whose decline he believed to be imminent, reviving in a period of general moral languor and reaction. He strove desperately to re-conquer Italy for his faith, but in spite of himself his efforts were now sectarian and divisive ; there were insurrectionary plots and hair-breadth escapes from the gallows, and in the eyes of the Moderates he became " Public Enemy No. 1." And yet in a very real sense he was still forcing the pace and directing the trend of events. " I took the portfolio of the Interior," confessed Cavour, " in order to combat Mazzini." It was true. But he discovered that, after all, the only way to combat him was to appropriate his programme of action and forestall him in its execution. This Cavour did. Mazzini's was the creative, Cavour's the manipulative and constructive, genius of the Unity movement which reached its climax in 1870. In that year, aged and stricken, Mazzini made his last desperate fling and lent his aid to a republican plot in the south. He was arrested, imprisoned, released. He had lived to see " Italy united with Rome for her capital "; but it was not the Italy of his dreams. " I have galvanised," he said, " a corpse."

Mazzini never married. The one serious romance of his life was his passionate friendship with Giuditta Sidoli, the noble and beautiful Lombard exile whom he met in Marseilles in the early days of " Young Italy." For the rest, Carlyle's judgment that Mazzini, had he withdrawn from politics, might have made a high place for himself in literature, is confirmed by the literary work he was able to produce (and considering the circumstances of his life his output was immense). During a brief sojourn in Corsica in 1831 he wrote a historical romance (*The Hermit of Sagunto*) which never saw, and apparently never deserved to see, the light ; but his biographical, philosophical and critical essays (for example, his essays on the Philosophy of Music and on Fatality as an Element in the Dramatic Art ; his studies of Dante, Paolo Sarpi, Victor Hugo, Byron and Goethe, and his two penetrating articles on Carlyle) have permanent value, while his longer studies and manifestos, *Faith and the Future*, *Thoughts upon Democracy in Europe*, *The Duties of Man*, and *From the Council to God* are still vital. There is an English translation of his works in six volumes ; the best reflection of his personality is found in the three incomparable volumes of his *Letters to an English Family*, edited by Mrs. E. F. Richards. The Italian National Edition of his works and letters, now numbering over fifty volumes, is still in process of publication.

III

Mazzini's value for us is, first of all, in his unique personality and inner life. As George Meredith declared of him, he saw far and grasped ends beyond obstacles ; he was nourished by sovereign principles and despised material present interests ; and though it is true that his methods were sometimes deplorable and that some of his theories are outmoded, there can be no question of his spiritual genius. He discovered " new lands and a new law," and lived by and for his vision ; and the man who, in such a world as this, and through an active and difficult life, has lived by a Higher Law and preserved within his own soul an embattled peace—such a man must always have significance for us. Such a man he certainly was. No doubt he was at times (to quote Meredith again) lifted " a deplorable half-inch " above the common earth ; but if he was a problem to others he was none to himself. He had " found peace " and inner unanimity. Moreover, he had a surer intellectual sanity than many of his kind (was it not " Mark Rutherford " who said of him that he was the only saint in whose face one could discern no strain of *foolishness* ?), and his mental isolation can be easily over-emphasised. " Without appeal to revelation, with only the afterthought of an appeal to history, he as it were discovered and lived by a theology of his own. He became the apostle and martyr of a view of the sum of things which simply occurred to him, of dogmas which no one taught him, and which, though he constantly preached them, he scarcely attempted to prove " (F. W. H. Myers). This is not wholly true. Mazzini's sources are plain enough. They may be found in Dante (especially *De Monarchia*), in Herder and the German writers of the Enlightenment, in the sacred literature of the East, and in the Christian Scriptures. God is One, says Dante, and Humanity is One. Civilisation also should be One—a civilisation of free nations united in one confederation with Rome as its moral centre. This doctrine of Dante's Mazzini took over. He did not spin it out of his inner consciousness any more than he invented his dogma of Progress or of Duty and the Moral Law. What he did with all these was to make torches of them and set them ablaze.

Yet withal, no doubt, he had the mystic's insight, the mystic's secret flame and something of the mystic's esoteric self-sufficiency. He believed that Europe, for lack of a true principle of Authority, was condemned to moral anarchy from which it could be saved only by a new creative word, a new unfoldment of the eternal religion of humanity, of which primitive Christianity was once the supreme expression. And he thought he divined something of the form of the coming faith. The relation of the individual to God had been the soul of primitive Christianity ; the relation of the individual to Humanity would be the new and completing principle ; under its empowerment the task of the future would be to supersede the Catholicism of Medievalism, effete in its hierarchy and obsolete in its dogma, by the " Catholicism of Humanity " ; and only out of these new heavens of religious faith could proceed the new earth in which humanity would be constituted as a moral and political fellowship.

And all this was related to his " worship of Rome." The European Question, he would insist, was at bottom a religious question and in Italy—in Rome—lay its solution. From a reformed Rome alone could proceed the initiative of the new order, as from a reformed Rome alone could come the effective abrogation of the old. A Word had once gone forth from Italy which had substituted a European spiritual unity—Roman Christianity—for the triumph of material force. A second time, at the Renaissance, Italy had diffused over the world the example of civilisation in art and literature. The third time her hand would remove the antiquated symbols of Medievalism and put in their place the new authority, the new unity, the new Catholicism. With Protestantism he had little sympathy. His thought was Catholic and collectivist throughout.

IV

Mazzini was a democrat, but he was no mere populist obsessed with the magical virtue of the ballot. " Give the suffrage," he wrote, " to a people governed by . . . reactionary passions . . . they will introduce instability into every part of the State ; they will render impossible those great combined views, those thoughts for the future, which make the life of a nation powerful and progressive." And for him, as much as for any modern ideologue of the Corporative State, " great combined views " and internal unity and stability were essential. He held them to be possible only when, in a national democracy, there was a real fusing of the classes, socially and economically, into one class—the People—only, that is to say, where there was genuine community of interest and of aim. Thus, while he advocated a League of Nations sixty years before it appeared, the League which he desired was one in which each national democracy would function as a real unit and not as a congeries of rival classes—not as a medleyed State criss-crossed with conflicting purposes and policies. And thus, too, what embittered his latter days was the spectacle of his Italian democratic revolution being captured by the Moderates, halted at the stage of political constitutionalism, cluttered up with class checks and safeguards, and made to subserve reactionary interests concealed behind Liberal phrases. It was a policy which he foresaw would postpone the real integration of Italy, alienate and embitter the working classes and lead in the end to revolution and counter-revolution and the dictatorship of force.

But Mazzini's State, because it was fundamentally democratic (he preferred the term " social government " because " democracy " had become too exclusively political in its significance)—Mazzini's State had nothing in common with coercive systems. He held that in a genuine democracy the economic fusion of the classes could proceed by voluntary means ; that by organising for co-operative industrial enterprises, concentrating its massed resources upon constructive effort, and co-ordinating its activities on a national scale, Labour had it within its own power gradually to conquer the economic field and win the confidence of the community. Here, of course, he clashed with Marx. Materialistic Socialism, he argued, offered to the oppressed classes only an exchange of tyrannies for which the fiction of " the State " as the embodiment of the general will was no adequate consolation. For if the voluntary and democratic principles were ruled out, the Socialist "State" meant no more than departments of individual officials charged with power to define the needs and organise and drill the life of the community, reducing it to " the life of the convent without its religious faith." " The best among Communists reply (he declared), ' You must devote yourselves.' Devote yourselves to whom ? Do you not impose the sacrifice of liberty upon all ? And if not upon all have you then a caste of masters—of directors—and a caste of labourers ? " But the word " devotedness " was, he added, " a sort of fatality " for all such schools. It reappeared, indispensable, inevitable, but meaningless so long as a materialistic philosophy " denied the sentiment of the infinite " and regarded human society as so many colonies of ants or beavers. On the other hand Democracy, he held, properly stood for a true reverence for human values in politics and statecraft. Its mission was not to create and impose a fixed, immobile system but to help carry human nature forward and society forward, and this could be done only through a high conception of human nature itself. (" You can elevate *men* only by elevating MAN ; by raising our conceptions of life, which inequality tends to lower.")

Marx dismissed Mazzini as " that everlasting old ass," but time has not yet shown that the errors and miscalculations were all on the Mazzinian side. For example,

Marx and his successors manifestly underestimated the force of national sentiment in Europe, and in dismissing the national principle they made a profound miscalculation. Mazzini was nearer political reality when he argued that the principle of nationality, though it might ultimately be superseded, could not be ignored ; that it was bound to receive recognition in the future reconstruction of Europe, and that the technique of internationalism lay, not in the attempted destruction of the national idea, but in its elevation into organic relationship with the idea of Humanity.

And here, in the realm of ultimate ideals, nothing has happened in the last hundred years to impair the cogency of Mazzini's democratic argument ; namely, that democracy, as " government freely consented to by all, and acting for all," is the only means of international association by which Humanity can at last be constituted as a real fellowship of the peoples. For democracy alone conserves the voluntary principle in collective action, and without that principle there can be no real and covenanted fellowship between consenting peoples, no true collective life, but only an artificial union imposed from without ; a union *made* and not *grown*, and therefore brittle and insecure.

V

And so, after all, it is in the region of *ends* that Mazzini's significance is supreme. Mussolini, for whom Liberalism means doctrinaire individualism, has said that Mazzini was no Liberal. Mazzini was certainly no individualist, but then, by the same token, neither was he a nationalist, in the modern (Fascist) sense. What would he have thought of a philosophy of nationalism which exalts the nation into an absolute, an end in itself, a god to itself, and which looks toward a future in which the world becomes a jousting-field for a medley of " absolute " States, an arena of warring gods, each inflamed with " the will to power " ? This is individualism with a vengeance.

It is here, then, in the region of ends, that Mazzini speaks to us. With the immense complexity of modern States he has nothing to do, but on the deeper issues of duty and purpose, of aim and goal, he searches us and challenges us, and his inquisition cannot be avoided.

" Your first duties—first in importance, because without understanding these you can only imperfectly fulfil the rest— are to Humanity . . . Those who teach morality, limiting its obligations to duties towards family or country, teach you a more or less narrow egoism and lead you to what is evil for others and for yourselves. Country and family are like two circles within a greater circle which contains them both ; like two steps of a ladder without which you could not climb higher, but upon which it is forbidden you to stay your feet." " The nations are the instruments of internationalism." " Our country is the fulcrum of the lever which we have to wield for the common good."

How familiar are these quotations to all Mazzinians ! But how strangely they clash with the preachments of our newest messiahs—how remote they sound amid our modern clamour, like a voice from a far-off star ! And yet it needs no special illumination to see that the anarchy of our time is due to the substitution of national egoism, political and economic, for the higher duty and the larger wisdom that Mazzini taught. Not, indeed, that all our elder—or our junior—statesmen are at pains to deny his doctrine. Many believe it, but they believe it feebly, and, in the presence of a generation that is not feeble and that does not believe it, they betray the cause with heavy homilies uttered in what George Meredith would have called the relapsing tone. They believe it as, in Mazzini's youth, Italians believed in the Unity of Italy—as a pious but sadly impossible ideal. We await a new European leader with Mazzini's divine genius for setting great ideas on fire and—in Morley's phrase concerning him—" for breathing a soul into democracy."

JOHN STUART MILL
1806–1873
by R. B. McCALLUM

JOHN STUART MILL
1806–1873
by R. B. McCALLUM

JOHN STUART MILL was one of the greatest of the rational advocates of democracy. Others have served the democratic cause more notably as leaders in action, others have preached with more emotional fervour the democratic faith. Mill's task was to teach his generation the reasoned arguments for democracy, to provide a logical defence both of its judgment and its wisdom. But his intellectual self-respect was too high for him to be blind to the dangers of democratic rule. He realised that it could only flourish in certain conditions; he uttered a warning against its possible abuses.

He received from his father, James Mill, a careful education for his task as a philosopher of democracy. He was trained like an heir-apparent for the succession to the radical leadership, in which his father had succeeded Bentham. Mill tells us in his autobiography that his father " was earnestly bent upon his escaping not only the corrupting influence which boys exercise over boys, but the contagion of vulgar modes and feeling." This exclusive education might well have bred conceit, but Mill attests that it did not. As young princes are disciplined by military exercise, Mill was disciplined by his father in learning and logic. " Both as a boy and a youth," he tells us, " I was incessantly smarting under his severe admonitions." At the age of three he began to learn Greek, passing on rapidly to arithmetic, history and later on Latin. Very soon he was far in advance of the average boy at school. His father was his sole instructor and after some years Mill had to become the teacher of his younger brothers and sisters, a disagreeable task which however consolidated his own progress in learning.

During the first years of his son's life, that is from 1806 onwards, James Mill was a hard-pressed journalist earning an income of perhaps £500. He had a growing family, nine in all, and some of his father's debts to clear off. He

had been born in Angus in Scotland in 1773 of a family
of small traders and farmers. He was educated at Edinburgh
University at the expense of a benevolent laird and licensed
as a preacher in the Church of Scotland. But he felt unable
to profess a religious faith, and came to London to seek his
fortune with his pen. This he did with some success, and
in 1818 he published a *magnum opus*, his *History of India*.
Although severely critical of British rule in his book, he
was given an appointment at India House by the directors
of the East India Company. From now on he was
moderately affluent. Beginning with a salary of £800 per
annum he rose to £2,000 before his death in 1836. But it
would be a mistake to think of the Mill family as belonging
to the upper middle classes in the ordinary sense. James
Mill had started from humble beginnings, he had a successful but desperate struggle against poverty. Such struggles
are not forgotten, even in the second generation. Both
father and son, by their social origins as well as by their
independent views, were imbued by that feeling of being
external to the conventional governing classes, which was,
and still is, so strong an element in English radicalism.

Mill followed his father in the service of the East India
Company. He became a junior clerk at the age of seventeen.
By 1828 he was earning a salary of £600 ; by 1836 £1,200 ; by
1856 £2,000. On the dissolution of the Company in 1858
he retired with a pension of £1,500. From that date till
his death in 1873 he was completely at leisure and sat in
the Parliament of 1865–1868, taking a prominent part in the
debates on the Reform Bills. It is important to remember
that for the better part of his life Mill was a busy civil
servant, working regular office hours with a month's holiday
in the year. His work as a writer was accomplished in
his spare time from the office. Unlike his father he was
free from the embarrassments of a family. He married
in 1851 a Mrs. Taylor, with whom he had kept up an
intimate friendship for twenty years during her husband's
life. This friendship with a married woman was frowned
on by his father and occasioned some scandal, but scandal
did not easily injure a man of Mill's sober, virtuous and
modest way of life. His wife's death in 1858 was a deep
personal loss, which is commemorated in eloquent language

in the dedication of the *Essay on Liberty*. " Were I but capable of interpreting to the world one half of the great thoughts and noble feelings which are buried in her grave, I should be the medium of a greater benefit to it, than is ever likely to arise from anything that I can write, unprompted and unassisted by her all but unrivalled wisdom." Mill's friends could never quite perceive such superlative qualities in Mrs. Mill, but she was by all accounts a talented and sympathetic woman and influenced him considerably in his opinions.

Mill never moved in fashionable circles, but from boyhood he was accustomed to the society of those able intellectuals who gathered round his father. He acknowledges that he and the younger members of the set were sectarian in their outlook. They decried " sentimentality " and upheld the standard of pure reason and analysis. Later, he tried to abandon this narrow view and to appreciate the importance of feeling as opposed to reason. He tells us that none of the later Utilitarians were prepared " to rely on the intellect and enlightened self-interest as the main motive powers for the amendment of human conduct." The amendment of human conduct was always his aim and the theme, directly or indirectly, of all his writings. These took the form of formal treatises such as his *Logic*, 1843 ; *Political Economy*, 1848 ; *Liberty*, 1858 ; *Representative Government*, 1861 ; *Utilitarianism*, 1863 ; *The Subjection of Women*, 1869. But in addition he was a frequent contributor to periodicals such as the *Westminster Review*. He was always glad, however, to have his secure position at India House, which made him entirely independent of his earnings in journalism and therefore under no temptation to trim his views to the public taste.

At the age of twenty he went through a spiritual or psychological crisis. He asked himself whether, if all his schemes for the betterment of mankind were fulfilled, he would then be happy, and an inner voice answered, " no." How then could he be happy in promoting such schemes ? Life lost all savour for him. The analytic habits of thought in which he had been brought up, seemed to him to undermine all living desires. He thought of himself as a well equipped ship with a rudder but no sail. His life had no motive power. " The fountains of vanity and ambition seemed to have dried up within me, as completely as those of benevolence." After a time this cloud lifted, but it left permanent effects. He did not abandon his utilitarian beliefs and his radical ideals, but he learned that happiness in life is obtained by making it not the direct end. It is better sought by aiming at another object than one's own happiness, the happiness of others or some art or pursuit followed as an ideal for its own sake. He also learned that a training in speculation was not the be-all and end-all of life. We must maintain " a due balance among the faculties," and cultivate " the passive susceptibilities." The emotions must be given their due place. From now on he began to appreciate poetry, music and the arts.

This conversion made Mill's thought and life more mellow and sympathetic than the bare rationalism of his father and Bentham. A severe reasoner and analyst he remained, but he was never the dry, didactic pedant that his opponents were inclined to picture. In his later years after his wife's death, he lived partly in the south of France at Avignon and partly at Blackheath, where he was the genial patron of a circle of younger rationalists. One of the most eminent of these, Lord Morley, has left us a description of Mill as he knew him.

" In bodily presence, though not commanding, at sixty he was attractive, spare in build, his voice low and harmonious, his eye sympathetic and responsive." Morley insists that Mill was never a pure theorist or ideologue. He always kept up a vivid and direct interest in practical problems ; he was indeed well-qualified to speak on them after a lifetime spent in the government of India. He gave his young disciples practical and invigorating advice. " Keep yourself in the fresh air of the world ; do your best in the world's affairs, study the active rather than the passive." Or again, " Do not expect from the world more than the world is capable of giving." Carlyle said of Mill's talk, that it was " rather wintry and sawdustish." So it may have been when compared with the lurid colours of Carlyle's speech and writing. But Mill was a responsible counsellor of statesmen ; he worked to achieve immediate and practical ends. It was not his mission to play the part of the prophet, crying out woe upon his generation, giving stimulus rather than nourishment. Morley tells us that "what Mill cared for in his own plans of work, was that the aim should be at least definite and in season." It is significant that he was accustomed to use the old-fashioned word "improvement" rather than the more showy catchwords of "progress" and "reform." Improvement suggests definite and limited objectives. Mill believed that the society in which he lived was ordered unintelligently and darkened by inhumanity. His zeal to make a better world was no less sincere than that of Carlyle, but it was a point of honour with him to concentrate his efforts and canalise his energy, never permitting it to overflow in exaggeration and rhetoric. Above all he was on his guard against deluding himself and others. He avoided the extremes of hope and fear, and whether attacking or defending, set up his rational judgment as a censor of all his actions.

It is of course possible to work for the improvement of society without being a democrat. A benevolent despot, or a wise and public spirited aristocracy, may serve the ends of the reformer. But Mill did not believe that benevolent despotisms, of a man or of a class, could ever achieve the ends for which he worked. Even if such governments could shower material benefits upon the masses, they could not give them, what he considered essential to the self-respect of a civilised people, a conscious and responsible share in the government of their State. But the virtues of despotisms were a mere question of theory to Mill. He saw that in practice self-interest placed strict limits to their beneficence. If improvement of the condition of the people was necessary for the fulfilment of democracy, democracy was an instrument without which social conditions could not be improved. For Mill was after all a Utilitarian. He believed that the only observable principle of human action is that men seek their own happiness. They do this in diverse ways; some find it in a simple, direct gratification of their immediate desires. Others find it indirectly by caring for others and serving society rather than themselves. In the long run both forms of pleasure are selfish, but that does not prevent us from recognising the latter class of pleasures, commonly called unselfish, as being superior to the former. They are superior because they are more enduring. As Mill says, " To those who have neither public nor private affections the excitements of life are much curtailed, and in any case dwindle in value, as the time approaches when all selfish interests must be terminated by death, while those who leave after them objects of personal affection, and especially those who have cultivated a fellow-feeling with the collective interests of mankind, retain as lively an interest in life on the eve of death, as in the vigour of youth and health." They are superior also because they are socially more valuable, and a society in which they are more freely pursued will be the happier.

The first purpose of society, therefore, is to make these superior pleasures available to as many people as possible, in fact to aim at the greatest happiness of the greatest number. This famous phrase of the Utilitarians has been much decried and misunderstood. It is often thought of as meaning the distribution of a certain store of happiness over a large number of people, transferring wealth or privilege from Peter to Paul, in order that all may share alike in the diluted nectar. But Mill did not hold any doctrine of a happiness fund; he had a more hopeful and creative ideal. He saw the productive powers of man increasing, and science providing new benefits for the human race. He hoped that the new wealth and the new powers of man would lighten the lot of the very poorest and open up prospects of a freer and fuller life for the masses. He believed that " there is absolutely no reason in the nature of things why an amount of mental culture sufficient to give an intelligent interest in objects of contemplation should not be the inheritance of every one born in a civilised country." Or again, " Most of the great positive evils of the world are in themselves removable and will, if human affairs continue to improve, be in the end reduced within narrow limits." Of these positive evils, poverty and disease are with us still, but their ravages have been much reduced since Mill's day. That they are still as serious as they are may be attributed to the failure of " human affairs " to improve. War, faction, and un-intelligent government have curtailed the use we can make of our great productive powers. If Mill's expectations of improvement have only been imperfectly fulfilled, it is because man is less of a rational creature than he supposed, and because the unreasoning and destructive forces in man are so difficult to tame.

This criticism of Mill has long been a commonplace. The discoveries of modern individual psychology, particularly those of Freud, have given us more insight into the problem. Mill assumed, that when the great positive evils were overcome, mankind could hope for happiness. Freud tells us, that, in one sense, man cannot hope for happiness at all. Even in his adult state he is governed by strong emotional desires, which in civilised life he can never satisfy. He learns to find substitutes which serve him well enough, but he is always unstable. Since the pleasures he aims at are substitutes for deeper desires, his conduct is marked by a strange waywardness, by inexplicable outbursts of ferocity and fanaticism. The problem of making man happy in society is many times harder than Mill supposed. Still we must remember that the great master of modern psychology recognises the pleasure principle as the governing factor of human action, in terms that are baldly utilitarian. If he fills us with new fears, he holds out to us as our only hope the strengthening of the rational element in man by analysis of the emotional springs of action within him. Freud has provided an instrument which Mill did not possess, but which he would have been the first to use.

While Mill did not believe that all men were selfish, in the ordinary sense of the word, he believed that it was fair to assume of any social class, that they were as a whole selfish. Some members of the class might pursue aims wider than the immediate interests of the class, but even then, without complete understanding of the outlook of other classes. The majority, however, will always look to their nearest interests. All human experience teaches us that the majority will have a sinister class interest, neither their intelligence nor their imagination will be equal to the task of comprehending the needs of the whole society.

This is the theme of the famous treatise *On Representative Government*, published in 1861. In it Mill argues, that the best possible form of government is that which gives due weight to the interests of all classes, so that none is left to the mercy of others. Speaking of the England of his own time he says : " In this country, for example, the working classes may be considered as excluded from all direct participation in the government. I do not believe that the classes who do participate in it have, in general, any intention of sacrificing the working classes to themselves. . . . Yet does Parliament, or any of the members composing it, ever for an instant look at any question with the eyes of a working man ? When a subject arises in which the labourers as such have an interest, is it regarded from any point of view but that of the employers of labour ? . . . On the question of strikes for instance, it is doubtful if there is so much as one of the leading members of either House, who is not firmly convinced that the reason of the matter is unqualifiedly on the side of the masters and that the men's view is simply absurd ? Those who have studied the question know well how far this is from being the case."

In this passage Mill places himself amongst the most frank and wholesale advocates of democracy. He waves away all theories of virtual representation, or of the trusteeship of one class for another. He was convinced that it was impossible to escape from the naked fact, that men in the mass would use political power, consciously or unconsciously, for the oppression of those who were without it.

But having laid down the general principle, that all men should have a share in the government, he was prepared to qualify this principle. For one thing, he did not believe that there were many countries where education and public spirit were strong enough to permit of such an extension of active citizenship. Where the people are servile or passive as in Russia, China or India, democratic institutions could not succeed ; or where there are racial divisions within a State, as in Austria ; or where religious passions or local interests deflect attention from the main issues of politics. With the spectacle of the French Empire before him, he even adds, that too great a concern for equality may prevent the people from obtaining political power. In short, before a people can enjoy democratic representative institutions, they must have a real desire to receive them, to preserve them and to discharge the many duties it imposes upon them.

These conditions ruled out most nations in Mill's day, but even with regard to Great Britain where conditions were favourable Mill was prepared to put limits to the extension of the suffrage, to exclude some persons from it and to concede extra votes to certain other classes. This laid him open to the charge of taking with one hand what he had given with the other. It is important, therefore, to be quite clear as to what kind of democrat Mill was. To some, democracy means the transfer of all social and political power from the propertied classes to the great mass of poor people and accepting all the consequences of this revolution. We may favour such a step, as Comte did, because he believed the working classes to be morally better than any other, because they are schooled by adversity and suffering to deeper sympathy and humanity. We may favour it, as Marx did, because it was inevitable, the next phase of human history. We may favour it, as Mr. Chesterton does, because it is a Christian duty on the part of the rich to submit to the poor. But it was absolutely foreign to Mill's temperament or doctrine to believe that any class of men was, *per se*, better than any other. The oppression of the few by the many was just as much an evil as the oppression of the many by the few. Neither of these two conditions fulfilled his ideal of the greatest happiness of the greatest number. Oligarchy means the exclusion of the masses from material prosperity and political liberty. Democracy may mean the trampling down of the most cultured and valuable elements in society. When he was first a candidate for Westminster, Mill was challenged at a meeting to say whether he had stated that the working classes of England were generally liars, and he replied bluntly, " I did." The same austere refusal to play the part of flatterer to the multitude pervades his theory of politics. If the masses should turn out to be a class, and have a sinister interest against other classes, whose only fault was to be a minority, then the scales must be adjusted to protect such minorities. Dealing with this subject, he wrote, " But is there not a considerable danger lest they (the majority) should throw upon the possessors of what is called realised property,

Q

and upon larger incomes, an unfair share or even the whole
of the burden of taxation, and having done so add to the
amount without scruple, expending the proceeds in modes
supposed to conduce to the profit and advantage of the
labouring class? Suppose again a minority of skilled
labourers and a majority of unskilled : the experience of
many trade unions, unless they are greatly calumniated,
justifies the apprehension that equality of earnings might
be imposed as an obligation, and that piece work, payment
by the hour, and all practices which enable superior industry
or abilities to gain a superior reward might be put down."

He therefore proceeded to suggest those limitations on
the suffrage, which horrified many of the ardent democrats
of his day. In the first place he was prepared to exclude
illiterates, on the ground that without reading and writing
a man could not be conversant with public affairs. Also,
since responsibility is of the essence of good democratic
government, recipients of poor relief must be excluded,
and those who bear no share of conscious direct taxation.
He proposed, however, to provide a wide scheme
of direct taxation so that all classes should feel its
burden, however small the payment. But this was not
enough. Certain classes should be given extra votes in
respect of superior education and what Mill calls " station,"
the occupation of positions of social responsibility. He
would even tolerate plural voting in respect of property
as being better than nothing. In addition to these adjust-
ments of the franchise he had other measures to propose.
Thus he opposed the radical cry for secret ballot, on the
ground that voting was a public duty and not a secret
act of registering a personal interest. A more fundamental
proposal was the scheme of minority representation of Mr.
Hare, the forerunner of modern methods of proportional
representation. This would save minorities from being
crushed in the rough and tumble of democratic politics,
and it would increase the diversity and the personal talent
available in the House of Commons. He could not of
course defend the House of Lords, but he advocated a
chamber recruited from those who had served the State in
high office. He seemed curiously blind to the fact that such
a body would be, in the conditions of his age, and indeed

of this, an essentially aristocratic assembly. The civil service was to be recruited by competitive examination instead of by patronage. This was a blow at aristocratic privilege, but at the same time was a guarantee of professional efficiency under a democracy. By all these methods the democratic impulse was to be harnessed to an aristocracy not of birth, but of personal merit. Yet when all his reservations had been made, he returned to his original utilitarian principle. The majority may be curbed but not subordinated. " The plurality of votes must on no account be carried so far that those who are privileged by it, or the class, if any, to which they mainly belong, shall outweigh by means of it all the rest of the community."

To this balanced and moderate scheme of representative government Mill added a postscript, which to most people in his day seemed madly radical. During the debates on Disraeli's Reform Bill in 1867, he proposed an amendment in favour of women's suffrage, for which he was able to muster seventy-three votes. Two years later he published his famous pamphlet, *The Subjection of Women*. Among the classes in society whose interests were ignored or disregarded was one half of the population, the female sex. In Mill's eyes women had as much claim as any other unenfranchised class to the consideration of Parliament, but in their case there was much more than the franchise to be won. It was necessary to amend the law which placed women at a disadvantage and made them little more than the chattels of their husbands. He made his appeal as challenging as possible, disdaining to argue for any partial concessions. He boldly threw on his opponents the onus of proving that there was any case at all for the legal discrimination which existed against women. Arguments based on the natural superiority of man left him unmoved. " Was there ever," he asked, " any domination which did not appear natural to those who possessed it ? " Nor would he admit any argument drawn from the actual condition of women as they then were. He denied " that anyone knows or can know the nature of the two sexes, as long as they have only been seen in their present relation to one another." Women were as men had made them, subjected by law to father and husband, deprived of intelligent

education, economic independence and public employment.
Grant that in spite of the law they enjoy great power, yet
this power is obtained by artifice rather than exercised as
a right. Grant that many husbands are kind and good, so
are many despotisms except for the one fact that, however
kind, they educate for servility. He reminded his readers,
that when accident placed women on a throne, they had
often showed conspicuous statesmanship. How great are
the benefits which society may expect from women when
the fruits of full emancipation can be reaped ?

Mill's writings on the subject of women are more
vehement and extreme than his other works. When we
consider the mountain of prejudice which lay before him
we may pardon him, if for once he lapsed from his wonted
moderation. No part of his writings has been more
successfully vindicated, and from the day of Mill's death
to the present the progress of women to civil and finally
to political liberty has been certain and rapid.

We have seen that Mill was concerned for the safety of all
minorities of opinion. Behind this question lies the ultimate problem of that minority of minorities, the individual.
This is dealt with in the famous *Essay on Liberty*, of which
Morley says, " I do not know whether then or at any other
time, so short a book ever produced so wide and so important
an effect on contemporary thought." It is a polished and
eloquent essay of little more than one hundred pages. He
begins by assuming that nothing is more important than to
permit human life to develop in its richest diversity. Yet
knowledge of history and experience of life show us that
the most fruitful minds and daring spirits, the most saintly
and virtuous characters, may be crushed by the dull average
majority of their fellows. Socrates and Christ were put
to death with the approbation of society ; Marcus Aurelius,
a monarch of singular wisdom and moderation, was a
persecutor. The moral is clear. We dare not arm society
with power to suppress opinions because they are unpleasing
to the generality of its members. The State may take
power to preserve public order and suppress sedition, it
may restrain individuals in those acts which harm others,
but there its legitimate power ends. The individual must
remain free in thought and speech and action. We need

not go over the well fought battle to which the *Essay on Liberty* gave rise. It can be shown that Mill's distinctions between what the State may or may not prevent are practically untenable or even inconsistent with his own views in his other works. The *Essay* remains as a permanent warning to rulers of the evils of persecution, and a permanent reminder to citizens lest they should make themselves rashly the judges and censors of their neighbours. If we think less of it now, it is because so much freedom has been won since it was written. There are not wanting signs that its principles may have to be invoked once more.

It remains to say a word about Mill's economic teaching in so far as it affects his position as a democrat. His book, *The Principles of Political Economy*, was published in 1848. He is often regarded as typical of the *laissez-faire* school which conceded all to the capitalist and left the wage-earner without any hope of advancement. It is true that Mill was strongly impressed by two dominant ideas of his day, the fear of over-population and the iron law of wages, which, if true, meant that workers' wages could only be raised at the expense of other workers. Yet while Mill believed that increase of population threatened to prevent any improvement in the standard of living he had great hopes of what might be done by checking population, hopes that have been in part fulfilled. At the end of his life too, he recanted his wages fund doctrine and admitted that an increase in the total amount of wealth payable in wages was well within the bounds of possibility. His view of economic science was not rigid and static. He says that he and his friends " did not overlook the folly of premature attempts to dispense with the inducements of private interest in social affairs, while no substitute for them has been or can be provided : but we regarded all existing institutions and social arrangements as being merely provisional, and we welcomed with the greatest pleasure and interest all socialistic experiments by select individuals (such as the Co-operative Societies)." He was also an advocate of one great democratic institution—peasant proprietorship, which is now the basic social fact in many European countries.

Since Mill's day the cause of formal democracy in Europe has succeeded to an extent which would have both surprised and alarmed him. It has risen in countries where the soil was unpropitious, and he, at least, would not be surprised at its many failures. In his own country the franchise has been extended without his safeguards, and yet the evils which he feared have not come to pass. The working classes are not the foes of learning and culture ; they demand, however, a share in the cultivated life of the more fortunate classes; to some extent they are obtaining it. They have the political machinery in their hands if they care to take it, and if in their use of it they remember some of Mill's counsels of prudence and moderation, they may hope to hold it.

WILLIAM MORRIS
1834–1896
by OLIVER BALDWIN

WILLIAM MORRIS
1834–1896
by OLIVER BALDWIN

ON March 24, 1834, at Walthamstow a boy was born into the family of a prosperous bill-broker named Morris. He was christened William after his father and was destined to become one of the most remarkable and gifted men of his age. At the age of four he was reading *Waverley* novels of his own accord and was even then showing signs of possessing an amazingly retentive memory. His family moved into the country when he was six and he immediately began to show a keen delight in natural history ; being particularly interested in bird life and peopling the woods with the romantic figures he had met with in the pages of the *Arabian Nights* or the works of Captain Marryat. At the age of thirteen he was sent to Marlborough College, where he was not unhappy.

In 1852, when he was eighteen, he passed into Exeter College, Oxford, and it was during the entrance examination in the College hall that he found himself seated next to the boy who was to become his life-long friend—Edward Burne-Jones. It was through Edward Burne-Jones that Morris came to find congenial company in his University life, for he introduced him to the little group that had come from his school in Birmingham, a group forgotten to-day but of great individual brilliance at that time—Fulford, Faulkner, Dixon, Cormell Price and Harry Macdonald. With these and Godfrey Lushington of Balliol, Vernon Lushington and Wilfred Heeley of Trinity College, Cambridge, he founded and contributed to the Oxford and Cambridge Magazine. All this time he was reading and learning. He revelled in Shakespeare and Milton and Alexander Smith's *Life Drama*. He visited English churches and gloried in the stained-glass windows, the brasses and the old church manuscripts. He made visits to Amiens, Beauvais and Chartres and chose the twelfth century as his ideal, a century in which his soul could find understanding and give him his fill of that beauty and romance for which

he always yearned. When he came of age he inherited
£900 a year and this enabled him to buy books he had long
coveted and to plan further expeditions to the great abbeys
and churches of France and Belgium. He began to write
poetry of a romantic character easily and fluently, showing
a good sense of rhythm and a love of short words. Much
of it betrayed the great influence of Sir Thomas Malory's
Morte d'Arthur. This love of the Middle Ages was Morris'
refuge from the ugliness of the early days of industrial
capitalism into which he was born and whose sordidness
was brought to his notice by conversations with his friends
from Birmingham. To combat this atmosphere of commercialism, Morris thought of founding a monastic brotherhood which would be more concerned with the arts and
crafts than with dogmatic religion, but the variety of his
interests increased so rapidly that the project faded into the
background towards the end of his time at Oxford. His
monastic order was to have Sir Galahad as patron and it
was to be founded with the purpose of enlisting a chosen
few " in this Crusade and Holy Warfare against the age."
As an undergraduate he was not politically conscious.
That was to come in later years; but it is interesting to recall
that whereas towards the end of his life he was to take a
prominent part in advocating action as a means of reform,
in his youth he advocated withdrawing from the possibility
of the struggle of protest by cutting himself off from the
world and sheltering himself within monastic life. Browning
and Tennyson were the two modern poets most read by
Morris and his circle, and Ruskin's influence as an art
critic led Morris and Burne-Jones to take an interest in the
Pre-Raphaelite school of painting, especially the work of
Holman Hunt, Millais and Rossetti. As physical recreation
in Oxford, Morris resorted to long walks and single-stick,
at which sport he was not only expert but ferocious and
dangerous, since his great physical strength was more than
a match for his adversaries. The visits which he and his
friends made to France enabled Morris to acquire that
amazing knowledge of ecclesiastical buildings and decoration which later was to make him so great an authority.
He learnt of brasses and stained glass, of illuminated church
manuscripts, of murals and even of campanology, and what

he learnt he remembered. When Morris first came up to
Oxford it had been his intention to take Holy Orders and
this, being also Burne-Jones's desire, had naturally drawn
them to one another; but at the age of twenty-two, when
walking with Burne-Jones on the quay at Havre, they both
decided to give themselves to art, the one as a painter, the
other as an architect. And by architecture Morris meant
the whole world of design and material creation, and not
the mere erection of a dwellinghouse or the mathematical
calculations necessary for the planning of a public building.
To him architecture was the greatest Art, all embracing
and all beautiful. So the decision was made and with it
the desire to go forth into the world on the great Quest for
beauty and creation—the new search for a more under-
standable San Grael. Five months later, having obtained
his B.A., he signed his articles with an architect named
Street in Oxford and began his work in close contact with
Philip Webb, the senior clerk, with whom he was so closely
connected in revolutionizing domestic architecture. Burne-
Jones at the same time began to work at painting under the
supervision of Dante Gabriel Rossetti, whom the two young
men had only lately met, but under the influence of whose
masterful personality they had completely fallen. It was
not long however before Mr. Street moved his offices to
London, whereupon Morris took rooms with Burne-Jones
in Bloomsbury and began, at the instigation of Rossetti, to
attend drawing schools in the evenings. So intent was
Morris on his new work that he was forced to drop his
contributions to the Oxford and Cambridge Magazine
and thereby sever all connection with his University life.
Rossetti urged him to paint above all things, for, as he told
Burne-Jones : " If any man has any poetry in him, he
should paint, for it has all been said and written and they
have scarcely begun to paint it." At this time in Oxford
the Union building had just been erected and the architect,
urged on by Morris, approached Rossetti and suggested
that the ceiling of the library might well be painted with
floral designs and large panels. This appealed mightily
to Rossetti and, without any knowledge of the actual
technique of mural decoration, he gathered together Morris
and Burne-Jones, Arthur Hughes and Spencer Stanhope,

Val Prinsep and Hungerford Pollen, and started on the work
right away. Morris designed the pattern for the ceiling
dome and also one of the panels which was of " How Sir
Palomydes loved La Belle Iseult with exceeding great love
out of measure, and how she loved not him but rather Sir
Tristram." But the paintings were left unfinished, for
the damp from the newly-built ceiling drew the colours
into the plaster and the whitewash on which the paintings
were laid began to flake off. It was during Morris' stay
in Oxford for the work on the Union ceiling that he first
met Swinburne, then an undergraduate at Balliol, and their
friendship became more intimate as time went on. Morris,
returning to London, began to experiment in different
forms of artistic creation, and between whiles he wrote
poems to be published the following year under the title of
The Defence of Guenevere and other Poems. This work was
much appreciated by a small but discriminating circle but
did not receive the wider appreciation accorded to *The
Dream of John Ball* or *The Earthly Paradise,* which were to
appear later and of which latter work Robert Browning
wrote : " It has been my delight ever since I read it . . .
and know you, of all the world, wrote it—you whose songs
I used to sing while galloping by Fiesole in the old days—
Ho ! is there any will ride with me ? " Although critics
were not kind to *The Defence of Guenevere* they made no
impression on Morris. " To think of a beggar making his
living by selling his opinion about other people," he said,
" and fancy anyone paying him for it." Just before his
twenty-sixth birthday William Morris was married in
Oxford to Miss Jane Burden whom he had met the year
before and whose striking and unusual form of beauty had
not only thrilled him but caused Rossetti to claim her for a
model in his usual imperious and not-to-be-gainsaid style.
The young married couple went to France, Belgium and the
Rhine for their honeymoon, and, full of schemes for building
and decorating, they returned and commissioned Philip
Webb to build them a house at Upton in Kent. It was to
be called the Red House and was built of brick and planted
in the middle of an orchard. Because of the extreme
difficulties he experienced in arranging for the making
of his house beautiful, he conceived, at the instigation of

Rossetti and Madox Brown, the idea of starting a firm of his own that should supply such things to the general public. Two years later, in 1861, he launched his enterprise with the help of Mr. Peter Marshall, a surveyor and friend of Madox Brown's, as Morris, Marshall, Faulkner & Co., on a capital of £107, and took premises at 8, Red Lion Square and engaged a few men and boys to help. The firm advertised themselves as Decorators and were prepared to make household furniture, table glass, jewellery ; to carry out painting, carving and metal work ; to design and execute mural decorations, stained glass, embroidery, stamped leather and ecclesiastical decorations. In 1862 the firm ventured forth into the designing of wallpapers, and the well-known trellis-work was produced—the rose trellis itself by Morris, the birds by Philip Webb. The daisy paper followed and this eventually led to the most famous design of all—the pomegranate.

Later the firm produced chintzes, carpets and dyed stuffs. Two daughters were born to him during his sojourn at the Red House, but in 1865 the expenses of his business became too great for him to bear and he reluctantly moved to Queen Square, Bloomsbury, and transferred his business to the adjoining out-buildings. Parting with the Red House was a great grief to Morris, but the fact that it was a very cold house in winter and he had had a bad bout of rheumatic fever helped him in his decision to move to London. Thither he brought some of his furniture, the remainder being sold or left to the purchasers of the Red House. From his new home he sent out his long narrative poem *The Life and Death of Jason* to the world, and this was well received. The immaturity of some of his past writing was no longer to be seen ; at the age of thirty-two he had established himself as a real poet. During the next ten years Morris' firm grew apace, and weaving, dyeing, and printing on cloth became its staple production. In 1867 the firm received its first important commission when it undertook the decoration of the Green Dining Room in the South Kensington Museum. The room is used to-day, but is far more in keeping with a mediaeval lady's tapestry work-room than with the modern habit of drinking tea. The excellence of the work is proved by the fact that it has

not yet needed re-decoration after nearly seventy years.
Morris' decorating craft was working hand in glove with
that of writing and he received especial praise from the
critics for his next publication *The Earthly Paradise*, a
three volume poetical work in the Chaucer manner mainly
based on the great Greek and Norse romances, but also
taken from French, Old English and Eastern sources.
This incursion into Norse romance drove him onward to
the study of the Icelandic language and he immediately
began the translation of the *Grettir Saga*, to be followed
a year later by the more famous *Volsunga Saga*.

In the intervals of this translation, which he carried out
with the help of Mr. Magnusson, he took up the illuminating
of manuscripts, and also returned to figure drawing in
Mr. C. F. Murray's studio.   The variety of his interests
was now amazing, and in every new craft which he took
up he became, in a short space of time, an expert.   Crafts
came easily to him.   Five years of living in London made
Morris yearn for the country, and finally he discovered a
grey-stoned Elizabethan house, situated on the upper
Thames, almost where the counties of Oxford, Gloucester
and Berkshire meet.   It was called the Manor House,
Kelmscott.   Since the only so-called sport that interested
him now was fishing, this house by the river suited him
well and he was destined to live in it till the end.   In
perhaps his best known prose work *News from Nowhere*,
the surrounding country, the haymaking and the river itself
were drawn from this out of the way part of England which
he grew to love so well.   Although all this time he was fully
occupied with his different interests he was always restless,
ever seeking for some new outlet for his great creative
energy and his great physical strength.   The fits of temper
to which he had been subject as a child still remained with
him, but whether he was crumpling a fork in his teeth
to prevent himself from being rude to a dinner guest, or
hurling the first thing that came to hand at one of his
workmen, or kicking in the panel of a door, he was always
beloved by those who knew him, and Kelmscott was a
guest house in a very real sense.   In 1871 he made his
first journey to Iceland and was captivated by the country.
It seemed as if he had found the cradle of his instincts in

this lonely land and he felt an affinity with it which was to
lure him back a second time. On his return Morris began
to study handwriting to enable him to do the actual work
of manuscripts and not only the illuminated letters and
surrounding decoration, and the result of his newly acquired
craft developed in him an interest in vellum which led
on to a study of printing and styles of type.

In 1872 Morris published a long romantic poem entitled
Love is enough, and the following year he gave up Queen
Square and took a London house on the Mall in Hammersmith. This was the beginning of other changes that were
to take place in Morris' life during the following three years,
for there arose an argument among the founders of the firm
which led to a dissolution of partnership and the renaming
of the Company—Morris & Co., under Morris' sole control.
The other event of importance was the final break with
Rossetti, who had been sharing Kelmscott.

1877 saw Morris moving for the first time into the
political arena. Up till then he had been a Liberal, merely
voting at elections, but taking no active part in the
propagation of his creed. Now, owing to his hatred of
vandalism, he rushed into the outskirts of the battle by
helping to form the Society for the Protection of Ancient
Buildings and thereby bringing himself into contact with
political authority. At the same time he joined the Eastern
Question Association and worked hard to draw the attention
of the people of England to the Turkish atrocities in
Bulgaria and appeal for their sympathy on behalf of Russia
when, taking the side of Bulgaria, she declared war on
Turkey. Because the Tory Party was pro-Turkish, he
decided to make his appeal " to the working men of
England," and he issued a manifesto in May, 1877, warning
them against any attempt on the part of " greedy gamblers
on the Stock Exchange, idle officers of the army and navy
(poor fellows !), worn-out mockers of the clubs . . . and
lastly, in the place of honour, the Tory Rump, that we
fools, weary of peace, reason and justice, chose at the last
election to represent us." The following year the shadow
of war that had passed returned with the Afghan campaign,
which was the revenge of the Tory war party on the success
of Russia over Turkey, and aimed directly at the power of

the great Slav Empire. Protest meetings were held, and
Morris' enthusiasm led him to write a political song—
Wake, London lads—which was distributed and sung at the
time.

This incursion into the radical circle of politics brought
him into contact with the leaders of the working classes,
and it was not long before the doctrine of Socialism made
its way into his heart and head as the only sane method of
economics and the best safeguard against international
strife. It was the vacillating policy of the Liberal Party
that finally caused him to cease supporting them : their
strange desire to ride two horses at the same time and
their invariable habit of falling between them. But while
the Tory war party was busy organizing their " peaceful
penetration " into other people's countries—and between
1877 and 1883 these countries included Egypt, the Trans-
vaal, Cyprus, Afghanistan and Zululand—Morris' workshops were growing to such an extent that he decided to
move them away from London. Kelmscott was too far
away from transport facilities and the higher Cotswold
country too far from London to suit his purpose, and
eventually in 1881 he moved his works to Merton, in Surrey,
where the water was ideally suited to his new dyeing
process. A circular issued at this time informs the public
that Morris & Co. design and execute painted glass windows,
Arras tapestry woven in the high warp loom, carpets,
embroidery, tiles, furniture, velvets and cloths and up-
holstery. Of these, the printed cotton goods, or " Morris
chintzes," became the most widely known and used.

By 1883 Morris, influenced by Mill, Henry George,
Toynbee, Owen, Marx and the Christian Socialism of Charles
Kingsley and Frederick Maurice—whose creeds were
constantly being expounded by his friends in radical circles
—definitely allied himself with Socialism and joined the
Social Democratic Federation on the same day that his old
College at Oxford honoured him by a unanimous election
to a Fellowship. During the next two years the cause of
Socialism so absorbed Morris that his output of literary
and manual work fell considerably. He began to lecture to
working-men's clubs on such things as " Art, Wealth and
Riches," basing his main plea for Socialism on the necessity

for giving beauty to the world. The position of the artist under Socialism, freed from commercialism, was one of his themes which was brought out so clearly in his *News from Nowhere*. These lectures met with a great deal of criticism from many of his listeners who held, as people do now, that whereas it was a pleasant thing for an artist to be free of commercialism, or even for a working man to be given education and decently housed, such things would invariably lead to the upsetting of the cherished preserves of private property and compound interest, to say nothing of the House of Lords and accepted charities. His expounding of the Socialist creed led also to many letters of abuse, such as the one from Mr. H. C. Donovan, suggesting that Morris was only fitted to be a candidate for the Zoo. To this Morris replied :

Dear Sir,
  I am obliged to you for your note inviting me to offer myself to the Greenwich Zoo as a possible candidate, but my principles as a revolutionary Socialist prevent my accepting your flattering offer.
  I am, dear Sir,
    Yours faithfully,
      WILLIAM MORRIS.

In 1884 Morris backed a new Socialist weekly called *Justice*, and continued to write for it until he separated from H. M. Hyndman and his Social Democratic Federation the following year on a question of policy, and started the *Commonweal*. This was the organ of the new Socialist League which he founded—of those who, like himself, had been antagonized by Hyndman's autocratic control of the S. D. F. Morris now began open-air propaganda and, although he was never a good public speaker, he had a fine presence and his blue reefer jacket and blue cotton shirt made him look more like a breezy sea-captain than an exponent of economics, as he stood before the people in the East End of London of a Sunday morning. At one of these meetings in Limehouse the police interfered and in the ensuing fracas eight persons were arrested and subsequently fined. Because Morris objected to the sentence he was also arrested for disorderly conduct, but discharged for lack of sufficient evidence. This brought the young Socialist movement to the fore and attracted many people to its banners who objected to police interference with the right of holding meetings. Political feeling was running high at this time owing to the projected Home Rule for Ireland Bill. In 1886 the crowds at open-air meetings were often unruly. Morris was arrested near Edgware Road for refusing to stop addressing a meeting. He was fined for obstructing the highway. This was his last personal encounter with the police in his efforts at open-air propaganda.

By 1887 Morris had completed his translation of the *Odyssey* into English verse. He followed this shortly after with *The Dream of John Ball*, a work full of fine description and deep vision. In the remaining nine years of his life, Morris published his prose romances : *The House of the Wolfings, Roots of the Mountains, News from Nowhere* (first in the *Commonweal*), *The Wood Beyond the World, The Well at the World's End* and *The Sundering Flood*. In 1890 he founded his own press, which he named after his country home, and designed special type for the printing. From this press came *The Story of the Glittering Plain*, and reprints of Caxton's *Golden Legend, Historyes of Troye, Reynard the Foxe, Order of Chivalry* and *Godefrey of Boloyne* ; *Biblia Innocentium, News from Nowhere* ; *Poems of William Shakespeare* ; Cavendish's *Life of Wolsey* and More's *Utopia*. In 1893 he also issued a translation of old French romances and a Chaucer of only two copies, bound in wood and vellum and clasped by silver bosses. After the death of Tennyson he was approached with an offer of the Poet Laureateship, but this he declined on the grounds that he was not a ceremonial writer of official verse. All this work was executed in the intervals of his continual advocacy of Socialism, which he preached in the open air, in lectures and within the growing Socialist organization. In 1887 he was present in Trafalgar Square on " Bloody Sunday " when a large Radical meeting, held to protest against the Government's dilatory Irish policy, was broken up by police and military ; and he spoke at the graveside of Alfred Linnell, who had died, from injuries received at the hands of the police, a month later. " Our friend who lies here," he said, " has had a hard life and met with a hard death ; and if society had been differently constituted, his life might have been a delightful, a beautiful and a happy one. It is our business to begin to organize for the purpose of seeing that such things shall not happen ; to try and make this earth a beautiful and happy place."

In 1889 Morris went as one of the English delegates to the International Socialist Congress in Paris, to celebrate the hundredth anniversary of the fall of the Bastille; that very Congress which was to mark the dividing line between Socialist and Communist, and finally lead to the triumph of Lenin over the whole of Russia.

The *Commonweal* failed in the following year as a result of the imprisonment of the writer of an article in defence of Anarchism, and with its failure ended the Socialist League. In order to rid Socialism of its liaison with Anarchism, Morris took this situation as suitable for the forming of a new society, and, having purged the ranks, he founded the Hammersmith Socialist Society ; but there was still too much mutual antagonism between H. M. Hyndman and himself to link up with the growing S. D. F. However, in 1893 he joined Hyndman and Bernard Shaw in drawing up a " Manifesto of English Socialists " which stands to-day as a fair and accepted statement of the aims of modern English Socialism, with the exception of the claim for universal suffrage which has already been granted. Although Morris' many Socialist songs have lost popularity owing to their lack of suitable accompanying music, the particular appeal for Socialism which he made during his life-time is still remembered, and I doubt whether any book, other than Robert Blatchford's *Merrie England,* has done more than his *News from Nowhere* in attracting people to the cause. To him Socialism was not only a common-sense creed, it was the only way out for the creative artist. He felt most strongly that art and beauty could not live hand in hand with commercialism and profit-seeking, and he turned to Socialism because that alone could free the artist not only from economic serfdom, but also from class-struggle with its lack of opportunity and its withering effect on all artists who may be devoid of the qualities that make for successful fighting against poverty and hunger.

Morris' Socialism and his attitude toward it is perhaps best expressed in his own words. In a series of letters to different friends who questioned him on his attitude, he is completely frank and sincere. To Mr. C. E. Maurice he wrote in 1883 : " For my part I used to think that one might further real Socialistic progress by doing what one could on the lines of ordinary middle-class Radicalism ; I have been driven of late into the conclusion that I was mistaken ; that Radicalism is on the wrong line, so to say, and will never develop into anything more than Radicalism ; in fact that it is made for and by the middle classes and will always be under the control of rich capitalists ; they will have no objection to its *political* development, if they think they can stop it there ; but as to real social changes, they will not allow it if they can help it ; you may see almost any day such phrases as ' this is the proper way to stop the spread of Socialism ' in the Liberal papers, the writer of the phrase never having taken the trouble to find out what Socialism meant, and also choosing to ignore the discontent, dumb indeed for the most part, which is widely spread even in England. Meantime I can see no use in people having political freedom unless they use it as an instrument for leading reasonable and man-like lives ; no good even in education if, when they are educated, people have only slavish work to do, and have to live lives too much beset with sordid anxiety for them to be able to think and feel with the more fortunate people who produce art and poetry and great thought. This release from slavery it is clear cannot come to people so long as they are subjected to the bare subsistence wages which are a necessity of competitive commerce ; and I cannot help thinking that the workmen will be finding that out for themselves ; it is certain that Henry George's book* has been received in this country and in America as a new Gospel ; I believe that Socialism is advancing and will advance more and more as education spreads and, so believing, find my duty clear to do my best to further its advance and in the same time, in what poor way I can, to soften the ruggedness and refine the coarseness which centuries of oppression have hammered into it, so to say." It is interesting that a little later on in

* *Progress and Poverty.*

the same letter Morris should attack the Liberal Party " for allowing itself to stiffen into Whiggery or practical Toryism, as it seems to me to be fast doing." To Mrs. Burne-Jones he wrote in the same year : " Meantime, I am sure it is right, whatever the apparent consequences may be, to stir up the lower classes (damn the word) to demand a higher standard of life for themselves, not merely for themselves or for the sake of the material comfort it will bring, but for the good of the whole world and the regeneration of the conscience of man ; and this stirring up is part of the necessary education which must in good truth go before the reconstruction of society ; but I repeat that without laying before the people this reconstruction, our education will but breed tyrants and cowards, big, little and least, down to the smallest who can screw out money from standing by to see another man working for him. The one thing I want you to be clear about is that I *cannot help* acting in this matter, and associating myself with anybody who has the root of the matter ; and you know, and it may ease your kind heart respecting me, that those who are in the thick of it, and trying to do something, are not likely to feel so much of the hope deferred which hangs about the cause as onlookers do." To Mr. Horsfall he wrote : " I have long felt sure that Commercialism must be attacked at the root before we can be on the road for these improvements in life which you and I so much desire. A society which is founded on the system of *compelling* all well-to-do people to live on making the greatest possible profit out of the labours of others must be wrong. For it means per-petuating the division of society into civilized and uncivilized classes ; I am far from being an anarchist, but even anarchy is better that this which is in fact anarchy and despotism mixed ; if there is no hope of conquering this, let us eat and drink, for to-morrow we die. Of course, I do not discuss these matters with you or any person of good-will in any bitterness of spirit ; but there are people with whom it is hard to keep one's temper ; such as the Philistine middle-class Radicals, who think or pretend to, that now at last all is for the best of all possible worlds." In 1890 Morris wrote in the *Commonweal:* " I say for us *to make Socialists* is *the* business at present, and at present I do not

think we can have any other useful business. Those who
are not really Socialists—who are Trades Unionists, disturbance breeders, or what not—will do what they are
impelled to do, and we cannot help it. At the worst there
will be some good in what they do ; but we need not and
cannot heartily work with them when we know that their
methods are beside the right way. Our business, I repeat,
is the making of Socialists, i.e., convincing people that
Socialism is good for them and is possible. When we have
enough people on that way of thinking, *they* will find out
what action is necessary for putting their principles in
practice. Therefore, I say, make Socialists. We Socialists
can do nothing else that is useful." And, finally, to an
American correspondent he wrote in 1896 : " Society (so
called) at present is organized entirely for the benefit of a
privileged class ; the working class being only considered
in the arrangement as so much machinery. This involves
perpetual and enormous *waste*, and the organization for the
production of genuine utilities is only a secondary consideration. This waste lands the whole of the civilized
world in a position of *artificial poverty*, which again debars
men of all classes from satisfying their rational desires.
Rich men are in slavery to Philistinism, poor men to penury.
We can none of us have what we want, except (partially
only) by making prodigious sacrifices, which very few men
can ever do. Before, therefore, we can so much as hope
for any art, we must be free from this artificial poverty.
When we are thus free, in my opinion, the natural instincts
of man towards beauty and incident will take their due place ;
we shall *want* art, and since we shall be really wealthy we
shall be able to have what we want." Thus we see Morris
had great faith in the inherent ideals of the people, and a
firm belief that education would encourage thought. He
did not foresee, however, the various soporifics that were
to be introduced the moment education became more general
—football matches, horse racing and the cinema.

To the post-war Socialist Morris is still a name to conjure
with, and his approach to Socialism through art and craft
has been one that has been followed by many hundreds
of men and women who have been struck by the ugliness
and brutality of the economic system as seen and felt in

our industrial centres. Although for some years past Morris had been troubled with gout and rheumatism—made worse by his public appearances on open-air platforms in inclement weather—in 1895 it appeared that there was something seriously wrong with his health. A gradual failure of his strength was noticeable and it was finally diagnosed as diabetes. He set out for Norway, hoping that the northern air would do him good, but he was restless and depressed and soon returned to Kelmscott. The following year congestion of the lungs set in and at the age of sixty-two he was a dying man. While he was in bed, music was played to him on the virginals, and his friends paid him daily visits. When someone mentioned the hard life of the poor, he burst into tears. He rapidly grew weaker, and on 3rd October, 1896, he died. He was buried in Kelmscott church-yard during a great rain-storm, a " sort of Viking, set down here," having made " art because there was nothing else to do." A plain grey stone lies over his grave, and it is still the scene of pilgrimages ; for fewer men were greater craftsmen or created more beauty in their lives. Wherever Socialism is preached in this country, Morris is remembered as a man who lived both after and before his time ; one who saw the way to a happier, saner world and did not hesitate to tell others of his vision.

our industrial centres. Although for some years past Morris had been troubled with gout and rheumatism—made worse by his public appearances on open-air platforms in inclement weather—in 1891 it appeared that there was something seriously wrong with his health. A gradual failure of his strength was noticeable and it was finally diagnosed as diabetes. He set out for Norway, hoping that the northern air would do him good, but he was restless and depressed and soon returned to Kelmscott. The following year congestion of the lungs set in and at the age of sixty-two he was a dying man. While he was in bed music was played to him on the virginals, and his friends paid him daily visits. When someone mentioned the hard life of the poor, he burst into tears. He rapidly grew weaker, and on 3rd October, 1896, he died. He was buried in Kelmscott church-yard during a great rain-storm, a "sort of Viking get down here," having made "art because there was nothing else to do." A plain grey stone lies over his grave; and it is still the scene of pilgrimages; for fewer men were greater craftsmen or created more beauty in their lives. Wherever Socialism is preached in this country, Morris is remembered as a man who lived better and before his time; one who saw the way to a happier, saner world and did not hesitate to tell others of his vision.

ROBERT OWEN

1771–1858

by C. E. M. JOAD

ROBERT OWEN

1771–1858

by C. E. M. JOAD

ROBERT OWEN
1771–1858
by C. E. M. JOAD

I

I PROPOSE to preface this study of Robert Owen, philosopher, humanitarian and democrat, with a brief account of his career. Robert Owen was born on May 14th, 1771, in the village of Newtown, Montgomeryshire. He was the sixth of seven children. His father, a saddler and ironmonger, sent him to the village school, whose master, Mr. Thicknesse, installed Owen as assistant usher at the age of seven ! Owen started to read early, and read widely ; he was particularly partial to works on religion. At the age of ten he was apprenticed at Stamford in the retail drapery establishment of a Mr. McGuffog, living for some years with the McGuffog family. Moving thence to London, when thirteen he accepted a situation in an old-established retail house on Old London Bridge, Borough, but finding the hours too long and the work too deadening, he went to Manchester and exchanged retail drapery for cotton spinning. Borrowing a hundred pounds from his brother, he started at eighteen in partnership with a mechanic, Jones, in a business for the making and selling of mules for spinning cotton. The cotton industry was at this time being revolutionised by the invention of Arkwright, and Owen, passing rapidly through the positions of manager of a mill in Stockport and managing director of the Chorlton Twist Company, became in 1798 manager and part-proprietor of a cotton mill at New Lanark. In this year he also married the daughter of the ex-owner of the New Lanark mill, David Dale.

From the first he interested himself in the conditions of the workpeople, his intention being, in his own words, " not to be a mere manager of cotton mills, as such mills were at this time generally managed, but to . . . change the conditions of the people, who were surrounded by circumstances having an injurious influence upon the character of the entire population of New Lanark." Owen built a model

village, instituted schools, drew up a standard set of factory
regulations, and made the New Lanark mills a place of
pilgrimage for reformers and humanitarians from all over
Britain.

Although the mills were a brilliant financial success,
Owen's partners, who were business men first and foremost,
took alarm at his philanthropic schemes, and two separate
partnerships were dissolved as a result of the ensuing
friction. Owen then appealed publicly for money to enable
him to establish a model manufacturing community. The
appeal was successful, Jeremy Bentham and William Allen,
the Quaker philanthropist, being among those who
responded, and Owen was henceforward given a free hand.

In 1813 Owen published his *New View of Society : or
Essays on the Principle of the Formation of the Human
Character*. This announced two main principles. First,
that man is primarily a gregarious being, and is completely
dependent therefore upon the community to which he
belongs for his happiness and welfare ; secondly, that his
character is formed not by him but for him by his education
and social environment. An effort was made to give
practical effect to these principles by the educational methods
adopted in the New Lanark schools.

In 1815 Owen called a meeting of Scottish manufacturers,
at Glasgow, to consider measures designed to improve the
condition of children employed in the cotton mills. At this
meeting he proposed a Factory Act, but failed to obtain
a seconder for his motion. In an intensive propaganda
campaign continued over the ensuing two years, Owen,
by means of pamphlets and addresses to conferences
pressed for a Government measure to regulate the employment of workpeople in factories, and drafted a Bill embody-
ing his proposals. The Bill was introduced into the House
of Commons and in 1818 (on its second introduction)
passed its Second Reading. Meanwhile, Owen's agitation
had induced Sir Robert Peel to secure the appointment in
1816 of a Government Committee to consider the employment of children in factories. Of this Committee Owen
was a member. The House of Lords, to which Owen's
Bill had been referred, appointed a further Committee on
the same subject in 1818. As a result the Bill which had

originated with Owen became law in 1819. It constituted
the first overt recognition by the State of its responsibility
for the conditions under which its citizens were employed.
But it had been so weakened during its passage through the
Houses of Parliament as to have lost most of its value.
For example, the provision of inspectors of factories
upon which Owen had insisted as a safeguard against
abuse of the Bill's regulations was entirely omitted.
Owen now turned his attention to international agitation,
and in 1818 addressed a memorial on the subject
of hours of work to the Congress of the Allied Powers.
The provisions of this memorial may be regarded as
the germ from which the International Labour Office
was subsequently to spring.

Owen had drawn up for the 1816 Committee a report
which he entitled *Plan for the Regeneration of the World,*
which contained a proposal for the formation of model
communities. In 1825 the first community was formed
on the lines of Owen's plan in the village of New Harmony,
Indiana, U.S.A. Organised and financed by Owen, it was
intended to put into practice the full principles of Communism. The members were to be one family; they were to
dress alike, share alike in the possession of the community's
property and govern themselves. No selection was exercised
in regard to potential members, and after two years the
community was driven by internal dissension to split into a
number of daughter communities, which quickly relapsed
into individualist practices. Two further communities, one at
Orbiston, near Glasgow, in 1821, and another at Queenwood,
in Hampshire, in 1839, of which only the latter was actually
founded by Owen, followed much the same course. Orbiston lasted for two years only, Queenwood for five. In
each case financial difficulties and dissension among the
members were the causes of failure. A few members only
were prepared to do their share of the work; many did not
work at all; as a consequence the communities lived hard
and poorly.

The latter part of Owen's life was devoted to a number of
economic and industrial experiments most of which proved
abortive at the time, though they have subsequently been
adopted in some form or other by most advanced industrial

communities. These included the formation of Co-operative
Societies, of joint stock enterprises, the goods produced by
the members being retailed from a common store—at least
a dozen were formed between 1820 and 1830—and of
Labour Exchanges, of which the first was opened in 1832.
These last were communal stores, designed to exclude the
middleman, at which a given number of labour hours entitled
the member to the receipt of a given amount of commodities.
Owen was also instrumental in the foundation of a number
of Trade Unions, of which the most impressive was the
" Grand National Consolidated Trades Union of Great
Britain and Ireland," which in a few weeks' time is said to
have enrolled between half a million and a million members,
with auxiliary branches in all the large industrial towns.
The Union aimed at securing control of the conditions under
which its members worked in all the leading industries and
contemplated the weapon of the strike against recalcitrant
employers. The Owenite Unions did in fact engage in a
number of strikes, which were uniformly unsuccessful; the
Labour Exchanges failed financially; and the Co-operative
Societies only succeeded at the cost of abandoning Owen's
ideals and becoming largely profit-making concerns. In
his later life Owen began to despair of political agitation, and
to rely upon direct action by the workers on Syndicalist
lines. It was presumably for this reason that he refused
to assist the Chartists. As an old man he became interested
in spiritualism and was in fact a professed spiritualist. He
died in 1858.

II

What sort of a man was Owen ? Pre-eminently he was
a self-made man. Self-made and self-educated, he possessed
the virtues and defects of his type. I take the defects first.

Like many self-educated men he was opinionated, dogmatic and self-assertive. He could not carry his knowledge
lightly, and he too often supplied the place of ignorance by
converting his conjectures into dogmas. Chief among his
dogmas was environmental determinism. This was not new,
and, in the form in which Owen maintained it, it was
almost certainly not true. Yet he announces it, as if it

were a divinely vouchsafed revelation which had only to be received to revolutionise the world. Men's characters, he believed, were made for them, not by them. Possibly, though probably not. But whether the doctrine of environmental determinism is true or false, to stigmatise the belief in free will and human responsibility as " this hydra of human calamity, this immolator of every principle of rationality, this monster which has hitherto effectually guarded every avenue that can lead to true benevolence and active kindness " seems, to say the least of it, excessive. Nor, one would have supposed, could there have been at any time much ground for Owen's prophecy that the " hydra," once dragged into the light of day by Owen's writings, would " conscious of its own horrid, loathsome deformity, instantaneously vanish, nevermore to appear."

Owen, in fact, took himself altogether too seriously. His sense of the force and the originality of his ideas led him to regard himself as the repository of absolute truth, and his fellow men as its delighted and grateful recipients. This was pardonable : but he goes further and often writes as if his fellow men were there for no other purpose than delightedly and gratefully to receive. All other systems having violated them, " we," he announces (in the Preface to *The New Moral World*), " undertake to explain the principles of nature," while the " truth " which he believed to lie at the basis of his educational theories, namely, that " the old collectively may teach the young collectively to be ignorant and miserable or to be intelligent and happy " is announced as " that great knowledge " with which it is Owen's privilege to enlighten the world.

Owen was in truth a comparatively ignorant man. He lacked not only a knowledge of philosophy, which would have saved him from the error of assuming that his environmental determinism was in any sense original and introduced him to its more obvious difficulties ; he lacked also the most elementary acquaintance with history. In writing of child labour, for example, he always assumes that it is a new growth, a product of the factory system and the Industrial Revolution, whereas it had been a perfectly normal feature of the textile industry as carried on under the domestic system. It was this lack of historical know-

ledge which, presumably, accounted for the excessive
optimism of his conviction that mankind had only to become
acquainted with his principles to begin immediately to
behave in accordance with them; that the publication of
his views would in fact coincide with their adoption. It was
the same lack which led him to adopt the common eighteenth-
century belief that men were " by nature " perfect, and that
that it was only improper environment and untoward
circumstances which had made them into the sinful, ignorant
creatures with whom Owen had to deal. The inference was
obvious : change the environment, alter the circumstances,
and human nature would go right of itself without rulers,
regulations or restrictions.

It is, I am afraid, impossible to avoid the conclusion
that ignorance and dogmatism combined so to bemuse
Owen as at times to blind him to the most obvious facts.
It is only on this assumption that we can interpret the
statement made in his memorial addressed in 1818 on behalf
of the working classes, " to the Allied Powers assembled
in Congress at Aix-la-Chapelle," on the threshold of
the biggest development of purely individualist enterprise
that the world has ever seen, that society was moving rapidly
to a state of harmony and co-operation, or comprehend the
almost pathetic faith with which he welcomed the break-up
of his community at New Harmony into five separate
villages as inducing " a belief that nothing can now prevent
the spread of the social system over the United States."

Owen remained to the last a confirmed and sonorous
optimist. He founded in 1834 the " Grand National
Consolidated Trades Union of Great Britain and Ireland."
In 1836 the Union was already in difficulties. Owen
proposed to meet the difficulties by changing the name of
the Union to " The British and Foreign Consolidated
Association of Industry, Humanity and Knowledge," and
thereupon proceeded to announce in the last number of
his magazine, *The Crisis*, that " the awful crisis " in human
affairs is now happily terminated. The old world, he
continues, will pass away, " through a great moral revolution
of the human mind, directed solely by truth, by charity and
by kindness."

Owen's language is no less excessive than his expectations.

Like many men who believe that they are the repositories of original truth which it is their duty to convey to their fellows, he must have been something of a bore. Leslie Stephen dubs him " one of those intolerable bores who are the salt of the earth." His writings make, it must be admitted, difficult reading. They are wordy, pompous, and given to exaggeration. Owen, in fact, writes in a perpetual hurricane of excitement. The world is perpetually being regenerated ; the millennium is always about to dawn; the name of the Grand National has only to be changed for the old world to pass away. Now in a hurricane you have to bawl to make yourself heard, and Owen is always talking at the top of his voice. The defect of the method is obvious. If you have to bawl in order to report a change in the name of an Association, you cannot raise your voice when you are announcing the millennium. Thus Owen deprives himself of all power of emphasis by constant over-exaggeration.

If he was something of a bore, he was also a martinet. It was all very well to draw up rules for the conduct of the villagers at New Lanark designed to maintain cleanliness and order ; but what are we to say of a regulation requiring all doors to be closed at 10.30, and forbidding anybody to be out in the street after that time without permission ? Such a regulation comes ill from an apostle of freedom, and the abstention from all alcoholic beverages which Owen at one time exacted from his workpeople, whatever view we may take of it on general grounds, is scarcely compatible with an exaggerated trust in human nature.

The tale of Owen's defects is told : it is time to turn to his virtues. I have already noticed that Owen was a self-educated man. It is only fair to give him credit for the fact, which represents an achievement carried through in the face of immense difficulties. At the age of seven Owen was serving as an assistant usher in a school. At the age of fifteen, when he was spending fourteen hours a day or more serving customers in a retail establishment in the Borough, he still found time for his books. At the age of twenty-five, when he was manager of a large mill, he was reading papers to the Manchester Literary and Philosophical Society, and discoursing on " religion, morals, and other similar subjects " with Coleridge. In short,

Owen was what we should now call an intellectual. He
cared, it is obvious, for the things of the mind, and insisted
on having them, whatever the difficulties which were placed
in his way.

Like most intellectuals, he was a humanitarian. He was
one of the first men in England to concern himself with the
welfare of the workers who were the source of his profits.
As a comparatively young man, he notices, in his *Autobiography*, the great attention given to the dead machinery
and the neglect and disregard of the living machinery.
This sense of contrast never left him. In 1813, in an
address which he drew up in connection with his campaign
for the regulation of factory conditions, he pleads with the
superintendents of factories, "Will you not afford some of
your attention to consider whether a portion of your time
and capital would not be more advantageously applied to
improve your living machines?" He sends copies of his
speech to Members of Parliament, goes to London, interviews them, addresses meetings up and down the country.
When we remember for what he was contending—that no
child should be employed in a factory or mill under the
age of ten, that no person under the age of eighteen should
be employed for more than twelve and a half hours a day, of
which only ten were to be given to work, half an hour to
instruction, two hours to rest and meals; and when we
remember that the ten-hour day did not become law until
1847, the prohibition of work by children under ten years
old until 1874, we can imagine the aspect of shocking, of
almost subversive novelty, that Owen's views must have
worn to the manufacturers and M.P.'s of his time, and
gauge the extent of the opposition which he must have had
to face.

Owen had the foresight—it was characteristic of him and
in no sense merely a bribe to placate hostile criticism—to
reinforce the humanitarian plea with a business argument.
He was, it is clear, a man of first-class business ability.
Here is a young man who comes to Stockport at the age of
eighteen with £100 in his pocket, completely ignorant of the
cotton industry, and proceeds with a single mechanic
partner to start on his own. Within a year he is installed as
manager of a mill and is in charge of 500 workpeople. Within

four years he is managing director of a company. Within nine he is manager and part-proprietor of the New Lanark Mills, and has taken marriage with the former proprietor's daughter in his stride. The mills under his management are a financial success to the tune of an annual distribution of £60,000 in dividends, in addition to the five per cent. paid on the capital. Owen's management becomes, indeed, so celebrated for its efficiency as well as for its novelty, that people come to see the mills from all over the country.

As a consequence, when Owen tells his fellow-manufacturers that shorter hours mean more efficient workmen and therefore better work, it might have been expected that they would have listened with attention and received with respect the opinion of a man who might be presumed to know what he was talking about. The complete incredulity with which Owen's contemporaries received a principle which has now become an industrial commonplace, affords gratifying evidence of our own comparative enlightenment.*

The same incredulity greeted Owen's educational proposals. In no department were Owen's views more enlightened than in that of education. Holding as he did that the human organism is in all respects the creature of its environment, he believed that you could shape men's minds and characters as you pleased by the environmental mould in which you cast them. The instruction of the young is, therefore, the foundation of his community system, his communities, like Plato's ideal State, being formed to embody his assumption that "the government of any community may form the individuals of that community into the best, or into the worst, characters."

III

Whatever view we may take of Owen's rather crude determinism, the educational moral which he drew from it was entirely salutary. When Owen went to New Lanark,

* Our gratification needs, however, to be qualified by the remembrance that precisely similar beliefs are entertained by mill-owners in India, and conditions not very different from those against which Owen inveighed obtain in their mills to-day.

he found working in the mills 500 children between the
ages of four and eight, labouring for thirteen (sometimes
more) hours a day, of which one and a half were set aside
for meals. The children received instruction from seven
to nine in the evening, but it is not surprising to learn that
they were too tired to do their lessons. One of Owen's
earliest acts was to discontinue the employment of children
under ten and to reduce the hours of work for those over
that age to twelve. The opposition of his partners alone
prevented more drastic reforms. In the schools which he
erected at New Lanark, the result of these changes was an
immediate improvement in the attendance of the children,
which rose in three months, in 1816, from 100 nightly to 396.

The attendance of children sufficiently awake to profit
by it having been secured, they received instruction according to Owen's peculiar principles. Since human beings
were in no sense responsible for their actions, prizes and
punishments were alike condemned as irrelevant. In Owen's
school there were neither. A child who did wrong was
thought to deserve pity for unfortunate instincts rather than
blame for moral turpitude. The pleasure of learning was
held up as the best incentive to industry, the joys of friendship as the best reward for kindness. Owen anticipated
the modern view that although punishment might produce
reform for the time, it effected no real transformation of
character. So long as it remained efficacious, the effect of
punishment was to add hypocrisy to obliquity ; so soon as
it was removed, the culprit relapsed.

In his methods of teaching Owen was also in advance
of his times. To make subjects interesting and attractive
was, he held, the best way to ensure that they would be
studied. We find him insisting, accordingly, that teaching
should be conveyed by means of visible, concrete objects,
that pictures, maps, and natural objects should, where
possible, take the place of books, and conversation between
teachers and pupils of instruction by teachers of pupils.
Special emphasis was laid upon the teaching of natural
science, history and geography. The children were asked
questions on what they had read, discouraged from learning by
rote and repeating from memory, and required to find their
own illustrations for the general principles they received,

the object being to train them in the habit of thinking for themselves. The maxim, train the child how to think rather than tell him what to think, and having trained him leave him to himself, would appear to summarise Owen's educational policy.

The reader of Robert Owen's discourses on the subject of education, of the accounts given by his son, Robert Dale Owen, of the New Lanark schools, or of the encomiums of the distinguished visitors who were continually visiting them, experiences inevitably a certain feeling of familiarity. He has, he feels, read all this before. As he searches his memory for its source, there comes to his mind the voluminous literature published by the sponsors of the advanced schools which have sprung up in England since the war. The statements of aim and intention are, allowing for the inevitable differences of terminology, almost identical. There is the same apparent pleasure on the part of the children in their lessons, the same difficulties to be experienced and overcome by the teachers, the same delighted reactions on the part of the visitors. When we remember the conceptions prevalent in Owen's time, that children were limbs of Satan, fit only for wrath and the rod, that education was a process of filling their heads with salutary but unpalatable facts, that it was natural and on the whole desirable that most of them should get no education at all, and that those who did were lucky to have acquired, in tears and travail, the arts of reading, writing and ciphering, it is difficult to withhold a tribute of surprised admiration from the man who, not content with being a pioneer in industry, a pioneer philanthropist in the treatment of his workpeople, a pioneer founder of model communities, Trades Unions, Labour Exchanges and Co-operative Societies, also contrived to anticipate many of the ideas of the most enlightened educationalists of our own time.

Owen, in fact, saw far and saw fast in many directions. " The grand question now to be solved is not how a sufficiency of wealth may be produced, but how the excess of riches which may be most easily created may be generally distributed throughout Society advantageously for all, and without prematurely disturbing the existing institutions or arrangements in any country." The words might be those of any economist dilating in the fourth decade of the twentieth century on the paradox of want in the midst of plenty. Man has not the wit, he would say, to learn to distribute what science has enabled him so embarrassingly to produce, and, he would be apt to continue—assuming him, that is, a member of the under-consumption school— one way out of the *impasse* is to give the working classes increased consuming power by raising their wages. Yet the quotation is not from the works of a twentieth century economist, but from the memorial on behalf of the working classes which Robert Owen addressed, in 1818, " to the Allied Powers assembled in Congress at Aix-la-Chapelle." Owen, in fact, was one of the first to grasp the enormous potential increase in production which the intensive use of machinery would entail. In this respect he was a good hundred years in advance of his time. It is no doubt true that, so far as the immediate future was concerned, he grossly exaggerated the increase of productivity which would accrue from the use of the machines then available ; so much so, that he looked to " wealth made abundant beyond the wants or the wishes of the human race " as a condition shortly to be realised for the universal spread of Communism. It was in the conviction that when money and goods are as plentiful as air and water, " any desire for individual accumulation or inequality of condition will consequently cease," that he founded his Communist communities, New Harmony and Queenwood, and he never seems to have been able quite to overcome his surprise at the failure both of the goods produced by the communal labour of the members to suffice for any but the most Spartan existence, and of the potential Communists to " outgrow the habits of the individual system." The Queenwood Socialists, work- ing from all accounts to the full extent of their power, fed on cauliflowers, turnips, potatoes and home-made bread. It is not perhaps surprising in the circumstances to learn that after a time the majority made the best of a bad job for themselves without reference to their neighbours, exploited the common property for personal profit, and shirking all the work which they could shoulder on to their more public- spirited fellows, played for their own hands and stomachs. Nevertheless, in spite of the exaggeration into which his

ebullient enthusiasm led him, Owen must take credit for
being one of the first to see that the introduction of machinery
had substituted the problem of distribution for that of
production as the chief concern of a modern community.
He was also one of the first, perhaps the very first, to realise
that it necessitated the regulation of industry by the State.
It was not enough, he saw, for the individual mill-owner
to improve conditions, raise wages, and shorten hours, to
become, in short, a model employer himself and then trust
the other employers to follow his model example. Let an
employer have the best will in the world to be " model,"
the pressure of competition was too great to permit him
to carry his intentions into effect. Under *laissez-faire*
conditions he would be driven to drive his work-people to the
last ounce of their energy, irrespective of their welfare and
his conscience, if he was to maintain his position against his
competitors. Therefore, the State must step in, not only
to protect workers against employers, but to protect employers against one another, and by prescribing minimum
rates, hours and conditions, and insisting on the maintenance
of what was prescribed, prevent the workers from being
sacrificed in the race for profits and the many decent employers from being blackmailed into squeezing their workpeople by the few who had no scruple about squeezing
their own. Owen, in fact, saw, and was one of the first
to see, why no State that wishes to keep its work-people
from revolution can afford a system of unrestricted *laissez-
faire* in industry.

IV

Owen seems to have been a sociable, gregarious sort of
man who liked and was liked by his fellows. I have
imputed to him above something of the character of a
martinet, citing his closing-hour regulations in New Lanark
village. Yet when he returned to New Lanark as one of
the proprietors of the mill, we are told that the workpeople were so pleased to see him that they took his horses
out of the traces and, harnessing themselves to his carriage,
drew him home ; while we hear of the children at the
New Lanark school taking Owen by the hand, plucking at

his coat, and insisting on his attending to them with a complete absence of awe or fear. He had, moreover, a flaming hatred of cruelty and oppression. When doctors were brought to testify to the House of Lords Committee, which sat in 1818, that it did not harm a child to work at night, to stand for twelve hours a day, or to eat its meals while standing, Owen's torrent of contemptuous protest seems to have been well worth hearing.

He not only liked his fellow-men, he trusted and believed in them. It was this trust and this belief that primarily entitle him to a place among the Great Democrats who are celebrated in the present volume. For the democrat is above all a man who is prepared to take the risk of rating average human nature high. If he did not, he would not be willing to invest it with the responsibility of the government of itself and of the community. Owen's trust in his fellow men was, indeed, so high that he believed that any chance collection of them could, if they were given a fair start and then left to themselves, found a Communist Utopia. This belief is a delusion. It is not the case that a civilised, still less a Communist State, can be made out of any sort of material, and the material attracted to Owen's communities fell so far short of even the average of human nature, that Robert Dale Owen is constrained to describe the potential Communists as " a heterogeneous collection of Radicals, enthusiastic devotees to principle, honest latitudinarians, and lazy theorists, with a sprinkling of unprincipled sharpers thrown in." Of many it seems to have been true that their only passport for the Utopia of Communism was their failure to succeed in the scramble of individualism ; the only ground for their conviction that they were good enough for the world as it might be, the obvious fact that they were not good enough for the world as it is. Owen, confronted with the unsuitability of his colonists, invoked his belief that " the government of any community may form the individuals of that community into the best, or into the worst characters " to back his assurance that even a ramshackle collection of visionaries and " down and outs " could, given suitable conditions, be transformed into the citizens of an ideal community.

Owen was so far right in that nothing can be more easily changed and moulded than human nature, provided that the material to be changed is taken in hand early enough. Agricultural labourers, aircraft mechanics, University dons, and film stars are so different one from another that they cannot endure one another's society for more than a few hours without gross discomfort ; it is even beginning to be doubtful whether they are intermarriageable. Yet these differences are artificial growths, the products of education, training, environment and habit.

But Owen was almost certainly wrong in thinking that such artificial growths can be produced in a night, and that a community of ideal, artificial growths can be formed out of already finished products. The fact is that, as the Russians have discovered, if you want to turn average individuals into Communists, you must catch them young and cultivate them intensively from birth onwards ; apart altogether from the fact that every normal human society contains, in addition to its mass of ordinary individuals, not only its percentage of saints, but its percentage of incorrigible scoundrels, who will wreck any community unless they are forcibly restrained or painlessly exterminated.

But the conclusion that Owen's optimism in regard to the potentialities of *adult* human nature for ideal self-government appears to have been excessive affords no excuse for lapsing into the pessimism of our contemporaries, who seem to think that of all things the most intolerable to the common man is liberty, liberty to form his own judgments and to decide his own actions, of all things the most necessary leadership, leadership to tell him what to think and how to behave. Owen belonged to the true tradition of nineteenth century democrats in respect of his conviction that human beings were in the last resort and in spite of all the evidence to the contrary rational creatures. Show them the truth and, he held, they will see it. And so they will, not perhaps quite as quickly as Owen supposed, but, nevertheless, sooner or later, provided that the truth is presented to them sufficiently often, sufficiently clearly and with a sufficient weight of arguments in its favour. Give them, he held further, adequate instruction and information, and they will prove capable of forming an enlightened and

R*

reasoned judgment on public affairs, and of giving effect
to their judgment through their chosen representatives.
Give them the opportunity of self-government, and they
will become through its exercise fit to govern themselves.

These beliefs lay at the bottom of Owen's multi-
tudinous schemes for workers' organizations. Owen was
a veritable fount of schemes for associations of workpeople for mutual profit and protection. There is, indeed,
scarcely any development of the British working-class
movement of which the germ cannot be traced in his
writings. And Owen's beliefs did not stop short with his
writings, they found expression in action. Thus his
persistent formation of Trades Unions, Co-operative
Societies and Labour Exchanges, proceeds from this same
fundamental faith in the ability of workpeople to run and
to manage their own affairs. He was the " father of English
Socialism " primarily because he was a believer in the
common people, not as they were, but as they might
become. For, give people, he held finally, reasonable and
equal environmental conditions, and they will grow into
reasonable persons, capable of living decent lives. As he
himself puts it, " the equality which belongs to the new,
true, and rational system of human existence is an equality
of conditions or of surroundings which shall give to each,
according to natural organisation, an equal physical, intellectual, moral, spiritual, and practical treatment, training,
education, position, employment according to age, and
share in local and general government, when governing
rationally shall be understood and applied to practice."

Such were Owen's fundamental beliefs. They led him
often into strange paths and the steps by which he sought
to embody them in concrete fact—communities of cranks
and ne'er do wells, Co-operative Trading Associations that
dispensed with money, Syndicalist Trade Unions that
dispensed with rules—may in retrospect seem wild and ill-
advised. But Owen was essentially a pioneer, and it is
unreasonable to expect of his experiments the balance and
solidity of established institutions.

Owen was one of a small group of humanitarians who,
in the fierce early stages of the Industrial Revolution,
nsisted that men should be treated as ends and not merely

as means. In a world mad for profits he claimed the attention of mankind for the human instruments that made the profits. Owen was a man who could see and could feel far better than he could think. If his ideas were often wild, his instincts were always sound. Where his views are the intellectual expression of his instincts, they are both wise and original. His conception of education, his views on the treatment of criminals, his concern with the welfare of work-people in factories, his conviction of the need for collective control to check the licence of *laissez-faire*—all these which seemed subversive and impracticable at the time are now accepted as the commonplaces of an enlightened society. Owen, like the other pioneers of his time, was a visionary and a dreamer. Inspired by a real hatred of the iniquities of the social system as he found it, he derived from this emotional source an unflagging energy in reform. It was the force of his sincerity which enabled him to appeal so strongly to the imaginations of men, suffusing his creed with an almost religious glow. What distinguished him from his contemporaries was his persistent determination to try out his ideas in practice. He not only conceived enlightened views as to the treatment of human beings working in factories ; he became a factory manager and put them into practice. He not only propounded theories as to the effects of environment on character and the importance of equality of opportunity and conditions, he founded communities where a chosen environment was free to form the characters desired, and opportunities and conditions were equal for all. If Owen was a dreamer, he was not content to dream his life ; he possessed the faith which enabled him to live his dreams.

THOMAS PAINE

1739-1809

by BERTRAND RUSSELL

THOMAS PAINE
1739-1809
by BERTRAND RUSSELL

THOMAS PAINE, though prominent in two Revolutions and almost hanged for attempting to raise a third, is grown, in our day, somewhat dim. To our great-grandfathers, he seemed a kind of earthly Satan, a subversive infidel rebellious alike against his God and his King. He incurred the bitter hostility of three men not generally united : Pitt, Robespierre, and Washington. Of these the first two sought his death, while the third carefully abstained from measures designed to save his life. Pitt and Washington hated him because he was a democrat ; Robespierre, because he opposed the execution of the King and the Reign of Terror. It was his fate to be always honoured by Oppositions and hated by Governments : Washington, while he was still fighting the English, spoke of Paine in terms of the highest praise ; the French nation heaped honours upon him until the Jacobins rose to power ; even in England, the most prominent Whig statesmen befriended him and employed him in drawing up manifestos. He had faults, like other men ; but it was for his virtues that he was hated and successfully calumniated.

Paine's importance in history consists in the fact that he made the preaching of democracy democratic. There were, in the eighteenth century, democrats among French and English aristocrats, among *philosophes* and Nonconformist ministers. But all of them presented their political speculations in a form designed to appeal only to the educated. Paine, while his doctrine contained nothing novel, was an innovator in the manner of his writing, which was simple, direct, unlearned, and such as every intelligent working man could appreciate. This made him dangerous ; and when he added religious unorthodoxy to his other crimes, the defenders of privilege seized the opportunity to load him with obloquy.

The first thirty-six years of his life gave no evidence of the talents which appeared in his later activities. He was born at Thetford, in 1739, of poor Quaker parents, and was educated at the local grammar school up to the age of thirteen, when he became a stay-maker. A quiet life, however, was not his taste, and at the age of seventeen he tried to enlist on a privateer called *The Terrible*, whose Captain's name was Death. His parents fetched him back, and so probably saved his life, as 175 out of the crew of 200 were shortly afterwards killed in action. A little later, however, on the outbreak of the Seven Years' War, he succeeded in sailing on another privateer, but nothing is known of his brief adventures at sea. In 1758, he was employed as a stay-maker in London, and in the following year he married, but his wife died after a few months. In 1763 he became an exciseman, but was dismissed two years later for professing to have made inspections while he was in fact studying at home. In great poverty, he became a schoolmaster at ten shillings a week, and tried to take Anglican orders. From such desperate expedients he was saved by being reinstated as an exciseman at Lewes, where he married a Quakeress from whom, for reasons unknown, he formally separated in 1774. In this year he again lost his employment, apparently because he organized a petition of the excisemen for higher pay. By selling all that he had, he was just able to pay his debts and leave some provision for his wife, but he himself was again reduced to destitution.

In London, where he was trying to present the excisemen's petition to Parliament, he made the acquaintance of Benjamin Franklin, who thought well of him. The result was that, in October 1774, he sailed for America, armed with a letter of recommendation from Franklin describing him as an " ingenious, worthy young man." As soon as he arrived in Philadelphia, he began to show skill as a writer, and almost immediately became editor of a journal.

His first publication, in March 1775, was a forcible article against slavery and the slave trade, to which, whatever some of his American friends might say, he remained always an uncompromising enemy. It seems to have been largely owing to his influence that Jefferson inserted in the draft of the Declaration of Independence the passage on this subject which was afterwards cut out. In 1775, slavery still existed in Pennsylvania ; it was abolished in that State by an Act of 1780, of which, it was generally believed, Paine wrote the preamble.

Paine was one of the first, if not the very first, to advocate complete freedom for the United States. In October, 1775, when even those who subsequently signed the Declaration of Independence were still hoping for some accommodation with the British Government, he wrote :

" I hesitate not for a moment to believe that the Almighty will finally separate America from Britain. Call it Independency or what you will, if it is the cause of God and humanity it will go on. And when the Almighty shall have blest us, and made us a people *dependent only upon him*, then may our first gratitude be shown by an act of continental legislation, which shall put a stop to the importation of Negroes for sale, soften the hard fate of those already here, and in time procure their freedom."

It was for the sake of freedom—freedom from monarchy, aristocracy, slavery, and every species of tyranny—that Paine took up the cause of America.

During the most difficult years of the War of Independence he spent his days campaigning and his evenings composing rousing manifestos published under the signature " Common Sense." These had enormous success, and helped materially in winning the war. After the British had burnt the towns of Falmouth in Maine and Norfolk in Virginia, Washington wrote to a friend (January 31st, 1776) :

" A few more of such flaming arguments as were exhibited at Falmouth and Norfolk, added to the sound doctrine and unanswerable reasoning contained in the pamphlet *Common Sense*, will not leave numbers at a loss to decide upon the propriety of separation."

The work was topical, and has now only a historical interest, but there are phrases in it that are still telling. After pointing out that the quarrel is not only with the King, but also with Parliament, he says : " There is no body of men more jealous of their privileges than the Commons : Because they sell them." At that date it was impossible to deny the justice of this taunt.

There is vigorous argument in favour of a Republic, and a triumphant refutation of the theory that monarchy prevents civil war. " Monarchy and succession," he says,

after a summary of English history, " have laid . . . the
world in blood and ashes. 'Tis a form of government
which the word of God bears testimony against, and blood
will attend it." In December, 1776, at a moment when the
fortunes of war were adverse, Paine published a pamphlet
called *The Crisis*, beginning :

" These are the times that try men's souls. The summer
soldier and the sunshine patriot will, in this crisis, shrink
from the service of their country ; but he that stands it *now*
deserves the love and thanks of man and woman."

This essay was read to the troops, and Washington
expressed to Paine a " living sense of the importance of
your works ". No other writer was so widely read in
America, and he could have made large sums by his pen,
but he always refused to accept any money at all for what
he wrote. At the end of the War of Independence, he was
universally respected in the United States, but still poor ;
however, one State legislature voted him a sum of money
and another gave him an estate, so that he had every prospect
of comfort for the rest of this life. He might have been
expected to settle down into the respectability characteristic of revolutionaries who have succeeded. He turned
his attention from politics to engineering, and demonstrated
the possibility of iron bridges with longer spans than had
previously been thought feasible. Iron bridges led him to
England, where he was received in a friendly manner by
Burke, the Duke of Portland, and other Whig notables.
He had a large model of his iron bridge set up at Paddington ;
he was praised by eminent engineers, and seemed likely to
spend his remaining years as an inventor.

However, France as well as England was interested in
iron bridges. In 1788 he paid a visit to Paris to discuss them
with Lafayette, and to submit his plans to the Académie des
Sciences, which, after due delay, reported favourably.
When the Bastille fell, Lafayette decided to present the key
of the prison to Washington, and entrusted to Paine the task
of conveying it across the Atlantic. Paine, however, was
kept in Europe by the affairs of his bridge. He wrote a
long letter to Washington informing him that he would find
some one to take his place in transporting " this early trophy

of the spoils of despotism, and the first ripe fruits of American principles transplanted into Europe." He goes on to say that " I have not the least doubt of the final and compleat success of the French Revolution," and that " I have manufactured a Bridge (a single arch) of one hundred and ten feet span, and five feet high from the cord of the arch."

For a time, the bridge and the Revolution remained thus evenly balanced in his interests, but gradually the Revolution conquered. In the hope of rousing a responsive movement in England, he wrote his *Rights of Man*, on which his fame as a democrat chiefly rests.

This work, which was considered madly subversive during the anti-Jacobin reaction, will astonish a modern reader by its mildness and common sense. It is, primarily, an answer to Burke, and deals at considerable length with contemporary events in France. The first part was published in 1791, the second in February, 1792 ; there was, therefore, as yet no need to apologise for the Revolution. There is very little declamation about Natural Rights, but a great deal of sound sense about the British Government. Burke had contended that the Revolution of 1688 bound the British for ever to submit to the sovereigns appointed by the Act of Settlement. Paine contends that it is impossible to bind posterity, and that constitutions must be capable of revision from time to time.

Governments, he says, " may all be comprehended under three heads. First, Superstition. Secondly, Power. Thirdly, The common interest of society and the common rights of man. The first was a government of priestcraft, the second of conquerors, the third of reason." The two former amalgamated : " the key of St. Peter and the key of the Treasury became quartered on one another, and the wondering, cheated multitude worshipped the invention." Such general observations, however, are rare. The bulk of the work consists, first, of French history from 1789 to the end of 1791, and secondly, of a comparison of the British Constitution with that decreed in France in 1791, of course to the advantage of the latter. It must be remembered that in 1791 France was still a monarchy. Paine was a republican and did not conceal the fact, but did not much emphasise it in *The Rights of Man*.

Paine's appeal, except in a few short passages, was to
common sense. He argued against Pitt's finance, as
Cobbett did later, on grounds which ought to have appealed
to any Chancellor of the Exchequer; he described the
combination of a small sinking fund with vast borrowings as
setting a man with a wooden leg to catch a hare—the longer
they run, the further apart they are. He speaks of the
"Potter's field of paper money"—a phrase quite in
Cobbett's style. It was, in fact, his writings on finance that
turned Cobbett's former enmity into admiration. His
objection to the hereditary principle, which horrified Burke
and Pitt, is now common ground among all politicians,
including even Mussolini and Hitler. Nor is his style in
any way outrageous: it is clear, vigorous, and downright,
but not nearly as abusive as that of his opponents.

Nevertheless, Pitt decided to inaugurate his reign of terror
by prosecuting Paine and suppressing *The Rights of Man*.
According to his niece, Lady Hester Stanhope, he "used to
say that Tom Paine was quite in the right, but then, he
would add, what am I to do? As things are, if I were to
encourage Tom Paine's opinions we should have a bloody
revolution." Paine replied to the prosecution by defiance
and inflammatory speeches. But the September massacres
were occurring, and English Tories were reacting by
increased fierceness. The poet Blake—who had more
worldly wisdom than Paine—persuaded him that if he
stayed in England he would be hanged. He fled to France,
missing the officers, who had come to arrest him, by a few
hours in London and by twenty minutes in Dover, where
he was allowed by the authorities to pass because he
happened to have with him a recent friendly letter from
Washington.

Although England and France were not yet at war, Dover
and Calais belonged to different worlds. Paine, who had
been elected an honorary French citizen, had been returned
to the Convention by three different constituencies, of
which Calais, which now welcomed him, was one. "As the
packet sails in a salute is fired from the battery; cheers
sound along the shore. As the representative for Calais
steps on French soil soldiers make his avenue, the officers
embrace him, the national cockade is presented"—and so

on, through the usual French series of beautiful ladies, mayors, etc.

Arrived in Paris, he behaved with more public spirit than prudence. He hoped—in spite of the massacres—for an orderly and moderate Revolution such as he had helped to make in America. He made friends with the Girondins, refused to think ill of Lafayette (now in disgrace), and continued, as an American, to express gratitude to Louis XVI for his share in liberating the United States. By opposing the King's execution down to the last moment, he incurred the hostility of the Jacobins. He was first expelled from the Convention, and then imprisoned as a foreigner; he remained in prison throughout Robespierre's period of power and for some months longer. The responsibility rested only partly with the French; the American Minister, Gouverneur Morris, was equally to blame. He was a Federalist, and sided with England against France; he had, moreover, an ancient personal grudge against Paine for exposing a friend's corrupt deal during the War of Independence. He took the line that Paine was not an American, and that he could therefore do nothing for him. Washington, who was secretly negotiating Jay's treaty with England, was not sorry to have Paine in a situation in which he could not enlighten the French Government as to reactionary opinion in America. Paine escaped the guillotine by accident, but nearly died of illness. At last Morris was replaced by Monroe (of the " Doctrine "), who immediately procured his release, took him into his own house, and restored him to health by eighteen months' care and kindness.

Paine did not know how great a part Morris had played in his misfortunes, but he never forgave Washington, after whose death, hearing that a statue was to be made of the great man, he addressed the following lines to the sculptor :

> Take from the mine the coldest, hardest stone,
> It needs no fashion : it is Washington.
> But if you chisel, let the stroke be rude,
> And on his heart engrave—Ingratitude.

This remained unpublished, but a long, bitter letter to Washington was published in 1796, ending :

" And as to you, Sir, treacherous in private friendship (for so you have been to me, and that in the day of danger) and a hypocrite in public life, the world will be puzzled to decide whether you are an apostate or an impostor ; whether you have abandoned good principles, or whether you ever had any."

To those who know only the statuesque Washington of the legend, these may seem wild words.   But 1796 was the year of the first contest for the Presidency, between Jefferson and Adams, in which Washington's whole weight was thrown into support of the latter, in spite of his belief in monarchy and aristocracy ; moreover Washington was taking sides with England against France, and doing all in his power to prevent the spread of those republican and democratic principles to which he owed his own elevation.   These public grounds, combined with a very grave personal grievance, show that Paine's words were not without justification.

It might have been more difficult for Washington to leave Paine languishing in prison if that rash man had not spent his last days of liberty in giving literary expression to the theological opinions which he and Jefferson shared with Washington and Adams, who, however, were careful to avoid all public avowals of unorthodoxy.   Foreseeing his imprisonment, Paine set to work to write *The Age of Reason*, of which he finished Part I six hours before his arrest.   This book shocked his contemporaries, even many of those who agreed with his politics.   Now-a-days, apart from a few passages in bad taste, there is very little that most clergymen would disagree with.   In the first chapter he says :

" I believe in one God, and no more ; and I hope for happiness beyond this life.

" I believe in the equality of man, and I believe that religious duties consist in doing justice, loving mercy, and endeavouring to make our fellow-creatures happy."

These were not empty words.   From the moment of his first participation in public affairs—his protest against slavery in 1775—down to the day of his death, he was consistently opposed to every form of cruelty, whether practised by his own party or by his opponents.   The Government of England at that time was a ruthless oligarchy, using Parliament as a means of lowering the standard of life in the poorest classes ; Paine advocated political reform as the only cure for this abomination, and had to fly for his life. In France, for opposing unnecessary bloodshed, he was thrown into prison and narrowly escaped death. In America, for opposing slavery and upholding the principles of the Declaration of Independence, he was abandoned by the Government at the moment when he most needed its support. If, as he maintained and as many now believe, true religion consists in " doing justice, loving mercy, and endeavouring to make our fellow-creatures happy ," there was not one among his opponents who had as good a claim to be considered a religious man.

The greater part of *The Age of Reason* consists of criticism of the old Testament from a moral point of view. Very few now-a-days would regard the massacres of men, women, and children recorded in the Pentateuch and the Book of Joshua as models of righteousness, but in Paine's day it was considered impious to criticize the Israelites when the Old Testament approved of them. Many pious divines wrote answers to him. The most liberal of those was the Bishop of Llandaff, who went so far as to admit that parts of the Pentateuch were not writtten by Moses, and some of the Psalms were not composed by David. For such concessions he incurred the hostility of George III and lost all chance of translation to a richer see. Some of the Bishop's replies to Paine are curious. For example, *The Age of Reason* ventured to doubt whether God really commanded that all males and married women among the Midianites should be slaughtered, while the maidens should be preserved. The Bishop indignantly retorted that the maidens were not preserved for immoral purposes, as Paine had wickedly suggested, but as slaves, to which there could be no ethical objection. The orthodox of our day have forgotten what orthodoxy was like a hundred and forty years ago. They have forgotten still more completely that it was men like Paine who, in face of persecution, caused the softening of dogma by which our age profits. Even the Quakers refused Paine's request for burial in their cemetery, although a Quaker farmer was one of the very few who followed his body to the grave.

After *The Age of Reason* Paine's work ceased to be important. For a long time he was very ill; when he recovered, he found no scope in the France of the Directoire and the First Consul. Napoleon did not ill-treat him, but naturally had no use for him, except as a possible agent of democratic rebellion in England. He became home-sick for America, remembering his former success and popularity in that country, and wishing to help the Jeffersonians against the Federalists. But the fear of capture by the English, who would have certainly hanged him, kept him in France until the Treaty of Amiens. At length, in October 1802, he landed at Baltimore, and at once wrote to Jefferson (now President) :

" I arrived here on Saturday from Havre, after a passage of sixty days. I have several cases of models, wheels, etc., and as soon as I can get them from the vessel and put them on board the packet for Georgetown I shall set off to pay my respects to you.   Your much obliged fellow-citizen,

THOMAS PAINE."

He had no doubt that all his old friends, except such as were Federalists, would welcome him. But there was a difficulty : Jefferson had had a hard fight for the Presidency, and in the campaign the most effective weapon against him —unscrupulously used by ministers of all denominations— had been the accusation of infidelity. His opponents magnified his intimacy with Paine, and spoke of the pair as " the two Toms." Twenty years later, Jefferson was still so much impressed by the bigotry of his compatriots that he replied to a Unitarian minister who wished to publish a letter of his : " No, my dear Sir, not for the world ! . . . I should as soon undertake to bring the crazy skulls of Bedlam to sound understanding as to inculcate reason into that of an Athanasian . . . keep me therefore from the fire and faggot of Calvin and his victim Servetus." It was not surprising that, when the fate of Servetus threatened them, Jefferson and his political followers should have fought shy of too close an association with Paine. He was treated politely, and had no cause to complain, but the old easy friendships were dead.

In other circles he fared worse. Dr. Rush of Philadelphia,

one of his first American friends, would have nothing to do with him : " his principles " he wrote, " avowed in his *Age of Reason*, were so offensive to me that I did not wish to renew my intercourse with him." In his own neighbourhood he was mobbed, and refused a seat in the stage coach ; in the last year of his life he was not allowed to vote, on the alleged ground of his being a foreigner. He was falsely accused of immorality and intemperance, and his last years were spent in solitude and poverty. He died in 1809. As he was dying, two clergymen invaded his room and tried to convert him, but he merely said " Let me alone ; good morning ! " Nevertheless, the orthodox invented a myth of deathbed recantation which was widely believed.

His posthumous fame was greater in England than in America. To publish his works was, of course, illegal, but it was done repeatedly, although many men went to prison for this offence. The last prosecution on this charge was that of Richard Carlile and his wife in 1819 : he was sentenced to prison for three years and a fine of £1,500, she to one year and £500. It was in this year that Cobbett brought Paine's bones to England, and established his fame as one of the heroes in the fight for democracy in England. Cobbett did not, however, give his bones a permanent resting place. " The monument contemplated by Cobbett," says Moncure Conway,* " was never raised. There was much parliamentary and municipal excitement. A Bolton town-crier was imprisoned nine weeks for proclaiming the arrival. In 1836 the bones passed with Cobbett's effects into the hands of a receiver (West). The Lord Chancellor refusing to regard them as an asset, they were kept by an old day-labourer until 1844, when they passed to B. Tilley, 13 Bedford Square, London, a furniture dealer . . . In 1854, Rev. R. Ainslie (Unitarian) told E. Truelove that he owned ' the skull and the right hand of Thomas Paine,' but evaded subsequent inquiries." No trace now remains, even of the skull and right hand.

Paine's influence in the world was twofold. During the American Revolution he inspired enthusiasm and confidence, and thereby did much to facilitate victory.

*Whose biography of Paine and edition of his works are a monument of patient devotion and careful research.

In France his popularity was transient and superficial, but in England he inaugurated the stubborn resistance of plebeian Radicals to the long tyranny of Pitt and Liverpool. His opinions on the Bible, though they shocked his contemporaries more than his unitarianism, were such as might now be held by an Archbishop, but his true followers were the men who worked in the movement that sprang from him—those whom Pitt imprisoned, those who suffered under the Six Acts, the Owenites, Chartists, Trade Unionists, and Socialists. To all these champions of the oppressed he set an example of courage, humanity, and single-mindedness. When public issues were involved he forgot personal prudence. The world decided, as it usually does in such cases, to punish him for his lack of self-seeking; to this day his fame is less than it would have been if his character had been less generous. Some worldly wisdom is required even to secure praise for the lack of it.

JOSEPH PRIESTLEY
1733–1804
by ANNE HOLT

JOSEPH PRIESTLEY
1733–1804
by ANNE HOLT

WHEN Joseph Priestley was born on the 13th of March, 1733, nearly forty-five years had passed since the Revolution of 1688 had put an end to arbitrary government, but to the Dissenters among whom he grew up the Revolution settlement did not appear, as it did to the great Whig families, to be the fulfilment of political wisdom but to be a starting-point in a struggle for better things. The amount of liberty which the Dissenters enjoyed was small in law, if greater in practice. The Test and Corporation Acts excluded all save Anglicans from service to the State. The Universities were the preserves of the Established Church. The so-called Toleration Act of 1689 required Nonconformist ministers to subscribe to thirty-six of the thirty-nine articles, while Unitarians and Roman Catholics were expressly excluded from its provisions. Meanwhile among the Nonconformists a new spirit was at work. In 1719 a synod of London Dissenting ministers, meeting at the Salters' Hall, by a majority refused to subscribe to any confession of faith, thus leaving the door open to progressive thought. This refusal to bind others, contemporaries or successors, to any dogma formed the most distinctive character of eighteenth century English Presbyterianism, and opened the way for its transition to modern Unitarianism.

Priestley's own family was Calvinistic but its mode of thought did not interfere with its charity of living. As a small child he was adopted by a well-to-do aunt whose house at Heckmondwyke in the West Riding was open to all ministers of a godly life irrespective of their beliefs. He was sent to school, probably to the Grammar School at Batley, and his education was supplemented by the teaching of various neighbouring ministers, one of whom at least taught him that the last word on ultimate reality had not been spoken by John Calvin. It was natural that a precocious child coming from such a home should be dedicated to the ministry, but difficulties occurred when the time came for him to enter an academy, as his opinions were already moving away from orthodoxy. He felt he could not enter that at Mile End where he would be required to sign assent to Calvinistic articles of faith. Fortunately the minister at home had little respect for the scholarship of orthodox Dissenters and so it was agreed that he should go to the Academy at Daventry.

It was the Age of Reason and the advanced Dissenters at least had come to see that controversy and argument, rather than fire and sword and prison, were the weapons with which they should fight. What their policy was outside, was also that within the Academy; and Priestley's description of life at Daventry makes it resemble a continuous debating society. On every subject of importance the staff of two and the students were evenly divided, and Priestley soon found that in every case he took the heterodox point of view.

On leaving the Academy in 1755 Priestley was called to the Independent Chapel at Needham Market where he stayed for three rather unhappy years. His congregation, which was orthodox, quite rightly suspected his views on the Trinity, for before leaving Daventry he had come to take up the Arian* position. Moreover, as he stammered, he had one serious drawback to success in the pulpit. From Needham Market he went in 1758 to Nantwich in Cheshire where he found a liberal congregation and where he was able to add to his income and interests by keeping school. So successfully did he do this that when, in 1761, a vacancy occurred on the staff of the Warrington Academy, he was called on to fill it. In the following year he married Mary, daughter of Isaac Wilkinson of Wrexham, a self-made ironmaster. It proved a completely happy marriage, and four children were born to them. He lectured and taught literature, history and politics. At the instigation of Benjamin Franklin and Richard Price he was already engaged on scientific work, and, in 1766, he was elected to the Royal Society. A year earlier his *Chart of Biography* had won him the degree of LL.D. from Edinburgh

---

* An Arian is one who, though admitting the pre-existence of Christ, denies his consubstantiality. A Socinian denies the deity of Christ.

University.   During all this time he continued his career
as a minister, preaching in the neighbouring chapels, and
being formally ordained.

In 1767 he left Warrington to become the minister of
the Mill Hill Chapel at Leeds, his reason for going being
the inadequacy of his stipend at the Academy to meet the
needs of a growing family.

Once more he took up the study of theology and became
a Socinian, or, as we should say, an Unitarian.   He founded
and edited a theological magazine.   In science he made
most of his important discoveries in gases, though it was
not until later that he discovered oxygen.   He also made
one of the important friendships of his life, that with
Theophilus Lindsey, the Catterick parson, who, at this
time, along with other clergymen of the Church of England,
was seeking relief from Parliament from the necessity of
assenting to the Thirty-nine Articles, a relief which was not
granted, and consequently led to Lindsey's leaving the
Church and founding the first avowedly Unitarian Church
in London.   Priestley had also begun his attacks on the
Church of England which were to win him its lasting ill-will.
His writings were quoted in the House of Lords, and, when
it was suggested that he should accompany Captain Cook
as naturalist on his second voyage, the appointment was
turned down by some clergymen on the Board of Longitude,
who objected to his theological opinions.

It was shortly after this disappointment that in 1773
Priestley became librarian and literary companion to the
Earl of Shelburne, later the first Marquis of Lansdowne.
The idea of a man of genius being the dependent of an
aristocratic patron had not yet become distasteful.
Priestley's relationship with Shelburne was much more
that of two friends and less that of master and servant
than that which existed a hundred years before between
John Locke and the great Earl of Shaftesbury ; for, it is said,
Locke walked by the side of his master's coach and stood
bareheaded while the great man got in and out.   There
were many inducements to Priestley to accept the position.
Shelburne was prepared to pay him £250 a year as against
the hundred guineas he had received at Mill Hill and to
promise him a pension of £100 when the arrangement

should end. During the seven years Priestley spent with Shelburne his time was divided between London and Calne, and it was at Calne that in 1774 he discovered oxygen. That same year he accompanied Shelburne on a tour of the Continent. They travelled through the Low Countries and came to Paris where Louis XVI had just become King, and where Turgot was installed as Controller-General and a last great effort was being made to avert catastrophe. Here Priestley met Lavoisier, the French chemist, who perished so miserably in the Revolution, and various economists of the Physiocrat school, but he did not care for France, and was shocked by the scepticism of the learned.

Priestley already had many friends in London, and now through his connection with Shelburne he must have met most of the interesting persons of the time. But the years were overshadowed by the American War. To him, as to most other Dissenters, the colonists were kinsmen and not aliens, and the struggle that was being fought out beyond the Atlantic seemed to be the same struggle against despotic government which had been fought at home in the preceding century. Priestley had been an intimate friend of Benjamin Franklin's at the time when he was the agent for Massachusetts, and both were members of the Club of Honest Whigs, as Franklin called it, which met at the London Coffee House. When Franklin's efforts to avoid bloodshed fell through, and he was determined to return home, he spent the last day reading the American papers with Priestley, and directing him as to what should be inserted in the English press. In politics Priestley was a follower of the Rockingham Whigs and Shelburne of the Earl of Chatham. Both parties deplored the War but while the former was prepared from an early date to grant independence, the latter believed that the loss of the colonies would be a blow from which the mother-country would never recover. It may have been this divergence in politics, or it may have been Shelburne's re-marriage which caused a break in the relations of the two men. In 1780 Priestley left Calne and moved to Birmingham, where shortly afterwards he became minister of the New Meeting.

At this time Birmingham was a scientific centre.
Boulton and Watt were turning out their steam engines.
Nearby, at Lichfield, Erasmus Darwin was embarked on
speculations which forecast those of his grandson Charles.
Priestley's erratic brother-in-law, John Wilkinson, was
sailing iron barges down the Severn. Josiah Wedgwood,
the great potter, had been intimate with Priestley ever
since the Nantwich days, and he now set about collecting
subscriptions which should defray the cost of his friend's
scientific experiments. But though Priestley continued
these experiments all his life, he discovered little more
that added to his fame. During the time he had lived
with Shelburne he had by no means neglected his theological speculations. His semi-philosophical works on
Matter and Spirit and *Philosophical Necessity* had further
heightened his unpopularity with the orthodox. These
works were followed in 1782 by his History of the *Corruptions
of Christianity*. His plan was to deal by the historical
method with the various corruptions which had invaded
the Christian Church and for this purpose he attempted
to trace the various doctrines to their sources. The principal
doctrine which he thus attacked was that of the Trinity.
It is not surprising that this challenge was taken up. The
next few years were filled with a bitter controversy between
him and Samuel Horsley, the Archdeacon of St. Albans.
The latter contented himself with pointing out the mistakes,
not a few, which Priestley had made, and thus the argument
was not conclusive. " Dr. Priestley," Horsley said, "forgets
that the main argument with him and with me goes to
different points. His point is the antiquity and truth of
the Unitarian doctrine. Mine is Dr. Priestley's incompetency in the subject." Horsley was rewarded for his
services with a bishopric, but Priestley, though he may shock
the modern historian by his preconceived theories, was,
by his appeal to history, pointing the way that the Higher
Criticism was to follow. At the same time that he was
attacking orthodoxy Priestley was also waging a battle against
the scepticism of Gibbon and Hume.

His speculations might have led to little excitement
had it not been for the outbreak of the French Revolution.
It was not the Dissenters alone who hailed it with

s

enthusiasm, for, to all liberal and humane minded men, it seemed a promise of better things to come when the lion should lie down with the lamb and the millennium be realized. For within a few short months, the French, with whom liberty had been almost non-existent, secured freedom in a degree far beyond that enjoyed by Englishmen. But to the Dissenters whose activities were curtailed by the Test and Corporation Acts there was something particularly touching in beholding the persecuted Huguenots obtain full civic rights as well as toleration. On the 5th of November, 1789, the Revolution Society met as usual to commemorate the landing of William III. Dr. Richard Price delivered the sermon on the text " Pray for the peace of Jerusalem. They shall prosper that love thee." In his final peroration Price thanked Heaven that he had lived to see thirty millions of people spurning slavery. It was this sermon which drew from Edmund Burke his *Reflections on the French Revolution*, and among the many who answered Burke was Priestley. Thus his opinions on the Revolution were well-known, and it was partly because of his radical sympathies and partly because of his attacks on the Church of England, that in July, 1791, he became the chief victim of the anger of the Birmingham mob and of the incompetency and criminal negligence of the magistrates. Priestley himself escaped to London, but his house with its library and valuable laboratory was destroyed. The Tory Government of the day refused to hold an inquiry into the conduct of the magistrates. George III expressed himself glad that Priestley had been made to suffer. The mob had done its work of destruction to the shout of " Church and King," and neither Church nor King seemed in the least ashamed of the association. The best criticism of this cry was made by Samuel Parr, a Whig and an Anglican clergyman. Being pressed to drink to it as a toast, he consented only if he might make his own comment. " Church and King," he said, " once it was the toast of Jacobites ; now it is the toast of incendiaries. It means a church without a gospel—and a king above the laws."

The three years which intervened between the riots and Priestley's emigration to America were spent in London.

Along with Bentham, Wilberforce, Romilly and others, he had had the honour of French citizenship conferred upon him, and in 1792 he was offered, but declined, a seat in the French National Assembly.

There were many reasons to lead him to leave England. Both his own and his wife's nerves had been badly shaken by the riots. The Government had started on its persecution of reformers and Priestley believed that he might be an intended victim. It was difficult for his sons to find work. In 1794 he sailed for the United States and eventually settled at Northumberland in Pennsylvania, a small town about 130 miles from Philadelphia. Here he built a house and continued his scientific and theological work. He spent two winters in Philadelphia where he founded the first Unitarian Church, which still flourishes. But his troubles were not yet over. His youngest and favourite son Henry died in 1795, and his wife the next year. Political disillusionment was added to personal sorrow. Like so many others Priestley had seen in the United States a promised land. In spite of the help which France had given the colonists in their struggle against England, in spite of the inspiration which the American Revolution had given the French, by 1798 animosity ran high between the two countries. It was not unnatural that the American Government should suspect the motives of those exiled from England on account of the Revolution, but it might also have remembered the exiles' earlier sympathies with the colonies in revolt. President Adams' Government talked of deporting Priestley under the Alien Act, and he had to consider the advisability of emigration to France. Fortunately, in 1801 Jefferson succeeded Adams. He was already a friend and correspondent, and now Priestley could say that for the first time in his life he was living under a Government truly favourable to him. But these halcyon days were not to last long. For some time he had been ailing, and on the 6th of February, 1804, he died.

Priestley was a typical product of the eighteenth century. Though others shared his interests in a diversity of subjects few reached his excellence in so many. His work in science, education, history and politics was carried on in the spare time he had left over from his daily work as a minister,

and though he loved all his other activities, he never thought
of them except as second to that of his calling. He was a
colossal worker in the days when working hours were
beyond what can now be realized. He could be a bitter
opponent but he never considered that difference of opinion
should interfere with friendship, and, even at the bitterest
time of the Unitarian controversy, he was on terms of
friendship with Anglicans and Roman Catholics as well
as with Quakers and orthodox Nonconformists. As a
young man he declared that all good citizens should learn
" to think with freedom, to speak and write with boldness,
to suffer in a good cause with patience, to begin to act
with caution, but to proceed with vigour." No one ever
fulfilled this more than he. At the time of the Birmingham
riots an onlooker noted that " not one hasty or impatient
expression, not one look expressive of murmur or complaint,
not one tear or sigh escaped him." His faults both as a man
and a worker were those which seem to go with his virtues.
He was impetuous. He was inaccurate. In rushing from
one kind of work to another, in never being idle, he did
not give himself the quiet time in which thought matures.
Thus, in science, he never saw the implications of his
discoveries, nor realized that it was his discovery of oxygen
that was upsetting the old theory of phlogiston. In later life
he was said to be fidgetty and difficult in small matters.
After the riots he was apt to see offence where probably
none was meant, but others have suffered from suspicions
of persecution with far less excuse.

   Priestley's political thought was, in many ways, the
outcome of his theological opinions. Behind all his reasoning
lay the belief in an omnipotent and wholly good God, the
First Cause of all our being, who was determining humanity
towards some glorious end. Matter and Spirit were not
two different and unrelated substances but were different
aspects of one. He believed in a future life in which a new
world should redress the balance of the old—a future life
which should involve the resurrection of the body. Pain
and evil are difficult problems to explain under any
philosophical system, and it cannot be said that Priestley
was particularly successful, but at least his doctrine of
philosophical necessity avoided the worst pitfalls of Calvinistic

predestination because, though he believed in future rewards and punishments, he did not believe in Hell.

When a tutor at Warrington he had been a pioneer in teaching the students such hitherto untaught subjects as Modern History, Political Science and Economics. He wished to see young men educated for life, " for it is certainly our wisdom to contrive that the studies of youth should tend to fit them for the business of manhood," and he thought that by introducing the living present into their studies much interest would be added. History, he held, should be the basis of politics, for the science of government could only be thus built soundly on a foundation of facts. In economics Priestley was far from a profound thinker, as he could use such opposite authorities as Sir James Steuart's *Principles of Political Economy* and Adam Smith's *Wealth of Nations*, but he did have the temerity to carry Smith's reasoning a step further and to see for himself the uselessness of the usury laws.

Neither the part on politics in his *Lectures on History and General Policy* nor his *Essay on Government* appear on the face of them to be momentous with change. Many years before Locke had written that government should be " directed to no other end but the peace, safety, and public good of the people." This idea runs through the whole Whig doctrine of trusteeship. Priestley re-stated it in his *Lectures* and again in his *Essay* when he declared that " the good and happiness of the members, that is, the majority of the members of any state, is the great standard by which every thing relating to that state must finally be determined." It was from this sentence of Priestley's that Jeremy Bentham took the idea of the Greatest Happiness of the Greatest Number, a rather humdrum slogan which has been instrumental in improving the condition of the people to an extent undreamt of by either author. But Priestley did not suggest, as Bentham did, that the people should be the judges of their own happiness, an idea involving in practice manhood suffrage. He considered that the franchise should at least be restricted to the literate.

Until the outbreak of the French Revolution Priestley's political efforts were rather confined to fighting the battles of the Dissenters than to general abuses. He was not a social reformer, and, like most of his contemporaries, he was more anxious to abolish bad laws than to make good ones. Perhaps it is of interest to note that the one occasion when he found himself in sympathy with other Birmingham ministers and clergy was when they were all united in preaching anti-slavery sermons. The liberty which he claimed for himself he was prepared to extend to others, and he pleaded for toleration of Catholics as well as of Dissenters. He saw no need to confine 'our neighbour' within the limits which satisfied us. " The wider we make the common circle of liberty, the more of its friends will it receive, and the stronger will be the common interest." The French Revolution evoked larger issues. Priestley's reply to Burke rapidly went through three editions. At the time of the American Revolution these two had been friends, and Priestley could not understand how Burke, who had befriended the American, should attack the French. He did not think Burke in a fit state of mind to enter into controversy. " Your imagination is evidently heated," he wrote, " and your ideas confused. The objects before you do not appear in their proper shapes and colours." As Sully and Burke himself had said, Priestley declared that " a whole people is not apt to revolt, till oppression has become extreme and been long continued, so that they despair of any other remedy than that desperate one." He held that people must retain the right of resisting an oppressive government, " that is, such as the people shall deem to be oppressive," and he believed that the execution of Charles I was justified. " The *thirtieth of January* was," he wrote, " (to use a phrase of Admiral Keppel's) a *proud day* for England, as well as the *fourteenth of July* for France ; and it will be remembered as such by the latest posterity of *freemen*. Let all tyrants read the history of both, and tremble. Good Princes will read it without any unpleasant emotion." He thought that the progress of democracy would lead to a better period in the world's history and that the extension of true principles would lead to the " extinction of all *national prejudice* and enmity, and the establishment of *universal peace* and goodwill among all nations " for, he goes on, " the empire of reason will ever be the reign of peace."

Priestley's service to democracy may thus be said to have been of an indirect nature. He did not organize the people. He did not harangue them from the hustings. His pamphlets on current politics were few. But he had a great faith in the common man and believed that he would be more easily led by the kindly light of reason than kings and the privileged few seeking only their own advantage.

He wished to liberate the people from bad and unequal laws, from unjust customs and from ignorance and the fears of superstition. No one who has ever read his letters written in exile can doubt of his love for his country, but love of country did not necessitate love of its rulers. If we admit that the patriot is one who serves his country rather than one who hates others, that a saint is one who through a lifetime works for his fellow-men and is not merely a stained-glass image, and that a sage is one who brings knowledge within the reach of all and not merely some scholar immured within library walls, then Coleridge's description of Priestley as " Patriot and Saint and Sage " must also be the verdict of posterity.

JEAN-JACQUES ROUSSEAU
1712-1778
by W. D. RUDLIN

JEAN-JACQUES ROUSSEAU
1712-1778
by W. D. RUDLIN

FEW of the men whom the world has called great have
exerted an influence as wide and profound as that of
Jean-Jacques Rousseau. Politics, religion, æsthetics,
literature, education—on all these remain the marks of his
impact; to all of them he gave new ideas and new tendencies
of which the significance for his own and subsequent ages
can hardly be exaggerated.

In religion, he was responsible for a great revival which
has not yet spent its force. To the teachings of the official
Church he opposed a religion of inner conscience, and to an
age which had lost itself in rational abstraction he recalled
the certainties of non-rational conviction.

In an artificial society where conduct had decayed into
cynicism and corruption he re-established the value of
sentiment and the simpler virtues. He restored the
forgotten sanctity of marriage, the delights of domestic life
and the ultimate satisfactions of a harmonious existence,
and demonstrated the possibility of their attainment in a life
lived according to the natural rules of conscience.

He changed the educational practice of his period,
bringing to bear on it what has been called a "magistral
commingling" of Plato, Locke and Condillac, and laying,
with the materials they had provided, the foundation of a
modern educational theory.

To his influence upon the theory and practice of politics
it is difficult to set a limit. Even those who, like Burke and
de Maistre, were most opposed to his doctrine, bear witness,
in the romantic quality of their thought, to the influence of
the movement which he inspired. Such men of the
Revolution as Marat and Robespierre were profoundly
affected by his teaching. And, since that time, men have
not ceased to use his name as a party cry. Some have seen
in him the prophet of extreme individualism, others have
hailed him as the high-priest of an all-embracing collectivism.
In their subordination of the individual to society the

teachings of Hegel and his disciples reflect the collective
aspect of Rousseau's thought. In its other aspect his work
has been urged as justification whenever men have sought
to substitute the authority of individual experience for that
of tradition.

Nor were they mistaken in seeing in Rousseau the
individualist *par excellence*. For, as his *Confessions* show,
what was fundamental in him was his insistence upon the
validity of his own experience and the final authority of his
own conscience. The essence of his doctrine was an
affirmation of his reactions to the world, of the emotions
aroused in him by contact with nature and human society.
That is why any study of that doctrine must be set in the
background of his personal history.

Jean-Jacques Rousseau was born in Geneva in 1712, of
French and Savoyard stock. His mother, a woman of
considerable talents, died in giving him birth, and for ten
years Jean-Jacques was brought up by his father—a watch-
maker by profession. Of outstanding importance in that
early upbringing was the elder Rousseau's habit of reading
with his six-year-old son the stock of romances left by his dead
wife. Perhaps no other influence did more to shape the
character of the later Rousseau than those evening sessions
which often lasted till " my father, hearing the swallows
begin to twitter in the early morning, would say, quite
ashamed,' Let us go to bed ; I am more of a child than
yourself.' "

Rousseau has told us in the *Confessions* what effect this
practice had upon him. "In a short time I acquired, by
this dangerous method, not only extreme facility in reading
and understanding what I read, but a knowledge of the
passions that was unique in a child of my age. I had no
idea of things in themselves, although all the feelings of
actual life were already known to me. I had conceived
nothing but felt everything. These confused emotions
which I felt one after the other, certainly did not warp the
reasoning powers which I did not as yet possess ; but they
shaped them in me of a peculiar stamp, and gave me odd and
romantic notions of human life, of which experience and
reflection have never been able wholly to cure me."

The legacy of romances being exhausted, father and son

turned to more substantial fare. While the elder worked at his trade, the younger read aloud Bossuet, Plutarch, Ovid, Fontenelle and Molière, who, he says, cured him a little of his taste for romance, and " formed in me the free and republican spirit, the proud and indomitable character unable to endure slavery or servitude, which has tormented me throughout my life in situations the least fitted to afford it scope."

This early education was brought to a close by the enforced departure of his father from Geneva, after a quarrel with an army captain, ". . . a cowardly and insolent fellow (whose nose happened to bleed during the affray) . . ." There followed for Rousseau five years of more normal childhood, first at the house of a Protestant minister at Bossey and later with his uncle Bernard at Geneva. At the end of that time he was apprenticed to a Town Clerk, a business which attracted him so little that he was dismissed as incapable. In his next post, as apprentice to an engraver, he was treated with great brutality and, having returned from a walk late one evening to find the city gates shut, he decided to avoid punishment by running away. So, at the age of sixteen, he embarked upon a period of restless wandering during which he was converted to Catholicism, became twice a lackey, studied for the priesthood, and taught music incompetently at Lausanne and Neufchâtel.

Throughout the record of this aimless wandering, there runs the thread of his intimate association with Madame de Warens, the woman who was to him both mother and mistress. Between 1728 and 1740 he spent much of his time at her country house, Les Charmettes, where, by providing him with books and leisure, she enabled him to increase his small store of learning. The days spent at Les Charmettes were the happiest of his life, and he never ceased to regret the conclusion of an association which gave him the greatest emotional and intellectual satisfactions he was ever to experience.

There came a day, however, when he returned to Les Charmettes to find his place filled by one whom he described as " vain, foolish, ignorant and insolent, he was in other respects the best fellow in the world." His attempts to restore the old harmony of life with " mamma " failed and in 1742 he set out for Paris in an effort to persuade the Academy of Sciences to adopt a new system of musical notation which he had invented. Failing in that venture he became secretary to the French Ambassador at Venice, where he acquired a passionate love of Italian music and formed those habits of political speculation which were later to culminate in the publication of the *Social Contract*.

Dismissal from the Embassy in 1745 sent him back to Paris where he made the acquaintance of such men as Diderot, d'Alembert and Condillac, visiting, in their company, the *salons* of the fashionably intellectual, but never knowing " how to find the thing he ought to say, nor the expression he ought to use."

Until 1749 then, his life had been, for the most part, a purposeless wandering from place to place and a profitless exchange of one occupation for another. He had reached the age of thirty-seven having achieved little besides the satisfactions of his association with Madame de Warens. Knowing himself to be endowed with natural talents and a capacity for happiness, wishing to lead a virtuous life, he had little to remember beyond the experience of talents ignored, happiness denied and virtue perverted. And knowing himself to be a failure he knew also where to lay the blame. He knew that the fault was with civilised society which had degraded him as it degraded all men who came beneath its corrupting influence.

His opportunity came in 1749 when he saw the offer, by the Academy of Dijon, of a prize for an essay on the subject, " Has the Progress of Sciences and Arts Contributed to Corrupt or Purify Morals ? " Fervently, he devoted himself to the task of showing that man is by nature good, that his departure from innocence and the degeneration of his moral qualities are the result of civilisation with its misplaced worship of intellectual progress.

The essay won the prize and Diderot undertook to get it printed. On its publication, the latter wrote to Rousseau ; " It has gone up like a rocket, such a success has never been seen before." The acclamation with which it was received gave him a real assurance of his abilities, which, in spite of his inner feelings, he had always previously doubted.

In 1755 appeared his *Discourse on the Origin and Foundation of Inequality Among Men.* In this work he preserved the basic opposition of the first *Discourse* between the natural state of men and the state of society and argued that a return to an intermediate stage between the natural and social states and abandonment of inequality would secure for men both the simplicities of nature and the advantages of society. This second *Discourse* shows Rousseau already feeling his way towards the philosophy of his greatest political work, the *Social Contract,* wherein he sought to state the ultimate principles of political right upon which civil society should be founded.

In 1755 appeared also his article *Sur l'Économie Politique,* in the *Encyclopédie* of the Philosophes—the great ones of that Age of Reason, who at first welcomed Rousseau as one of themselves, but who later came to regard him, more correctly, as hostile to that insistence upon the value of reason which was the centre of their teaching. In the following year he was able, to his intense joy, to leave Paris and go to the country, where for six years he remained. These were the years of his greatest productive effort; they were also the years of his greatest persecution. Against his pleasure on finding himself once more in natural surroundings and his delight in the company of the Madame d'Houdetot, who inspired the *Julie* of his *Nouvelle Héloise,* must be put the active envy and persistent criticism of what he called the Holbachian clique, chief among whom were his former friends Grimm and Diderot. In 1761 appeared the *Nouvelle Héloise* and with it the height of his popularity. In the following year he published the *Émile* and the *Social Contract.* The *Émile* outraged the Church, which accused its author of heresy, and the Parlement, which ordered his arrest. The Sorbonne denounced it, and, for Rousseau the bitterest blow of all, the Government of Geneva had it publicly burned.

Coming at the end of that long period of bad treatment at the capable hands of the Holbachian clique, these fresh attacks drove him once more upon his wanderings. After vainly seeking asylum in Switzerland he found protection under Frederick the Great at Motiers, where he wrote the *Letters from the Mountain.* These caused a fresh outcry and forced him eventually to accept Hume's invitation to stay

in England. Returning to France he wandered from
place to place, eventually being allowed to return to Paris
on condition that he wrote nothing against religion or
the Government. In May, 1778, he went to a cottage at
Ermenonville and died there a month later.

Those last years saw the intensification of the two afflic-
tions, one physical and one mental, which had done so much,
all through his life, to determine his outlook upon the world.
From the age of thirty he had been the victim of a painful
disease which became more acute as he grew older. And
with failing health there came increasing mental suffering.
His last years were darkened by the tortures of that habit
of introspection which was the root of his genius. It was
his great gift to be able to question and dissect his own
emotions, to report upon the state of his soul and to set
out with no trace of evasion or reticence the record of his
conflicts with society and with himself. This ability, while
it was the secret of his success in a world which had lived
too much with the precept *toujours méfiez vous l'enthousiasme*,
was also inevitably fatal to his peace of mind. It poisoned
many of his social contacts and much of his self-communion.

An understanding of that lack of harmony with himself
and with society is fundamental to an appreciation of
Rousseau's philosophy. When he first arrived in Paris
he was inarticulate, embarrassed and unhappy ; he was
also ambitious, sensitive and proud. With the sense of
failure, therefore, came bitterness with his fellows and
disgust with himself. And not even the knowledge of
success could make it easy for one who put the imperative
demands of sentiment and conscience before the claims of
reason to be at peace with the formal, rationalistic atmosphere of Parisian society. And it must, moreover, be
remembered that if he was by nature a romantic he was by
birth a citizen of Geneva. Whatever the weaknesses of
character which he has described for us, he always retained
that firmly embedded streak of simple puritanism, that
heritage from the city of Calvin, which was always distressed and often moved to judgment by the complexity
and materialism of the world of Holbach and Voltaire.

Nothing, indeed, could have been further removed from
the intellectual temper of the Age of Reason than those

bursts of intuitive revelation which were, for Rousseau, the approach to truth, nor the sweeping affirmations in which they were proclaimed. The method of the time was that of ordered, logical analysis and systematic statement. But with Rousseau truth was personal, coming from the heart rather than the head as an assertion of himself. The essence of that personal affirmation was the conviction that man was made for happiness, goodness and freedom. But in contrast to that natural ordinance he found that his own experience and the common experience of humanity was of a life of unfreedom, misery and evil. What had been ordained by nature was denied by civilisation, the life intended for man corrupted by social institutions. That is the doctrine of the First Discourse. The Second Discourse goes further. The evils of society and civilisation spring from the inequality upon which they are based. That inequality destroys the natural goodness in man, allots misery to the many and pleasure to the few and makes of society an ever-increasing disharmony.

The basic theme of Rousseau's teaching is, therefore, the abolition of inequality. It cannot be achieved by a return to primitive conditions of life, man has already gone too far. What is possible is for man to take advantage of his present powers in order to rectify his early mistakes and to return to an intermediate stage between the natural and social state. In such a condition man might preserve the simplicities and delights of nature while securing the advantages of early society. But in order to do so he must readmit the natural impulses and realise that society and civilisation can confer blessings only if they do not deny those impulses. With the Second Discourse, then, we are already in possession of Rousseau's central idea and on the threshold of his greatest constructive work, the *Émile*, the *Nouvelle Héloise* and the *Social Contract*, in which he sought to rebuild social institutions and, thereby, to increase man's moral stature.

In the *Émile* he set out a system of education which would allow the natural and therefore good impulses to develop within the child before they are stifled by contact with society. By nature, man is solitary, a creature of instincts, learning by the experience of his desires. The child, therefore, must have no contact with society, nature rather than reason must direct its instincts, books are to be withheld until a natural character has been formed which will not succumb to the dangers of civilisation contained in the printed word. So, also, with religion. A knowledge of God is permitted to the child because natural man is familiar with the idea. Ritual and dogma, however, are corrupt social devices and must be withheld. In short, everything which might interfere with the free operation of nature is to be excluded in order that when the child eventually enters society it may, by strength of natural character, be armed against the moral perils of civilised society.

So to be armed is to be like the Julie of the *Nouvelle Héloise* who found in a return to natural impulse the moral solution of the problems of personal relationships. Rousseau's heroine surrounded by the cynicism and corruption of fashionable life is able, by withdrawing from society and entering upon a "natural" relationship, to avoid the moral dangers of an adultery which that society would permit. By entrusting herself to the natural dictates of conscience she is able to re-establish the institution of the family and through it to experience happiness and genuine feeling instead of the falsity and hypocrisy of civilised life. Long before his critics Rousseau was aware that such a solution was but a partial one. The great mass of men cannot escape into that well-provided isolation in which Julie was able to devote herself exclusively to the discovery of conscience. Nor can they enter the world equipped, like Émile, with a character again built up in seclusion. Rousseau knew that what he had written was a description of what ought to be : even of what in fact might be, given favourable circumstances. It remained, therefore, for his third great work, the *Social Contract*, to state the social solution of the same problem of human happiness and freedom to which the *Émile* and the *Nouvelle Héloise* were the individual approach. It remained to state those principles of political right upon which society must be founded if the good life is to be realised ; to make possible a civil society wherein the benefits of natural virtue might be obtained without the disadvantages of social evil.

This can be achieved only by the abolition of inequality and its consequent oppression of the common people. In order to achieve the state of virtue man must emancipate himself from his passions and selfish interests and identify his particular will with the will of society. That is possible only if the will of society is such that the individual man can harmonise himself with it without sacrificing his moral freedom. The will of society must, that is, be a General Will, the sum of the wills of all the members of society in a state of virtue—a state to be achieved by a common sacrifice of right and a common will to government prescribed to and submitted to by all in equal degree. When that has been achieved every man will be free since the weight of authority will be self-imposed and voluntarily borne in equal measure. Such a solution of political problems must depend, however, upon the strict maintenance of religion. The power of religion must be present to provide a sanction for the observance of the new principles. For those principles are rooted in the sacrifice by which man gives up his individual rights in order to participate in the common will and the common sovereignty. And only upon conditions of the closest association with the idea of God is that self-sacrifice possible.

Rousseau's whole system, therefore, begins and ends with an appeal to individual morality. His concern is always with the individual and his freedom—the freedom which comes from self-liberation. The community is brought forward as the instrument which is to make possible that liberation, but it is never the end of Rousseau's thinking. Essentially he is concerned with the problem of individual freedom, in terms of a civil society so organised as to maximise the possibility of its attainment.

The State, for Rousseau, has, it is true, a certain priority, in practice, over the individual. But such priority can only derive its justification to the extent to which the State does in fact promote the moral and political freedom of the individual. This emphasis on the individual he carries over from his philosophy to his system of political institutions. The duty and right of the citizen to play his part in the determination of the General Will of the State means the continual exercise of individual judgment, and in terms

of institutions its implication is that the actual working of the
General Will is only realisable in the small city State, where
all citizens can have a direct voice in legislation. His
insistence was not upon the exaltation of the State at the
expense of the individual, but upon the realisation of a
democratic State based, not upon force or even upon consent,
but upon an active will for universal law and an active
participation of all citizens in the ordering of the State.
In the unfettered will of the people Rousseau saw the only
possibility of social justice. His essentially democratic
faith in the people as the legislative power springs from the
belief that the people as a whole, given equality and the
sanction of religion, will live according to the universal law
as revealed by conscience.

There is no place in this system for traditional or
hereditary rights, no function for the monarch, aristocrat
or priest. It is the creation of a plebeian bred in the city
State of Geneva ; one who had faith, not in governing
classes but in his own people. On their behalf he forced
on his generation claims to recognition and power which
seemed to men like Burke and de Maistre a declaration
of war against society. For such men the sovereignty of
the people was an impossibility ; the reliance upon spontaneous morality a direct incitement to anarchy. But for
Rousseau, natural law is " graven on the heart of man in
characters that cannot be effaced, and it is there it speaks to
him more strongly than all the precepts of the philosophers."
The natural goodness of man was the fundamental theme
of all his teaching ; the point of departure and the final goal
of his thought in education, politics, religion and ethics.
It was the concept by which he gave an infant Romanticism
its letters of credit, and enabled it in his own and subsequent
generations to exert its profound and many-sided influence.
With Molière, La Fontaine and Saint Évremond there had
already developed a Romanticism which, denying the
validity of criteria imposed from without, saw in deep
feeling the criterion of truth and human conduct. But
with Rousseau's addition of the dogma of the natural goodness of man that movement took on a new force. It became
harder to deny the dictates of the heart after Rousseau had
demonstrated with passion that the heart is the seat of

virtue ; the supremacy of rationalism was shaken after Rousseau had transformed a half-conscious feeling of the inadequacy of reason into an ardent faith in the morality of sentiment. Thus to exalt the dictates of the heart is to make of equality the essential social dogma. For if the final judgment upon a man's conduct is to be made by his own conscience, no other man may be his master. Law must be justified not by its origin nor by its content, but by its success in satisfying the demands made upon it by the individual. Social institutions must be judged by their success in making equal rights available to all. Authority must take its title from its ability to identify its ideals with those of the people as a whole.

Natural virtue demands equality and equality demands the sovereignty of the people. In this aspect, therefore, Romanticism becomes an insistence upon democracy, begetting a movement which furnished the western world of the nineteenth century with its experience of the major political freedoms. That, certainly, is not its only aspect. There is in Rousseau an undeniable emphasis upon political obedience and social unity, an emphasis which became, in the hands of Hegel, the theoretical justification of an extreme conservatism. That was, however, a later development of his theories and one for which he would have denied all responsibility. The inheritance of the essential Rousseau belongs less to Hegel than to Babeuf and Fourier, to Shelley and Godwin, to Karl Marx and all those of the revolutionary tradition who have heard his passionate plea for equality.

JOHN RUSKIN
1819–1900
by J. HOWARD WHITEHOUSE

JOHN RUSKIN
1819–1900
by J. HOWARD WHITEHOUSE

IT is not difficult to justify the inclusion of Ruskin in a book devoted to great democrats. He could only be excluded under a pedantic definition of what constitutes a democrat. I am guilty of no exaggeration when I say that Ruskin had more influence in the middle and later part of the nineteenth century in the inspiration of democracy and of democratic movements than any other man.

No one would be satisfied to-day with the definition of a democrat as being simply one who believed in a particular form of the machinery of government. We think of the word as standing not only for one who believes in liberty and self-government, but for one whom we should describe as a servant of the people, possessing the qualities necessary for that position.

Ruskin is greatly misunderstood. This is partly due to a temporary neglect of his books. I say temporary, for it is not easy to understand why it should have arisen at all. It is partly due to the fact that much of his teaching has now become the accepted faith of innumerable disciples, and that his constructive suggestions have, in many cases, been carried into effect, often during his lifetime. It is partly due to the Great War, which altered men's habits of reading in a way we still do not fully recognise. It is partly due to the new method of biography, based partly upon Lytton Strachey and partly upon Freud. This has resulted in a number of books being issued about Ruskin in recent years which fail to give any adequate or accurate picture of him. For the most part they are written by men who fail almost entirely to realize the position of Ruskin as the greatest social reformer of modern times. They give us instead a kind of *pseudo*-psycho-analysis, leading to the real character of his work and teaching being hidden under sensational theories having no basis of truth.

Let me also here refer to the frequent charge that his

writings are contradictory. Those who make such a charge appear unable to realize that there must be development in the teaching of a great original mind. Ruskin began to write when a boy of seven, and continued until after the age of seventy. The library edition of his works extends to thirty-nine volumes.

He was born in 1819. His childhood was one of very remarkable interest. The significance of the influences which helped to mould his character has frequently been lost by those who write about him. A study of these influences is essential to an understanding of Ruskin.

His life as a boy was extraordinarily happy. The relations between him and his parents were marked by singular understanding on both sides. Although great care was taken of the boy's health he was not under domination in the narrow sense of the word by either his father or his mother. They cared for him deeply, and did everything they could to encourage his great gifts and aptitudes.

In the last working years of his life Ruskin wrote a short biography, *Praeterita*. It gives a picture of his life as a boy which is singularly attractive.

Let me quote his own words :

" In the afternoons, when my father returned (always punctually) from his business, he dined at half-past four, in the front parlour, my mother sitting beside him to hear the events of the day, and give counsel and encouragement with respect to the same ; chiefly the last, for my father was apt to be vexed if orders for sherry fell the least short of their due standard, even for a day or two . . . After that in summer time we were all in the garden as long as the day lasted ; tea under the white-heart cherry tree ; or in winter and rough weather, at six o'clock in the drawing-room—I having my cup of milk and slice of bread and butter, in a little recess, with a table in front of it, wholly sacred to me ; and in which I remained in the evenings as an idol in a niche, while my mother knitted, and my father read to her—and to me so far as I chose to listen.

" The series of the Waverley novels, then drawing towards its close, was still the chief source of delight in all households caring for literature ; and I can no more recollect the time when I did not know them than when I did not know the Bible ; but I have still a vivid remembrance of my father's intense expression of sorrow mixed with scorn, as he threw down Count Robert of Paris,

after reading three or four pages ; and knew that the life of Scott
was ended : the scorn being a very complex and bitter feeling
in him—partly indeed of the book itself, but chiefly of the
wretches who were tormenting and selling the wrecked intellect,
and not a little, deep down, of the subtle dishonesty which had
essentially caused the ruin."

Ruskin goes on to record his " deeper gratitude " to
his mother for having so exercised him in the Scriptures
" as to make every word of them familiar to my ear in
habitual music." This early training in the music and
meaning of the Scriptures had a profound influence upon
Ruskin's literary style, and upon his thought. " It is
strange," he writes in *Praeterita*,

" that of all the pieces of the Bible which my mother thus taught
me, that which cost me most to learn, and which was to my child's
mind chiefly repulsive—the 119th Psalm—has now become of
all the most precious to me, in its overflowing and glorious
passion of love for the law of God, in opposition to the abuse
of it by modern preachers of what they imagine to be his gospel."

In counting the blessings of his life up to the age of seven
years he puts first the fact that he had been taught the
perfect meaning of peace, in thought, act, and word. He
never saw an angry glance in the eyes of either his father
or his mother. He never heard a servant scolded. He
never saw a moment's trouble or disorder in any household
matter. He learnt also, he tells us, obedience and faith,
and the habit of fixed attention.

There were other wonderful influences which his parents
deliberately brought into his life. His father, as is well
known, was a wealthy wine merchant, and preserved the
old custom of visiting his customers personally. These
journeys were done in a horse-drawn carriage and took
him through a great part of England, Wales and Scotland.
His wife and young son went with him. In this way Ruskin
became as a boy familiar with a large part of England and
Wales, and the lowlands of Scotland. His father was a
man of considerable cultivation, a lover of art and literature,
and a man of sound critical judgment. On these journeys
old houses and castles were visited, and many places famous
for their beauty or for their literary associations.

Let me carry the story of Ruskin's life with his parents a little further. On his fourteenth birthday he was given a copy of Rogers' *Italy* by his father's partner, Henry Telford. The book was illustrated by Turner's vignettes. Ruskin had known nothing of Turner before and was fascinated by his drawings. Shortly afterwards his father obtained for him Prout's *Sketches in Flanders and Germany*. The cumulative influence of these two books persuaded Ruskin's father to widen the scope of his travels and to take his wife and son abroad. This first foreign journey took place in 1833, when Ruskin was fourteen years old. The party went by Calais and Brussels to Cologne, up the Rhine to Strasburg, across the Black Forest to Schaffhausen, through North Switzerland, and over Splügen to Como, Milan and Genoa.

It is worth while recalling the great passage in which Ruskin describes the influence which the first sight of the Alps had upon him. The party had reached Schaffhausen, and, walking out in the evening, John had suddenly come within sight of the mountains :

" Infinitely beyond all that we had ever thought or dreamed— the seen walls of lost Eden could not have been more beautiful to us; not more awful, round Heaven, the walls of sacred Death.

" It is not possible to imagine, in any time of the world, a more blessed entrance into life for a child of such a temperament as mine. True the temperament belonged to the age : a very few years—within the hundred—before that, no child could have been born to care for mountains, or for the men that lived among them, in that way. Till Rousseau's time, there had been no sentimental love of nature; and till Scott's, no such apprehensive love of ' all sorts and conditions of men ' not in the soul merely, but in the flesh. St. Bernard of La Fontaine, looking out to Mont Blanc with his child's eyes, sees above Mont Blanc the Madonna ; St. Bernard of Tallories, not the Lake of Annecy, but the dead between Martigny and Aosta. But for me the Alps and their people were alike beautiful in their snow, and their humanity ; and I wanted neither for them nor myself, sight of any thrones in heaven but the rocks, or of any spirits in Heaven but the clouds.

" Thus in perfect health of life and fire of heart, not wanting to be anything but the boy I was, not wanting to have anything more than I had ; knowing of sorrow only just so much as to make life serious to me, not enough to slacken in the least its sinews ; and with so much of science mixed with feeling as to make the sight of the Alps, not only the revelation of the beauty of the earth, but the opening of the first page of its volume— I went down that evening from the garden terrace of Schaffhausen with my destiny fixed in all of it that was to be sacred and useful. To that terrace, and the shore of the Lake of Geneva, my heart and faith return to this day. In every impulse that is yet nobly alive in them, and every thought that has in it help or peace."

The first foreign journey taken by Ruskin at the age of fourteen profoundly affected his life. He remained for the rest of his active life an eager traveller, and frequently spent a great part of each year abroad.

In any attempt to sum up the advantages to Ruskin of his parents' attitude to him as a boy, we should have to add many things to those which Ruskin calls attention to in *Praeterita*. He was given every encouragement to study art, literature, and natural beauty. His desire to express himself in creative activities was given every opportunity to develop. He was encouraged to write and above all to draw. His father's good taste brought him early into touch with great painters. He acquired a genuine love of beauty and a true appreciation of it. His standards of taste and criticism were wonderful in so young a boy. He was enabled to travel in an age when this was comparatively rare, and to do so under the happiest conditions. The sympathy which brought all these things into his life was based upon a passionate love for him on the part of both his parents, yet it was a love which on the whole was wisely exercised.

Ruskin entered Christ Church, Oxford, in 1837, at the age of eighteen. He was already a writer. He had kept long diaries of his visits to many places both in this country and abroad. He had written some poems. Above all he had been taught to draw. It would perhaps be more accurate to say that he had taught himself. He had had some lessons, but as a young boy he had developed a remarkable gift for drawing with great fidelity and sympathy buildings and landscapes. He also knew a lot about pictures and about architecture.

He continued writing during his undergraduate years, and won the Newdigate Prize at the age of twenty. After taking his degree in 1842 he pressed forward with his art studies, and began *Modern Painters*, the first volume of which was published in 1843, when he was twenty-four years old. He did not complete *Modern Painters* until 1860, when at the age of forty-one he published the last volume. Between the publication of the first and fifth volumes, a period of seventeen years, Ruskin had done a vast amount of work. He had not only studied for long months abroad, preparing to write the later volumes of *Modern Painters*, but he had written *The Seven Lamps of Architecture, The Stones of Venice*, and many other books of great importance. He had lectured in many parts of the country ; he had co-operated in the foundation of the Working Men's College, and had taught there ; he had thrown himself into many public movements ; he had done a great amount of hard work on the superb collection of Turner drawings at the National Gallery ; he had defended the Pre-Raphaelites and influenced a not inconsiderable body of public opinion in their favour ; he had become the greatest influence in the country on art questions.

The position of influence to which he had attained when at the age of forty-one he published the last volume of *Modern Painters* was not wholly due to his eminence as an authority on art. It was generally felt that a new creative force had arisen. His books on art went far beyond the titles they bore. They made a deep human appeal. *Modern Painters* is not only a study of ancient and modern art, with biographies and interpretations of the great masters of the Renaissance, it is a profound piece of philosophy dealing with most of the vital problems of life. It also gives an exposition of the beautiful which in its main features has never been challenged. *The Stones of Venice* is not a glorified guide-book to the famous city. It is a scholarly historical work almost unique in character, for it explains the faith and nature of a great people through an examination of the works of their hands. It contains also a very noble inquiry into the functions of the workman. The chapter on the nature of Gothic had an immediate influence on the thought of this country. The book, and this chapter in particular, increased the number of his disciples amongst the social workers of England.

It is well to remember all these things, because we have now reached a period in Ruskin's life when for the most part he was to cease to write upon art, and to turn his attention almost exclusively to social questions and experiments. It is often thought that this change in the subject of Ruskin's books marked a violent break with his past interests. Nothing could be further from the truth. When at the age of forty-one Ruskin began to write books on social questions which placed him in a position of commanding influence, it was a natural transition from his earlier work. In this latter he had tried to interpret the eternal laws of beauty, to define the principles of individual and national greatness, to set forth the basis of noble labour. As he wrote on these questions he became increasingly conscious of the squalor and ugliness of our cities, of our false competitive system, of the degradation of great masses of our people. The eternal principles of beauty which he pursued in his earlier books were not something to be confined to buildings and pictures. They affected every aspect of our lives. Ruskin, therefore, deliberately resolved to attempt to point the nobler way in our national life. The year which saw the publication of the final volume of *Modern Painters* saw too the appearance of *Unto This Last*, the most famous and the most influential book on political economy of which we have any record.

Its early history is well known. Ruskin sent the first three chapters of the book to Thackeray in the form of articles for the *Cornhill*. Thackeray began to publish them. They created a storm in all orthodox and conventional minds, and especially in those who represented the established order of things. The outcry was so great that Thackeray was intimidated. He told Ruskin that he would publish one more article, and that then the series must close. The four papers which appeared in the *Cornhill* were issued in book form eighteen months later, in 1862. The first edition consisted of 1,000 copies. It took about twelve years for his publisher to dispose of this edition, but when it was republished under Ruskin's

own supervision the annual sale for at least thirty years
was never less than 2,000 copies.

Unto This Last was the first of a noble series of books
on social reform and political economy. His views were
to be developed in such works as *Time and Tide, The Crown
of Wild Olive, Fors Clavigera,* and *Munera Pulveris.* His
election in 1869 as Slade Professor of Art at Oxford
gave him an additional platform for the utterance of his
views.

This then is a convenient point briefly to consider Ruskin's
social teaching and especially his position as a pioneer
force in modern life. It must be remembered that we are
thinking of a man whose great prophetic appeal was made
seventy-five years ago. Labour had not entered the House
of Commons, the Education Acts had not become law,
none of the great political parties had discussed the great
measures of social reform passed in the present century.
There was no representative franchise; trade unions had
not the organisation nor the power, nor the legal position
which they now hold. Ruskin was not the mouthpiece
of any party in the State, he was a solitary teacher, and at
first stood almost alone. The keynote of Ruskin's work
may be given in one sentence from his pen:

" There is no wealth but life ; life including all its powers
of love, of joy and admiration. That country is the richest
which nourishes the greatest number of noble and happy
human beings. That man is richest who, having perfected
the functions of his own life to the utmost, has also the
widest possible influence both personally and by means
of his possessions over the lives of others."

His books are a remorseless exposure of the industrial
system, and the economic dogmas upon which it was based.
He demanded the principle of co-operation for that of
competition, and he put forward no vague definitions, but
exact proposals for the reform of society. In these proposals
he anticipated many of the great social questions which
were to be brought to an issue later.

Thus he proposed the limitation of the hours of labour,
but he went much farther than this. Not only were the
hours of labour to be shortened, but those which remained
must not be competitive and oppressive to the workman.

The employer was to suppose that the workman was his son, and to act accordingly.

He appealed for old age pensions. " It ought to be quite as natural and straightforward a matter for a labourer to take his pension from his parish because he has deserved well of his parish, as for a man in higher rank to take his pension from his country because he has deserved well of his country."

It was fifty years later when Mr. Asquith's government carried out the precise proposals of Ruskin.

The widest response to the teaching of Ruskin came from the working classes. His language made the same appeal as did the prose of the Bible to an earlier age. It gave working men a new vision of life. The humblest factory worker could understand passages like this :

" The great cry which rises from all our manufacturing cities, louder than the furnace blast, is all in very deed for this ; that we manufacture there everything except man. We blanch cotton and strengthen steel and refine sugar and shape pottery ; but to brighten, to strengthen, to refine, or to form a single living spirit never enters into our estimate of advantages. And all the evil to which that cry is urging our myriads can be met only in one way . . . by a right understanding on the part of all classes of what kinds of labour are good for men, raising them and making them happy ; by a determined sacrifice of such convenience or beauty or cheapness as is to be got only by the degradation of the workmen and by an equally determined demand for the products and results of healthy and ennobling labour."

He appealed before anyone else for the minimum wage. When the first wages board was set up in this country the government were but carrying out the precise proposal made decades before by Ruskin. He has left on record the fact that no competitive system could justify sweating. When the labour exchanges were established they sought to deal with the vital problems of fixity of employment in the constructive spirit in which Ruskin had brought that problem forward.

In connection with land reform Ruskin was ahead of all others. We sometimes associate with this cabinet minister or that the popular indictment of slums and their owners,

T

and the social system which enables them to exist. The first indictment came from Ruskin. He appealed for their abolition, for fair rents, for fixity of tenure, for the elimination of profiteering. Persons who owned land or houses must observe the principles of personal responsibility and personal service. The proper use of the land was taught by him long before there was any popular discussion of the subject in political life. We were wasting land, and using it for degrading purposes. He told us how to get more food from it. We were to break rock, exchange earth, drain the moist, and water the dry. We were to increase facilities of carriage. We were to reclaim waste land and practise national afforestation.

Ruskin set forth principles of taxation which have since been carried out. It was he who first suggested the graduated income tax and super-tax. He was a pioneer in the cause of the reform of the mines. We find him three-quarters of a century ago calling attention to the conditions under which miners worked, and insisting upon those conditions being made safe.

Ruskin was a great educational reformer. His teaching was constructive and has also been carried out in many vital aspects. All that he taught was based upon his definition of education. It was not the acquisition of knowledge, it was primarily the cultivation of noble character. It was not to teach people something they did not know before, it was to make them something which they were not, to persuade them to act as they would not have acted. He attacked the narrow conception shown in all forms of education. It did not consist at any stage in acquiring the art of reading, writing or arithmetic. Foolish and ignorant conceptions controlled the elementary schools. In 1857 he pleaded for drawing to be taught as an integral part of education. He pleaded for the inclusion of music and noble literature as essential things in education. He desired all schools to be beautiful, and in beautiful surroundings. He would try to form standards of taste by surrounding children with beautiful things. He made a noble plea for the value of the outdoor life and scenes of natural beauty in education.

There is not one of these constructive suggestions which

has not in part been carried out, and carried out under the influence of his teaching. The attempt has been made to provide better educational buildings. Pictures, sculpture, architecture, colour, are now realised to be instruments of education. Drawing was made a compulsory subject in elementary schools in 1890, and many reforms have been introduced, too numerous now to mention.

Perhaps the greatest contribution which Ruskin made to education was his insistence on the value of handicrafts. He desired to see these used as a method of moral and intellectual training. He was not speaking of something to be regarded as a hobby for young children. He desired education to be associated with practical work, the tilling of the land, the management of sailing boats, the knowledge and care of living animals, all the activities of a natural outdoor life. Ruskin believed that to give a child the opportunity of studying a wide range of arts and crafts not only gave him a greater power of self-expression, but also cultivated his moral and intellectual qualities, giving him new interests in life, with new standards of taste and judgment.

Ruskin's teaching in this connection has made considerable progress. Some of the modern public schools of England have adopted his principles. There are great numbers of our secondary schools, now purely academic in their curriculum, which could with advantage apply the principles of Ruskin. The State schools are experimenting more and more widely in this direction. The schools which still neglect the value of manual activities include many of the public schools.

No account of Ruskin's life would be complete without some reference to his social experiments. He was not content to write and to lecture. Whenever possible he tried to demonstrate the rightness of his views.

During his professorship at Oxford a body of his students under his leadership constructed a road to enable Ferry Hinksey to be reached by carts which were cutting into ruts for want of a road a piece of green on which cottages bordered. He wrote " I want to show my Oxford drawing-class my notion of what a country road should be . . . I want to level one or two bits where the water lodges, to get the ruts out of the rest, and sow the banks with the wild flowers that ought to grow on them." He went on to add that his chief purpose, however, was to let his pupils feel the pleasures of useful, muscular work, and especially of the varied work involved in getting a human pathway rightly made through a lovely country. It was a good object lesson, and a social experience for the men who took part in the experiment. At a later period of his life he protested against the neglect of local authorities to keep the streets of London clean. He organized some of his old servants and others, and for some time these swept a certain road and kept it fit for walking across.

His words often expressed burning indignation at the way the poor are exploited. One aspect of the injustice they suffer he tried, in some little degree, to put right. He opened a tea shop. He put in charge of it two of his mother's old servants. Arthur Severn painted a sign for it, and Ruskin announced that he would sell tea there in tiny quantities to the poor at the same proportionate price that the wealthy paid for large quantities.

These enterprises were all small things. He did bigger ones. He put the properties that he had inherited in London into the hands of Miss Octavia Hill. This devoted social worker looked after the properties and the tenants and applied the rents to necessary repairs.

Ruskin's benefactions were princely. At Oxford he founded the Ruskin Drawing School, and handed to the University authorities a capital sum of money to provide the salary of the drawing-master. (The first to be appointed was Alexander Macdonald, himself an artist of no little merit.) He gave to Oxford University drawings of great value by Turner and many others. They form some of the richest treasures of art in the country. Similarly he made a noble gift of drawings to the University of Cambridge, and he gave liberally of his drawings and books and minerals to a great number of schools and colleges in this country, in Scotland and in Ireland.

His private benefactions were marked by extraordinary sympathy and understanding. Sick friends received gifts to go abroad and recuperate. Promising young men were sent to study abroad and to sketch. He organized a not inconsiderable band of painters and set them to work to make records of beautiful buildings and scenes in Europe, and financed them from his own pocket. He bought at liberal prices the works of the young Pre-Raphaelites and others in the days when they were despised and neglected. His life is a long record of generous deeds.

Most important of the social experiments for which he was responsible was the foundation of the Guild of St. George. He appealed for the support of all people of good will. The scheme of the Guild was to acquire land, farms and houses and to encourage people to live healthy lives away from the cities, working at the noble forms of labour. His scheme included the foundation of schools, and a great range of plans for noble study. In connection with the Guild he founded at his own cost the Museum at Sheffield, and he placed there many of the treasures which he had collected. Some of his friends and disciples made gifts to the Guild. Mrs. Talbot gave some cottages on the mountain side at Barmouth. A Birmingham alderman, George Baker, gave some woodland in the Midlands. But it would be true to say that there was little popular response, and the scheme was looked upon as Utopian and impractical. It would be a mistake to dismiss it as a failure. It inspired some very noble writings by him. It brought together a band of sincere people, the survivors of whom have kept in touch since they were first brought together under Ruskin's influence. The Museum at Sheffield is still in existence, and its treasures are now becoming more generally appreciated. It will play an increasing part in the wider education of the people of the city.

The great fortune which Ruskin inherited from his father was all spent in the service of the great causes to which Ruskin devoted his life. In this connection his generosity to the Severn family should be recorded. His father died in 1864, and his cousin Joan Agnew, who later became Mrs. Andrew Severn, came to live with his mother at Denmark Hill. When Ruskin bought Brantwood Mrs. Severn and her family came to live there also as Ruskin's guests. They lived there until his death, and then inherited the property.

Ruskin had married Miss Effie Gray in 1848. The marriage was not a happy one, and was annulled in 1854. Mrs. Ruskin became a little later the wife of Sir John Millais.

Ruskin bought Brantwood, on the banks of Coniston Water, in 1871, and for the last twenty-nine years of his life, when he was not abroad, he lived and worked there. The beauty of its surroundings soothed a mind tired with exertions attempted by few. He wrote many books here, including his touching autobiography. He ceased to write about 1890, and died at Brantwood in 1900, at the age of eighty-one.

No account of Ruskin would be complete without some reference to his amazing draughtsmanship, and his powers as an artist. Most of his works were illustrated with his own drawings. *Modern Painters*, *The Stones of Venice*, *The Seven Lamps of Architecture*, and a great number of others, contain drawings of singular beauty, illustrating his arguments. Ruskin's powers in this direction have never received due recognition. He had the gift of drawing buildings, landscapes, trees and flowers, in a supreme degree. His drawings are marked by extraordinary delicacy, fidelity and sympathy. If Ruskin's work in life had simply consisted of the production of these beautiful things his fame would have been secure. He did not set out to make a finished picture. In the vast majority of his drawings he simply wanted to record some beautiful detail—a growing plant, a Gothic arch, a mass of roofs, a carved capital, a cathedral tower, a momentary cloud effect, a cluster of leaves. They were details, but they were also things of enduring beauty.

He also spent long months copying pictures or parts of pictures by the great masters. In the Sistine chapel of the Vatican he had a great scaffolding erected, and for weeks worked at copies of Botticelli's frescoes and others. He has given us some glorious copies of Tintoretto, Carpaccio, and many others. He has drawn exquisitely many of the monuments of Italy.

His drawings not only make an immediate appeal by reason of the beauty of their execution. They also show us some of the most interesting things in nature, art and all the works of man. He made at least fifteen thousand drawings. Of this great total there is not one without its own charm.

What was the religious faith of Ruskin ? In his childhood under the influence of his mother he had been a careful reader of the Bible. Its style had greatly affected his own. Its poetry and imagery entered into his life. If his Biblical references were collected they would form in themselves a great interpretation both of the Old and the New Testament. They are marked by extraordinary eloquence and originality, and by a fearless devotion to truth. His social appeal is based upon the principles of justice which he finds set forth so clearly in the pages of the New Testament. But Ruskin was far too great a man to be limited by the dogmas or creed of any sect. It would be idle to attempt to place him in any religious category. It is sufficient to record that he was a profoundly religious man, that the spiritual world was to him as real as the material world, and that his vision was so great and sincere that he desired here and now to erect the visible kingdom of God.

In his personal character Ruskin observed the standards of a modern St. Francis. He was beloved by everyone who came within reach of his influence. He loved children, and to a great number of friends, young and old, he wrote letters of singular charm and sincerity. He was the last of the great letter writers. Few would dispute the beauty of his prose, for he ranks with the greatest masters.

He brought new music to our language. He opened the eyes of countless thousands to the beauty as well as the mystery of life. He inspired many disciples to carry on his work and to extend it in many directions. He performed for Italy what no man has ever before accomplished for any nation. He interpreted her history and her treasures in a manner which inspired thoughtful people all over the world. Physical memorials to his memory are to be found in many far distant places—the high Alps, the shores of Derwentwater, Oxford, Cambridge, Sheffield, unknown schools in Ireland, Boston in the United States, the little house at Venice where he wrote that city's immortal story.

Even greater memorials are to be found in the societies, and foundations, and movements, created to carry out some at least of the things he fought for. Greater still is

the memorial for ever enshrined in the hearts of those
who knew him and who believe that wherever people are
gathered together in the pursuit of peace and beauty,
freedom and justice, and a national and international life
under which these things are possible, the name of John
Ruskin will be honoured.

PERCY BYSSHE SHELLEY
1792-1822
by JOHN MIDDLETON MURRY

T*

PERCY BYSSHE SHELLEY

1792-1822

by JOHN MIDDLETON MURRY

WILLIAM GODWIN'S *An Enquiry Concerning Political Justice* culminates in a sustained and searching attack, from the standpoint of an idealist morality, on the existing property system. He portrays the superior humanity of a society of individuals who have emancipated themselves from the sordidness of production for profit, and among whom the principle " From each according to his ability, to each according to his need " is naturally operative. For all its occasional naivety of individualism—for instance in his expectation that members of this future society would refuse to compromise their integrity as individuals by performing music in concert or by speaking words not their own in theatrical plays—Godwin's vision is singularly impressive. It has been derided ; it has been forgotten, until it has become one of the major mysteries of literary criticism that a book, whose chief title to remembrance is that it enabled its author to sponge on the ardent and youthful Shelley, should have been the inspiration of Coleridge and Wordsworth and Southey and Hazlitt, long before Shelley took the contagion.

Few things, it appears, are more congenial to the inertia of human nature than the discomfiture of an idealist. That idealists are fools is common knowledge ; that they should be proved knaves as well is no common satisfaction to human complacency. And, of course, it needs no demonstration that Godwin was a knave. He sponged on Shelley. If one were to suggest that Jesus of Nazareth likewise sponged on the devoted women who maintained him, it would be reckoned blasphemy or bad taste. Yet the cases were not so different. Both these idealists believed and proclaimed that there could be and should be a new relation of loving kindness among men, and that in a humane society one individual's need should be a sufficient and peremptory claim on another's superfluity.

That expectation will never be wholly banished from the hearts of men; nor, even in the barren times when hope is dimmed, will there be lacking men who, even if they cannot conceive felicity within their time, will feel sympathy and tenderness and gratitude towards those in whom the desire of it is strong and the expectation near.

To these belonged William Godwin. That he believed that he had only to put his imagination of a nobler order of society before men's minds for them to embrace it, was a weakness which all great prophets have shared, from Jesus to Karl Marx included. If it is an illusion, it is an illusion inevitable to the mind which conceives such an ideal. For evidently it is impossible for the same man to believe in the possibility of universal love, and to believe that the majority of men are incapable of responding to the doctrine. It is a condition of his own sanity that he should believe that such a conception is latent in the hearts and minds of all mankind ; for without that assumption the ideal of universal love is the chimera of a madman's brain. What is it then that prevents men from responding to it ? Since, by hypothesis, the ideal is natural to man, the obstacle must lie in some malign influence which thwarts or perverts man's nature. This malign influence Godwin found in " positive institutions "— in government, in monarchy, in established religion, in the family, in property. The apparent concreteness of this notion of Godwin's was deceptive : in fact, it was curiously abstract, and could hardly have been conceived save by a remarkably innocent mind. But the beauty and the unconscious purpose of Godwin's idea was that it placed the responsibility for the depravity of human nature, or the darkening of human reason (which were, for Godwin, the same thing) on a power external to man himself. " Positive institutions " were, in Godwin's view, the Devil : and he said so. As Shelley, who was Godwin's life-long disciple in these matters, put it : mankind had incurred " the mighty calamity of Government."

Manifestly, though Godwin did not see it, this was a religious mythology. The Godwinian Fall of Man consisted precisely in his submission to " positive institutions " ; the occurrence of " the mighty calamity of Government " was Man's expulsion from Paradise. Whereas the legend of

Genesis offered some poetic cause for this primal catastrophe, Godwin's mythology offered none at all. Since he refused to accept the new myth of the Social Contract, for him the original of Government was a mystery : not very different from " the mystery of iniquity," which has perplexed sensitive Christian thinkers. But it was not a weakness in Godwin's thinking that the origin of evil, which was synonymous with Government, should have remained a mystery. No doubt the orthodox Christian doctrine of Original Sin is truer to the facts of average human nature. But Godwin was not really concerned with average human nature. The idealist cannot be. The true idealist is one who feels in himself the capacity to live in accord with a higher morality than that of the human average. Inevitably, he seeks to express this capacity of his nature, and he is bound to universalise it, since no imaginative man can accept the notion that he is essentially superior to his fellows. Thus true idealism depends on turning a blind eye to human inertia. That gives an opening to the cynic, whether political or religious, to deride what he calls the cheap optimism of the idealist ; but the derision itself is cheap. A larger imaginative view will comprehend how necessary, if human society is to be saved from moral stagnation and the human mind from spiritual despair, is the leaven of men who will believe, and live by the belief that—as Shelley put it in *Queen Mab*—a happy Earth is the reality of Heaven.

Godwin was not unaware of the distance that separated a society of true freedom and true equality from the society in which he lived—a society controlled by an aristocracy panic-stricken by the French Revolution, wherein wealth accumulated and men decayed, and the simple equation of Government and Evil was by no means remote from the facts. His final chapter—" On the Means of Introducing the Genuine System of Property "—opens with the quaint sentences :

Having thus stated explicitly and without reserve the great branches of this illustrious picture, there is but one subject that remains. In what manner shall this interesting improvement of human society be carried into execution ?

It is urged, he goes on, that the propagation of such

doctrines as his will lead to bloody revolution. Even if it
were so, he says, we should not shrink from the prospect :
a brief convulsion is no outrageous price to pay for future
felicity. Anyhow, the duty of the philosopher is to promul-
gate the whole truth without diffidence or reserve. The
clash, if clash there is to be, will only come from " one body
of men in the community outstripping another in their ideas
of improvement and becoming impatient of the opposition
they have to encounter." This will be the moment of
crisis. It is incumbent then on the promulgators of truth
to refrain from inflammatory language.

The tidings of liberty and equality are tidings of good will
to all orders of men. They free the peasant from the iniquity
that depresses his mind, and the privileged from the luxury and
despotism by which he is corrupted. Let those who bear these
tidings not strain their benignity by showing that that benignity
has not yet become the inmate of their hearts.

So much for the evangelists themselves. But what of the
privileged ? Those of them who are actuated by self-
interest alone (Godwin argues) will surely see the folly of
anything more obstinate than a temperate and yielding
resistance. If they do not, on them will fall the responsibility of convulsion. But there are generous minds among
them : above all among the youthful aristocracy.

The same spirit that has led forth the young nobility of
successive ages to encounter the hardships of a camp might
easily be employed to render them champions of the cause of
equality ; nor is it to be believed that the circumstance of
superior virtue and truth in this latter exertion will be without
its effect.

That was the appeal to which Shelley responded. Godwin's *Political Justice* had been published in 1793. Despite
its fame and its influence on an earlier generation, so complete was the obscurity into which its author had been
thrust, that in 1811 Shelley learnt with " inconceivable
emotion " and manifest surprise that Godwin was still
alive. Godwin was fifty-five ; he had endured much.
The defection of Wordsworth and Coleridge and Southey
who had made their peace with reaction, and comfortably
persuaded themselves that the triumph of Napoleon ab-

solved them from loyalty to their youthful belief in human
equality; the continued failure of his own indefatigable
efforts to earn a living; the death of Mary Wollstonecraft:
these had been more than a fair share of the burdens of
life. The declaration of impassioned discipleship by a
young aristocrat of genius must have warmed his heart.
And there was this vital difference between Shelley and his
former disciples, that Shelley really had absorbed his ideas.
They had become part of the fibre of his intellectual being;
and Shelley was to be faithful to them to his death.

Nevertheless, though it is to Godwin that we must go to
find the clue to much in Shelley, it would be a mistake to
call Shelley a Godwinian; still more mistaken to imagine
that the Godwinian elements in Shelley's work are an alien
excrescence which can be detached by a neat effort of
critical surgery, leaving the pure essence of Shelley intact
and uncontaminate. Shelley was an *anima naturaliter God-
winiana*. He was not, as it is still often represented, the
unfortunate victim of the influence of a second-rate mind.
Godwin's was not a second-rate mind; and his thought
did not so much influence Shelley's as give intellectual
expression to the tendencies of Shelley's own idealistic
nature.

The religious mythology which underlay Godwin's
political thought was completely congenial to Shelley. The
conflict between aspiration and circumstance, the contradiction between the ideal and real, which tormented
Shelley all his life, seemed to be explained by Godwin's
theory of the malign effect of " positive institutions." That
the explanation was illusory and, in fact, no more than a
re-statement of the contradiction, dawned only gradually
upon him. For a blissful period of enthusiasm it seemed
that Godwin's political theory had solved the problem of
evil itself. All the inertia of existence, all the reluctance of
the material world to be informed by spirit, was segregated
into " the mighty calamity of Government "; so that the
everlasting struggle between soul and body, the incessant
warfare between the spiritual and animal allegiances of man,
was comprehended in the warfare between political liberty
and political tyranny. Hence what appears to us the strange
extravagance of Shelley's early writing. He pours into

what is, on the surface, the theory of a political conflict, the passion that belongs to the struggle between absolute Good and absolute Evil, with a vehemence baffling to a generation like our own. For, even to the extreme idealists among us, Government is no longer a natural symbol of absolute Evil. On the contrary, we tend to regard it, with some justification, as the vehicle of potential or actual good ; and its function is increasingly held to be less that of a weapon to defend an inequitable property-system than an instrument for a gradual redistribution of property.

The strangeness to a modern mind of Shelley's identification of Government with absolute Evil, and of the metaphysical and demonic significance with which he invests " positive institutions," is a measure of the vastness of the change which has been wrought in English political and social life in the hundred and thirty years since Shelley wrote *Queen Mab*. Yet that identification, which is become so unnatural to us, was eminently natural to an imaginative genius to whom the Revolutionary Terror in France was a vague memory, and the repressive system of Pitt and Sidmouth and Castlereagh a grim actuality. Government in those dark days was, perhaps, as near as it had ever come in English history to being absolutely evil. And Religion was its handmaid. Even a sincerely religious man, like Wilberforce, whose labours for the abolition of slavery are justly remembered, was eloquent in defence of the rigours of political repression and a main supporter of the tyrannous anti-combination laws. And, if this was the attitude of a sincere Evangelical Christian, it needs no effort to conjecture the attitude of the average parson who prospered on his tithe of corn, while the peasant and the worker starved. Shelley's fierce denunciations of religion and his abhorrence of Christianity were as natural as his detestation of Government. Repressive government and established religion were twin manifestations of a single iniquity. It seemed as though the aristocracy and clergy of England, even with the example of the French before them, were being driven by a destiny to a similar doom. In his *Philosophical View of Reform*, written shortly after Peterloo, Shelley passionately depicts the increasing degradation of the worker and the peasant.

They eat less bread, wear worse clothes, are more ignorant, immoral, and desperate. This then is the condition of the lowest and largest class, from whose labours the whole materials of life are wrought, of which the others are only the receivers or the consumers. They are more superstitious, for misery on earth begets a diseased expectation and panic-stricken faith in miseries beyond the grave.

For this inhuman condition Government and Religion, the instrument of Government, were responsible. Abolish them !

At such a time, we repeat, it was natural that Godwin's gospel that positive institutions were the only obstacle to the true liberty of mankind should appear to Shelley as the good tidings indeed. It was the solution to the mystery of life, the concrete dramatisation of the struggle between the powers of Light and the powers of Darkness, and the guarantee that the Good would prevail. The metaphysical conflict was embodied in the political struggle. And Shelley, we may guess, did not pause to reflect that twenty years had passed since Godwin's gospel had been given to the world, and all that had happened was that things had gone from bad to worse. It scarcely occurred to him that *Political Justice* had a human author : *e cœlo descendit*. And this, we imagine, was the real cause of the strange surprise and " inconceivable emotion " with which Shelley heard that Godwin was still alive. Perhaps it stirred him hardly less than one might be stirred to learn that the author of the *Sermon on the Mount* was in the land of the living.

Shelley had believed that a universal change was imminent. The reign of universal benevolence was at hand. To meet Godwin in the flesh was to realise that the miracle had not happened. Godwin was not the Legislator of the new Republic ; he was an obscure and battered journalist, struggling to keep a family alive. He had spoken the veritable word, but men's ears were dull and their hearts were hardened.

It is impossible to separate Shelley's political faith from his religious faith. Even in the case of Godwin himself the separation is not really possible. The society of " universal

benevolence " is hardly to be distinguished from the Kingdom of Heaven on earth.   Godwin believed in its ultimate
inevitability.   Possibly he was right ; and his only mistake
was in miscalculating the speed of its coming, and the
nature of the process by which it would arrive.   But Shelley's
conception of the true condition of man was more trans-
cendent even than Godwin's, inasmuch as his ideal was
metaphysical.   Shelley desired the absolute Good and the
absolute Beauty ; and if for a time he projected these into
some condition of human society, which he believed or
hoped to be quickly attainable, he outgrew that illusion.
The conclusion of *The Ode to Liberty* is already despondent.

> Comes she not, and come ye not,
>   Rulers of eternal thought,
> To judge, with solemn truth, life's ill-apportioned lot ?
> Blind Love, and equal Justice, and the Fame
>   Of what has been, the Hope of what will be ?
> O Liberty ! if such could be thy name,
>   Wert thou disjoined from these, or they from thee ;
> If thine or theirs were treasures to be bought
>   By blood and tears, have not the wise and free
>   Wept tears, and blood like tears ?

But this Liberty, we feel, is already almost a liberation from
the bondage, not of mere tyranny, but of material existence
itself.   And in the final chorus of *Hellas* the doubt is
more explicit still.   The fearful thought of the eternal
recurrence rises in Shelley's mind to give an aching
poignancy to his vision of felicity.

> Another Athens shall arise
>   And to remoter time
> Bequeath, like sunset to the skies,
>   The splendour of its prime ;
> And leave, if nought so bright may live,
> All earth can take, or Heaven can give.

It is magnificently said.   Never was Shelley's utterance of
his own essential thought more crystalline.   And what does
it mean ? That the Athens of the future, the City of the
Soul, the *civitas Dei*, will be a visitant from another realm.
For one supreme moment of consummation the white
radiance of Eternity will dissolve into its own incandescence

the many colours of the dome of glass. But the moment will pass. The Many will re-conquer the One. The memory of that future earthly city will be as the memory of the heavenly city which now haunts men's minds : for they are the same city.

> But Greece and her foundations are
> Built below the tide of war,
> Based on the crystálline sea
> Of thought and its eternity.

This is a city which was, and is, and ever shall be. But who shall imagine it established in the life of nations ? Does it not belong to the moment when there shall be no more Time, to the eternal moment when there *is* no more Time ? Between this abiding city and the flux of existence is there not a mortal enmity ? At the last, Shelley must confess it.

> Oh, cease ! must hate and death return ?
> Cease ! must men kill and die ?
> Cease ! drain not to its dregs the urn
> Of bitter prophecy.
> The world is weary of the past,
> Oh, might it die or rest at last !

Maybe the moment will come when men shall not kill ; but they shall die. Shelley's cry is that the wheel of existence should cease its motion, and Time be dissolved into Eternity. The thought of incessant Becoming is like an arrow in his heart. For how can Becoming not be the enemy of Perfection ?

That metaphysical anguish is of the essence of Shelley ; it distinguishes him absolutely from his great coeval, Keats, whose mind was naturally bent to discover the supreme of Beauty in the process of Becoming itself, in

> Joy, whose hand is ever at his lips,
> Bidding adieu.

And, at the critical moment of his spiritual development, shortly before writing those lines, Keats faced the problem in intellectual terms, and declared his belief that " the nature of the world would not admit " of the kind of perfection of which Shelley dreamed. The difference between

them was that Keats believed, or came to believe, that the
eternal element in the human soul was created by the
resolute contemplation and endurance of the conflict
between the desire of the heart and the knowledge of the
mind, whereas for Shelley the desire of the heart was itself
the eternal element, and the knowledge of the mind the
oil on the wings of the soaring bird.

One cannot judge between them ; to which of them
goes out our greater sympathy depends on personal temperament and experience.   But, in the matter of the
relation between the philosophies and the politics of these
two great poets, it is to be noted that Keats was, by his
philosophy, better prepared to face the basic inertia of
mankind. His vision did not blench at the realisation that
men and women were, in the main, instinctive and animal
still. " The creature hath a purpose, and his eyes are
bright with it." For Shelley, on the other hand, this
admission was painful ; and so far as he might, he avoided
it. His belief in the natural goodness of man was too
precious to suffer him to reflect that the belief was self-
destroying. His metaphysical mind demanded the great
separation between absolute Good and absolute Evil and
he saw these powers embattled in the political field :
absolute Evil embodied in the tyrants, absolute Good in the
oppressed. But in that case what became of the natur
goodness of Man ? for the governors were also men.

But this very compulsion which was upon him to see the
political struggle as a struggle of metaphysical absolutes
gave Shelley a double force and vehemence as a political
writer, and at the same time safeguarded him from the
facile doctrine of violence. If the oppressed people represented, as they did in his imagination, the absolute Good,
then it followed that they must be loyal to the principle
which was incarnate in them. Thus it is that Shelley
presents the superficial paradox of extreme violence in his
denunciation of the iniquity of the ruling-class, and a
resolute insistence on the necessity of a non-violent resistance
to it. That seems strange to the political "realist," but
it is a necessary consequence of the metaphysical passion
which inspired Shelley's political attitude. The people
must be worthy of the perfection of their own Idea.

Because of this metaphysical idealism Shelley's championship of democracy is a permanent inspiration ; and, still more remarkably, by reason of the moral restraint which this idealism imposed upon his search for a solution to the conflict, his actual treatment of the political problem is splendidly sane. Moreover, he is perfectly consistent with himself. *The Masque of Anarchy* agrees at all essential points with his *Philosophical View of Reform.* The former is simply the imaginative and poetic utterance of the same conviction which the latter expounds in argument. The poem opens with the spectacle of Anarchy, like Death on the pale Horse, trampling underfoot " the adoring multitude." It is the vision of Peterloo, transfigured into universal and symbolic significance. Hope alone is left to confront him in his bloody and triumphal march, and she prepares deliberately to immolate herself before him. At that voluntary sacrifice the miracle happens.

> Between her and her foes
> A mist, a light, an image rose,
> Small at first, and weak, and frail
> Like the vapour of a vale.

It grows ; it gathers strength ; with wind-soft step it passes over men's heads, and wakens new thoughts in their minds. They look up. They see Hope walking quietly, and Anarchy dead. Then a mysterious voice speaks to them. It tells them what Freedom is : not a superstition and a name, but

> Clothes and fire and food
> For the trampled multitude——

equal Justice, true Wisdom, Peace, Love. Science, Poetry and Thought are its lamps.

> Spirit, Patience, Gentleness,
> All that can adorn and bless
> Art thou—let deeds not words express
> Thine exceeding loveliness.

This is no freedom that politics could ever win ; or rather, the politics which could win such a freedom must be made by men who have already won it. Nevertheless, Shelley is no dreamer; for it is because it contains the germ of such a freedom that democracy is precious. All other systems of government deny the possibility of this condition : democracy asserts it as a human potentiality. When, therefore, Shelley imagines a great gathering of those who suffer oppression and those who feel the sufferings of others, declaring that they are " as God has made them—free," though he is imagining the impossible—since no body of men, and few individuals, have ever been in this sublime sense " free," and certainly God did not make them so— he is also positing the inward and spiritual grace of which the action he bids them take is the outward and visible sign.

> Stand ye calm and resolute,
> Like a forest close and mute,
> With folded arms and looks which are
> Weapons of unvanquish'd war . . .
>
> And if then the tyrants dare,
> Let them ride among you there,
> Slash and stab and maim and hew :
> What they like, that let them do.
>
> With folded arms and steady eyes
> And little fear and less surprise,
> Look upon them as they slay,
> Till their rage has died away.

Such action is sacramental. Men capable of it are capable of the " freedom " which Shelley imagines. The means is attuned to the end.

And for that reason, as Shelley knew, this is the only practical politics which can lead men to the condition which he meant by " freedom." In so far as that high ideal has expression in the politics of to-day, it is in " the classless society " of which Socialists dream. And it is as true to-day as it was when Shelley wrote, that it is inconceivable that such a society should be achieved by violence. Shelley's grasp on spiritual truth was firm ; he saw, what many Socialists have failed to see, that although it might be true that history had been a struggle between classes and that the political dispossession of one class by another had always been attended by violence, it does not follow that the final class-struggle must be violent. On the contrary, if this final class-struggle was indeed to bring men into a new *kind* of society, then it was impossible that violence should be the midwife of the new order. Into a truly classless society men will enter peacefully or not at all. And this, as Shelley also saw, is not due to any miraculous virtue of non-violent resistance. It is involved in the nature of political democracy. " Ye are many : they are few."

Shelley was more than a democrat ; he was a champion and apostle of the democratic social revolution. But because he was a true visionary, he saw that the social revolution could be achieved only through democratic process, even though that meant centuries of apparent delay.

" The first principle of political reform is the natural equality of men, not with relation to their property, but to their rights. That equality of possessions which Jesus Christ so passionately taught is a moral rather than a political truth and is such as social institutions cannot without mischief inflexibly secure . . . Equality in possessions must be the last result of the utmost refinements in civilization ; it is one of the conditions of that system of society towards which, with whatever hope of ultimate success, it is our duty to tend."

Many to-day, intoxicated by the doctrines of scientific Socialism, believe that equality of possessions, so far from being primarily a moral truth, is something more material even than a political truth, namely, an economic one ; and that its advent is either economically inevitable, or can be enforced by " positive institution." They will be disillusioned ; they will discover that Shelley was right. Before equality of possessions comes to be in a democratic society, there will have to be a majority of people who *believe* in such equality as a moral or religious truth. Nothing less will serve to establish it. The mere political rule of the working-class as such will not : only the democratic self-government of men to whom economic equality is a Faith.

Shelley's insight into fundamentals which are too easily forgotten guided him to a true political wisdom. In *The Philosophical View of Reform* he warns the advanced democrats against making even the demand for universal suffrage immediately. Any sudden attempt at universal suffrage would lead, he says, to "an immature attempt at a Republic."

"It is no prejudice to the ultimate establishment of the boldest political innovations that *we temporize so that when they shall be accomplished they shall be rendered permanent.*"

Those who have the conventional view of Shelley as one for ever beating his luminous wings in vain, may rub their eyes at this, and ask : Can this be he ? But it is Shelley, and Shelley of the purest. It is the politics of a man whose mind is imbued with the moral beauty of his ideal. The path to a society of peace must be itself peaceful ; to a humane community the advance must be humane. The choice is simple to one who sees as clearly as Shelley saw : either a peaceful growth spurred on by men devoted to an ideal and subdued to its quality, or a sudden snatching at a premature amelioration which must either be lost, or maintained by violence. If the latter, " the mighty calamity of Government " is once more renewed.

Ultimately, in all his political thinking, Shelley was a democrat of the rarest and noblest type. Democracy was the vital atmosphere of his political thought. His mind, in these matters, could breathe no other air. And so far from being a limitation, this was his strength. Political Democracy was for him—as surely it must be for any man who shares his ideals—the only system of government congruous with the condition of mutual love that he dreamed that men might attain. Of that condition Democracy might be a crude symbol, a clumsy paradigm ; but it alone pointed towards it, though tremulously, steadfast as the needle to the Pole. Better, therefore, a furlong won through Democracy and peace, than a mile by absolutism and violence.

" Let us be contented with a limited *beginning*, with any whatsoever opening ; let the rotten boroughs be disfranchised and their rights transferred to the unfranchised cities and districts of the nation ; it is no matter how slow, gradual and cautious be the change ; we shall demand more and more with firmness and moderation, never anticipating but never deferring the moment of successful opposition. . . . . . If reform could begin from within the Houses of Parliament as constituted at present, it appears to me that what is called moderate reform, that is, a suffrage whose qualification should be the possession of a certain small property, and triennial parliaments would be a system in which all reformers ought to acquiesce."

But, were this moderate reform to be obstinately refused, then the complete democratic demand for universal suffrage must be pressed ; and pressed by the method of non-violent resistance which he imaginatively depicted in *The Masque of Anarchy*. Not that Shelley absolutely repudiated violent revolution He does not condemn the violence of the French Revolution, which was in his eyes " an additional proof of the necessity of the long-delayed change which it accompanied and disgraced." But the responsibility for violence is not on the revolutionaries, but on those cruel defenders of privilege who make it necessary. England, he believed, might escape this destiny, for " the will of the people to change their government is an acknowledged right in the Constitution of England." Thus, in the conclusion of *The Masque of Anarchy* the Voice bids the assembled people invoke " the old Laws of England " as arbiters in the dispute.

Despite his metaphysical anguish as a poet, Shelley as a politician made his peace with the world of reality. Strange though it may sound, I believe that, if he had lived, he might have been a great political leader ; even as he still may be a great fountain of true political inspiration. For though he underestimated the inertia of humanity in the mass, he appealed to the element in men which alone is capable of conquering that inertia. It is a matter of familiar knowledge to those who deal with men in the mass, that they are capable of acting either far below their level as individuals, or far above it. And that is an index of the potentialities of a nation. The average man is, in reality, an abstraction. Man in reality is below the average, or above it ; and the same man is capable of either. He is either a creature of self-interest or self-sacrifice. And the way to arouse him from the instinct of self-interest is to appeal to the nobler instinct of self-sacrifice. But both alike are instinctive. Thus the two great opposed religious maxims, that man is naturally bad, and that man is naturally

good, are both true : whereas the non-religious maxim
that man is a reasonable creature is false.   So in the realm of
politics, the pure appeal to the natural goodness of man
which Shelley made, and from which he never flinched,
has lost nothing of its power with the lapse of generations.
By his absolute refusal to allow the end to be compromised
in the means, his political gospel retains the unsullied
purity of a high religious faith ; and likewise its efficacy.
For there is no point at which we can say :   Here, in
Shelley's doctrine, the Ideal is degraded by its contact with
the real.   If in his politics he does, as we have said, make
his peace with reality, it is because in his politics the Ideal
itself is at peace with reality.   For the politics which has
the courage to use self-sacrifice for its only weapon is more
than politics ; it is itself an education into a new order of
humanity, and its adepts the vanguard of a society to be.

CARL VOM STEIN

1757-1831

by ERNST TOLLER

CARL VOM STEIN
1757-1831
by ERNST TOLLER

CARL FREIHERR VOM STEIN was born in 1757 at Nassau, a little town on the Rhine. His family were " reichsunmittelbar," that is to say, subject only to the Emperor, and not to any territorial prince. This class of knights, immediately subject to the Emperor, stood in natural opposition to the despotisms of the German princes. They were natural supporters of those tendencies which made for the unity of the German Empire. The territorial princes, anxious to establish their sovereignty securely, to deprive their subjects of rights and to weaken the power of the Emperor, frequently allied themselves with the enemies of the Empire. The Imperial knights considered it their task and duty to strengthen the power of the Emperor. Many of them served him in distinguished positions. The Imperial High Court of Justice and the Imperial Council, the two most important institutions of the disintegrating imperial power, were scenes of their activity. In their work they were supported by the free towns of the Empire, which opposed the internal dissolution of the Empire.

Carl vom Stein grew up amidst moderate wealth. His mother was a woman of spirit and character. From the beginning she directed the thoughts of her children to ethical values. Her letters, which are written with a complete command of language, are an indication of the high level of civilisation which noble families could reach in Western Germany at that time.

The boy was violent and unruly, only to be controlled with difficulty. At sixteen he was sent to the University of Göttingen. He was accompanied by a private tutor, a jurist from Alsace named Salzmann, a man of superior intellectual powers. But Carl rebelled against any tutelage. With every resource of his irony and sarcasm he opposed this man and made his life a torment. In vain did his mother attempt to control him. In a letter which illustrates the distinction of her powers of expression and the breadth of her knowledge, she says : " From my love of you I beg you, my dear son, to leave these harsh ways and these answers which are not fitting for a man who knows a little of the duties of good breeding. Must I repeat to you that when one offends against another, one offends against oneself ? And against whom, now ? Against one who loves you, who is devoted to your good, who desires only to see you perfect, who joins his good name with yours. And how do you reward him for all that ? Ask your conscience ! I implore you not to cherish that mischievous idea that through submission you humiliate yourself, and that you do not show yourself a man unless you oppose everything that is put to you . . ." And sadly this mother adds : " Mothers are only phantoms for their sons. They forget that one deserves at least a certain consideration, even if our tenderness, our care and our trouble are not rewarded. Thus we do well to step back from this stage on which we have played our part."

The mother's efforts were in vain—Salzmann had to give way.

But Stein's unruliness, once brought under control, was to prove of the highest value to the common good. Democracy is not only a form of social constitution ; the essence of democracy shows itself in the style and conduct of a man's life.

Carl vom Stein completed his studies without obtaining an academic degree, and so turned away from the middle-class careers which made an examination an essential preliminary. He practised in the Imperial Supreme Court at Wetzlar, a few years after Goethe had left. He went on the " Grand Tour," and visited France, Baden and Württemberg. Finally, he sought for a post in the Prussian state service. His normal course would have been to enter the service of the Emperor. Probably he had been repulsed by the miserable conditions of the broken-down institutions of the Empire and attracted by the fame of Frederick II (the Great). But as he pursued his plan somewhat negligently, he did not succeed, and again went travelling, this time to Vienna, the Steiermark, Hungary.

Meanwhile his mother had been active on his behalf.

She negotiated with the Prussian Minister Heinitz, an enlightened, liberal man, who was connected with the Imperial nobility by marriage. Stein went to Berlin, entered the Department of Mines, studied zealously at the Academy of Mines at Freiberg, and investigated mining conditions in Poland and later in England. English life presented him with a picture of aristocratically organised self-government which always remained his ideal.

His official activity during this first part of his career took place exclusively in the western possessions of Prussia. The conditions of western Prussia were fundamentally different from those in the east. There the system of estates of the realm was suppressed, while in the west it was maintained by the self-governing knights, towns and free peasants. The west was a fruitful land, its citizens were distinguished for their self-consciousness and self-assurance. Here an officialdom developed that was free and broad in its views. The Prussian kings did not succeed in extending the recruitment of their army to their western possessions. For the higher culture of the western provinces the Prussian kings showed no understanding. Frederick II was ready for any opportunity to sell them or to exchange them for districts in the east. He complained of his western subjects that they were drunkards, stupid and lazy, and of no use to their King.

In the east, on the other hand, reigned the long-established despotism of the Prussian central power, which was based entirely upon the nobility. The rights of the towns were completely suppressed. But even the nobility had no rights in the state. The King ruled them as he wished, and they ruled as absolute sovereigns over their peasants.

The Hohenzollern policy of conquest was based upon this despotism of the King over his nobles and of the nobles over the peasants. The hereditary subjection of the peasants was pure slavery. The peasants were called " subjects," the knightly landowners, " their lordships " (Herrschaft). The peasants had to give their master their sworn vow of fealty and submission. They could not leave the estate nor even marry without permission of the master. The master had the right of inflicting corporal punishment and could throw the peasants and their wives into prison at will. The peasants were bound to the state only by crushing taxes and their military service. This was the hide-bound squirearchy beyond the Elbe that vom Stein so much despised.

Stein writes of a journey through Mecklenburg, where conditions were much the same as in East-Elbe Prussia : " The dwelling of the Mecklenburg nobleman, who keeps down his peasants instead of improving their position, reminds me of some beast of prey which lays waste everything about it, and surrounds itself with the stillness of the grave."

The superior institution in Prussia, the first estate in the realm, was the corps of officers. Through it the King ruled. Soon Stein came into conflict with the military. A colonel wanted to recruit men in the district Stein governed. Stein was at once on the defensive.

Corn, which he should have put at the disposal of the military, he turned over to the needs of the population. Another dispute. Unhesitatingly, he fought the military gentlemen with all his lively irony.

Whatever he undertook he carried out with the deepest seriousness, delegating little to his subordinates. Always he sought to penetrate into the heart of a matter, and never feared hard work. In silence a fine character was being formed.

Looking at the portrait of Stein in his maturity one is struck by the broad face from which juts a strong, characterful nose ; his features are as though carved in wood.

Stein's talent and knowledge of affairs were too great and too well known for him not to come to the top. And so Frederick William III was full of prejudices against him. He considered him " eccentric " and " original." He feared that Stein would bring a predisposition in favour of the constitution of the Westphalian provinces to Prussia, which would be harmful to the state.

The King was right. When Stein became minister in 1804, his feelings for the German Empire came into violent opposition to the particularism which inspired the ruling class in Prussia.

When the National-Socialists nowadays quote Stein's famous remark : " I know only one Fatherland, called

Germany," and call upon Stein as a witness to their nationalism, they falsify his meaning. The nationalism of his time was spiritually the contrary to the nationalism of our day. It was liberal, democratic, it was cosmopolitan ; it never forgot the European community of states and was based upon union, not upon separation. Further, among the liberal nationalists the belief ruled that with the fulfil-ment of national claims the era of cabinet wars and of wars in general would come to an end.

Napoleon's victory over Prussia brought the country to the brink of ruin. The Prussian fortresses and army detachments were surrendered. The King had to flee to East Prussia. A decisive cause of the collapse of Prussia was the despotic power over the affairs of state which Frederick II had introduced. This over-praised monarch believed he could conduct every affair of state himself. He saw his ministers only once a year. He ruled through his secretaries of state, who alone had access to him and who conveyed his commands to the ministers. His successors, with less capacity, continued this method of government. And thus the army and the administration completely collapsed, and proved themselves incapable of putting up any sort of significant resistance.

Carl vom Stein could not continue to work in such circumstances. If a state has no constitution, he declared, then it must have at least an administrative constitution. The King must stand in direct relationship with his ministers, must preside at the ministerial council and must base his decisions upon immediate interchange of opinions with it. The Ministers, however, must have the right, in exceptional cases, to examine the position of the monarchy and must be seriously concerned to investigate and remove the causes of a bad situation. " To neglect this," he wrote, " is as culpable as to betray the cause of the good and noble. The consequences are the same." He thought that he could carry through his plan if several respected state officials proposed to the King the need for change, and, in the event of the proposal not being accepted, handed in their resigna-tions.

But the King was opposed to any diminution of his authority. He was not to be thought a blockhead, he

v

replied, and he described as insolent the idea that he might yield to a council contrary to his will. " From all this I have perceived with great sorrow that, unfortunately, I made no mistake in you at the beginning, but that you are even more to be considered as a contrary, defiant, obstinate and disobedient servant of the state ; one who, presuming upon his genius and talent, is far from keeping before him the good of the state, is led only by caprice and acts only from passion and personal hatred and bitterness . . . so that if you are not minded to change your disrespectful and unseemly conduct, then the state cannot put any great value upon your future services."

Stein's answer was to ask for permission to resign. In his application he repeated with malicious sarcasm the complaints which the King had showered upon him. The King's reply was brief : " As Baron vom Stein, by his letter of yesterday's date, has pronounced his own sentence, I know of nothing to add to it."

Stein departed. The Tsar offered him a ministerial post. Meanwhile Prussia suffered one defeat after another. The King, confined to the province of East Prussia, without any prospect of improvement, sent again for Stein. And Stein returned unconditionally to the Prussian service.

From October 1st, 1807, to November, 1808, he served as Minister. In these months he was at last able to carry out what he had long planned. He reformed the whole life of the Prussian state which had for a century lain torpid. The freeing of the peasants was due to him. He improved the patrimonial jurisdictions and the rural estates police, despite the bitterest opposition from the Junkers against any change in the agrarian system.

Even his liberal advisers and officials, influenced by Kant and Adam Smith, were dissatisfied with him. They wanted the complete dissolution of all agrarian ties. Stein resisted them : he wanted to free the peasants, but at the same time to protect them and their right of property.

He was certainly no democrat in the middle-class sense. He was a feudal democrat who always remained conscious of his origin. He might raise up the lower classes, but at the same time he wanted to create a rich and great aristocracy. The North German petty nobility was unsympathetic to him; he described it as greedy, small-minded and uncultured. He wished to do away with the nobility in general, and limit it to a few great families who, through their independence, could watch over and promote the common interests of the state.

Simultaneously with the emancipation of the peasants he began the reform of the towns. The Prussian kings had suppressed the old German rights of the towns, and had made of them taxable domains and garrisons. A tax-collector, usually a former military official or officer, ruled despotically in the cities, in so far as he himself was not under the despotism of the garrison commander. For a long while the towns had had no self-governing authorities. The Municipal Council was appointed by the King. Where the hand of the King was not heavy upon them, they had to support the encroachments of the Junkers in trade and business. No industries could be developed. Thus the towns were oppressed.

Stein freed the corporations and gave every propertied citizen the right to vote. At the same time he carried on the difficult reparations negotiations with the French, and had to defend himself against the intrigues of the reactionary higher officials and against the attacks of the Junkers. His most bitter enemy was Queen Luise, who wanted to solve the national crisis with *coquetterie*. She had endeavoured in vain to bewitch Napoleon, and now she set everything on a flirtation with Tsar Alexander. She wanted to travel with the King to St. Petersburg, but Stein explained that he could not afford the cost of the journey. The money was wanted for the repair of ruined buildings.

There was hardly a single sphere in which Stein did not begin and carry through legal reforms. Corporal punishment was abolished in the army. An edict permitted the admission of middle-class men to the ranks of the officers. Hitherto the officers had come from the military academies of the nobility, those " hatcheries of class pride and noble haughtiness." By reform of the army the defence of the state was placed on the widest foundation. Without the help of the military reformers, Stein could only have carried through with the greatest difficulty the freeing of the peasants and the towns. From the King he got little help.

But, contrary to the previous occasion, the King did not dare to oppose him seriously. Stein knew that. " I can only be satisfied," he wrote once, " with the fear the King has of me."

But the Junkers went on with the struggle. They were then, as they are to-day, only concerned about their own interests. National tasks might demand sacrifice; never-the-less they were readier to betray the nation than give up their interests. " Rather three lost battles of Auerstädt, than one October decree freeing the peasants," was the opinion of one Junker, Baron von Reck.

When there came into the hands of the Junkers a letter of Stein's in which he declaimed fiercely against the French Government, the Junkers placed this letter in the hands of Napoleon, and succeeded in their aim—that Napoleon should demand Stein's dismissal. This dismissal found Stein in the midst of new plans. He was about to begin on a constitution for Prussia.

After Stein's dismissal, General York, now a national hero of the Nazis, wrote : " One mad head has been cut down. The other brood of vipers will die of its own poison."

Stein lived now as an *émigré* in Prague and Brünn (Brno). The Tsar once more sent for him. Stein would not accept office, but remained the Tsar's adviser.

After Napoleon's first defeat, Stein returned to East Prussia—the King was in Berlin—roused the province, summoned the Diet, ordered the mobilisation of the army. All this was done without any instruction from the King, without his having any Prussian office, and was, in reality, rebellion. When at last the King had called upon the people with promises of a constitution—which promises he afterwards shamefully broke—and had collected the army at Breslau, Stein himself arrived there. But how was he treated ? The King scorned him, the Junkers and court circle avoided him. He could not find a decent lodging and had to live in the loft of an inn, ill and alone. His family were still in banishment, his property was seized by Napoleon who denounced him and outlawed him as an enemy of the Empire. Was it not his work that now approached completion ? Had he not for years and years bent all his energies to the saving of Germany and Prussia, to the restoration of the power of the King ? Now he learned what was the gratitude of the King of Prussia.

The King thought no more about giving the people the promised constitution. The union of Germany was further off than ever. After the downfall of Napoleon came a period of violent reaction. All reformers were dismissed from the Prussian army and the civil service. Stein and his friends were spied upon by the police, were denounced as " Jacobins." The emancipation of the peasants ended in the Junkers seizing a great part of the peasants' land. The constitution of the towns was continually encroached upon by new decrees, continually countermanded and cut away. The nation, deceived and betrayed, was held down and oppressed by the old methods of despotic power.

Stein retired to live on his estates. In Frankfurt he founded the *Monumenta Germaniae* collection. Only once did he re-enter politics. As a member of the Westphalian provincial Diet he proposed the convocation of a united Parliament—that is, the granting of the promised constitution. Once again he received a sharp reprimand from Berlin.

During his time in Prussia, Stein acquired a deep hatred for the country and its Junkers. " Those desolate steppes," he wrote, " are capable only of dragging down one's spirits, and making any exaltation impossible." The Prussian nobility and the Prussian middle class were indeed incapable of enthusiasm for Stein's reforms. They lacked initiative, were altogether too egotistical and small-minded. The middle classes had in fact never attained any real life. To preserve their independent existence at all, they had been forced, in the words of Franz Mehring, to flee into the ethereal caverns of the Idea. The 200 year old military despotism had subjected and subdued the country. To march was more important than to think, obedience was more important than free responsibility.

The profound effects of this subjection and this oppression are perceptible right down to our own time. They showed themselves in the November revolution of 1918, when the nation, unaccustomed to responsibility, showed itself unable to hold and use the power it had won. They showed themselves when Hitler seized power and middle-class democracy was swept away by a stroke of the pen, without making the least resistance. For democracy must live in the hearts of its supporters, or it remains but a scrap of paper. A land without free citizens will, at a crisis, throw itself into the arms of any dictator. It will never understand the spirit of the time, and will follow tyrants because of its fear of the new social divisions it sees opening out.

What Stein did was often imperfect and uncompleted. Nevertheless, whatever Prussia obtained in the way of modern state organisation may be traced back to that one-year ministry of Stein's, to that late successor of the Imperial Knights Hutten and Sickingen with his hatred of princes and clerkly souls. No revolutionary, but a character was Karl vom Stein.

" A Government that wastes the blood and the ability of the nation," said Stein in his diary, " that treats men as tools and not as aims, that suppresses freedom of thought, will not last any longer as soon as it slackens or suffers misfortunes."

Often in history it happens that reforms are undertaken by members of those classes which stand to lose by them. Enlightened, active, progress-loving men, by turning their energies to some great task, can lead humanity forward a little. But when reforms touch the roots of society and thus become revolutions, then they can only hope for lasting success if they are fought for, not by individuals, but by the great classes and divisions of society which are their supporters.

GUSTAV STRESEMANN
1878-1929
by RUDOLF OLDEN

GUSTAV STRESEMANN

1878–1929

by RUDOLF OLDEN

GERMANY'S contribution to democracy has not been great. In the Free Cities of the Empire, the city-states of the Middle Ages, there persisted at one time a strong tradition of self-government and a high cultural *niveau*, but no sooner had the territorial princes consolidated their power than those traditions died away. Germany was parcelled out into a number of despotic states, whose lack of dignity only gave rise to amusement. In the South and West alone, where the civilization of the towns had flourished, there still remained a keen desire for civil liberty.

The political focus shifted to the North, where the military despotism that grew up in Prussia aroused not so much amusement as horror. It was founded on the absolute sway that landowners of noble birth exercised over their serfs. It has been doubted whether the Junkers can really be classed with the nobility. They were chiefly grain-growers, but at the same time dealt in grain, brewed it and distilled it. Between them and the Hohenzollerns there existed a permanent alliance, of which the citizens bore the cost. The towns were robbed of their rights by the Electors and of their livelihood by the agrarian party. In Prussia the towns lost their prosperity, the population its intellectual and social birthright. In their place the smartest, the best disciplined and the most obedient army in the world was created. The Junkers furnished the officers, the peasantry the men.

The Prussian army became the groundwork of the new German Reich. The ruling class in Prussia was not nationalistic, but particularist and hostile to the Reich, and Prussia herself, a traitor to the cause of German unity, had grown powerful in the struggle against the Emperor. The National State, of which liberalism had dreamed, was

made a reality by Prussia.   In Versailles, in the presence of
the army, outside the besieged capital of its " auld enemy,"
the new Reich was proclaimed. The representatives of the
" People " had come all the way from Berlin, but played a
trivial and subordinate part, while the head of the secret
police grudgingly did them the honours. Hindenburg,
who as a lieutenant was present at the great ceremony,
writes, fifty years after the event, that the Germans from the
South had been more openly enthusiastic. " In this respect
we Prussians showed greater restraint, on historical grounds ;
we had recognised our own worth at a time when Germany
was no more than a geographical concept." The King
himself was out of temper, would not countenance so
ill-founded a scheme, refused the title of Emperor and, on
the day he was made Emperor, despite himself, was offended
with Bismarck, who had forced the office on him.

Bismarck himself, however, made the Reich into a Greater
Prussia, swept the administration clear of the last remnants
of liberalism, heeded no qualms on the score of humanity,
and, although he ruled with cunning and deceit rather than
with force, made the people believe in " Blood and Iron "
as the only possible, wholesome and natural executive
system. When he was dropped by an Emperor whose
mind had been shaped in the officers' mess at Potsdam, he
regretted that he had not done more for the political
education of the country.

Delayed schooling is the hardest. The Prussian army
fell to pieces on the battlefields of France. The republic
was left with the Herculean task of enforcing a policy without
military support—and no nation was made for this less
than the Germans. They had learnt from Frederick
the Great that God himself fights on the side of the
big battalions. The Great Elector's last legacy to his
country had been the warning that no ruler was menaced
more than the overlord of Prussia. Frederick William I,
who built up the Prussian army and organised the State
as the army's commissariat, had been a neurotic who lived
in perpetual fear for his throne, looking on his formidable
army as his only safeguard.

Germany had acquired wealth and strengthened her
position in the world, but inherited sensibilities live on.

William II had brandished his "gleaming arms" and strained his neighbours' nerves to breaking point. To compel England, the object of his unrequited affections, to return his love, he had built the fleet that could not but make her Germany's enemy. Germany disarmed, stripped of the protection which alone she had learnt to trust, was like a child whose mother has died. She saw a world full of malicious goblins waiting to swallow her up. And this was the moment when she was faced with the task of framing a democratic programme. What does such a programme imply? Among other things, a policy of self-confidence and self-reliance, clear-headed and independent.

At a time when the National-Socialist party is master of Germany, when every democratic institution has been wiped out, when the German people are being pressed to strain every fibre in the cause of re-armament, we have to confess that the German nation has been defeated by this task. Defeated for the moment, as those will urge who refuse to give up hope for the future and who decline absolutely to envisage Germany's and Europe's future as the relapse into barbarism, the utter extinction of all culture, a reversion to the Bronze Age.

Fifteen years stand between Germany's defeat and Hitler's victory. The end of this period does not see Germany back at that stage in its inner evolution where it was cut short by the ravages of the Great War ; the clock has been set back to the epoch that saw the first rise of Prussia. Germany is experiencing the phenomenon known by psychologists as "infantile regression," a not uncommon symptom of derangement.

But there has been one brief period of political progress not backed by force of arms, a period of intellectual *rapprochement* with the world, a time of optimism and hope for the future of democracy in Germany. Europe seemed to be standing on the threshold of an epoch of social and cultural growth. This is the period which we associate with the name of Stresemann. At a superficial glance this short period and the fifteen years of the German republic seem to be one and the same. We may guess now at the fairy tale that the schoolmasters of the future will repeat to our grandchildren. They will identify the time during which Germany lived at peace with the rest of the world with the years between the Armistice and Hitler's rise to power. But this is a mistake.

The war was not at an end for Germany when, in the Forest of Fontainebleau, Erzberger received the Armistice stipulations at Foch's hands, nor when two Ministers signed the peace treaty of Versailles. So, too, war did not break out afresh only after the Storm Troops took up arms and opened hostilities against the pacifists, or when Germany resigned from the League of Nations. The war ended with the suspension of " passive " resistance in the Ruhr. It broke out anew when Brüning set to work to plunge Germany into poverty in order to blot out the " humiliation " of reparation payments, and when Curtius announced the " tariff union " with Austria and defiantly showed all Europe that treaties and agreements had no binding force on Germany.

The intervening time is very short, lasting from 1923 to 1929, six years in all, from the day Stresemann became Chancellor to the day of his death. For six years he was the leader of the nation, for six years he imposed his will on varying and generally recalcitrant majorities in the Reichstag, for six years he fought down again and again the incessant opposition of his own party, for six years he accustomed Germany to Western methods in the sphere of international relations, for six years he breathed life into the democratic system of government in Germany.

Lord d'Abernon, then British Ambassador in Berlin, a man scarcely prone to fulsome judgment of his fellow-men, at a time when Stresemann was making his first hesitant approach to executive power, noted in his diary : " He is without doubt a great personality, and knows it." One cannot say that Stresemann was often flattered by appreciative recognition of his character. He roused prejudice rather than sympathy. Great men are often inhibited by the antipathy of others, but Stresemann's powers grew through breaking antipathies down. To-day, even among supporters of his policy, disparaging judgments are still quite often heard. The period of his influence was brief and has left no trace. For it happened to be a time of peace. The historians, who create popular legends, grant unstinted praise only to conquerors. Bismarck once expressed himself on this subject with splendid irony. " One may say in general," he writes in the third volume of his *Thoughts and Reminiscences*, " that the greatest affection and popularity are reserved for kings who have won for their country the bloodiest laurels, often only to lose them again . . . Love of peace and devotion to the people's welfare normally rouse the Christian nations of Europe to less enthusiasm than a successful gamble in war, with the citizens' lives and fortunes at stake." He quotes Charles XII and Louis XIV as instances, but he has Prussian Germany in mind. One need not be surprised if in these few years Stresemann's name has already been half forgotten.

Germany's public policy during this time, which fittingly can only be called the period of Stresemann, represents a break in her evolution. In its conception as a whole, as well as in its details and in the method with which it was pursued, it marks a reversal of tradition. Any attempt to define the unusual elements in Stresemann's policy must rest on a study of the unusual elements in the career of the man who framed it.

In Imperial Germany, posts in the government service were filled from among the members of a restricted circle, which included only the nobility and the small part of the *bourgeoisie* it had assimilated. The sifting process took place in the army and in certain students' societies, in the various " corps " which in practice had an exclusive claim to official posts. The Reichstag was not a high road to the civil administration. The opposite rather was true, for intensive pre-occupation with politics tended to injure members of the ruling class, while it did nothing to help outsiders. It was a harder matter to be received into the ruling class in the relatively upstart Prusso-German kingdom than it is in countries with an old and exclusive aristocracy. When, during the war, attempts were made at introducing a more democratic spirit, the government's slogan, " Make Way for Ability," evoked a powerful response. What then were the restrictions of rank that still stood in the way of advancement from below ? None, indeed, were prescribed by law or constitution. But practice defies legal regulations. The circle of those admitted was in fact still a narrow one,

and the requirements as to birth and belief, never clearly
stated, were well understood in official circles.

Young Stresemann had had to travel a long way. He had
grown up in a public house in the heart of old Berlin. His
father and grandfathers had been *petits bourgeois* of moderate
means, men of narrow ideas who could think of nothing
except their scanty livelihood and who shared in the flat
dullness that lies rooted in the unbroken plains of the
Marches, in the hideous barrenness of the towns, in the
whole Prussian character. No cathedrals, no running
streams, no green hills helped to lift his youthful spirits.
His craving for romanticism had to be met by books.

Satisfaction at the restoration of Germany's world power
was the keynote of the intellectual life of the times, and even
the schools did everything to strike the same chord. But
while this tendency in education brought up the sons of the
ruling caste to fix their thoughts on nothing higher than a
successful public career along the usual groove and to
attach a little more importance to " correctness," turning
them into very suave, determined and polished young
people, entirely without feeling and regarding sensibilities
as an obstacle to success, it filled the studious boy who sat
in the little parlour behind the bar with a burning interest
in Germany's past and with great visions of the glory of
the Reich, the earth that his children were to inherit. As
a young man he was an enthusiastic follower of the parson-
politician, Friedrich Naumann, the " people's imperialist,"
who tried to win the working classes for a programme of
Weltpolitik and naval construction.

We see him appearing in public for the first time as,
with two companions, flaunting the bright caps of the
students' corps to which they belonged, he laid a wreath
on the graves of the martyrs of the " March Days," the
victims of the street fighting in the Year of the Revolution,
1848. The police, whose duty it was to keep a sharp
watch on workers' demonstrations at this spot, looked on
with astonishment as the young undergraduates lingered
round so unlikely a place. The year 1848 had seen the
revolt against the despotic military absolutism of the King
of Prussia, and now the first public act of faith performed
by this shy, unathletic boy was dedicated to the citizens and

workers who had been trampled down by the Prussian
Guards. But they had been more than this : they had
been the first soldiers in the fight for a strong and united
Germany. We cannot tell with certainty for whom the
young student made his demonstration, whether for the
rebels against a petty tyranny or for the forerunners of
German unity.

It is not easy for a stranger to realise that in Germany
there exist two kinds of imperialism, one cherished by
liberals and democrats, the other by militarists and Junkers.
Germans themselves sometimes fail to see the line that
divides them. Nevertheless, there is here a clear and
ineradicable difference, as well as a separate historical
tradition.

Frederick the Great and William I rank with the conservatives, while the liberals can lay claim to Freiherr vom
Stein and the members of the National Assembly of 1848.
The older official class look on subordination and the
division of the nation into master and man as the prime
necessity, while the leaders of the newer trends of thought
prefer equality before the law, self-determination and free
expression of public opinion. The former are agrarians,
the latter industrialists ; these militaristic, the others
academic ; the first German in the narrow sense and
Prussian, the second German in the wider sense, that is,
South German and Austrian.

Problems that bring the two schools of thought out into
the open always arise sooner or later. Under the Republic
the desire for the *Anschluss* with Austria was given expression by the liberals, led by Paul Löbe, the Social-Democratic
President of the Reichstag. The conservatives thought it
more important to win back the Polish Corridor, Schleswig,
Upper Silesia and Alsace-Lorraine and to rebuild the Reich
as it had existed under the Hohenzollerns. What was
Austria to them ? What prospects of conquest did she
offer ? They were more concerned to bend foreign powers
to their will than to unify the German world. They
preferred to leave Austria outside the gates. The Austrians
were too individualistic for them, too soft, far too little
given to militarism. It was hard enough to make the
Bavarians toe the line. On the far side of the Inn there is

no " human material " that can be adapted to Prussian methods.

The two kinds of German nationalism have to be considered, too, without relation to territorial questions. The conservatives want a strong army, because they regard the maintenance of power, internally as well as abroad, as a matter of principle ; and they refuse to acknowledge defeat. The honour of arms must be restored. The liberals, on the other hand, strive for a strong policy in home affairs. They look for their appeal and glamour to literature and the arts, to scientific and technical achievement. Full harmony between all citizens seems to them to be Germany's best protection.

The conservatives are pessimists. They hold that nothing is secure unless defended by rifles and cannon.

The liberals are optimists. They believe in the power of ideas.

Sometimes the two currents merge, and then only those who know Germany's national complexities most intimately can tell one from the other. This is the case in time of war, when in Germany, as in all other countries, the much vaunted " unity of the nation " comes true.

Stresemann's camp was that of the liberal imperialists. He had agitated untiringly for a large fleet and the acquisition of colonies. After all, the first act of the 1848 Parliament had been to order warships flying the black, red and gold flag, to the unspeakable horror of the old Prussians. Stresemann aimed at cosmopolitanism, the expansion of world trade, the securing of sources for raw materials and of new markets. His political convictions coincided with his profession, for he was at that time on the board of the " Industrialists' Union," which represented the interests of the manufactured goods industry and the export trade. In Parliament he was fond of attacking the feudal forces in diplomacy that showed no comprehension for the world of commerce.

But in war there can be no question of a divided imperialist camp ; the only thing that matters is victory over the enemy. There was a rationalist party in opposition that did not believe that Germany would defeat the whole world. It was a picturesque group and counted the German Crown

Prince among its members. Stresemann in no sense belonged to it. He was a keen admirer of Ludendorff and a bitter opponent of the defeatist, of the weak in faith who had doubts about "ultimate victory." As late as the summer of 1918, when many clearly enough foresaw the inevitable end, he travelled up and down the country whipping up the nation's spirits and cursing everyone who did not share his faith.

The disappointment he experienced when Germany collapsed was all the more terrible. It came over him in stages. The first occasion was when it was announced in parliamentary circles that the manufacture of munitions was far behind that of the Western Powers, and an officer attached to the War Department shrugged his shoulders and said : "Yes, if only we had a Lloyd George !" The second time was when the Supreme Command asked for the Armistice. The third when, years later, Helfferich, who had been Vice-Chancellor during the war, made it clear to him that the submarine war had been begun without preparation and without prospect of success. Each of these events made a deep and lasting impression on him and shook a belief that is firmly rooted in the hearts of nearly all Germans—his confidence in the Prusso-German military command. A German may be an anti-militarist on principle and loathe the officer caste, but he rarely doubts the infallibility of the General Staff. A series of successful campaigns—the Silesian wars of Frederick the Great, the Wars of Liberation in 1813, the wars against Denmark in 1864, against Austria in 1866, against France in 1870-71—had surrounded the army commanders with a divine nimbus.

His loss of this belief marked an important stage in Stresemann's development. He said later that he had thought the German army invincible. "It was an unheard of disappointment that we had to admit ourselves beaten by the English and Americans, who are mere amateurs at warfare." It was not the opinion of Mirabeau alone that war is Prussia's real industry. This is what the Prussians themselves have always learnt and taught in their schools. Stresemann was inclined to listen to popular catchwords, but he never lent credence to the slanderous legend of the "stab in the back" which served to defame the Social-

Democratic party. That the generals and admirals alike
had failed to have an adequate number of shells manufactured, that they had not had submarines built in time,
that they had refused to listen to any talk of tanks, that they
had countenanced the shady practices of war profiteers, that
they had given assurances that America's support of the
Entente would be valueless, that victory had been promised
even after all was lost—these were realisations that greatly
influenced and advanced Stresemann's development. Advanced, because the collapse of his belief in the traditional
authorities strengthened his belief in himself. To believe
in himself and to believe in democracy—that was one and the
same thing for the politician of a middle-class party. The
antithesis did not at that time present itself in different
terms. After the failure of the upper classes and of the
system under which Germany had formerly flourished, only
democracy, which had been victorious in the war, could take
their place. At first, the fall of the gods whom he had
unquestioningly worshipped plunged Stresemann in profound depression. But afterwards it served to deepen and
extend his self-reliance. He felt that he would have
succeeded where they had failed. " He is so certain of his
own strength that he thinks nothing impossible," Lord
d'Abernon writes in his diary on another occasion.

When Sir Austen Chamberlain was about to meet
Stresemann for the first time, he was warned : " There's
your real Junker ! " The bull neck, the bald round head,
the small eyes, the powerful shoulders—these he had ;
but the warning was unjust. The Junker looks different,
firmer in his carriage, at once smoother and more sinister,
less lively in expression and slower in perception. Moreover, he is not an admirer of Napoleon nor a tireless reader
of Goethe, as Stresemann was all his life. We need only
recall his politics as a young man. No Junker ever thought
of the revolutionaries of 1848 except as rebels steeped
in shame who, worked up by Jews and Poles, sinned against
the God of Prussia.

Nor was Stresemann ever accepted by the Junkers.
They looked on him as an upstart, as an ambitious inter-
loper without legitimate claims to office. Many persons
at that time appeared in high positions who clearly had no

business to be there. But this man not only forced himself to the fore, but settled down and succeeded. He would not allow himself to be overawed. He was no Junker; that might pass in such troubled times. But he felt himself the equal and even the superior of the Junkers; that was dangerous. Behind his back the Junkers' animosity towards him was very pointedly expressed.

During the war the line that separated liberal from conservative imperialism was barely distinguishable. But fate placed Stresemann at a cross-roads where the two branches diverged sharply, where one led to the right, the other to the left, that of the pessimists to fatalistic self-destruction, that of the optimists to courageous reforms.

It is conceivable that events might have taken another course and that Stresemann might never have helped to accentuate this difference. We can imagine him as a man twenty years older, a typical liberal leader, an amiable *frondeur* occasionally asking for a few official posts for members of his party, indulging in mild polemics against the reactionary agrarians, but in other respects a faithful ally of the conservatives, agreeing to the demand for new army corps and sleeping soundly only as long as Germany is the strongest military power on the continent.

Fate gave him a position where a distinction that at times seemed little more than a difference of accent became a deep rift. When in autumn, 1918, the country veered round to new ideas, the democratic party broke with Stresemann, as a man who had compromised himself, a whole-hogger, a submarine enthusiast, " one of Ludendorff's young men." Embittered at his rejection by a party that was re-shaping liberalism, he moved once again towards the right. Overnight he founded a new party, the *Deutsche Volkspartei*. For five years longer he remained in opposition. He did not take up the reins of government until the last attempt of the " unyielding front " and of unconditional resistance had failed. " The continuation of the war with other weapons " was Stresemann's name for the Ruhr struggle. Germany had lost the war a second time. The condition of the country was far worse than in 1918. Production was completely disorganised, agriculture was sabotaged, separatists were agitating in the west, there was rebellion in Bavaria, Communists were taking up arms in Saxony and Thuringia, the Black Reichswehr was rising in the Mark, Hitler was organising his first *Putsch* in Munich. And worst of all, the *danse macabre* of the paper millions. Germany had lost her most important, most productive and most tenacious class ; the educated middle classes were dispossessed and pauperised.

The heroes of history are victorious generals and the statesmen who have made victory possible for them. But it can be a more heroic task to deal with a defeat for which others are responsible. That was Stresemann's task. He did not hesitate, he did not look for excuses, he did not involve the Reich in new adventures ; he took the straight path which was traced out for him by his predecessors' mistakes. He put an end to the fighting and turned from war to politics.

Directly after the armistice on the Ruhr Stresemann began preliminary negotiations for a real peace. There followed the London conference, Locarno (which will give its name to this phase in European history), Germany's entry into the League of Nations, the luncheon at Thoiry, the Dawes Agreement, the Kellogg Pact, the Young Plan, the conference at The Hague, the evacuation of the Rhineland. The last of these Stresemann only foresaw in spirit. He did not live to see the victory he had won in the good fight for peace.

The last foreign soldier had left German soil, the reparations payments went on, the Reich was on the best of terms with the Great Powers that had defeated it, world trade again began to flourish. It was a great moment, not only for Germany but for Europe, a time on which to-day, five years after, we can only look back with envy.

Stresemann was the first man of the middle class to achieve solid political results for Germany. It would be absurd to imagine that he was the only German citizen to show such understanding. There were not a few who shared it. But before his time, and once more after his death, they were without a leader. He alone had had the courage of his convictions.

Bismarck once said that the Germans lacked " civil courage." This judgment reveals deep insight into the

German character. They had for too long had every step prescribed for them by the Prussian autocracy. Sometimes they were granted the right of free criticism. But they had never been given the chance of gaining self-confidence, of exercising responsibility, of summoning up the courage to carry their ideas into practice. The main virtue of democracy, that of independent decision, they were never allowed to practise. This is true above all of the Prussians, the Junkers and those brought up under the Junker hegemony. When a new despotism arose in Germany, it was the work of foreigners : Hitler and his friends came from every corner of Europe to revive the old Prussian tyranny.

The highbrows smiled pityingly at Stresemann's enthusiasm for Goethe : it was not sufficiently literary and polished for them. Perhaps they were right. But the vitality of Goethe's influence on Stresemann the statesman was manifest when he appeared for the last time before the European public. In his farewell speech at Geneva in September, 1929, one month before his death, he spoke of the union of the countries of Europe that he believed would be realised in the near future. "All great ideas seem mad at first," he quoted. And then : "Why has Europe no European currency and no European postage stamps ? " These are ideas that Germany owes to Goethe. The words are almost the same as those Stresemann quoted a few years before in a lecture on Goethe's German policy : "Germany shall be one country, and the German *Thaler* and *Groschen* shall have the same value in the whole Reich. One country, and my trunk shall pass unopened through all thirty-six states. . . . Germany shall have one weight and one measure, one trade and traffic, and uniformity in all things."

A coincidence that is no accident has made it impossible for us to overlook the source of the liberal imperialism to which Stresemann adhered. When Freiherr vom Stein, who in Goethe's day organised Prussia's resistance to Napoleon, said "I know only one Fatherland, and that is Germany," he meant that Prussia was for him an obsolete concept. And immediately afterwards he mentioned a league of European nations that a later age would have the good fortune to see.

Stresemann was an isolated figure among his social equals, among his own countrymen, in his whole environment. Not in his ideas, which were part and parcel of Germany's heritage of all times, shared by thousands of good Europeans in Germany. He was alone in his self-confidence, in his independence of traditional forces, in the bravery that Bismarck called civil courage.

He had long been ill. He was sensitive and thin-skinned. The attacks on him grew in severity and made his condition worse from day to day. His influence in his own party vanished ; they could no longer be moved by persuasion and became more and more difficult to carry along.

The overwhelming majority of the *bourgeoisie*, distrusting their own strength, were assailed by an ever stronger urge to seek refuge in the old militaristic forces. The flow of liberal imperialism was too meagre ; it dried up among the pebbles of fear and pessimism and worship of force. Germany was actually winning back her old position and greatness, making its weight felt in the centre of Europe, protecting German minorities in other countries. But conquest—without arms ? The conservatives would not stand for this. A proverb that has profoundly affected the character of the German *bourgeoisie* runs : " The pen destroys what the sword has won." And was the pen now to make good what the sword had destroyed ? Impossible ! This ran counter to all the old moral ideas of Prussian Germany. Politics in place of war ? No, they would rather have war, even if for the time being it had to be a bloodless war.

Stresemann's last plan, of which he spoke with enthusiasm, was to travel the length and breadth of Germany, and in a great campaign to win back the German people to his side. It is impossible to prophesy for the past and to say how the fate of Germany and Europe would have fallen out, had he lived, had he defended himself and the peace of Europe and democracy. It is certain that his temperament, his sincerity, his self-assurance would not have been without influence.

He had scarcely closed his eyes before the reaction set in ; all who had unwillingly and despite themselves bowed to his will breathed freely again. At this time the two

German flags had become symbols. Stresemann had in
his later years spoken in public only when the black, red
and gold colours decorated the hall. His party held their
memorial service for him under the black, white and red
flag. It became a matter almost of indifference who took
over the Ministry or who was in charge of foreign affairs.
It was the government offices that framed policy, not the
politicians. The officials wrested back their old authority,
the generals again began to make demands ; democracy
had not the courage to put them in their place. Stresemann
had been an isolated figure and he had not laid lasting
foundations. The same chairs were occupied by the same
men as before his time ; the same principles, the same
traditions, the same authorities that had for centuries
ruled in the same halls were welcomed back again.

The same fear of invasion, the same distrust, the same
belief in force, the same pessimism reigned.

Barely three years after the evacuation of the Rhineland,
the President of the Reich summoned Hitler to the
Chancellorship. The German Government announced
its programme of re-armament. That moment saw the
death of German democracy.

JOSEPH STURGE

1793–1859

by STEPHEN HOBHOUSE

JOSEPH STURGE

1793–1859

by STEPHEN HOBHOUSE

I

THE name at the head of this chapter will be unfamiliar, indeed probably unknown, to many readers of this volume. Nevertheless, the influence of Joseph Sturge was far-reaching and at times perhaps decisive in more than one field of social and democratic endeavour—adult suffrage, international peace, and the liberation of the slave. It is by no means always the men whose names are conspicuous on the pages of history, who deserve the greatest credit for creating the spiritual atmosphere which makes the improvement of social conditions possible. Sturge's rugged figure stands out from early Victorian days as one of the strongest representatives of the evangelical fervour to which modern England owes so much.

Joseph Sturge was born during the period of the French Revolution in a Gloucestershire farmhouse. Both his parents came of a healthy stock of yeomen and farmers who had been Quakers from the seventeenth century. Up to the age of ten he lived a happy open-air life with his brothers and sisters, and only attended school between ten and fourteen. For the next seven years he worked on the farm under his father's skilled guidance. He thus laid the foundations of a sound constitution which carried him through long periods of incessant and often harassing activity without serious illness until he was well over sixty. He was a powerful, broad-shouldered man of intense energy and vitality, and to the end of his life a lover of children and animals, of the pleasures of his garden, and of horsemanship. In spite of his slender education he became a competent, though not a brilliant public speaker and writer, as well as an expert merchant. He was a constant student of the New Testament, and in later life he read few other books save those that had a direct bearing on his public interests.

At the age of twenty-one Sturge set up in trade as a corn-

factor at Bewdley, in Worcestershire, and thence removed
to Birmingham, where the corn-dealing business of the
brothers Joseph and Charles Sturge, in spite of periods of
serious losses, grew to great prosperity. Thus was Joseph
enabled to devote large amounts of money and time to
public interests, and he had, like his friend John Bright, the
inestimable advantage of a sympathetic brother who was
willing to liberate him very largely from the conduct of
his business. For many years too, both before and after
the early death of his first wife, he lived with a sister who
was in full sympathy with his political activities.

Sturge was generally loved and honoured by those
whom he employed. There were many instances of his
extreme conscientiousness in business. He was a generous
friend and a patron of many good causes. " Have you a
California of your own," wrote Cobden to him, " or is the
miracle of the widow's cruse performed by you in sovereigns
instead of oil, or how do you contrive to give away five
times more than other people, and still keep up your credit
in Mark Lane ? "

It is impossible to appreciate correctly the career of this
democrat without some understanding of the peculiar
character of the religious community in which he was
nurtured, and to which, in spite of his wide political
associations, he remained devoted throughout his life.

The religious Society of Friends (as the Quakers call
themselves) had been originally dominated in the seventeenth century by an intense missionary enthusiasm. But
when persecution ceased and their thrift and honesty
brought them wealth, they gradually crystallised into an
almost closed community of birthright members centring
round a nucleus of quiet, devout traditionalists, whose
chief care was to keep pure the fountains of inward piety
and to maintain the various Quaker testimonies directed
against military service and the taking of oaths, against
the paid ministry and " priests' demands," or against
music and other diversions. Most Friends used the " plain
language " (" thou and thee ") and many wore (as Sturge
always did) the " plain dress," this meaning in the case of
the men a collarless coat of sober hue and a broad-brimmed
hat.

From the time of Fox and Penn onwards many of the
Friends have always been alive to the need of social reform,
a concern which was a necessary (though not always recognised) outcome of their central doctrine of the " Inner
Light," or the divine principle in every man. Nevertheless during the eighteenth century work for social reform
and even philanthropy was regarded with hesitation by
the Society as a whole, if it meant co-operation with others
outside their own borders. Participation in politics was
definitely discouraged. Towards the close of the century
a partial exception to this non-political principle was made
in the case of the anti-slavery movement; and the door
thus opened was gradually and in spite of much opposition
in the Society made wider during the first half of the
nineteenth century by the conversion of many Friends
to the evangelical enthusiasm, which was revivifying the
other religious bodies. The larger spirits of that time,
like Elizabeth Fry, Joseph Pease, the first Quaker M.P.,
and Joseph Sturge, were able in a remarkable way to combine
a constant fervour for the spread of Christianity and for
social reform with a faithful observance of the old traditions
and testimonies, and a practice of inward retirement and
meditation which enabled them to preserve a spirit of
goodwill and serenity in the midst of the storms of
controversy.

Sturge is described by his contemporaries as a man of
inflexible will, when once his determination was formed,
and of a restless activity of mind and body. Cobden said
that he was equal in energy to any three men that he had
ever known. Yet he left upon his associates the impression
of an unfailing serenity of soul, which was especially marked
in times of discouragement. " It is always a comfort,"
wrote one of them, " to see Joseph Sturge's face, ever so
full of benignity and hopefulness. It is always a cordial
to meet him, he is so full of gentleness, courage, and hope."
Sturge's mind was not one of a diplomatic cast that foresees
difficulties and tries to overcome them by pulling wires and
making concessions. His strength lay in his undeviating
aims and in the intense moral convictions, resting on his
Christian faith, that drove him on in unwearied efforts.
Those who disagreed with him often thought him obstinate,

extreme, and unpractical, though more than once the issue proved him right.

He was not an eloquent speaker, but he could state his case clearly and convincingly before the largest audiences, and had a singular power of impressing them with a sense of his perfect sincerity and courage. He was a good organiser and indefatigable as a travelling missionary for his cause.

II

Apart from one important period of some two years, when he concentrated his efforts upon the reform of the franchise, the two great causes into which Sturge threw himself wholeheartedly during middle and later life were the liberation of the negro slave and the struggle against war. As a young man he took the lead in organising a new branch of the Bible Society, and afterwards one of the Peace Society, founded by a few enthusiasts shortly after Waterloo. Later on he became Secretary of the influential Birmingham Anti-Slavery Society, soon after the emergence of the national movement from the partial eclipse which had overtaken it since the abolition of the slave trade in 1807.

In the campaign which led up to this achievement a leading part had been taken by the Quakers, who had already by about 1763 (and by 1784 in America), through the labours of John Woolman and others, cleared their own body of all complicity in slave-owning. In the attack upon slave-owning (as distinct from slave-trading) it was upon Fowell Buxton especially in Parliament that the mantle of the aged Wilberforce had fallen ; in the country Sturge and his future father-in-law, James Cropper of Liverpool, were among the first and most prominent of the leaders to insist that emancipation should be both immediate and complete.

The anti-slavery movement, from about the year 1825, was in effect (apart from O'Connell's Catholic agitation in Ireland) the first organised campaign for a political object in these islands. It served in some respects as a model for the more systematic agitation of the Anti-Corn-Law League. Before 1832 no statesman of the front rank, except O'Connell and the erratic Lord Brougham, supported

Negro emancipation. But the demand in the country was becoming so insistent that the first Ministry of the reformed Parliament was compelled to bring forward a measure to effect it. Not however in a form satisfactory to abolitionists of the type of Sturge. They thought that it was to the slaves rather than to their masters that compensation was due and were deeply distrustful of the seven years' " apprenticeship " which was to act as a transition to freedom.

When the Emancipation Act of 1834 was passed, Buxton and almost all the other leaders accepted the position and refused to consider the question of shortening the apprenticeship. Not so Joseph Sturge. With a Quaker companion he went off to the West Indies and brought back a volume of convincing evidence which showed the innumerable injustices and cruelties which were being inflicted on the Negro " apprentices " and the risk of the transition period being used to forge a system of coercion which would retain them in a servile status.

In this second campaign, which was looked at askance by the old leaders, Sturge was the inspiring and guiding personality. He addressed crowded audiences in all parts of the country and was examined at great length by a House of Commons committee (of which the young Gladstone, as son of a leading slave-holder, was a member). Petitions bearing more than a million signatures were presented to Parliament and the crusade compelled the Whig Ministry and the West Indian legislatures reluctantly to yield. On the 1st of August, 1838, legal slavery in the British colonies finally ceased.

This was the great achievement of Sturge's life. Buxton generously confessed his error of judgment. O'Connell wrote to Sturge that, if it had not been for his efforts, it was " clear beyond any doubt " that at the very least " two years of more and more aggravated cruelty " would have been inflicted on over half a million Negroes. And Brougham told Cobden soon afterwards that Joseph Sturge, by his West Indian journey and the resulting campaign, " won the game off his own bat."

If only as one of the chief organisers and spokesmen of the first nation-wide and successful democratic campaign for an entirely worthy objective, Sturge deserves a niche in the temple of history.

III

In one phase of the British artisan's long struggle to win the vote Sturge also took an important part. Here he had to face the strong disapproval of the majority of his own friends and intimates reared in the traditions of the Quaker body to which reference has been made. " We trust Friends may desire ever to be found of those who are quiet in the land " was the rebuke implicitly directed against Joseph Sturge and John Bright by the Friends' " Yearly Meeting " in the agitating year 1843. Had not the " infidel " Tom Paine been a renegade Quaker, and was he not the author of the *Age of Reason* as well as of the *Rights of Man* ? Eleven years earlier Sturge had been driven to justify himself publicly before his fellow Quakers for joining the Birmingham Political Union, which played so large a part in securing the passing of the Reform Bill. He took part also, both passively and actively, in the fight against the compulsory Church-rate (which was successful in Birmingham at a comparatively early date). As one of the first directors of the London and Birmingham railway he led a campaign against the Sunday employment of the staff, by no means as a narrow Sabbatarian, but because he considered that every workman needed a day on which he could secure rest and refreshment and see something of his family. Both the efforts last mentioned were essentially outcomes of Sturge's faith in democracy.

Sturge was in 1838 made an alderman of the newly-incorporated borough of Birmingham and it was then that he became drawn into sympathy with the movement for a democratic suffrage which was sweeping across industrial Britain. Very soon divergence began to manifest itself between the " physical force " Chartists under Feargus O'Connor's fiery leadership and the apostles of moral force, of whom several of the finest, Collins, Lovett, O'Brien, O'Neill, and Vincent, were connected with Birmingham.*

* Studies of O'Connor, Lovett, O'Brien, and other leaders, together with a survey of the whole Chartist Movement, will be found in the chapter by Alfred Plummer on pages 161–190 of this volume.

The town was selected for the Chartist National Convention and the magistrates in alarm imported one hundred of the new Metropolitan police. Their provocative and brutal conduct created more disorder than it allayed. Alderman Sturge was often present among the excited crowds in the Bull Ring, attempting with varying success to counter the incitements to violence. He took the lead in petitioning for a reprieve of the death sentences inflicted on some of the rioters ; he was chairman of an investigating committee of the Town Council which censured the conduct of the police, and he headed the opposition to the measure by which the Government for a time compelled the citizens of Birmingham to maintain police, armed with cutlasses, over whom they had no control.

Meanwhile Sturge had been led to the conclusion that the agitation for the six points of the People's Charter, if it could be divorced from the threats of violence of some of its advocates, was one worthy of his whole-hearted support. This was the time when Cobden and Bright were setting on foot the anti-corn-law campaign. Cobden, an intimate friend and admirer of Sturge, made every effort to secure the co-operation and experience of the anti-slavery veteran for his new League. We have his testimony that Sturge's influence was decisive in securing the adoption of " total and immediate repeal " as the principle of the League and in basing its successful seven years' activities " on the rock of abstract truth and justice."

But Sturge felt that the first necessity for the improvement of the miserable condition of the working classes was to obtain for the people " a just and permanent control over their own affairs." Thus it was that in November, 1841, at a gathering of anti-corn-law delegates and others in Manchester, with the Radical master-tailor, Francis Place, in the chair, the " Complete Suffrage Union " was formed. The Union had a remarkable, though meteoric career of not much more than a year, before it entered upon a rapid decline. Branches were formed in forty or fifty of the big towns. The six points of the Charter were advocated in all but name, and the Union endeavoured to unite upon a common platform both middle class and working class citizens, and to draw them away from the

w

temptations of the "physical force" propaganda. For a time even O'Connor and his associates appeared to be tamed. Sturge was indefatigable in his efforts, the prophet and the pivot of the movement. As its representative he only just failed, after a by-election campaign that was unprecedented—on his side—for its "purity," to persuade the middle class electors of the corrupt borough of Nottingham to reject in his favour a strong Whig candidate.

But at this moment a wave of chaotic strikes and rioting spread over the country. Feargus O'Connor's disruptive leadership reasserted itself. Most of the other working class leaders fell away from the Complete Suffrage Union. Many of its members were diverted into the anti-corn-law agitation. The movement split on the question of adopting the Charter in name as well as in substance. Sturge's efforts at reconciliation were of no avail. He had sorrowfully to admit that he had failed in his attempt to unite in the cause of democracy the middle class progressive and the thoughtful working man.

Yet there is good evidence that many of the seeds sown by Sturge during 1841–3 bore fruit. Some of the men (and especially several who suffered imprisonment for their faith) who best served the cause of the people in after years came under his influence. The closing months of his life were brightened by the election campaign of his friend and fellow Quaker, John Bright, who was triumphantly chosen as Birmingham's M.P. in 1859 on a programme in the forefront of which was franchise reform.

Henry Vincent, the "Chartist Demosthenes," was one of the popular leaders, whose arrest in 1839 had led to something like civil war. These are his words written some twenty years later :

"The suffrage movement of which Joseph Sturge was the soul did good in everything. It brought about a better feeling between the middle and working classes and allayed the fierce exasperation of the people, by proving that men of Christian character were willing to risk popularity with the wealthy and powerful in their desire to serve them. It pushed men of high character into prominence. It raised many in sobriety by its moral appeals . . . Many men there are, whom I need not name, now living useful lives, who may be called Joseph Sturge's political children."

It is relevant to this tribute of Vincent's to add here that Sturge was one of the founders of the modern Adult School movement which developed mainly under Quaker leadership. He started in his own town " First-Day " Schools for men and women, where they learned to read and write and study the Bible.* To the end of his life he himself, wherever possible, presided at the seven o'clock Sunday breakfast for men teachers and opened the School, often characteristically choosing a Scripture reading from either Romans XII or 1st Corinthians XIII.

The spread of popular education, in this and in other fields, was promoted by Sturge as his contribution to democracy as well as to Christianity. The same twofold motive underlay his constant enthusiasm for the cause of total abstinence.

For Joseph Sturge's democratic convictions were rooted in his Christian faith. He believed wholeheartedly in the essential equality of all men, of whatever class or race ; that all are of equal, that is of infinite value, in the sight of God, their Creator, and of Christ, their Redeemer. To the objection that extension of the franchise was wrong, in that it gave votes to the ignorant and vicious, he would reply, " No, that is not God's method ; for God first gives the privileges of a son to them that are ignorant and out of the way, and after that comes all the training that fits them for their high vocation " ; and he would have added that it was not only among the poor that ignorance and vice were to be found.

IV

Amid the recurrent phases of Sturge's activities, political, civic, educational, pacifist, faithfulness to the cause of the oppressed Negro was the most persistent. It took many forms. There was the promotion of the welfare of the liberated West Indians, some of whom adopted the " Sturge " hat with a broad brim in honour of their benefactor. There were the protests against the

---

* Sturge seems to have founded his schools largely as the result of a visit to the " Shakesperean School " conducted at Leicester by the Chartist, Thomas Cooper. (See page 179 of this volume.)

use of armed cruisers to hinder the export of African slaves to America—a matter in which the pacifist Sturge had another painful difference with his old ally, Fowell Buxton. There were the deputations to foreign Governments that still allowed slavery. And the Quaker-Chartist was a strange figure in the Paris of 1848 presenting a congratulatory address to the poet Lamartine, at that time Foreign Minister of the revolutionary Government that had just abolished both capital punishment and colonial slavery. Above all there was the stimulation of the fluctuating anti-slavery movement in the United States.

After the World Anti-Slavery Convention of 1840 (in which we unfortunately find Sturge opposing the admission of *women* delegates) he secured the company of the poet Whittier on a tour of the Northern States. Their principal aim was to stir up the American Quakers (who had indeed long ceased to hold slaves themselves) to abandon their widespread attitude of indifference to or disapproval of any vigorous prosecution of the abolitionist cause. A characteristic incident was the personal appeal which Sturge addressed to a large Baltimore slave-dealer whose establishment he had inspected.

The chief anti-slavery preoccupation of Sturge's later years was the " free labour " movement. It was a heroic, though not directly successful, attempt to make slavery unprofitable by increasing both the production and the consumption of free-labour produce, sugar, rice, coffee, tobacco, and particularly Indian cotton, in substitution for the slave-grown American material. Here he had the co-operation of John Bright, himself a cotton-mill owner. So great was their zeal for the cause that in many Quaker and Evangelical families there was an almost complete abstention from the use of articles tainted with the " sin of oppression," although free-labour substitutes were often either scarce or unsatisfactory. In this respect the Sturge household was very strict.

Sturge's zeal for Negro emancipation is not open to the same criticism as was that of many of his fellow abolitionists. For, as we have seen, unlike most of that party he also strove valiantly for the greater freedom of the British worker. Moreover it is right to regard the liberation of the Negro slave as a blow struck against the imposition of more servile conditions at home. If the capitalists of Europe and America had succeeded in frustrating the anti-slavery movement, the slave system would in all probability have spread like a plague all round the tropics and, combining with an intensification of servile industrialism in Europe and Northern America, might have revived the economic conditions of the Roman Empire with the added horrors entailed by the scientific developments of industry. In this way the abolitionist party were true servants of British democracy.

V

Yet another leading strand that ran through the crowded web of Sturge's life was his hatred of war in all its manifestations. Though he was ready enough to promote the effectiveness of the Peace Society and of International peace conventions, he was much more than a talking pacifist.

Joseph Sturge as a young man suffering the distraint of his sheep rather than find a substitute for the militia ; Alderman Sturge in middle life remonstrating with would-be rioters at a tumultuous Chartist demonstration ; or losing his watch in an attempt to stop a prize fight and refusing to prosecute the thief ; or again chafing at the sight in his garden of a policeman with a sabre and withholding his rates, since they went to the support of such armed police —these incidents prepare us for the remarkable interventions into European political conflicts of the same unyielding lover of peace.

The first of these was an episode which in its more modern guise reminds one of Froissart's attractive picture of the peace-making French Cardinal on the eve of the battle of Poitiers trotting to and fro on his palfrey between the marshalled antagonists. During the third of the World Peace Congresses (at Frankfurt in 1850) war was going on between Denmark and the Duchies of Schleswig-Holstein. Sturge felt a strong Quaker " concern " to go with two companions and endeavour to persuade the opposing Governments to cease fighting and submit their differences to arbitration. After surmounting many obstacles they were more than once received courteously by the leading

Ministers on both sides, and it seemed probable that a
reasonable settlement through neutral arbitrators would
reward their efforts, when the Great Powers stepped in
with results that were ultimately disastrous. " By your
startling expedition," wrote Cobden, " you have done good
service in breaking down the flimsy veil with which the
diplomatists of the world try to conceal their shallow craft
and in penetrating into their mysterious domain."

Four years later the scoffers had a still greater opportunity
to hold up to ridicule the irrepressible Quaker. In the
tense days immediately preceding the Crimean War the
small Quaker body was deeply disturbed over the situation,
and mindful of the interest in their religious practices
shown by several of the Russian Czars they made an attempt
to move Nicholas I in the direction of conciliation. Sturge
and two others volunteered to go. A fortnight's journey
by rail, carriage, and sledge amid the rigours of a German
and Russian winter was no light thing for a man of sixty.
They reached St. Petersburg and were courteously received
by the Czar and members of his family. The English
newspapers, after being surprised into something like
admiration, covered the outrageous pacifists with ridicule
and invective, and at least one historian, without a shred
of evidence, asserted that the visit of the three Quakers
helped to precipitate the outbreak of hostilities.

During the conflict with Russia in the Crimea Sturge,
in common with his friends Bright and Cobden, had to
suffer the abuse which in war-time pursues all advocates
of peace. It was therefore a great happiness to him to be
able to register in the course of the year following the
war two considerable achievements in peace-making.
The first constitutes a landmark in the history of international arbitration. Lord Palmerston had given a sharp
rebuff to a deputation headed by Cobden, which urged
upon him and his Government the inclusion in the treaty
of peace of the principle of arbitration. Sturge, almost
alone, refused to be deterred. He and two others posted
off to Paris and, by influencing Lord Clarendon and the
other plenipotentiaries, they played a considerable part in
securing the protocol to the Treaty of Paris emphasising
the benefits of arbitration—a declaration, which, as

Gladstone said in the House, was " a very great triumph, and perhaps the first time that the representatives of the nations had agreed to disapprove a resort to war and assert the supremacy of reason, of justice, humanity, and religion."

Very soon after his Paris visit Sturge was in Russian Finland on a mission for the relief of war-victims that was probably the first of the kind ever organised by citizens of an enemy country. The British fleet had burnt and plundered the Finnish coastal towns, and the Quakers felt that here was both an opportunity and a duty of reparation. Inevitably Sturge once more took the lead in this enterprise. He visited the devastated districts and set up local relief committees, which were generously supplied from a British fund raised under Quaker auspices. As his American friend, Whittier, put it (in one of four poems devoted to his memory), it was his achievement

> " to build the old waste places,
> . . . and sow with England's daisies
> The moss of Finland's moors."

No sooner was he back from Russia than what Cobden described as his friend's " inexhaustible energy—he could run a dozen young men off their legs—" re-asserted itself. Facing the ordeal of again being hissed by the people of his own town, he was on the platform protesting against the new wars in Persia and China and the massacre of natives in Borneo. And amid the wild cries for vengeance which followed on the news of the Indian Mutiny he was with difficulty persuaded by anxious friends from visiting India to report on matters requiring redress.

Sturge's magnificent constitution was by now nearly worn out through years of almost incessant activity. He died of sudden heart failure, at the age of sixty-five, happy in being able to work in harness up to the end in the service of the causes that meant so much to him. One of his last tasks was a campaign of speaking in the interests of inter-national peace in the big northern towns. In one large respect he was fortunate in the occasion of his death—*felix opportunitate mortis*. For it is not difficult to imagine what would have been his feelings during the terrible

four years of war which soon afterwards broke out over
the body of the American slave, when so many of his fellow
pacifists forgot, in their enthusiasm for emancipation, the
principles of their faith.

Joseph Sturge is said to have expressed a wish to be
buried, not in the Friends' own graveyard, but in the great
borough cemetery among the nameless green mounds of
the working people. The last thing that he would have
desired would have been a memorial in Westminster
Abbey. But there is in the Abbey one inscription, in
honour of Canon Barnett, a more recent disciple of the
same Master, which would have been singularly appropriate
to the staunch old Quaker :—

> *Believing that we are all members one of another,*
> *he laboured unceasingly to unite men in the service*
> *of God, and, by his counsel and example, inspired*
> *many to seek for themselves and for the nation the*
> *things that are eternal.*

WALT WHITMAN
1819–1892
by GERALD BULLETT

WALT WHITMAN
1819–1892
by GERALD BULLETT

T HE equality of men, the root idea of democracy,
is a doctrine which superficial philosophers take
much pleasure in deriding. With dazzling wit they
ask us if we have not observed that this man is tall and that
man short, this man clever and that man stupid, this man
generous and that man mean, this man Shakespeare and
that man John Smith. One answer to this sally is to say
that equality does not imply sameness ; but perhaps a
better answer is to say that equality *does* imply sameness,
a fundamental sameness underlying superficial differences.
All circles are round, all squares are square, no matter
what their size. All water is wet, all fire is hot, and all men
are human. The Atlantic Ocean is larger and possibly
more impressive than the Round Pond in Kensington
Gardens, but it is no wetter : in size and shape they differ,
but in respect of their essential quality they are equal.
The same may be said, with equal confidence and triteness,
of Shakespeare and John Smith. To say then that all men
are equal is merely to state a truism in terms of a paradox :
it is merely a provocative and perhaps ill-advised way of
saying that all men are men. I suppose, in its historical
context, it meant, first of all, that all men are hungry :
to-day it means that all men, by virtue of their humanity,
have an equal right to civil liberty, social opportunity, and
the means of life. It is precisely this right that is being
everywhere challenged in the world to-day.

But though the democratic doctrine can be justified by
logical argument, it is not by argument that a man is persuaded of its truth. This idea of human equality is at
bottom a religious idea. It has been affirmed—by saints
rather than by politicians—in all times and places ; and
it is by intuition, not by taking thought, that men have
perceived its truth. I would say " by spiritual intuition,"
did not that seem a rather high-flown phrase for what is
after all as natural a human instinct as the instinct for
mating and parenthood. The thing is obvious common

sense, but it has to be felt to be believed. It is in the realm of the human spirit that all great events happen and all great ideas have their birth. It is possible, in the interests of a false religion (such as Nationalism or Fascism), to avert one's eyes from the plain fact of human brotherhood; but the fact stubbornly remains, and we ignore it at our peril. We are all in the same boat, and we live in the shadow of a common doom. " Carlyle," remarks Mr. Chesterton, " said that men were mostly fools. Christianity, with a surer and more reverent realism, says that they are all fools. This doctrine is sometimes called the doctrine of original sin. It may also be described as the doctrine of the equality of men. But the essential point of it is merely this, that whatever primary and far-reaching moral dangers affect any man, affect all men. All men can be criminals, if tempted; all men can be heroes, if inspired."

A little over a hundred years ago, on Paumanok or Long Island, there was born a man in whom this sense of democracy burned like a consuming flame. Biographers have conjectured that Walt Whitman was in the direct line of descent from an Elizabethan yeoman-farmer, Abijah Whitman, whose two sons in 1640 sailed west in the *True Love*. His father was Walter Whitman, carpenter and spare-time farmer; his mother was Louisa van Velsor, of Cold Spring, a few miles west of the Whitman farm, herself the daughter of Major Cornelius van Velsor, " jovial, red, stout, with sonorous voice," and Naomi Williams, a woman of Quaker stock. Whitman senior was a warm admirer of Elias Hicks, the latitudinarian preacher who was expelled from the Quaker communion, and soon after this expulsion the three of them—Walt, now ten years old, and his parents—went to hear Hicks preach in the ball-room of Morrison's Hotel on Brooklyn Heights. He preached that doctrine of Immanent Deity which, in varying form, is common to all mystical philosophies; and there can be little doubt that he made a great and permanent impression on the boy's mind. Of Walt's mother we have no intimate or vivid record. He himself tells us that as a young woman she was a daring rider; she was a good wife and a superb mother; and her death was a bereavement that shook Walt, at the age of fifty-four, to the very

foundations of his vital being. That fact alone says much
for her. " Out from these arrières of persons and scenes,"
writes Walt, in his clumsy idiom, " I was born." Continuously for his first four years, and for long periods of
his youth and early manhood, he lived in Paumanok, the
long island that stretches " east through King's, Queen's
and Suffolk counties, a hundred and twenty miles altogether.
On the ocean side the great south bay dotted with countless
hummocks, mostly small, some quite large, occasionally
long bars of sand out two hundred rods to a mile and-a-half
from the shore." He spent many an hour " on Turtle Hill
by the old lighthouse, on the extreme point, looking out
over the ceaseless roll of the Atlantic "—at the age of ten
or eleven a profound and rich experience indeed. His
schooling, in the public schools of Brooklyn town, was
homely rather than luxurious. He learned no language
but his own : it was no schoolmaster who provided him
with those scraps of French—*arrière, en masse, allons, élève,
chef-d'œuvre*—with which the style even of his major work
is disfigured. At the age of eleven he was acting as office-
boy to a firm of lawyers named Clarke, a father and two
sons ; at thirteen he began an apprenticeship in the printing
office of *The Long Island Patriot*. Later, in his home
country or in New York, he worked as compositor, as schoolmaster, as editor. He was dismissed from *The Eagle*, a
Brooklyn paper, in 1848, for failing to cut his politics to the
pattern designed by the proprietors ; and so went south,
to New Orleans, to join the staff of a new daily. A few
months later, however, for reasons not fully known, he
was back in Brooklyn, where he soon became publisher-
editor of yet another newspaper. Fortunately for us, this
enterprise was short-lived. Walt joined his father, became
a master-carpenter, and prospered in body and soul.
Released from journalism his mind now ruminated at its
abundant leisure upon his tremendous project, the book that
was to be the living microcosm of himself and America. He
had already, in New York, written sketches, stories, poems,
and a temperance novel (of all fantastic things !) called
Franklin Evans ; but these were conventional pieces, callow
and melodramatic, the green fruits of his immaturity.
Leaves of Grass, which he began writing at the age of

thirty-seven, is something either more or less than a piece
of literature. From the merely literary point of view much
can be urged against it, and too much has been claimed for
it, though Emerson told only the sober truth when he
declared that it contains " incomparable things, said incomparably well." Whitman himself put the matter in a single
sentence : " Who touches this book touches a man." Let
us see what we can make of this man.

Was Whitman original ? What is his contribution to
thought ? There have seldom lacked philosophers and
mystics eager to affirm their conviction of what, for want
of a better term, we must call divine immanence. But
Whitman differed from the philosophers in that he felt
intensely what they held intellectually, and from the general
run of religious mystics in that he accepted passionately,
voluptuously, the gross as well as the spiritual aspects of
that universal life. " I find letters from God dropt in the
street," he wrote, " and every one is sign'd by God's
name." A cloistered saint might have said no less ; but few
cloistered saints would endorse his further avowal :
" Copulation is no more rank to me than death is. . . I
believe in the flesh and the appetites." He has indeed no
use at all for the crude dualism of the puritan. " I have
said that the soul is not more than the body, and I have
said that the body is not more than the soul." And I
think he must have applauded (if he encountered it) the
suggestive aphorism of Blake : " Man has no Body distinct
from his Soul ; for that call'd Body is a portion of Soul
discern'd by the five Senses, the chief inlets of Soul in
this age." This is a doctrine that Whitman reiterates
again and again. He was in love with life, and would hear
no ill of it. Men, women, animals, birds, trees, flowers,
mountains, rivers, tram-cars, " the awl and knee-strap,
the pint measure and quart measure, the counter and stool,
the cart of the car-man, the omnibus, the ponderous dray "
—he was enamoured of them all, and nothing short of a
list of all the things in the universe would satisfy his longing
to celebrate his great passion. That is why he indulges
so riotously in mere catalogue, like a warehouse clerk gone
mad in the middle of the half-yearly stocktaking. The best
of him is perhaps to be found in *Song of Myself*, that long

rhetorical discourse to which, in his first edition, he gave pride of place. He has often been criticised, and with some justice, for egotism and arrogance ; but it was no personal arrogance that made him claim, for himself and all his kind, the august attributes of deity. He celebrates himself, and sings himself, but " what I assume you shall assume, for every atom belonging to me as good belongs to you." Again and again he strikes this note : it is the key-note of the whole. " These are really the thoughts of all men in all ages and lands, they are not original with me. If they are not yours as much as mine they are nothing, or next to nothing." And again : " All I mark as my own, you shall offset it with your own, else it were lost time listening to me." Affirming by inference his personal identity with all created things and with all created spirit, he claims not only to see the whole human drama, but to act in every part of it. He shares the hopes and fears, the ecstasies and the anguish, of every member of the cast. For him the light in which the whole material universe is bathed shines out at him from animal no less than from human eyes :

> Oxen that rattle the yoke and chain or halt in the leafy shade,
>   what is it that you express in your eyes ?
> It seems to me more than all the print I have read in my life.

And the prostitute, no less than the President holding his cabinet council, has a place in Whitman's religious communion :

> The prostitute draggles her shawl, her bonnet bobs on her
>   tipsy and pimpled neck,
> The crowd laugh at her blackguard oaths, the men jeer and
>   and wink to each other,
> (Miserable ! I do not laugh at your oaths nor jeer you).

To another of her kind he cries, in a later poem : " Not till the sun excludes you do I exclude you—Not till the waters refuse to glisten for you and the leaves to rustle for you, do my words refuse to glisten and rustle for you." He declares himself independent, standing aloof from all environing things :

> Battles, the horrors of fratricidal war, the fever of doubtful
>   news, the fitful events ;

These come to me days and nights and go from me again,
But they are not the me myself.

Apart from the pulling and hauling stands what I am,
Stands amused, complacent, compassionating, idle, unitary.

Yet he is the "caresser of life," and calls himself proudly "the mate and companion of people, all just as immortal and fathomless as myself." In spirit he visits all sorts and conditions of men, an endless diversity of scenes, understanding each, sharing the experience of each, finding in all the sweetness and clarity and eternal security that is in his own soul. The carpenter dressing his plank, the butcher boy in the market sharpening his knife, blacksmiths with grimed and hairy chests, the negro with his team of horses, the sharp-hoofed moose of the north, the cat on the house-sill, the chickadee, the prairie-dog, the pilot seizing the king-pin, the harpooner—it seems an interminable catalogue. Lists were meat and drink to Whitman, as were classical allusions to Milton. He surveys mankind from China to Peru and with the eye of a dramatist selects significant scenes; conjures up a hundred pictures, all moving pictures. He tries to sketch in his pages the scenario of the whole drama of human existence, and, tedious or not, it is all germane to his purpose. And he does, by this very profusion, demonstrate the immense range of his sympathies. It is as though he took to himself the injunction given to Caedmon of old, and sang of all created things. American as he is, and devoted to America, his is a universal vision and a universal song :

Swiftly arose and spread around me the peace and knowledge
    that pass all the argument of the earth,
And I know that the hand of God is the promise of my own,
And I know that the spirit of God is the brother of my own,
And that all the men ever born are also my brothers, and the
    women my sisters and lovers,
And that a kelson of the creation is love,
And limitless are leaves stiff or drooping in the fields,
And brown ants in the little wells beneath them,
And mossy scabs of the worm-fence, heap'd stones, elder,
    mullein and poke-weed.

Contemplating the flight of the wood-drake and the wood-duck, he says : " I believe in these winged purposes, and acknowledge red, yellow, white, playing within me . . . and do not call the tortoise unworthy because she is not something else ! " This last sentence is one that the critic of literature may profitably ponder.

Categories, moral or intellectual, are often arbitrary and sometimes vicious. Nevertheless, all advancement has been won by choosing one thing at the expense of others. If we seek to move in all directions at once we get nowhere ; if we insist that all impulses are equally valuable, we are saying in effect that all impulses are equally without value ; and when we find Whitman announcing : " I am not the poet of goodness only, I do not decline to be the poet of wickedness also," we are forced to conclude that he is expressing himself imperfectly. The remark undoubtedly means something, but it cannot mean precisely what it says. It means, perhaps, that " good " and " wicked " are terms ridiculously crude and of purely subjective content. But if that is so, why use them at all ? He continues scornfully :

What blurt is this about virtue and about vice ?
Evil propels me and reform of evil propels me, I stand indifferent,
My gait is no fault-finder's or rejecter's gait,
I moisten the roots of all that has grown.

Did you fear some scrofula out of the unflagging pregnancy ?
Did you guess the celestial laws are yet to be work'd over and
    rectified ?

The letter killeth ; the spirit maketh alive. To moisten the roots of all that has grown is to deprive oneself of daily bread by encouraging the tares to compete with the wheat. But this moralizing misses the spirit of the lines. Whitman extolled a spontaneous and abundant life, free from niggardly restrictions, not subject to footrule measurement by this or that code. But he had not always patience enough to propound his doctrine lucidly. His own truculence, his aggressiveness, got in the way of clear expression and sprinkled his work with positive defects. And yet we shall do well to accept him, gratefully, with all his imperfections. If we had the power to wish away from him the personal faults that are too faithfully reflected in his writings, we should do well not to exercise the power lest by some mischance it should strip him also of the strength, the courage, and the high vision, that are his title to fame.

And even though the singer does occasionally strike a gawky attitude or sing a false note, *Leaves of Grass* is a work of great cumulative power. " Logic and sermons never convince," cried Whitman. " The damp of the night drives deeper into my soul." And if, as the sceptic might retort, reiteration is an equally fallible instrument, Whitman's reiterations do at least convince us that he was tremendously in earnest and that he had something important to share with all who would break with him the bread of communion.

I believe a leaf of grass is no less than the journey-work of the stars,
And the pismire is equally perfect, and a grain of sand, and the
    egg of the wren,
And the tree-toad is a *chef-d'œuvre* for the highest,
And the running blackberry would adorn the parlours of heaven,
And the narrowest hinge in my hand puts to scorn all machinery,
And the cow crunching with depress'd head surpasses any statue,
And a mouse is miracle enough to stagger sextillions of infidels.

Of sentences pregnant as these he is master, when the tide of his inspiration flows strongly. " Cycles ferried my cradle," he writes, in four words expressing a vast idea and speeding the imagination on an endless voyage. " Now on this spot I stand with my robust soul." This robust soul was his gift to mankind. " I do not," he said, " give lectures or a little charity. When I give I give myself." If you are impotent, loose in the knees, he will blow grit within you, not waiting to ask who or what you are, for that is not important. " To cotton-field drudge or cleaner of privies I lean. On his right cheek I put the family kiss, and in my soul I swear I will never deny him." In lines prophetic of his years to come, when in the hospital-wards he became literally a saviour of men, he declares that to anyone dying he will bring new life, his own life. He will turn the bedclothes back, send home the physician and the priest, and seizing the dying man, raise him with resistless will. " O despairer, here is my neck. By God, you shall not go down ! hang your whole weight upon me. I dilate you with tremendous breath, I buoy you up."

We have to remember that Whitman was a mid-Victorian, a contemporary of Emerson, before we can begin to understand the storm of scurrility that greeted his book. " Muck," " obscenity," " egotism," " vulgarity," " nonsense," " bombast "—these are a few of the epithets hurled at it by godly reviewers. But he was not cast down ; he received encouragement as well as abuse ; he had unbounded confidence in himself ; and Emerson sent him a letter that would have turned the head of a far more modest man. He began a furious campaign of self-exploitation, even going so far as to write anonymous laudations of himself in the press. A second edition, issued without a publisher's imprint, by Fowler and Wells, of New York, appeared in the following year. Upon its cover gleamed the gold lettering of Whitman's culminating indelicacy : " I Greet You at the Beginning of a Great Career : R. W. Emerson." The whole of Emerson's letter was included in an appendix, together with a reply from Whitman boasting of the sales of the first edition. Mr. Bliss Perry (in *Walt Whitman : His Life and Work*) tells us that this account of the sales was mendacious, very few copies having in fact been sold. This second edition, which contained more cause of offence to the prudish, fared even worse ; for the publishers, alarmed at the outcry, withdrew it from the market. Whitman, however discouraged, was not confounded. Distinguished men of his day, among them Thoreau, visited him. " It is as if the beasts spoke," said Thoreau, of the more physiological of the poems ; but of Whitman's work as a whole he added : " It sounds to me very brave and American, after whatever deductions. I do not believe that all the sermons, so called, that have been preached in this land put together are equal to it for preaching. We ought to rejoice greatly in him." This, with Emerson's " I give you joy of your free and brave thought," must have been balm to his vanity. But vanity, though he had it, was perhaps the least of his qualities. All who met and knew the man were won by his personal charm and personal power. The distinguished men who visited him went away to write letters in his praise to other distinguished men ; and the simpler folk with whom he mostly associated regarded him, not as an author at all, but as a good fellow, remarkable only for the warmth of his affections and the depth of his understanding. He was never captured by a literary coterie : ferry pilots and omnibus drivers were always more to his mind. " Broadway Jack, Dressmaker, Balky Bill, George Storms, Old Elephant, his brother Young Elephant, Tippy, Pop Rice, Big Frank, Yellow Joe, Pete Callahan, Patsey Dee, and dozens more ; for there were hundreds. They had immense qualities, largely animal—eating, drinking, women—great personal pride, in their way—perhaps a few slouches here and there, but I should have trusted the general run of them, in their simple good-will and honour, under all circumstances. Not only for comradeship, and sometimes affection—great studies I found them also." It adds little to our picture of him to know that he became the (unmarried) father of six children and that he died in his seventy-third year.

My prose quotations are taken from *Specimen Days*, a volume of discursive autobiography which, for those who wish to know all they can discover about Whitman, is a valuable complement to *Leaves of Grass*. These straightforward reminiscences assure us that the eloquent if sometimes strident prophet was after all no doctrinaire, but a man full-blooded and brotherly, unselfconscious in his democracy and genuinely at ease with all kinds and classes. The universe, he says (in the superb piece called *I sing the Body Electric*), is a procession in which everyone has a rightful place :

The man's body is sacred and the woman's body is sacred,
No matter who it is, it is sacred—is it the meanest one in the
    laborers' gang ?
Is it one of the dull-faced immigrants just landed on the
    wharf ?
Each belongs here or anywhere just as much as the well-off,
    just as much as you,
Each has his or her place in the procession.

(All is a procession,
The universe is a procession with measured and perfect
    motion.)

Do you know so much yourself that you call the meanest
    ignorant ?

Do you suppose you have a right to a good sight, and he or
   she has no right to a sight ?
Do you think matter has cohered together from its diffuse
   float, and the soil is on the surface, and water runs and
   vegetation sprouts,
For you only, and not for him and her ?

In April, 1861, the American Civil War broke out.
Whitman had already begun to write his war-poems,
Drum Taps, before he saw the vanquished regiments
pouring into Washington after the battle of Bull Run :

The sun rises, but shines not. The men appear, at first sparsely
and shame-faced enough, then thicker, in the streets of Washington—appear in Pennsylvania Avenue, and on the steps and
basement entrances. They come along in disorderly mobs,
some in squads, stragglers, companies . . . During the forenoon
Washington gets all over motley with these defeated soldiers—
queer-looking objects, strange eyes and faces, drench'd (the
steady rain drizzles on all day) and fearfully worn, hungry,
haggard, blister'd in the feet . . . Amid the deep excitement,
crowds and motion, and desperate eagerness, it seems strange
to see many, very many, of the soldiers sleeping—in the midst
of all, sleeping sound. They drop down anywhere, on the steps
of houses, up close by the basements or fences, on the sidewalk,
aside on some vacant lot, and deeply sleep. A poor seventeen
or eighteen year old boy lies there, on the stoop of a grand house ;
he sleeps so calmly, so profoundly. Some clutch their muskets
firmly even in sleep. Some in squads ; comrades, brothers,
close together—and on them, as they lay, sulkily drips the rain.

Returning to Washington he plunged heart and soul into
the work for which nature and disposition alike had peculiarly
fitted him, the work of saving life. In the hospital wards
his superabundant vitality waged incessant war upon the
weakness around it. He spent himself generously, making
no distinction between friends and enemies. He fought a
hundred battles ; and to these battles he marched, not with
flags flying and drums beating, but silently, in his own
strength. Many years earlier he had written :

Agonies are one of my changes of garments,
I do not ask the wounded person how he feels, I myself become
   the wounded person,
My hurts turn livid upon me as I lean on a cane and observe.

And now he was to pay the price of that sensibility, being
called upon not to lose his life by sudden violence (he made
no effort to join the army) but to spend it surely day by day
in the service of a greater cause, supporting himself the
while by doing clerical work in a paymaster's office. It is a
story very apt to the occasions of our modern world. The
same problems engage us, together with others which Whitman did not live to encounter. And equally relevant to
our tragic times is the beautiful poem called *Reconciliation* :

Word over all, beautiful as the sky,
Beautiful that war and all its deeds of carnage must in time be
    utterly lost,
That the hands of the sisters Death and Night incessantly softly
    wash again, and ever again, this soil'd world ;
For my enemy is dead, a man divine as myself is dead,
I look where he lies white-faced and still in the coffin—I draw
    near,
Bend down and touch lightly with my lips the white face in the
    coffin.

Enough has been said to indicate the greatness of the
man, a greatness that was personal rather than intellectual,
and spiritual rather than literary. In the profoundest sense
of the term, Whitman was a great lover ; all his exuberant
vitality was spent in the service of a love as large as the
world. His influence is incalculable ; for no one who reads
him with understanding can fail to be vitally affected by
him. Disquieting, rough, boisterous, and cleansing, like
a wind ; intense, fierce, like a flame ; he is an elemental force.
If there is loquacity in his collected works, there is also
sublimity, " the echo of a great soul." He will always
attract his spiritual kindred, the passionate, the affectionate,
the turbulent, the preachers of an all-inclusive charity ; and
he will continue to repel the ultra-fastidious, the finicking,
those who wear in season and out the blinkers of expedient
morality. I will scatter myself, he promised—

I will scatter myself among men and women as I go,
I will toss a new gladness and roughness among them.

And he was as good as his word.

JAMES WOODROW WILSON
1856–1924
by NORMAN HAPGOOD

JAMES WOODROW WILSON
1856–1924
by NORMAN HAPGOOD

URING the year in which Lee surrendered, which
was the same year in which Lincoln was shot by
a madman, Woodrow Wilson reached nine years of
age. Both Lincoln and Lee were democrats, in the sense
of wishing power to reside in all the people and to be able
to find expression according to law, and both regretted the
belated institution of slavery. The question settled at
Appomattox, as far as it related to the nature of government,
was answered by the decision that the unit of control in the
United States was to be expressed by the adjective rather
than by the noun ; that the sovereignty of the thirteen free
colonies had been merged by the constitution in the united
government they had created.

It was in Georgia and South Carolina, both secession
states, that Wilson was a child, and his later boyhood years
were spent under the régime of reconstruction and carpet-
bagging ; under the régime, in other words, of suppression
of local initiative, control from Washington, punishment,
and general departure from that natural adaptation to the
inevitable that Lincoln had mapped out before his death.
It was the region for which the greatest of political prophets
was Thomas Jefferson, who had stressed state rights in the
struggles that ended in the compromise of the Constitution ;
Jefferson who, since that question was reduced manyfold
by the Civil War, still remains, for the country as a whole,
the foremost of political prophets.

In young Wilson's blood mathematically the most
important strain was Scotch, which was also the strain that
expressed itself from the beginning predominantly in his
character. The consistent resolve of the statesman was
harmonious with the ethical sternness of the Presbyterian
minister who was his father.

When the youth entered Princeton College, in 1875, his
course was set ; not indeed, toward action, which caused his
fame, but toward the study and elucidation of democratic

government, as practised under the American Constitution, the proper distribution of powers, and their effective use toward the general welfare. He himself sometimes would quote, as we are told by his official biographer, these lines :

> It is the generous spirit, who, when brought
> Among the tasks of real life, hath wrought
> Upon the plan that pleased his boyish thought.

Mr. Baker also gives us a glimpse of Wilson, when only sixteen, busily teaching himself shorthand while sitting at a desk under a portrait of which, to a little cousin, he explained : " That is Gladstone, the greatest statesman that ever lived. I intend to be a statesman, too."

In Princeton, where he was a student from 1875 to 1879, he continued this interest, for in the year after graduation an article by him was printed in the *University of Virginia Magazine* under the title of " Mr. Gladstone : A Character Sketch." He underscored the pages of Macaulay, Bagehot, and Green, as well as *The Federalist*. Burke and John Bright were on the list of the books to which he gave serious attention. Debating and English were always topics in which he came out well, and both lent themselves to his later triumphs, and they both were, from the beginning, used to express political principles. It was while he was still in college that he wrote an essay called *Cabinet Government in the United States*, the basis of his first book, *Congressional Government*, than which nothing he ever wrote is to-day held in higher esteem. The central idea is that the decline in American statesmanship, and in the oratory expressing it, was due to the change from fighting out decisions on the floor of Congress, as (he pointed out) was done still in England, to a deadening mechanism of committee government. And while he was writing on so high a plane he was going into the woods around Princeton to pour out the orations of Gladstone, Bright, Patrick Henry, Daniel Webster, and even Demosthenes. In an article on oratory, in the *Princetonian*, to some of these names he added Cicero, Burke, Fox, and Canning. He was elected to the highest office of the Whig Society, and he himself organized the Liberal Debating Club, of which the constitution, written by Wilson, gave to the Secretary of State far more powers and responsibilities than the American President; bills were to be presented, and the Secretary of State and his Government were to be sustained or turned out as in the British Parliament. He wrote a prize essay on Chatham, and of Green he said : " It is a grateful thought that this *History of the English People* is a history of the American people as well ; it is a high and solemn thought that we, as a lusty branch of a noble race, are by our national history adding lustre or stain to so bright an escutcheon."

Graduating, he turned to the law, which in the United States had always been the best road to politics. His studies were at the University of Virginia, founded by Thomas Jefferson, and located near his home ; yet in his sojourn there Wilson never once visited Monticello. In spite of his early surroundings, and in spite of his later emphasis on Jefferson, he then looked upon himself as something of a Federalist—as veering toward the party of Hamilton—because of his intense belief in the need of national unity. Before he left the University, however, he became President of the Jefferson Society.

Although he studied the law faithfully he made no intermission in his study of government, and of democracy as the best method of governing. His reading included : Stubbs' *Constitutional England*, Lecky's *Eighteenth Century*, the *Congressional Globe*, and Goodrich's *British Eloquence*.

While taking his law course he delivered an oration on John Bright, in which, a Southerner himself, he disagreed entirely with Bright on the Civil War, declaring that *because* he loved the South he rejoiced in the failure of the Confederacy. Had the Southern states won the war, he argued, they, weakened by slavery, would have remained ever in danger from their stronger neighbour. " Even the damnable cruelty and folly of reconstruction," he declared, " was to be preferred to helpless independence."

Actual practice of the law did not continue long. His bent was too strong, and in 1883 he wrote to a friend the reasons that had led to his determination to leave Atlanta, Georgia, where he had begun to practise, and to pursue his studies at Johns Hopkins, in Baltimore. To help in the expression of these reasons he called on Burke, who says that the law does more to quicken and invigorate the under-

standing than all other kinds of learning put together, but
that it is not likely, except in persons very happily born,
to open and to liberate the mind in exactly the same proportion. His new departure, Wilson thinks, is brought
about by his passion for original work, love of composition,
keen desire to become a master of philosophic discourse,
and " to become capable and apt in instructing as great a
number of persons as possible."

From the age of twenty-nine, when he became associate
professor of history at Bryn Mawr, the new college for
women, to the age of fifty-four, when he first ran for office,
Wilson's intellectual life was in academic shades. Among
his articles in periodicals, one in the *Political Science
Quarterly*, for June, 1887, contains sentences which must
be considered in any study of the origin of the League of
Nations : " There is a tendency—is there not ?—a tendency
as yet dim, but already steadily impulsive and clearly
destined to prevail, towards, first the confederation of
empires like the British, and finally of great States themselves. Instead of centralization of power, there is to be
wide union with tolerated divisions of prerogative. This is
a tendency toward the American type—of Governments
joined with Governments for the pursuit of common purposes, in honorable equality and honorable subordination."

In presenting a man for membership among Great
Democrats, we inevitably have in mind some standards of
greatness, and also—what is more difficult—some definition
(or definitions) of democracy. On this second and more
exacting task—one not to be met by a mere consultation
of a dictionary—Wilson helps us by an essay published
in 1889. " Democracy," says he, " is of course wrongly
conceived when treated as merely a body of doctrine, or
as simply a form of government. It is a state of development . . . Its process is experience, its basis old wont,
its meaning national organic unity and effectual life . . .
America has democracy because she is free ; she is not
free because she has democracy. A particular form of
government may no more be adopted than a particular form
of character may be adopted : both institutions and character
must be developed by conscious effort and through trans-
mitted aptitudes." Also : " The government which we

founded one hundred years ago was no type of experiment in advanced democracy, as we allowed Europe and even ourselves to suppose; it was simply an adaptation of English constitutional government."

So vivid was his belief that Americanism was but English tradition across the ocean that he criticized even in Jefferson the strain that was in him of philosophy from the French. This exotic philosophy, Wilson says, runs like a false and artificial note through all his thought. It was un-American in being abstract, sentimental, rationalistic, rather than practical. In the writings of Jefferson, Wilson therefore found a lack of hard and practical sense. The first man to show what Wilson thought true Americanism, and show it " with an unmistakable touch of greatness and distinction," was Benjamin Franklin. But, in spite of Wilson's origin in the South, the " supreme American " was Abraham Lincoln. " He never ceases to be a common man : that was his source of strength. But he was a common man with genius, a genius for things American, for insight into the common thought, for mastery of the fundamental things of politics that inhere in human nature and cast hardly more than their shadows on institutions ; for the practical niceties of affairs ; for judging men and assessing arguments. . . . The whole country is summed up in him : the rude Western strength, tempered with shrewdness and a broad and humane wit ; the Eastern conservatism, regardful of law and devoted to fixed standards of duty. He even understood the South, as no other Northern man of his generation did." In those words we have a picture, which Wilson never surpassed, of what to his mind a great American democrat ought to be.

His notable service as President of Princeton University, from 1902 to 1910, helped to show greatness as an administrator and idealistic drive toward higher standards, but what most illustrates the unswerving nature of his democracy was his endeavour to check what he deemed the movement of Princeton away from democracy to club life. " I found myself obliged to fight for a return to democracy all along the line, or else know that the young men in the University were not being properly prepared for American life or imbibing American ideals." Whether, in a controversy that centred about where certain buildings were to be placed, Wilson was right, or whether reason lay with opponents who included Grover Cleveland, could not be treated without going afield into details. The principle, on the other hand, in the light of which Wilson saw the facts, was one that was central in his whole life.

With the governorship of New Jersey, from 1910 to 1912, the democratic statesmanship of Wilson changed its medium of expression from unimpeded theory to theory expressed in bills, forced through legislatures, and applied to the improvement of specific conditions. Had he died at the end of his governorship he would never have appeared in history as one of the Great Democrats, because his books, while admirable, are not great, and because the stage at Trenton was not conspicuous or long occupied, and some of the Governor's work was hasty. However, direct primaries, a Corrupt Practices Act, employers' liability, a public utilities commission, an Act for the reform of municipal administration, added to a programme, not expertly carried out, but significant, to check exploitation by monopolies, earned him the Presidency.

This legislation, combined with explanatory speeches and open defiance of the " bosses," and of the corporate interests behind them, brought to Wilson's support the more liberal elements in the West and South, including the most powerful leader in the party, William Jennings Bryan. Many progressive conservatives (there are no established names for such groups in the United States) in the East were considering him seriously for the Presidency before the more discontented and radical parts of the country turned toward him.

The largest intellectual change that had been coming over him, since his early manhood, was one of emphasis. In all the most important American statesmen since Jackson there has been some combination of elements taken from Hamilton with others taken from Jefferson. When the Civil War was close to him Wilson had felt like emphasizing the need of national unity, and therefore he emphasized thought which he shared with Hamilton, but as that issue grew further away, and his attention became more fixed on the controversies then before the nation, his Jeffersonism became more pronounced. On the other great issue between the two early statesmen—the one trusting basically the influence of wealth and wishing an aristocracy, the other seeking to realize the popular will and trusting to the soundness of popular thought and feeling—Wilson stood entirely (sometimes even to the extent of ingenuousness) with Jefferson.

In supporting movements that were departures from that representative government expressed in the Constitution towards more direct government by the masses Wilson ran into no inconsistency. It was to the intent of the Constitution rather than to its literal forms that he was permanently devoted. In his own words : " What we must devote ourselves to now is, not to upsetting our institutions, but to restoring them. . . . If we felt that we had genuine democratic government in our State legislatures no one would propose the initiative or referendum in America." It was because the men chosen to represent the people did not in fact represent them, but instead represented, and were often actually chosen by, the prevailing money powers, that Wilson favoured devices for putting the power back where he believed it should rest. He continued to believe what he had said earlier, that democracy was not a system but a spirit.

Reasoning on such a basis he had perhaps realized more fully than at his earliest period the truth behind Jefferson's objections to centralized governmental power. It was of Jefferson himself that Wilson said : " His principles were the right of the individual to opportunity and the right of the people to a development not monopolized by the few," and under that general purpose he went on : " If we would act now in the spirit of Jefferson, we must be careful not to depend too much upon the federal government or turn too often from the remedy which is at hand in the power of the States. It is easier to apply morals in limited communities than in vast States."

Already he was laying the foundation for one of the major efforts of his first term as President when he said : " Banking is founded on a moral basis and not on a financial basis. The trouble to-day is that you bankers are too narrow-minded. . . . You take no interest in the small borrower and the small enterprise which affect the future of the country, but you give every attention to the big borrower and the rich enterprise which has already arrived."

Nominated for the Presidency at Baltimore, in 1912, in a hard and definite fight between advanced liberalism (to choose words that come as near as may be to expressing the idea) and a decayed money-controlled conservatism that Hamilton himself might well have repudiated, Wilson had no hesitation about the issues he was to put forward in the campaign. President Taft was the candidate of the regular Republicans, and as he had signed the Payne-Aldrich Tariff Bill, the latest example of tariff schedules drawn up in the back offices of trust, he was indeed vulnerable. Still more helpless was he made by the fact that Theodore Roosevelt, disappointed in not having the Republican nomination himself, and also indignant that Mr. Taft had allowed his favourite policy of the conservatism of natural resources to be betrayed in his own Cabinet, ran on a third ticket, his followers being called Progressives. Their platform was kept from any outspoken declaration on the real issues by the influence of George W. Perkins, himself a trust magnate, who was the chief money-raiser of the Progressive campaign, and they endeavoured to arouse public enthusiasm for a platform made up mostly of humanitarian planks familiar abroad.

Next in intellectual importance to Wilson was a lawyer widely known to the nation for a long series of valuable suggestions and constructive reforms in city public utilities, railroads, banking, and insurance, whose conduct of the case against Ballinger, the Cabinet member who had betrayed the conservation movement, had shown a magnificent grasp of the principles involved. Where Mr. Brandeis counted most in the campaign was in his unequalled mastery of the monopoly problem, in the wealth of detail which he brought to the issue of regulated competition, as recommended by him and by Mr. Wilson, against the regulated monopoly supported by the Roosevelt party. When, later, President Wilson put this expert and inventive constitutional reformer on the Supreme Court of the United States he expressed in action the cause he had most at heart—the shackling of those forces that interfere with free and disinterested action for the general welfare. " The difficulty," the President once said to the writer of this chapter, " I got into when I put Brandeis on the Court is that I shall never again be able to live up to that appointment. Never again shall I find a lawyer, among those very successful in handling ordinary big money cases, who can be counted on to use his talents and experience for the people's causes."

The tariff question had its separate side, on which Wilson had been long a student, but also it was inseparable from the issue of control by trusts, since it was the most flagrant illustration of that control. To the attentive student, few of the accomplishments of Wilson's first term rank higher than the success with which he drove the lobbyists out of Washington, by making it clear that any attempt to influence legislation in behalf of specific business enterprises would bring about the President's open and bitter opposition to the proposal urged.

Dishonesty and venality apart, a high protective tariff was against that prevailing side of Wilson's philosophy that derived from Jefferson. It fostered big cities, big business, special interests, money influence, all the evils of size and monopoly against the steadiness and freedom of natural growth and smaller units. Wilson sought no such drastic step backwards as withdrawal from the corporate form of doing business. He knew that a few activities were monopolistic in their very nature. His belief in growth and the unwisdom of sudden change made him realize that a tariff for revenue only, the right principle on Jeffersonian grounds, had been made impossible by the building up of the country under protection. His plan of revision was severe, but it did not amount to complete reversal.

To the carrying out of the Democratic promises Wilson gave that firm leadership that he, going on the analogy of the British Prime Minister, felt the executive ought to exercise. Also he took over certain planks from the Progressive platform, the most important being the formation of a Federal Trade Commission (which is still active and influential) for the regulation of business, especially through enforcing knowledge of the facts, but also for passing on breaches of the laws against monopoly.

x

The Federal Reserve Act was planned to modernize a woefully obsolete system of currency and credit. To make the system less rigid, more adjustable to need, both as to expansion of credit and as to retrenchment of it, the first steps had been prepared in the preceding administration by the Aldrich Bill, but the side of the new Act that was looked upon with horror by those who had drawn the Aldrich Bill consisted of those provisions intended to decentralize credit and those intended to give to government representatives, rather than to bankers, the management of the new system.

There is no doubt among American students that in constructive measures to make the country more success-fully democratic, in leadership to give purpose, clearness, and unity to the party programme, and efficiency to the administration, Wilson's first term has a higher record of accomplishment than any other since the Civil War ; many would say, than all the others taken together. Yet in the campaign for re-election, in 1916, this constructive record counted for little with the general public. What gave Wilson his re-election, by a very slight margin, was the slogan, " He kept us out of war."

When we discuss a Great Democrat, do we discuss his democracy, and his general greatness, or only his greatness as a democrat ? It is an irony of the problem, in the case of Wilson, that the most important question about his place in the future must for many years remain unanswered. There is little doubt that as an American democrat he stands first since Lincoln ; second among the leaders of his own party since Jackson ; but whether in general stature the future will see him in the first rank of all American statesmen, along with Washington, Franklin, Hamilton, Jefferson, Madison, and Lincoln, must depend on the fate that shall ultimately befall such efforts as have their centre in Geneva.

It is true that his executive and administrative ability, applied to the contribution of the United States to the fighting, was of a high quality, but it seems apart from our subject. What of the relation of American entry into the war to democracy, and of the strife for world co-operation to Wilson's life principles ?

He had for some years been interested in such peace movements as the Hague Court, but only in a general sense, without special study, his whole life-work having been concentrated on political principles on the Anglo-American scene. Early in his Presidency, when the present writer asked him if anything was worrying him, he replied : " Only Mexico. What worries me is what I do not understand." The relations of the United States to Colombia, Nicaragua, Haïti, the Dominican Republic, the Philippines, found him in a territory new to his thought. He interpreted democracy as including the greatest possible amount of self-determination, but what is the greatest amount possible ? Even Jefferson, as Wilson himself pointed out, found his passion for peace abate " when he saw the mouth of the Mississippi about to pass into French hands." It was shortly before he assumed the Presidency that he said : " It would be the irony of fate if my administration had to deal chiefly with foreign affairs." It was not until sixteen months later that he had to face a problem that, in the view of history, was to overshadow all his domestic constructive leadership.

It will never be possible to say dogmatically how far his change in regard to entering the war was motivated by technical duties in defence of American rights ; how much by unwillingness to see victory rest with a powerful oligarchy, when the two leading countries on the other side were democracies ; how much by being led to believe that if the Entente were victorious the terms could be made to rest on principles laid down in advance by him. But it seems reasonably certain that without the acceptance by Great Britain and France of his Fourteen Points the country would have remained aloof from the war.

Unquestionably the end was hurried, if not determined, not only by American entrance, but also by the intensive propaganda carried on by Wilson to convince the German people that if they should lay down their arms there would be a peace as generous and an acceptance into fellowship as complete, as was offered to the South by Lincoln and by Grant.

Wilson's failure to secure the treaty he wished ; his acceptance of one he deemed in important aspects a failure to carry out the agreement with him ; his success in making the League of Nations an integral party of the treaty ; his

limitations as a politician, that caused his defeat in the
Senate on ratification; these matters are still too con-
troversial for our purpose, and of a bearing too remote on
democracy. Far above them in its relation to any guess
at his greatness—to the challenging question, in history
how heroic are his proportions?—is the future fate of
regular co-operation of the nations, in open discussion, to
prevent war, by removing causes, and when necessary by
exercising police control.

It has been correctly said, by Mr. Baker in the *Life and
Letters*, that " Wilson, in his international policies, was
Jeffersonian in his demand for ' self-determination,' Hamiltonian in his struggle for a union of the States of the world."
Such a combination harmonizes with his career, and the
harmony will be complete if in the end some kind of regional
devolution is worked out, throwing less inclusive responsibility on the central body at Geneva. If, by some such
route, the nations in control of the world become free,
democratic, and co-operative, then indeed will Wilson
stand among the great democratic leaders, not only of his
own country but of the world.

MARY WOLLSTONECRAFT

1759-1797

by EVELYN SHARP

MARY WOLLSTONECRAFT

1759-1797

by EVELYN SHARP

MARY WOLLSTONECRAFT, like most thinkers in advance of their age who find themselves in revolt against existing institutions, provoked during her lifetime such extremes of hero-worship and antagonism that contemporary criticism is of little use to us in the formation of our own judgment of her. Horace Walpole's well-known allusion to " that hyena in petticoats," and Hannah More's comment—" How many ways there are of being ridiculous ! "—on Mary's great book, which she was " invincibly resolved " not to read, probably sum up the average polite prejudice of the period against a woman who not only demanded freedom for others, for oppressed men as well as oppressed women, but dared to be free herself.

There were others among her contemporaries whose praises were hardly less extravagant. " She was a delightful woman," declared Southey ; " I never saw a woman who would have been better fitted to do honour to her sex . . . Of all the lions I met in London her countenance was the best, infinitely the best." An anonymous writer in the *Gentleman's Magazine* concluded an article on her, written after her death, with the unqualified tribute—" For soundness of understanding and sensibility of heart she was, perhaps, never equalled." All this fails, as completely as Shelley's famous lines about her, to suggest Walpole's hyena. Shelley never knew her ; she died too soon to be his mother-in-law ; but it is significant that, seeing her only in relation to his wife, her daughter, Mary Godwin, he wrote of her as one

> Whose life was like a setting planet mild,
> Which clothed thee in the radiance undefiled
> Of its departing glory.

Mary Wollstonecraft herself gives us a clue to much of this conflicting evidence in a letter she wrote to her sister announcing her intention of earning her living as a writer, then almost an unprecedented thing for a woman to do.

" I am thus going to be the first of a new genus," she says ;
and again, elsewhere—" I am not born to tread the beaten
track." But it is possible that she would not have roused
either antagonism or admiration in such intensity if her only
achievement in life had been the exposure of the wrongs of
women. She was not only a champion of oppressed
women, she was also a champion of the oppressed poor ;
and the inequalities in the distribution of wealth troubled
her fully as much as the inequalities in the position of the
sexes. It is important to remember what is often overlooked, that her first notable publication was not her
Vindication of the Rights of Woman, on which her fame rests,
but her *Vindication of the Rights of Men,* an answer to
Burke's attack upon the French Revolution. As a feminist,
which she never was in the narrow sense of the word, she
might have been dismissed for a harmless crank ; but as
champion of the mob, whose wretched condition seemed to
her some justification for the excesses of the Revolutionists,
she became dangerous. The history of democracy is full
of similar instances of intellectual ostracism.

In making a study of Mary Wollstonecraft it is impossible
to separate her life from her work ; she lived too intensely
to succeed in detaching her art from her human experience,
as some writers, more often men than women, seem able to
do. All through her childhood and youth her spirit was
bound and her genius thwarted by poverty and by the
inferior position of women in the home. There was nothing
in her up-bringing to make her think well of the marriage
tie, or of the way men were able to use their power over
their wives and daughters, or of the protection afforded by
society to women thrown upon it by misfortune or by lack
of means. If she had really been the hyena in petticoats,
the uncompromising exponent of women's rights she is
still often imagined to have been, there was clearly abundant
excuse for it. That she was nothing of the sort, but retained
to the end her inner faith in the beauty of family relationships and in the importance of building a nation's happiness
upon the happiness of its homes, and, further, that she even
converted Godwin to this view of hers, after first living with
him unmarried, is a testimony to her power of rising above
personal experience in her search for truth.

She was born in Essex, probably in Epping Forest, in 1759, and was the eldest daughter and the second of six children. Both her parents were unsatisfactory ; her father, as improvident as Micawber, drank into the bargain and ill-treated her mother, who was a weak creature and in her turn bullied Mary. " How can women be just or generous when they are the slaves of injustice ? " she wrote, years later ; and one result of her home life was the discovery, an important one for a reformer, that good and bad qualities were pretty equally distributed between the sexes. Another was that there was something to be said for running wild with her brothers and escaping regular lessons, for, in a passage advocating co-education, she afterwards wrote : " Most of the women, in the circle of my observation, who have acted like rational creatures or shown any vigour of intellect, have accidentally been allowed to run wild."

Some idea of her sufferings during those early years of struggle may be gathered from her two works of fiction, not great books in themselves, but of some autobiographical value. In 1778, she gained further bitter experience from two years spent as companion to a rich and tyrannical woman at Bath, then returned home to nurse her mother, who had now come to lean upon the daughter she formerly oppressed ; and when, after her mother's death, her father married again, she almost wilfully asked the worst of fate by going to live with the family of her great friend, Fanny Blood, whose home life was a dreadful repetition of her own. Her first defiance of the conventions occurred when she carried off her sister and helped her to hide from a husband who wanted to put her in an asylum ; but it was characteristic of Mary that she still saw the husband's unhappy point of view, and, owing to this impartiality, was able finally to arrange an amicable separation between the two. When, soon after, she set up a little school for the support of her own and Fanny Blood's relations, it looked as though she was at last going to find some peace of mind in this outlet for her original views on education.

Again came one of those demands upon her sympathies that she never refused to meet. The unfortunate Fanny, now married and dying in Lisbon, sent her an urgent call ; and off went Mary just in time to see her before she died.

x*

On her return she found the school had gone to pieces in her absence, and two sets of relatives were again waiting to be helped. It was little wonder that she wrote later to her lover Imlay that, "fatigued during my youth by the most arduous struggles . . . not merely pleasures escaped me, I mean the simple pleasures that flow from passion and affection, but the most melancholy views of life were impressed by a disappointed heart on my mind."

These perpetual interruptions to her career would not be worth dwelling upon if it were not for their bearing upon her character. Moving amid these human failures, she retained by some superhuman strength of will the driving force of her purpose in life, and at last secured her independence. She met the publisher Johnson to whom she afterwards owed so much, earned her first ten guineas from him with a little book, *Thoughts on the Education of Daughters*, used it to send the Bloods to Dublin whence they fortunately never returned, and then, in 1788, after a year spent as governess in Ireland, returned at Johnson's suggestion to London, where she settled down to a literary career in rooms in George Street, Southwark.

The next four years were years of happiness and development. She was at last fulfilling herself, winning recognition, doing the work she liked, mixing with her intellectual equals ; and it was probably a matter of indifference to her that she had to hand out her hard-earned money to subsidise her father, train her brothers and keep her sisters in their periods of unemployment, so long as she was left in comparative peace to live her own life. She learned German and Italian, translated from both and from French for Johnson, reviewed books for his *Analytical Review*, and wrote her two finest works—the more famous of the two in six weeks. She dined with the Johnsons once or twice a week, met Tom Paine, Mrs. Trimmer (the founder of Sunday Schools), Fuseli the painter, and many others. She was at her best among these congenial people, was now able to dress better, and people discovered that she was a beauty. She made her mark before her books appeared.

Enjoying that comradeship with men on which she always set so much store, not yet enslaved by a love affair or distracted by the cares of motherhood, and deeply stirred

by the French Revolution which awakened all her natural
enthusiasm for liberty, Mary was free to put her emotional
vitality as well as her literary ability into her work ; and in
those eventful four years she wrote, first, *Mary : a
Fiction* ; and *Original Stories from Real Life, with
conversations calculated to regulate the affections and form
the mind to truth and goodness* (both in 1788) ; then
*The Vindication of the Rights of Men : A Letter to
Burke occasioned by his Reflections on the Revolution
in France* (1790) ; then her *Vindication of the Rights
of Woman, with strictures on Political and Moral subjects*
(1792). Later there followed other publications ; in 1794,
the first volume of her *Historical and Moral View of the
Origin and Progress of the French Revolution, and the effect
it has produced in Europe,* unfortunately never finished ; and
lastly her second novel, *The Wrongs of Woman, or Maria*
(published posthumously) ; and she left behind her a
collection of letters, some private, and some written definitely
for publication during her tour in Scandinavia, which alone
would have brought her considerable notice. But most
critics would agree that her highest accomplishment as a
writer was reached in the work she did during the
years, 1788-92, when she enjoyed almost complete immunity
from domestic anxiety and was still untouched by the violent
emotions that seem to have characterised her more intimate
relationships with men.

Her friendship with Fuseli was the first of these affairs.
Whether it ever became anything warmer than friendship
must always remain a matter for speculation. It certainly
meant so much to her that she made the extraordinary
proposition to his wife that she should live with them
in order to enjoy his uninterrupted companionship ; and
when his wife declined to concur in this arrangement,
and Mary soon afterwards went to Paris, there were naturally
some who saw in her journey abroad a proof that she had
something to run away from. But it is at least equally
possible that to a woman of her independence and pride
the rumour that she was in love with Fuseli (if she was not)
would have been enough to make her want to avoid for a
time the set in which such things were being said about her,
apart from her very natural desire to go to the centre of the

events that were stirring as much controversy then as we
have seen roused in our own time by similar events in
Russia. In any case, it does not concern us here whether
she was or was not in love with Fuseli. It is surely time
that we approached with more detachment the love affairs
of Mary Wollstonecraft, which have been allowed too long
to obscure her importance as a prophet of democracy.
Had she been a man, they would have been regarded as
natural accompaniments to imaginative genius. Or had
she been a conventional woman who concealed both her
sentimental intrigues and her outrageous opinions from a
censorious world, she would have caused less turmoil in
respectable circles, both during and after her lifetime. But
Mary was not that sort of woman. She scorned hypocrisy
as she insisted on freedom of thought and action—and
human affection was indispensable to her. " I cannot live
without some particular affection—I am afraid not without
a passion," she wrote to Imlay in 1795 ; " and I feel the
want of it more in society than in solitude " ; and this is
a revealing statement, especially the last sentence of it.

If Fuseli was her first lover, he was soon replaced by
another—Gilbert Imlay, a captain in the American army
during the war of Independence, and author of the first
American novel, *The Emigrants*. She met him in Paris and
her letters leave no shadow of doubt as to her passion for
him. It absorbed her while it lasted ; she refused to
believe in his inconstancy when it was patent to all the
world ; when she could no longer doubt it, she tried to drown
herself. The birth of their child at Havre in 1794, the ill-fated
Fanny who afterwards took her own life, only increased
her infatuation for the father. She was, undoubtedly,
at this period of her life an absurd woman in love,
though not more absurd than any man or woman who is
reduced to unreason by an overmastering affection for some
one who has ceased to return it. But she showed greater
strength of character than some women might in her ability
to take up her life again when her love for Imlay died, and
to absorb herself in her work and her child, to whom she
appears to have been an ideal and adorable mother ; so that
finally, when she again met William Godwin after her
rupture with Imlay, there was nothing to stand in the way

of their yielding to their natural affinity for one another. In 1797, after living with him openly for some months, she married him legally within a short time of the birth of her second child, the daughter who afterwards married Shelley and was the author of *Frankenstein*. When this baby was born, Mary insisted on being attended only by a midwife, a dangerous concession to feminism in those days of primitive midwifery, and it cost her her life. Ten days later, she died at the early age of thirty-eight.

Mary Wollstonecraft's unconventional attitude towards the relations of the sexes undoubtedly created a prejudice against her in the minds of many who would otherwise have hailed her as a prophet. This seems to be the only explanation of the neglect of her written works by those who, whether social, political or educational reformers, ought to have drawn from her books in the century-and-a-half that followed her death ample support for their democratic views. From this standpoint, and because the economic position of the wife and mother creates a problem in democracy that only Soviet Russia among modern States has so far attempted frankly to face (and along lines that Mary Wollstonecraft herself might have laid down), her opinions on the subject of what is called free-love, if they can be discovered, are worth consideration here. Her actual conduct does not tell us very much, for accomplishment rarely matches endeavour in anybody's life. There is a doubt whether she was in love with Fuseli at all, so her flight from him, if it was flight, cannot be taken as a proof of chastity. In Paris, owing to the unsettled conditions of the time, there were obstacles in the way of her marrying Imlay ; if they had been removed, or if he had remained faithful to her after their return to England, we do not know what she would have done ; nor do we know whether she would have taken another lover if she had lived long enough to outgrow her passion for Godwin. There is no real evidence for or against promiscuity in the actual story of her love affairs.

In her writings we find expressions of opinion that point to certain broad principles. She certainly thought that no conventional considerations should stand between two people who really loved each other ; it was always the

substance and not the shadow that she pursued through
life. "What is termed virtue is only want of courage,"
she writes; and again—"We should never perhaps have
heard of Lucretia had she died to preserve her chastity
instead of her reputation." Too much importance, she
felt, was attached to constancy, and in women's constancy
as such she frankly disbelieved, saying that "A mistaken
education, a narrow uncultivated mind and many sexual
prejudices tend to make women more constant than men."
In a letter to Imlay she drew a distinction between fidelity
and constancy, to the advantage of the former, adding that
"Two people who mean to live together ought not to be
long separated." And of one thing we can be absolutely
certain ; she denied that love and marriage were the only,
or even the chief business of women, saying delightfully in
one passage on the subject—"How women are to exist in
that state where there is neither to be marrying nor giving
in marriage we are not told."

Everything that Mary Wollstonecraft wrote was interesting,
and not least attractive among her miscellaneous writings
is a fragment called *Lessons*, which she wrote for her little
girl Fanny. It is a charming witness to the intelligent way
she approached the upbringing of children at a period when
such ideas were more or less without precedent. But
indisputably, her best and most characteristic work is to
be found in the two *Vindications*, and it is upon them that
her claim rests for inclusion among the early preachers of
democracy.

In *The Vindication of the Rights of Men* all her indignation
is concentrated upon a defence of the oppressed classes, with
no reference to the special wrongs of women. She pours
scorn upon Burke for his inconsistency, for upholding
American independence and the abolition of slavery while
he condemns the French Revolution ; for praising the British
Constitution as a model of liberty—"Security of property !
Behold in a few words the definition of English liberty ! " she
scoffs—; for lamenting the griefs of a Queen of France when
the miseries of poor mothers in his own country leave him
unmoved ; and above all, for his "contemptible hard-
hearted sophistry" in commending to the downtrodden
labourers of town and country a "submission to the will

of Heaven." She draws a touching picture of the landless peasant, and an astonishingly modern picture of the workless mechanic rendered unemployable by the inability to get work, and goes on to say scornfully—

It is, Sir, *possible* to render the poor happier in this world, without depriving them of the consolation which you gratuitously grant them in the next . . . Is the human heart satisfied with turning the poor over to another world, to receive the blessings this could afford ?

Finally, referring to Burke's condemnation of the Royal executions and comparing these with the way the poor live always, she asks dramatically : " What were the outrages of a day to these continual miseries ? " It is true that to some extent her admiration for the French Revolution was theoretic, like Burke's for the British Constitution ; and her personal contact with it in Paris, in 1794, certainly tended to modify her revolutionary enthusiasm. But nothing ever changed her passion for freedom and her conviction that neither class nor sex should set up an artificial barrier to freedom ; and in this early publication we have evidence of that passionate faith.

But others at that time were also defending the French Revolution. Mary Wollstonecraft stands at this period almost alone as champion of the emancipation of women. Her *Vindication of the Rights of Woman* is incomparably her greatest work, not only because it is far in advance of its time in regard to the position of women, but also because it is far in advance of its time in other matters as well. On education on peace and war, on economics, on the treatment of animals and of children, it reveals her as a pioneer, and especially in education, which she thinks should be national, free to younger children, and open to all, irrespective of class. There should be public day schools ; for ' schoolboys infallibly lose that decent bashfulness which might have ripened into modesty at home " ; and girls and boys should be taught together, " to improve both sexes," the curriculum to be the same for both and to include botany, mechanics, astronomy, reading, writing, arithmetic, natural history and some simple experiments in natural philosophy—" but these pursuits should never

encroach on gymnastic plays in the open air." She comes
directly into line with our enlightened educationalists of
to-day with her suggestion of self-government in schools—
" They should be tried by their peers "—and even antici-
pates the co-operation of parents and staff by proposing
a committee of teachers in each parish to which the former
could bring complaints. She has, too, a great saying about
animals :

Humanity to animals should be particularly inculcated as a
part of national education. . . . Justice, or even benevolence,
will not be a powerful spring of action unless it extend to the
whole creation ; nay, I believe that . . . those who can see
pain unmoved will soon learn to inflict it.

After this, one is not surprised to find her saying that defensive war " is the only justifiable war in the present advanced
state of society . . . I sincerely wish to see the bayonet
converted into a pruning-hook " ; and, with regard to
political emancipation :

I may excite laughter by dropping a hint . . . I really think
that women ought to have representatives, instead of being
arbitrarily governed without having any direct share allowed
them in the deliberations of government.

It is only by understanding Mary Wollstonecraft's
conception of human freedom that one can understand her
plea for the freedom of women. Those who have
dismissed her as an atheist because she denounces " slavery
to forms that makes religion worse than a farce " are
equally ready to see in her an opponent of the marriage tie
because she says bluntly—" Marriage will never be held
sacred till women, by being brought up with men, are
prepared to be their companions rather than their mistresses."
Her *Vindication* will remain a feminist tract for all who do
not read it carefully enough to discover that in her own
words—" It is an affection for the whole human race that . . .
leads me earnestly to wish to see woman placed in a station
in which she would advance and not retard progress." No
woman-hater of either sex could be harder on women's
faults than is the writer of the *Vindication*, but she never
fails to point out that their subjection and their lack of a

liberal education are the causes of those faults. " The
whole tenor of female education tends to render the best-
disposed romantic and inconstant, and the remainder
vain and mean," she says : but a better education
" might save many from legal and common prostitution,"
since " women would not then marry for a support."

In the same spirit she refuses to attribute any special
qualities to men or to women, so long as their upbringing
remains different :—

I here throw down my gauntlet and deny the existence of
sexual virtues, not excepting modesty. For men and women
truth must be the same . . . Women, I allow, may have different
duties to fulfil, but they are *human* duties . . .

It is vain to expect virtue from women till they are in some
degree independent of men. . . . Virtue will never prevail
in society till the virtues of both sexes are founded on reason,
and till the affections common to both are allowed to gain their
due strength by the discharge of mutual duties.

Finally, she sees in women's subjection infinite harm
resulting to the home and thence to the whole nation. She
refers to the " brutish affection " that the subject-woman
shows for her own children, " forgetting the common
relationship that binds the whole family on earth together."
And the democrat in her speaks out again when she
maintains that the freedom of the race depends upon the
freeing of women, who, " denied all political privileges, and
not allowed as married women, except in criminal cases,
a civil existence, have their attention naturally drawn from
the interest of the whole community to that of the minute
parts."

It is always the whole community that concerns this broad-
minded idealist. " For a small number of distinguished
women I do not ask a place," she insists ; and—" It is
not for the benefit of society that a few brilliant men should
be brought forward at the expense of the many."   But
quotation can give only a limited idea of Mary Wollstonecraft's breadth of vision. The only way to arrive at the
truth about her, by adjusting the balance between her
intellectual aims and her very human attempts to carry them
out in her own life, is to read without prejudice what

she wrote and to study the few facts of her life that are actually established as facts. These will tell their own story and it will be found the fascinating story of one of those rare spirits that appear now and then in the course of centuries, to disturb our equanimity and shock our complacency, but stirring us nevertheless to new endeavour and never quite leaving the world as they found it.

As a mortal life, Mary Wollstonecraft's might be said to be incomplete. She was only thirty-eight when she died; it is impossible to say in what directions she might have developed or modified her theories of love and marriage, of economics and sociology, of politics and the humanities, had she lived her full threescore-and-ten, though it is fairly safe to assume that her fundamental sincerity and her passionate regard for freedom and justice would never have allowed her to abandon one jot of her basic principles. Still, to judge her accomplishment as we should judge that of one who had lived to be old might appear to be unfair.

This theory would be challenged, however, by those who believe in some guiding purpose behind all the groping and the endeavour, the rising and the falling of the human race. Mary Wollstonecraft was neither the first nor the last of the world's artists and teachers to die prematurely young. Byron, Burns, Raphael, Mozart, leaving behind them names unforgettable in the minds of men, all died before the age of thirty-eight; others, and some greater than they, have died still younger. We may then see equally in the life of one whose name and work have won fame in many countries besides our own (the *Vindication of the Rights of Woman* is widely read in America and on the Continent, and has been translated more than once) a similar indication that Mary Wollstonecraft was the chosen instrument for just the message she did bring and the task she did accomplish; and so a career which seems to have been cut short was in reality a completed career.

That seems to explain in some degree Mary Wollstonecraft's tremendous vitality and the immediate impression, pleasing or the reverse, that she made on every one with whom she came in contact. She was the " hyena in petticoats ", or she was unequalled " for soundness of understanding and sensibility of heart "; no moderate estimate of her seemed possible. She did everything with the whole of herself, whether she threw up her prospects to rush across the sea to a dying friend, or wrote a work of genius in six weeks, or lavished a torrent of affection upon an average man incapable of realising the woman she was. She was a great lover and friend and mother, as well as a great writer and pioneer; and, glancing at her meteoric passage across a world that was not nearly ready for the message of genius that she brought, and in some ways is not ready for it yet, we see the inevitability of her early death. She loved too much, she fought too hotly, she felt too intensely. She had to burn herself out at an age when most of us are still short of our prime. But the flame of her burning will lighten the path, down through the ages, of all rebels, all visionaries, who help to pave the way to that democracy which, some day, will bring freedom to humanity.

EPILOGUE :

DEMOCRATIC LEADERSHIP
by A. BARRATT BROWN

I

A study of the portraits that are included in this volume yields rich matter for consideration in the light of the happenings of our own time. We are passing through a period in which Democracy is under a cloud, and in which once again it needs faith and courage to be a Democrat. Where once men accepted all too complacently the democratic label, to-day they are timid and dubious if not frankly sceptical.

A defeatist attitude is to be found among those who have been the most stalwart supporters of Democracy in the past. They are chary of exposing candidly their change of mind ; they prefer to speak of Democracy (following Mr. Wells) as "under revision" rather than frankly dismiss it as effete ; or they refer vaguely (following Mr. Laski) to Democracy being "at the crossroads" when the situation they really envisage is a precipice.

It would appear that the outbreak of Dictatorships since the war has had the effect of paralysing men's minds and beclouding their faith in principles they once held unquestionable. But Dictatorships have no enduring principle to sustain them, and Democracy is not discredited because in countries, not one of which has had a long-established democratic constitution, Dictatorship prevails. Dictatorships are born of ignorance and despair, a miserably unsatisfactory parentage. Until recently they were confined to comparatively illiterate and peasant populations, and it is only the sense of frustration and desperation in Germany that has brought a largely educated and largely industrial nation under the sway of Hitler.

Meanwhile mere denunciations of Dictatorship are not enough. Democracy must be shown to be capable of adjusting its methods of government to the needs of a world that is far more complicated and far more closely interlocked than the world in which it first grew up. That its earlier advocates were not blind to the defects and dangers of popular government is shown by more than one of the accounts in the preceding chapters. The peculiar danger to which John Stuart Mill called attention—" the tyranny of the majority "—was one which de Tocqueville foresaw when he visited America a century ago. " Faith in public opinion becomes in such countries a species of religion, and the majority its prophet." A profound distrust of leaders and elected representatives is much older than Walt Whitman's fear of " the never-ending audacity of elected persons," and might almost be said to be a settled matter of doctrine among some of the founders of Democracy both in England and America. The checks and balances which the English and still more the American Constitution have provided, as well as the later adoption of the devices of ' direct government '—the referendum and initiative and recall—represent an elaborate machinery of mistrust.

A charge against parliamentary Democracy that is still more frequently heard to-day is again one of long standing and no mere post-war phenomenon. That is the charge that Parliament is a futile waste of time in mere talk. It reminds us of the name by which both Carlyle and Ruskin disrespectfully spoke of the Mother of Parliaments—" the talking-shop at Westminster." It is tempting to retort that the charge was manufactured in the writing-shops of Chelsea and Denmark Hill. It is no solution to withdraw, as Matthew Arnold was tempted to withdraw, from " the sterile hubbub of politics," nor to abandon constitutional methods for various forms of " direct action." Among the supporters of " action "—whether Communist or Fascist— I have not indeed observed any the less disposition to idle and even recriminatory talk. The anti-parliamentary tendencies of to-day revive (it may be noted) a controversy that has raged throughout the history of the democratic movement in Europe. It is interesting to recall that Karl Marx supported parliamentary action against the anarchism of Bakunin.

Of more weight, however, than the charge of idle talk, is the indictment of Democracy as inefficient. M. Faguet's phrase " the cult of incompetence " has been repeated with

variations by Mr. H.G. Wells in his *After Democracy* and by
Mr. Bernard Shaw in his *Apple Cart*. Yet on the score of
sheer competence, a close examination of the actual working
of government, and especially of local government, in
democratic countries like our own as compared with that of
similar institutions in countries that have come under
Dictatorship, would show that Democracy has nothing to
fear from the comparison.

That is not to say that democratic institutions do not
require revision and reorganisation to meet the needs of the
present day, and especially with a view to applying the
machinery of government to the supervision of financial and
industrial affairs. The Manifesto and Further Statement on
Liberty and Democratic Leadership published in the winter of
1933-1934 over the names of some 150 distinguished
representatives of politics, economics, religion, art, science
and education, indicate not only the strong hold that the
democratic principle still retains over the minds of forward-
looking citizens, but also the extent to which they are aware
of the defects of democratic institutions, and the extent to
which they are agreed on the main lines along which they
may be improved and rendered adequate to the increasing
quantity and changing quality of the work they have to
undertake.

II

I am not here concerned, however, with institutions and
machinery, but with the persons who control them. The
problem which Dictatorship throws into relief is the problem
of leadership in the modern State. It is sometimes assumed
that Democracy is incompatible with leadership, that the
recognition of the need for strong and enlightened leadership
involves us in the embarrassing position of having to choose
between Democracy and Dictatorship. But neither the
history of Democracy nor the analysis of the kind of
leadership that is required to-day will be found to justify
this assumption. Democracy, ever since the days of
Pericles, has thrown up its leaders, and the foregoing studies
of Great Democrats have sufficiently shown that in the last
150 years leaders have not been wanting either to inspire the
thought of popular movements or to direct the working of

popular institutions. The leadership has needed to be, and has been, of two kinds. We may distinguish, following a suggestion of Mr. Walter Lippmann, the pioneer and the routineer, the orator and the administrator, the politician and the expert. Most of the figures in the foregoing chapters are representative of the former type. The Great Democrats have been hitherto the pioneers of popular movements, speakers and writers who have inspired their aims and made articulate their demands. In part this is due to the fact that the democratic movement is a comparatively young and recent growth, and that in the early stages more attention has been given to the proclamation and champion-ship of the democratic ideal. But in part it is due to the fact that greatness is more readily recognised in the persons who achieve public prominence on the platform and in Parliament, or through books and plays and pamphlets that are widely known and circulated. The work of the administrator, no less important in the building up of democratic government, is less open to the public eye and to popular recognition and applause. Yet here, too, Democracy has been well served by a host of men and women whose names are for the most part unknown, but whose work—in the Civil Service, in local councils, in the trade union and the co-operative movement, and in the numerous committees which are the training-ground and indispensable if tiresome mechanism of Democracy—is of incalculable value. Here and there a great public servant or a trade union official has not only left his mark on democratic institutions but imprinted an imperishable signature, and the names of men like Edwin Chadwick and Dr. Southwood Smith among the Benthamites, of Dr. John Simon in the later development of Public Health and Sir Robert Morant in that of Education, or again of Robert Applegarth and Alexander Macdonald, of William Newton and Thomas Burt in the trade union movement, remind us of leaders of this type who will be long remembered and held in honour.

III

But at the root of Democracy and giving life and strength to all its forces is an attitude of mind that I can only call the democratic faith. It is not easy to define but it is not difficult to discern. It accounts for the fact that Democracy is not only a form of government but a principle of government. That principle has been best expressed in a saying of John Stuart Mill : " All human beings have the same interest in good government ; the welfare of all is alike affected by it, and they have equal need of a voice in it to secure their share of its benefits." The Master of Balliol in his little book *The Essentials of Democracy* quotes a remark which Colonel Rainboro' the Leveller made to Cromwell in 1647 : " I think the poorest he that is in England hath a life to live as the richest he." Bentham, though not himself a thoroughgoing equalitarian, laid down the same principle when he said that " the happiness of the worst man of the species is as much an integrant of the mass of human happiness as is that of the best man."

The democratic principle, then, declares that all human beings have a value such that they should be consulted in matters which affect their interest or welfare. In small and likeminded groups it is possible to ensure that every member not only consents but contributes to all that is done. But direct Democracy with its popular assembly and rotation of office is not practicable under the conditions of the large-scale modern State. Here all that can be ensured is that there shall be :

(1) A central representative assembly.

(2) Local governing bodies—provincial or municipal.

(3) Full and free use of all the organs of opinion and discussion—the public meeting, the conference, the press, the wireless, and every form of publication.

(4) Consultation with representatives of the varied interests affected by legislation and administration.

In this way as many circles of discussion touching as many persons as possible may be drawn into effective collaboration, but the final deliberation and decision are left to a responsible Parliament and Executive.

The Master of Balliol suggests that the two most important qualities of a representative system are sensitiveness and efficiency. The first depends in part upon the mental attitude of representatives and public officials, in part upon the machinery of consultation ; the second depends in part upon the sagacity of electors in choosing their representatives and in part upon the methods by which appointments to positions of leadership and responsibility are made.

But the statement of the democratic principle as Mill defined it covers a wider field than that of political affairs, and demands application to all human affairs and relationships in which some kind of organisation and government is necessary ; and although the forms of its expression may be very different, the principle remains the same : that the people most intimately concerned in any activity—political or industrial, or (it may be) educational or religious—" have equal need of a voice in it." This is not to say that they have need of an equal voice in it. Democracy does not require that every leader or official shall be directly responsible to the whole people or to his immediate subordinates. It does require that the field of selection shall be open and not confined to any privileged class—whether hereditary or propertied ; and that the decisions and actions of those appointed shall not be arbitrary but subject to proper scrutiny and unimpeded discussion.

It is clear from what has been said that the democratic principle has not yet found complete and satisfactory expression even in political government, where it is often assumed to prevail, still less in the sphere of industrial relations ; and the failure of Democracy, in so far as its failure is admitted, is to be ascribed not to any weakness in the principle but to its incomplete expression hitherto. In other words, the cure for the defects of Democracy is to be sought not in less opportunity for the democratic principle but in more and better facilities for its application.

IV

Its wider application, however, is not so much a matter of machinery as of a mental and spiritual attitude. What I have called the democratic faith springs from certain profound beliefs that are common to Christian and Democrat alike. They may be stated under three heads :

1. The belief in the value of the individual personality.
2. The belief in the equality of all men before God.
3. The belief in collaboration and the method of persuasion.

And these may be seen largely to correspond to the revolutionary trinity—Liberty, Equality and Fraternity.

(1) The respect for the individual personality is fundamental to the democratic idea and the democratic method. It underlies the principle of Liberty—personal, civil, religious and political—not as the mere assertion of individual rights but as the obligation to respect the other man, to listen to his arguments and to take into account his point of view. Its classical expression is to be found in the saying attributed to Helvetius :" I detest your opinions, but I will contend to the death for your right to utter them." It is this principle which is most decisively violated by the authoritarian and totalitarian methods of Dictatorships, with their monopoly control of educational and propagandist agencies and their rigid repression of dissentient opinion. " The University in Fascist Italy " says an Italian Professor of Political Science, " is working . . . to create a definite type of Italian—' the Italian of Mussolini,' whose character and personality must be perfectly adapted to the ideal and practical necessities of Italy." " The entire educational effort of the state ," says Hitler, " must be to brand the sense of race into the hearts and brains of youth " so that " when the youth leaves school he shall not be a half-and-half Pacifist or Democrat but German through and through."

But not only education in school and university is directed to a uniform result ; every agency and organ of thought and opinion is *gleichgeschaltet* or assimilated to a prescribed pattern—the press, the wireless, the stage, the cinema, and even the production of books and pamphlets. And this curtailment and censorship of opinion is reinforced by the stamping out of minorities and heresies by methods which recall those of the Inquisition.

" Government," says a Fascist enthusiast, " has not only the right but the positive duty, in accordance with such lights as it possesses, to aim at stamping out—even if prudence dictates that the process should be gradual—by the sanction of its laws every form of activity which is anti-social, anti-patriotic, anti-moral and anti-religious."*

The Communist Dictatorship, while allowing more

* Major H. S. Barnes : *Fascism.*

freedom of discussion in the initial stages, is equally ready to suppress opposition when once decisions have been taken. By the method of what is euphemistically called "liquidation" the formation of organs of opposition, even within the working-class movement, is discouraged. As M. Tomsky frankly stated :

" Certainly two or three or four parties may exist under the conditions of working-class dictatorship, but only provided that one party is in power and all the rest in prison."*

The contrast with the conditions of our own parliamentary system, in which the status of the Opposition parties is indicated by the phrase " His Majesty's Opposition," need not be emphasised. The principle of Liberty, though threatened and at times infringed by laws against blasphemy and sedition, is safeguarded under our democratic institutions as under no others.

(2) Liberty is necessarily linked with Equality, for it is not the personality of a few élite individuals but of all men and women without distinction that the Democrat is asked to revere. Equality, however, is a vague and misleading word, which gives rise to frequent misunderstandings. It is unnecessary to labour the obvious fact that equality of nature or endowment does not exist, and that equality in the sense of stereotyped similarity is as undesirable as it is happily unattainable. It takes all sorts to make a world and it would be a poor and colourless world that did not contain all sorts.

Nor is identity of treatment demanded by the principle of Equality. Equality must indeed be interpreted in terms of the previous principle of the value of personality, and it will then be seen to stand for the worthwhileness of men and women everywhere and the consequent demand that they should be enabled to develop to the best of which they are capable. Equality will then mean the denial of every kind of artificial privilege or prescriptive rights, and of every kind of exploitation—of race, or class, or sex.

(3) And this brings us to the third principle—the principle of Fraternity, whose expression demands the extension of

* *Pravda*, Nov. 19, 1927.

love and fellowship to embrace the whole of mankind, and the preference for the method of persuasion over that of force and repression. Here again, terms like love of humanity are often used with a vagueness that leads to ridicule. " You cannot love," it has been said, " an indefinitely extended Post Office Directory," and humanity must be defined in terms of the men and women with whom we are brought in contact. But the principle implies an imaginative insight and sympathy which overleaps the differences of nationality and colour, of language and religion, of class and upbringing. It accounts for the energy and conviction with which reformers have flung themselves into movements for the abolition of slavery, the reform of the penal system, the furtherance of international peace and the promotion of social justice and welfare. It is significant that among the Great Democrats whose lives appear in this volume so many have given themselves not alone or even mainly to the extension of parliamentary Democracy but to the redress of injustice and inhumanity of every kind.

The democratic faith and the democratic temper reach to wider issues than those of political method and machinery. And they are found, perhaps supremely, in men and women whose political influence has been slight. John Woolman, the eighteenth Century American Quaker, who pioneered the cause of anti-slavery a hundred years before the Abolition, is an outstanding example of a man whose whole life was an expression of this faith and temper, but who confined himself to methods of persuasion and influence brought to bear on individuals and groups rather than on Governments. A New Jersey tailor, he had occasion as a young man to be called upon to make a bill of sale for the owner of a Negro woman. It was suddenly brought home to him that the transaction was inconsistent with his Christian faith. From that time he gave himself to the work of persuading his fellow-members in the Society of Friends to abandon the practice of slave-holding. He is said to have visited the owners of eleven hundred slaves, and he did not rest until he had succeeded in securing not only the almost complete cessation of the practice within the Society, but the support of its members for a campaign against the institution outside their borders. His appeal both in his personal dealings with individuals, and in his writings on slavery and other social questions, is always to the spirit of " universal love."*

In a time of illness John Woolman had a vision which showed him that he was to consider himself identified with all men.

" I saw a mass of matter of a dull gloomy colour . . and was informed that this mass was human beings in as great misery as they could be, and live, and that I was mixed with them, and that henceforth I might not consider myself as a distinct and separate being."

John Woolman's identification with his fellows has had few parallels, but it is the key to the meaning of Democracy as it was understood by Walt Whitman and Edward Carpenter.

Whitman's declaration in *Leaves of Grass* :

" I speak the password primeval, I give the sign of Democracy, By God ! I will accept nothing which all cannot have their counterpart of on the same terms,"

is repeated in Carpenter's *Towards Democracy* :

" If I am not level with the lowest, I am nothing ; and if I did not know for a certainty that the craziest sot in the village is my equal, and were not proud to have him walk with me as my friend, I would not write another word—for in this is my strength."

And again :

" You cannot violate the law of Equality for long.
" Whatever you appropriate to yourself now from others, by that you will be poorer in the end ;
" What you give now, the same will surely come back to you. If you think yourself superior to the rest, in that instant you have proclaimed your own inferiority."

When Eugene Debs was brought before an American court on a charge of sedition during the war, he said to the judge :

" Your Honour, years ago I came to the conviction that I was not one whit superior to anyone on earth. And I said

---

* His tract, *A Word of Remembrance and Caution to the Rich* (1793) was republished by the Fabian Society in 1897 (last reprinted in 1921).

then as I say now, that while there is a lower class I am in it, while there is a criminal class I am of it, while there is a soul in prison I am not free."

Extravagant words these may seem, and wild and unconvincing they would be from most men's lips, but Woolman, Whitman, Carpenter and Debs had earned their right to utter them. And at least it must be said that something of this spirit of universal fellowship and identification with others is required both to explain and to inspire the democratic faith.

> And now abideth these three, Liberty, Equality and Fraternity,
> But the greatest of these is Fraternity.

V

The democratic faith which I have attempted to define and illustrate has not been characteristic of all democrats. Few of them indeed have exhibited more than a portion of its features. Moreover it has been, as I have suggested, most fully embodied in men who were not politically active. It is noticeable that the adjective "democratic" has come to have a wider significance than the noun " Democracy." Yet Democracy as a constitutional form and a political method (and that is the proper scope of the term) carries with it an implicit if not conscious reference to the faith and temper which I have described. For the acceptance of the method of free discussion and readiness to consult the persons most nearly affected implies a recognition of the value of the common man and an unreadiness to override minorities. And this gives rise to the kind of leadership which is appropriate to democratic government. Here again the leaders of Democracy will be seen to vary greatly in the degree to which they possess the qualities that are truly democratic. The demagogue will be found to resemble the Dictator in attitude and temper, since he relies on a kind of mental coercion which is as foreign to Democracy as the rule of force under a Dictator. It is significant that the Dictators of our time employ all the arts of demagogy to accompany their exercise of forcible methods of domination and repression. They exploit mass-suggestion by the emotional appeals of symbols and uniforms, of mass-oratory and mass-broadcasting. Herr Ludwig in his recent book on *Leaders in Europe* distinguishes between statesmen whom he calls " servants of the people " and statesmen whom he calls " rulers of the people." Among the first he includes Nansen, Masaryk, Briand, Rathenau and Motta, and among the latter not only Mussolini and Stalin, but also Venizelos and Lloyd George, because though " democrats by principle and education " they are " dictators by temperament." The distinction helps to explain the contradictions which are observable in some of the Great Democrats included in this volume. It is illustrated by a comment of Bruce Glasier's in his book on William Morris, in which he contrasts Morris with Ruskin and Carlyle. " With Ruskin," he says, " the people are always ' you ' ; with Carlyle they are even further away, they are ' they ' ; but with Morris the people are always ' we '."

The comrade-leader is rarely found but singularly influential. A striking phrase of Jesus draws an ironic contrast between the autocracy of pagan Dictators " who are called forsooth benefactors " and the unassuming leadership of the servant of the people who comes " not to be served but to serve." " Let him who would be leader be as one that serveth." *Imperator*, Protector, *Duce*, *Führer*—that is one kind of leader ; but another kind is represented by the Carpenter of Nazareth, by the " little Poor Man of Assisi " and by the Quaker tailor of New Jersey. And among the Great Democrats the greatest have been those who have combined initiative and leadership with a belief in the common man and a readiness to enlist his co-operation. The leadership which Democracy requires is a leadership that is itself democratic, a leadership of persuasion and friendly guidance, and not a leadership of force and domination. It is the leadership not of Dictators nor of spell-binders, but of those who seek the " collaboration of the led." And such leadership is infinitely more effective in the long run than the short-lived triumphs of Dictatorship.